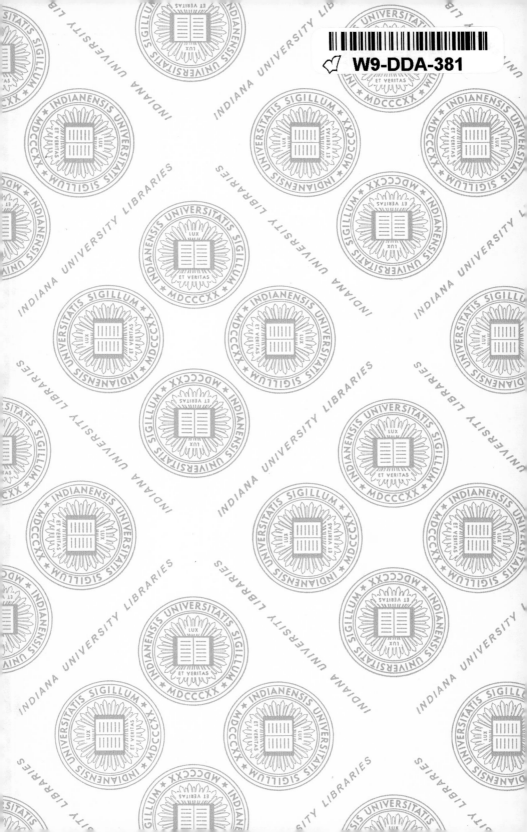

THINKING: CURRENT EXPERIMENTAL STUDIES

THE LIPPINCOTT COLLEGE PSYCHOLOGY SERIES
Under the Editorship of
Dr. Carl P. Duncan, Northwestern University
and Dr. Julius Wishner, University of Pennsylvania

THINKING: CURRENT EXPERIMENTAL STUDIES

edited by Carl P. Duncan
Northwestern University

J. B. LIPPINCOTT COMPANY
Philadelphia and New York

Copyright © 1967 by J. B. Lippincott Company
Library of Congress Catalog Card Number: 67–15515
Printed in the United States of America

Preface

This collection of articles is intended to be a core reading list for an advanced undergraduate or graduate course in the psychology of thinking. The book is also intended as a supplementary text for courses in learning and educational psychology. The emphasis is on experimental research on the environmental and task variables that influence performance of human adults in the areas of problem solving and concept learning. Because of this, other topics in the broad area of the psychology of cognition, such as the development of thinking and individual difference approaches to thinking, are not covered.

The articles selected for each chapter or topic are intended to give the student some knowledge of the best and most recent research on the topic. For almost every topic in concept learning, choice of articles was difficult because a number of studies seemed to be equally good candidates. This was not the case in problem solving, where it was often difficult to find enough acceptable studies, an indication that both experiment and theory are more advanced and more systematic in concept learning than in problem solving.

For permission to reproduce copyrighted material, thanks are due to Academic Press, *The American Journal of Psychology*, the American Psychological Association, *The Quarterly Journal of Experimental Psychology*, *The Scandinavian Journal of Psychology*, and Southern Universities Press.

EVANSTON, ILL. CARL P. DUNCAN

Contents

PART ONE

Problem Solving

The first five sections in this part deal with factors involved in problem solving or response discovery behavior, in tasks in which there is one (rarely more), clearly specifiable solution. Although research in this area began before 1900, the rate of research has always been, and continues to be, low. There is very little theoretical work, and most of the empirical research is unsystematic (although very recently anagram solving has begun to be investigated systematically). Because of this, the papers included in a section are in some cases only very generally related to each other. Occasionally, a paper is the only one of its kind and is included partly because it has a method or approach that should be followed up.

Recently considerable interest has developed in the area of creative thinking or problem solving. The tasks used in this area typically permit a number of "solutions," and the solutions may have to be judged for degree of acceptability. As yet there is very little experimental research on creative thinking. Section Six includes nearly all the experimental papers dealing with performance on task where several solutions may be judged to have varying degrees of acceptability.

SECTION ONE

Problem-Solving Theory

The paper by Maltzman, in which he extends Hull's theory of the habit-family hierarchy to problem solving, is one of the few theoretical papers in the area that has stimulated experimental research. An example is the series of studies on set by Maltzman and his associates, one of which is reprinted in Section Two. This response hierarchy approach to problem solving has also been presented, in one form or another, by several other writers cited in the Duncan article.

The paper by Duncan does not present new theory. It summarizes attempts to apply response hierarchy theory to a variety of tasks. It appears that in tasks in which it is possible to achieve considerable knowledge and control of the hierarchy, it can be demonstrated that response discovery behavior is predictable, in part, from the hierarchy. However, attempts to manipulate, experimentally, response hierarchies that subjects are only presumed to have are not always successful.

The Restle and Davis paper presents a different theoretical approach to problem solving. It is one of the very few attempts, so far, to develop a mathematical theory in this area. Mathematical theories in problem solving have tended to develop from comparisons of individual versus group problem solving. This area is not specifically covered in this book, but some references to the literature are given by Restle and Davis. It is also worth comparing their view of stages of problem solving tasks with Johnson's analysis of stages in Section Five.

1.   Thinking: from a Behavioristic Point of View

Irving Maltzman

Hull (10) has demonstrated that the habit family hierarchy and related principles may generate many hypotheses concerning behavior in
relation to objects in space such as might occur in the *Umweg* problem
or simple kinds of novel behavior. He has thus shown that the elementary
laws of behavior may be applicable to behavior of non-speaking organisms
in so-called reasoning situations.

The purpose of this paper is to demonstrate that the principles formulated by Hull and by Spence may also be applicable to the problem
solving of articulate humans. In this respect the present analysis has much
in common with the important formulations concerning mediated generalization and problem solving by Cofer and his associates (2, 3), Dollard
and Miller (5), Doob (6), and Osgood (19). The behavior theory involved may be outlined as follows. Behavior is a function of effective
reaction potential ($_s\bar{E}_R$), which in turn is a multiplicative function of
habit strength ($_sH_R$) and the effective drive state (D) minus the total
inhibitory potential (I_R). The latter represents the summation of reactive
(I_r) and conditioned ($_sI_R$) inhibition. It is assumed here that the effective
drive state represents the summation of the anticipatory goal response
(rg-sg) as well as the primary and secondary drives (23). Furthermore,
the multiplicative effect of the anticipatory goal response is restricted to
its associated class of instrumental responses.

The principal theoretical conception necessary for our account of problem solving is an extension of Hull's spatial habit family hierarchy (9, 10).
The great complexity of human thinking requires the formulation of what
might be called compound temporal habit family hierarchies. In the spatial habit family hierarchy, alternative locomotor responses are elicited
as a function, in part, of spatial and temporal distance from a goal. But
in adult human problem solving, responses in changing spatial relations
to a goal are not usually elicited, although there are problems involving
motor skills in which this may be the case. A typical performance change
in problem solving is in terms of verbal responses, and the change is solely
a temporal one (4). Nevertheless, it is assumed that the principles operating in the spatial habit family hierarchy will to a large extent operate
in the temporal hierarchy. Recent evidence in support of this assumption
has been obtained by Rigby (21).

The conception of a compound temporal habit family hierarchy is based

Reprinted with permission of the author and the American Psychological Association from *Psychological Review*, 1955, 62, 275–286.

upon the prior assumption that the elementary laws of behavior derived from conditioning and applicable to trial-and-error and discrimination learning are also applicable, at least in part, to primary problem solving or reasoning, and thinking in general. That different kinds of behavior are observed in conditioning, trial-and-error, discrimination, and problem-solving situations is not to be denied. But these different behaviors need not necessarily involve fundamentally different laws. Different behavior is observed in these situations because the initial conditions are different, and the situations represent varying degrees of complexity in the sense of the number of different variables and principles operating in

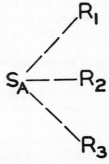

Fig. 1. A divergent mechanism. The stimulus has varying tendencies to elicit the alternative responses.

them. Nevertheless, it is reasonable to assume that at least some of the elementary laws derived from conditioning will lead to the development of the composition laws operating in human problem solving.

As Hull (10) has demonstrated, these elementary laws can account for many of the phenomena of simple trial-and-error learning. A hierarchy of responses elicitable by a given stimulus, in which the correct response is relatively low in the hierarchy, characterizes this form of behavior, as shown in Fig. 1. Learning is said to be complete when the order of the response hierarchy has so changed that the correct response is now dominant in the hierarchy. Hull has called this hierarchy of responses, elicitable by a given class of stimuli, the divergent mechanism (9).

As Spence (22) and Hull (10) have demonstrated, the elementary laws of behavior derivable from conditioning situations can also account for many of the phenomena of simple discrimination learning. A hierarchy of stimuli eliciting a given response in which the correct cue is relatively low in the hierarchy characterizes this form of behavior, as shown in Fig. 2. Such learning is said to be complete when the order of the stimulus hierarchy has so changed that the correct cue is dominant. Hull has called this

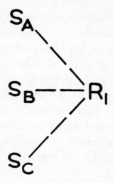

FIG. 2. A convergent mechanism. The alternative stimuli have varying tendencies to elicit a given response.

hierarchy of stimuli eliciting a given response the convergent mechanism (9).

A synthesis of the divergent and convergent mechanisms gives rise to the habit family hierarchy involved in behavior sequences in relation to objects in space (9, 10). A hierarchy of this sort is shown in Fig. 3.[1]

As seen in this figure, S_A (the external stimulus) and S_D (an internal drive stimulus) are capable of eliciting a given habit family hierarchy and equivalent responses leading to a given goal. Common to all responses in the hierarchy is a fractional anticipatory goal response (rg_a-sg_a) which is associated with both the external and internal sources of stimulation. Responses in the hierarchy may be elicited directly by either the external or internal stimuli, or by both. The effects of reinforcement or extinction of individual members of the hierarchy generalize to other members through the mediating mechanism of the anticipatory goal response and its stimulus. It therefore follows that the principles of conditioning and trial-and-error learning should also apply, at least in a general way, to the habit family hierarchy.

For example, if the reaction potential of the correct response leading to a goal is low in the hierarchy, then the generalized conditioned inhibition from the repeated failures of the dominant incorrect responses may reduce its effective reaction potential below the response threshold. Attainment of the goal would never occur under the conditions present. Or,

---

[1] There have been a few minor deviations from Hull in the manner of diagramming the stimulus-response relationships in order to simplify their presentation. Instead of having a dashed line between the stimulus and each response member of the divergent mechanism, a single dashed line leading to a bracket is used. All bracketed responses are associated with the stimulus. The number and length of the response sequences have also been reduced. A dashed line between a stimulus and a response signifies a learned association, while a solid line between a response and the cue it produces indicates an unlearned association.

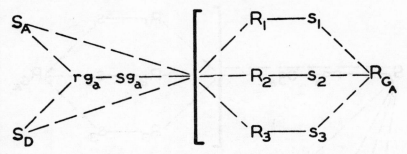

FIG. 3. A habit family hierarchy produced by a divergent and a convergent mechanism.

if the subject has a high degree of an irrelevant need such as anxiety, aside from the possible interfering effects coming from the competing responses aroused by this drive, failure to attain the goal under the above conditions would be even more pronounced. The increased effective drive state multiplying the habit strengths for the dominant incorrect responses and the weak correct responses would increase the absolute difference in reaction potential between the two.[2] Such a condition would produce a greater amount of conditioned inhibition generated through the repeated extinction of incorrect responses. This in turn would increase the probability of failure.

Another way in which changes in the habit family may occur is through the arousal of the fractional anticipatory goal response (rg_a-sg_a). Its arousal may produce an immediate increase in effective reaction potential for the related responses. This effect occurs because it presumably enters into a multiplicative relationship with habit strength in the determination of reaction potential.

A synthesis of habit family hierarchies gives rise to the compound habit family hierarchy involved in human problem solving. A hierarchy of this sort is shown in Fig. 4. It is formed when the stimulus of a divergent mechanism becomes a member of a convergent mechanism as well. By the same learning process, responses of the divergent mechanism in question become responses in convergent mechanisms. In the compound habit family hierarchy not only does S_A have the disposition for arousing its habit family hierarchy, but to varying degree the habit family hierarchies

---

[2] For illustrative purposes we may substitute numerical values in the formula for reaction potential ($_sE_R = {_sH} \times D$). The $_sH_R$ value for the dominant incorrect response is 5; the $_sH_R$ value for the weaker correct response is 2; drive has a value of 1. The absolute difference in reaction potential between the correct and incorrect responses is therefore 3. If the drive state is increased to a value of 2, then the absolute difference between response becomes 6. A greater difference in reaction potential must now be overcome before the correct response can become dominant in the response hierarchy.

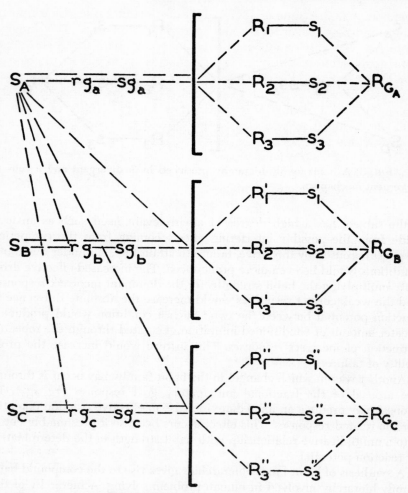

Fig. 4. A compound habit family hierarchy produced by a combination of habit family hierarchies.

of S_B and S_C as well. There is a hierarchy of habit families elicitable by S_A. An analogous condition holds for the other stimulus complexes, S_B and S_C. They have varying amounts of reaction potential for the elicitation of the other habit family hierarchies. These relations as well as the drive stimuli have been omitted in Fig. 4, in order to avoid confusing details.

When the compound hierarchy is formed, R_1, for example, originally only a member of the divergent mechanism elicitable by S_A, becomes a member of a convergent mechanism. There is now a hierarchy of stimuli, S_A, S_B, S_C with differing amounts of effective reaction potential for its elicitation. A similar state of affairs exists for the other response members of a hierarchy, as well as for the anticipatory goal responses. The stimulus complex S_A has varying amounts of reaction potential for the elicitation of the anticipatory goal response rg_b-sg_b and rg_c-sg_c as well as its original anticipatory response. We now have a hierarchy of habit family hierarchies or a class of classes of stimulus-response relationships.[3] Thinking in general, and problem solving in particular, thus may involve the selection of habit family hierarchies as well as the selection of specific response sequences within a hierarchy.

If the selection of response classes or habit family hierarchies obeys the same principles as the selection of individual responses, then the task of discovering the principles of problem solving may be greatly facilitated. The laws derived from conditioning could then be used to account for changes in the compound hierarchy, without, of course, necessarily excluding other principles. Maltzman and his associates have obtained some experimental evidence in support of this assumption (16, 17, 18).

An additional basis for such an assumption is that the difference between instrumental conditioning and problem solving in this respect may not be as great as it seems. In problem solving the members of a response class are qualitatively different—for example, different verbal responses. Effects upon one member may influence other members through mediated generalization, as previously indicated. In instrumental conditioning, changes in a response class, however, are also involved, because precisely the same response may not occur on successive trials (10). There are differences in intensity and, perhaps, in quality in the successive bar-pressing responses in the Skinner box. Nevertheless the rate of bar pressing increases with successive reinforcements. Learning occurs even though a given response is not precisely repeated, because a class of similar responses is reinforced as a result of simple stimulus and simple response generalization. The limits and the precise manner in which generalization occurs in the two situations are probably different. But because of its important theoretical implications for a theory of problem solving, the similarity between the two situations in this respect should not be discounted.

Changes in the order of dominance in the compound hierarchy may occur as a result of either or both of two effects. First, the effective reaction potential of the incorrect dominant habit families and their individual members may be decreased as the result of extinction. The initial

[3] This presentation of the compound habit family hierarchy is an oversimplification. For one thing, it does not indicate that individual response members of a habit family may potentially serve as the anticipatory goal response for other habit families. Also, the stimulus aspects of the compound hierarchy, and how they are related to concept formation and perception are not developed here.

Theories of problem solving by Duncker (7), Duncker and Krechevsky (8) and by Wolters (25), although stemming from different points of view, have a number of characteristics in common with the compound habit family hierarchy.

response elicited in a given problem situation would tend to be the dominant response in a dominant habit hierarchy. If this response does not lead to a solution, as by definition it would not, it would receive an increment in inhibitory potential, and responses next in the order of dominance would tend to occur. There would be temporary extinction and spontaneous recovery of these incorrect responses. Eventually the inhibitory potential of these responses would reduce their effective reaction potential below that of the responses contained in the hierarchy next in the order of dominance, and so on. Each response in the hierarchy need not be elicited and extinguished, however, since mediated conditioned inhibition may generalize from one member of a hierarchy to another. The anticipatory goal response of this hierarchy presumably would also acquire inhibitory potential, thereby further reducing the effective reaction potential of the related class of responses.

A second general way in which changes in the order of dominance in a compound hierarchy may occur is by increasing the effective reaction potential of the habit family or families initially low in the hierarchy which contain the correct responses. One way in which this may come about is as a result of previous reinforcement of individual members of the hierarchy in that situation. Through mediated generalization all members of the hierarchy would receive an increment in reaction potential.

Another way in which a habit family may be raised in the compound hierarchy is through the arousal of the anticipatory response of the habit family. Elicitation of the anticipatory goal response produces an immediate increase in effective reaction potential for the related class of responses, for the reason previously mentioned (15). The antecedent condition for the anticipatory goal response is assumed to be commerce with a goal or a substitute, often symbolic, for the goal. In adult human problem solving the latter is the typical condition. Recent research indicates that verbal instructions given by the experimenter provide an important condition determining the arousal of the anticipatory response (2, 15). The consequent condition of its arousal is an increased probability of occurrence of responses instrumental in attaining the goal in question.

These different ways in which changes in the compound habit family hierarchy may occur are related to the different kinds of problem solving distinguished by certain writers. As Hull (10) has pointed out, any learning situation other than classical conditioning involves problem solving of some sort. The essential characteristics of a problem-solving situation are that an organism is motivated, and that attainment of some goal object satisfying that drive is dependent upon the organism's performing in a given manner. It is characteristic of problem solving that the appropriate response leading to goal attainment does not immediately occur. This is true to some extent in instrumental conditioning, and to a greater extent in trial-and-error learning and in what has traditionally been called problem solving.

Further distinctions between different kinds of problem solving have also been made. Maier (13, 14) has repeatedly distinguished between different functions responsible for problem solving, and has classified problem solving as either productive or reproductive. The latter kind of thinking according to Maier involves the application of previously acquired experiences which lead to a correct solution in a new situation. It is problem solving based on the transfer of training, or equivalent stimuli. Productive thinking on the other hand is the consequence of the integration of previously unrelated experiences. The integration is produced by a direction which is an "outside" force not itself a habit.

The present treatment of problem solving, as previously indicated, makes use of the concept of the fractional anticipatory goal response. Certain functional characteristics of the anticipatory goal response appear to make it an analogue of Maier's concept of a new direction. However, among other things, we do not accept Maier's restriction that only productive thinking involves the combination of previously isolated habit segments, to use Hull's terminology. To some extent this is the distinguishing characteristic of all thinking. It is the feature that sets it off from simple retention, and trial-and-error learning. All forms of thinking involve mediated generalization, and hence compounding of previously isolated habit segments.

Nevertheless, there are differences between reproductive and productive thinking. Situations eliciting reproductive thinking often involve the presentation of a succession of problems. The solution of each of these requires the elicitation of different response members of the same habit family hierarchy. This habit family will then become dominant in the compound hierarchy, as the result of reinforcement of its response members and the extinction of responses belonging to different habit families. As previously indicated, the increase in reaction potential of the entire class of responses as the result of reinforcement of individual members would occur as a consequence of mediated generalization. For example, subjects given a series of anagrams whose solutions all belong to the same word category will have a greater frequency of success on subsequent anagrams of the same category than subjects without such prior experience (20). However, failure on individual problems may occur because a solution is still dependent upon selection of particular responses within this one habit family.

The occurrence of reproductive thinking in situations where only a single problem is presented is also the consequence of the factors outlined. As a result of past training the dominant habit family in the compound hierarchy contains the correct response. Solution of the given problem depends upon extinction of the initially dominant incorrect responses within this one hierarchy.

In productive thinking, on the other hand, a habit family initially low in the compound hierarchy must become dominant before a correct solution can be attained. This occurs as the result of the extinction of the dominant incorrect response hierarchies. Once the appropriate habit family is dominant a solution will occur, provided that the correct responses within that hierarchy in turn become dominant. The protocols of subjects in Duncker's radiation problem exemplify this mode of thinking (7).

If a subject incorrectly anticipates the goal or solution to the problem— e.g., "destroy the tumor by means of rays sent over a path as free as possible from healthy tissue"—the proposed solutions are alternative responses within the same dominant habit family, and are all attempts to achieve this end. Repeated failure of these proposals will produce extinction of the anticipatory goal response and its related instrumental responses. As a consequence, another habit family may become dominant. The subject will now anticipate a different kind of solution, such as "reduce the intensity of radiation." As a result, all potential response sequences in the subject's habit family leading to this goal are facilitated. If the correct solution (converging rays from different angles) is not the dominant response in this hierarchy, extinction of incorrect responses must occur before the solution will be attained.

In an actual protocol this orderly progression from one habit family to another is probably an infrequent occurrence. The more typical case would be one in which the reaction potentials of two or more habit families overlap. This would probably be the case after the first few responses from the dominant hierarchy have been extinguished. Thus reproductive and productive thinking differ with respect to the kinds of changes which must occur in the compound hierarchy before a correct solution can be attained. In reproductive thinking the habit families containing the correct responses are dominant at the outset of the problem, as the result of training and generalization from other situations. Or they rapidly become dominant in the compound hierarchy through the reinforcement of individual response members of the habit family. In productive thinking the habit families containing the correct responses are initially low in the compound hierarchy. They become dominant following the extinction of the dominant habit families which lead to incorrect solutions.

Experiments on the effects of direction in the pendulum problem by Maier (12) and by Weaver and Madden (24) are a special case of productive thinking, in that instructions and demonstrations are employed to increase the reaction potential of the anticipatory goal response and individual response members of the habit families leading to a correct solution. The problem is to construct two pendulums which would make chalk marks on two different places on the floor. In Maier's experiment (12) one group of subjects was given only the statement of the problem. Other groups received the statement of the problem plus various additional instructions or demonstrations. One of these groups was given three different demonstrations of operations on the material which were necessary for solution of the problem. They were shown how to make a plumb line, how to combine poles by using a clamp, and how to wedge poles against a surface. A third group was given these demonstrations and told that they must combine them for a solution of the problem. A fourth group was told that it would be advantageous if the pendulum could hang from the ceiling. They were given a "direction." The fifth group received the demonstrations and the direction. All of the problem solutions except one occurred in this last group.

According to the present formulation the experimenter's statement that it would be advantageous to hang the pendulum from the ceiling tended to elicit an anticipatory response for this goal. A wide variety of equivalent responses instrumental in leading to this goal therefore received an immediate increment in reaction potential. However, for a correct solution to occur, certain specific responses must be elicited. The three demonstrations given the last group increased the tendency of these responses to occur within their respective habit family hierarchies. The increased frequency of solutions under these conditions would follow from the differential increase in reaction potential of the relevant responses and the lawful nature of trial and error learning. However, since a large number of responses belong to a given hierarchy, and the correct responses may still not be dominant, extensive extinction of incorrect responses must occur. If the correct responses are very low in the dominant hierarchy, a solution may not occur at all because of the extensive generalization of the effects of extinction of the incorrect responses. Another basis for failure in this group is that despite the instructions tending to arouse the appropriate anticipatory goal response, some subjects, presumably as the result of self-instructions, induce different anticipatory goal responses. These are the subjects that adopt an inappropriate approach to the problem, according to Maier.

Groups 2 and 3, which are not given the directional instructions but receive the demonstrations, also have an increase in reaction potential for the three response sequences necessary for a solution. However, the anticipatory goal response and the related class of responses necessary to suspend the pendulum from the ceiling are not increased in strength, which is presumably why these subjects failed to solve the problem. However, contrary to Maier, Weaver and Madden (24) found no difference between the performance of groups 3 and 5.

Their experiment implies that the appropriate habit family for suspending the pendulums from the ceiling may be elicited by self-instructions, or that the increase in habit strength of the three necessary response sequences by itself may be sufficient for the solution of the problem in some individuals. Why there was this discrepancy between the two studies, however, is not at all apparent.

Throughout the previous discussion the systematic and theoretical status of the concept of thinking has only been implied. We shall now try to make it more explicit. According to the present systematic position, thinking is a defined concept or hypothetical variable. The specific definition that is given to it is the problem of theory, and will be discussed presently. Now we must explore further the consequences of the assumed systematic status of the concept. For one thing, thinking is not a response, verbal or otherwise, just as learning is not a response, and just as electricity is not the temperature of a conductor. All of these are dispositional concepts that are given empirical meaning by statements referring to their antecedent as well as their consequent conditions (1). They are not equivalent to their manifestations or consequent conditions. The insistence that thinking *is* a verbal response, a contraction of certain muscles, or activity in the central nervous system, is thus based on an inappropriate use of language. The verbal response, for example, is just one of several different kinds of responses that may be taken as a criterion or manifestation of thinking. Other response criteria might be gestures, mimicry, motor skills, etc. Questions as to which ones may be taken as criteria, and under which conditions, as well as how they are related to thinking, are to be answered by experiments and theory.

The present systematic position with respect to the relationship between thinking and verbal responses (the most frequently used criterion of thinking) may be made clearer by using the analogy of bar pressing in the Skinner box. The assumptions here are analogous to the assumption that bar pressing is a function of other variables besides learning. If a bar depression does not occur, it need not necessarily imply the absence of learning. The rat's motivation may have been reduced to a minimum; there may be temporary extinction of the response, or inhibition due to the arousal of competing responses by extraneous stimuli, etc. Similarly, the absence of a verbal or some other kind of response does not necessarily mean the absence of thinking. It may be due to the absence of effective reaction potential for that particular response; perhaps the relevant motivation is absent; or other response tendencies inhibit its appearance, etc. On the other hand, the presence of bar pressing does not necessarily imply that learning has occurred. It may be an operant level, some unconditioned response strength—in Hull's terminology, $_sU_R$. Likewise, verbal responses may occur in the absence of thinking. One aspect of this condition will be discussed shortly.

In the foregoing we have tried to explicate the systematic status of the concept of thinking. We shall now turn to the more specific problem of how it may be treated within the framework of Hull's theory of behavior.

Since it is assumed that thinking as well as learning is a disposition or hypothetical variable, the problem now is to distinguish between the two concepts. If the two are defined in terms of the same operations and consequences, they have the same empirical meaning and the distinction is purely a verbal one. As commonly employed, the term learning refers to the acquisition of a hypothetical state, $_sH_R$, as a result of antecedent conditions such as the number of reinforcements. The consequent conditions are changes in some response criteria such as decreased latency, increased rate of responding, etc.

The term thinking as it is employed here refers to the utilization of new combinations of habit strength by articulate organisms. In other words, we assume that thinking is equivalent to a complex form of effective habit strength which is produced by mediated generalization. The reason for arbitrarily restricting the usage of "thinking" to humans is the belief that extensive mediated generalization is necessary for the recombination of habit strengths to occur, and complex mediated generalization of this sort is made possible primarily by linguistic responses.

We have stated that thinking involves the utilization of learning in new combinations, as distinguished from the acquisition of learning. A further problem is to distinguish between thinking and retention, since the latter also involves the utilization of habit strength.

The distinction is not always easy to make, and at times may be arbitrary. But so is the commonly accepted distinction between learning and retention (11). As previously noted, learning refers to the acquisition of a hypothetical state as a function of the number of reinforcements. Retention is a term referring to the persistence and subsequent manifestation of that hypothetical state. In a learning experiment, performance on trials after the first is a function of the persistence of previous learning, or retention, from earlier trials. Only on the first trial is nothing more than the acquisition of habit strength involved. This entire process, however, is called learning even though much of it is actually retention. After the subject has reached some predetermined criterion, he is required to utilize in some manner the habit strengths previously acquired. He is asked to recall the material previously learned, recognize, or relearn it, etc. In every case the responses originally acquired are elicited again to some extent. This implies that the habit strengths utilized in the test of retention are substantially the same as that originally acquired. Retention has as its consequent condition the elicitation of some previously acquired response, presumably as a result of the persistence of previously acquired habit strength. The term thinking has as its consequent condition the elicitation of a response other than the previously acquired response as a result of past learning. Habit strength previously acquired has entered into new compounds, has changed as the result of mediated generalization.

A fundamental problem for a behavioristic psychology of thinking is to determine the laws governing these combinations and recombinations of habit strengths. Hull's equations (10) for combining habit strengths in generalization and compound stimulus situations are approximations of such composition laws. But they are only first approximations, because the generalization and compounding of habit strengths occurring in thinking are undoubtedly a good deal more complex than those that Hull has treated. A basic problem in this respect would be the development of the laws of mediated generalization which, theoretically, produce the new compounds of habit strength, and empirically, produce the formation of new stimulus-response classes. It is likely that the close connection between language and thinking (or even their equating) in certain theories results from the fact that language permits the greatest degree of mediated generalization and therefore thinking.

Admittedly the theory of thinking and problem solving outlined here is loosely formulated and incomplete. Nevertheless, it at least has the merit that it relates human problem solving to behavior in simpler situations. It is an attempt to integrate the two, as distinguished from the usual gestalt approach which treats problem solving as divorced from the relatively large number of principles derived from conditioning and trial-and-error learning. Although many of the principles derived from conditioning may not entirely apply to human problem solving, this is certainly an empirical question worth investigating. At the very least, these principles should yield significant hypotheses as to the factors determining problem solving.

Summary

A theory of human problem solving has been outlined, based upon the concept of a compound temporal habit family hierarchy, which is assumed to function, at least in part, according to the principles of conditioning and trial-and-error learning. Some of the characteristics of the compound hierarchy were noted, and its role in different kinds of problem-solving situations was indicated.

The systematic status of thinking from a behavioristic point of view was described as a disposition or hypothetical state of the organism. Within the present theory it is equivalent to a new combination of habit strengths produced, primarily, by mediated generalization.

References

1. Carnap, R. Logical foundations of the unity of science. *Int. Encyc. unif. Sci.*, 1938, 1, 42–62.
2. Cofer, C. N. Verbal behavior in relation to reasoning and values. In H. Guetzkow (Ed.), *Groups, leadership and men.* Pittsburgh: Carnegie Press, 1951. pp. 206–217.

3. COFER, C. N., & FOLEY, J. P., JR. Mediated generalization and the interpretation of verbal behavior: I. Prolegomena. *Psychol. Rev.*, 1942, 49, 513–540.

4. COHEN, J. The concept of goal gradients: a review of its present status. *J. gen. Psychol.*, 1953, 49, 303–308.

5. DOLLARD, J., & MILLER, N. E. *Personality and psychotherapy.* New York: McGraw Hill, 1950.

6. DOOB, L. W. The behavior of attitudes. *Psychol. Rev.*, 1947, 54, 135–156.

7. DUNCKER, K. On problem solving. *Psychol. Monogr.*, 1945, 58, No. 5 (Whole No. 270).

8. DUNCKER, K., & KRECHEVSKY, I. On solution-achievement. *Psychol. Rev.*, 1939, 46, 176–185.

9. HULL, C. L. The concept of the habit-family hierarchy and maze learning. *Psychol. Rev.*, 1934, 41, 33–54, 134–152.

10. HULL, C. L. *A behavior system.* New Haven: Yale Univer. Press, 1952.

11. McGEOCH, J. A., & IRION, A. L. *The psychology of human learning.* New York: Longmans, Green, 1952.

12. MAIER, N. R. F. Reasoning in humans: I. On direction. *J. comp. Psychol.*, 1930, 10, 115–143.

13. MAIER, N. R. F. The behavior mechanisms concerned with problem solving. *Psychol. Rev.*, 1940, 47, 43–58.

14. MAIER, N. R. F. Reasoning in humans: III. The mechanism of equivalent stimuli and of reasoning. *J. exp. Psychol.*, 1945, 35, 349–360.

15. MALTZMAN, I., & EISMAN, E. Two kinds of set in problem solving. Paper read at Amer. Psychol. Assoc., New York, September, 1954.

16. MALTZMAN, I., FOX, J., & MORRISETT, L., JR. Some effects of manifest anxiety on mental set. *J. exp. Psychol.*, 1953, 46, 50–54.

17. MALTZMAN, I., & MORRISETT, L., JR. Different strengths of set in the solution of anagrams. *J. exp. Psychol.*, 1952, 44, 242–246.

18. MALTZMAN, I., & MORRISETT, L., JR. The effects of single and compound classes of anagrams on set solutions. *J. exp. Psychol.*, 1953, 45, 345–350.

19. OSGOOD, C. E. *Method and theory in experimental psychology.* New York: Oxford Univer. Press, 1953.

20. REES, H., & ISRAEL, H. An investigation of the establishment and operation of mental sets. *Psychol. Monogr.*, 1935, 46, No. 6 (Whole No. 210).

21. RIGBY, W. K. Approach and avoidance gradients and conflict behavior in a predominantly temporal situation. *J. comp. physiol. Psychol.*, 1954, 47, 83–89.

22. SPENCE, K. W. The nature of discrimination learning in animals. *Psychol. Rev.*, 1936, 43, 427–449.

23. SPENCE, K. W. Theoretical interpretations of learning. In C. P. Stone

(Ed.), *Comparative psychology*. New York: Prentice-Hall, 1951, pp. 239–291.

24. WEAVER, H. E., & MADDEN, E. H. "Direction" in problem solving. *J. Psychol.*, 1949, 27, 331–345.

25. WOLTERS, A. W. On conceptual thinking. *Brit. J. Psychol.*, 1933, 24, 133–143.

2.   Response Hierarchies in Problem Solving

Carl P. Duncan

The theory of the habit-family hierarchy, as developed by Hull (1934, 1952), was extended to the area of human thinking by Maltzman (1955), Osgood (1953), and Cofer (1957). Although Maltzman especially dealt with more than one kind of hierarchy, we shall be concerned here only with the divergent, or the response, hierarchy. This is the case in which a stimulus may elicit any one of several different responses. Since the responses will usually vary in probability of occurrence to the stimulus, the responses may be said to form a hierarchy. Viewed in this way, a problem to be solved is a stimulus, and the solution to the problem is a response that is low in the hierarchy of responses elicited by the stimulus.

The response-hierarchy approach to problem solving taken by Osgood and by Cofer particularly emphasized verbal response hierarchies, not only as being worthy of study themselves but also as mediators to instrumental response hierarchies. I will mention first a group of studies that was devoted to this kind of mediation.

A number of investigators have assumed that the response hierarchy of an instrumental problem might be changed, thereby influencing probability of solution of the problem, by manipulations carried out on a verbal response hierarchy presumably related to the instrumental response hierarchy. A typical method was to have subjects list uses for various objects, some of them relevant objects, some of them irrelevant, to problem solution, then attempt to solve the problem. This method or variants of it has been used by Saugstad (1955); Saugstad and Raaheim

Presidential Address to the Midwestern Psychological Association, Chicago, May 1966. My thanks to I. David Isaacs, Roger Dominowski, and Gordon Wood. The work was supported in part by grant HD00901 from the Institute of Child Health and Human Development, National Institutes of Health, United States Public Health Service.

(1957); Maltzman, Brooks, Bogartz, and Summers (1958); Staats (1957); and in several experiments in our laboratory (Duncan, 1961). Cofer and his students (Judson, Cofer, & Gelfand, 1956) had their subjects first learn lists of words among which were included names of objects relevant to problem solution, then attempt to solve the problem. The problem used in most of these studies was one of the Maier (1933) problems, the favorite one being the two-string problem with pendulum solution.

The great majority of the many experiments reported in these several studies were negative; problem solution was not facilitated by elicitations or manipulations of verbal response hierarchies. In a few cases minimal success was reported, but these have not stood up in replication. It seems fair to say that we have been unsuccessful in facilitating the solution response to these Maier-type problems by manipulations of verbal response hierarchies.

We now turn to the study of verbal problems and verbal response hierarchies themselves, where considerable success has been attained. I will deal with a number of different kinds of verbal response hierarchies and some of the experiments based on each of them.

First, there are the verbal norms developed by Underwood and Richardson (1956a) for use in concept learning or concept discovery studies. To obtain these norms, subjects were presented with a number of names of objects. The subjects were asked to give a sensory impression to each name. Each sensory impression was given by a different percentage of subjects. Therefore, Underwood and Richardson obtained a hierarchy of responses which are sensory impressions to the particular object. It has been repeatedly demonstrated in a variety of ways that concept learning and discovery vary directly as a function of the strength of these impression responses in the hierarchy (e.g., Freedman & Mednick, 1958; Schulz, Miller, & Radtke, 1963; Underwood & Richardson, 1956b).

The second verbal hierarchy I want to consider is the Russell and Jenkins (1954) norms for Kent-Rosanoff word association. We have used these materials for several experiments, and I will present some of the data. Most of our experiments are based on the first forty Kent-Rosanoff stimulus words, as listed in the Russell and Jenkins publication, together with the five most frequently occurring associates for each stimulus word. Since most of the results to be presented are based on the mean of these forty items, a figure has been prepared showing the over-all mean hierarchy.

Fig. 1 shows the mean per cent occurrence of each of the five strongest responses, number 1 being the strongest or first associate given by Russell and Jenkins' subjects, and number 5 being the weakest one, that is, the weakest one that we have used. The means are based on an N of 40, the first 40 stimuli. It can be seen that the mean per cent occurrence of associate 1 is about 39 per cent. That is, whatever word was given as the most

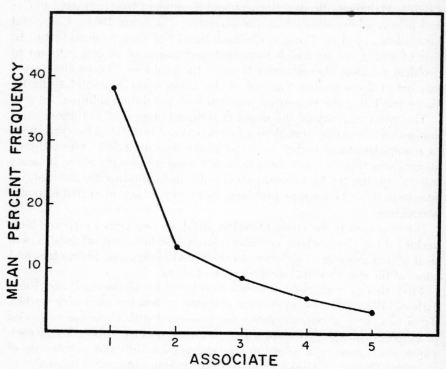

FIG. 1. Mean percent frequency of the five strongest associates to the first 40 Kent-Rosanoff stimuli from the Russell and Jenkins norms. By permission of the authors.

frequent associate to these 40 stimuli, it was given on the average by something like 390 of Russell and Jenkins 1008 subjects. It can also be seen that the average strength of the fifth associate is below 5 per cent. Summing over the five associates yields almost 80 per cent. In other words, although every one of the stimuli elicited very many more than five associates, on the average the first five associates account for the responses of approximately 800 of the subjects.

In the several experiments that I will present, the over-all purpose was the same. We were trying to measure to what extent problem solving, or response discovery behavior, as it is exhibited in a verbal response hierarchy, is influenced by the hierarchical nature of the responses. We were interested in the effect of the hierarchy both on the solution response and on the error responses.

In one experiment (Exp. I) the procedure was as follows: A subject was handed a 5 × 8 card on which one of the Kent-Rosanoff stimulus words was printed on the left, and its five strongest associates were printed

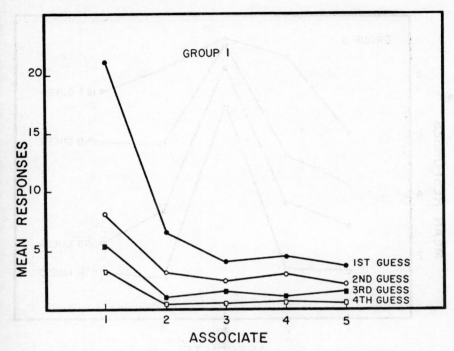

FIG. 2. Mean responses to each associate on each guess of Group 1 in Experiment I.

in a horizontal row on the right. The responses were not printed in order of strength but in one of several random orders. The subject was told that each of the five words on the right of the card was associated, but not equally associated, with the word on the left. The instructions went on to explain that the five response words represented five different degrees of association with the stimulus word, one of the words being the strongest associate, one the second strongest, and so on to the fifth or weakest associate. The subject was told to look at the stimulus word, then look at the five words on the right and try to guess a particular associate. The particular associate that he was to guess varied depending on the group to which he had been assigned. Subjects in Group 1 were told that they were to guess the strongest or first associate of the word on the left. Subjects in another group were told to guess the third strongest associate. We shall call this Group 3. And subjects in still another group were told to guess the fifth or weakest associate. This will be Group 5. There were 20 subjects in each group. On each of the 40 items, subjects were required to keep guessing until they finally guessed the correct word, so subjects could make up to four errors on each item. Each of these items, consist-

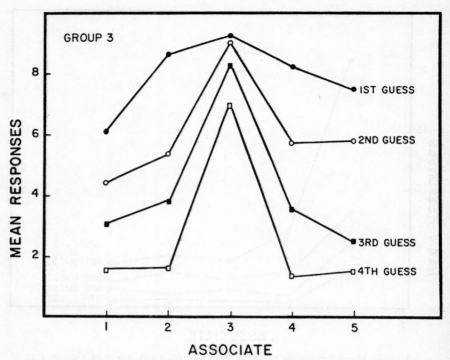

FIG. 3. Mean responses to each associate on each guess of Group 3 in Experiment I.

ing of a stimulus word and its five hierarchical responses, may be considered a problem, or at least an analogue of a problem, in which subjects must discover a solution response among a hierarchy of responses attached to the problem stimulus.

Fig. 2 shows mean responses over the 20 subjects and over the 40 items for Group 1, the group that was to guess the strongest associate. The graph shows the way in which each of the four possible guesses was distributed over the five associates. The top curve shows that on the first guess, a mean of about 21 of the 40 items was guessed correctly, that is, associate 1 was the guess that was made. The curve shows that the *error* responses on the first guess, that is, guesses of associates 2, 3, 4, and 5, tend to be distributed to some extent according to the hierarchical strength of those associates. If the first guess was incorrect, subjects were allowed a second guess; and the curve marked *second guess* indicates the way in which these responses were distributed over the five associates. The pattern is similar to that for the first guess, that is, most of those second guesses were of associate 1, so they were correct. The error responses were distributed over the remaining associates, although now the curve is rela-

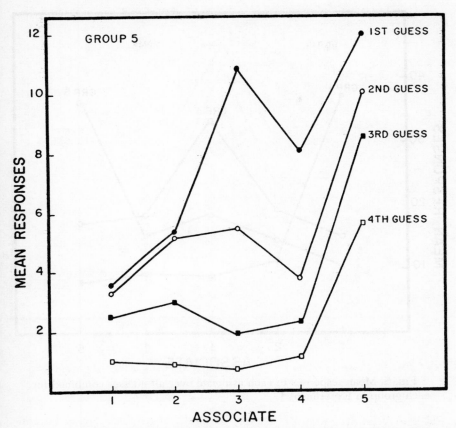

FIG 4. Mean responses to each associate on each guess of Group 5 in Experiment I.

tively flat. The pattern for the third and for the fourth guesses is much the same.

Let us now turn to the group that was asked to guess the third strongest associate. Fig. 3 shows the effect of having to discover a response in a hierarchy when there are present both responses stronger than, and weaker than, the response to be discovered. Note that on the first guess, the correct associate, number 3, is guessed slightly more frequently than the associates on either side of it, but not to any great extent. The task, at least on the first guess, is considerably harder than it was for Group 1. As we go to the second, third, and fourth guess, the inverted V-shaped pattern becomes more pronounced, at least through the third guess. Guess 3 is the most clear-cut case of showing that the errors are distributed according to what one would expect for a response hierarchy.

Let us now turn to Group 5, the group asked to guess the weakest asso-

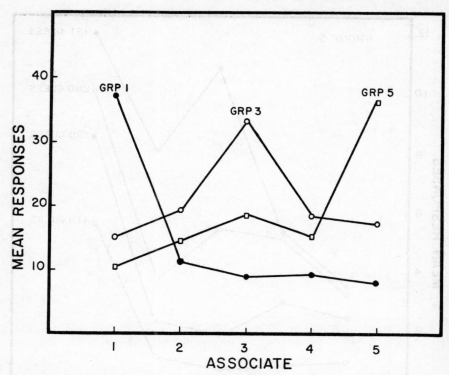

FIG. 5. Mean responses to each associate over all guesses combined for each group in Experiment I.

ciate. Here again, as shown in Fig. 4, the over-all pattern is much the same as for the previous two groups. For each of the four guesses, the most frequent response made is the correct response, associate 5. The remaining responses within that guess tend to be distributed at least roughly in accord with the strength of the associates 4, 3, 2, and 1.

We may now compare the three groups. In Fig. 5 all four guesses have been combined for each of the three groups. The figure shows that Group 1 had the somewhat easier task. Their point above associate 1 is, by a small amount, the highest point on the curve. However, their task was not greatly easier than that of Group 5. The most difficult response to discover was the associate in the middle, the third one. The distribution of error responses in a hierarchical fashion is probably clearest in Group 3, next in Group 5, and least in Group 1, although even in Group 1 there is some tendency for guesses of associate 2 to be slightly greater than those for associate 3, and so on. In general, this experiment shows fairly well that to the extent that a number of responses associated with the same

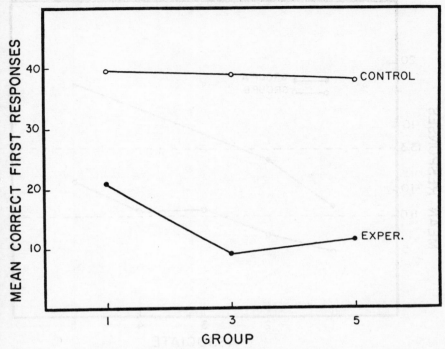

Fig. 6. Mean correct responses on the first guess of the three groups in the Control Experiment. The curve labeled "experimental" shows corresponding data from Experiment I.

stimulus exist in a hierarchy of relative strengths, both correct and incorrect guesses, in a response discovery situation, will bear some relationship to the hierarchy.

The experiment just described suggests that whatever associate is defined as correct, the discovery of that associate is interfered with by the other associates. Presumably this is because the other associates also tend, in varying degrees, to be elicited by the stimulus word. In the next experiment (Control Experiment) we attempted to eliminate or at least minimize interfering associations, while maintaining the ratio of four wrong responses and one correct response. For each of the 40 items we replaced four of the associates to the stimulus word with four other common English words which, insofar as we could judge, had no particular associative connection with the stimulus word. The four filler words were different for every item. The remaining Russell-Jenkins associate left for each item was, for different groups, the strongest, the third strongest, or the fifth strongest. In this experiment the instructions for each of the three groups

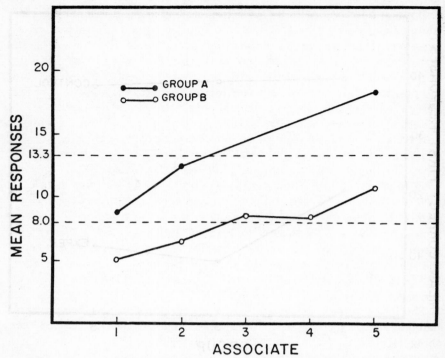

FIG. 7. Mean responses to each associate on the first guess by each group in Experiment II.

were simply that the subject was to guess which word of the five words on the right of each card was associated with the word on the left. There were 20 subjects in each group. All groups went through all 40 items, and all groups were allowed to guess on every item until they got it correct. The results are shown in Fig. 6.

As it turned out, the task was so easy that only the data for the first guess are reported. Performance was so high that little information could be obtained from subsequent guesses. The top curve shows the performance of the three groups in this Control Experiment. For comparison, performance on the first guess only is shown for the three groups in Exp. I, in the lower curve labelled "experimental." If one looks closely at the point for Group 1 in the Control Experiment, it can be seen that performance is not quite perfect. In a total of 800 first guesses (20 subjects × 40 items), there were two errors. Reading the mean for that group as 39.9 and going along the curve to Group 3 and Group 5, one can see that there is, numerically, a slight gradient. The mean for Group 3 is 39.1, and for Group 5 is 38.5. Comparison of the control curve with the experimental curve suggests very clearly that discovery of any solution response is interfered with by other responses that are associated with the stimulus and that are present with the solution response. When interfering responses are present, as in the experimental curve, the curve suggests that discovery of the correct response is a function of some combination of the absolute strength of the particular response defined as correct and the position of the correct response relative to the interfering responses. Later I will compare this experimental curve with another set of data.

Earlier it appeared that the words that most interfered with discovery of the correct response were those most similar in strength to the correct response. We decided to check this out a bit further. In the experiment (Exp. II) there were two groups, of 40 subjects each, and both groups were to guess the fifth associate. For one of the groups, all five associates were on the card. So this group was run in the same way as Group 5 of Exp. I. For the other group, associates 3 and 4 were removed for each item. There were only three associates on each card, the strongest, the second strongest, and the weakest. Both groups were instructed to guess the weakest associate among the three or five associates on each card, and both groups were given repeated guesses on each item until they got it correct. The results are shown in Fig. 7.

The figure shows performance for the first guess only. Since Group A had only three associates and Group 5 had five associates, the dashed lines show the chance baseline for each group. Since there were 40 items, Group A might have gotten a mean of 13.3 items correct by chance, and Group B a mean of 8 items, on the first guess. It can be seen that both groups guessed the weakest associate, which is what they were instructed to do, better than chance. Both of the points above associate 5 are significantly greater than the appropriate chance baseline; $t = 8.81$ for Group A, 6.69 for Group B, $p < .01$.

Comparing the two groups, Group A guessed associate 5 significantly better than Group B, after correction for chance ($t = 3.27$, $p < .01$). Removing associates 3 and 4 definitely made the task easier for Group A. Some indication of the interfering effect of associates 3 and 4 can be gained by noting that in Group B, those two associates were guessed at a rate slightly above chance. In both groups, the two strongest associates, 1 and 2, but farthest removed from associate 5 in strength, were guessed at rates below chance.

Fig. 8 shows the detailed pattern of guessing for each of the first four guesses by Group B, with 5 associates, of Exp. II. This group replicates Group 5 of Exp. I, and the hierarchical pattern of guessing is replicated quite well.

In the experiments reported so far, all of the responses from which the subject must guess the correct response have been present. The subject's task was one of response *selection;* he was not required to *produce* the correct response. We have also undertaken experiments in which a cer-

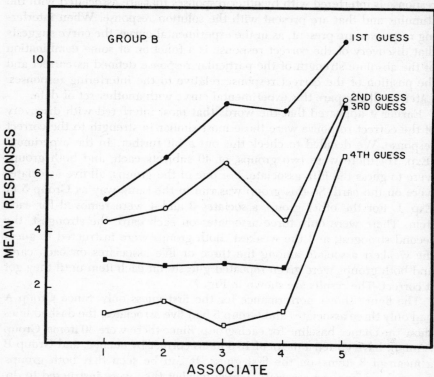

FIG. 8. Mean responses to each associate on each guess of Group B in Experiment II.

tain amount of response production was required of the subject, and I will report some of those data.

In one experiment (Exp. III), the subjects were first told about the procedure used by Russell and Jenkins to obtain associations to the Kent-Rosanoff stimulus words. The fact that each stimulus word had elicited a number of associations and that these associations varied in frequency of occurrence was explained, and it was made certain that the subjects understood this before proceeding further. The subjects were then given the 40 stimulus words and were asked to guess a particular associate, the associate varying for different groups, that the subjects *thought* Russell and Jenkins subjects had given, *not* the association that they themselves might give to the stimulus words. In order to reduce somewhat the great variety of responses that are usually elicited in response production situations, subjects were given the first letter of the associate that they were to guess. There were three basic groups, which will be identified as 1, 2, and 3. Group 1 was asked to guess the first associate, Group 2 the second, and Group 3 the third. For each item, in each group, subjects were shown

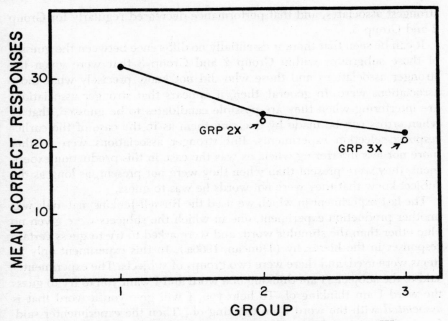

FIG. 9. Mean correct responses by each group in Experiment III.

the stimulus word and the first letter of the particular associate they were to guess. Since we were, as usual, interested in the effect, if any, of stronger responses when one is trying to guess weaker responses in the hierarchy, Groups 2 and 3 were subdivided. Half of the subjects in Group 2, who were to guess the second associate, had the first associate printed on the sheet for them, and they were told: "In order to help you, this is the strongest associate; it is your job, given the initial letter, to guess the second strongest associate." For the other half of the subjects in Group 2, Xs were typed on the sheet in place of the strongest associate. In Group 3 half of the subjects had both the first and the second associate printed on the sheet for them. They were told what these words were and that they were to guess the third associate. The other half of the subjects in Group 3 had Xs replacing the first and second associates. There were 40 subjects in Group 1 and in each subgroup of Groups 2 and 3.

Fig. 9 shows mean correct responses, where correct response is defined as giving the word in the Russell-Jenkins norms, for each of the three groups, or three associates, 1, 2, and 3, plotted on the base line. In Groups 2 and 3 the solid dots are the means for those subgroups for which the stronger associate or associates were printed on the sheet. The open circles are for those subgroups where those associates were replaced by Xs. The figure shows that Group 1 guessed a mean of about 32 out of the 40 strongest associates, and that performance decreased regularly for Group 2 and Group 3.

It can be seen that there is essentially no difference between the guesses of those subgroups within Group 2 and Group 3 that were given the stronger associations and those who did not know precisely what those associations were. In general, then, it appears that stronger associations are interfering when they are possible candidates to be guessed, that is, when errors can be made by guessing them as in the case of the earlier response-selection experiments. But stronger associations were neither more nor less interfering when, as was the case in this production experiment, they were present than when they were not present, as long as the subject knew that they were not words he was to guess.

The last experiment in which we used the Russell-Jenkins materials was another production experiment, one in which the subjects were given no clue other than the stimulus word, and were asked to try to guess certain responses in the hierarchy (Duncan, 1966a). In this experiment only 20 items were used, and there were two groups of subjects. The experimenter said to the subject, "I am thinking of a word and I want you to try to guess the word I am thinking of. To help you, I will give you a word that is *associated* with the word I am thinking of." Then the experimenter said, for the first item, "The word that is associated with the word I want you to guess is . . . ," at which point the experimenter gave the subject the Kent-Rosanoff stimulus word. This was done for each of the 20 items. Subjects were allowed three guesses. One group was told correct if they guessed the strongest associate of the stimulus word. The other group was told correct if they guessed the second strongest associate. In this experiment we should be able to predict to some extent what will happen. The first guess should be of responses high in the hierarchy. Subsequent guesses should tend to be of responses lower in the hierarchy. Therefore, a group that is trying to guess the strongest associate should do well on the first guess; but in cases where these subjects make errors and are given subsequent guesses, such subsequent guesses should not do a great deal to improve their performance. On the other hand, a group that is trying to guess the second strongest associate should not do very well on its first guess, but subsequent guesses should improve its performance.

Fig. 10 shows mean correct responses for the first guess, and for guesses 2 and 3 combined. As expected, Group 1, guessing the strongest associate, does very much better than Group 2, trying to guess the second strongest associate, on the first guess. But on guesses 2 and 3 combined their performance is reversed, although not by a large amount. In any case, the interaction here between performance on guess 1 and performance on the combined subsequent guesses is highly significant, $F = 142.9$, p .001, 1 and 98 df.

Over-all, both the earlier selection experiments, in which subjects had

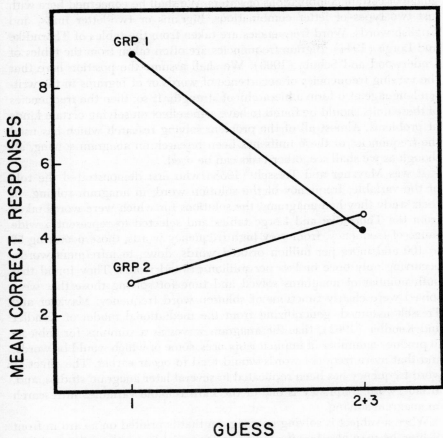

FIG. 10. Mean correct responses on the first guess and on guesses 2 and 3 combined for each group. Data taken from Duncan, 1966a. By permission of Psychonomic Press.

to try to pick a response among several presented to them, and the later production experiments, in which subjects had, to some degree, to come up with the correct response, suggest that if the population of responses elicited by the stimulus situation is organized in a hierarchy of relative strengths, then the subjects' response discovery behavior will tend to be ordered to some degree in accordance with the hierarchy. Others, such as Margaret Peterson (1956), Coleman (1964), and Flaugher (1965) have also found this associative hierarchy useful for response-discovery experiments.

I turn now to a third kind of verbal response hierarchy. The hierarchy that I shall deal with is the frequency of occurrence in the written language of certain combinations of letters. We shall be concerned here with just two types of letter combinations, bigrams or two-letter units, and English words. Word frequencies are taken, from the tables of Thorndike and Lorge (1944). Bigram frequencies are often taken from the tables of Underwood and Schulz (1960). We shall assume the position here that the varying frequencies of occurrence of words or of bigrams in the written language also form a hierarchy of strength. If so, then the frequencies of these units should be found to have some effect on solving certain kinds of problems. Almost all of the problem solving research which has used the frequencies of these units has been research on anagram solving, although as we shall see, other tasks can be used.

It was Mayzner and Tresselt (1958) who first demonstrated the role of the variable, frequency of the solution word, in anagram solving. In their study they had anagrams, the solutions for which were words taken from the Thorndike and Lorge tables and selected to represent a wide range of frequency, from very high frequency words, those occurring 50 to 100 and more per million printed words, down to infrequent words, occurring only once or less per million printed words. They found that both number of anagrams solved and time for solving those that were solved were clearly functions of solution word frequency. Mayzner and Tresselt assumed, generalizing from the mediational model of Kendler and Kendler (1962), that the anagram serves as a stimulus for subjects to produce a number of implicit responses, some of which would be words, and that more frequent words would tend to occur earlier. The effect of word frequency has been replicated in several later anagram studies, and, in fact, word frequency is one of the most reliable variables in research on anagram solving.

When a subject is solving an anagram that is printed on a card in front of him, he may also be affected by letter variables, such as the positions of letters and the frequencies of occurrence of individual letters or bigrams, etc. So in one of our experiments we attempted to minimize the effects of letter variables and to maximize the effect of frequency of the word as a whole by using more of a production method (Duncan, 1966b). We chose 20 pairs of consonants. Each pair consisted of the first letter and of the last letter of a group of five-letter English words taken from Thorndike and Lorge. For each pair of letters the group of available words ranged in frequency over almost the entire range of 100 or more occurrences per million words, down to words of considerably less than one occurrence per million words. The subject was told to think of a five-letter English word that was not a capitalized word or a proper name, that began with the first letter the experimenter would give him and ended with the last letter. The subject was given one minute to try to think of a word for each pair of letters. Each subject attempted to guess a word from each

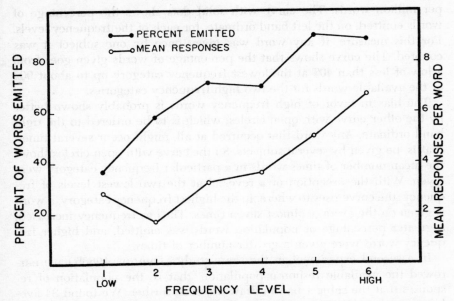

Fig. 11. Percent of words emitted (left ordinate) and mean responses per word (right ordinate) for each six levels of word frequency. Adapted from Duncan, 1966b. By permission of Academic Press.

of the twenty letter pairs. In this situation the subject is free to give any five-letter English word, that meets the criteria of the correct first letter and last letter, that occurs to him. We would therefore expect that the Underwood and Schulz (1960) *spew* principle would operate, that is, that the order of emission of verbal units should be in accord with their frequency of occurrence.

The results showed that by any measure, high frequency words were given more often than low frequency words. For example, the mean frequency (28.60) of the words emitted by the subjects was significantly higher than the mean frequency (22.97) of the population of words that they had to draw on, $t = 2.39$. Another way of looking at the data is shown in Fig. 11. The population of words available to the subjects (very few words are given by subjects that are not in the Thorndike and Lorge tables) consisted of 266 five-letter words, that is, the twenty letter pairs included a total of 266 words. These population words were categorized into six frequency levels, with about 40 to 50 words at each level. In Fig. 11, the low frequency level, level one, includes words of less than one per million frequency. The high frequency level, level six, includes words at the A and AA level, so called, that is 50 to 100 and more occurrences per million words. The curve with solid dots shows the percentage of words emitted, on the left hand ordinate, for each of the frequency levels. For this measure, if any word was given once by one subject it was counted. The curve shows that the percentage of words given goes from a low of less than 40% at the lowest frequency category up to about 90% of the available words for the two high-frequency categories.

The bias in favor of high frequency words is probably shown better by the other curve with open circles, which is to be ordered to the right hand ordinate. Any word that occurred at all, might occur several times, that is, be given by several subjects. So the curve with open circles shows the mean number of times words in a particular frequency category were given. With the exception of a reversal at the two lowest levels of frequency, the curve rises to where, in the highest frequency category, a word is given on the average almost seven times. Thus as frequency increased, a greater percentage of population words was emitted, and higher frequency words were given a greater number of times.

In a second experiment in the same study (Duncan, 1966b) we narrowed the available response population, that is, the population of responses that the subject had to draw on, even further. We found 34 five-letter words in the Thorndike and Lorge tables where for each of the 34 words there was one and only one other five-letter word that began with the same letter and ended with the same letter. Thus, for each of the 34 sets of letters there were just two words available. Within each of these pairs of words, one of the words was of higher frequency than the other. We predicted that if subjects were given the first and the last letter, and asked to think of a word, they would tend to think of the higher frequency member of the pair. This was the case. For the 34 pairs of words, significantly more higher frequency members of the pairs were thought of within the one minute allowed for each item than low frequency words.

In a third experiment, in that study (Duncan, 1966b) we used items consisting of two, and only two words that began with the same letter, were the same length (3 to 6 letters), and were names of objects from the same class, for example, two trees, *willow* and *walnut*. In this experiment one group was given the name of the category, the initial letter, and the length of the words and was allowed to try to guess a word, with either word being acceptable. There were also two groups in which subjects were given the same information and then were told by the experimenter, "I will give you an example of such a word," thereby leaving only one word left to be guessed. One group was given the higher frequency word of each pair; another group was given the lower frequency word. The results were that for the group allowed to guess either word, again higher frequency words occurred significantly more often than lower frequency words. In the group that was *given* the higher frequency words, there was a significant increase in the number of low frequency words emitted.

However, in the group *given* the lower frequency words, there was no increase in the number of high frequency words emitted. Thus, it was possible to increase guessing of low frequency words, but not of high frequency words.

In these three experiments, in which we assumed that reordering of letters was minimized and word production was maximized, the role of past experience in the form of various strengths of responses, as measured by frequency of occurrence, has been quite clear and quite strong. The Underwood and Schulz spew hypothesis was well supported by these results. It was also supported by a study of anagram solving recently reported by Johnson and Van Mondfrans (1965). They used anagrams that had three or more solutions. The solution words varied in Thorndike and Lorge frequency of occurrence. Order of occurrrence of solution words was a direct function of word frequency.

We now turn to the hierarchy of bigram frequency. The frequencies with which pairs of two letters occur in the written language have been tabulated by Underwood and Schulz (1960) and by Mayzner and Tresselt (1965), and others. Mayzner and Tresselt (1959) were the first to measure whether bigram frequencies would play a role in solving anagrams. Their original measure of bigram frequency, which has been used by most investigators since, was to sum the frequencies of successive bigrams in any set of letters. Thus, in a five-letter word or five-letter anagram there would be four successive left-to-right bigrams. The tabled frequencies of the bigrams would be summed for a total bigram frequency. One can get a total bigram frequency for a word that is a solution of some anagram. This is the solution bigram frequency total. One can also get a total bigram frequency for the letters of an anagram. This is the anagram bigram total frequency. Mayzner and Tresselt found that anagrams with low total bigram frequencies were easier to solve than anagrams with high totals. They reasoned that to the extent that solving anagrams involves rearranging of letters, letter combinations with low frequencies would be easier to break up and rearrange. In a later study, Mayzner and Tresselt (1962) found that solution words which had high bigram totals were solved more rapidly than those with low. This finding suggests that in rearranging letters, the letter combinations that the subject comes up with are more likely to be high frequency combinations.

Dominowski and I (Dominowski & Duncan, 1964) became interested in determining whether there would be interaction between anagram and solution word bigram frequencies, in addition to the main effects reported by Mayzner and Tresselt in their two separate studies. So we carried out three experiments, all of them quite similar, in which we had words with high bigram frequency totals and words with low totals. Each word was arranged into two anagrams, one with high bigram frequency total and the other with low total, so that we had two sets of anagrams for each set

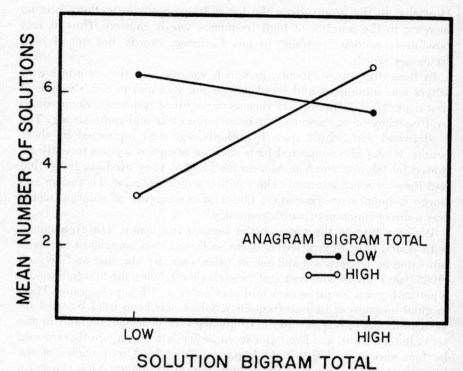

FIG. 12. Mean number of anagram solutions as a function of total bigram frequency of solution words with total bigram frequency of anagrams as the parameter. Data taken from Dominowski and Duncan, 1964. By permission of Academic Press.

of words. The results were that anagram bigram frequency was not significant as a main effect in any of the three experiments. Solution word bigram frequency was not significant as a main effect in two out of the three experiments. In all three experiments there was a highly significant interaction between anagram total and solution word total. Since the interaction was much the same in all three experiments, the experiments have been combined to show the interaction in Fig. 12. In the graph, mean number of words solved is plotted as a function of solution bigram total on the base line, and anagram bigram total is shown as the parameter. The interaction looks much like this if plotted for each experiment separately. In these combined data, neither of the two main effects, anagram or word bigram frequency total, is significant, but of course the interaction is highly significant. Our description of these findings, a description which we realize can easily be challenged, is something like this, namely, that there are perhaps three levels of performance in the graph. The poorest performance, represented by the open circle point in the lower left hand corner, occurred when subjects were presented with ana-grams having high bigram totals and had to solve those for words that had *low* bigram totals. An intermediate level of performance, represented by the right hand solid point, occurred when these extreme conditions were reversed, that is, when subjects had to proceed from anagrams with low totals to words with high totals.

The best performance occurred when both anagram and word totals were low, shown by the left-hand solid point, or when both were high, shown by the right hand open circle. Concerning this interaction, it is possible that low frequency bigrams, when present in an anagram, tend to suggest to S other low frequency bigrams and that high frequency bigrams in an anagram many tend to suggest to S other high frequency bigrams. If this hypothesis is correct, it would account for the interaction found. Concerning our failure to replicate Mayzner and Tresselt's main effects, I can only say that some unpublished work from our laboratory has also failed to find significant main effects, and this has also been true in a published study by Stachnik (1963). However, very recently Mayzner and Tresselt (1966) again reported finding significant main effects of bigram frequencies, both word and anagram.

At the moment we are forced to say that the role of bigram frequencies in solving anagrams is complex and unclear. But, Dominowski (1965) has shown that bigrams of different frequencies do in fact form a response hierarchy which acts in predictable ways in a problem solving situation. He made up ten problems, each problem consisting of five bigrams of different frequencies. Subjects were given as many guesses as they needed to guess the correct bigram in each problem. Each of the five levels of frequency was correct, in different groups. The results were strikingly similar, at least from my point of view, to the data I reported earlier for five varying-strength Russell-Jenkins associates of a stimulus word. Difficulty increased directly from the first to the second to the third most frequent bigram, then dropped for bigrams fourth and fifth in frequency. Thus for the three positions, 1, 3, and 5, for which we have data on Russell-Jenkins associates, the results were the same. The most frequent position was easiest, the intermediate or third position hardest, and the fifth or weakest response next hardest. This is shown in Fig. 13 where Dominowski's bigram data are compared with the experimental (lower) curve for word associations taken from Fig. 6. (In Fig. 13 the word association curve is plotted in terms of errors rather than correct responses.) So there appears to be some generality to this finding that when a subject is confronted with the problem of selecting a correct response among five responses, varying in relative strength, the most difficult problem for him is to pick the intermediate or third response, not the response of lowest absolute strength.

In summary, we have seen that the first systematic experimental effort

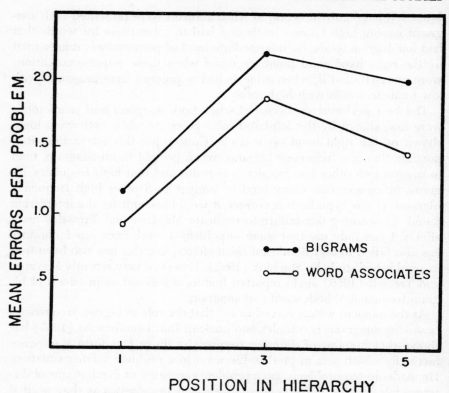

FIG. 13. Mean errors per problem as a function of position of problem solution in the response hierarchy. Data for the bigrams curve taken from Dominowski, 1965, and by permission of Psychonomic Press. The curve for word associates is the curve labeled "experimental" in Fig. 6, here plotted in terms of errors.

to apply response hierarchy notions to problem solving consisted of a group of studies in which an attempt was made to facilitate solution of some instrumental problem, that is, to influence the instrumental response hierarchy assumed to exist for that problem, by the indirect procedure of eliciting or reinforcing words in a verbal response hierarchy presumed to have some relation to the instrumental response hierarchy. This effort was largely, perhaps entirely, unsuccessful. It may be that responses even within the same hierarchy are sufficiently independent of each other, though all attached to the same stimulus, that elicitation of various responses in the hierarchy will have little effect on the probability of occurrence of any *specific* member of the hierarchy. We also know too little about transfer between presumably related verbal and instrumental response hierarchies. As often seems to be the case when one is dealing with transfer, one is optimistic and overestimates the amount of transfer that actually occurs.

In contrast, several measured or scaled verbal response hierarchies that are now available for research, such as the sensory impression norms, word association norms, tables of word frequencies, and frequencies of various letter combinations, as well as others not discussed here, have been of major help in research in learning, in concept formation, and in problem solving. In particular, two kinds of response discovery, selection and production, have been shown to be, in part, functions of the hierarchical structure, when it is known, of the population of responses to be searched.

REFERENCES

COFER, C. N. Reasoning as an associative process: III. The role of verbal responses in problem solving. *Journal of General Psychology*, 1957, 57, 55–68.

COLEMAN, E. B. The association hierarchy as a measure of extraexperimental transfer. *Journal of Psychology*, 1964, 57 (2), 403–417.

DOMINOWSKI, R. L. Problem difficulty as a function of relative frequency of correct responses. *Psychonomic Science*, 1965, 3, 417–418.

DOMINOWSKI, R. L., & DUNCAN, C. P. Anagram solving as a function of bigram frequency. *Journal of Verbal Learning and Verbal Behavior*, 1964, 3, 321–325.

DUNCAN, C. P. Attempts to influence performance on an insight problem. *Psychological Reports*, 1961, 9, 35–42.

DUNCAN, C. P. Problem solving within a verbal response hierarchy. *Psychonomic Science*, 1966, 4, 147–148. (a)

DUNCAN, C. P. Effect of word frequency on thinking of a word. *Journal of Verbal Learning and Verbal Behavior*, 1966, 5, 434–440, (b)

FLAUGHER, R. L. Detection Value: A measure of verbal relatedness applied to free association. *Journal of Verbal Learning and Verbal Behavior*, 1965, 4, 309–314.

FREEDMAN, J. L., & MEDNICK, S. A. Ease of attainment of concepts as a function of response dominance variance. *Journal of Experimental Psychology*, 1958, 55, 463–466.

HULL, C. L. The concept of the habit-family hierarchy and maze learning. *Psychological Review*, 1934, 41, 33–54, 134–152.

HULL, C. L. *A behavior system.* New Haven: Yale Univer. Press, 1952.

JOHNSON, T. J., & VAN MONDFRANS, A. P. Order of solutions in ambiguous anagrams as a function of word frequency of the solution words. *Psychonomic Science*, 1965, 3, 565–566.

JUDSON, A. J., COFER, C. N., & GELFAND, S. Reasoning as an associative process: II. "Direction" in problem solving as a function of prior reinforcement of relevant responses. *Psychological Reports*, 1956, 2, 501–507.

KENDLER, H. H., & KENDLER, T. S. Vertical and horizontal processes in problem solving. *Psychological Review*, 1962, 69, 1–16.

MAIER, N. R. F. An aspect of human reasoning. *British Journal of Psychology*, 1933, 24, 144–155.

MALTZMAN, I. Thinking: from a behavioristic point of view. *Psychological Review*, 1955, 62, 275–286.

MALTZMAN, I., BROOKS, L. O., BOGARTZ, W., & SUMMERS, S. S. The facilitation of problem solving by prior exposure to uncommon responses. *Journal of Experimental Psychology*, 1958, 56, 399–406.

MAYZNER, M. S., & TRESSELT, M. E. Anagram solution times: a function of letter order and word frequency. *Journal of Experimental Psychology*, 1958, 56, 376–379.

MAYZNER, M. S., & TRESSELT, M. E. Anagram solution times: a function of transition probabilities. *Journal of Psychology*, 1959, 47, 117–126.

MAYZNER, M. S., & TRESSELT, M. E. Anagram solution times: a function of word transition probabilities. *Journal of Experimental Psychology*, 1962, 63, 510–513.

MAYZNER, M. S., & TRESSELT, M. E. Tables of single-letter and diagram frequency counts for various word-length and letter-position combinations. *Psychonomic Monograph Supplements*, 1965, 1, No. 2.

MAYZNER, M. S., & TRESSELT, M. E. Anagram solution times: A function of multiple-solution anagrams. *Journal of Experimental Psychology*, 1966, 71, 66–73.

OSGOOD, C. E. *Method and theory in experimental psychology.* New York: Oxford, 1953.

PETERSON, M. J. Verbal response strength as a function of cultural frequency, schedule of reinforcement, and number of trials. *Journal of Experimental Psychology*, 1956, 52, 371–376.

RUSSELL, W. A., & JENKINS, J. J. The complete Minnesota norms for responses to 100 words from the Kent-Rosanoff word association test. *Office of Naval Research*, 1954.

SAUGSTAD, P. Problem-solving as dependent upon availability of functions. *British Journal of Psychology*, 1955, 46, 191–198.

SAUGSTAD, P., & RAAHEIM, K. Problem solving and availability of functions. *Acta Psychologica*, 1957, 13, 263–278.

SCHULZ, R. W., MILLER, R. L., & RADTKE, R. C. The role of instance contiguity and dominance in concept attainment. *Journal of Verbal Learning and Verbal Behavior*, 1963, 1, 432–435.

STAATS, A. W. Verbal and instrumental response-hierarchies and their relationship to problem-solving. *American Journal of Psychology*, 1957, 70, 442–446.

STACHNIK, T. Transitional probability in anagram solution in a group setting. *Journal of Psychology*, 1963, 55, 259–261.

THORNDIKE, E. L., & LORGE, I. *The teacher's word book of 30,000 words.* New York: Columbia Univer. Press, 1944.

UNDERWOOD, B. J., & RICHARDSON, J. Some verbal materials for the study of concept formation. *Psychological Bulletin*, 1956, 53, 84–96. (a)

UNDERWOOD, B. J., & RICHARDSON, J. Verbal concept learning as a function of instructions and dominance level. *Journal of Experimental Psychology*, 1956, 51, 229–238. (b)

UNDERWOOD, B. J., & SCHULZ, R. W. *Meaningfulness and verbal learning.* Philadelphia: Lippincott, 1960.

3. Success and Speed of Problem Solving by Individuals and Groups

Frank Restle and James H. Davis

The problem solving process, which begins with the presentation of a problem, is terminated when the subject arrives at a correct solution, when he arrives at an incorrect solution he believes correct, or when the experimenter arbitrarily ends the experimental session. Performance on a problem is usually summarized by the proportion of subjects who solve, or by the mean or median time to solution. A more complete description of the data gives the success of each subject (whether he obtained the correct answer or not) and the time taken; that is, a distribution of solution times or times until terminal error. One purpose of this paper is to show how the full distributions can be used to answer theoretical questions about the structure of the problem.

Small ad hoc groups of subjects can work together on verbal puzzles. Such cooperation seems natural and is appropriate to the nature of the problem and the usual behavior of college students. Generally speaking, small groups solve problems more rapidly and surely than individuals from the same population (Faust, 1959; Husband, 1940; Lorge, Fox, Davitz, & Brenner, 1958; Lorge, & Solomon, 1955; Marquart, 1955; Shaw, 1932; Taylor & Faust, 1952; Thorndike, 1938; and Watson, 1928). The advantage of groups may be a simple effect of pooling, "two heads are better than one," for in cooperative problem solving the group gets credit

Reprinted by permission of the authors and the American Psychological Association from Psychological Review, 1962, 69, 520–536.

for the first individual insight. Other factors such as interference between group members or emergent group facilitation of thinking must be measured as deviations from the simple "pooling" hypothesis. The second aim of this paper is to formulate the pooling hypothesis so that it applies to distributions of solution times.

MODEL OF THE DISTRIBUTION OF SOLUTION TIMES

Suppose that time is divided into short equal intervals of duration h. In any interval the subject may either solve the problem or not. [Imagine that there exists a probability φ that the problem is solved in the nth interval given that it has not been solved previously.] The probability φ is taken by hypothesis to be constant over intervals. Then the probability that the problem is actually solved in exactly the nth interval is the probability that it is not solved in any of the first $n - 1$ intervals (an event with probability $(1 - \varphi)^{n-1}$) times the probability that it is solved in the nth interval. That is,

$$P(n) = \varphi(1 - \varphi)^{n-1} \qquad [1]$$

the geometric distribution. This is a positively skewed (J-shaped) distribution with mean $1/\varphi$ and variance $(1 - \varphi)/\varphi^2$.

To say that φ is constant over trials, that the probability of solving is independent of how many times the subject may have failed to solve the problem, is in effect to say that problem solving is a one-stage, or all-or-nothing process. This assertion is frequently unreasonable in that some problems clearly seem to involve more than one stage.

MULTI-STAGE PROBLEMS

Suppose that to obtain the final solution the subject must actually solve a sequence of stages. The stages may be solved in fixed order, or it may be that the order of stages can be inverted, but suppose that the subject actually can work on only one stage at a time. Furthermore, suppose that the time to solve an individual stage has the geometric distribution, and that the distribution of times to solve Stage 2 is independent of how long it took to solve Stage 1, etc. (Of course, it is assumed that work on Stage 2 does not even start until Stage 1 is completed.) The distribution of times to solution for a k stage problem can be determined; it is a random variable, and the sum of the k random variables which are the times to complete the k stages. If the k stages have the same probability of solution per interval, φ, then the probability that the kth stage (and the whole problem) are completed as just trial N, is given by the negative binomial (Pascal) distribution,

$$P(N; k, \varphi) = \binom{N-1}{k-1} \varphi^k (1 - \varphi)^{N-k} \qquad [2]$$

An intuitive justification of this formula is given by Bush and Mosteller (1955, Ch. 14) and its derivation is discussed by Feller (1957, pp. 155–157). Note that Equation 2 reduces to Equation 1 when $k = 1$. The expected number of time intervals to solution, the expectation $E(N)$, and the variance of number of intervals, are given by

$$E(N) = k/\varphi \qquad [3]$$
$$\text{Var}(N) = k(1 - \varphi)/\varphi^2 \qquad [4]$$

Although it is not likely that the various stages of a given problem would be equally difficult (have equal values of φ), there is great difficulty in estimating φ's of separate stages unless one has direct observations of the completion of various stages. Such analyses can sometimes be done but it is helpful to be able to deal directly with total solution time. For this purpose it is expedient to use the simplifying hypothesis that all stages are equally difficult, so as to be able to estimate the number of stages in the problem.

CONTINUOUS TIME

The above remarks deal with short intervals of time, yet time to solve a problem may be measured continuously. If the interval h is taken smaller and smaller, then the probability of solution within the interval h, φ (h), also decreases but the ratio $\psi(h)/h$ will (in any application of the present theory) approach a limit. Let

$$\lambda = \lim_{h \to 0} \left(\frac{\varphi(h)}{h} \right)$$

and it can be shown by standard methods that for a one-stage process, the density function describing the distribution of problem solving times is

$$f(t; \lambda) = \lambda e^{-\lambda t} \qquad [5]$$

the exponential distribution; and in the case of k equally difficult stages,

$$g(t; \lambda, k) = \frac{\lambda}{(k-1)!} e^{-\lambda t} (\lambda t)^{k-1} \qquad [6]$$

the gamma distribution. The mean and variance of the gamma distribution are

$$E(t) = k/\lambda = \mu \qquad [7]$$
$$\text{Var}(t) = k/\lambda^2 = \sigma^2 \qquad [8]$$

The exponential and gamma distributions are conceptually just like the geometric and Pascal distributions given above; in fact they are limits taken by going to continuous time (intervals of duration zero).

ESTIMATES OF PARAMETERS

A gamma distribution with parameter k (k stages) is the distribution of the sum of k exponentially distributed, independent, random variables. An exponentially distributed variable has mean equal to standard deviation, $\mu = \sigma = 1/\lambda$, from Equation 7 and 8. When one adds independent random variables, the mean of the sum is the sum of the means, and the variance of the sum is the sum of the variances. With more stages, accidental fluctuations tend to cancel out somewhat, so that the standard deviation becomes smaller relative to the mean, the more stages are involved. With increasing k, the gamma distribution becomes more nearly symmetrical, and narrower. This property can be used to estimate the parameter k. Note that from Equations 7 and 8,

$$\mu^2 = \frac{k^2}{\lambda^2}$$

and

$$\sigma^2 = \frac{k}{\lambda^2}$$

so that

$$\mu^2/\sigma^2 = k \qquad\qquad [9]$$

Given large samples of observations, it is possible to substitute the obtained mean and variance, $\bar{t}$ and s_t^2 for the parameters, obtaining the estimation equation

$$\hat{k} = (\bar{t})^2/s_t^2 \qquad\qquad [10]$$

The authors have used this estimate, an example of the method of moments, instead of possible maximum likelihood or minimum chi square estimates. The method-of-moments estimate seems relatively insensitive to imperfections in the experimental procedure, and its general significance remains sensible even if the actual stages of the problem are not exactly equal in difficulty. If the stages differ in difficulty, then $\hat{k}$ can be considered as follows; the actual problem is represented by a model problem with equally difficult and independent stages, and k is the number of stages in the model. The interpretation is like one common in information theory; if a certain system transmits just 3 bits, it can be represented by a system which perfectly discriminates exactly 8 equally probable signals. The value of 3 bits may actually be derived from a system which makes imperfect discriminations of 24 categories which are not equally probable, but the model gives a general impression of the behavior of the system. Similarly, our use of a gamma distribution gives a general impression of the number of stages in a problem, of its "complexity," without necessarily being correct about the detailed structure of the problem.

APPLICATION

Davis (1961) gave three problems to 178 undergraduates, and timed each subject on each problem. The order of the three problems was changed from subject to subject. A sizable fraction of the subjects arrived at wrong answers on some problems, and the wrong answers will be set aside; even if there are exactly k stages to solution of the problem, there is no assurance that it also takes k stages to arrive at a wrong answer.

On the basis of subsidiary measurements, a relatively constant "reading time" could be subtracted from the total time consumed on each problem. When this was done, means and standard deviations of net solution time were calculated on each of the three problems.

The first (Rope) problem described a prisoner attempting to escape from a tower, who found in his cell a rope which was half long enough to permit him to reach the ground safely. He divided the rope in half and tied the two parts together and escaped. How could this have been? The answer is that the rope is divided lengthwise. This problem was taken to be a "one-stage" problem in that the solution seems to depend on a single idea.

The net mean time was 131.3 seconds, the standard deviation was 115.5, whence the estimated number of stages is $(131.3)^2/(115.5)^2 = 1.3$ stages, not far from the one stage predicted. In fact, it is possible that the time taken to write the solution might produce the modest discrepancy.

The second (Word Tangle) problem was a more complex one: "If the puzzle you solved before you solved this one was harder than the puzzle you solved after you solved the puzzle you solved before you solved this one, was the puzzle you solved before you solved this one harder than this one?" Subjects were to answer yes or no and why. The answer (yes) requires canceling of several mutually defeating phrases. Net mean time was 264.8 seconds, with a standard deviation of 154.1, so that the estimate of k is 3.0 stages.

The third (Gold Dust) problem was a more complex version of the standard water-jug problem. Given containers of 163, 14, 25, and 11 ounces, obtain exactly 77. Solutions are to subtract, from 163, either $2(25) + 14 + 2(11)$, or $25 + 2(14) + 3(11)$, i.e., either five or six manipulations. The net mean time was 373.0 seconds, standard deviation 166.7, whence the estimated number of stages is $\hat{k} = 5.0$.

The estimates of number of stages of these problems seem, to the present writers, quite in accord with our intuitive judgments of number of stages. When a group of students, after having solved the problems, were asked to estimate the number of stages in the three problems, their mean judgments were 2.8, 4.0, and 6.3, respectively. These judgments are consistently higher than those obtained from the distributions of solution

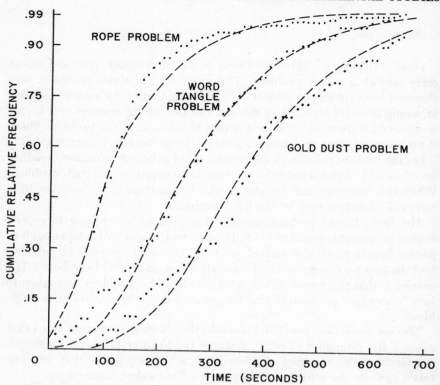

FIG. 1. Cumulative relative frequency of individual solvers and fitted gamma distributions with $k = 1.3$, 3.0, and 5.0 for Rope, Word Tangle, and Gold Dust Problems, respectively.

times, but the correlation is remarkable and indicates that our judgments as to the relative number of stages in the three problems agree in substance with judgments of student solvers.

In addition, it was found that the gamma distributions (Equation 6) give satisfactory fits to the obtained distributions of solution times on the three problems. The obtained cumulative distribution of time to correct solution of the three problems are shown in Figure 1, along with fitted gamma distributions. An investigation of overall goodness of fit of the theoretical gamma distribution was made separately for each problem, using the Kolgomorov-Smirnov one-sample test. The maximum discrepancies between theoretical and observed distributions were all well within the .05 acceptance region for all three problems.

MEANING OF THE MODEL FOR DISTRIBUTION OF SOLUTION TIMES

The model for the distribution of solution times assumes that the times subjects take to solve a problem vary widely because solving a problem involves having only one or a few ideas, in sequence; and the time to an idea is taken to be a random variable. [This seems a natural consequence of thinking of such a problem solving process as "insightful."] The detailed model includes other, less attractive, simplifying assumptions. One is that the stages of a problem are all equally difficult. Another is that the same parameter λ applies to all members of the population tested. These assumptions are probably wrong in detail, though small deviations may not be easily detectable from the kind of data we have used. It is emphasized that they are only simplifying assumptions which are made, in this model, because we were not able to separate and measure the stages of solution of the problems (because we did not, originally, know what they might be, and we are not sure now), and we did not have good individual differences predictors for our subjects.

POOLING OF ACCOMPLISHMENTS IN GROUPS

In the usual experiment on problem solving by groups, groups are better than individuals. If "Eureka" problems are used, the group is likely to solve successfully as soon as the first group member arrives at the correct solution. If it is assumed that group members are just as effective in groups as they would be working alone, then it is possible to predict group from individual performance, provided that individuals and members of group are sampled randomly from the same population of subjects, and groups are formed randomly.

The one model available for such predictions is by Lorge and Solomon (1955) who divide the population into "solvers" and "nonsolvers," use tests of individuals to estimate P_1 (the proportion of solvers among individuals) and then predict that the probability of finding at least one solver in a group of size r will be $P_r = 1 - (1 - P_I)^r$. Using this theory it is possible to transform the cumulative distribution of individual solvers, which gives P_I as a function of t, into a cumulative distribution for groups of size r, though Lorge and Solomon do not do so.

Lorge and Solomon also note that if a problem has more than one part or stage, it is possible that a group will solve it though no individual in the group can solve it. Different group members may be able to solve different parts, and then pool their abilities to obtain an emergent solution. If the abilities to solve the various parts are equally frequent in the population and are independent, this gives a decided extra advantage to groups.

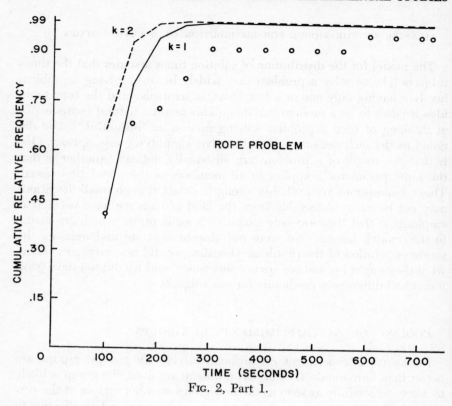

FIG. 2, Part 1.

FIG. 2. The solid and broken lines represent cumulative relative frequency at 50-second intervals, predicted by Lorge-Solomon Model ($k = 1$, $k = 2$, respectively) for groups of Size 4. (Observed group performance, for the same intervals, is given by solid points.)

With k equally probable stages the probability of a group solution with r people is:

$$P_r = [1 - (1 - P_I^{1/k})^r]^k \qquad [11]$$

Equation 11 also can be used to generate a distribution of group solution times given a distribution of individual solving times, for any given value of k.

The use of the waiting-time model for the distribution of solution-times yields an estimate of k for a problem, from the distribution of individual solution times. That estimate can be inserted for k in Equation 11, and group performance can be predicted from individual performance. Davis (1961) performed the appropriate experiment. In addition to the 178

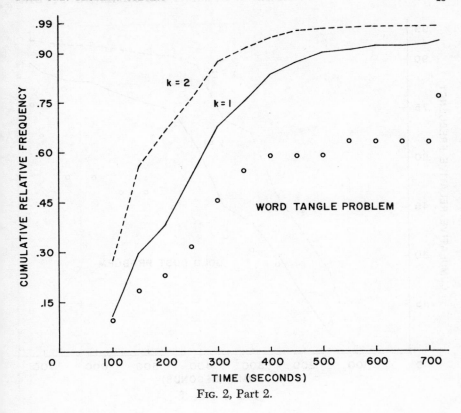

FIG. 2, Part 2.

individuals, he had 22 four-person groups work on his three problems. Recruitment of subjects, working conditions, instructions, etc., were closely comparable for individuals and groups. When Equation 11 is used to predict group from individual solution times, the results are very inaccurate. Figure 2 shows the predicted group performance (from Equation 11) and the obtained distributions on the Rope, Word Tangle, and Gold Dust problems for $k = 1$ and $k = 2$. The actual estimates of k were 1.3, 3.0, and 5.0, which would obviously give extremely inaccurate estimates.

However, deeper consideration shows that the Lorge-Solomon model is not the proper one to be used with the waiting-time model developed. Lorge and Solomon begin by dividing the population into solvers and nonsolvers. To obtain more complete predictions, we extended the idea to "solvers by time t" and "nonsolvers at time t," which seems a legitimate extension of the ideas of Lorge and Solomon. However, we earlier had generated the distributions of solution time from the assumption that solution was a random event, and all subjects had equal probability of solu-

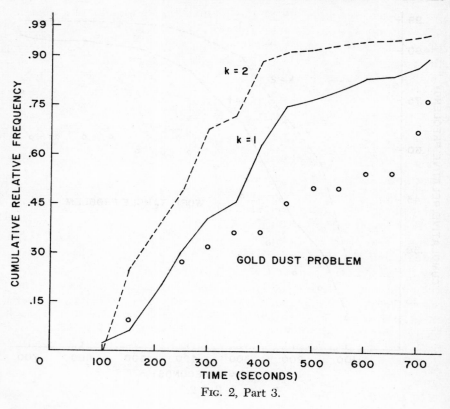

FIG. 2, Part 3.

tion in a given interval. The Lorge-Solomon model takes the individual performance as a fixed fact which identifies solvers and non-solvers, assumed to be individuals with different abilities. The random waiting-time model leads to a different, combination-of-*contributions* model.

COMBINATION OF CONTRIBUTIONS

Consider a group of subjects none of whom misinterprets the problem or arrives at a wrong solution. Suppose that for each subject the problem involves the same k stages each of which has an exponential distribution of time-to-completion of $\lambda e^{-\lambda t}$. With r subjects in a group, it can be shown that the distribution of group performance is given by the gamma distribution,

$$g(t; r\lambda, k) = \frac{r\lambda}{(k-1)!} e^{-r\lambda t}(r\lambda t)^{k-1} \qquad [12]$$

which is precisely the same gamma distribution derived for individual performance except that the rate (λ) is increased by a factor of r, the size of the group. Part of the proof is given. Within a short interval h, given that no one has solved a certain stage, the probability that some one in the group will solve is $1 - (1 - \Psi)^r$. As h is taken small, Ψ becomes small, in which case

$$1 - (1 - \Psi)^r = 1 - 1 + r\Psi - \binom{r}{2}\Psi^2 + \cdots \pm \binom{r}{r}\Psi^r$$

approaches $r\Psi$. The reason is that all terms involving Ψ^2, Ψ^3, etc., become relatively negligible when Ψ becomes small. Hence, in the limit, the distribution of time to a given stage approaches $r\lambda$.

This calculation provides a prediction of group problem solving if no subjects arrive at wrong solutions. Preliminary results of an experiment by R. Hoppe at Michigan State University [1] give some support for this model. Hoppe used Rokeach's (1960) "Doodlebug" problem and tested individuals, and groups of Size 2 and 3. In Hoppe's study the subjects could ask the experimenter questions and were, in the main, redirected when they had made a serious mistake, so that all subjects and groups either solved the problem correctly or ran out of time. The data were in agreement with the hypothesis that all time distributions were of the same shape (it is not possible to make a good test of the gamma distribution since a substantial proportion of subjects failed to finish) and that the rate of solution is roughly proportional to the number of people in the group.

In Davis' (1961) experiment the subjects received no redirection from the experimenter, and about half of the individuals arrived at wrong answers on the two harder problems (Word Tangle and Gold Dust). The effect of wrong answers in the group situation is not directly known, since observations did not enable the experimenter to tell which members of groups had solved the problem. However, two plausible hypotheses can be formulated, and they lead to two quite distinct predictions regarding group performance.

Hierarchical model. It is possible that subjects going "off the track," referred to here as nonsolvers, are nonfunctional in their groups. If so, a group with two solvers and two nonsolvers will solve the problem just as rapidly, on the average, as a group of two solvers alone. (It is assumed that in Eureka problems, groups will not agree on a wrong solution.) Nonsolvers would be nonfunctional if, for example, the solvers suppress nonsolvers and form an intellectual hierarchy within the group.

If a group of size r has A solvers and $B = r - A$ subjects who are nonsolvers, then by the Hierarchical model the distribution of time to solution should be gamma distribution, $g(t; A\lambda, k)$. If a proportion a of individual

---

[1] Ronald Hoppe, personal communication, 1961.

workers solve the problem, then the probability that a group of size r has exactly A members who will solve is

$$P(A) = \binom{r}{A} a^A (1 - a)^{r-A}, \qquad [13]$$

a binomial distribution.

The distribution of solution times of a collection of groups will then be described by the density function,

$$f_H(t) = \sum_{A=0}^{r} P(A)g(t; A\lambda, k) \qquad [14]$$

if the hierarchical model is correct.

Equalitarian model. Another possibility is that those subjects who go off the track, the nonsolvers, continue to take full part in group discussion though they do not arrive at solutions. This idea leads to the hypothesis that the nonsolvers would consume their share of the group's time, slowing up the other members of the group. This would mean that the probability that a solver in the group solves in unit time is reduced from λ to $[A/(A+B)]\lambda$, when there are A solvers and B nonsolvers present. The distribution of solution times for such a group is, by the argument leading to Equation 12,

$$g\left(t; A\,\frac{A}{A+B}\,\lambda, k\right) = g\left(t; \frac{A^2}{A+B}\,\lambda, k\right) \qquad [15]$$

Given that the probability of an individual's solving is a, the distribution of solution times of a collection of groups will be described by the density function,

$$f_E(t) = \sum_{A=0}^{r} \left[P(A)g\left(t; \frac{A^2}{A+B}\,\lambda, k\right) \right] \qquad [16]$$

if the equalitarian model is correct.

The evidence of Davis' (1961) experiment is that the hierarchical model is seriously in error, and the equalitarian model yields predictions which are quite close to the data, not seriously in error. The Kolgomorov-Smirnov one-sample test leads to rejection of the distribution calculated from the Hierarchical Model, for the word tangle and gold dust problems, at the .05 level of significance. The distribution derived from the Equalitarian Model is accepted at the .05 level for all three problems. Of course, with only 22 groups, the statistical acceptance is not decisive. Predictions from these two combination-of-contributions models, along with the distributions of group performance, are shown in Figure 3.

Subsidiary evidence in the form of sociometric choices and communication frequencies (Davis, 1961) was collected, and the results agree in substance with the assumption of an equalitarian group structure.

DISCUSSION

STRUCTURE OF PROBLEMS

The estimates of number of stages of the Rope, Word Tangle, and Gold Dust problems would be very impressive evidence, except that we have no strong independent measurement of the number of stages in such problems. The intentions and judgments are suggestive but not decisive. The number of stages in a problem is the number of distinct ideas required to obtain the solution. The number of stages is the number of ideas which must be conjoined to obtain the solution—the subject must have Idea 1 *and* Idea 2 *and* . . . , etc. If there were alternative answers, the subject could have Idea 1 *or* Idea 2 *or* . . . , and these would not be stages. This analysis makes it possible to compare stage-estimates from the data with the logical structure of the problems; and the agreement is good. Unfortunately, we are not sure how to identify "ideas" in the sense used above, hence the logical analysis is not sure of its elements.

What is needed, obviously, is an experimental separation of stages in problem solving. Hoppe's work, mentioned above, attempts such an analysis. A difficulty is that one can hardly separate the stages of a problem, experimentally, unless he knows what those stages are. Verbal protocols of problem solving process are useful for identifying parts, but they present difficulties of interpretation. The writers do not forsee any easy and immediate answer to the question of problem structure.

Stages versus parts. In the special model above it was assumed that the stages are to be accomplished in sequence. If there are simply k parts which must be accomplished, in any order, then the distribution of times may be changed. If the subject is thought to work on only one stage at a time, solving the stages in some irregular order, then the gamma distribution model applies. However, if ideas for different parts of the problem can arise freely and independently, a new distribution arises. Solution time of any part will be exponentially distributed, but until the subject has solved the first part there are k parts which may be solved. Hence the rate until the first part-solution is $k\lambda$. After one part is completed, there are $k-1$ parts left and the rate until the second part is $(k-1)\lambda$. Finally, when there is only one part left, the rate is λ. These "rates" can be defined as above if the distribution of times until the next stage is assumed to be exponential.[2]

---

[2] The writers are indebted to Herman Rubin for the formulation and solution of this mathematical problem.

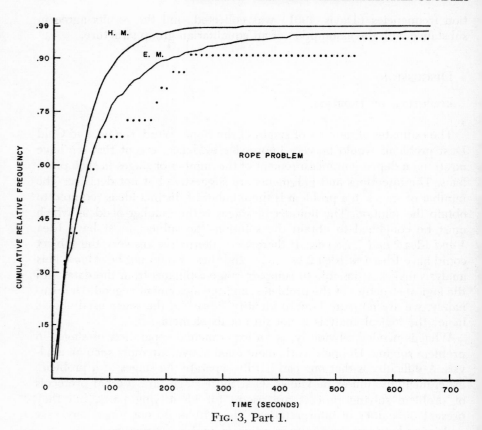

FIG. 3, Part 1.

FIG. 3. The solid lines represent cumulative relative frequency predicted by the Hierarchial and Equalitarian Models for groups of Size 4. (Observed group performance is given by solid points.)

The resulting distribution is rather complicated, but its mean and variance can be developed easily. Since the mean of each of the waiting times is independent of the others by hypothesis, the total mean is the sum of k waiting times with means $1/\lambda$, $1/(2\lambda)$, ..., $1/(k\lambda)$. Hence the mean total time to solution, $E(T)$, is

$$E(T) = (1/\lambda) \times (1 + 1/2 + 1/3 + \cdots + 1/k) \qquad [17]$$

By a similar argument, the variance of total times is

$$\mathrm{Var}(T) = (1/\lambda^2) \times [1 + (1/2)^2 + (1/3)^2 + \cdots + (1/k)^2] \qquad [18]$$

Table 1 shows how mean and standard deviation, and also the value

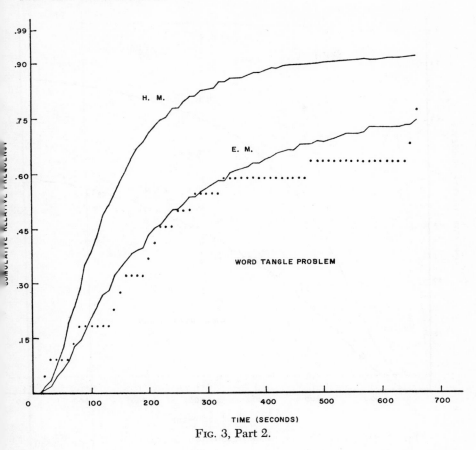

TIME (SECONDS)

FIG. 3, Part 2.

of μ^2/σ^2, progress with more and more parts. Comparable values for "stages," i.e., parts which must be solved in succession, are shown for contrast.

Possible effects of wrong solutions. The Equalitarian model for predicting group from individual performance was chosen because it seemed to take proper account of the fact that some subjects may arrive at wrong but self-satisfying answers. However, wrong solutions may distort the distribution of times to correct solution. In estimating the number of stages to solution and working out the waiting-time model, subjects who arrived at wrong solutions were eliminated from the data. This seems reasonable, for the number of stages to a wrong solution may be different from the number of stages to a correct solution. However, this conditional distribution of times (times to solution given that a correct solution is reached) may be misleading. The difficulty is that a subject who happens to take

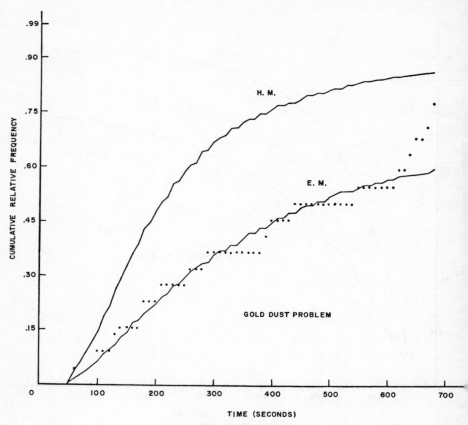

FIG. 3, Part 3.

a long time to get the correct answer has an increased vulnerability to error, whence long times to correct solution may be systematically less frequent when errors occur than they would be if the whole distribution were known.

The difficulties can be studied by investigating the properties of random systems with more than one outcome. The most general model available to the present writers is that proposed by LaBerge (1960)[3] which permits any of several responses which involve k_1, k_2 . . . stages respectively. La Berge derives the distribution of times to completion of the k_1 stages of Outcome 1 provided that Outcome 1 occurs.

One special model may be called the "misreading" model, in which it is supposed that the subject may, at the very beginning, make a choice which leads to a wrong solution. The subject either enters into a process

[3] LaBerge, D. A. A statistical theory of discrimination behavior. (Prepublication draft, December 1960.)

TABLE 1

SOME STATISTICS OF PROCESSES WITH PARTS
(Which May Be Solved Concurrently)
AND PROCESSES WITH STAGES
(Which Are Solved Successively)

Number of parts or stages	$\mu\lambda$		$\sigma\lambda$		μ^2/σ^2	
	Parts	Stages	Parts	Stages	Parts	Stages
1	1.00	1.00	1.000	1.000	1.000	1.00
2	1.50	2.00	1.108	1.414	1.800	2.00
3	1.83	3.00	1.117	1.731	2.469	3.00
4	2.08	4.00	1.119	2.000	3.049	4.00
5	2.28	5.00	1.210	2.238	3.562	5.00
6	2.45	6.00	1.221	2.452	4.025	6.00
7	2.59	7.00	1.229	2.642	4.447	7.00
8	2.72	8.00	1.236	2.828	4.836	8.00
9	2.83	9.00	1.241	3.000	5.198	9.00
10	2.93	10.00	1.245	3.161	5.536	10.00

which leads to success (with the gamma distribution of Equation 8), or onto some other which leads to failure. The conditional distribution of times to correct solution, given that a correct solution and not an error is attained, is the original gamma distribution.

A third possibility is that the subject may at any time before solution make a decision which leads to a wrong answer. Consider that this wrong decision is a unitary event which has a constant probability of happening at any time, given it has not already happened, up until the problem is solved. Then the accidental event will have an exponential distribution. The density (probability per time interval) of solution of the problem will be the product of the original gamma density, $g(t; \lambda, k)$ and the probability that the accidental event has not occurred. If the constant probability-per-unit-time or rate of the accidental event is α, the probability that it has not occurred by time t (provided the problem is not solved before t) is $e^{-\alpha t}$. The conditional density of solution at time t, given that a correct solution is attained, is

$$f(t; \lambda, \alpha, k) = \frac{g(t; \lambda, k)e^{-\alpha t}}{\int_0^\infty g(t; \lambda, k)e^{-\alpha t}\, dt} \qquad [19]$$

$$= \frac{\dfrac{\lambda}{(k-1)!}\, e^{-(\lambda+\alpha)t}(\lambda t)^{k-1}}{\int_0^\infty \dfrac{\lambda}{(k-1!)}\, e^{-(\lambda+\alpha)t}(\lambda t)^{k-1}\, dt} \qquad [20]$$

The numerator is simply

$$g(t; \lambda + \alpha, k) \left(\frac{\lambda}{\lambda + \alpha}\right)^k \qquad [21]$$

and the denominator is

$$\left(\frac{\lambda}{\lambda + \alpha}\right)^k \int_0^\infty g(t; \lambda + \alpha, k)\, dt = \left(\frac{\lambda}{\lambda + \alpha}\right)^k \qquad [22]$$

The step from Equation 20 to Equation 21 is accomplished by noting that $g(t; \lambda + \alpha, k)$

$$= \frac{\lambda + \alpha}{(k-1)!} e^{-(\lambda+\alpha)t}[(\lambda + \alpha)t]^{k-1}$$
$$= (\lambda + \alpha)^k e^{-(\lambda+\alpha)t} t^{k-1}$$

If this is multiplied by $[\lambda/(\lambda + a]^k$ one obtains the numerator of Equation 20.

Hence the conditional distribution of solution times is

$$f(t; \lambda, \alpha, k) = g(t; \lambda + \alpha, k) \qquad [23]$$

a gamma distribution with the original number of stages, k, but with rate increased to $\lambda + a$. The probability of a correct solution is $[\lambda/(\lambda + a)]^k$.

In summary, three effects of wrong solutions were mentioned; they might distort the distribution from a gamma to some other distribution (if the subject works concurrently on stages of several different processes leading to several answers), it might leave the conditional distribution of solution times unchanged (if errors arise only through an initial wrong decision such as misreading the problem), or it might leave the conditional distribution a gamma, still with k stages, but increase the rate of solutions, if entry onto an erroneous path is thought of as a unitary random event.) Of these, the third seems most in accord with the problem solving situation in Davis' (1961) experiment.

Unhappily, we do not have the data needed to decide which of these possibilities, if any, occurred in the Davis (1961) experiment. As we understand it, the LaBerge formulation could be fit to the data exactly only if we knew what all the wrong solutions were and could estimate the number of stages and the rate parameters of each. Davis' experiment was not designed to facilitate such an investigation, and the necessary analysis is not feasible. Since LaBerge's model involves parameters we cannot estimate, it cannot be compared with the other models validly. The misreading model and the accidental event model do not require analysis of the inner structure of erroneous solutions, hence can be applied to the present data. Since both lead to gamma distributions of correct solution, both agree with Davis' results. Only a detailed qualitative analysis of protocols, or a technique for eliminating wrong solutions without otherwise disturbing performance, would indicate which model is correct. In fact, some subjects might misread and others err through an accidental random event, and the conditional distribution of correct solution time would still be a gamma distribution.

This theoretical result increases the plausibility of the gamma distribution as an hypothesis by showing that it might, under reasonable conditions, characterize data from problems with quite different frequencies of wrong solution.

OTHER MODELS FOR OTHER KINDS OF GROUPS

The predictions of group performance in Davis' experiment were for ad hoc groups of equivalent members, with no discernible social inequalities. Furthermore, the nature of the problems was such that ideas were pooled with little controversy over the correctness of a correct proposal. In a "team" it sometimes happens that all members must solve their parts of the problem before the group succeeds. Then the probability of group solution is the joint probability that all members have completed their tasks by time t. If the individual assignments are unitary problems with the same difficulty, and all members of the group can work concurrently (as in servicing an automobile) then the model leading to Equation 17 and 18 should describe the situation. If one stage of the process must wait upon completion of another stage, then combining the individual contributions can lead to a gamma distribution. If solution of the problem is mainly a matter of decision rather than invention, then the probability of decision by time t may be the probability that all group members accept the same idea at that time. Changes of opinion, persuasion, and the invention of compromises are the events of primary interest, and the main results of the present paper do not apply.

These remarks emphasize that the mathematical theory used in this paper is not a general theory of group problem solving, but is a careful and precise formulation of some hypotheses about one particular kind of group problem solving. The hypotheses depend both upon the constitution of the groups and the nature of the problems.

RELATION TO OTHER AREAS OF PSYCHOLOGY

The mathematical forms discussed in this paper have applications elsewhere in psychology. The notion that an individual stage of problem solving will have an exponential distribution of solution time, is essentially the same as the hypothesis that a unitary learning event will occur on a geometrically distributed trial. Both arise from the statement that the event has constant probability of occurring, until it does occur. In learning theory, this is the hypothesis of "all-or-nothing" learning (Bower, 1962; Estes, 1960; Restle, 1961b, 1962). A truly unitary process, indivisible and independent of other processes, should have a constant probability of occurrence. If an event is not unitary but a compound, then every effort should be made to tease apart the stages involved in it. Hence the geometric and exponential distributions (for trials and continuous time, respectively) give a theory for any event which can properly be left unanalyzed.

The only compounds which do not require detailed analysis into parts are those made up of equivalent parts. A beam of light can be thought of as a compound of unitary emissions of photons, but the only interesting question about such a beam is the number of photons, since separate photons are all alike. Thus, an ideal compound event must be one made up of equivalent, identically distributed parts. The gamma distribution describes compounds of the type used in this paper. Previous applications of gamma distributions include Bush and Mosteller (1955, Ch. 14) on the time rats take to traverse a runway, and Restle (1961a) on simple reaction time.

Similarly, the simplest kind of model for comparing group with individual performance is one which assumes that people in a group are, in all ways possible, just like people working alone. In a nonevaluative sense one can say that the Lorge-Solomon models, and the variations given in the present paper, are all versions of this ideal hypothesis.

Any deviations between model and data suggest the actions of factors more complex (and perhaps more interesting) than the very simplest possibilities discussed here. For example, since Davis' groups did not reach the level predicted by Lorge-Solomon models, it became possible to introduce the hypothesis that individuals who have entered on a wrong interpretation of the problem take up their share of group time and interfere with the progress of others. Discrepancy from one model became a measurement of a previously unmeasured factor.

Summary

A waiting-time model was developed to give a distribution of times to solution, for word puzzles. The distribution depends upon the number of stages involved in solving the problem. Experimental results showed that the theoretical distribution (gamma distribution) gives a good fit to the data, and the estimated number of stages agrees well with intuition and judgments. A theory of "pooling of contributions" was developed to describe the superiority of groups over individuals in solving word puzzles. Experimental results suggested that subjects who have misunderstood the problem and will arrive at wrong answers, nevertheless consume their share of group time. With this addition, the pooling of contributions theory accurately predicts group problem solving data. Some alternative models, resulting from different problem structures and different kinds of groups, were discussed, and the waiting-time theory was shown to be related to the concept of "all-or-nothing" learning.

REFERENCES

BOWER, G. H. An association model for response and training variables in paired associate learning. *Psychol. Rev.*, 1962, 69, 34–53.

BUSH, R. R., & MOSTELLER, F. *Stochastic models for learning.* New York: Wiley, 1955.

DAVIS, J. H. Models for the classification of problems and the prediction of group problem-solving from individual results. Unpublished doctoral dissertation, Michigan State University, 1961.

ESTES, W. K. Learning theory and the new "mental chemistry." *Psychol. Rev.*, 1960, 67, 207–223.

FAUST, W. L. Group versus individual problem solving. *J. abnorm. soc. Psychol.*, 1959, 59, 68–72.

FELLER, W. *Introduction to probability theory and its applications.* New York: Wiley, 1957.

HUSBAND, R. W. Cooperative versus solitary problem solution. *J. soc. Psychol.*, 1940, 11, 405–409.

LORGE, I., FOX, D., DAVITZ, J., & BRENNER, M. A survey of studies contrasting the quality of group performance and individual performance, 1920–1957. *Psychol. Bull.*, 1958, 55, 337–372.

LORGE, I., & SOLOMON, H. Two models of group behavior in the solution of eureka-type problems. *Psychometrika*, 1955, 20, 139–148.

MARQUART, DOROTHY I. Group problem solving. *J. soc. Psychol.*, 1955, 41, 103–113.

RESTLE, F. *Psychology of judgment and choice.* New York: Wiley, 1961. (a)

RESTLE, F. Statistical methods for a theory of cue learning. *Psychometrika*, 1961, 26, 291–306. (b)

RESTLE, F. The selection of strategies in cue learning. *Psychol. Rev.*, 1962, 69, 329–343.

ROKEACH, M. *The open and closed mind.* New York: Basic Books, 1960.

SHAW, MARJORIE E. Comparison of individuals and small groups in the rational solution of complex problems. *Amer. J. Psychol.*, 1932, 44, 491–504.

TAYLOR, D. W., & FAUST, W. L. Twenty questions: Efficiency in problem solving as a function of size of group. *J. exp. Psychol.*, 1952, 44, 360–368.
THORNDIKE, R. L. On what type of task will a group do well? *J. abnorm. soc. Psychol.*, 1938, 33, 408–412.
WATSON, G. B. Do groups think more efficiently than individuals? *J. abnorm. soc. Psychol.*, 1928, 23, 328–336.

SECTION TWO

Set

If a subject has a tendency to respond to a problem with some response that is not the solution response, he is said to have a wrong set. Sets can also be facilitating. Typically, two tasks, viz, anagrams and water jars (arithmetic) problems have been used to study what is sometimes called simple set in problem solving. The Maltzman and Morrisett paper is one of a series by these authors in which both facilitating and interfering effects of set in anagram solving were shown to be functions of both instructional conditions and training procedures.

The Gardner and Runquist study with water jars takes somewhat the same learning approach to set as do Maltzman and Morrisett. Set with water jars has also been studied systematically, primarily by Luchins; see in particular the book: Luchins, A. S. and Luchins, E. H. *Rigidity of Behavior*. Eugene: University of Oregon Press, 1959.

Set also appears in the form called functional fixedness. The task employed is some instrumental problem which can be solved only by using a familiar object in an unfamiliar way. Wrong set as functional fixedness is induced prior to the problem by having subjects use the problem-relevant object in its common use.

The Adamson and Taylor paper is included chiefly because of their first experiment, showing that functional fixedness decreases with time. However, it is worth noting that in their second experiment, the water jars series used is more typical of Luchins' approach to set than is the Gardner and Runquist study.

Functional fixedness also appears to vary with drive level. In Glucksberg's study, different strengths of functional fixedness were first produced by variations in the appearance of the problem object. Then when incentive was increased, already-strong functional fixedness became, relatively, even stronger.

4. Effects of Task Instructions on Solution of Different Classes of Anagrams

Irving Maltzman and Lloyd Morrisett, Jr.

Previous experiments by the writers have explored implications of Hull's principle of habit strength and related corollaries for directed thinking (5, 6). The conditions under which habit strength plays a differential role in determining the direction of thinking are characteristic of those described as mental set. However, numerous experiments have shown that the course of thinking may be directed under conditions other than those producing the growth of habit strength (4). In particular, the instructions or task given S may have such an influence. According to the present formulation these conditions may give rise to a nonassociative factor contributing to the effective reaction potential determining the problem-solving behavior.

Rees and Israel (7) attempted to study the effects of task instructions on the solution of different five-letter anagrams. However, their study involved possible differences in training effects as well as the difference in instructions administered to experimental and control groups.

Although it does not appear possible to determine directly the effects of task instructions as distinguished from training in a problem-solving situation, this may be done indirectly. If the effects of task instructions plus training on set solutions are determined, and the effects of training alone are also observed, the approximate effects of instructions alone may be inferred. In an experimental study of this nature it would also be desirable to precede the set test trials by a training session so that increments in habit strength occurring during the test session would be relatively small.

The purpose of the present experiment was to determine the effects of task instructions upon the percentage of set solutions for different classes of anagrams by this indirect procedure, and to study the summation of the effects of training and task instructions.

Reprinted by permission of the authors and the American Psychological Association from *Journal of Experimental Psychology*, 1945, *45*, 351–354.

METHOD

Subjects.—Fifty volunteers from introductory psychology classes served as Ss in the experiment. There were ten Ss in each of the five experimental conditions.

Procedure.—The training series for all conditions consisted of 20 five-letter anagrams having only one word as a solution which were typed in lower case on 3 × 5-in. index cards. A test series followed of 15 five-letter anagrams possessing several different words as solutions. Only one of the alternative solutions was a set solution related to the given class of training anagrams.

In the nature-training or N condition the solution of each of the anagrams in the training series was a word referring to some aspect of nature, for example, "fruit." The test anagrams had one solution referring to some aspect of nature and at least one other solution not directly or obviously related to nature. For example, the words "peach" or "cheap" would be solutions for the same anagram, but only the former would be a set solution. An attempt was made to increase the homogeneity of the nature class, and thereby avoid the development of competing sets (6), by employing only anagrams referring to plants and their habitat. The different anagrams in this condition were in no consistent letter order or arrangement.

A second condition was the order-training or O condition. The training anagrams in this condition had only one possible solution and all were in the same letter order, 32145. The third letter in the word was the first in the anagram, and so on. The anagrams were not consistently related to each other in any other obvious manner. Anagrams in the test series all had multiple solutions one of which was in the 32145 letter order.

A third condition was the nature-instructions or NI condition. Anagrams in the training and test series were the same as those in the nature-training condition. This condition differed from the N condition only in the addition of special instructions. The fourth condition was the order-instructions or OI condition. It differed from the O condition only in the instructions administered. These four conditions formed a 2 × 2 factorial design.

A fifth condition was employed which was the compound of the first two conditions, order- and nature-training. Anagrams in the training and test series were the same as those in the N condition. In addition they were in the letter order of the O condition for the training series. In the test series the nature-word solution was in the 32145 letter order. The alternative solutions in the test series were in no consistent letter order.

Words used to form anagrams for the different conditions are shown in Table 1. Most of the words were obtained from lists used by Rees and Israel (8). A 2-min. time limit was enforced for each anagram in the training and test series of all conditions. During the training series, if S failed

TABLE 1

Words Employed as Anagrams
Practice: brick, chair, erase

Nature Training				Order Training			
peony	birch	plant	ferns	child	cigar	comes	cream
lotus	herbs	fruit	tulip	fresh	cards	waken	house
lawns	grape	pansy	hedge	towel	mouth	write	uncle
grain	prune	phlox	stems	dozen	lends	scarf	lunch
bough	daisy	beans	onion	hands	learn	party	match

Nature Test	Order Test
aster, stares, tears, rates, tares	cause, sauce
range, anger	least, steal, stale, tales, slate
plums, slump, lumps	march, charm
peach, cheap	satin, stain, saint
pears, spear, pares, rapes, spare,	baker, break, brake
parse, spear, reaps	board, broad
petal, leapt, pleat, plate	broth, throb
thorn, north	teach, cheat
stalk, talks	trace, crate
cedar, cared, raced	gates, stage
palms, lamps	sword, words
pines, spine, penis, snipe	lamed, medal
straw, warts, swart	waits, waist
dates, stead	wrote, tower
weeds, sewed	worth, throw
trees, steer, terse, reset	

to obtain a correct solution in the allotted time, or gave an incorrect solution, E gave the correct solution. This correction technique was not employed during the test series. If S did not solve a test anagram within the allotted time or gave an incorrect solution, E presented another anagram without comment. Three practice anagrams were presented prior to the start of the experiment. They were in random letter orders and were not directly related to the class of nature anagrams. Instructions to the different groups were as follows: "This is an experiment on thinking. We want to find out how anagrams are solved. The results will in no way affect your class grades. You are to solve the five-letter anagrams that I will present to you as quickly as possible. A five-letter anagram is simply five scrambled letters. Your solution must use all the letters, that is, it must be a real five-letter word. It must not be a proper noun or slang. As soon as you have the answer, call it out to me and I will give you another to solve, but be sure your word fits the five letters before you name it. If you can't find a solution within two minutes, we will go on to another. Here is an example. What word can you make out of these five letters: c-i-k-b-r? The solution is brick. Now solve this one . . . and now this one. . . . Are there any questions? Do not ask any questions once the experiment has begun. Remember, call out your answer as soon as you find one."

After the presentation of the three practice anagrams, condition NI received the following additional task instructions: "During the experiment it will help you to look for words referring to flowers, growing things or their habitat. If you find some other solution you will also be credited with a correct answer."

Condition OI received the following task instructions after presentation of the practice anagrams: "During the experiment it will help you to look for a particular letter order. If you find some other solution you will also be credited with a correct answer."

RESULTS AND DISCUSSION

The mean percentages of set solutions in the test series obtained under the first four experimental conditions are presented in Table 2. Bartlett's test of homogeneity gave a chi square of 1.45, $df = 3$, $p < .50$. The results of the analysis of variance of these four conditions are summarized in Table 3. The main effects of instructions and anagram class were significant beyond the .05 and .01 levels of confidence, respectively. The latter findings is in accord with the results of a previous study of the writers (6). The interaction of anagram class and instructions was not significant. Thus the results indicate that task instructions may produce a significant increase in the percentage of set solutions independently of training effects.

The task instructions produced an increase of 6% in the nature condition and 12.7% in the order condition. These increases due to instructions are considerably less than the increments reported by Rees and Israel (7), indicating that the latter study may have confounded training and instruction effects.

The percentage of set solutions obtained in Cond. ON was 85.3, $s^2 = 225.6$. The significance of the difference between Cond. ON and N was tested by means of the t test, giving a t of 5.25, $df = 18$, $p < .01$. A comparison of Cond. ON and O yielded a t of 3.30, $df = 18$, $p < .01$. The letter t is greater than that obtained in a previous study, (6).[1]

A comparison of Cond. ON with Cond. OI and NI would indicate the relative effects of the summation of two habit structures in Cond. ON with the summation of associative and non-associative factors in Cond. OI and

---

[1] The percentages of set solutions obtained in Cond. ON, O, and N were substituted in Hull's shrinkage index (2, 6). The index was 85.3/63.3 + 54.7 = 72.3. This value of the index is slightly higher than that previously obtained (6).

TABLE 2

MEAN PERCENTAGE OF SET SOLUTIONS FOR DIFFERENT CLASSES
OF ANAGRAMS AND INSTRUCTIONS

Measure	Training		Task Instructions	
	Nature (N)	Order (O)	Nature (NI)	Order (OI)
Mean	54.7	63.3	60.7	76.0
S^2	106.9	219.7	162.3	219.2

TABLE 3

ANALYSIS OF VARIANCE OF SET SOLUTIONS

Source	df	Mean Square	F
Anagram class	1	1441.20	8.14**
Instructions	1	871.43	4.92*
Interaction	1	111.89	
Within groups	36	177.04	
Total	39		

* Significant at the .05 level.
** Significant at the .01 level.

ON. The comparison of Cond. ON and OI gave a t of 1.39, $df = 18$, $p = .20$. The comparison of Cond. ON and NI gave a t of 3.97, $df = 18$, $p < .01$.

According to Hull (2, 3) habit strength is a function of the number of reinforcements, and possibly other variables. Habit strength is the associative factor determining performance and has the characteristic of a state variable. It persists relatively unchanged with the passage of time. The present S-R formulation assumes that the phenomena described as mental set in directed thinking can be accounted for by the principle of habit strength and related corollaries in Hull's theory of behavior. However, the direction of thinking may be influenced by variables other than those producing habit strength. This study has demonstrated that task instructions may increase significantly the percentage of set solutions independently of the effects of training. This increase is assumed to be due to an increased amount of reaction potential produced by increments contributed by a nonassociative factor. In classical psychology this factor was the determining tendency or the Aufgabe (4). An analogous concept in Hull's theory of behavior is that of the fractional anticipatory goal response (1). On the basis of the present study, however, it is not possible to determine the characteristics of this nonassociative variable, or how it may be related to other intervening variables in Hull's theory. These are all problems of future research.

SUMMARY

It was found that both instructions and anagram class significantly influenced the percentage of set solutions. The summation of order and nature classes of anagrams produced significantly more set solutions than either component class. The summation of order and nature produced significantly more set solutions than the summation of nature and task instructions but not order and task instructions.

The results of the experiment were discussed in terms of Hull's theory of behavior.

REFERENCES

1. HULL, C. L. Goal attraction and directing ideas conceived as a habit phenomena. *Psychol. Rev.*, 1931, 38, 487–506.
2. HULL, C. L. *Principles of behavior*. New York: D. Appleton-Century, 1943.
3. HULL, C. L. *Essentials of behavior*. New Haven: Yale Univer. Press, 1951.
4. HUMPHREY, G. *Thinking*. New York: Wiley, 1951.
5. MALTZMAN, I., & MORRISETT, L., JR. Different strengths of set in the solution of anagrams. *J. exp. Psychol.*, 1952, 44, 242–246.
6. MALTZMAN, I., & MORRISETT, L., JR. The effects of single and compound classes of anagrams on set solutions. *J. exp. Psychol.*, 1953, 45, 345–350.
7. REES, H., & ISRAEL, H. An investigation of the establishment and operation of mental sets. *Psychol. Monogr.*, 1935, 46, No. 6 (Whole No. 210).

5. Acquisition and Extinction of Problem-Solving Set

R. Allen Gardner and Willard N. Runquist

The behavioral changes commonly observed in reasoning or problem solving have much in common with those observed in simple associative learning. No experiment or series of experiments can exclude entirely the possibility that qualitatively different processes, such as insight or mental set, distinguish reasoning or problem solving from other classes of behavior. Nevertheless, it is possible to demonstrate the logical and descriptive advantages of analyzing problem-solving behavior by the paradigms of simple associative learning. The experiment described here represents an attempt at such a demonstration.

The Water-Jar Problem, which has been described in detail elsewhere (2, 3), was selected as a convenient means of studying typical human problem-solving behavior. Briefly, it is a simple arithmetic problem involving three jars each with a different maximum volume. The task consists of measuring out a required fourth volume by suitable manipulation of the three known volumes. It is possible to construct a series of different problems all of which can be presented in the same form and can be solved by the same steps. Let these steps be called Solution A. If S is required to solve a series of problems, which can be solved only by Solution A, then his performance would be expected to improve with each succeeding problem as in the acquisition of other instrumental responses. Similarly, if acquisition of Solution A is followed by extinction to a given criterion, then resistance to extinction would be expected to vary directly with the number of acquisition problems solved. Such an extinction criterion could be provided by a problem of the same kind which could be solved only by a Solution B which is incompatible with Solution A. Assuming that Solution A must be extinguished to some specific level before Solution B is attempted, the time required by S to solve a Solution B problem will depend upon the acquisition level of Solution A. Thus, resistance to extinction of Solution A can be measured by performance on a Solution B problem.

Such an analysis of problem-solving set in terms of competing responses is unequivocal in its predictions and economical in its assumptions. It enables the incorporation of problem-solving behavior into a larger body of information. In addition, its assumptions can be made explicit and subjected to direct test. For example, if it is correct to assume that S must extinguish Solution A to a given criterion level before he can solve a So-

Reprinted by permission of the authors and the American Psychological Association from *Journal of Experimental Psychology*, 1958, 55, 274–277.

lution B problem, then it follows that groups which were at different pre-extinction Solution A performance levels will be equated by forcing them to solve a single Solution B problem. That is, regardless of the differences in Solution A performance created by solving different numbers of Solution A problems, performance on a postextinction Solution A problem will be equal.

Three consequences of the thesis that Water-Jar Problem behavior conforms to a paradigm of simple associative learning can now be stated: (*a*) During acquisition, the time required to solve a problem by a given solution, A, will vary inversely with the number of problems previously solved by Solution A. (*b*) During extinction, the time required to solve a problem by a given solution, B, incompatible with Solution A, will vary directly with the number of problems previously solved by Solution A. (*c*) After extinction to a criterion of one problem solved by Solution B, the time required to solve a Solution A problem will be independent of the number of Solution A problems solved during acquisition.

METHOD

Problem materials.—Each Water-Jar problem used in this experiment could be solved by only one of two solutions corresponding to Solution A and Solution B in the above discussion. Solution A required filling the largest jar and emptying once into the second largest jar and twice into the smallest jar. It is referred to elsewhere (1, 2, 3) as the *b-a-2c* solution, the Einstellung solution, or the indirect solution. Solution B required filling the second largest jar and emptying it once into the smallest jar. It has been referred to as the *a-c* solution or the direct solution.

Procedure.—Undergraduates enrolled in introductory psychology courses at Northwestern University served as Ss in this experiment. No S served in more than one condition. Each S was tested individually seated at a table facing E. The problems were presented one at a time on 3 × 5-in. cards. Each card bore three numbers labeled A, B, and C representing the given jar volumes, and a fourth number labeled X representing the volume to be obtained. A supply of scrap paper was provided for preliminary calculations and S indicated each solution by writing it on a separate page of a special pad. Both the problem card and the final solution were removed by E after S produced a correct solution. Time to solve was measured from the presentation of the problem card by E to the completion of the correct solution on the special pad by S. Instructions included four practice problems whose solutions were demonstrated by E. Among the practice problems were one example of Solution A and one of Solution B. Instructions also included the information that performance would be timed and urged S to work as quickly as possible. If S gave evidence of not understanding the instructions within the first 2 min. of work on the first problem, the instructions were repeated and the trial was started again.

Experimental conditions.—There were three experimental groups of 36 Ss each. They received a training series of 6, 11, or 21 Solution A problems, followed by an extinction test which consisted of one Solution B problem. This was followed by a postextinction test which consisted of one Solution A problem. The last training problem, i.e., Problem 6, 11, or 21, was designated as the pre-extinction test. The same two Solution A problems were used for the pre- and postextinction tests. Half of each group received one of these as a pre-extinction test and the other as a postextinction test while this order was reversed for the other half. There were 22 Solution A problems in all. Two of these served as pre- and postextinction problems in the manner described above. The remaining 20 problems were divided into four blocks of five problems. Each block was used as training for an equal number of 6-problem Ss. For the 11- and 21-problem groups, the blocks were counterbalanced so that each block appeared equally often as the first or last block of training problems. The same Solution B problem was used as the extinction test for all Ss.

Controls.—There were two control experiments, a Forgetting Control and a Practice Control. The Forgetting Control consisted of two replications of the experimental conditions with 12 Ss in a group and one alteration in procedure. In place of the extinction problem, these groups were given cartoon books to read between the pre-extinction test and the postextinction test problems (in this case, the pre- and postforgetting problems). One replication read cartoon books for 5 min. and the other for 10 min. The Practice Control consisted of one replication of the 6- and 11-problem conditions with 36 Ss in a group, and the following alteration in procedure. These groups were practiced on several simple addition and subtraction problems prior to the training problems in an attempt to compensate for the extra arithmetic practice of the 21-problem group. The 6-problem group was given 45 of these problems, and the 11-problem group, 30. This equalized the actual number of addition and subtraction operations which each S had made at the end of the training series.

Results

The time to solve for each problem was recorded to the nearest .1 sec. In order to normalize the highly skewed distributions, raw scores were converted to logarithms. The mean log time to solve for the pre-extinction, extinction, and postextinction tests is plotted for all three groups in Fig. 1. A separate analysis of variance was performed on the log scores for each of the three test problems. For the pre-extinction test, F was 23.33 and for the extinction test F was 5.52. Both are significant with

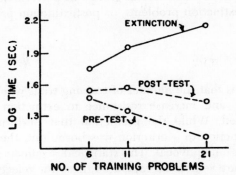

FIG. 1. Mean log time to solve the three test problems as a function of the number of acquisition problems.

$P < .01$ for 2 and 105 df. For the postextinction test F was 2.51, which is not significant ($P = .10$).

The Forgetting Control experiment yielded a measure of the loss in Solution A performance which might be attributed to the time intervening between the pre-extinction test and the postextinction test at the three acquisition levels. The differences were obtained by subtracting time to solve for the pretest from time to solve for the posttest. The raw difference scores were then converted to logarithms for analysis. The means of these log scores appear in Table 1. None of these mean differences is significantly different from zero. The largest t was 1.39 for the 11-problem, 5-min. interval group. Moreover, analysis of variance yielded F's of less than 1.00 for time interval, number of training problems, and interaction. Thus it would seem unreasonable to attribute any significant amount of the post-extinction losses of the experimental groups to the time intervening between the pre-extinction test and the post-extinction test.

The Practice Control also yielded negative results. After equalizing pretraining practice in arithmetic, these groups were indistinguishable

TABLE 1

MEAN LOG LOSS (SEC.) FOR GROUPS GIVEN NO
EXTINCTION PROBLEMS

| Number of | Time Interval (min.) | |
Problems	5	10
6	− .203	.387
11	.490	.009
21	.256	.329

from the comparable experimental groups in performance on pre-extinction problems, extinction problems, or postextinction problems.

DISCUSSION

The predictions that the number of training trials would improve training performance and increase resistance to extinction both seem adequately confirmed. While the prediction that performance would be equated by extinction to a criterion was borne out, the confirming data is somewhat less unequivocal. The statistical arguments for accepting a null hypothesis are seldom as cogent as those for rejecting one, and this prediction must be confirmed by accepting a null hypothesis. Furthermore, the F value did approach significance, and the most deviant point was the superior performance of the 21-problem group which is the one that would be expected to be superior on a common-sense basis in the absence of any specific hypothesis. At the same time, this prediction is more crucial to the theoretical argument in the sense that it is the one least likely to be arrived at by extrapolation of other data or alternative paradigms of problem-solving behavior. Also, it represents an internal check upon the assumption which permits us to use the Solution B problem performance as a measure of extinction to a criterion. The conclusion that extinction to a criterion equated performance is supported by these data more than any other conclusion. The present authors can only suggest further experimentation which provides data for points from 11 problems to 21 problems and beyond in order to determine the stability of the weak trend shown in these data.

There is very little data in the literature of suitable design and technique to offer results comparable to those presented here. The results of an unpublished experiment performed by R. P. Youtz at Barnard College have been made available to the authors by personal communication. As in the present experiment, each problem had only one solution and time to solve was the response measure. Youtz presented 5, 10, 20, and 40 Solution A problems and followed these with 10 Solution B problems. He reports that performance on the first Solution B problem differed significantly while performance on the second and all subsequent Solution B problems did not. This could indicate that all, or nearly all, of the differential extinction of Solution A takes place during the first Solution B trial which would be in accord with the interpretation presented here.

Kendler, Greenberg, and Richman (1) present an analysis of the Water-Jar Problem behavior and supporting data which suggests that the greater part of problem-solving behavior consists of weakening or extinguishing alternative responses which are incompatible with a required solution. This would seem to agree with the data presented here.

Please pass

Christine Taylor

to Attendance

Office

2-4-74
8:45

M. Cuzzo

Teacher's Daily Attendance Report

CLASS		BOYS	GIRLS	CHECK ONE

PUPILS	Cl. No.	1 2 3 4 5 6 7 8	TEACHER

1
2
3
4
5
6
7
8

Reg. Tr.   Date   Captain

SUMMARY

Three groups ($N = 36$) were trained on 5, 10, or 20 Water-Jar problems which required the same solution. They were then given a pre-extinction test which consisted of one more problem requiring the same solution, an extinction test which consisted of one problem which required a new solution incompatible with the first solution, and a postextinction test which consisted of still another problem which required the first solution.

The results were: (a) Performance on the pre-extinction test was a positive function of the number of training problems ($P < .01$). (b) Performance on the extinction test was a negative function of the number of training problems ($P < .01$). (c) Performance on the postextinction test was not demonstrably unequal for the three groups ($P = .10$). (d) Controls for differential forgetting effects and differential practice effects yielded negative results.

REFERENCES

1. KENDLER, H. H., GREENBERG, A., & RICHMAN, H. The influence of massed and distributed practice on the development of mental set. *J. exp. Psychol.*, 1952, 43, 21–25.
2. LEVITT, E. E. The Water-Jar Einstellung Test as a measure of rigidity. *Psychol. Bull.* 1956, 53, 347–370.
3. LUCHINS, A. S. Mechanization in problem solving. *Psychol. Monogr.*, 1942, 54, No. 6 (Whole No. 248).

6. Functional Fixedness as Related to Elapsed Time and to Set

Robert E. Adamson and Donald W. Taylor

Duncker (3) originally proposed the hypothesis that problem solving may be inhibited by the functional fixedness of solution objects. That is, owing to previous use of the object with a function dissimilar to that demanded by the present problem, S is inhibited in discovering the appropriate new use. In a series of six experiments he obtained results supporting the hypothesis. An earlier paper (1) reported a repetition of

Reprinted by permission of the authors and the American Psychological Association from *Journal of Experimental Psychology*, 1954, 47, 122–126.

three of Duncker's experiments, using a larger N and with more carefully specified experimental conditions. The results essentially confirmed those of Duncker, and, together with evidence from a study by Birch and Rabinowitz (2), offer convincing proof of the existence of functional fixedness. The present study follows two lines of investigation designed to clarify the nature of the phenomenon: (a) determination of conditions influencing its occurrence, and (b) exploration of its relation to other kinds of set in problem solving.

It would appear that the fixedness of an object results from its association with a particular function. As a result of this association it becomes more difficult to utilize the object with a new function. One inference from this is that anything which weakens the association between an object and a specific function will lessen the amount of functional fixedness for that object. Duncker has stated, along these lines, that "separation of the two functions F_1 and F_2 in two independent problem situations about eliminates the disturbing functional fixedness of the crucial object" (3, p. 96). But the Birch and Rabinowitz study (2) incorporated such a change of context and still demonstrated fixedness for the solution objects. One factor which might clearly be expected to weaken the association between an object and a specific function would be lapse of time following the use of that object with that function. This expectation suggests the hypothesis that functional fixedness will decrease with increasing time following initial usage of the object. Experiment I was designed to test this hypothesis.

Studies by Luchins (5, 6) and Guetzkow (4) have been concerned with the operation of set in problem solving, where set is defined as the continued attempt to use a previously successful method in problems where the method is no longer adequate. Both functional fixedness and set thus defined involve the limiting effect of past experience; in both the variability of approach to a problem is reduced. This similarity suggests that individuals susceptible to functional fixedness would also tend to be susceptible to such set. Guetzkow (4) has distinguished susceptibility to set from the inability to overcome set. Experiment II was designed to test the hypothesis that susceptibility to functional fixedness is positively related to susceptibility to set and to inability to overcome set.

EXPERIMENT I: THE INFLUENCE OF ELAPSED TIME ON FUNCTIONAL FIXEDNESS

Procedure. Five experimental groups, including 16, 16, 14, 11, and 10 Ss, respectively, participated in the first experiment. The Ss were randomly assigned to the various groups and all were undergraduate students in general psychology at Stanford University.

The procedure employed was a modification of that introduced by Birch and Rabinowitz (2), a procedure which allows the introduction of a varying time interval between the initial usage of an object and its use in the test problem. The members of the experimental group were first "given practice" in completing electric circuits with either a switch or a relay. In the present study, each S in the experimental groups was initially given a "speed test" requiring the construction of an electric circuit following a drawing. For half of the Ss in each group the circuit incorporated a microswitch; the other half completed a circuit using a small relay.

Between this initial task and the test problem, a period of uncontrolled activity occurred, the length of time being different for each of the five groups (see Fig. 1). Following this interval all Ss were given Maier's "two-string" problem (7). This problem consists of tying together the ends of two strings which are too far apart to be reached simultaneously unless one of the strings is moored or swinging. Since the method of presenting the problem prevented the mooring of either string, the only solution was to swing one of them while procuring the other. The oscillations of either string dampened too rapidly for it to swing by itself, and a weight attached to the end of the string was necessary. The S was presented with a number of possible solution objects, among them being the switch and the relay, the only two heavy enough to serve as a pendulum weight for the string. The purpose was not to determine whether S could solve the problem; rather it was to determine which of the two objects would be used to solve the problem, the one used in the initial task or the one not used in the initial task. If S had not solved the problem at the end of 3 min., E brushed against one of the strings so as to start it swinging. No S failed to solve the problem within the time allotted.

Results. In the initial task, half of the Ss in each experimental group had been given the switch and half the relay to use in completing the circuit. Therefore, in the two-string problem the null hypothesis would be that by chance 50% of each group would use the object previously used and 50% the one not previously used.[1] Occurrence of functional fixedness would

---

[1] In choosing the microswitch and relay to be used in the experiment, the attempt was made to select two objects whose physical characteristics would make them equally appropriate for use as pendulum weights. A group of 16 Ss were given the two-string problem, but not the initial task involving completion of the circuit using the switch or relay. In solving the two-string problem, eight Ss chose the switch and eight the relay.

It should be noted, however, that the null hypothesis does not depend on this finding that no preference was exhibited for one of the objects. Since in the initial task half of each experimental group received the microswitch and half the relay, the null hypothesis in the two-string problem would be that half would choose and half avoid the obect previously used even though the group as a whole exhibited a preference for the microswitch (or relay) as a pendulum weight. Suppose, for example, that of 100 Ss in an experimental group, 70 chose the microswitch and 30 the relay. The null hypothesis would be that of the 70, 35 would be from the group of 50 given the switch in the initial task and 35 from the group of 50 given the relay. Similarly, of

result in more than 50% of a group choosing the object not used in the initial task. The results obtained are presented in Fig. 1.

Of the 16 Ss in each of the first two experimental groups, 11 (69%) used in solving the two-string problem the object not used in the initial task. If these two groups are combined and the significance of the difference between the obtained 69% and the expected 50% computed, a critical ratio of 2.13 is obtained which with a one-tail test is significant at the .02 level. Experience in the initial task did produce functional fixedness.

The experiment was designed, however, to test the more specific hypothesis that functional fixedness decreases with increasing time. Figure 1

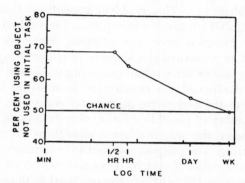

Fig. 1. Functional fixedness as a function of log time.

shows that the five groups rank in the order predicted, with the exception that the first two groups are tied. Computation of tau for the correlation between the predicted and the obtained rank orders yields a value significant at the .02 level (8). Thus, the hypothesis is confirmed.

Discussion. The conclusion that functional fixedness decreases as a function of time is not to be interpreted as assigning causal significance to time as such. This decrease is probably best interpreted in terms of the concept of retroactive inhibition. It appears likely that the activity during the period between the initial task and the two-string problem tends to interfere with the retention of the association formed during the initial task. The longer the interval, the larger the amount of intervening activity,

the 30, 15 would be from the group given the switch and 15 from the group given the relay. Thus, even though a definite preference is exhibited for the microswitch, the null hypothesis is that 35 + 15 or 50 will choose and 35 + 15 will avoid the object previously used. It should be noted further, however, that in the case of such a preference, a maximum of 80 of the 100 Ss could choose the object not previously used. The two-string problem will be most sensitive as a measure of functional fixedness if the two objects are equally appropriate for use as pendulum weights.

the greater the degree of retroactive inhibition, and hence the smaller the amount of functional fixedness obtained. The nature of the activity during the intervening interval was uncontrolled in the present experiment. It would be expected that the decrease in functional fixedness with time would be a function of the kind of intervening activity. Additional experiments will be necessary to test this hypothesis.

EXPERIMENT II: THE RELATION BETWEEN FUNCTIONAL FIXEDNESS AND SET

Procedure. All except one of the 46 Ss from the first three experimental groups in Exp. I were also given a series of 11 problems devised by Luchins (5). In each problem, the task is to explain how a stipulated quantity of water could be obtained by using jars of given sizes; e.g., given an empty 14-qt. jar, an empty 36-qt. jar, and an empty 8-qt. jar; measure 6 qt. water. Problem 1 involves only two jars and is given to illustrate the nature of the task. Problems 2 to 6 are all solved in the same way: first fill the second jar, then subtract from it the amount necessary to fill the first jar once and the third jar twice. Problems 7, 8, 10, and 11 can also be solved in this way or, more directly, in one step which does not involve the second jar. Problem 9 can be solved only by the more direct method. The time allowed for each problem was 1.5 min.

Luchins (6) has pointed out that two types of behavioral rigidity should be distinguished in performance on the water-jar problems. Use of the indirect instead of the simpler direct method in solving Problems 7 and 8 may be taken as evidence of one kind of behavioral rigidity. Since use of the indirect method, even though less efficient, does result in solution, designating such behavior as rigid may be questioned. In any case, this kind of rigidity should be distinguished from that involved in Problem 9 where failure to use the direct method results in failure to solve the problem.

Guetzkow (4) has used somewhat different terminology in making the same distinction. Use of the indirect method in solving Problems 7 and 8 is taken as evidence of susceptibility to set. Failure to solve Problem 9 is evidence of inability to overcome set.

Results. The first hypothesis to be tested was that susceptibility to functional fixedness is related to susceptibility to set. Data presented in Table 1, however, show that no significant relation was obtained between the choice of solution objects in the two-string problem and the method used in solving Problems 7 and 8.

In contrast, the results clearly support the second hypothesis that susceptibility to functional fixedness is related to inability to overcome set. As shown in Table 1, those who solve the two-string problem by using the object not used in the initial task are more likely to fail Problem 9. The argument may be plausibly made that this analysis should include only those Ss who solve Problems 7 and 8 indirectly: if performance on Problem 9 is to be a criterion of ability to overcome set, its use must be limited to those Ss for whom the existence of set has been demonstrated on Problems 7 and 8. A plausible counterargument would be that those Ss who solve Problems 7 and 8 directly have done so in the face of the same

TABLE 1

χ^2 CONTINGENT TABLES: FUNCTIONAL FIXEDNESS, SUSCEPTIBILITY TO SET, AND INABILITY TO OVERCOME SET

| Luchins Problems | Nature of Solution | Two-String Problem | | χ^2 | p^* |
		Object Previously Used	Object Not Previously Used		
7 and 8	Both indirectly	10	23	.13	—
	One or both directly	5	7		
9	Failed	3	20	6.95	< .005
	Solved	12	10		
10 and 11	Both indirectly	4	17	2.51	< .06
	One or both directly	11	13		

* Since the direction of the relations was predicted, a one-tail test was employed, i.e., the square root of χ^2 was interpreted by means of the normal curve table. Yates's correction was employed in all computations of χ^2 in this article.

set-inducing experience on Problems 2 to 6 and have thereby demonstrated their ability to overcome set. In any case, the analogous fourfold table including only the 33 Ss who solved Problems 7 and 8 indirectly yielded a χ^2 of 11.61, significant at the .0004 level.

The relation between choice of solution objects in the two-string problem and the method used in solving Problems 10 and 11 approaches significance, p being .06. Actually, if the analysis is limited to the 41 Ss who solved Problems 10 and 11 both directly or both indirectly, a χ^2 of 3.10 and p of .04 are obtained.

Discussion. The distinction between two types of behavioral rigidity, or in other terms between susceptibility to set and inability to overcome set, is apparently an important one. Luchins (6) found that behavioral rigidity measured by performance on problems like Problem 9 is positively related to concreteness of thinking as measured by the Similarities subtest of the Wechsler-Bellevue Intelligence Scale. No significant relation was found between behavioral rigidity of the kind measured by performance on problems like Problems 7 and 8 and concreteness of thinking. Guetz-kow (4) obtained a significant difference between men and women in inability to overcome set, but found no such difference in susceptibility to set.

The present finding that susceptibility to functional fixedness is related to inability to overcome set, but not to susceptibiliy to set confirms the importance of the distinction. Continuing to use an effective indirect method, even though a more direct method is available, does not have the same significance psychologically as does continued use when the method is inappropriate.

The fact that the relation between susceptibility to fixedness and per-formance on Problems 10 and 11 approaches significance is not in conflict with the statement just made. It is highly probable that performance on Problems 10 and 11 was affected by performance on Problem 9. Those who solve Problem 9 become aware of the direct method and may be expected to use it in solving Problems 10 and 11; in fact, of the 22 who solved Problem 9, only 1 person solved both 10 and 11 indirectly. The obtained relation between fixedness and performance on Problems 10 and 11 may be best interpreted as owing to the effects of experience with Problem 9.

Attention should be called to an important limitation of the measure of functional fixedness employed here. The 30 of the 45 Ss who in the two-string problem employed the object not previously used were in the analyses of the data of Exp. II all classified as susceptible to functional fixedness. This classification is open to question. As pointed out in the analysis of Exp. I, the null hypothesis would be that by chance 50% use the object not previously used. Hence the 30 Ss include those who by chance chose the object not previously used as well as those susceptible to functional fixedness. Unfortunately, there is no way to discriminate be-tween them. For the purposes of Exp. II, therefore, the measure of func-tional fixedness employed must be regarded as a relatively insensitive one. The fact that in spite of this insensitivity a highly significant relation be-tween functional fixedness thus measured and inability to overcome set was obtained deserves emphasis. This insensitivity must also be kept in mind in interpreting the fact that no significant relation was obtained between functional fixedness and susceptibility to set.

SUMMARY

Five groups including a total of 67 Ss participated in Exp. I designed to test the hypothesis that functional fixedness decreases as a function of time. All Ss were first given the task of constructing an electric circuit. For half of the Ss in each group, the circuit employed a micro-switch and for the other half a small relay. Following an interval of uncontrolled activity, all Ss were given Maier's two-string problem. Among the objects available for possible use as a pendulum weight, the only two which would work were the microswitch and the relay. The purpose was to determine which of the two objects would be used in solving the problem. The length of the interval between the initial task and the two-string problems was varied, being 1 min., ½ hr., 1 hr., 1 day, and 1 week for the five groups, respectively. Functional fixedness, as measured by the percentage of the Ss using as a pendulum weight the object not used in the initial task, did decrease as a function of time. The relation was significant at the .02 level.

In Exp. II, concerned with the relation of functional fixedness to set, 45 Ss from the first three groups in Exp. I were given a Luchins series of water-jar problems. Problems 2 to 6 are all solved by the same indirect method. Performance on Problems 7 and 8, which can be solved either by this indirect method or by a more direct method, was used as the criterion of susceptibility to set. Performance on Problem 9, which can be solved only by a direct method, served as the criterion of inability to overcome set. Susceptibility to functional fixedness, as defined by the Maier two-string problem, was found to have a significant relation to inability to overcome set, but no relation to susceptibility to set, as defined by the Luchins problem series.

REFERENCES

1. ADAMSON, R. E. Functional fixedness as related to problem solving: a repetition of three experiments. *J. exp. Psychol.*, 1952, 44, 288–291.
2. BIRCH, H. G., & RABINOWITZ, H. S. The negative effect of previous experience on productive thinking. *J. exp. Psychol.*, 1951, 41, 121–125.
3. DUNCKER, K. On problem-solving. *Psychol. Monogr.*, 1945, 58, No. 5 (Whole No. 270).
4. GUETZKOW, H. An analysis of the operation of set in problem-solving behavior. *J. gen. Psychol.*, 1951, 45, 219–244.
5. LUCHINS, A. S. Mechanization in problem solving. *Psychol. Monogr.*, 1942, 54, No. 6 (Whole No. 248).
6. LUCHINS, A. S. The Einstellung test of rigidity: its relation to concreteness of thinking. *J. consult. Psychol.*, 1951, 15, 303–310.
7. MAIER, N. R. F. Reasoning in humans. I. On direction. *J. comp. Psychol.*, 1930, 10, 115–143.
8. STILLITO, G. P. The distribution of Kendall's coefficient of rank correlation in rankings containing ties. *Biometrika*, 1947, 34, 36–40.

7. Problem Solving: Response Competition and the Influence of Drive

Sam Glucksberg

Abstract. *A functional fixedness problem was constructed which con-*
sisted of two sub-tasks. The initial sub-task, termed problem perception,
was designed to involve minimal response competition. The second, a
functional fixedness sub-task, involved both high and low response com-
petition. Drive level did not influence problem perception time. High
drive impaired problem-solving performance by increasing functional
fixedness strength when response competition was high. When response
competition was low, drive did not influence functional fixedness strength.
The obtained interactive effect of drive level with problem difficulty, pre-
dicted by Spence's drive theory, was attributed to the interactive effects
of drive upon functional fixedness strength.

Glucksberg (1962) applied Spence's drive theory (1956) to a functional fixedness problem. Using Duncker's candle problem (Duncker,
1945), a predicted interaction between drive level and problem complexity was obtained. High drive impaired performance when the response
designated as correct was low in the response hierarchy, but tended to
facilitate performance when the correct response was high in the response
hierarchy.

The measure of functional fixedness strength used in the earlier study
was total time to solve the problem. Total time to solve, however, represents more than just functional fixedness strength. In the candle problem,
S must use a small pasteboard box in order to solve the problem of mount-
ing a candle on a vertical surface. The time score employed included the
time from the beginning of the problem until S became aware of the nature of the problem, *viz.*, that something was needed to support the candle.
This particular portion of solution time can be described as problem perception time. A measure of the strength of functional fixedness is the time
from problem perception until the functionally fixed object is used. This
portion of total solution time can then be described as functional fixedness
time, representing the strength of functional fixedness. These two measures, problem perception time and functional fixedness time, can, in simple problems, comprise total solution time.

Can drive level influence problem solving by influencing the strength of

Reprinted by permission of the author and of Southern University Press from
Psychological Reports, 1964, *15*, 939.

functional fixedness *per se?* According to Spence's drive theory, high drive impairs performance in competitional response situations when the dominant response is incorrect and facilitates performance when the dominant response is correct. If, however, the dominant correct response can be executed rapidly and easily, then the influence of drive level is negligible (Glucksberg, 1962). By controlling the position and nature of the correct responses in the response hierarchies in each of the two stages of functional fixedness problems, it would be possible to control and predict the influence of drive level on performance in each of the two stages posited: problem perception and functional fixedness.

This study investigated the influence of strength of drive on functional fixedness strength. A problem was devised in which problem perception does not involve response competition, and in which functional fixedness could be either high or low with respect to response competition. The effect of drive could then be tested under two conditions. When the correct response is low in the response hierarchy (high response competition, strong functional fixedness), a high drive should increase functional fixedness strength, and thus impair problem-solving performance. In contrast, a high drive should have a negligible effect when functional fixedness is weak and the correct overt response can be executed rapidly. Furthermore, the influence of drive should be confined to the functional fixedness portion of the problem only.

Method

Subjects. Ss were 42 male undergraduates enrolled in psychology courses at Princeton University. Two Ss were excused when they professed complete ignorance of electrical wiring and refused to try to solve the problem.

Design. The 2×2 factorial design involved two levels of drive and two different response hierarchies in a functional fixedness problem. A description of the problem follows. S is required to construct a simple circuit consisting of a pair of flashlight batteries, a DPDT switch, and a 6-v bulb so that operation of the switch turns the bulb on and off. All components are presented mounted on an 8-in. $\times$ 12-inch. rectangular masonite pegboard. The batteries and bulb are pre-wired to four plastic binding posts mounted on the board, so that S must make connections between the binding posts and to screw terminals on the switch. Available to S are 4 wires of varying lengths. The wires, added together, are 1¼ in. too short to complete the desired circuit. Also available are a coil of Plasticene modelling clay, 12 in. long, and one of two screwdrivers. In Cond. Dm+ (dominant response correct) the screwdriver supplied was 9 in. long, with a bright silvery blade 6 in. long and a red plastic handle identical in hue and texture to the plastic binding posts. When the screwdriver was supplied, the wires available were not insulated and resembled the screwdriver blade in brightness, gloss, and hue. In Cond. Dm— (dominant response incorrect) the screwdriver was 3¼ in. long, with a 1½-in. blade. This screwdriver had a dark wooden handle and the metal blade was not shiny. The wires available in this condition were insulated with yellow plastic, stripped ¼ in. on each end. Both forms of the problem could be solved in only one way: by using a screwdriver blade to make up for the short wires.

Procedure. The materials for the problem were placed in standard positions on a table and covered with a flexible sheet of opaque plastic. Posted on a wall to S's left was a simplified diagram of the circuit to be constructed. Ss were seated at the table and asked to explain the circuit diagram. When they had indicated that the diagram made sense to them they were told: "Under this cover is a board with batteries, a bulb, and a switch mounted on it. The problem is to complete the circuit so that operation of the switch controls the bulb. You may not move any of the components mounted on the board. You may use any of the materials on the table."

In addition to these instructions, high drive Ss were told: "As an incentive we are offering a prize of $10.00 for the fastest solution to the problem." Low drive Ss were told: "We are interested in finding out how long people take to solve problems of this type." E then said, "ready," and started two Standard Electric timers upon removal of the cover.

One measure taken was problem perception time. This was the time taken for S to indicate awareness of the nature of the problem (wires too short). The time at which any of the following was first observed served as this measure: any verbalization by S that there was not enough wire available, including requests for more wire, any attempts to use modelling clay as a conductor, or any attempt (despite instructions) to move components mounted on the board. The second measure was total time to solve. This was the time at which S placed the screwdriver blade into the circuit, irrespective of whether or not the wiring was correct. A score of 20 min. was assigned to Ss failing to use the screwdriver blade as part of the circuit. The difference between these two time scores (net solution time) served as the measure of functional fixedness strength.

RESULTS AND DISCUSSION

Seven Ss in Cond. Dm+ (two low drive and five high drive) placed the screwdriver blade into the circuit without prior indication that they were aware that the wires were too short. Each of these S's total solution time was considered as the best estimate of problem perception time, yielding net solution times of zero for these seven Ss. The means of problem per-

TABLE 1

MEAN PROBLEM PERCEPTION TIME

Group		Problem Perception Time (min.)	
Nature of Dominant Response	Drive Level	M	SD
Dm+	High	2.29	1.43
	Low	2.60	1.66
Dm−	High	3.96	1.43
	Low	2.70	1.00

ception times are presented in Table 1. Analysis of variance applied to these scores indicated that neither main effects nor interaction of drive × conditions was significant. Neither drive level nor functional fixedness response hierarchies influenced problem perception time.

Net solution time means, together with number of failures per group, are presented in Table 2. Even though solution time scores were skewed, analysis of variance and t tests were applied to the net solution time scores (Boneau, 1960). A significant effect of Conditions ($F = 18.84$, $df = 1/36$, $p < .001$) was obtained. The Dm+ form of the problem, as expected, was easier than the DM− form. As expected, the over-all effect of drive level was not significant, while the predicted interaction of drive and nature of the dominant response was obtained ($F = 10.75$, $df = 1/36$, $p < .01$).

Differences between the means of high and low drive groups within response hierarchy conditions were evaluated by t tests. The difference was significant ($t = 3.45$, $p < .01$) in Cond. Dm−, but not in Cond. DM+. Identical conclusions are reached using the total solution time scores. The influence of drive level on total problem solving performance parallels precisely the influence of drive on functional fixedness.

These data clearly show that drive level can influence functional fixed-

TABLE 2

FUNCTIONAL FIXEDNESS STRENGTH: NET SOLUTION TIME SCORES

Group		No. Failures	Net Solution Time (min.)	
Nature of Dominant Response	Drive Level		M	SD
Dm+	High	0	1.92	3.33
	Low	0	4.39	4.55
Dm−	High	7	13.13	4.54
	Low	1	5.95	5.04

ness strength *per se* and that the influence of drive level upon problem-solving performance was attributable solely to the effect of drive on functional fixedness strength. This is in accord with Spence's drive theory which predicted that the effect of drive would be confined to that aspect of the problem involving high response competition. In this case, this was the functional fixedness sub-task. Given a more difficult and complex problem perception sub-task, i.e., involving high response competition, drive would be expected to influence problem perception in the same way it influenced functional fixedness.

REFERENCES

BONEAU, C. A. The effect of violations of assumptions underlying the *t* test. *Psychol. Bull.*, 1960, 57, 49–64.

DUNCKER, K. On problem-solving. *Psychol. Monogr.*, 1945, 58, No. 5 (Whole No. 270).

GLUCKSBERG, S. The influence of strength of drive on functional fixedness and perceptual recognition. *J. exp. Psychol.*, 1962, 63, 36–41.

SPENCE, K. W. *Behavior theory and conditioning.* New Haven: Yale Univer. Press, 1956.

Task Variables and Past Experience

Problem solving performance is usually found to vary as a function of independent variables that consist in some change in the problem task itself. Changes in the number, kind, or arrangement of elements of the problem, changes that induce differing associations in subjects, and others, are examples of manipulations that effectively vary problem difficulty. Anagrams are a particularly useful class of problems for studying task variables since they lend themselves to many kinds of variations both among letters and among words.

Problems involving production or rearrangement of letters or larger verbal units such as bigrams, in order to discover other verbal units (bigrams, words, etc.), have also turned out to be one of the most useful devices for studying the role of past experience in problem solving. There are now available tables of the frequencies of occurrence in the written language of several verbal units: letters, bigrams, words, and others. To the extent that these frequencies are a measure of long-term past experience and, therefore, of subjects' habit strength for verbal units, such tables (see citations in the references of articles in this chapter) are useful aids in selecting problem variations that will tap differential past experience.

In the Dominowski and Duncan study, frequencies of the bigrams within the anagrams presented to the subjects and frequencies of the bigrams within the words that were the solutions of the anagrams were varied independently. These two variables were also used in the Mayzner and Tresselt paper. In addition, another task variable, letter order, appears in their study. The variable of solution-word frequency has been consistently found to reflect the effects of differential past experience with the language.

Another task variable, word versus nonsense anagrams, is the concern of the Beilin and Horn paper. This study is also an example of the necessity, and sometimes the difficulty, of equating anagrams on task variables other than the independent variable.

In anagram solving, the subject has all the letters of the anagram and, therefore, of the solution word presented to him. In principle, the subject could solve simply by rearranging letters (although the evidence suggests that this is not the chief solution process). In the Duncan study, the role of past experience, as tapped by word frequency, is demonstrated with problems in which subjects must produce a word without having all letters available. It may also be noted that in this study the size of the population of words that the subject must search varies across the three experiments from several words down to one word in some cases, yet the tendency to emit higher frequency words remains consistent.

8.   Anagram Solving as a Function of Bigram Frequency

Roger L. Dominowski and Carl P. Duncan

Any sequence of letters may be considered to be composed of successive two-letter combinations (bigrams). Counts are available indicating the frequency of occurrence of bigrams in the English language. By summing the frequency counts for successive bigrams in left-to-right sequence, a total for that sequence may be obtained. The bigram frequency total for an anagram will be referred to as *anbitot*, and the corresponding total for a solution-word will be called *solbitot*; both have been found to affect the difficulty of anagram solution. Mayzner and Tresselt (1959) found that low anbitot anagrams resulted in faster solutions than high anbitot anagrams. High solbitot was associated with significantly shorter solution times than low solbitot (Mayzner and Tresselt, 1962). Contradictory evidence was gathered by Erlebacher (1962), who found no difference between high and low anbitot but found that low solbitot words were produced in less time than high solbitot words.

The present investigations were conducted to gather further information

Reprinted by permission of the authors and the Academic Press from *Journal of Verbal Learning and Verbal Behavior*, 1964, 3, 321–325.

concerning the role of bigram frequency in determining difficulty of anagram solution. In addition, an attempt was made to replicate the O'Connell and Duncan (1961) finding that anagrams with 10 typewriter spaces between letters were solved more rapidly than those anagrams with one space separating letters.

GENERAL METHOD

Materials. Two lists of 12 five-letter words each were selected, one containing words with high bigram frequency totals, the other composed of words with low bigram frequency totals. These constituted the high and low solbitot conditions. The Total Count of bigram frequency reported in Underwood and Schulz (1960) was used to compute solbitot values. All words were drawn from the "known to all adults" section of the *English Vocabulary Builder* (O'Connor, 1948). The words are listed in Table 1 in order of decreasing solbitot. For the high solbitot words, the mean bigram frequency total was 7093, ranging from 5792 for *beach* to 10065 for *linen*. For the low solbitot words, the mean bigram total was 2583; the range was 1087 (*foggy*) to 3634 (*sugar*).

For each word a high anbitot anagram and a low anbitot anagram were constructed. The anagrams are given in Table 1. In the formation of these anagrams the attempt was made to maximize or minimize the anbitot value while making the anagram as different as possible from the solution-word. For the high solbitot words, the high anbitot anagrams had a mean anbitot of 6662, range: 3585–10,019); the low anbitot anagrams had a mean anbitot of 950 (range: 32–1792). For the low solbitot words, the high anbitot anagrams had a mean anbitot of 4122 (range: 1148–8337); the low anbitot anagrams had a mean anbitot of 653 (range: 73–1361).

Letter order and word frequency have been found to affect anagram difficulty (Mayzner and Tresselt, 1958). The letter orders employed in the current experiments were in the "hard" range, requiring either two or three letters to be relocated (disregarding distance moved) in order to form the solution word. The high and low solbitot lists were similar in word frequency (Thorndike and Lorge, 1944); both contained words with frequency counts in the following ranges: 1–49, 50–99, and 100 or higher. The median frequency count was in the 50–99 category. Erlebacher (1962) found that solution words beginning with consonants were solved more readily than those with initial vowels. No difference existed between the present lists regarding this characteristic.

Each of the four sets of 12 anagrams was typed with one space between letters and also with 10 spaces between letters. Thus, there were 8 conditions, each a combination of high or low anbitot, high or low solbitot, and wide or narrow spacing.

TABLE 1

THE WORDS AND THE ANAGRAMS FOR EACH

| | High solbitot | | | Low solbitot | |
| | Anagrams | | | Anagrams | |
Word	High anbitot	Low anbitot	Word	High anbitot	Low anbitot
linen	nilen	lnnie	sugar	grasu	srgua
onion	inono	nnooi	lunch	huncl	uhcnl
river	reriv	eivrr	enjoy	yenoj	njyeo
bring	ngirb	rgnbi	tribe	iterb	eibrt
cream	mearc	aemcr	brook	korob	rbkoo
train	ranti	rtnia	cocoa	oocac	oaocc
ranch	harcn	crhna	snack	cansk	scnka
drink	ndirk	ikdnr	fruit	tirfu	iufrt
stage	gseat	tsgae	swamp	maspw	wpmsa
bacon	canob	cnbao	knife	finek	ekifn
write	teriw	eiwrt	fudge	geduf	duefg
beach	hecab	aebhc	foggy	ggyof	gfygo

General Instructions. The Ss were told that an anagram is a sequence of letters which can be rearranged to form an English word. An example with four letters was demonstrated. It was indicated that there was a time limit (but not its duration) and that no foreign words, plurals, or proper nouns were admissible as solutions. With these restrictions, there was only one solution to each anagram.

EXPERIMENT I

Procedure. The Ss were 152 students enrolled in introductory psychology. Group presentation of the materials was employed, with each S working on a list of 12 anagrams representing a single anbitot × solbitot × spacing condition. The 12 anagrams were typed on one sheet of paper. The total time allowed was 3 min. for all 12 anagrams. The score recorded for each S was the number of solutions produced within 3 min.

Results. Three-way analysis of variance indicated that significant effects were due to solbitot ($F = 7.04$, $df = 1/144$, $p < 0.01$), there being more solutions of high solbitot words, and to the anbitot × solbitot interaction ($F = 10.10$, $df = 1/144$, $p < 0.005$). The effect of spacing was not significant thus groups in different spacing conditions have been combined in computing the means shown in Table 2.

Because of the very short time limit employed, the possibility existed that the anagrams which were solved had required little "manipulation"

TABLE 2

MEAN NUMBER OF SOLUTIONS UNDER THE FOUR
ANBITOT × SOLBITOT CONDITIONS

| Exp. | Anbitot | Solbitot | |
		Low	High
I	High	2.53	5.05
	Low	3.95	3.71
II	High	5.04	6.28
	Low	7.15	5.35
III	High	2.53	8.58
	Low	8.50	7.62

and that this was responsible for the lack of effects due to anbitot and spacing. A second experiment was conducted to determine if time was a factor.

EXPERIMENT II

Procedure. The Ss were 184 students enrolled in introductory psychology. The materials and procedures used in the first experiment were repeated, with the exception that the total time allowed was 5 min. for all 12 anagrams. Again the score recorded was the number of solutions produced within the time limit.

Results. In the analysis of variance only the effect due to the interaction of anbitot and solbitot was significant ($F = 10.67$, $df = 1/176$, $p < 0.005$). With slight variation, the form of the interaction was consistent with that found in Exp. I (Table 2).

Since the results of the first two experiments were at variance with the findings of Mayzner and Tresselt (1959, 1962) and Erlebacher (1962), it seemed possible that procedural differences were responsible for the lack of consistent results. Mayzner and Tresselt had used individual presentation, with S given one anagram at a time; Erlebacher had run Ss in groups. Her Ss worked on a list consisting of one experimental anagram surrounded by buffer anagrams. Therefore, a third experiment was conducted to determine if the finding of the anbitot × solbitot interaction and the lack of main effects were an artifact of the method employed in the group experiments. In addition, by running Ss individually, control over the time spent on each anagram was established, and information not available from group experiments was obtained.

Experiment III

Procedure. The materials employed in the previous experiments were used, with the exception that only the narrow spaced condition (one space between letters) was presented. Thus, there were four conditions: high and low anbitot within each of the sets of high and low solbitot words. Each S served in only one condition. To assign Ss to conditions, 12 random orders of the four conditions were constructed. This sequence of 48 was used for the first 48 Ss, then repeated for the second 48 Ss.

Each anagram was typed on a 3 × 5 card. Within each condition, the 12 anagrams were presented in 12 completely different orders such that each anagram appeared in each ordinal position. One min. was allowed on each anagram.

The Ss were students from introductory psychology classes. There were 12 men and 12 women in each of the four conditions.

Results. Based on the number of anagrams solved by each S, analysis of variance indicated that the only significant effect was due to the anbitot × solbitot interaction ($F = 6.73$, $df = 1/92$, $p < 0.025$). The form of the interaction was consistent with that found in the preceding experiments (Table 2).

For each word the median solution time was determined for the low and high anbitot conditions separately (24 Ss per condition). For the 12 high solbitot words, the median of these 12 medians was 25.2 sec in the low anbitot condition, and 12.0 sec in the high anbitot condition. For the 12 low solbitot words, the median of medians was 14.8 sec in the low anbitot condition and 60.0 sec in the high anbitot condition. Thus, both methods of scoring, number solved, and median of median solution times yielded the same ordering of the four conditions.

Each S had worked a series of 12 anagrams. Based on the number of solutions at each ordinal position, there was no evidence of a practice effect in any of the four conditions.

A comparison of the number of solutions by the 48 females and 48 males indicated no sex differences either in over-all performance or in the effects of the variables.

Discussion

None of the three main variables, spacing, anbitot, or solbitot, had reliable effects on performance. For spacing, it may merely be noted that, in the O'Connell and Duncan (1961) study of spacing, each anagram was on a separate card and Ss were run individually, whereas in the present study (Exps. I and II), all anagrams were on one sheet and Ss were run in groups. Concerning anbitot, neither the present study nor the experiments of Erlebacher (1962) or Stachnik (1963) have replicated Mayzner and Tresselt's (1959) finding that anbitot was an effective variable. However, none of these studies has exactly duplicated Mayzner and Tresselt's experiment. Regarding solbitot, Mayzner and Tresselt (1962) found high solbitot words were solved more easily. Erlebacher (1962) found the opposite, while the present study confirmed Mayzner and Tresselt in Exp. I but found no effect of solbitot in Exp. II or III. Again, no one of these several experiments used a procedure identical to that of any other experiment.

The one consistent finding in the present study was the interaction between anbitot and solbitot. Table 2 shows that the interaction can be described as follows. In all three experiments, poorest performance was obtained when Ss were presented with anagrams having high bigram totals which had to be solved for words having low bigram totals, i.e., solving high anbitot for low solbitot. Intermediate levels of performance were obtained when these extreme conditions of total bigram frequency were revised, i.e., when Ss had to proceed from low anbitot to high solbitot. Best performances occurred when both anbitot and solbitot were low, or when both were high. These latter two conditions, low-low and high-high, varied from each other (numerically) in one direction in Exp. I, in the opposite direction in Exp. II, and were not different in Exp. III; taking the results as a whole, these two conditions will be considered equal.

Assuming that the experimental conditions do produce three levels of performance, the results might be interpreted in this way. Low-frequency bigrams tend mainly to elicit, as implicit responses, other low-frequency bigrams while high-frequency bigrams tend chiefly to elicit other high-frequency bigrams. So when S works on a low anbitot problem, he is more likely to solve it if the solution word also contains low-frequency bigrams than if the word is made up of high-frequency bigrams. However, if the anagram has a high bigram total, S is more likely to solve if the solution word also has a high, rather than a low, bigram total. This suggested principle (low evokes low, high evokes high) would alone produce the interaction between anbitot and solbitot. In addition, there was the finding that anagrams with low bigram totals tended to be solved for words with high totals more readily than the opposite (high to low) case. Thus, in this qualified respect, there is some support for Mayzner and Tresselt's (1962) finding that words containing bigrams frequently occurring in S's past experience (high solbitot) are more easily solved than low solbitot words.

Recently, Mayzner and Tresselt (1963) have recomputed bigram frequencies taking into account both the length of words and the position of bigrams in the word. They reported that correlations between bigram total and solution difficulty of words were increased when the new totals were used. Taking the data for Exp. III of the present study, rank-order correlations between ranks based on the number of solutions were computed for the high and low solbitot words. When the bigram totals were computed from Underwood and Schulz's (1960) Total Count, the correlations were −0.29 and 0.34 for low and high solbitot words, respectively. When totals were computed from Mayzner and Tresselt's tables, the corresponding values were 0.28 and 0.42. Correlations between ranks based on the two types of bigram totals were 0.40 and −0.09 for low and high solbitot words, respectively.

As a final point, one may note the importance of the word itself, what might be called "word uniqueness" as a variable. From Exp. III, correlations were computed from ranks based on solution difficulty, between low and high anbitot forms of words. For low solbitot words, rho was 0.71; for high solbitot words, rho was 0.86. Thus, a word's relative difficulty was not greatly changed even when its anagrams were markedly different. In this connection it may be worth noting that inspection of the low and high solbitot words in Table 1 reveals that the two classes of words differ in certain respects. The low solbitot words have more O's, U's, and Y's; the high solbitot words have more A's, E's, and I's. The two sets of words also differ somewhat in the positions that vowels and consonants occupy. These differences, acting in conjunction with possible letter-sequence habits among Ss, may have contributed to the anbitot × solbitot interactions.

SUMMARY

In three experiments on anagram solving, the variables were high vs. low total bigram frequency both of the anagrams and the solution words. In two of the experiments, spacing between letters of the anagrams was varied. Subjects were run in groups with all anagrams presented at once in two experiments and individually with one anagram at a time in the third experiment. The time allowed for solving was varied from experiment to experiment.

With the exception that more anagrams were solved as more time was allowed, no main variable had any consistent effect across experiments. The consistent finding over all three experiments was a highly significant interaction between bigram frequency total of anagram and word. Anagrams with low totals were solved more easily for words with low than for words with high totals. Anagrams with high totals were solved more easily for words with high than with low totals. Certain interpretations of this interaction were discussed.

REFERENCES

ERLEBACHER, A. Parameters of anagram tasks. Unpublished doctoral dissertation. Univer. of Wisconsin, 1962.

MAYZNER, M. S., AND TRESSELT, M. E. Anagram solution times: A function of letter order and word frequency. *J. exp. Psychol.*, 1958, 56, 376–379.

MAYZNER, M. S., AND TRESSELT, M. E. Anagram solution times: A function of transition probabilities. *J. Psychol.*, 1959, 47, 117–125.

MAYZNER, M. S., AND TRESSELT, M. E. Anagram solution times: A function of word transition probabilities. *J. exp. Psychol.*, 1962, 63, 510–512.

MAYZNER, M. S., AND TRESSELT, M. E. Anagram solution times: A function of word length and letter position variables. *J. Psychol.*, 1963, 55, 469–475.

O'CONNELL, E. J., JR., AND DUNCAN, C. P. Anagram solving a function of letter spacing. *Psychol. Rep.*, 1961, 8, 117–118.

O'CONNOR, J. *English vocabulary builder.* Boston: Todd, 1948.

STACHNIK, T. Transitional probability in anagram solution in a group setting. *J. Psychol.*, 1963, 55, 259–261.

THORNDIKE, E. L., AND LORGE, I. *A teacher's word book of 30,000 words.* New York: Teacher's College, Columbia Univer., 1944.

UNDERWOOD, B. J., AND SCHULZ, R. W. *Meaningfulness and verbal learning.* Chicago: Lippincott, 1960.

9. Anagram Solution Times: A Function of Multiple-Solution Anagrams

M. S. Mayzner and M. E. Tresselt

Abstract. *4 groups of 20 Ss each were presented with a set of 21 multiple-solution anagram problems and 2 additional groups of 20 Ss each received 21 single-solution problems, in which the anagram was itself a word. An S–R mediational model of problem-solving behavior was employed to make predictions concerning the effects of 4 variables, viz., anagram letter order, solution-word Thorndike-Lorge frequency, anagram digram frequency, and solution-word digram frequency, on anagram solu-*

Reprinted by permission of the authors and the American Psychological Association from *Journal of Experimental Psychology*, 1966, 71, 66–73.

tion times. All predictions of the model were confirmed and the results showed that for multiple- as well as single-solution anagram problems, solution times are faster for easy letter orders, high solution-word Thorndike-Lorge frequencies, low anagram digram frequencies, and high solution-word digram frequencies.

A series of earlier studies (Mayzner & Tresselt, 1958, 1959, 1962, 1963; Mayzner, Tresselt, & Helbock, 1964) examined anagram problem solving within the framework of an S-R mediational model of problem-solving behavior (Kendler, 1961; Kendler & Kendler, 1962). In these studies four variables, viz., anagram letter order, solution-word frequency, anagram transition probability, and solution-word transition probability, were identified and related to anagram solution times. Since the anagrams employed had only a single possible solution, predictions concerning the effects of these four variables had to be related to differences in solution times between different sets of anagrams which varied in a systematic way along the dimensions of these variables.

The present study, in contrast, employs anagrams with multiple solutions, which allows for predictions to be made concerning the effects of these four variables within the same anagram problem. For example, in one of the earlier studies (Mayzner & Tresselt, 1958), it was shown that solution-word frequency, as measured by the Thorndike-Lorge (1944) counts, has a highly significant effect on anagram solution times. More specifically, anagrams whose solution words have high frequencies of occurrence in English, such as CHAIR, SUGAR, TRAIN, etc., were solved from three to five times faster on the average than anagrams whose solution words have low frequencies of occurrence, such as TANGO, PEONY, TRIAD, etc. In the present study anagrams (e.g., LTAEB) will be employed which have two solutions, i.e., TABLE with a high Thorndike-Lorge count and BLEAT with a low Thorndike-Lorge count. For such anagram problems, an S-R mediational model would predict that solution words with the higher Thorndike-Lorge count (e.g., TABLE) would occur first and of necessity have shorter solution times than solution words occurring second (e.g., BLEAT). Expansion of S-R model predictions to multiple-solution anagrams will provide additional tests for the model and if confirmed will extend the model's generality of application from single- to multiple-solution problem situations.

METHOD

Subjects. The Ss were 120 students from introductory psychology classes at New York University. No S had served in any previous anagram study.

Stimulus material. The stimulus material consisted of 21 anagram problems, each problem having two solutions with one exception where through an oversight one problem had three solutions (ELBOW, BELOW, and BOWEL). Since the third and overlooked solution (BOWEL) was given by only 6 of the 120 Ss participating in the study, data for this solution were not included in the analyses that were made. In 10 of the 21 problems, both solution words had high and approximately equal Thorndike-Lorge (1944) frequency counts and in the remaining 11 problems, one solution word had a high-frequency count while the other solution word had a low-frequency count. All solution words and associated Thorndike-Lorge frequency counts are presented in Table 2.

Procedure. The 120 Ss in the study were assigned randomly to one of six different experimental conditions (EC), each consisting of 20 Ss. In EC I and II, S was presented with one of the two solution words associated with each anagram problem and required to obtain the other solution word. These conditions were employed to determine the effects on solution time, when the anagram is itself a word rather than a meaningless array of letters. In EC III and IV, S was presented with anagrams having low or high digram-frequency totals (Mayzner & Tresselt, 1959), respectively, and required to obtain both solution words. These conditions were employed to determine if the effects on solution time resulting from differences in anagram diagram-frequency totals are the same with multiple-solution anagrams as with single-solution anagrams (Mayzner & Tresselt, 1959). In EC V and VI, S was presented with easy letter order anagrams (Mayzner & Tresselt, 1958), having three of the five letters in the anagram in the same letter position as in one or the other of the two solution words, respectively, and required to obtain both solution words. Thus, for EC V, three letters were fixed in position in the anagram favoring one of the two solution words, while for EC VI, three letters were fixed in position in the anagram favoring the alternate solution word. These conditions were employed to determine if the effects on solution time resulting from easy vs. hard anagram letter orders are the same with multiple-solution anagrams as with single-solution anagrams (Mayzner & Tresselt, 1958).

Four variables (i.e., anagram letter order, solution-word frequency, anagram transition probability, and solution-word transition probability) were examined in the present study and Table 1 presents a summary of the six experimental conditions and all of the relevant measures employed in constructing the 21 anagram problems, and shows how these conditions and measures apply to a particular problem. As may be seen, each problem is presented in a different anagram form for each of the six experimental conditions, and associated with each anagram form is a digram-frequency total which represents the summed value of the four sequential digrams (e.g., AE, EP, PH, and HS) constituting that particular anagram form (i.e., AEPHS). These digram-frequency counts are based on tables

TABLE 1

SUMMARY OF EXPERIMENTAL CONDITIONS AND RELEVANT MEASURES
EMPLOYED IN CONSTRUCTING THE ANAGRAM PROBLEMS

Experimental Cond.	Anagram Problems	Solution Words	Digram-Freq. Totals
I—Solution Word to Solution Word	SHAPE	PHASE	1872
II—Solution Word to Solution Word	PHASE	SHAPE	2497
III—Low Digram-Freq. Anagram to Both Solution Words	AEPHS	SHAPE-PHASE	123
IV—High Digram-Freq. Anagram to Both Solution Words	HESAP	SHAPE-PHASE	4081
V—Three Letters Fixed in Anagram Favoring Solution Word SHAPE (HPE)	AHSPE	SHAPE-PHASE	404
VI—Three Letters Fixed in Anagram Favoring Solution Word PHASE (HSE)	AHPSE	SHAPE-PHASE	685

Solution-Word Digram-Position Frequencies

Solution Words	T-L Freq.	1	2	3	4	1 + 2	1 + 2 + 3 + 4	Digram-Freq. Total
SHAPE	AA	62	33	8	2	95	105	1872
PHASE	15	9	33	48	149	42	239	2497

(Mayzner & Tresselt, in press) involving a sample of 20,000 words and represent the total frequencies with which these digrams occur in this 20,000 word sample. In EC III and IV, the letters were ordered so as to yield low (123) and high (4081) summed values or digram-frequency totals, since interest is focused on the effects of anagram digram frequencies. In contrast, in EC V and VI, where interest is focused on easy vs. hard letter orders with three of the five letters in the anagram in the same position as in the solution word, anagram digram-frequency totals are kept relatively equal (404 vs. 685) for the two conditions, allowing only anagram letter order to vary. For example, the anagram AHSPE represents an easy letter order for the solution word SHAPE, since the letters "H," "P," and "E" are in the same letter position in the anagram as in the solution word, while with the anagram AHPSE, the letters "H," "S," and "E" are in the same letter position in the anagram as in the alternate solution word PHASE.

It may also be seen in Table 1 that the two solution words (SHAPE and PHASE) have a number of values listed. The Thorndike-Lorge frequency (T-L Freq.) shows values for these words, with SHAPE occurring more than 100 times per million words (i.e., AA) and PHASE occurring 15 times per million words. The values appearing under Digram-Position Frequencies refer to the frequency counts, taken from the Mayzner and Tresselt (in press) tables, with which the four sequential digrams, e.g., SH, HA, AP, and PE, or, PH, HA, AS, and SE occur in the tables in the first and second, second and third, third and fourth, and fourth and fifth positions of five-letter words. The columns headed $1+2$ and $1+2+3+4$ are merely the sums of digram positions $1+2$ (i.e., $62+33=95$) and $1+2+3+4$ (ie., $62+33+8+2=105$). The final column headed Digram-Freq. Total refers to the summed frequencies for the four sequential digrams based on the total 20,000 word sample. The importance of the distinction between digram-position frequencies, which take word-length and letter-position variations into account, and digram-frequency totals which do not was examined in a previous study (Mayzner & Tresselt, 1963). All of the frequency values listed in Table 1 were employed in the various analyses that were made and their specific relationship to the S-R model being employed will be explained subsequently.

All anagrams were typed in caps on 3×5 in. cards. All Ss were tested individually and the order of problem presentation corresponds with the ordering of the 21 pairs of double-solution problems shown in Table 2. In EC I each S received as his anagram problem the second word of each of the 21 pairs and was required to obtain the first word as a solution, while in EC II, each S received as his anagram problem the first word of each of the 21 pairs and was required to obtain the second word as a solution. In EC III, IV, V, and VI each S received an anagram, appropriate to his experimental condition, and was required to obtain both solution words. In all six conditions S was allowed 240 sec. to reach either a single solution, as in EC I and II, or two solutions, as in EC III, IV, V, and VI. In those conditions where double solutions were possible and S solved both problems within 240 sec., he received two time scores, with the time score for the second solution equal to the time taken to obtain the first solution plus the additional time needed to obtain the second solution. If S solved only one problem, he received the time score required to solve this problem and he received 240 sec. as his time score for the unsolved problem. If S failed both problems, he received two time scores, each of 240 sec. On all failed problems, S was given the solution or solutions before preceding to the next problem. All solutions were given by S verbally (i.e., S had no paper or pencil) and solution times were recorded with a stopwatch.

RESULTS

Table 2 presents the principal findings of the study and shows the median solution times for each of the solution words under all six experimental conditions. Median rather than mean solution times were selected

TABLE 2

THORNDIKE-LORGE FREQUENCIES (T-L) AND MEDIAN SOLUTION TIMES
FOR ALL SOLUTION WORDS FOR ALL SIX EXPERIMENTAL CONDITIONS

T-L	Solution Words	Median Solution Times					
		Cond. I	Cond. II	Cond. III	Cond. IV	Cond. V	Cond. VI
AA	EARTH	44.0		240.0	240.0	228.5	225.0
AA	HEART		14.5	28.5	168.5	34.5	9.5
AA	SHORE	11.0		8.5	39.0	6.5	78.5
AA	HORSE		10.5	26.5	105.0	27.5	21.0
A	TRIAL	218.0		93.5	149.5	2.5	240.0
A	TRAIL		47.0	7.0	153.0	49.0	7.0
A	CHARM	12.5		84.0	27.0	40.0	146.0
AA	MARCH		8.5	82.5	24.0	45.0	53.0
AA	BOARD	61.0		19.5	22.0	16.0	3.5
A	BROAD		22.5	40.5	25.0	51.0	28.0
AA	THING	50.0		9.0	16.0	9.0	131.0
AA	NIGHT		47.0	17.0	42.0	4.0	3.0
A	ANGER	131.5		240.0	122.0	83.0	114.0
A	RANGE		9.0	46.0	56.0	21.0	8.0
AA	TIRED	44.0		23.0	35.5	47.5	45.0
AA	TRIED		25.0	18.0	71.0	65.5	43.0
AA	WRONG	24.0		15.0	23.5	1.5	23.5
A	GROWN		16.0	6.0	10.5	39.5	6.5
A	TOWER	105.5		119.0	163.5	2.0	73.5
AA	WROTE		81.0	16.5	9.0	15.0	5.0
AA	SHAPE	15.0		7.5	6.0	5.5	14.0
15	PHASE		59.5	11.0	115.5	79.5	21.0
A	BRUSH	7.5		12.0	8.0	1.5	14.5
17	SHRUB		12.5	10.5	15.5	18.5	2.0
AA	OCEAN	240.0		240.0	69.0	98.5	240.0
32	CANOE		240.0	142.5	240.0	240.0	30.5
A	BREAD	23.0		4.0	31.0	2.0	1.5
32	BEARD		41.5	28.5	70.0	125.0	9.5
AA	BELOW	79.5		69.5	117.0	18.0	159.0
26	ELBOW		31.5	103.5	68.5	112.0	104.5
AA	DRIVE	14.5		10.5	27.5	2.0	53.0
25	DIVER		32.0	32.5	49.0	76.0	5.0
A	TRACE	19.0		19.0	38.5	30.5	184.0
7	CRATE		22.0	18.0	48.5	37.0	60.0
AA	TABLE	38.0		13.0	17.5	6.5	26.0
7	BLEAT		53.5	65.5	101.0	206.5	240.0
A	FLESH	16.0		15.5	11.0	16.5	30.5
11	SHELF		6.0	4.0	14.0	8.0	2.5
AA	TRADE	52.0		6.5	22.0	27.5	133.5
26	TREAD		116.5	92.5	58.5	45.0	30.5
AA	CAUSE	9.0		28.5	123.5	5.5	30.5
27	SAUCE		32.5	100.5	240.0	55.0	15.5

as most representative of the distribution of scores obtained from the 20 Ss under each condition, since most distributions were skewed as well as having an artificial ceiling imposed of 240 sec.

In previous studies (Mayzner & Tresselt, 1958, 1952, 1962) predictions derived from an S-R mediational model were made of anagram solution times based on the combined results for groups of anagram problems and no attempt was made to make predictions for individual anagram problems. However, in the present study each anagram problem will be treated as representing an individual test of the various hypotheses deduced from the model. In adopting this procedure the sign test (Siegel, 1956, p. 68) will be employed to evaluate the degree to which model predictions are confirmed by the pattern of individual anagram solution times.

Since the effects of anagram letter order appear to be among the strongest effects examined, this analysis will be presented first. In EC V the model predicts that the first solution word of each of the 21 pairs should be solved faster than the second solution word, since the first has three of the five letters of the associated anagram in the same letter position as in the solution word. The opposite obtains for EC VI, and therefore, the second solution word of each pair should be solved faster than the first. In both EC V and VI, 17 of 21 pairs yield differences in the predicted direction for the respective conditions, and a 17–4 split as evaluated with the sign test yields $p < .004$.

Comparing EC III with IV, the model predicts that all solution times under EC IV should be higher than the associated solution times under EC III, since the digram-frequency totals associated with the anagrams under EC IV are all higher than the digram-frequency totals associated with the anagrams under EC III. Since 21 problem pairs are available, 42 individual tests of the prediction are possible, and excluding the one tie occurring with the solution word EARTH, 30 of the remaining 41 comparisons are in the predicted direction, yielding a $p < .003$.

The effects of Thorndike-Lorge solution-word frequency on anagram solution times for the last 11 problem pairs (i.e., SHAPE-PHASE through CAUSE-SAUCE) may be examined most clearly in EC I–IV. In EC V and VI solution-word frequency and anagram letter order are confounded and therefore, the effects of the two variables cannot be separated. For EC I–IV the model predicts that the first solution word of each pair, with the higher T-L count, should be solved faster than the second solution word of each pair, with the lower T-L count. Comparing EC I and II, excluding the tie that occurs with the OCEAN-CANOE pair, 8 of the remaining 10 pairs are in the predicted direction ($p < .055$). In EC III 7 of the 11 pairs are in the predicted direction ($p < .274$) and in EC IV 10 of the 11 pairs are in the predicted direction ($p < .006$).

In examining the effects of solution-word digram frequencies on anagram solution times, an analysis technique was employed that was developed in a previous study (Mayzner & Tresselt, 1963). In this technique anagram solution times were correlated with various measures which reflect digram-frequency characteristics of the solution words. As was previously indicated, Table 1 presents instances of seven such measures for the problem pair SHAPE-PHASE and Table 3 presents the rank-difference correlations between these seven measures, associated with solution-word digram-frequency characteristics, and anagram solution times, for EC I–VI. Since T-L solution-word frequency is a variable affecting anagram solution times, the correlations presented in Table 3 were calculated separately for the three solution-word T-L frequency subgroupings (i.e., F-F, the words derived from the word pairs in which both solution words of each pair have high T-L counts, F, the frequent T-L words, and I, the infrequent T-L words, derived from the word pairs in which one solution word has a high T-L count and the other solution word has a low T-L count).

The results shown in Table 3 confirm the findings of the earlier mentioned study (Mayzner & Tresselt, 1963), which had found that anagram solution times show much higher correlations with digram-frequency measures that reflect word-length and letter-position variations than with measures that do not take such variations into account. For example, in Table 3, 12 of the 15 correlations based on summed sequential digram-position frequency counts (i.e., the values under $1 + 2 + 3 + 4$) are higher than the correlations based on total counts, with a 12 out of 15 split, as evaluated with the sign test, yielding a $p < .018$.

Table 3 also permits comparisons to be made between the correlations obtained when each sequential digram frequency is correlated separately with anagram solution times as well as when only the first two sequential digrams are summed and the summed values are then correlated with anagram solution times. Comparing, e.g., the values under $1 + 2$ with those under $1 + 2 + 3 + 4$ (excluding the one tie of .56), 12 of the 14 comparisons show higher values under $1 + 2$ than under $1 + 2 + 3 + 4$ ($p < .006$) and comparing $1 + 2$ with total, 14 of the 15 comparisons show higher values under $1 + 2$ than under total ($p < .001$). These results strongly suggest that digram frequencies $1 + 2$ are the "best" predictors of anagram solution times. Carrying this analysis one step further, anagram solution times were correlated with the digram frequencies associated with each of the four separate sequential digram positions, as shown under 1, 2, 3, and 4. These results reveal a pattern of decreasing correlation values from Digram Positions 1 through 4, with a marked break in values occurring between Digram Positions 2 and 3. If all digram-position comparisons are made, i.e., 1 vs. 2, 1 vs. 3, 1 vs. 4, 2 vs. 3, 2 vs. 4, and 3 vs. 4, splits of 9–6, 11–4, 13–2, 15–0, 13–2, and 11–4, respectively, are obtained for the number of high correlations vs. low, for each of the respective comparisons. These six splits, as evaluated with the sign test, yield p values of

TABLE 3

RANK-DIFFERENCE CORRELATIONS (RHO) BETWEEN SOLUTION-WORD
DIGRAM-POSITION FREQUENCIES AND ANAGRAM SOLUTION TIMES
FOR THE SIX EXPERIMENTAL CONDITIONS

Experimental Cond.	(N)	\multicolumn{7}{c}{Solution-Word Digram-Position Frequencies}						
		1	2	3	4	1 + 2	1 + 2 + 3 + 4	Total
I								
F	(21)	.40	.23	.11	−.18	.29	−.03	−.18
II								
F	(10)	.22	−.10	−.28	.29	.01	.26	.60
I	(11)	.19	.10	−.35	−.25	.19	.11	−.36
III								
F-F	(20)	.27	.52	.37	−.16	.52	.10	−.34
F	(11)	.60	.72	−.14	−.29	.76	.03	−.07
I	(11)	.43	.46	.17	−.07	.56	.56	.18
IV								
F-F	(20)	−.06	.21	.06	−.14	.06	−.10	−.27
F	(11)	.37	.23	−.30	−.48	.16	−.46	−.21
I	(11)	.55	.48	.07	−.36	.57	.35	.02
V								
F-F	(20)	.06	.21	.12	.27	.13	.29	−.10
F	(11)	.40	.20	−.16	−.02	.31	−.12	−.13
I	(11)	.47	.36	−.14	−.19	.46	.28	−.04
VI								
F-F	(20)	−.27	.21	.17	−.30	.11	−.15	−.53
F	(11)	.57	.22	−.16	−.19	.34	−.19	.08
I	(11)	.47	.40	−.04	−.11	.53	.45	.03

Note.—N refers to the number of anagram problems on which the rhos are based and for Ns of 10, 11, 20, and 21, values of rho significant at the .05 level are .69, .65, .47, and .45, respectively. F refers to frequent T-L words, I refers to infrequent T-L words, and F-F refers to the two groups of frequent T-L words combined.

less than .304, .059, .004, .001, .004, and .059, respectively, and again strongly suggest that Digram Positions 1 and 2 are the best predictors of anagram solution times, with Digram Positions 3 and 4, in general showing negative correlations with solution times.

Discussion

In the present study an S-R mediational model of problem-solving behavior (Kendler, 1961; Kendler & Kendler, 1962) was employed to make predictions concerning anagram solution times for multiple-solution anagram problems. The results presented in Table 2 provide strong support for all model predictions and extend the model's generality of application from single- to multiple-solution anagram problems. These results also indicate that if multiple-solution anagrams are used to test, e.g., certain aspects of mental-set phenomena as has been done by Maltzman and Morrisett (1952, 1953), confounding of set variables, with such variables as solution-word T-L frequencies, solution-word digram frequencies, etc., may occur unless explicitly controlled.

The results presented in Table 3 deserve special comment, since while they confirm previous findings (Mayzner & Tresselt, 1963), the results also suggest an important modification in the manner in which this variable affects solution times. It would appear from the pattern of decreasing correlation values shown in Table 3, from Digram Positions 1 through 4 and from $1 + 2$ to $1 + 2 + 3 + 4$ for all six experimental conditions, that the first and second digram positions in the solution word are the critical elements leading to either fast or slow solution times, rather than all the digrams constituting the solution word. This result poses an interesting extension for the model to anagram problems consisting of more than five letters. It might be found, e.g., that as the length of the anagram problem increases from five to nine letters, that the sharp break which occurs in correlation values between Digram Positions 2 and 3 with five letters would occur between Digram Positions 3 and 4 or 4 and 5 with nine letters. Such a finding would suggest that as the anagram letter array is increased in length S correspondingly increases the size of the letter "chunk" he chooses for his implicit letter rearrangements.

Closely related to the size of a letter chunk selected by S for rearrangements, and the letter position at which a sharp break occurs in correlation values, is the size of letter group employed to characterize solution-word structure. In the present study and in all previous work on anagram problem solving by the authors, two-letter groups or digrams were used exclusively, however, in further extending the range of application of the model to include longer anagram letter arrays, it might also be fruitful to characterize solution-word structure in terms of sequential trigram or tetragram frequencies and additional effort should be directed to this issue.

REFERENCES

KENDLER, H. H. Problems in problem solving research. In, *Current trends in psychological theory: A bicentennial program.* Pittsburgh: Univer. Pittsburgh Press, 1961.

KENDLER, H. H., & KENDLER, T. S. Vertical and horizontal processes in problem solving. *Psychol. Rev.*, 1962, 69, 1–16.

MALTZMAN, I., & MORRISETT, L., JR. Different strengths of set in the solution of anagrams. *J. exp. Psychol.*, 1952, 44, 242–246.

MALTZMAN, I., & MORRISETT, L., JR. The effects of single and compound classes of anagrams on set solutions. *J. exp. Psychol.*, 1953, 45, 345–350.

MAYZNER, M. S., & TRESSELT, M. E. Anagram solution times: A function of letter-order and word frequency. *J. exp. Psychol.*, 1958, 56, 376–379.

MAYZNER, M. S., & TRESSELT, M. E. Anagram solution times: A function of transition probabilities. *J. Psychol.*, 1959, 47, 117–125.

MAYZNER, M. S., & TRESSELT, M. E. Anagram solution times: A function of word transition probabilities. *J. exp. Psychol.*, 1962, 63, 510-513.

MAYZNER, M. S., & TRESSELT, M. E. Anagram solution times: A function of word length and letter position variables. *J. Psychol.*, 1963, 55, 469–475.

MAYZNER, M. S., & TRESSELT, M. E. Tables of digram and single-letter frequency counts by word-length and letter-position for a sample of 20,000 words. *Psychon. Monogr. Suppl.*, in press.

MAYZNER, M. S., TRESSELT, M. E., & HELBOCK, H. An exploratory study of mediational responses in anagram problem solving. *J. Psychol.*, 1964, 57, 263–274.

SIEGEL, S. *Nonparametric statistics for the behavioral science.* New York: McGraw-Hill, 1956.

THORNDIKE, E. L., & LORGE, F. *The teacher's word book of 30,000 words.* New York: Teachers College, Columbia University, Bureau of Publications, 1944.

10. Transition Probability Effects in Anagram Problem Solving

Harry Beilin and Rheba Horn

It has been proposed that if certain gestalt assumptions about perceptual and cognitive organization are true, meaningful letter groups such as words should resist reorganization more than meaningless letter aggregates when these are the materials of anagram problem solving experiments (Hollingworth 1935, 1938). Hollingworth and others (Nissenson & Sargent, 1941; Sargent, 1940), however, have found words to be no different from nonsense letter arrangements in resisting alteration. Up to the

Reprinted by permission of the authors and the American Psychological Association from *Journal of Experimental Psychology*, 1962, *63*, 514–518.

time of Johnson's (1955) review only Devnich's (1937) findings suggested that a difference exists. This was sufficient for Johnson to consider the question still open.

In the main, the technique used in these experiments required that S discover the word (e.g., KANGAROO) that could be made from either related or unrelated word groups (e.g., AGO, KORAN) in contrast with meaningless letter arrangements (e.g., OAG, KRNOA). More recently, Mayzner and Tresselt (1958, 1959) have tested the aforementioned thesis employing meaningless letter aggregates as anagrams. They establish that anagram solution time is a function of anagram letter order, solution word frequency (Mayzner & Tresselt, 1958), and transition probability (Mayzner & Tresselt, 1959). By contrasting the solution times of anagrams of high transition probability total (from summed digram frequencies of sequential letter pairs) with those of low transition probability total a positive relationship is established between the two variables. In other words, the higher the transition probability total of a letter aggregate the more difficult it is to alter the letter arrangement and the longer the solution time. Although Mayzner and Tresselt (1959) do not directly infer from these results that the difficulty of altering letter arrangements in words, in contrast to nonsense letter arrangements, is a function of transition probability they do conclude that well patterned letter groups (which they illustrate with words) are more difficult to reorganize than loosely patterned letter groups (which they illustrate with nonsense arrangements) if patterning is defined in terms of transition probabilities.

In the foregoing experiments two variables are considered and to some extent confounded. Words and nonsense letter arrangements used as anagrams differ both in meaning and organization (or patterning). These variables require independent treatment since it is not at all difficult to have nonsense letter arrangements which are more highly patterned than words (if patterning is taken as the equivalent of transition probability total, as Mayzner and Tresselt propose). In the Mayzner and Tresselt studies only nonsense letter arrangements of greater and lesser patterning (transition probability totals) are employed. It is dubious therefore whether the transition probability hypothesis can be applied as an explanation for solution time differences between word and nonsense anagrams, without a test in which words and nonsense arrangements are employed.

The present experiment offers a test of the hypothesis that solution time differences between highly and loosely patterned anagram letter arrangements are a function of transition probability. This is achieved by utilizing both five-letter words and nonsense five-letter aggregates as anagrams, keeping transition probability, letter order, and solution-word frequency constant.

Method

Subjects. Sixty students, primarily in their junior year, at Brooklyn College served as Ss; 30 were randomly assigned to each of two groups which differed in the presentation order of the materials.

Materials. The stimulus materials consisted of 10 five-letter nonsense aggregates (e.g., OBAVE) typed in capital letters on plain 3 × 5 in. index cards and another set of 10 five-letter words (e.g., FROTH) typed in identical fashion on index cards. Both words and nonsense letter aggregates are used as anagrams in the experiments.

Experimental design. One group was first given the 10 nonsense letter anagrams and then the 10 word anagrams; the other group the reverse. The presentation order of individual anagrams was rotated so that every anagram arrangement occurred in each serial position and in a different combination with its counterpart in the other anagram group (i.e., 1, 1; 2, 3; 3, 5; . . . 10, 10).

The solution words for both nonsense and word anagrams were selected from the Thorndike-Lorge (1944) word list and equated for frequency. The mean frequencies of nonsense and word anagram solution words are 74.4 and 74.3, respectively.

The traditional anagram problem was modified so that only *two* letters of the nonsense or word anagram were to be interchanged to produce the solution word (keeping the remaining letters in order). The "letter switching order" of the nonsense and word anagram sets was matched to control letter order alteration (i.e., there is one 1–3 switch in each group, one 1–4, one 1–5, etc.). This is necessary since some letter orders are more difficult than others (Hunter, 1959); limiting the altering task to two letters controls the unscrambling necessary to solve the anagram.

The anagram sets were also equated for transition probability. The nonsense anagrams were arranged to yield mean transition probability totals equal to the mean totals for the word anagrams. Transition probability totals are derived from summed digram frequencies of sequential letter pairs (Pratt, 1942). For example, the total for the anagram OBAVE is the total of OB, BA, AV, and VE = 4 + 10 + 10 + 29 = 53. The mean transition probability total for nonsense anagrams is 153.8; for word anagrams, 151.7 (the difference is not significant).

The use of transition probability totals from summed digram frequencies is based upon S's supposed knowledge (of probabilities of occurrence) of pairs of letters in his native language. Since S may be equally affected by his knowledge of three-letter, four-letter, and five-letter groupings and single letter expectancies in his attempts at solution it suggests that the total transition probability of an anagram should be a composite of digram, trigram, quadragram, and pentagram frequencies, as well as initial and terminal letter frequencies. Pentagram and quadragram frequency tables were not available to us, although trigram frequency tables were (Pratt, 1942). We have computed the mean total of summed trigram frequencies for word and nonsense anagrams. The mean for word anagrams is 204.2 ($SD = 392.2$); for nonsense anagrams, 164.8 ($SD = 355.8$). The difference between these means is not significant. In addition the difference of mean initial letter frequencies is not significant (word mean $= 63.0$, $SD = 63.1$; nonsense mean $= 67.4$, $SD = 58.5$), nor the difference between terminal frequency means (word mean $= 122.6$, $SD = 72.5$; nonsense mean $= 72.7$, $SD = 81.7$).

Procedure. The Ss were told they were to make meaningful words from the nonsense and word anagrams by interchanging two of the letters and keeping the remaining three in the same location. Only one correct solution is possible for each anagram. One example (i.e., CAUSE-SAUCE, ERTEN-ENTER) and one sample problem (i.e., SPOON-SNOOP, FALSH-FLASH) was given before each anagram list. The Ss were also told there would be 10 anagrams in each list with a maximum 2-min. solution time per anagram, after which the solution word would be given before continuing to the next anagram. Solutions were given by S verbally with no aids permitted. Solution times were recorded with a stop watch. Testing was individual and the experiment proper was followed by asking Ss how they obtained the solutions.

RESULTS AND DISCUSSION

Medians of S's solution times for each anagram set and median group ($N = 30$) solution times per anagram were computed. Table 1 gives the major results expressed as the means and SDs of individual medians. Within this design it is possible to evaluate the effects upon solution time of the word-nonsense letter arrangement differences, as well as possible practice effects. The word-nonsense arrangement effect was tested with the Friedman two-way analysis of variance by ranks (Siegel, 1956). Word anagram solution time was significantly slower than nonsense anagram solution time ($P < .001$). (First and second order presentations were combined, on the basis of the analysis which follows.)

The effects of practice were assessed separately for the word and nonsense letter arrangement groups. A Mann-Whitney U test was applied to the first and second order solution times within each task. The values indicated are not significantly different ($P > .10$).

To assess further the relationship between transition probability and solution time (since transition probability total is already controlled) Kendall τ's were computed between nonsense anagram solution times and their associated transition probability totals. The same was done for the word anagram solution times. The τ's for nonsense anagrams, first and second order presentations, were −.06 and −.16, respectively. For words, these τ's were .11 and .08. These correlations are not significant. On the other hand, τ between solution times for the first and second presentation of word anagrams was .62, and the comparable τ for nonsense anagrams was .63 ($P < .05$).

The anagram problem solver has two kinds of data to take into account; the anagram and the solution words he generates. If he requires knowledge of the transition probabilities of the letter pairs in his language to

TABLE 1

SOLUTION TIMES (SEC.) FOR NONSENSE ANAGRAM AND WORD ANAGRAM TASKS

Presentation Order	Word Anagrams			Nonsense Anagrams			Total		
	N	Mean	SD	N	Mean	SD	N	Mean	SD
First	30	18.23	21.45	30	8.37	11.19	60	13.30	17.68
Second	30	15.17	12.01	30	10.46	12.75	60	12.81	12.41
Total	60	16.70	17.33	60	9.42	11.83			

Note.—Means and SDs are based upon medians of S's solution times for 10 nonsense anagrams and 10 word anagrams.

treat adequately the letter pairs of the anagrams (Hunter, 1959) the same should apply to the solution words. This is evident from those Ss who put correct combinations together but do not recognize them as words. (We might be tempted to say that the process of solving anagrams is one of testing varieties of possible letter combinations and then recognizing the combinations as words, were it not that many Ss produce solution words and *then* check the correctness of the letter combinations.) We tested to be certain the transition probability totals for *solution* words were not different, even though word frequencies were equated. The difference between averaged transition probability totals (from summed digram frequencies) for solution words is not significant (word mean = 145.1, $SD = 63.9$; nonsense mean = 151.4, $SD = 75.3$).

The Ss divide into those who solve nonsense anagrams faster and a smaller group who solve word anagrams faster. To test whether these represent stable S capactices, we first hypothesized that the S trait represented here is the ability to deal with embedded figures (viz., letters embedded in words). Such an S capacity might be related to an ability to deal with geometric figures embedded in complex designs as represented by the Gottschaldt figures.[1] No such relationship, however, was found to exist.

As Mayzner and Tresselt (1958) and Hunter (1959) show, by different methods, the production of solutions per unit time comes very quickly at first and then tapers off. By applying the method used by Hunter, which indicates the average rate of correct solution production, to a 10-sec. interval, we find the same solution production pattern except that the production rate for word anagrams is slower than for nonsense anagrams. Examination of Ss' retrospective reports suggests why this may be so. Some Ss comment that word anagrams often bind them whereas nonsense anagrams do not. These Ss perseverate on the word anagrams to such an extent that problem solution is interfered with. Whether perseveration is due to attention to the meaning associated with the word or to its sound is not clear.

Word anagrams are more difficult to alter than nonsense anagrams. This supports the findings of Mayzner and Tresselt (1958) and Devnich (1937). Since transition probability was controlled the Mayzner and Tresselt explanation of the difference may be rejected. The low correlation between solution time of individual anagrams and their transition probability totals further supports such rejection. Although solution time differences due to patterning may be accounted for by transition probability it does not follow that it will similarly account for differences in meaning.

Although it has not been possible to compute composite transition probability values for the anagrams, we may conclude that anagram solution time differences between words and nonsense arrangements are not due to averaged digram, trigram, or initial and terminal letter frequencies.

Two possibilities remain to account for the anagram solving differences. The first is the perseverative effect generated by word anagrams and the second, organization or patterning effects independent of transition probabilities of successive letter arrangements.

Summary

An experiment tested the effect of transition probability of successive letter sequences upon the solution time of word and nonsense anagrams. Transition probability totals (from summed digram frequencies of sequential letter pairs), solution word frequencies, and letter switching orders were equated for word and nonsense anagrams.

Solution time is significantly longer for word anagrams than nonsense

[1] We therefore administered the Thurstone Concealed Figures Test (Thurstone, 1944, 1951) on a group basis to 40 of the 60 Ss still available to us. The mean correct solutions were 81.9 for nonsense anagrams ($SD = 15.5$) and 84.2 for words ($SD = 17.2$) ($P > .05$). We are indebted to Aaron Carton for suggesting this possibility to us.

anagrams. This difference is not accounted for by transition probability totals from summed trigram frequencies, initial and terminal letter frequencies, or transition probability totals of solution words.

Word perseveration effect is offered as a possible explanation of the solution time difference as well as organization effects not accounted for by transition probabilities of successive letter arrangements.

REFERENCES

DEVNICH, G. E. Words as "Gestalten." *J. exp. Psychol.*, 1937, 20, 297–300.

HOLLINGWORTH, H. L. The conditions of verbal configuration. *J. exp. Psychol.*, 1935, 18, 299–306.

HOLLINGWORTH, H. L. Verbal Gestalt experiments with children. *J. exp. Psychol.*, 1938, 23, 90–95.

HUNTER, I. M. L. The solving of five-letter anagram problems. *Brit. J. Psychol.*, 1959, 50, 193–206.

JOHNSON, D. M. *The psychology of thought and judgment.* New York: Harper, 1955.

MAYZNER, M. S., & TRESSELT, M. E. Anagram solution times: A function of letter order and word frequency. *J. exp. Psychol.*, 1958, 56, 376–379.

MAYZNER, M. S., & TRESSELT, M. E. Anagram solution times: A function of transition probabilities. *J. Psychol*, 1959, 47, 117–125.

NISSENSON, M., & SARGENT, S. S. Words as configurations. *J. exp. Psychol.*, 1941, 28, 85–89.

PRATT, F. *Secret and urgent.* New York: Blue Ribbon, 1942.

SARGENT, S. S. Thinking processes at various levels of difficulty. *Arch. Psychol., N.Y.*, 1940, No. 249.

SIEGEL, S. *Nonparametric statistics for the behavioral sciences.* New York: McGraw-Hill, 1956.

THORNDIKE, E. L., & LORGE, I. *The teacher's word book of 30,000 words.* New York: Columbia University, Bureau of Publications, 1944.

THURSTONE, L. L. *A factorial study of perception.* Chicago: Univer. Chicago Press, 1944.

THURSTONE, L. L. An analysis of mechanical aptitude. *Psychometer. Lab. Bull.*, No. 62. Chicago: Univer. Chicago Press, 1951.

11. Effect of Word Frequency on Thinking of a Word

Carl P. Duncan

Abstract. *Three experiments were performed to determine the effect of word frequency on thinking of a word. In all experiments Ss were given certain characteristics of words, such as the first letter, the last letter, the number of letters, or the class of the object named by the word, and were asked to think of a word fitting the given characteristics.*

In all experiments, more words of higher frequency were emitted than were words of lower frequency. In general, the tendency to emit words of relative frequencies held throughout the whole range of absolute frequencies. Not all high-frequency words that could have been emitted were emitted. The findings were interpreted in terms of a combination of the spew hypothesis, and of incomplete sampling from a population of words.

In certain kinds of problem solving, S must search among a population of possible responses until he hits upon, if he does, the particular response defined as the solution. As S emits responses, often implicitly, in his search, what variables determine which responses occur and which do not occur? It seems reasonable to assume that one such variable will be the frequency, in S's past experience, with which he has encountered the responses. In general, responses known or assumed to have occurred more frequently in S's experience should be more likely to occur to him during searching or thinking.

This hypothesis concerning the effects of response frequency on thinking derives chiefly from two sources. One is the spew hypothesis of Underwood and Schulz (1960), according to which verbal units are emitted in the order of frequency of experience with the units. These authors summarize a number of studies in which the spew hypothesis was supported in relatively free responding situations such as free association. The other source is the study of Mayzner and Tresselt (1958) in which anagram solution times vary inversely with Thorndike-Lorge (1944) frequency of the solution words. It is Mayzner and Tresselt's theory that in attempting to solve an anagram, S generates implicit responses as some function of frequency.

With an anagram, S has all the letters of the solution word presented to him. Letter hypotheses (Rhine, 1959), letter orders (Mayzner and Tresselt,

Reprinted by permission of Academic Press, Inc. from *Journal of Verbal Learning and Verbal Behavior*, 1966, 5, 434–440.

1958; Teraoka, 1959), and frequencies of letter combinations (Dominow-ski and Duncan, 1964; Mayzner and Tresselt, 1959) become variables in-fluencing solution. In the present study, an attempt was made to minimize the effects of letter variables and to maximize the frequency of the word as a whole. The S was asked to think of a word that meets certain specifi-cations. The specifications served both to narrow the response population to be searched to the point where there was some probability that S would discover the word, and also to restrict, sometimes to a single word, the number of words that met the specifications. Problems of this type should be solved more readily if the solution is a high-frequency rather than a low-frequency word.

EXPERIMENT I

METHOD

Words. The source of words was the five-letter words from Thorndike and Lorge (1944). The set of words to be used was obtained by select-ing 20 subsets of words. The words in each subset had the same first letter and the same last letter. The 20 pairs of initial and final letters were: *bd* (thus including such words as *brand, beard, blind,* etc.), *bh, bn, ck, cl, cp, fk, fr, ln, mh, pk, pr, rl, rt, sk, sm, td, tr, wh, wt.* These subsets ranged in number of five-letter words available (i.e., listed in Thorndike and Lorge) from six words (both *ln* and *pk*) to 36 words (*sk*). The total number of words, all 20 subsets combined, was 266. Within each subset there was one or more words of T-L frequency of less than one per million words (Thorndike and Lorge General Count). Also within each subset there was one or more words of frequency of A (here taken as 50) or AA ('here taken as 100), except for *fk*, where the highest-frequency word was 44, and *pk*, highest frequency 28. The mean frequencies of the 20 subsets ranged from 11.4 to 39.1. The 20 median frequencies ranged from 1.5 to 26.0. For all 266 words in the population the mean frequency was 22.97, the median frequency 8.8.

Subjects. The Ss were 60 students from introductory psychology classes in which students are required to serve in experiments.

Procedure. After E and S had sat down facing each other across a table, E said to S, "I want you to guess some five-letter English words. I will give you the first letter and the last letter of one of these words. Then you try and tell me what the five-letter word is. None of the words which you are to guess is in plural form, and none is capitalized such as proper names or brand names. O.k., here is the first one." The E then gave the first let-ter of a problem item, paused a moment, then gave the last letter. The S was given 60 sec. in which to respond. If S gave an unacceptable response, e.g., not a five-letter word, E pointed out the error and S was allowed the remainder of the 60-sec period to make another response. After S had responded with an acceptable response, or after 60 sec had elapsed, E said, "Let's try another one." The E continued until all 20 letter pairs had been presented to each S. The 20 letter pairs were presented in a different haphazard order for each S.

RESULTS

Of the total possible 1200 responses (60 Ss × 20 guesses), 806 usable responses were obtained, for a mean of 13.43 ($\sigma_M = .44$) words per S. In addition, there were 58 responses consisting of words, e.g., *boxed*, for which a T-L frequency is not available. These responses are not included in the data.

For each S separately, both the mean T-L frequency and the median frequency of the words S gave were determined. Over all Ss, the mean of the means was 41.91, $\sigma_M = 1.13$. The mean of the medians was 35.07, $\sigma_M = 2.02$; the median of the medians was 32.0. The mean frequency of the population of words was 22.97; thus, it can be seen that either of the obtained means is higher by a t-value of at least 5. For 58 of the 60 Ss, the mean frequency of S's responses was higher than the population mean; for 59 Ss the median frequency of their responses was higher than the population median frequency (8.8).

Another comparison is obtained by examining not total responses, but only the number of different words emitted. Over all Ss, 186 words out of the population of 266 words were given at least once, 80 were not given. Of the 133 words above the median frequency (8.8) of the population, 113 were given. Of the words below the median, only 73 were given. For the 186 emitted words, the mean T-L frequency was 28.60, $\sigma_M = 2.38$ (median frequency was 15.3); thus, though this is a fairly large sample of the population, the mean frequency is significantly higher ($t = 2.39$) than the population mean frequency (22.97). For the 80 words not emitted, the mean frequency was 8.79, $\sigma_M = 2.04$ (median frequency was 2.1).

In Table 1, frequency classes (first column) have been set up that contain roughly equal numbers of population words (second column). Column 3 shows the number of different words emitted, and Column 4 shows total responses, for each of the frequency classes. It is clear that both number of different words emitted and total responses decrease as frequency decreases. For all 266 population words, the correlation between frequency of the word and number of times it was emitted was .44; for the 186 words that were given at least once, the correlation was .40.

TABLE 1

POPULATION WORDS, EMITTED WORDS, AND TOTAL RESPONSES
IN VARIOUS FREQUENCY CATEGORIES IN EXP. I

Frequency class	Population words	Emitted words	Total responses
A and AA	52	46	311
18–49	44	40	202
8–17	43	30	108
3–7	41	29	96
1–2	41	24	41
Less than 1	45	17	48

EXPERIMENT II

In Exp. I, each of the subsets of words associated with a letter pair contained several words. The S was free to give any one of the words in a subset that he could think of. Since even the smallest subset contained six words, while the largest contained 36 words, the task was something of a "free response" situation like those in which Underwood and Schulz (1960) found evidence for the spew hypothesis. The purpose of Exp. II was to test the effect of T-L frequency in a task where the number of acceptable responses was severely restricted.

METHOD

Words. The words were 34 pairs of words from Thorndike and Lorge (1944). Each of the 68 words had five letters. The two words within each pair had the same initial letter and the same final letter (initial and final letters were themselves identical in only two of the 34 pairs). The two words of a pair had different T-L frequencies. Hereafter, the word of higher frequency in a pair will be called the HF (high frequency) word and the other word will be called the LF (low frequency) word, regardless of the absolute frequency. The presence of a difference in frequency between the words of a pair is the independent variable; the expectation is that the HF word will be more readily emitted when S is required to think of a word.

Among the 68 words there were words of high absolute frequency (A or AA), and words of low absolute frequency (less than one per million). The difference in frequency between the words of a pair also varied, e.g., earth (AA) vs. epoch (5), until (AA) vs. usual (A), borax (2) vs. beaux (1).

Pilot work had revealed that there were pairs of words (from Thorn-

dike and Lorge) for which Ss could think of too many alternative responses; the 34 pairs finally used do not include such pairs. It was also
discovered that Ss found the task difficult. Because of this, the 34 pairs
were divided into two sets, A and B, of 17 pairs each, and any one S
worked on only one set. (To obtain an equal number of pairs in each set,
one pair of words was used in which the two words had the same frequency, viz., *outdo* and *outgo*, both having frequency of one.) The two
sets were roughly equivalent in absolute frequencies of words and in differences of frequency between words of a pair.

Subjects. The Ss were 80 students from introductory psychology courses.
Half were assigned Set A, and half Set B.

Procedure. After E and S sat down facing each other across a table,
E said, "I want you to guess some five-letter English words. I will give
you the first and the last letter of one of the words. Then you try to tell
me what the five-letter word is. None of the words that you are to guess
is plural form, and none is capitalized, such as proper names or brand
names. O.k., here is the first one." The E then gave the first letter, paused
momentarily, and gave the last letter. If S said either of the words in a
pair, E gave him the next item. If S had not responded after 60 sec had
elapsed, E said, "Let's try another," and gave S the letters for the next
item. A different haphazard order of presentation of the 17 items in a set
was used for each S. For each item, there were only two words available,
one being of higher frequency than the other.

RESULTS

Since there was little difference in response to Sets A and B, the data
were combined. For all 80 Ss, the mean total number of responses was
4.13. Since the maximum possible was 17, the task was rather difficult.
(The Ss gave a total of 28 responses that were not counted, either because
they were not clearly words, or do not appear in Thorndike and Lorge.)

For each S, the total number of responses was broken down into those
that were HF responses, i.e., where S gave the higher-frequency word
from a pair, and those that were LF responses. The mean number of HF
responses was 2.69 ($\sigma_M = .21$). The mean number of LF responses was
1.44 ($\sigma_M = .13$). The difference between these means yields t (related
measures) $= 4.77$, $p < .001$.

For the 34 HF words, the median frequency was 10.5. Over all 80 Ss,
a total of 215 responses was given which were HF words: 144 were responses of words above the median frequency, 71 were responses of words
below the median frequency. For the 34 HF words, the correlation between T-L frequency and number of responses was .47.

For the 34 LF words, the median frequency was 1.0. A total of 115 responses was given which were LF words; 84 of these were of words above

the median frequency, 31 of words below the median. The correlation between T-L frequency and number of responses to LF words was .56.

For all 68 words, the median T-L frequency was 3.0. Of the total 330 responses made, 233 were of words above the median frequency, 97 of words below the median. For all 68 words, the correlation between T-L frequency and number of responses was 55.

EXPERIMENT III

In Exp. II the task was rather difficult; the mean number of words given was small in comparison to the total possible. So in Exp. III another set of pairs of words was used, a set that pilot work indicated would elicit more responses.

Experiment III was also designed to obtain certain other kinds of information. The following question was asked: When S is required to guess a word from a pair of words, one of them higher T-L frequency than the other, will the probability of guessing one of the pair change if S is told the other word? If S is told one of the two possible words just as he starts trying to think of a word that will meet the specifications given him, then he no longer has a choice, since only one word remains to be guessed. Also, knowing one of the words might either facilitate or inhibit guessing the other. If such a transfer occurs, it may vary depending on whether S is given the higher-frequency word and must guess the lower-frequency word, or vice versa.

Experiment III was also designed to determine the effect of frequency on guessing when S is encouraged to try to think of more than one word per item. In Exps. I and II, S was not required to produce more than one word per item. In Exp. III, the question is raised whether more higher-frequency words would be guessed than lower-frequency words if S were given an opportunity to produce both the higher- and the lower-frequency word for each item.

METHOD

Words. The words were 17 pairs of words from Thorndike and Lorge (1944). Both words in a pair were names of objects that belonged to the same class, e.g., trees (*willow and walnut*). Both words in a pair began with the same first letter and had the same number of letters (3, 4, 5, or 6 letters). Within each pair, one of the words had a higher T-L frequency than the other, and again will be identified as the HF word and the LF word. Over the 17 pairs, 13 different classes of objects were represented; trees, musical instruments, vegetables, and birds were represented twice each (the two pairs for each of these latter four categories began with different letters and differed in length of words). The 17 HF words ranged in frequency from 3 per million to AA; the median frequency was 22. The LF words ranged in frequency from 1 to 19; the median was 5.

Conditions. There were four groups, differentiated on the basis of the word or words that Ss were to emit.

In Group E (either), S could give either the HF or the LF word for each item. After a word was emitted, or after 60 sec had elapsed with no response, E gave S the next item; thus, Group E is a replication, with the new items, of Exp. II.

In Group L (low frequency), E gave S the HF word for each pair (see Procedure), leaving S with only the LF word remaining to be guessed (though S would not know that this was the case). Group H (high frequency) is the opposite of Group L. Group H Ss were given the LF word of each pair, and thus had only the HF word left to be guessed. In Group B (both), Ss were asked to give two words (i.e., both the LF and HF words) for each item.

Subjects. There were 30 Ss, students from introductory psychology classes, in each of the four groups. Students were assigned to groups in turn.

Procedure. After E and S had sat down facing each other across a table, E gave the general instructions for all groups. These were to the effect that S was to guess words that were names of objects, and that E would give S the class of object (such as Animals, or Part of the Body), the number of letters in the word, and the first letter. Groups L and H were also told they would be given an example of a word that fit the specifications. Group B was given the general instructions and told that they were to think of two words that fit the specifications.

In Groups E, L, and H, Ss were allowed 60 sec per item. The Ss in Group B were allowed 2 min per item. It is recognized that these Ss were free to take either more than or less than 1 min to think of one word, thereby leaving less than or more than 1 min to think of another word. The data will suggest that this was probably not a serious problem.

A different haphazard order of presentation of the 17 items was used for each S.

RESULTS

Table 2 shows the mean number of words (HF, LF, or both) given by the four groups. Among the groups, three comparisons of HF and LF means can be made: within Group E, between Groups L and H, and within Group B. In all three cases the HF mean was significantly higher than the LF mean. Within Group E, the t (related measures) between the means was 7.68. Between Groups L and H, t (independent measures) was 5.83. Within Group B, t (related measures) was 11.12. As expected, the items used in Exp. III were easier than those used in Exp. II, as suggested by higher means in Group E for both HF and LF words in Exp. III, while the advantage of HF over LF words is, if anything, greater in Exp. III.

Comparisons across groups may be made to determine if the different methods of eliciting HF and/or LF words did in fact produce differences in mean number of words emitted. The HF means will be considered first. Comparison of HF means of Group E, H, and B yielded $F(2,87) = 14.71$, $p < .01$. The difference between the HF means of Groups E and H is not significant ($t = 1.48$); thus, giving S the LF word in Group H, leaving only the HF word to be guessed, did not increase the number of HF

TABLE 2

MEAN NUMBER OF HIGH-FREQUENCY AND OF LOW-FREQUENCY
WORDS GIVEN BY EACH GROUP IN EXP. III

Group	HF	σ_M	LF	σ_M
E	8.80	.41	3.83	.31
L			6.33	.36
H	9.60	.43		
B	11.63	.28	7.27	.34

words. However, the procedure used with Group B did increase the number of HF words. The HF mean for Group B is significantly higher than the HF means for Group E ($t = 5.25$) and for Group H ($t = 3.77$). The mean (11.63) for Group B is, of course, based both on those items where the *first* response was an HF word, plus those items where S, after giving an LF word as his first response, managed to give the HF word as a second response. An HF mean for Group B that should not be greatly different from the means of Groups E and H would be the mean of first responses only. This HF mean for Group B was 9.73, and it does not differ significantly from Group E ($t = 1.83$) or from Group H ($t = .25$). Thus, an increased total number of HF words was obtained only by allowing another guess (Group B) on those items where the first response was an LF word. It may also be noted that although the experimental procedure permitted Ss in Group B up to 2 min. (vs. 1 min in all other groups) to think, this did not increase the number of HF words that were first responses.

The $F(2,87)$ for the three LF means was 27.72, $p < .01$. Comparison of Groups E and L yields $t = 5.25$; thus, giving the Group L Ss the HF words, leaving only the LF words to be guessed, significantly increased the number of LF words emitted. Group B also produced significantly more LF words than Group E ($t = 7.23$), and Group L ($t = 1.97$). If the

Group B mean is reduced by including only those LF words that were the first responses (Mean = 4.17), then Groups B and E do not differ ($t = .74$), but now Group L is significantly higher than Group B ($t = 4.36$).

Comparison of Groups E and B revealed that the interaction of groups with frequency was not significant (F less than 1.0).

The preceding analyses of the HF and LF means yield the following conclusions: (a) no procedure significantly increased the number of HF words given as first responses; (b) giving Ss the HF words (Group L) significantly increased the number of LF words thought of as first responses; (c) when Ss were allowed to attempt a second response (Group B), both the numbers of HF and of LF words guessed were significantly increased.

So far, the words emitted have simply been classed as HF or LF, and the results have been analyzed in terms of numbers of such words in each class. Since the mean number emitted, shown in Table 2, was less in every case than the number possible (17 HF and 17 LF), it is of interest to examine the actual T-L frequencies of the words that were emitted. The mean T-L frequency of the 17 HF words was 28.71. The HF words emitted by Groups E, H, and B had mean T-L frequencies of 34.05, 34.72, and 32.07, respectively. The standard errors in these three means were 1.68, 1.54, and 1.36, respectively; thus, in all cases the sample (HF words emitted) mean frequencies were higher than the population mean frequency by t's of at least 2.4 (even though in Group B, the mean number of HF words emitted, 11.63, is 68% of the available words).

The mean T-L frequency of the 17 LF words was 6.47. The mean frequencies of the LF words emitted by Groups, E, L, and B, were 7.76, 8.27, and 7.73, with standard errors of .51, .37, and .34, respectively. Thus the LF words emitted also tended, by t's of at least 2.5, to be those of higher frequencies.

DISCUSSION

Mayzner and Tresselt (1958) found that solution time of anagrams varied as a function of the Thorndike-Lorge frequency of the solution words, a result which has been confirmed by O'Connell and Duncan (1961). Mayzner and Tresselt suggested that the anagram stimulus generates implicit responses by S, and that words of higher frequency in S's past experience should occur earlier among the implicit responses. This notion that order of occurrence of words should vary directly with word frequency is what Underwood and Schulz (1960) called the spew hypothesis.

The spew hypothesis, as applied to problem solving, may be considered to be a part of response-hierarchy theory, a more general approach to problem solving that has been discussed elsewhere (Duncan, 1959; Maltz-man, 1955). Briefly, a problem is assumed to elicit several responses vary-ing in habit strength, a response hierarchy. The order of responses in the hierarchy will be determined by a number of variables, e.g., recency, set, frequency, etc. The spew hypothesis refers only to the frequency variable.

Applied to the present study, the spew hypothesis seems adequate to account, in part, for the main findings. In all three experiments, the in-structions restricted, to varying degrees, the response space or word population that S had to search. However, S was still free to make a num-ber of implicit responses while searching. If it can be assumed that im-plicit words of higher T-L frequencies occur either earlier, or in greater numbers, or both, as compared to lower-frequency words, then one may say that if the solution to a problem is a high-frequency word, the prob-ability of occurrence of the solution is increased.

At the same time, it is worth noting that the spew hypothesis, if true, only assures that *some* high-frequency words will occur prior to low-frequency words. In a problem-solving situation, where the number of responses acceptable as solutions may be limited to a few or only one, S's implicit responses may be in accord with spew, but still not include the solution response. In the present Exp. I every S failed to give a word to at least one, and usually to several, of the items, even though all the items included one or more high frequency words. In Group H of Exp. III, only one of two words was allowed as the solution for each item. Since the lower-frequency word of each pair was given to these Ss, only the higher-frequency word remained to be guessed. Some of these words were also of high absolute frequency; even so, not all of them were guessed. These were failed problems. Thus, the spew hypothesis alone cannot account for the fact that some one-solution problems will not be solved even if the solutions are high-frequency words. It also cannot account for the fact that with multiple-solution problems, some of the solutions will be low-frequency words, even when high-frequency words are available and acceptable.

The spew hypothesis may be limited by inadequate sampling. When S samples words in attempting to think of a solution word, the sample apparently includes more high-frequency words than low-frequency words, but probably does not include all possible high- or low-frequency words in the population specified by the problem stimuli. Thus, it is sug-gested that when S is trying to think of a word, a combination of sampling and spew determine that (a) only part of the words, of high or of low frequency, that might occur do occur, and, (b) of those words that do occur, high-frequency words occur earlier and in greater number than low-frequency words.

Finally, it is worth noting that the tendency to emit words of higher frequency (relative to some other words) held in general throughout the entire range of absolute frequency. This is suggested in part by the data in Table 1. Another indication comes from Exp. II and III. In these experiments, all of the following numerical differences were found (regardless of whether one or two words were available to be guessed): (a) the higher-frequency word of a pair of words was emitted more often than the lower-frequency word, (b) among the higher-frequency words that were emitted, more of them were words with absolute frequencies above the median frequency of their own distribution than below the median, (c) in those cases where the lower-frequency word of a pair was emitted, more of such words had absolute frequencies above the median frequency of their own distribution than below the median.

REFERENCES

DOMINOWSKI, R. L., AND DUNCAN, C. P. Anagram solving as a function of bigram frequency. *J. verb. Learn. verb. Behav.*, 1964, 3, 321–325.

DUNCAN, C. P. Recent research on human problem solving. *Psychol. Bull.*, 1959, 56, 397–429.

MALTZMAN, I. Thinking: From a behavioristic point of view. *Psychol. Rev.*, 1955, 62, 275–286.

MAYZNER, M. S., AND TRESSELT, M. E. Anagram solution times: a function of letter order and word frequency. *J. exp. Psychol.*, 1958, 56, 376–379.

MAYZNER, M. S., AND TRESSELT, M. E. Anagram solution times: a function of transition probabilities. *J. Psychol.*, 1959, 47, 117–126.

O'CONNELL, E. J., JR., AND DUNCAN, C. P. Anagram solving as a function of letter spacing. *Psychol. Rep.*, 1961, 8, 117–118.

RHINE, R. J. The relation of achievement in problem solving to rate and kind of hypotheses produced. *J. exp. Psychol.*, 1959, 57, 253–256.

TERAOKA, T. Effects of letter-orders and material words on the anagram solution. *Jap. J. Psychol.*, 1959, 30, 253–263.

THORNDIKE, E. L., AND LORGE, I. *The teacher's word book of 30,000 words.* New York: Teachers Coll., Columbia Univer. Press, 1944.

UNDERWOOD, B. J., AND SCHULZ, R. W. *Meaningfulness and verbal learning.* Chicago: Lippincott, 1960.

SECTION FOUR

Information

The term information can refer to a number of variables or approaches in problem solving. The three papers included in this chapter represent three meanings or uses of the term. In the article by Goldbeck, Bernstein, Hillix, and Marx, a trouble-shooting procedure, the half-split technique, is examined. This technique is one that can be used in some problems to acquire information, usually of the kind that narrows the population of responses yet to be searched, i.e., the population containing the solution. The half-split technique might also be considered an example of what is sometimes called a problem solving process, as considered in Section Five.

Information provided to the subject can also be varied by manipulating the amount or the kind of feedback. In Donahoe's study, it appears that increasing the amount of feedback is not necessarily helpful. It seems likely that detailed informational feedback may not be assimilated or remembered. It may be mentioned that feedback, both informative and misinformative, has been studied in several experiments in concept learning, but it was not possible to include this area in this book.

Another meaning of information is given in terms of information theory. Brush's study applies this theory to both the stimuli and the responses of a problem solving task. A basic concept of the theory is uncertainty. Both stimulus and response uncertainty are shown to be inversely related to the rate of information transmitted. The measure of information referred to in the Brush and Donahoe papers, viz., bits, is also sometimes used on the stimuli in concept experiments. The Brush study is somewhat of a combined problem solving and concept learning experiment since it uses both the technique of more available responses than stimuli (response discovery or problem solving) and more stimuli than responses (grouping or concept learning).

12. Application of the Half-Split Technique to Problem-Solving Tasks

Robert A. Goldbeck, Benjamin B. Bernstein, W. A. Hillix, and Melvin H. Marx

The need to maintain complex electronic equipment has stimulated interest in a class of problem solving called trouble shooting. Faulty components in electronic systems must be located on the basis of the performance of the system and its parts. Solution of a problem may be considered to have two parts: the determination of a set of possible faulty components, and the elimination of all but the component that is actually faulty through some checking procedure.

Miller, Folley, and Smith (3) have presented a logical demonstration of the superior efficiency of the half-split technique for problems so considered. Each check eliminates half of the alternatives. However, there has been no empirical examination of this solution method, the effectiveness of which will depend upon human capability to use it.

First, a set of trouble alternatives (possible faulty components) must be determined. Then check points which divide the set of alternatives into halves must be located. If the trouble alternatives are directly given and have a simple structure which can be easily divided into halves, empirical results should follow closely the mathematics of information theory. But if either of these two aspects of the method is complicated by complexities in the structure of the system, method effectiveness should be more intimately related to the capabilities of Ss.

The two experiments reported here were designed to provide empirical tests of application of the half-split method. The major purpose of our first experiment was to examine the effects of problem complexity upon the efficiency of solution for Ss instructed in the half-split method and for Ss not so instructed. Specifically, the experiment was designed (a) to test the hypothesis that half-split instruction increased efficiency for simple problems, and (b) to determine half-split efficiency for more complex

Reprinted by permission of the authors and the American Psychological Association from *Journal of Experimental Psychology*, 1957, 53, 330–338.

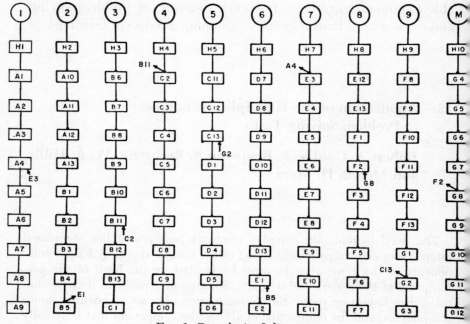

FIG. 1. Complexity I diagram.

problems. As implied in the preceding paragraph, it was expected that the half-split instructions would improve efficiency for the simpler problems, but not necessarily for the more complex.

The second experiment was designed to determine whether additional practice, different methods of instruction, and more complex training materials would produce an improvement in S's ability to arrive at a set of alternatives, and, if so, whether the half-split method would then be more efficient. Four different training methods were tested for effectiveness.

EXPERIMENT I

METHOD

Apparatus. The problems were presented to S by means of an apparatus designed to simulate an electronic system, and a diagram of the system relationships. The system consisted of 10 display items and 100 connected components. The apparatus is described elsewhere (2) in more detail.

The diagram of the simplest system is shown in Fig. 1. Each of the 10 display items terminated a signal chain consisting of 10 units connected in series. Each signal chain was connected to one of the other signal chains at a random point in the chain. Thus each simple chain had one remote connection; this was either an input to the chain or an output from it. This system diagram, used in Exp. I at Complexity I, formed the skeleton for the other two diagrams. For the Complexity II diagram, an additional remote connection was made for each of the chains. For Complexity III, a third connection was made. As complexity increased, the signal network feeding the display items became more complicated and a faulty unit caused more symptoms (display items that were off) in the symptom array.

The display items were presented as nine lights and a meter on a panel. When operating properly, the components transmitted a signal to the display items connected to them, causing the nine lights to be on and the meter to give a specified reading.

A second panel consisted of switches and an associated light. By throwing the switch representing the check point of any one of the 100 components under the display items, S could find out whether or not the signal was present at the output of the component. If it was, the light would come on; if not, the light would remain off.

There was a third panel which also had a switch for each of the 100 components. When S thought he knew the faulty component, he could throw the associated switch on this third panel, thus effectively replacing this component. If that component was really the faulty one, the items on the display panel that had been off would now come back on, thus showing S that he had solved the problem.

The Ss were given a problem-solving test (PST) designed to measure ability on those aspects of the trouble shooting that concerned the deduction of the set of trouble alternatives. It consisted of 20 questions requiring S to count units that had specified relationships to other units in the network printed on a diagram. The 64 units were identified by pairs of letters.

Subjects. The Ss were 90 male university students drawn from a general experimental psychology class. Thirty Ss were assigned to each of the three complexity levels; 15 were given each method of instruction.

Procedure. On Day 1, S was given a diagram for the complexity level to be used during testing, but with remote connection inputs and outputs at different points in the simple signal chains, in order to prevent specific transfer effects. The S listened to recorded instructions covering the general functioning of the system. He was told that a trouble-shooting problem would be presented as a pattern of on-and-off display items called the symptom array. A faulty component would cause whichever display items were connected to it to be off. By tracing the relevant connections on the system diagram, S could determine which units might cause the given pattern of symptom items to be off. He could also determine the most efficient place to check. He could check points in the system by means of switches on the checking panel. Finally, the checking information would enable him to locate the trouble source. The problem was solved when he threw the replacement switch for the faulty component, and the display items came back on. After hearing the instructions, S was allowed to ask questions and then required to answer a list of questions to check his comprehension of the task. These questions required S to perform and interpret correctly specified checks and replacements.

On Day 2, Ss were given a second set of check-out questions to insure retention of the instructions. The Ss in the half-split (HS) groups listened to a 5.5 min. recording of instructions on the half-split method and were asked if they had any questions about the method. Check-out questions followed which required S to correctly apply the half-split method, step by step, to two simple problems. The S was to examine the symptom array and the associated interconnected units. For any given array, there were several units whose malfunctioning could produce that array. These were called trouble-possible units. The S was to locate these and successively halve them by making the appropriate checks until the faulty unit was isolated and replaced.

The Ss in the control groups received no special method instructions, but were given those parts of the check-out questions that did not involve the HS method as such. All Ss were told that their task was to find the trouble in the least number of checks possible; 20 min. would be allowed for each problem, but otherwise time was not a consideration. A total of 12 Ss failed to finish a total of 17 problems within the 20-min. time limit. Estimates of times and checks to solution were made for these incompleted problems, based upon the degree of solution and the average rate at which S progressed toward solution.

The first problem given each S at all three complexity levels was a trouble with only one symptom—the simplest type of problem. For the next five problems all Ss were given the same five troubles (i.e., the same five "faulty units" were used regardless of method or complexity level). The symptom array for a given trouble varied with complexity level. Trouble order was counterbalanced according to a latin square arrangement with three replications in each cell of the factorial design.

Following testing on the electronic system Ss were given the PST.

RESULTS

Checking scores and times. The over-all method difference was not significant ($F < 1$) for a simple analysis of variance using method, complexity, and within-Ss variance. The Method × Complexity interaction was also significant ($F < 1$). As was expected, the complexity difference was significant ($F = 3.89$, $P < .05$ for $df = 2$, 84); the number of checks was positively related to complexity.

Since a difference in favor of the HS group had been predicted at Complexity I, a separate analysis was carried out for Complexity I only. Here the method difference was significant ($F = 4.68$, $P < .05$ for $df = 1,24$).

The solution time for the HS groups was significantly longer than for the control ($F = 7.44$, $P < .01$ for $df = 1, 84$). This reflects the additional covert solution behavior associated with the attempt to reduce checking responses by means of the half-split procedure. With increasing complexity the times increased ($F = 18.60$, $P < .001$ for $df = 2, 84$), and the obtained HS-control difference became more marked.

PST analysis.—In order to assess the effects of levels of PST performance in conjunction with the main variables, Ss were divided into three levels according to the upper, middle, and lower third of the PST score distribution for each group.[1] An analysis of variance was performed using these levels as an additional variable. The results agreed with those of the previous analysis and produced two additional findings. PST level had a highly significant effect ($F = 9.20$, $P < .001$ for $df = 2, 72$), as did the PST Level $\times$ Complexity interaction ($F = 3.49$, $P < .05$ for $df = 4$, 72). Increasing complexity resulted in increased check scores only for Ss scoring low on the PST.

It would seem that the difficulty of complex problems was in large part dependent upon S characteristics which were measured by the PST.

The product-moment correlations between PST and checking scores at the three complexity levels were as follows: for the half-split group, $+ .16$, $- .31$, and $- .80$; for the control group, $+ .24$, $- .63$, and $- .80$. The increase in correlation with complexity indicates a greater role for PST ability on complex problems. High PST scores and low checking scores represent good performance, producing negative r's.

Since the PST was administered to Ss in Exp. I after they had performed the apparatus problems, it was possible that differential transfer from the apparatus problems to the PST occurred for the different experimental groups. To test this possibility, an analysis of variance was carried out on the PST scores classified according to the complexity and method variables used for the apparatus problems. There was no evidence for differential transfer ($F < 1$ for M and C, 1.48 for M $\times$ C with $df = 2, 84$ for the latter).

Reliability.—The reliability of the total-checks scores for each of the major experimental groups was determined by an analysis of variance technique developed by Hoyt (1). For the HS groups the reliability values

---

[1] The levels breakdown of PST scores by groups, some analysis of variance tables mentioned in the text, the instructions for both experiments, and certain tabulations data from both experiments, have been sent to the American Documentation Institute. Order Document No. 5145 from ADI Auxiliary Publications Project, Photoduplication Service, Library of Congress, Washington 25, D.C., remitting in advance $2.00 for microfilm or $3.75 for photocopies. Make checks payable to Chief, Photoduplication Service, Library of Congress.

were .62, .72, and .53 for Complexities I, II, and III, respectively. For the control groups the reliability values were .50, .99, and .74. These values indicate reasonably high reliability for the experimental situation. The split-half reliability using an odd-even breakdown on the PST was .83.

Half-split performance measures.—The Ss were unable to benefit from instruction in the logically superior HS method, at least at the higher complexities. It is then appropriate to examine the reasons for this failure and to determine which aspects of the method present difficulty.

Since the HS Ss were instructed first to determine the units which if faulty could cause the symptom array presented (trouble-possible units), the number of times each S's first check was among the trouble-possible units was scored. The HS groups showed a slight advantage in beginning their responses in the trouble-possible area, but the methods effect was not significant ($F = 2.29$ for $df = 1, 72$).

It is surprising that Ss who have been told how to go about limiting the scope of trouble alternatives were not significantly better at this part of the task. A strong effect of PST levels ($F = 5.66, P < .01$ for $df = 2, 72$) indicates that there was an important ability factor involved in determining trouble-possible units.

A significant complexity by PST level interaction ($F = 2.50, P < .05$ for $df = 4, 72$) resulted from a steeper decline in trouble-possible first checks with increasing complexity for low PST-scoring Ss than for middle- or high-scoring Ss. However, for the high PST level the complexity difference was still significant ($F = 4.24, P < .05$ for $df = 2, 20$). These results, plus the significant complexity effect ($F = 10.04, P < .001$ for $df = 2, 72$), indicate that increasing complexity had the effect of preventing Ss from accomplishing the first step in the half-split method used in this experiment. At the higher complexities Ss were limited by an ability factor in arriving at the trouble-possible set of alternatives by an interpretation of the symptom array.

The second part of the HS method concerned making half-split checks among the trouble-possible units. Scoring each S for the number of perfect half-split checking sequences used in the trouble-possible area resulted in the superiority of the HS groups. The method difference was highly significant ($F = 30.65, P < .001$ for $df = 1, 72$). Here there was no significant complexity difference. However, with increasing complexity the number of trouble-possible units was generally smaller, requiring fewer steps in the half-split checking sequence.

To eliminate this bias, only the first check in the trouble-possible area was considered. An analysis of variance using this measure showed a significant method effect ($F = 71.12, P < .001$ for $df = 1, 72$) and a Complexity by Method interaction ($F = 4.57, P < .05$ for $2, 72$). This resulted from a reduction, in half-split checks, with increased complexity by the HS group. Since the trouble-possible units were contained in simple lines at all complexities (except for two troubles at Complexity II where two lines were involved), this reduction in half-split checks can be attributed to the difficulty in the first step of getting a set of alternatives. If the trouble alternatives cannot be recognized as such, they cannot be split in half.

Correct solutions. Although primary emphasis has been placed upon the number of checks used to solve a problem, consideration of whether or not Ss' first solution was a correct one is of some importance. When each S was scored for the number of correct first replacements for the five problems, only PST level showed a significant effect ($F = 5.99$, $P < .01$ for $df = 2, 72$). This indicates that this aspect of performance was determined by the characteristics of S rather than by the situational variables.

In addition, each S was scored for the average number of checks used for finding troubles where he made no incorrect replacements. There was a significant method effect ($F = 23.47$, $P < .001$ for $df = 1, 72$) and significant Method $\times$ Complexity interaction ($F = 5.77$, $P < .01$ for $df = 2, 72$). The HS group was most superior at Complexity III. Where S avoided any incorrect solutions, the half-split method was more effective.

The results of Exp. I may be summed up as follows: (*a*) The increase in number of checks required with increased complexity indicates the importance of being able to deduce the trouble-possible units correctly, especially since the number of trouble-possible units decreased with increasing complexity. If Ss could have conceptualized system relationships perfectly, fewer checks would have been required. (*b*) The HS method cannot in general be said to be superior. (*c*) There is evidence that it is superior under certain conditions, such as with diagrams of low complexity, where Ss apparently had little difficulty in finding the trouble-possible units, and where Ss avoided incorrect replacements.

This latter finding gave some hope that if all Ss could be given increased training on working with the system relationships, then the HS method would be superior even with more complex diagrams. Experiment II was an attempt to improve the effectiveness of the HS method by improving instruction and giving extended practice.

EXPERIMENT II

METHOD

Apparatus. The same apparatus was used as in Exp. I, except that only the system diagram of greatest complexity (three remote connections) was used during test trials. The training diagram was different, being the previous test diagram of intermediate complexity (two remote connections).

Subjects. The Ss were 40 male students from a general experimental psychology class at the University of Missouri. Ten Ss were randomly assigned to each of the four instructional groups.

Procedure. Before beginning either the instructions or the experimental sessions in trouble-shooting, all Ss were given the PST for use in analysis of covariance. The basic instructional procedure was similar to that of Exp. I. However, all Ss had 2-hr. sesssions on the first day, rather than the 1-hr. session of Exp. I. All Ss had additional practice with the diagram of intermediate complexity, with special conditions of practice for each group.

Group C (control) was essentially like the control group of Exp. I, except for the additional practice. During this practice, E asked S to specifiy the check he wanted made. If it did not violate any basic instructions, S was allowed to make the check.

Group DHS (Deductive Half-Split) was like the previous Group HS, with additional practice on the more complex diagrams. During the supervised practice for this group, S was allowed to make the check only if he had correctly deduced the trouble-possible items, and if the check correctly half-split those units. If it was an incorrect check, S was told only that it was incorrect because it was not a half-split check, whereupon S kept trying until the correct check was made.

Group DA (Deductive Alternatives) differed from the groups previously used. The rationale for setting up this new group is as follows: It is not necessary to arrive at the *minimum* set of trouble-possible units in order to find the trouble, so long as the set arrived at contains the faulty unit. It may be that S can do better where he is required only to find *some* set of alternatives that includes the trouble spot, if finding the minimum set would strain his capabilities, as happened in Exp. I. Thus, Group DA was instructed in three alternative ways of conceiving of the set of alternatives, and allowed to choose any one of them for half-split application during the test. The minimum set consisted *only* of the trouble-possible components, just as in Group DHS. The maximum set consisted of all components in the lines beneath display items that were off. The intermediate set was obtained by eliminating those lines in the maximum set which did not have components feeding into other off-display items. For example, if there were three display items off, all the components beneath the off-display items (30 components) would constitute the maximum set. If one of the three lines involved did not have components feeding into either of the other two off-display items, it could not possibly contain the faulty component and thus could be eliminated from consideration for the intermediate set, which would then consist of 20 components. Further considerations might allow elimination of further components for the determination of the minimum set. During the practice session for this group, E told S what kind of set to split and allowed only a half-split check of the designated set.

Group HS (Half-Split) received varied practice in half-splitting sets of components, but was given no practice in determining the sets of alternatives. The symptom array was not used during practice for this group. The E told S which units to split, and corrected him only if checks did not correctly half-split the given set of alternatives.

Test procedure was like that in Exp. I. There were two trouble-by-trial latin square arrangements in each group. The Ss were allowed 25 min. to finish a problem.

RESULTS

Checking scores and times. Both the mean number of checks required to find the five troubles and the mean number of times S's first check was among the trouble-possible units are shown in Table 1, along with the

TABLE 1

Group Means for Performance and PST Measures, Exp. II

Measure	Group			
	C	DHS	DA	HS
Mean checks to solution	57.1	22.3	39.1	60.8
Mean trouble-possible first checks	1.4	3.8	1.8	0.1
Mean PST scores	11.4	14.1	12.4	8.9

group means on the PST. The groups scored in the same order on all three measures, and the group difference on the PST was almost significant ($F = 2.62$, with 2.86 required for $P = .05$, $df = 3, 36$), despite the fact that Ss were randomly assigned.

Therefore, an analysis of covariance was used to determine whether the groups differed due to treatments, in addition to the variation correlated with the PST. Since the means and variances for number of checks to solution were correlated, and the variances were significantly heterogeneous ($x^2 = 10.99$, $P < .02$), a log transformation was used and successfully corrected for the heterogeneity. The method difference for the transformed scores was significant ($F = 6.75$, $P < .01$ for $df = 3, 35$). The adjusted log means for the groups were as follows: C, 1.68; DHS, 1.39; DA, 1.59; and HS, 1.66. Tests of these means, using a generalized error term of .069 derived from the analysis of covariance, showed that Group DHS was superior to each of the other groups at the .01 level. None of the other comparisons was significant.

The analysis of covariance of the trouble-possible first check scores yielded a highly significant treatment difference ($F = 13.22$, $P < .001$ for $df = 3, 36$). The adjusted means for the four groups were: C, 1.44; DHS,

3.50; DA, 1.71; and HS, .46. The t tests showed the DHS group superior to all other groups at beyond the .001 level. The HS group was inferior to all other groups at beyond the .05 level. The only insignificant difference was between Groups DA and C. This result indicates that the different instructions and conditions of practice differed in their effectiveness in helping S to accomplish the first step of the trouble-shooting process. The difference in number of checks to solution seems attributable to differences in ability to deduce a set of trouble-possible units, rather than to differences in ability to half-split alternatives, once determined. The analysis of covariance on time to solution did not yield any significant results.

Another subsidiary measure of efficiency was the number of times S "replaced" a unit on the replacement panel. Perfect efficiency would involve using only as many replacements as there were troubles, five in this case. The average numbers were: C, 9.0; DHS, 8.0; DA, 10.1; and HS, 12.1. The analysis of covariance of the scores did not approach significance.

PST scores. Product-moment correlations between number of checks to solution and PST scores for the four groups were as follows: C, $-.46$; DHS, $-.59$; DA, $-.56$; and HS, $-.59$. The required r for significance at the .05 level is .60 for the small N of 10. The correlations were, of course, negative since low check scores indicate better performance than high check scores.

Comparison with Exp. I. Groups C and DHS from Exp. II were combined with the two groups from Exp. I in an analysis of covariance with PST scores as the predictor variable. This use seems justified despite the fact that PST was administered *after* the apparatus test in Exp. I, and *before* the apparatus test in Exp. II, since there was no evidence of differential transfer in Exp. I.

The analysis showed a significant study × Method interaction ($F = 6.34$, $P < .02$ for $df = 1$, 45). Since the variances were again heterogeneous ($\chi^2 = 12.85$, $P < .01$), a conservative interpretation is necesasry. Even so, this comparison tends to support the observation that the instructions and practice given Group DHS in Exp. II were more effective in reducing the number of checks than were the less extensive instructions in Exp. I. The mean number of checks for Exp. I at the high complexity were C, 47.8; HS, 45.3; for Exp. II, C, 57.1; DHS, 22.3.

The analysis of covariance of the trouble-possible first check scores for the two studies also showed a significant Study × Method interaction ($F = 6.09$, $P < .02$ for $df = 1$, 45). Here the variances were not heterogeneous ($\chi^2 = 5.30$, $P > .10$). The method of instruction seemed to produce a dramatic change in the ability to deduce a set of trouble-possible units as well as in the ability to locate a faulty unit in a minimal number of checks.

DISCUSSION

Although the half-split method has been demonstrated to be logically superior (3), the results of the two experiments herein reported indicate that its empirical superiority is a function of the nature of the task, and the degree and type of training given the trouble shooter. The S's checks more closely approximate those which would be expected logically when task complexity is low or instruction in deducing trouble-possible units is high.

There seem to be two components in the empirical process of trouble shooting. The first component involves finding the trouble-possible units. The second component involves half-splitting the trouble-possible units at each stage by some checking operation, or at least eliminating part of the units from consideration. In the present experiments the second step was relatively simple. Those Ss who were able to locate the trouble-possible units, as measured by the occurrence of the first check in the trouble area, were able to perform efficiently in finding the troubles.

Wherever a significant difference in number of checks was found between groups, there was an accompanying difference between the number of initial checks in the trouble-possible area to help explain it. In Exp. I, failures to find expected differences were correlated with difficulty in isolating trouble-possible units. Also, half-split Ss who avoided making any incorrect replacements were more efficient than comparable control Ss. The importance of the deductive component was further substantiated by the marked superiority of DHS Ss in Exp. II as compared to HS Ss. This difference seems attributable to their greater practice in the deductive component.

It appears then that the failure to find a general superiority for the half-split method is the result of S's inability to perform efficiently in the more fundamental deductive task of isolating sets of trouble units. This result suggests that it will be more profitable in future research on training methods to emphasize the more basic deductive phase rather than the relatively mechanical half-splitting aspect of the process.

SUMMARY

This is a report of two experiments on the use of the half-split method of locating trouble sources in malfunctioning equipment. The experiments were carried out using apparatus and diagrams designed especially for this purpose. Experiment I investigated the effects of differing complexity of system and differing instructions on efficiency in locating trouble sources. Experiment II was a further investigation of the effects of instruction and practice for the high complexity condition.

Both sets of results indicated that where the system relationships were easily mastered by a given S the half-split method was an aid to efficiency. However, S needed either relatively high ability or instructional aid to overcome the load put on his capacities by the more complex systems. He had to be able to deduce from the symptom complex which units might be faulty in order to use the half-split method efficiently. It is probable that this ability also indicated that these Ss were better able to understand the meanings of the checks made. It was concluded that deductive ability is a prerequisite for application of the half-split technique, and indeed may play a preponderant role at each stage of the trouble-shooting task.

REFERENCES

1. HOYT, C. J. Test reliability estimated by analysis of variance. *Psychometrika*, 1941, 6, 153–160.
2. MARX, M. H., GOLDBECK, R. A., & BERNSTEIN, B. B. An apparatus for investigating the methods humans use in solving complex problems. *Amer. J. Psychol.*, 1956, 69, 462–465.
3. MILLER, R. B., FOLLEY, J. P., JR., & SMITH, P. R. Systematic trouble shooting and the half-split technique. Lackland Air Force Base, Texas: Human Resources Research Center, July, 1953. (*Tech. Rep.* 53–21).

13.   The Effect of Variations in the Form of Feedback on the Efficiency of Problem Solving

John W. Donahoe

The present experiments were designed to study problem-solving behavior as a function of the manner in which information regarding prior performance was fed back to S. A geometrical game was employed as the task.

Reprinted by permission of the author and the American Psychological Association from *Journal of Experimental Psychology*, 1960, 60, 193–199

Experiment I

METHOD

Subjects. For the initial experiment, 24 Ss were selected from the laboratory sections of introductory psychology. The work was required as part of the course.

Procedure. By means of a random procedure, the 24 Ss were assigned to two subgroups of 12 Ss. All Ss were given a *map* of the ocean. This map consisted of a piece of white cardboard on which was drawn a 7 × 7 grid with the grid lines spaced 1 in. apart. The maps ranged from A to G in latitude and from 1 to 7 in longitude. Of the 49 intersections, 12 were distinctly marked with a large black dot. The Ss were told that the dots corresponded to the possible locations of enemy ships. The primary purpose of Exp. I was to study differences in performance as a function of the form of information presentation irrespective of the latitude-longitude correlation. Accordingly, 12 pairs of maps were constructed with the dot positions independently and randomly determined for each. One map of each pair was assigned to a subgroup.

The S was then shown the *fire control panel*. On this panel were located 12 lever action switches corresponding to the 12 possible ship locations represented on the map. Depending upon the experimental condition to which S had been assigned, either one or two pairs of lights were located above the switches. In any case, one of each pair of lights were marked *nearer*, while the other was marked *farther*.

Each S given information from a single pair of lights was instructed to fire (by raising a switch) until he hit the enemy ship, but to choose wisely in order to sink the enemy with as few shots as possible. After a shot was made, the fire control panel signaled whether the present guess was *nearer*, *farther*, or the *same* distance away from the enemy ship as the previous shot. The signal, *same*, was represented by the condition in which neither light of the pair was illuminated. All replies were based upon the Euclidean distance between the relevant positions in two-dimensional space. This method is known as the *combined* condition since both latitude and longitude were considered together in the reply.

In the condition in which two pairs of lights were present, the instructions were similar with one exception. Here, the machine gave two signals after each guess, one signal with respect to latitude (letters), and one with respect to longitude (numbers). As S was told about each dimension separately, this method of presenting information was known as the *separate* condition. Half of the Ss served under the separate condition (two sources of information) and half under the combined condition (one source of information). In both conditions, Ss were allowed to proceed at their own pace and to take notes if they desired. Also, the meaning of the three possible machine signals was clarified with illustrations from the maps.

All Ss played 10 games, a game being completed when the target ship was sunk. The onset of a buzzer and a light signified this event. The location of the ship was randomly determined for each game. The number of guesses required to sink the enemy was recorded as the criterion variable.

Apparatus.[1] Each of the 12 switches on the fire control panel introduced a predetermined resistance between the grid and ground of an electronic bridge circuit. The magnitude of resistance was proportional to distance in the map. One control grid of a dual triode tube was biased in accord with the resistance placed between it and ground by S's previous guess, while the bias on the other grid reflected the present guess. A single-pole, double-throw polarized relay was put in one arm of the bridge. If the negative bias of the grid associated with the previous guess was greater than that of the grid associated with the present guess, the relay turned on a light which indicated that S was nearer. If the reverse was true, S was farther. Finally, in the case where the grid had equal negative bias, the relay remained in the null position and no light went on, indicating that S was the same distance away from the target as on the previous guess. Two such bridge circuits were built. One served in the combined information condition and also represented latitude in the separate condition where it represented longitude. The resistance associated with each switch was governed by a rotary switch on the back of the panel. By this technique, an entire game could be played with one setting of the rotary switches.

RESULTS

An analysis of variance was used to evaluate the guessing data. Because it was possible for the target to be discovered on the first guess 1 time in 12 by chance alone, the 10 games per S were grouped into blocks of 2 games in order to secure a more representative estimate of variability. As there were no Ss treated alike, the pooled Maps interactions were used as error variance.[2]

Although it can be shown, using a locus principle, that the separate

---

[1] The author is indebted to Ralph Albers for suggesting the circuit used in the apparatus.

[2] The summary tables for all analyses of variance have been deposited as Document Number 6377 with the ADI Auxiliary Publications Project, Photoduplication Service, Library of Congress, Washington 25, D.C. A copy may be secured by citing the document number and by remitting $1.25 for photoprints, or $1.25 for 35-mm. microfilm. Advanced payment is required. Make checks or money orders payable to: Chief, Photoduplication Service, Library of Congress.

method always leads to a logical elimination of at least as many positions as does the combined method, Ss in the separate condition did not require significantly fewer guesses to attain the target ship. In fact, the prediction verged on significant *reversal* ($F = 4.31$; $1/11$ *df*; $P < .10$). The mean number of guesses for Ss in the separate method was 7.1, while that for the combined condition was 4.0. Furthermore, no reduction in the number of guesses occurred as a function of games.

An empirical check on the information superiority of the separate condition was obtained by tallying the number of points logically eliminated by the first guess for each game. On the average, 7 positions were eliminated under the combined condition as opposed to 9 positions under the separate method. Thus, for some reason, Ss were unable to use to full advantage the information as fed back to them from two sources. Only the variance associated with the maps variable was significantly different from error ($F = 2.92$; $11/11$ *df*; $P < .05$) in the analysis of the guessing data. One interpretation of this finding is that the latitude-longitude correlation, which was allowed to vary randomly, was critical in determining the ability of Ss to assimilate the information. Experiment II was directed to this point.

EXPERIMENT II

METHOD

Subjects. Thirty-six Ss were used in Exp. II. Again, they were recruited from the laboratory sections of the introductory psychology course.

Procedure. The original 36 Ss were randomly subdivided into three groups of 12 Ss each. The map for Group 1 possessed a .00 latitude-longitude correlation, and hence, a low redundancy between sources of information in the separate condition. Groups 2 and 3 were characterized by maps with .86 and 1.00 correlations, respectively. Thus, for Group 3, the amount of information imparted by the combined and separate conditions was exactly the same (one source completely redundant). One half of each of the redundancy groups was given information by the combined method, one half by the separate method.

Groups 2 and 3 were further partitioned into two equal subgroups, one of which was given a positive and the other a negative longitude-latitude correlation. Within each correlation-sign combination were three randomly selected sets of 10 target locations. The instructions used were the same as in Exp. I. However, in Exp. II the maps varied from A to L in latitude and from 1 to 12 in longitude in order that a correlation of 1.00 might be represented. All Ss were given 10 games, and the number of guesses and the amount of time required to discover the target were recorded.

RESULTS

Number of guesses. Two analyses of variance were performed, one for the .00 correlation group and one for the .86 and 1.00 groups. This was necessitated by the absence of the sign variable in the .00 group. In the first analysis conventional error terms were possible due to the presence of more than one S per group. For the second analysis, target interactions (pooled where homogeneous) were used as error.

With the .00 map, the method of presenting information to Ss was not a significant source of variance. However, once again, numerically fewer guesses were required by Ss under the combined condition (see Table 1).

TABLE 1

NUMBER OF GUESSES AND RATE OF RESPONDING AS A FUNCTION
OF SOURCES AND LATITUDE-LONGITUDE CORRELATION

Latitude-Longitude Correlation	Mean Guesses		Mean Rate (Sec.)	
	1 Source	2 Sources	1 Source	2 Sources
.00	4.2	4.7	24	33
.86	4.6	3.5	22	35
1.00	3.6	4.2	23	15

The number of guesses to target attainment decreased significantly ($F = 3.87$; $4/24$ df; $P < .025$) from 5.4 to 3.1 guesses.

The analysis of the data obtained under .86 and 1.00 correlations revealed a significant interaction ($F = 5.75$; $1/12$ df; $P < .05$) between the map correlation and the method of information presentation. Two sources of information were inferior to one source with a 1.00 latitude-longitude correlation, but superior with a .86 correlation (see Table 1). The sign of the correlation also was a significant factor in determining the effect of the method of presenting information ($F = 4.81$; $1/12$ df; $P < .05$). An inspection of the appropriate means revealed that a positive correlation led to the fewest number of guesses with a 1.00 map (3.6 vs. 4.1 guesses), while a negative correlation was most beneficial with a .86 map (3.6 vs. 4.5 guesses). Unlike the .00 correlation, a significant decrease in the number of guesses did *not* occur as a function of trials.

Rate of guessing. The interval between the first guess and the attainment of the target was recorded. This time was divided by the number of guesses in the game and evaluated by two analyses of variance analogous to those used to appraise the guessing data.

The rate of responding increased in all three map correlations. In the

1.00 map, the rate increased over the five blocks of games from 24 to 15 sec. ($F = 6.06$; $4/24$ df; $P < .01$). The average time per guess fell from 36 to 26 sec. in the .86 map and from 34 to 27 sec. in the .00 map ($F = 1.00$ map, the rate increased over the five blocks of games from 24 to 15 sec. ($F = 6.06$; $4/24$ df; $P < .01$). The average time per guess fell from 36 to 26 sec. in the .86 map and from 34 to 27 sec. in the .00 map ($F = 2.94$; $4/64$ df; $P < 05$). Generally, responding was slower under the separate method (see Table 1). However, there was a significant inter-

TABLE 2

ANALYSIS OF THE DEPENDENCIES BETWEEN RESPONSES

Source	df	F
Between Ss	17	
Correlation (C)	2	1.21
Between Ss, same group	15	(150.07)
Within Ss	90	
Order of dependency (D)	2	85.44**
Measures (M)	1	199.83**
D × M	2	3.50*
D × C	4	1.64
M × C	2	1.88
D × M × C	4	.06
Pooled Ss interactions	75	(54.61)
Total	107	

* $P < .05$.
** $P < .01$.

action with map correlation ($F = 4.89$; $1/14$ df; $P < .05$), the highest rate occurring with the 1.00 map and two sources of information. The rate of responding with one source of information was relatively invariant over the correlations sampled.

Dependencies between guesses. In order to examine the sequential relationships between responses more closely, the games were simulated on an IBM 650 digital computer.[3] The Ss' guesses were read into the computer and the number of points logically eliminated by each guess was determined. (Only the data from the combined condition were analyzed in this manner due to limitations imposed by the computer. Thus, the following results are probably overly generous estimates of Ss' information processing ability.) The data were tallied in three ways: (*a*) for each guess singly, (*b*) in conjunction with the immediately preceding guess, and (*c*) in conjunction with the immediately preceding two guesses.

[3] The author is indebted to the Computing Center of the University of Kentucky and especially to J. W. Hamblen for assistance in the following analyses.

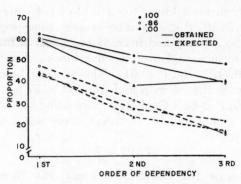

Fig. 1. The proportion of obtained and expected *good* guesses as a function of the order of response dependency.

There was a significant gain in the amount of information presented in these three combinations. The respective values were 6.6, 8.6, and 9.9 points. There were no differences between the correlation groups with regard to this measure.

To estimate the *goodness* of a guess, where a good guess is defined as guessing a position which has not been logically eliminated on the first; first and second; or first, second, and third guesses preceding the one under consideration, the following comparisons were made. The average number of points remaining after a guess was divided by 11 (S could not choose the same point on successive guesses) to secure an estimate of the probability of making a good guess by chance alone. This was the expected proportion of good guesses. The obtained proportion was arrived at by dividing the number of good guesses by the total number of guesses of the type under concern (first, second, or third order of dependency). In this manner, three expected and three obtained proportions were secured for each S. The analysis of these values (neglecting the sign variable in the .86 and 1.00 maps) is presented in Table 2. As shown in Fig. 1, Ss performed at better than chance expectancy unaffected by the map correlation. There was a significant decrease in the proportion of good guesses as a function of the order of dependency indicating a retention loss. However, this drop was not as sharp as that indicated by the expected values (D × M significant).

DISCUSSION

As the average amount of information per guess (number of points logically eliminated) was greater with two sources than with one source, it was expected that the number of guesses required to attain the target would be less in the former condition. Generally, this expectation was not upheld. Inferior performance with two sources of information was demonstrated with random correlation maps and with .00 and 1.00 maps. Only in the case of a .86 latitude-longitude correlation was the prediction upheld. It would appear that the ability to combine informational outputs was, in this task at least, contingent upon a moderate degree of redundancy between sources. Some precedent for this finding is provided by an eight-cue, probability learning study conducted by Calvin and Curtin (1958). Two of the eight cues were relevant to the two-choice response required of S. With uncorrelated relevant cues, all Ss were found to use only one of the two cues to a significant degree although some Ss were given over 2,000 trials. In the map game, however, the difficulty presented by the .00 map was largely surmounted as the number of guesses per game decreased with continued play.

Not only did the magnitude of the latitude-longitude correlation significantly affect performance, but also its sign. Further inquiry into the role of this variable is needed as the present results may be an artifact of the unequal strengths of associative connections between certain numbers and letters (A with 1, B with 2, etc.).

For all but the 1.00 correlation, the rate of guessing was highest with one source of information. Nevertheless, the slower rate with two sources in the .00 map condition did not lead to fewer guesses. The trend toward more rapid responding where one source of information was completely redundant (the 1.00 map) may have its counterpart in a visual discrimination study reported by Eriksen (1954). He found 4.1 bits transmitted per stimulus when the stimuli varied simultaneously in size, brightness, and hue; whereas, variation in any of these attributes singly resulted in the transmission of only 2.7 bits. This was in spite of the fact that the attributes were perfectly correlated (i.e., two were completely redundant).

Under what was the most favorable method of presenting information (one source), the proportion of good guesses was .60 with respect to the information afforded by the immediately preceding guess. This value dropped to .50 and .42 for the second- and third-order dependencies, respectively. A clue to the mechanisms underlying this borderline performance can perhaps be supplied by Ss' spontaneous comment during the games. Rather than regarding the signals *nearer* and *farther* as objective methods of providing information, these stimuli apparently acquired differential reinforcing properties. This was particularly evident when the fire control panel signaled *farther*. Many Ss retraced their steps after this reply, a strategy which, needless to say, resulted in no new information but did insure the occurrence of *nearer*.

SUMMARY

Subjects played a two-dimensional geometric game under two conditions of feedback concerning the consequences of their responses. One group was informed about a response from a single source which collapsed the two-dimensional character of the game by means of Euclidean distance measures. A second group received information from two sources which separately reflected each dimension of the game. Despite the greater amount of information available per response in the latter condition, performance, as measured by the number of steps required to complete the game, was inferior. Only in the case of a moderate degree of redundancy between the two sources did relative amount of information and performance covary as expected. This was accompanied, however, by a decrease in the rate of responding.

REFERENCES

CALVIN, J. S., & CURTIN, M. E. Learning of a probable-cue judgment. Paper read at Southeastern Psychol. Assoc., April 1958.

ERIKSEN, C. W. Multidimensional stimulus differences and accuracy of discrimination. *USAF WADC tech. Rep.*, 1954, 54–165.

14. Stimulus Uncertainty, Response Uncertainty, and Problem Solving

F. Robert Brush

As an experimental method, the variety and uses of problem solving situations seem limited only by the ingenuity of the investigator. In its various forms, problem solving has been employed in the measurement of intelligence and the study of individual differences (1, 4, 5, 13, 14, 15), and in the investigation of the effects of stress on performance (1, 2, 6, 7, 8, 9). The process of problem solving has also been an area of investigation in its own right, and as many interpretations of problem solving have been offered as there are theorists of learning and perception. How-

Reprinted by permission of the author and the *Canadian Journal of Psychology*, 1956, *10*, 239–247.

ever, there has been little systematic investigation of the basic dimensions of problem solving.

Common sense and fashion suggest that an application of the Shannon-Weaver theory of communication may be useful in delineating these basic dimensions. We may, for example, imagine a situation in which the problem for the subject is to discover, by trial and error, the S-R code which assigns each of the possible stimuli to one and only one of the possible responses. If the S-R code is such that a given response may be assigned to more than one stimulus, the number of alternative stimuli and the number of response alternatives may be varied independently of each other. Shannon (12) has defined a subject's uncertainty as $\log_2 n$, where n is the number of equiprobable alternatives from which one is to be drawn. In the experimental situation just described, stimulus uncertainty is defined by $\log_2$ of the number of equiprobable stimuli, of which only one is presented at a time. Similarly, the response uncertainty is defined by $\log_2$ of the number of equiprobable alternative responses, from which one is preselected by the experimenter to be the "correct" response for each stimulus. Thus, in this situation, an S-R code is employed, but is unknown to the subject, and stimulus and response uncertainty are independently manipulable.

The Shannon-Weaver theory is useful in so far as it suggests this relatively simple and pure form of the problem solving situation and eliminates the variability and low generality of findings from problem solving experiments where substantive content is involved. There are serious limitations to the application of the information model to human behaviour, since it was designed to describe the properties of inanimate communication channels. However, it may provide a reasonably adequate model for describing the problem solving process. It does provide a method of statistically analysing non-metric data.

The present experiment employs an experimental situation like the one described, in an effort to investigate the effects of stimulus and response uncertainty on problem solving behaviour.

METHOD

Apparatus. From S's point of view, the apparatus consisted of a wooden box, the front panel of which is schematically represented in Figure 1. On the right side of the panel was an array of buttons, each of which was individually removable. To the left of the buttons a red pilot light was mounted. This served as an indicator of the occurrence of a "correct" response. To the left of the red light was a white screen behind which was mounted a small loudspeaker for delivering auditory stimuli. Directly above the speaker opening was a white pilot light which served as a sig-

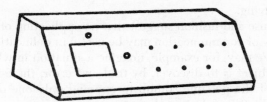

FIGURE 1. Schematic drawing of apparatus.

nal, warning S of the imminent onset of the stimulus. In addition to this panel, three Hunter timers, an audio oscillator, and a chronoscope were employed.

Procedure. A trial consisted of a fixed sequence of three time intervals which were controlled and repeated by the Hunter timers. The first interval was 2 sec. in duration, during which the white light was illuminated. At the end of the 2 sec., the light was extinguished. Simultaneously with this event the second interval, which lasted for 5 sec., was begun. At the onset of this interval, the chronoscope was started and a tone was presented. The chronoscope was stopped and the tone terminated by pushing any one of the available buttons. Pushing the "correct" button illuminated the red light for the remaining portion of the 5-sec. interval. If no response was made, the tone and the chronoscope remained on until the end of the 5-sec. period. The buttons were activated only during this period and a latching relay circuit prevented the occurrence of more than one response during a given trial. Simultaneously with the end of the 5-sec. interval, the third time period began. This interval lasted for 10 sec., during which the apparatus was inactivated to allow time for E to record the observations and to make the necessary adjustments for the next trial. At the end of the 10-sec. period the cycle was repeated, starting with the presentation of the 2-sec. warning signal. Total time per cycle was therefore 17 sec.

Experimental design. Table I provides a diagram of the experimental design. Four groups of 28 Ss each were presented with problems having either 1, 2, 3, or 4 tones. Thus the rows of Table I represent independent groups. Each of these groups received three problems, with 4, 6, and 8 buttons in counterbalanced order.[1] The columns of the table, therefore, represent dependent subgroups.

Subjects and Instructions. The Ss were 112 male and female McGill University students enrolled in an elementary psychology course. After

[1] The groups with 1 and 2 tones also received additional problems with 2 buttons. These data are not included in this report since the groups having 3 and 4 tones did not receive problems with 2 buttons. The order in which the problems were presented appeared to have little or no effect on performance.

assuring the Ss that the experiment was not a test of their intelligence or personality, they were instructed as follows:

"This is an experiment in guessing behavior, and it goes something like this. When this white light comes on you are to get ready to respond. Shortly after that, the light will go off and you will hear a tone of a given pitch. Your problem is to guess which one of these buttons is the correct one for the (each) tone. You simply indicate your guess on each trial by pushing the button which you think is going to be the correct one. If your guess is correct, the tone goes off and this red light comes on. If your

TABLE I

EXPERIMENTAL DESIGN

No. of tones	No. of Ss	No. of response alternatives		
		4	6	8
1	28			
2	28			
3	28			
4	28			

guess is incorrect, the tone goes off as before, but that's all for that trial. You are permitted, then, just one guess on each trial, but we shall continue running trials in each experiment until you have found the correct button for the (each) tone.

"Now, I determine in advance which button is the correct one for the (each) tone. That is, I don't change anything while you are working on the problem. Thus this all boils down to an initial shot in the dark, but then becomes a problem in elimination. There is only one correct button for the (each) tone, but a given button may be the correct one for more than one tone. . . .[2] Since I am interested in your reaction time, would you try to make your guess on each trial as quickly as you can, but don't knock yourself out over it."

In order to obtain stable latency measures, preliminary trials were run during which the S-R code was provided for S. These data, of course, provide an empirical measure of the subjective stimulus uncertainty. During both the preliminary and the actual problem solving trials, the order of occurrence of the tones, in the three groups where more than one tone

[2] This usually required amplification. When necessary, the instruction was repeated and an example where more than one tone was assigned to a given button was described.

was employed, followed a fixed scrambled order which assured equal probabilities of occurrence. The "correct" buttons were selected in a similar manner, so that the frequencies with which each button was the "correct" one were roughly equal. The tones employed in this experiment had the following frequencies: 200, 400, 2,000, and 4,000 cps. When only one tone was used, it was the 200 cps. tone. The group with two tones received the 200 and 400 cps. tones, and so on.

On each trial, the latency of response, measured from the onset of the tone, and S's choice among the available buttons were recorded.

TABLE II

MEAN TRIAL NO. OF FIRST CORRECT RESPONSE

No. of tones	No. of response alternatives		
	4	6	8
1	2.4	3.4	5.4
2	2.7	3.4	5.0
3	3.0	3.8	5.4
4	3.3	4.4	6.1

RESULTS

Table II presents the mean trial number of the first correct response for each group. The cell entries in this table were obtained by computing the mean for all tones for each S, and then obtaining the mean for all Ss. This method was employed since we view the problem presented to the 8 group having four tones and eight buttons, for example, as a two bit choice followed by a three bit choice. We deal with the average response uncertainty of three bits rather than with the sum of the four response uncertainties, twelve bits. This follows from the fact that in this case $4 \times 8 = 32$ alternative responses at the outset are reduced to $4 \times 1 = 4$ at solution, a reduction equivalent to three binary choices or bits.

The data presented in this table indicate that the mean trial number of the first correct response is a direct function of both stimulus uncertainty and response uncertainty. Analysis of variance indicates that both of these main effects are significant well beyond the 0.01 level; interaction between them is negligible. In order to determine the relative effectiveness of each variable, the partial regression equation for this measure as a function of $H(x)$ and $H(y)$ (stimulus and response uncertainty, respectively) was computed. This partial regression equation is as follows: Trial of first CR $= -.353 + .124\ H(x) + .253\ H(y)$. The two regression coefficients are significantly greater than zero, but not different from each other, indicating that both stimulus and response uncertainty have a significant and roughly equal effect on the trial number of the first correct response.

Table III presents the mean number of repetition errors made before the first correct response. A repetition error is defined as a choice of an incorrect button after the first choice of that button. Again, the mean presented in the table are across tones and subjects. The frequency of repetition errors is found to be directly related to both stimulus and

TABLE III

MEAN NO. OF REPETITION ERRORS BEFORE THE FIRST CORRECT RESPONSE

No. of tones	No. of response alternatives		
	4	6	8
1	0.0	0.0	0.5
2	0.1	0.3	0.6
3	0.4	0.6	0.8
4	0.9	1.0	2.0

response uncertainty. Analysis of variance on these data indicates that both main effects are significant beyond the 0.01 level, and again there are no interaction effects. The partial regression equation is as follows: R.E. $= -1.070 + .550 \ H(x) + .432 \ H(y)$. Again, the regression coefficients are greater than zero but not different from each other.

Analysing these data with the aid of information statistics requires that we view response uncertainty, $H(y)$, as the input and $H(z)$, based on the distribution of responses, as the output of the communication channel. $T(y;z) = H(y) + H(z) - H(y,z)$ is the amount of transmitted information, and this quantity is computed for successive trials. As a function of trials, $T(y;z)$ begins roughly at 0 and increases to $H(y)$ at the limit, at which time all Ss have solved the problem. As response uncertainty varies from group to group, so the asymptotic value of $T(y;z)$ varies from group to group. The quantity $D(z:y) = T(y:z)/H(y)$ is an expression for the exhaustiveness of transmission, or the relative amount of $H(y)$ transmitted on a given trial. This measure takes on values between 0 and 1; 0 before the first trial, and 1 on whatever trial solution is reached by all members of the group. The slope, b, of this line over the first ten trials per tone in each group is presented in Table IV. A large number indicates a relatively high rate of information transmission per trial; a small number indicates a relatively low rate of assimilation of the available information per trial. Analysis of variance on these data indi-

TABLE IV

SLOPE (b) OF D(z:y) VS TRIALS

No. of tones	No. of response alternatives		
	4	6	8
1	0.240	0.176	0.090
2	0.175	0.103	0.076
3	0.110	0.095	0.078
4	0.085	0.064	0.036

cates that both stimulus and response uncertainty bear a significant inverse relationship to the rate of transmission per trial. The partial regression equation follows: $b = .281 - .048\ H(x) - .047\ H(y)$. Again, both coefficients are significantly different from zero but not from each other.

Turning to the latency data, Table V presents the mean latency over all trials for each of the groups. Latency of response is directly and significantly related to stimulus uncertainty, but the similar, more tenuous, relationship between latency and response uncertainty is not significant. The partial regression equation also expresses this:

$$RT = .616 + .275\ H(x) + .026\ H(y).$$

TABLE V

MEAN LATENCY OVER ALL TRIALS

No. of tones	No. of response alternatives		
	4	6	8
1	0.687	0.689	0.769
2	0.872	0.878	0.890
3	1.093	1.069	1.135
4	1.241	1.271	1.278

Bricker and others (3) have defined the rate of gain of information $\dot{T} = 1/b$, where b is the slope of the regression line relating transmitted information to reaction time. $\dot{T}$ is expressed in units of bits per sec. In the present experiment, we have two measures of the rate of gain of information, $\dot{T}_x = 1/.275 = 3.64$ bits per sec., and $\dot{T}_y = 1/1.026 = 38.46$ bits per sec.

Discussion

In problem solving, as in test construction and scaling, the usual measure of difficulty is in terms of the proportion of Ss failing a test or test item. Use of percentage scores requires rather large samples if relatively small effects are to be measured. Miller (10), Rogers and Green (11), and others have made considerable progress in establishing the sampling distributions of information measures. Even with small samples, the expected variance of uncertainty measures is rather small. It is felt that while the usual measure of difficulty is satisfactory for many purposes and has the advantage of simplicity, the measures of information employed here have the advantage of greater stability and sensitivity, in addition to providing a model for describing the process of problem solving itself. The use of these measures has the further advantage of permitting a meaningful combination of both time and error scores, for example, rate of gain of information.

From the point of view of problem solving, the present experiment indicates that both stimulus and response uncertainty are important variables for controlling problem solving behaviour. The majority of experiments in the literature have tended to ignore the response side of the picture. While manipulation of these two variables is useful for controlling problem solving behaviour, only future research can indicate whether the distinction between stimulus and response uncertainty will be useful in predicting the effects of other variables such as rewards, punishments, stress, etc., on problem solving. Preliminary data from our current research suggest that this distinction may indeed have considerable utility in making such predictions.

Experiments on disjunctive reaction time have confounded variation in stimulus uncertainty with concomitant variation in response uncertainty. The direct relation between reaction time and stimulus and/or response uncertainty was generally attributed to the effects of stimulus uncertainty. The present experiment helps confirm this interpretation of the obtained relationship. However, the value for $\dot{T}_x$ obtained in the present experiment is somewhat lower than that found in other experiments on disjunctive reaction time. Bricker (3) has reviewed these experiments and reports that in many of them $\dot{T}_x$ varies between 5.5 and 7.5 bits per sec., but remains relatively constant over a fairly wide range of experimental variation. However, these experiments all employed visual-spatial discriminations. The tones employed in the present experiment are certainly not as discriminable from each other as are the positions of an illuminated light. It is suggested, therefore, that in addition to stimulus uncertainty *per se*, the discriminability of stimuli may be another important variable influencing the rate of gain of information and problem solving in general.

Although auditory reaction times are generally shorter than visual ones, the inequality between visual-spatial and auditory acuity probably accounts for the lower rate of gain of stimulus information obtained in the present experiment. The high rate of gain of response information we obtained also suggests that under the present conditions Ss have little difficulty in discriminating one button from the other, although they have some difficulty in remembering which buttons have been tried on previous trials.

From the point of view of ascertaining the effects of other variables, for example stress, on problem solving, the results of the present experiment provide rather clean and reliable control data. As indicated above, preliminary findings suggest that the information statistics employed here are more sensitive to the effects of stress than are the more usual measures of performance. Although they involve somewhat more labour, measures of uncertainty seem to have a utility and sensitivity which is lacking in the standard measures of trials to solution and frequency of errors.

SUMMARY

The present experiment was concerned with the effects of variation in stimulus uncertainty and response uncertainty on problem solving. Shannon's definition of uncertainty was employed. Four groups of 28 Ss each were presented with problems having one, two, three, or four auditory stimuli, to each of which E had pre-assigned a "correct" response. A response consisted of pressing one of several buttons available to S. S's problem was to find the "correct" button for each stimulus by eliminating "incorrect" buttons on successive trials. Each group of Ss received three problems, in which the "correct" responses had been selected from four, six, and eight buttons, respectively. The following results were obtained:

(1) The mean trial number of the first correct response for each stimulus is directly related to both stimulus and response uncertainty.

(2) The mean frequency of repetition errors (more than one choice of an incorrect button, for each stimulus) is also directly related to both stimulus and response uncertainty.

(3) The relative rate of gain of information per trial is an inverse function of both stimulus and response uncertainty.

(4) The rate of gain of information per sec. is directly related to stimulus uncertainty but is unaffected by response uncertainty.

These results were discussed and it was suggested that the distinction between stimulus and response uncertainty might be of some value in predicting the effects of other variables, e.g., reward, punishment, stress, on problem solving behaviour.

REFERENCES

1. ADAMS, C. R. Individual differences in behavior resulting from experimentally induced frustration. *J. Psychol.*, 1940, 10, 157–176.
2. BARKER, R., DEMBO, T., & LEWIN, K. Frustration and regression: an experiment with young children. *Univ. Ia. Stud. Child. Welf.*, 1941, 18, No. 1.
3. BRICKER, P. D. Information measurement and reaction time: a review. In QUASTLER, H. (Ed.), *Information theory in psychology*. Glencoe, Ill.: The Free Press, 1955, pp. 350–359.
4. GOLDSTEIN, K., & SCHEERER, M. Abstract and concrete behavior: an experimental study with special tests. *Psychol. Monogr.*, 1941, 53, No. 2.
5. HANFMANN, E., & KASANIN, J. A method for the study of concept formation. *J. Psychol.*, 1937, 3, 521–540.
6. HUTT, N. L. A clinical study of "consecutive" and "adaptive" testing with the revised Stanford-Binet. *J. consult. Psychol.*, 1947, 11, 93–103.
7. KENDLER, T. S. The effect of success and failure on the recall of tasks. *J. gen. Psychol.*, 1949, 41, 79–87.
8. LAZARUS, R. E., & ERIKSEN, C. W. Psychological stress and its personality correlates: Part I. The effects of failure stress upon skilled performance. *J. exp. Psychol.*, 1952, 43, 100–105.
9. McKINLEY, F. Certain emotional factors in learning and efficiency. *J. gen. Psychol.*, 1933, 9, 101–116.
10. MILLER, G. A. A note on the bias of information estimates. In QUASTLER, H. (Ed.), *Information theory in psychology*. Glencoe, Ill.: The Free Press, 1955, pp. 95–100.
11. ROGERS, M. S., & GREEN, B. F. The moments of sample information when the alternatives are equally likely. In QUASTLER, H. (Ed.), *Information theory in psychology*. Glencoe, Ill.: The Free Press, 1955, pp. 101–108.
12. SHANNON, C. E., & WEAVER, W. *The Mathematical theory of communication*. Urbana, Ill.: University of Illinois, 1949.
13. TERMAN, L. M., & MERRILL, M. A. *Directions for administering forms L and M: revision of the Stanford-Binet tests of intelligence*. Boston: Houghton Mifflin, 1937.
14. THORNDIKE, E. L., & WOODYARD, E. The influence of the relative frequency of successes and frustrations on intellectual achievement. *J. educ. Psychol.*, 1934, 25, 241–250.
15. WECHSLER, D. *Wechsler-Bellevue Intelligence Scale: Form II. Manual for administering and scoring the test*. New York: Psychol. Corp., 1946.

SECTION FIVE

Processes and Language

The oldest type of research in human problem solving, beginning before 1900, consists of attempts to find out how subjects solve problems, i.e., what behavioral processes are involved. Unfortunately, the older studies, which are usually very long and unrelated to each other, have not produced either an agreed-upon body of knowledge, nor have they led to a systematic area of research.

Recently, studies of processes have begun to use experimental methods, rather than the observational techniques characteristic of the earlier literature. Two such papers, by Johnson and by Hayes, are included here.

Johnson shows that of the great variety of processes that have been suggested, one set at least, those involving stages of thinking, can be brought under experimental control. Having done so, he finds that in fact there are identifiable stages and that the stages are differentially affected by various independent variables. Johnson's method of serial analysis can be adapted to a variety of problems, as his paper suggests, and should prove to be an increasingly fruitful technique.

Since so much of thinking is implicit, behavioral methods of measuring quantitatively what goes on in the head are particularly needed. An example of such a technique appears in the Hayes study (see also the method used by Ranken, in this section, and Underwood's procedure, in Section Nine). As Hayes' paper shows, his mental maze problems are quite amenable to variations in such task characteristics as number of elements, branching, etc. And it is clear that his method yields a considerable amount of quantitative data about implicit behavior in thinking.

154

The role of language in thinking is one of the oldest topics in philosophy and psychology. Nevertheless, until very recently there has been no clear-cut experimental study of what part, if any, words play in thinking. Ranken's paper provides such a study. A particularly worthwhile aspect of his study is that the effect of the presence or absence of words, as names, is examined in wholly implicit behavior, i.e., in a problem that can be done entirely in the head (compare with Hayes' problem). His study shows clearly that words can facilitate or can interfere with thinking, depending upon the nature of the problem.

Glucksberg and Weisberg indicate that a verbal label can eliminate functional fixedness. Furthermore, they were able to find transfer from symbolic (verbal and pictorial) presentation of problem stimuli to the instrumental responses needed for solution. As noted in the Duncan paper in Section One, such symbolic-to-instrumental transfer has rarely been achieved in problem solving, short of telling the subject what to do.

15. Serial Analysis of Thinking

Donald M. Johnson

As the other papers in this monograph demonstrate, there are many ways to study thinking. In large part, it seems that we are trying to understand what happens during those brief episodes of concentrated intellectual activity that occur when some kind of problem interrupts the routine activities of ordinary life. It is not altogether necessary, of course, to analyze such a problem-solving episode. There is much to be learned by treating it as an undifferentiated whole and using over-all measures of outcome, such as type of solution and time required, for comparison with antecedent variables. Attempts at analysis usually promise some additional information not obtainable from these conventional measures and should be evaluated in respect to this promise.

Reprinted by permission of the author and the New York Academy of Sciences from Harms, E. (Ed.) *Fundamentals of Psychology: The Psychology of Thinking.* *Annals of the New York Academy of Sciences*, 1960, *91*, 66–75.

The most familiar analysis in the past was that by John Dewey (1910), who analyzed reflective thought into five steps, preparatory to explaining to school-teachers how thought may be studied. Then Graham Wallas (1926) published a similar analysis reducing thought to four stages, of which "preparation" and "incubation" are perhaps the best known today. In later research on thought processes investigators have requested the thinkers to talk as they worked and then tried to classify the verbal output in categories of functional significance. Whereas the early writers seemed to assume that the real thought processes would be revealed by the introspections of an astute psychologist, current methodology views such research as attempts to demonstrate the consistency and utility of a coding system (Johnson, 1955).

Other analyses have been based on sequences of overt behavior. At first the experimenter simply watched the movements of his subjects and reported that he observed trial and error, insight, or perseveration. More recently the rules for identifying a response sequence have been written in advance, and the frequency of such a sequence compared with chance frequencies or with frequencies under other conditions. It is not common in experimental psychology today to attempt a complete description of problem-solving activities; rather the experiments are usually planned so that only those patterns of activity pertinent to a particular hypothesis are observed, and such patterns are not called thought processes because this research stems from a different tradition. However, in a broader sense the aim is the same, that is, to describe problem-solving activities in functional units that are larger than the single response and smaller than the whole problem-solving episode.

A sophisticated example of this approach is the study of concept attainment by Bruner et al. (1956) in which the subjects selected cards one after another in an attempt to discover the concept that the experimenter considered to be correct. From the mathematics of the case and the limitations of human memory, the investigators were able to describe certain ideal strategies, such as focussing and scanning, and then to observe how frequently such strategies were followed under different conditions and with what success. The apparatus used by John (1957) required his subjects to press buttons in sequence, and the records thus obtained permit description of the subjects' activities in several respects, such as the time at which the problem-solving activity shifts from a process of analysis to one of synthesis.

The experiments to be reported here also analyze problem-solving sequentially but follow the ideal of the older speculations and attempt to describe the whole problem-solving enterprise in terms of sequential thought processes. Nevertheless, the early analyses attempted too much, identification of four or five separate processes, with an inadequate method, introspection. The present attempt is more modest and more objective. The most manageable number larger than one is two, thus the analysis is a two-part analysis. The problems are simple ones that are solved in less than a minute, and this brief episode is divided into two intervals by control of the exposure of the problem material during which two different intellectual activities are presumed to take place serially. A general description of thinking, outlined several years ago (Johnson, 1955), suggested that the first step, commonly called preparation, was the locus of many errors and was often overlooked by researchers, hence preparation was selected for special study and the remainder of the problem-solving episode was designated "solution." A simple model of cognitive dynamics attempts to describe the two processes preparation and solution, especially the dependence of the second on the first, and to make predictions that can be tested by the serial-exposure method.

The methodological problem of separating one activity from the next has not been discussed to any extent by psychologists, but two extreme possibilities can readily be imagined. We can imagine these two activities as completely different and completely separated in time and, if we knew where to draw the line, we could divide them clearly. Also, we can assume that the problem-solving episode is undifferentiated and that wherever a division is made the events in one group would be indistinguishable from those in the other. However everything we know about living organisms suggests that the most likely possibility is neither complete separation of the two processes (———- ----), nor no separation (⁼⁼⁼⁼), but partial overlapping (———- ----). Reading aloud, for example, includes a perceptual process and vocalization process, and the first no doubt precedes the second, but the two overlap to the extent of the eye-voice span. Regressive eye movements when the material is difficult indicate even greater overlap. Preparation for problem-solving may likewise precede solution and continue after solution attempts have started. It is an empirical question whether, in any particular type of problem, the overlap is too great to permit temporal separation of the two activities. The problems of the following experiments were chosen to show in which cases separation of the two processes is possible and, where it is possible, to describe the preparation process and the variables that influence it. Some of the individual experiments will be described in more detail elsewhere.

Apparatus and Method

The serial-exposure box consists of two chambers separated by a partition and separately lighted. The side toward the subject includes a half-silvered mirror about 7×9 inches, and on the back side is a holder for 5×8 cards positioned so that when the light in the left chamber is turned on the left half of the card is visible and when the light in the right chamber is turned on the right half of the card is visible. The problem material is separated in two parts and typed on the card as follows:

What number turned on	the letter
its side looks like	m

The answer to each problem is a letter from A to E or a number from 1 to 5, which is expressed by pushing one of five appropriately labeled buttons. A system of interval timers, relays, and clocks permits considerable flexibility of exposure conditions and timing. The experimenter can expose each side for a fixed interval of time or the subject can expose each as long as he wishes, and various combinations of these exposure conditions have been used in these experiments.

The main assumption of the method is that the thinker in his effort to solve the problem operates serially on the material that is presented serially. While the material on the left half of the card is exposed to view, the thinker has no problem to solve, but he is presumably getting ready for the material to be presented next and his activity is called preparation. His activity during the next period, which eventuates in selecting a solution and pressing a button, is called solution.

The subjects of the experiments were all college students, recruited in the usual way from elementary psychology classes.

EFFECTS OF DISTRACTION

The first experiments explored the effects of distraction on preparation in order to see if anything of consequence takes place during this period. The problem is actually solved during the solution period and one would certainly expect that distraction during this period would interfere with solution but, if preparation is important to the solution, distraction during the preparation period would interfere also. To test this hypothesis 15 short problems were constructed, similar to those that appear on intelligence tests, and each was divided into two installments, the first giving the orientation to the problem, the second being a key word, letter, or number, as in the illustration above. The first or preparatory part of the problem was exposed for 5 sec., then the solution material was exposed until the subject indicated his solution by pressing a button. Distraction in the form of a loud doorbell under the exposure box extended for the duration of the preparation period, or for the duration of the solution period. Two experiments with about 100 subjects showed that distraction in either period increased the number of errors compared to control conditions. In one experiment preparation seemed to be more vulnerable to distraction than solution, but in another the direction of the difference was reversed.

It was clear that preparation is worth serious study but that better control of exposure conditions was needed.

Controlled and Uncontrolled Exposure

The possibility of controlling both exposures was next explored. Thirty short problems of variegated verbal, numerical, and spatial content were given to 5 groups of 15 subjects each, equated as to mean scores on a standard intelligence test. Each subject was allowed 12 sec. for each problem, but the 5 groups differed in the way this 12-sec. episode was divided between the two exposures. One group had 2 sec. for preparation and 10 for solution, another had 4 and 8, another 6 and 6, another 8 and 4, and finally 10 sec. for preparation and 2 for solution. The interval timers and relays exposed the right half of the problem immediately after the left half, with no blank between exposures and no overlap of exposures. Under these conditions there was a significant difference between the groups in number of errors. The 2/10 group made a mean of 13.7 errors, the 4/8 group 10.7, the 6/6 group 13.1, the 8/4 group 13.5, and the 10/2 group 18.3. Hence the optimal condition was 4 sec. for preparation and 8 for solution, and the worst were the two extreme conditions. Evidently, with these brief heterogeneous problems, the 12-sec. problem-solving episode is not entirely undifferentiated. A certain minimal time is necessary for each operation, perhaps about 3 sec., and extra time for one cannot be substituted for a shortage of the other.

Another way to assess the data of this experiment is to describe each of the 30 problems in respect to the relative difficulty of preparation. Many investigators have commented on the lack of standardization of problems used in problem-solving research and have asked for a method of comparing problems in some dimensions other than errors and time of solution. It is possible to scale these problems by dividing the number of errors made with short preparatory exposures (2/10 and 4/8) by the number of errors made under all exposure conditions. These indices range from 0.20 to 0.67, showing that some problems are much more vulnerable to short preparatory exposure than others or, alternatively, that some are more vulnerable to short solution exposure.

The latest method that we have developed for presenting such problems in the serial-exposure box is called uncontrolled or self-paced exposure. The subject has control of a centrally mounted double-throw switch that he uses when he is ready to switch the lights from the preparatory side to the solution side. He pushes a response button when he has selected a solution. Thus we have a record for each problem of time spent on the left side (preparation time), time spent on the right side (solution time), and the solution selected. When this method is used to scale problems in respect to relative difficulty of preparation, the times are converted to logarithms and the index is preparation time divided by total time. With 40 subjects and the same 30 heterogeneous problems these indices ranged from 0.32 to 0.70, indicating that the subjects spent much more time preparing for some problems than for others.

We now have two indices of relative difficulty of preparation for each of these 30 problems. If the two methods of scaling problems in this respect are dependable, the scale values should agree, and in fact the correlation between them is 0.68. Hence we can say that those problems that are failed most often when the preparatory exposure is short are generally the same problems on which other subjects spend the largest amount of their time in preparation. The uncontrolled or self-paced method of presenting the problems is simpler and more convenient than controlled-exposure, and it seems more natural in that it offers less interruption to the continuity of the problem-solving enterprise. After one demonstration the subjects flip the switch as automatically as they turn the pages of a book or look from one side of the page to the other.

THE QUESTION OF ARTIFICIALITY

At this point the question of artificiality was considered. It seemed possible that exposure of the problem material in two parts, serially, makes the problem a peculiar one, and that the method does not study genuine problem solving. This critical question was answered in three ways.

An intelligence test was used to match the groups in the above experiment by the controlled-exposure method, and scores on this test correlated 0.47 with number of problems solved. This correlation based on all 75 subjects is an underestimate for several reasons, but it does show that problem-solving performance under these conditions has something in common with the solution of the problems on a standard test of intelligence.

These problems were given to another group with both chambers of the serial-exposure box lighted so that the whole problem was visible for 12 sec. Under these more natural conditions of complete exposure, mean performance was only slightly better than under the optimal serial exposure, and the difficulty values for the 30 problems correlated 0.64 with difficulty values from controlled exposure and 0.72 with difficulty values from uncontrolled exposure.

When these problems were printed in the usual format without any separation and presented to psychologists for subjective estimates of relative difficulty of preparation, their mean estimates correlated reasonably well with comparable scale values obtained by the two objective methods: with controlled exposure 0.42, with uncontrolled exposure 0.56.

These three checks demonstrate, therefore, that the separation of the problem material into two parts for serial exposure does not distort the problem very much, that the indices of relative difficulty of preparation have something in common with psychologists' understanding of preparation, and that the self-paced method is generally the better of the two.

INDUCTION AND DEDUCTION

Now that we have a method for studying preparation time that yields results of some stability and significance, we are in a position to investigate the determinants of preparation time. The verbal analogy seems to be a convenient problem for this purpose because the four terms of the analogy divide themselves naturally into two and two and because different types of analogies can be constructed and predictions about preparation times can be made in advance. In the case of analogies, preparation consists mostly of induction, that is, formulating the relation between the first pair of words, and solution consists mostly of deduction, that is, applying this relation to the second pair.

A block of 25 analogies was constructed with the first pair of words more difficult than the second pair, for example, *Visit* is to *Invade* as *Friend* is to *Enemy*. Another block of 25 was constructed with the second pair of words more difficult than the first pair, for example, *Lose* is to *Win* as *Liability* is to *Asset*. If the first pair of words is more difficult, the analogy problem may be said to emphasize induction and, if the second pair is more difficult, it may be said to emphasize deduction. Hence we would predict that the index of relative difficulty of preparation will be higher for those analogies that emphasize induction.

The first pair of words was presented in the left side of the serial-exposure box and the first word of the second pair in the right side. The subject was instructed to think of the solution word, which always began with a letter from A to E, and to press the appropriate button. The two types of analogies were mixed in irregular order in a list of 50 problems and given under controlled exposure to four groups of 10 subjects each, matched as to mean score on the Terman Concept Mastery Test. The exposures were 2/10, 4/8, 6/6, and 8/4. The corresponding mean errors were 20.1, 22.0, 21.5, and 22.6, and the variance due to exposure conditions was not significant. Evidently a preparatory exposure of as little as 2 sec. will suffice for perception of two words, and the relation between them can be formulated during the solution period if necessary. The overlap between the two operations can be so large a portion of the whole that separation is not possible by this method. Correspondingly, the indices of relative difficulty of preparation, computed by taking errors under short preparatory exposures as a fraction of all errors, did not differ significantly between the two types of analogies.

When the same list of analogies was given to 20 subjects by the self-paced method of exposure, a better differentiation between the two types of analogies was obtained. Log mean preparation time was greater for the analogies emphasizing induction, and log mean solution time was greater for those emphasizing deduction. Likewise the time index of relative difficulty of preparation differentiated the two types of problems significantly. Thus we can conclude that in the case of analogy problems the method of controlled exposure is not adequate because the thinkers can remember such a small amount of preparatory material and work on it during the solution exposure, but that the self-paced method is adequate. When the thinkers are allowed to control the exposures, the mean times do reflect the relative difficulty of the two different logical operations. Any method that does not fractionate the problem-solving episode could not obtain such a differentiation because the two types of analogies were practically the same in respect to mean errors and total time.

Amount of Information

In problem solving and any other task in which one operation depends on a preceding one the amount of information presented is probably an important variable. In the heterogeneous problems of the intelligence-test type the number of words in the preparatory material was not controlled and in the analogy problems the number was always two. In order to study the influence of amount of information on time required for preparation, we need a task in which the number of items can be systematically varied. The type of problem most suitable for this purpose asks the subject to think of a solution that meets specifications stated in terms of discrete items, such as adjectives. This type is common in real life and is convenient in the laboratory because such problems can be constructed with varying numbers of specifications and because exposure of the specifications can be separated from exposure of the alternative solutions. A problem with four specifications is illustrated below:

gummed	1. map
descriptive	2. book
flat	3. label
readable	4. paper
	5. globe

The subject is instructed to study the material on the left side and to be prepared to find an object on the right that meets these specifications. The number of specifications was varied from 3 to 11 in order to get data on both sides of the span of immediate memory. Preparation for a problem of this type presumably consists of memorizing or organizing the specifications in some way and one may confidently expect that preparation time will increase with an increase in the number of specifications. The effect of this variable is something like what Bruner *et al.* called "cognitive strain." The number of alternative solutions was held constant at five, so if time spent on selection of solutions does not increase similarly, we may conclude that preparation is complete when solution commences, that preparation does not overlap solution.

Another variable was introduced in this experiment in order to make our description of problem-solving more complete. In problem-solving and many serial perceptual tasks, when the subject has difficulty making progress, he turns back if possible to a re-examination of the problem material, then searches again for a solution. Regressive eye movements in reading are a familiar indicator of difficulty and an analogous indicator in the self-paced serial-exposure situation would be switching the lights from the solution exposure back to the preparatory exposure. It would be expected that the number of such switchbacks would increase with the increase in number of specifications.

Four problems of each number of specifications from 3 to 11 were constructed, making 36 in all, and given to 20 subjects with switchback permitted and 20 without switchback. Those who were permitted to switch back had one switchback forced during the practice problems. The timing arrangements separated switchback time from solution time and added it to time of initial preparation.

The results turned out as expected. In the group not permitted to switch back median preparation time increased regularly from 5 sec. for problems of 3 specifications to 17 sec. for problems of 11 specifications. The group permitted to switch back showed the same regular increase but took somewhat more time in preparation for problems of more than 5 specifications —because of the increase in switchbacks upon reaching 5. In both groups solution time remained constant around 10 sec. in spite of variations in number of specifications on the preparation side. Thus for problems of 3 and 4 specifications solution time was longer than preparation time, while for problems of 6 or more specifications preparation time was longer than solution time. This appears to be reasonable in the light of previous discussion. When the preparatory material consists of only a few adjectives, one glance will suffice, and the thinker quickly switches to the other side to look for a solution, organizing these few specifications during the solution period if necessary. When there are 6 or 7 specifications, these cannot be grasped immediately but must be memorized or processed in some way. This addition of specifications requires more time and is not always done thoroughly and switchbacks occur if permitted. In this experiment preparation and solution are clearly different processes in that their durations are differentially influenced by the independent variable, the number of specifications.

Returning briefly to the question of artificiality, we ran a group of 20 subjects on these problems with both sides of the problem exposed, but these subjects did not differ significantly from the serial-exposure subjects in respect to either time or errors. We surmised that they used a serial procedure even with complete exposure; at least whatever they do that is different from a serial procedure is not more efficient.

FORMULATION AND REFORMULATION

The next experiment attempts to push the analysis beyond time comparisons toward a description of preparation. It is not possible, of course, to observe the preparation process, but it is possible on the basis of previous research to write a hypothetical description or model of cognitive dynamics and make predictions from it that can be tested by the serial-exposure technique. If the problem presents more material than can be easily grasped and retained during the search for a solution, the thinker memorizes or organizes this material in some way before attempting solution. If, in addition, the problem material is ambiguous or complicated, the thinker surveys the material selectively, ignoring some features and emphasizing others, and assembles those features that he has emphasized into a structure or formulation that he can retain and use in the search for a solution. Once the thinker has achieved a formulation of the problem, he prepares to search for solutions of the type that fit this formulation, hence it is possible to predict from formulation to solutions. It follows also that, if the thinker does not find the type of solution he is looking for, he will reformulate the problem and prepare for another type of solution. If the problem is an abstract one, like a concept-formation problem, reformulation changes the cognitive side of the set, for example, from observing colors to observing shapes, while the motor side of the set remains constant.

To test this simple model of cognitive dynamics and validate this mediating cognitive construct that we call formulation, we need problems that permit two distinct formulations and two correspondingly distinct solutions, and an independent variable that slants formulation toward one or the other. Figure concepts were used because it is easy to draw many sets of figures that can be conceptualized in terms of their shape, many others that can be conceptualized in terms of their markings or texture, and many ambiguous ones that can be conceptualized either way. Ten figures were drawn on the left half of a card and ten others on the right. With such a card in the serial-exposure box the instructions are to observe what the figures on the left have in common, then to switch to the right and find another illustration of this concept.

Ambiguous problems were constructed for the first group of 24 subjects.

That is, the preparatory material consisted of ten figures that were similar in respect to both shape and texture and could therefore be formulated either way, and the solution figures included one that fit the shape formulation and one that fit the texture formulation. When the problems are ambiguous in this sense, selection of the shape solution indicates that the problem was formulated in terms of shape similarities and selections of the texture solution indicated that it was formulated in terms of texture.

The independent variable intended to slant formulation toward either shape or texture was pretest experience. Rees and Israel (1935) and Luchins (1942) have demonstrated that a set for a certain type of solution can be induced by previous experience with a series of problems for which such solutions are obvious. The hypothesis is that the pretest experience slants the formulation toward a general class of similarities, for example, shape, then, when the preparatory material of a test card is presented, the subject will be set to observe shape similarities. If he finds a similarity of shape, for example, triangles, he adopts a more specific set for this subclass, switches to the solution side, and looks for a triangle, ignoring many other things along the way. Half the subjects had 8 easy pretest shape problems and the other half had 8 easy texture problems. Then all subjects had the same three ambiguous test problems, and the number of set solutions was 89 per cent, far above chance levels. Those who had had the pretest shape series selected shape solutions and therefore must have formulated the test problems in terms of shape, while those who had had the pretest texture series selected texture solutions and therefore must have formulated these same problems in terms of texture similarities. Thus we have demonstrated the role of previous experience in formulation and we have a technique of manipulating formulation for the next experiment.

Now suppose the subject, having formulated a problem, looks confidently for a solution that fits his formulation, but does not find one. Everyone is familiar with this sequence of events. Our model of cognitive dynamics would predict that, when the amount of preparatory material exceeds the memory span, the disappointed thinker will switch back to the preparatory material and reformulate the problem, then return and look for a solution to fit this new formulation. In the case of the concept-formation problem this reformulation would consist of trying to find a different dimension of similarity among the 10 figures. The switchback is an observable indicator of reformulation, so the hypothesis is simply that, when the test problems do not have a solution that fits the formulation developed during the pretest series, the subjects will switch back, then return and find a correct solution.

The pretest series were the same as before, but the 12 subjects who had pretest shape problems now had test problems with a texture solution only, and the 12 who had pretest texture problems had test problems with a shape solution only. The results were as expected. Every subject switched back to the preparatory material at least once, and the total number of switchbacks was 43, to be compared with 9 for a control group. The percentage of correct solutions was 83, to be compared with 57 for a group given the same sequence of problems but not allowed to switch back. The data on preparation time and solution time are also congruent with this analysis. The evidence is clear, then, that we can describe and experimentally manipulate not only formulation and solution of these concept problems but also failure, reformulation, and solution on the second try.

LIMITATIONS

These studies have been concerned with the solution of short problems finished, for the most part, in less than one half of one minute. Obviously if the times were much longer, the activities could shift back and forth, and serial analysis might be unprofitable. Also, these problems have been solved by selection from a display of solutions. In the experiments planned next the subject will produce his own solutions.

CONCLUSIONS

These assembled studies justify the following conclusions:

It is worthwhile to analyze thinking serially, by serial-exposure of portions of the problem, and the data obtained are more descriptive than the conventional data on total time and errors.

The overlap between one thought process and the next is smaller when the thinker himself controls the presentation of the material.

Efficiency of problem-solving under serial-exposure differs little, if at all, from efficiency under complete exposure.

It is possible by this serial-exposure technique to identify, in the solution of a variety of types of problems, a preparation process that precedes the actual selection of alternative solutions.

Preparation, as thus identified, differs from solution in respect to the functional relation between the time spent on each and certain independent variables, such as type of problem and amount of preparatory material.

There is a large class of problems, preparation for which consists of formulating the problem in terms of a dimension of similarity among the items and, when there are alternative dimensions of similarity, this formulation is influenced by immediately preceding experience with similar problems.

The difficulty in solving a problem may be quantitative when there is too much preparatory material to remember, and in such cases the thinker is likely to switch back to the preparatory material for more adequate preparation and to be more successful on the next try.

The difficulty may be qualitative when the formulation does not fit the available solutions, and in such cases also the thinker will switch back to the preparatory material to reformulate the problem and is likely to be more successful on the next try.

REFERENCES

BRUNER, J. S., J. J. GOODNOW & G. A. AUSTIN. 1956. A Study of Thinking. Wiley. New York, N. Y.

DEWEY, J. 1910. How We Think. Heath. Boston, Mass.

JOHN, E. R. 1957. Contributions to the study of the problem-solving process. Psychol. Monogr. 71 (447).

JOHNSON, D. M. 1955. The Psychology of Thought and Judgment. Harper. New York, N. Y.

LUCHINS, A. S. 1942. Mechanization in problem solving. Psychol. Monogr. 54 (248).

REES, H. J. & H. E. ISRAEL. 1935. An investigation of the establishment and operation of mental sets. Psychol. Monogr. 46 (210).

WALLAS, G. 1926. The Art of Thought. Harcourt, Brace & Co. New York, N. Y.

16. Problem Topology and the Solution Process

John R. Hayes

Duncker (1945) has described problem solving as proceeding from an initial problem situation to a goal in a sequence of solution phases, each phase being generated by the phase preceding it and, in turn, generating the one following it. Bartlett (1958) has defined problem solving (and thinking in general) as " . . . the extension of evidence in accord with that evidence so as to fill up gaps in that evidence: and this is done by moving through a succession of steps. . . ." Both Duncker and Bartlett seem to propound a rather common sense view of the solution process

Reprinted by permission of the author and the Academic Press, Inc. from *Journal of Verbal Learning and Verbal Behavior*, 1965, 4, 371–379.

which may be reformulated as follows: A problem solution is a sequence of linked phases or steps which form a chain or path connecting the initial conditions of the problem with its goal. If this view is correct, then information relating the topological properties of problems, e.g., length and degree of branching, to the solution process should be basic to the study of problem solving.

In solving a problem S may retrace a path or enter a blind alley. A particular solution may contain some unnecessary steps, i.e., steps which could be deleted without destroying the solution. A solution which has no unnecessary steps will be called a "minimal chain." A problem may have several minimal chain solutions, and they need not all be of the same length.

This paper will be concerned with problems which have only one minimal chain. The properties of the solution process will be related to the length of the minimal chain and to the number and length of side chains or blind alleys attached to it.

If all the steps within the test problem were of equal difficulty, the effects of length and branching would be easier to observe than if successive steps varied in difficulty. Two common causes of such variability are (a) that successive steps are not of the same type, e.g., the first step may be logical and the second arithmetic, and (b) that required information may be retrieved from memory more easily for one step than for another. Therefore, a problem type in which both of these factors can be controlled, the "spy" problem, was especially designed for the present investigation.

EXPERIMENT I

The first experiment was designed to determine the relation between problem solution time, the length of the minimal chain, and the number and length of branches on the minimal chain.

METHOD

Subjects. The Ss were 12 Regis College students paid to serve as subjects.

Procedure. In all of the experiments described here, Ss solved "spy problems." The instructions for these problems covered the following points.

(a) The S was to imagine that he was running a spy ring and that for security reasons not all of his spies could talk to each other. (b) Before each problem, the E would give S a list of spy-name pairs which would designate the spies who could talk to each other. A pair "x-y" for example, indicated both that x could talk to y and that y could talk to x. The list of pairs will be called the "connection list." (c) The S was required to learn the list to a criterion of three successive error-free trials. Any change in the order of pairs or in the order of spies within a pair was scored as an error. (d) The S would be allowed to study the list for as long as he wanted to and a learning test would be administered whenever S requested it. (e) When the learning criterion was met, E would state the problem verbally to S, e.g., "Get a message from Tango to China," and simultaneously hand S a card on which was written the initial state, e.g., "Tango," and the goal, e.g., "China." (f) The S was to solve the problems aloud, without aid of pencil and paper, and he was to tell E everything he was thinking, including rote recitations of the connection list.

The E then guided S through two practice problems and answered his questions about the procedure before the experimental trials began.

Materials. The spy names used in constructing the problems were drawn from a set of 480 items, divided into 24 categories, e.g., presidents, countries, rivers, etc., each containing 20 familiar members.

To construct a problem, first a diagram was drawn representing the desired problem structure. Spies were represented by circles, and communication links between spies by lines connecting the circles. Eight such structural diagrams are shown in Fig. 1. A spy name was then written in each circle, each spy name being chosen from the spy-name set so that no category was represented more than once in any problem.

The connection list consisted of all pairs of spy names which were connected by a line. In ordering the items *within the pairs*, the item nearest to the initial state of the problem was always placed first. The pairs were printed on a card in a column, one pair to a row. The ordering of the pairs in the column was randomized separately for each problem. The connection list for any specified problem was presented to all Ss in the same randomized order.

Problems. The eight problem types used in this experiment are shown in Fig. 1. The "I's" designate initial states and the "G's" goals.

The problem types will be designated by a three-digit code. The first digit will designate the length of the minimal chain, the second digit, the number of blind alleys attached at each point of the minimal chain, and the third digit the length of the blind alleys. Thus "900" represents an unbranched problem of length nine, and "312" a length-three problem with one length-two blind alley at each point of the minimal chain.

Problem types 300, 500, 700, 900 and 311 each contain a subgroup of spies unconnected to the minimal chain. These subgroups were added as "filler" so that each of the eight problem types would have exactly 11 communication links or spy pairs to be learned.

Solution time, i.e., the time elapsed from the instant at which E designated the goal to the instant at which S completed the last problem-solv-

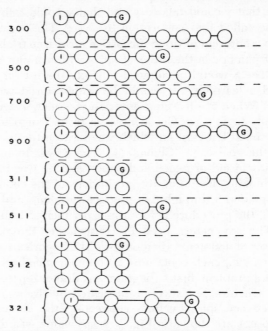

FIG. 1. The structures of the eight problem types in Exp. I.

ing step, was measured by stop watch. The E recorded the sequence of steps leading to solution as S announced them.

Each S solved 40 problems, five problems of each of eight problem types, at the rate of approximately three problems per day. About 3 min elapsed between problems within a session. The tests were arranged in five groups of eight tests each, each group containing one of each of the eight problem types. At no time did E give S information which would allow him to anticipate the type of problem he was about to solve.

RESULTS

A general description of spy problem solutions. The protocols of Exp. I, with the exception of a few comments, consist of pairs drawn from the connection lists. The pairs occur in sequences each of which describes a connected path through the problem structure, (e.g., *shower* to *beef*, *beef* to *larynx*, *larynx* to *tree*, etc.). The 480 protocols collected in Exp. I contain 1000 separate paths. Almost all of these (987), start either at the initial state or at the goal. The two starting places represent two general strategies available to S. That is, he may attempt to solve forward, from the initial state, or backward, from the goal. In Exp. I, 25% of all paths

were executed in the backward direction. The use of the backward strategy has been widely noted (cf. Duncker, 1945; Johnson, 1955; Newell,
Shaw and Simon, 1958; and Polya, 1957). The backward strategy appears
to be a secondary one, being used most often after the forward strategy
has failed. This may be seen by examination of the paths according to
the sequence in which they occurred in the problem. Of the first paths,
only 12% were backward; of the second paths, 40%; of the third paths,
35%; and of the remaining paths, 38%.

Usually, when S constructs a path, he simply announces the pairs of
the path in sequence without intervening comment. In some cases, how-

TABLE 1

RELATIONS AMONG MEAN SOLUTION TIME, T; PROBLEM LENGTH, L;
AND MEAN NUMBER OF STEPS TO SOLUTION, N

Problem type	T	T/L	N	N/L	T/N
300	23.3	7.79	3.23	1.08	7.23
500	42.2	8.44	5.73	1.15	7.36
700	86.4	12.16	9.27	1.32	9.33
900	144.0	16.00	12.83	1.43	11.22
311	35.5	11.84	4.10	1.37	8.66
511	117.9	20.24	8.35	1.67	14.13
312	64.7	21.58	5.61	1.87	11.53
321	44.0	14.07	4.25	1.42	10.36

ever, after announcing a pair, S will either recite the connection list aloud
from the beginning until he comes to the next pair in the path, or he will
announce that he is silently reciting the list. This behavior, which will be
called list searching, occurs relatively infrequently—55 times in the 3200
steps of Exp. 1. It is important to note the occurrence of list searching in
the protocols despite its low frequency, because, as will be shown below,
steps which involve list searching take much more time than steps which
do not.

Solution time and length of solution chain. This section and the two
following will be concerned with three quantities and the relations among
them; T, the total solution time for a problem, L, the length of the minimal chain solution, and N, the number of steps actually taken for solution. N may be much larger in a particular problem than L.

The second column of Table 1 shows that solution time, T, increases
with the length of the minimal chain, L, both for unbranched problems
(problem types 300, 500, 700, and 900) and for branched problems (problem types 311 and 511). The significance of the differences in T (and of

all of the results of Exp. I) was tested by two-tailed matched Pitman test (Moses, 1952) with a .05 level of confidence. All of the differences among the unbranched problems and the difference between problem types 311 and 511 were found to be significant. A significant interaction between length and branching was found by Pitman test on the quantity $(T_{511} - T_{311} - T_{500} + T_{300})$.

Table 1 also shows that T increases more than proportionately with increases in L. While problem type 900 is only three times as long as problem type 300, it takes more than six times as long to solve. The disproportion is best seen in the T/L ratio, shown in the third column of Table 1. All of the differences in T/L among the unbranched problems are significant except for the difference between problem types 700 and 900. The difference between problem types 311 and 511 is also significant.

Solution time and branching. The effect of branching on T may be seen by comparing solution times among problem types 300, 311, 312, and 321 and among problem types 500 and 511. All of these comparisons yielded significant differences in solution time.

While T increased roughly linearly with number of blind alleys (compare problem types 300, 311, and 321), it increased more than linearly with length of blind alleys (compare problem types 300, 311, and 312). The nonlinearity was found to be significant by Pitman test on the quantity $(T_{312} - 2T_{311} + T_{300})$.

The fact that problem type 312 required significantly more time to solve than problem type 321 means that one double-length blind alley had more effect in impeding solution than two single-length blind alleys.

Number of steps and time per step. In the last two sections it was shown that increases in length, whether of the minimal chain or of the blind alleys, cause more than proportional increases in T. Essentially the same relation was found for N, the number of steps taken for solution. Examination of the fourth column of Table 1 shows that the three major sequences of problem types, 300, 500, 700, 900; 311, 511; and 300, 311, 312, 321, are ordered in the same way whether one considers T or N. The pattern of significant differences was also the same for these two variables. Further, the ratio N/L increases with L as did the ratio T/L (see Table 1, column five).

However, in spite of the close relation of the two variables, increases in T from one problem type to another are not completely accounted for by the corresponding increases in N. The sixth column of Table 1 shows that the ratio T/N is not constant, but rather varies in much the same way as T and N. The ratio T/N is significantly smaller for problem type 300 than for problem types 500, 312, and 321, for problem type 500 than for problem types 700 and 900, and for problem type 311 than for problem type 511.

The results indicate, then, that increases in length of minimal chain or

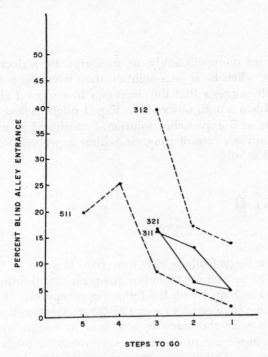

FIG. 2. Percent of blind-alley entrance as a function of the number of steps to go to solution.

of the blind alleys cause decreases in problem solving efficiency whether that efficiency is measured by T/L, N/L, or T/N.

Blind-alley entrances. Blind-alley entrances were analyzed as follows: (a) While S sometimes passed through a specified choice point more than once, only the first choice at each choice point was scored. (b) The choices were categorized by "steps to go," that is, by the number of steps on the minimal chain which S had not yet completed.

Figure 2 shows that for all problem types, Ss entered the blind alleys much less than would be expected by chance (chance levels—50% for problem types 311, 312, and 511, and 67% for problem type 321). The results indicate that S accomplishes this by responding both to the properties of the correct paths and to the properties of the blind alleys. As the steps-to-go decrease (a property of the correct path), the proportion of blind-alley entrances decreases for all problem types. When steps-to-go are held constant, the double-length blind alleys of problem type 312 are entered more frequently than the single-length blind alleys of the other problem types.

DISCUSSION

The S operates more efficiently, as measured by a decrease in blind alley entrances, when he is near solution than when he is far from solution. This result suggests that the decreases in temporal efficiency, with increasing problem length observed in Exp. I might reflect an increasing rate of progress as S approaches solution. Experiment II was conducted to determine how S's rate of progress within a problem changed as he worked toward solution.

EXPERIMENT II

METHOD

Subjects. Five Regis College girls were paid to serve as Ss.

Procedure. The procedure, including the problems and the instructions, was the same as in Exp. I with the following exceptions: (a) Acquisition time, i.e., the time between S's receipt of the connection list and his successful completion of the learning test, was measured by stop watch. (b) Each problem-solving protocol was tape recorded for later transcription and timing. (c) Following each problem solution S was interviewed concerning list searching, blind alleys, and backward solution process.

RESULTS

Acquisition time. Table 2 shows the mean acquisition time for each problem type. Acquisition was faster for any of the branched problems than for any of the unbranched problems. The connection list of the branched problems differed in two ways from those of the unbranched problems: (a) They contain more pairs which have the same initial item. A moderate amount of negative transfer would be expected between such pairs (Osgood, 1953). (b) They contain fewer pairs in which the final item of one is the same as the initial item of another. Since a large amount of negative transfer would be expected between pairs of this kind (Pri-

TABLE 2

MEAN ACQUISITION TIMES (SEC) IN EXP. II

Problem type							
300	500	700	900	311	511	312	321
306.4	289.4	319.9	297.4	246.5	255.1	275.4	246.6

TABLE 3

MEAN SOLUTION TIMES (SEC) IN EXP. II

Problem type							
300	500	700	900	311	511	312	321
30.8	61.84	89.72	163.24	44.48	139.24	98.56	63.92

moff, 1938) the present result is in consonance with the literature on paired-associate learning.

Solution time. Examination of Table 3 shows that differences in solution time observed in Exp. II exactly paralleled those found in Exp. I. In this sense, Exp. II was a successful replication of Exp. I.

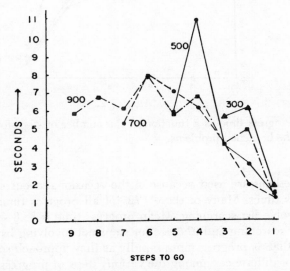

FIG. 3. Progress time as a function of the number of steps-to-go to solution for the unbranched problems.

Progress time. The S was scored as making a "step of progress" whenever he took a step along the minimal chain, whether in the forward or backward direction, which he had not taken before. The "progress time" for a given step of progress was the interval of time elapsing between the occurrence of that step and the occurrence of the previous step of progress. Figure 3 shows the median progress time for each step of progress as a function of the number of steps remaining for solution for the unbranched problems. Figure 4 shows the same function for the branched

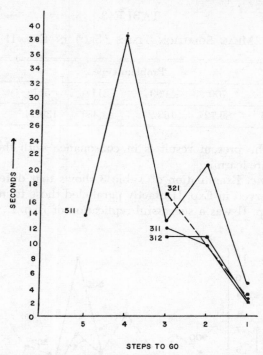

FIG. 4. Progress time as a function of the number of steps-to-go to solution for the branched problems.

problems. Medians are used because of the occasional occurrence of very
long progress times. Many of these (72% of all progress times of 1 min.
or more) involve list searching. Mean progress time is 88.8 sec for steps
involving list searching and 07.5 sec for steps not involving list searching.

It is clear that Ss progress more rapidly as they approach solution. The
significance of differences among the various steps of progress was tested
by matched two-tailed sign test (Moses, 1952) with a .05 confidence level
on the 25 problem solutions within each problem type. For all problem
types, the last step of progress was significantly faster than each preceding step with the single exception that in problem type 312, the last step
was not significantly different from the next-to-last step. The only other
significant differences involved the two steps preceding the last. In problem type 500, the third step was significantly quicker than the second,
and the fourth, or next-to-last step, was significantly quicker than the first
and second. In problem type 700, (Fig. 3) the fifth step was significantly
quicker than the third and fourth, and the sixth, or next-to-last step, was
significantly quicker than all preceding steps except the first.

In the connection list, the ordering of spies within pairs corresponds to the order in which they would be encountered by S solving in the forward direction. When solving in the backward direction, however, S may invert this order.

In Exp. II,[1] when S was solving in the backward direction, 66% of the pairs were inverted, but when he was solving in the forward direction, none was inverted. The pairs seem to be readily available to S in either ordering, a result in consonance with Asch and Ebenholtz' principle of associative symmetry (1962).

Post-solution interviews. The post-solution interviews were conducted to check on the completeness of the problem-solving protocols. Only the results concerning list searching will be presented here. Immediately after solution, S was asked whether or not he had performed any list searching and, if so, at what points in the solution process. In the 200 interviews, 87 list searches were reported. These included all 55 list searches appearing in the protocols with an additional 32 not appearing in the protocols. Both the list searches which appeared in the protocols and those which did not were associated with long progress times. Thus, the post-solution interviews can provide a valuable supplement to the information obtained in the protocols.

DISCUSSION

In Exp. I, it was found that increases in problem length cause more than proportional increases in solution time. Two results of the second experiment provide the basis for an explanation of this finding.

(a) The solution process accelerates as S approaches solution. The final step was markedly accelerated in all problem types, and the two steps before the final one showed acceleration in some problems. (b) As Fig. 3 shows, when steps to go are taken into account, progress time does not seem to vary with problem length. Thus, S's rate of progress depends not on how far he has come in the problem, but rather on how far he has to go.

Long problems contain as many quickly executed steps, i.e., steps close to solution, as short problems, but they contain more steps which are executed slowly, i.e., steps far from solution, than do short problems. For this reason, long problems take longer to solve in proportion to their length than do short problems.

It is tempting to compare the present results concerning solution acceleration and blind alley entrances with similar results obtained in experiments on animal maze-learning (cf. Munn, 1950). Such a comparison would be misleading, however. The present studies are concerned with S's use of previously acquired information in his first traversal of the solution path. Maze-learning experiments, on the other hand, are concerned

---

[1] Inversions were not consistently recorded in Exp. I.

with S's acquisition of information in successive traversals of the solution path. Maier (1940) has effectively argued that fundamentally different processes are involved in these two types of experiments.

A theory of the terminal acceleration which has frequently been suggested to the author concerns the number of alternative pairs or connections available to S at each step of the solution. Briefly, the theory holds that the solution process "uses up" connections and that as solution proceeds the rate of progress increases because the number of alternatives from which the next step must be chosen decreases.

This theory does not cover the facts. Since all of the problems have the same number of learned pairs (eleven), the theory must predict that the third step from the beginning of problem type 900 would take as much time as the third step from the beginning of problem type 300. Examination of Fig. 3 shows that this is not the case.

Two theories are advanced here which do offer some promise of explaining the acceleration. Both theories postulate covert planning by S; one theory postulates "local" planning and the other "remote" planning. An example will help to clarify the distinction between local and remote planning.

Suppose that in working through a chain A–B–C–D–E–F, S announces steps in the order A–B, B–C, etc. The S will be described as working from A to F.[2] According to the remote-planning theory, S, in working from A, notices connections in the neighborhood of F, specifically "E–F." When S gets from A to E, the step "E to F" occurs rapidly because it has been planned. Remote planning may of course, involve more than one step. Remote planning could also explain the reduction in blind-alley entrances as S approaches solution. In the example above, S is unlikely to enter a blind alley at E, since he knows that the path "E–F" leads to a desired position.

According to the local-planning theory, S covertly explores alternative paths in the neighborhood of his present position to a depth of one or perhaps more steps. If S recognizes that a path is a blind alley, he rejects it. If S recognizes that a path leads to a solution, he stops exploring and executes the path overtly. If S explores a path but fails to find either that it is a blind alley or a "solution," he may execute it overtly in the absence of a better alternative. According to the local-planning theory, blind-alley entrances decrease and rate of progress increases as the number of steps to go decreases, because with fewer steps to go, S is more likely to discover a solution path in his local covert exploration. Whether planning is local or remote, the length-two blind alleys should be entered more fre-

[2] It is irrelevant to the theories whether the direction from A to F is toward the initial state or toward the goal. Neither local planning nor remote planning, therefore, can be subsumed under Duncker's (1945) concepts of "analysis of the goal" or "analysis of material."

PROBLEM TYPE

A and B

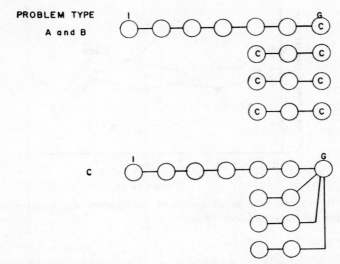

FIG. 5. The structures of the three problem types in Exp. III.

quently than the length-one blind alleys, because S is less likely to plan two steps into a blind alley than one.

On the basis of present evidence, either of these processes or both of them may operate in the problem solutions. Experiment III was conducted to obtain further information relevant to these theories. Specifically, Exp. III was designed to show the effects on problem solution of preventing remote planning.

EXPERIMENT III

METHOD

Subjects. Nine Northeastern University students were paid to serve as Ss.

Procedure. The method was the same as for Exp. II with the following exceptions: The list of pairs was presented on an ordered deck of cards, one pair to a card.

The Ss solved five problems in each of three problem types—a total of 15 problems per S. The structures of the three problem types are shown in Fig. 5.

In the control problem, A, S's task was to get from a specifically named initial state to a specifically named goal, e.g., "Get from Joe-to-cow." In problem B, S was prevented from planning remotely by concealing the

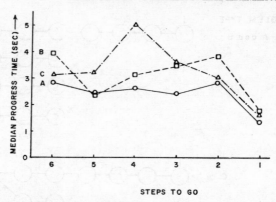

FIG. 6. Progress time as a function of the number of steps-to-go to solution for the three problem types.

specific identity of the goal from him. The S's task was to get from a specifically named initial state to a goal which was specified only by a category, e.g., "Get from Joe to an animal." Each problem contained several
spy names in the goal category (in the positions marked with Cs in Fig. 5),
but only one of them could be reached from the initial state. Thus,
S could not identify the goal until he reached it and, hence, could not plan
remotely. The three blind alleys in problem type C were intended to reduce the effectiveness of remote planning by reducing the probability that
any given plan would involve the solution chain. In all problem types,
S was instructed not to work backward.

RESULTS

As Fig. 6 shows, the course of progress was essentially the same in all
three problem types. Progress was accelerated on the last step in all three
cases. Differences were computed between the various steps within each
of the 45 solutions obtained for each problem type and tested by two-
tailed sign test (Moses, 1952) with a .05 confidence level. In each of the
three problem types, the last step was significantly faster than all previous
steps with the single exception in problem type B of the second step. Only
two other significant differences were observed; the difference between
step 2 and step 5 in problem type B, and the difference between step 1
and step 3 in problem type C. No significant differences were observed in
the overall solution times of the three problem types.[3]

[3] In a supplementary experiment, 10 Ss solved 10 type B problems and five type C
problems. For both problem types, the last step was executed significantly more
rapidly than any of the preceding steps.

DISCUSSION

The results clearly indicate that acceleration of progress can occur even when remote planning is prevented. The acceleration, however, was restricted to the last step rather than extending over the last three steps as in Exp. II. This restriction may be taken as indirect evidence that both remote and local planning contributed to the acceleration observed in Exp. II.

Contrary to expectation, the acceleration in problem type A was no more extensive than in problem types B and C. Remote planning may have been suppressed in problem type A either (a) because it was presented in a context of problems in which remote planning was difficult or impossible, or (b) because of the instructions not to work backward.

REFERENCES

ASCH, S. E., AND EBENHOLTZ, S. M. The principle of associative symmetry. *Proceed. Amer. Philos. Soc.*, 1962, 106, 135–163.

BARTLETT, F. *Thinking, an experimental and social study.* London: Allen and Unwin, 1958.

DUNCKER, K. On problem-solving. *Psychol. Monogr.*, 1945, 58, No. 270.

JOHNSON, D. M. *The psychology of thought and judgment.* New York: Harper, 1955.

MAIER, N. R. F. The behavior mechanisms concerned with problem solving. *Psychol. Rev.*, 1940, 47, 43–58.

MOSES, L. E. Non-parametric statistics for psychological research. *Psychol. Bull.*, 1952, 49, 122–143.

MUNN, N. L. *Handbook of psychological research on the rat.* Boston: Houghton Mifflin, 1950.

NEWELL, A., SHAW, J. C., AND SIMON, H. A. Elements of a theory of human problem-solving. *Psychol. Rev.*, 1958, 65, 151–166.

OSGOOD, C. E. *Method and theory in experimental psychology.* New York: Oxford, 1953.

POLYA, G. *How to solve it.* New York: Doubleday, 1957.

PRIMOFF, E. Backward and forward association as an organizing act in serial and in paired associate learning. *J. Psychol.*, 1938, 5, 375–395.

17. Language and Thinking: Positive and Negative Effects of Naming

Howard B. Ranken

Abstract. *Subjects instructed to think of novel shapes in terms of relevant names made fewer errors in recalling a serial ordering of the shapes, but more errors in solving a mental jigsaw puzzle and in drawing the shapes from memory, than subjects instructed to visualize the shapes without using words.*

Is it easier to think about objects, and to manipulate them "in one's head," if one has names for them than if one does not? Spiker (1) found that performance in the delayed-reaction experiment, often considered to depend on representational processes, was facilitated when subjects had names for the stimuli. He suggests that during the delay period the subject repeats the name of the baited stimulus, and that the name then serves to guide his choice. This hypothesis assumes that names do in fact perform this representational function more effectively than non-verbal representations, such as images. On the other hand, Saltz and Newman (2) found that while learning the names of the parts to a low criterion before doing a mechanical assembly problem led to fewer errors, learning to a high criterion resulted in more errors than no name learning at all. Thus names yielded no consistent advantage in the kind of mental manipulation required in the assembly problem. These findings suggest that the effect of prior name learning on thinking depends on the nature of the problem. Pretraining which leads a subject to think of objects in terms of names, rather than, say, in terms of images, may facilitate performance in one problem but interfere with performance in another.

The relative effectiveness of nominal (verbal) and imaginal representations will presumably depend, among other things, on the kind of information about the stimulus objects which is needed to solve the problem. The evidence from the delayed-reaction experiments and from studies of the effect of name learning on serial learning (3) suggests that names will be advantageous when the task involves short-term retention of specific items or of sequences of items, as do many reasoning tasks. If, on the other hand, problem solution specifically depends on figural properties of the stimuli (as opposed to such properties as weight, number, or sequence), as is true in the mechanical assembly problem, we might expect imaginal representations to be at least as effective as names. If, as seems likely in

Reprinted by permission from *Science*, Vol. 141, No. 3575, July 5, 1963. Copyright © 1963 by the American Association for the Advancement of Science.

view of the effect of labels on reproduction of visual forms (4), introduction of names results in loss or distortion of figural information, the imaginal representations should be more effective in such problems. Such a finding would be contrary to Prentice's conclusion (5) that names do not affect what is remembered but only the way it is reproduced.

Two groups of 16 undergraduates each, the "Named" and "Unnamed" groups, were given training designed to induce the formation of, respectively, nominal and imaginal representations of a set of novel shapes. Half the subjects in each group then attempted to solve, in their heads, a "mental jigsaw puzzle" composed of the shapes. The other half of each group

TABLE 1

Errors and Logarithmic Solution Times

Condition	Errors		Log t (sec)	
	Mean	σ	Mean	σ
Jigsaw problem				
Named	4.9	1.5	2.52	0.24
Unnamed	2.6	1.6	2.54	0.29
Memory task				
Named	2.5	1.6	1.45	0.18
Unnamed	4.6	1.2	1.66	0.30

were given a memory task in which they had to reconstruct, in their heads, a novel ordering of the shapes, after seeing the novel ordering only once. The jigsaw puzzle could be solved only if the subject's representation of the shapes encoded their figural properties. The memory task provided a direct measure of short-term retention of sequences at the ideational level.

The stimulus objects were eight shapes, each consisting of a 2-inch square with the top and bottom sides replaced by randomly constructed three-segment contours. Four such contours were used, each appearing as the top of two shapes and the bottom of two others (Fig. 1). Starting from any shape, the eight shapes could be fitted together in several different ways, one under the other in jigsaw-puzzle fashion, to form a vertical column. Subjects were first shown each shape for 30 seconds. Those in the Named condition were given an animal name for each shape (Fig. 1), and the way in which the shape resembled the named animal was pointed out to them. Subjects in the Unnamed condition were instructed "to study each shape carefully . . . and try to remember what it looks like," but "to think of each shape just as a shape, without using words in any way."

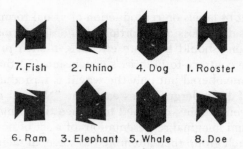

FIG. 1. Stimulus shapes, with names, grouped vertically by bottom contour and horizontally by top contour. Numbers indicate position in ring, running clockwise, with No. 8 at the top.

All subjects then received training in a recognition task, designed to provide an opportunity for subjects in the Named condition to practice naming the shapes, while requiring subjects in the Unnamed condition to attain the same degree of proficiency in discriminating the shapes, without using words. A test shape was shown for 2 seconds and then, after a 2-second pause, all the shapes were presented, and the subject pointed to the test shape. In the Named condition, subjects, prompted by the experimenter if necessary, said the name of the test shape when it was first shown on each trial, and were instructed to "try to remember the shape by keeping the name in mind." In the Unnamed condition, subjects were told to "try to remember the shapes by visualizing them to yourself, without using words." Subjects in both Named and Unnamed conditions continued recognition training until they had given correct recognitions for all eight shapes on four consecutive trials. Accuracy of naming the shapes did not enter into this criterion. The shapes were so constructed that the subject had to use information from both top and bottom contours of each shape to respond successfully in the recognition task, whether he was in the Named or Unnamed condition. In this sense, the cues used to discriminate the shapes, and the level of discriminative ability represented by the recognition criterion, were the same in the two conditions.

All subjects next learned to associate each shape with a different position in a ring consisting of eight small circles arranged to form a large circle. After a demonstration trial, the experimenter pointed to the positions in random order, and the subject pointed to the shape which belonged in each position. Training continued to a criterion of four consecutive perfect trials. Instructions concerning the use of names were similar to those in recognition training. [A more detailed description of these training procedures is given elsewhere (3, "experiment IV").]

In the jigsaw problem, the experimenter indicated the shape, randomly assigned, from which the puzzle was to start. The subject's task was to pick another shape that would fit under the first one (that is, one whose top contour would match the bottom contour of the first shape), then a third shape which fitted under the second, and so on. The subject did not see the shapes at any time during the problem. The starting shape, and the subject's subsequent choices, were indicated by referring to the corresponding positions in the blank ring, and numbering them to indicate the order in which the shapes should be arranged to form the jigsaw column. An error was scored for each instance in which two nonmatching contours were placed adjacent to one another in the subject's final ordering of the shapes.

In the memory task, the shapes were shown one at a time for 2 seconds each, in a random order, different for each subject. A test for recall of this new order followed immediately. As in the jigsaw problem, the experimenter indicated the first shape, and the subject indicated his choices, by numbering the corresponding positions on the blank ring. An error was scored for each incorrect two-shape sequence in the final ordering. Nothing was said about the use of names in the presentation of either problem.

Mean errors and mean logarithmic solution times are shown in Table 1. Subjects in the Named condition made fewer errors on the memory task, but more errors on the jigsaw problem, than those in the Unnamed condition. This interaction between effect of names and type of problem is highly reliable (2×2 analysis of variance, $F = 15.19$, $df = 1/28$, $p < .001$). The Named-Unnamed difference is reliable both on the jigsaw problem (overall within-groups mean square used as error estimate, $t = 2.91$, $df = 28$, $p < .01$) and, in the opposite direction, on the memory task ($t = -2.66$, $p < .05$). The only reliable effect on solution times is the overall difference between jigsaw and order problems ($F = 100.17$, $df = 1/28$, $p < .001$). The fact that solution time for the jigsaw problem was slightly longer for the Unnamed than for the Named group raises the question whether the Unnamed group made fewer errors simply because they spent more time on the problem. When the effect of this difference in working time is removed by means of covariance analysis, however, there is still a reliable difference in errors in favor of the Unnamed condition ($F = 7.62$, $df = 1/27$, $p < .05$).

The assumption that the Unnamed group would form representations which encoded more information about figural properties of the shapes than the representations used by the Named group was tested directly by having all subjects draw the shapes from memory, in their positions in the ring, at the end of the experiment. An error was scored for each of the eight line segments of each shape that was omitted, drawn slanting in the wrong direction, or connected to the wrong end of an adjacent segment. The mean number of such errors was 20.2 in the Named condition and 14.8 in the Unnamed condition ($t = 3.10$, $df = 30$, $p < .01$).

The results are consistent with the assumption that the Named and Unnamed conditions induced the formation of verbal and imaginal representations, whose relative merits depend on the problem to be solved. An alternative possibility is that subjects in the Unnamed condition verbalized the figural properties of the shapes, or the relations between them, and that these verbalizations facilitated the jigsaw and drawing tasks. Analysis of post-experimental reports does not support this interpretation. Those subjects in the Unnamed condition who reported doing the most verbalizing made more errors in the jigsaw problem and fewer in the memory task than those reporting less verbalizing. Subjects who reported that they did not notice during training that any of the shapes fitted together showed as strong an interaction between naming and type of problem as those who reported noticing such relations. These findings support the interpretation that the interaction reflects a difference in the properties of nominal and imaginal representations.

REFERENCES AND NOTES

1. C. C. SPIKER, *J. Exptl. Psychol.* 52, 107 (1956).
2. E. SALTZ AND S. E. NEWMAN, *Am. J. Psychol.* 73, 91 (1960).
3. H. B. RANKEN, *Psychol. Repts.*, in press.
4. L. CARMICHAEL, H. P. HOGAN, AND A. A. WALTER, *J. Exptl. Psychol.* 15, 73 (1932).
5. W. C. H. PRENTICE, *Am. J. Psychol.* 67, 315 (1954).

18. Verbal Behavior and Problem Solving: Some Effects of Labeling in a Functional Fixedness Problem

Sam Glucksberg and Robert W. Weisberg

Abstract. *3 differently labeled illustrations of Duncker's candle problem were exposed to Ss as they worked on that problem. In the first of 3 experiments, the picture which elicited the name of the functionally fixed object also elicited correct initial solutions in a verbal form of the*

Reprinted by permission of the authors and the American Psychological Association from the *Journal of Experimental Psycholgy*, 1966, 71, 659–664.

problem. In Experiments II and III, Ss were given manipulative forms of the same problem. Time to achieve criterion solution, choice of initial solution object, and within-group variability were each a function of the labeling procedures. The functional fixedness effect in specifically to the functionally fixed object, either in terms of labeling or attending.

Duncker (1945) cites, as one of the factors involved in functional fixedness, a lack of "signalling of the perceptual properties of the object [p. 92]." Failure to solve the candle problem, in which S must use a box originally filled with tacks in order to solve the problem of affixing a candle to a vertical surface, is represented in perceptual terms. The S is said to perceive only the container properties of the box and not its platform properties. Saugstad (1958), as well as Staats (1957), in essential agreement with Duncker's analysis, views the problem as one in which the novel function of the fixed object is not available.

The three experiments reported were performed to test a different interpretation of the functional fixedness phenomenon. In an earlier study (Glucksberg, 1964b), Ss were required to solve the candle problem while blindfolded, and each time the box was touched an observing response was recorded. Problem solution occurred upon manual contact with the functionally fixed object, the tack-filled box. This finding suggests that it is not a function that is unavailable to S, but rather the functionally fixed object itself.

Two additional bits of evidence are consistent with this interpretation. First, the problem is trivially simple when the box is presented empty (Adamson, 1952; Duncker, 1945; Glucksberg, 1962). Second, when S's are asked to recall the objects available in the problem situation, solvers report the box earlier in their lists of recalled objects than do nonsolvers. Further, and perhaps more important, solvers report the box as a separate verbal unit, e.g., "a box." Nonsolvers often must be prompted before they report the box, sometimes cannot report it at all, and when they do report it, refer to it in a verbally undifferentiated manner, such as "a box full of tacks," or "a tack box" (Glucksberg, 1964a).

There is little doubt that the verbal behavior associated with the problem-solving situation is an important determinant of problem-solving behavior. Judson, Cofer, and Gelfand (1956) have demonstrated that relevant patterns of verbal associations, including verbal chains, may facilitate performance in the Maier two-string and hatrack problems. In relatively simple tasks like the candle problem, complex verbal behavior may be unnecessary. All that may be necessary for problem solution is the label of the functionally fixed object. The three experiments reported test this hypothesis: Exp. I in a verbal form of the candle problem, and Exp. II and III in manipulative forms of the same problem.

EXPERIMENT I

An immediate solution to a functional fixedness problem should occur if the stimulus situation initially elicits the name of the functionally fixed object. If it does not elicit that name initially, then solution may still occur if repeated solution attempts are permitted. This is because of the hierarchical nature of word associations. If the object name is not elicited as a dominant response, it may be elicited at some later time during the course of problem-solving activity. When the name is elicited, then problem solution should occur.

Accordingly, we should expect initial problem-solving performance to vary as a function of the initial label-eliciting properties of the stimulus situation. Differences between different label conditions should be minimized, however, when overall performance is considered.

METHOD

Subjects. One hundred, sixty-five undergraduate college students served as Ss. Ninety Ss performed a word-association task in three groups of 30 each. An independent sample of 75 Ss, divided into three groups, was given one of three paper-and-pencil forms of Duncker's candle problem.

Procedure. A simple line drawing illustrating the candle problem was constructed. The drawing contained a table next to a wall, with the following materials on the table: a candle, a box filled with thumbtacks, and a book of matches (see Fig. 1). This drawing was presented as a word-association stimulus in three different forms: (*a*) all objects in the picture labeled, including the critical object, the box (Picture 1); (*b*) no labels (Picture 2); and (*c*) just one label, the word TACKS printed in capital block letters on the side of the box (Picture 3). Each group of 30 Ss was given one of these pictures and instructed to write, immediately under it, the first words that came to mind. After 5 min. had elapsed Ss were told to stop, and then were asked to identify all objects portrayed in the picture. The relevant objects were correctly identified by all Ss. The word-association lists were scored for inclusion of the word BOX in the list of words obtained.

The three pictures were then used as illustrations for a paper-and-pencil group form of the candle problem. The instructions were printed and bound into a pamphlet including one of the three pictures. An answer sheet, on a separate page, had spaces for four numbered solutions, with instructions to turn back to the picture after each solution had been written. The instructions provided an unambiguous criterion for solution: "the problem is considered solved when the candle can be firmly affixed to the wall, burn properly, and does not drip wax on the table or floor." Each

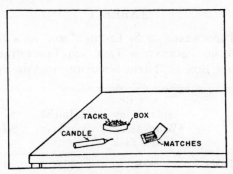

Fig. 1. Candle problem illustration used in the three experiments. (The all labeled form is shown.)

group received one picture as an illustration of the problem. Group 1 ($N = 20$) had Picture 1 (all labeled), Group 2 ($N = 20$) had Picture 2 (no labels), and Group 3 ($N = 35$) had Picture 3 (TACKS label).

Two response measures were employed: number of Ss in each group writing a solution using the box as Answer No. 1, and number of Ss in each group writing a solution using the box in any answer.

RESULTS AND DISCUSSION

The word-association and problem-solving data are presented in Table 1, where the frequency data have been expressed in percentages. A chi-square test applied to the distribution of frequencies of BOX responses indicated reliable differences between the three groups, $\chi^2 (2) = 29.80$, as well as between each pair of groups ($p < .02$ in each case).

Considering the initial solution data (answers in the No. 1 position on the answer sheet), the difference between the groups are in the predicted direction. The differences between the three groups are reliable at the .01 level, $\chi^2 (2) = 9.82$. Only Group 1, however, differs reliably from each of the other two groups ($p < .02$).

When solutions, irrespective of sequence of entry on the answer sheet, are examined, the differences between the three groups are no longer reliable. Chi-square applied to these scores yielded a value of only 5.32 ($df = 2$, $p > .05$). This finding points up a difficulty in attempting to relate word-association data to problem-solving behavior. Typically, word-association responses are obtained in a stimulus situation that is not changed by S while he performs the task set for him. Problem solving, however, is quite different in this respect. Indeed, one of the salient features of problem-solving behavior is the restructuring of the stimulus situation by S as he works on the problem (Duncker, 1945). Viewed in this light, it is not surprising that the relatively close parallel between word-

TABLE 1

Exp. I: Percentage of Ss Listing "box" as a Response
in the Word-Association Task, and Percentage of Ss
Using the Box in Their Solution to the Problem

Group	% box Responses in Word-Association Task	% Initial Solutions	% Total Solutions
All Labeled	90.0	95.0	100.0
No Labels	63.3	65.0	85.0
TACKS Label	20.0	54.3	77.1

association data and problem-solving performance breaks down as time
spent on the problem increases.

This particular effect should be even more pronounced if the same
problem were to be given in manipulative form, in which S physically
alters the stimulus situation. Experiment II was performed to test this
hypothesis, and to extend the findings on initial solutions to a problem requiring a nonverbal solution.

Experiment II

METHOD

Subjects. Twenty-four male college students enrolled in introductory
psychology courses served as Ss.

Procedure. The 24 Ss were randomly assigned to one of three groups of
8 each. Each S was seated at a table, on which, under a cover, were a
candle, a pasteboard box filled with thumbtacks, and a full book of safety
matches. These materials were placed in the same relative positions as the
objects in the pictures used in Exp. I. On the wall to the left of S was a
cardboard "wall" which was replaced for each S. A translucent projection
screen was in place on the table 3 ft. in front of S, with a standard lantern
slide projector behind it. Tape recorded instructions were played to
each S:

> We are investigating several kinds of simple problems. Each can be
> solved in several ways. We are going to give you one of these prob-
> lems. On your left is a cardboard wall. Directly in front of you is a
> projection screen. While you are listening to these instructions, watch
> the screen, because the problem will be illustrated for you on that
> screen. This is the problem. Under this cover (E pointed) are a candle
> and several household objects. The task is to affix the candle to the

cardboard wall using any of the objects under the cover. The problem is considered solved when the candle is affixed to the wall, burns properly, and does not drip wax on the table or floor. This picture (Picture 1, 2, or 3 projected onto the screen from behind) illustrates the materials you will have available.

The picture was displayed on the screen for 10 sec., during which time E removed the cover. As in Exp. I, the three groups of Ss differed in terms of the labels printed on the picture displayed. The standard lantern slides used were prepared by photographing the pictures used in Exp. I. Each time S succeeded in affixing the candle to the wall and had lit it he was asked to try additional methods of solving the problem until the box had been used. Time to use the box as a support for the candle was recorded, as well as the solution object selected for the initial solution attempt. The Ss failing to use the box within 15 min. were assigned a terminal score of 15 min.

RESULTS AND DISCUSSION

Solution-time scores are presented in Table 2. Only two Ss failed to use the box, one each in Groups 2 and 3. Only one S in Group 3 solved faster than the slowest S in Group 1. The distribution of scores in Group 2 did not overlap with the distribution in Group 1. The differences in solution-

TABLE 2

Exp. II: Solution-Time Scores (Min.)

Group	Mdn.	M	SD
All Labeled	0.59	0.61	0.40
No Labels	10.86	8.82	4.49
TACKS Label	5.01	5.69	4.48

time scores between the three groups were evaluated using a Kruskal-Wallis one-way analysis of variance by ranks. The H (2) value obtained was 723.43, $p < .001$. Median tests applied to the differences between Groups 1 and 2 and between 1 and 3 indicated reliable differences between these pairs ($p < .01$).

Of particular interest are the differences in variability between Group 1 and the other two groups ($p < .001$). It seems clear that, in this form of the problem, supplying S with the verbal label of the functionally fixed object as he begins to work effectively destroys functional fixedness, and drastically reduces variability between Ss. Indeed, seven of the eight Ss in Group 1 offered the box solution as their initial solution. In neither of the other two groups did this occur.

The difference between the means of Groups 2 and 3 is not reliable. These two groups did differ, however, in their choice of initial solution object. Consistent with the labeling procedures, Group 3 displayed more frequent initial, as well as total, use of tacks as a sole solution object. More frequent use of tacks increases the number of opportunities to touch, and thus to notice, the functionally fixed object, the box.

Duncker (1945) cited contact with the functionally fixed object as a factor facilitating solution. Glucksberg (1964b) has found that candle-problem solution may be triggered by observation of the box. The TACKS label, by indirectly increasing the number of box contacts, may have offset the possible advantage of Group 2 over Group 3 that might have been predicted on the basis of the word-association data.

Consistent with our hypothesis about the persistence of the labeling effect, the groups did not differ reliably in terms of total number of Ss solving the problem. During the course of problem-solving activity, the box is touched, handled, sometimes emptied and put aside, and eventually noticed, whether or not the picture presented at the beginning of activity elicited the word BOX. The criterion for solution demanded the box (so that wax would not drip) and Ss did, sooner or later, use it.

The question arises, will the differently labeled pictures influence the choice of a functionally fixed solution object even when the object is not required by the solution criteria? Experiment III examines the effect of labeling in a form of the candle problem which does not require the use of the box for solution.

EXPERIMENT III

METHOD

Subjects. An independent sample of 24 male students, again randomly assigned to three groups of eight each, served as Ss.

Procedure. The procedure used in Exp. II was followed except that the phrase "and does not drip wax on the table or floor" was deleted from the tape-recorded instructions. This change effectively permitted any solution which resulted in the candle staying up on the wall and burning. The same scoring procedures were followed.

RESULTS

Median time to use the box, along with the number of Ss in each group failing to use the box, are presented in Table 3. The same pattern of results obtained in Exp. II was obtained here. The picture eliciting the word BOX now influences Ss to choose the box as a solution object despite

TABLE 3

Exp. III: Median Solution-Time Scores (Min.) and No. of Ss Who Failed to Use the Functionally Fixed Object within 15 Min.

Group	Mdn.	No. of Failures
All Labeled	6.48	1
No Labels	15.00	6
TACKS Label	15.00	6

Note.—$n = 8$/group.

the availability of alternative solutions. A Kruskal-Wallis one-way analysis of variance applied to the solution-time data was significant, $H(2) = 13.60$, $p < .01$. Fisher exact probability tests between each of the three pairs of groups indicated that Group 1 differed reliably from each of the other two groups ($p < .025$). Again, as in Exp. I and II, Groups 2 and 3 did not differ reliably with respect to their use of the box.

Initial choice of solution object was again influenced by the labels presented. Group 3 used tacks initially more often than did Group 2, and again, this may have accounted for the failure of Group 2 to show a greater preference for the box despite the expected word-association effects.

General Discussion

The three experiments presented strongly support the interpretation of functional fixedness offered. The problem solver simply does not have the functionally fixed object available as an effective stimulus. In nontechnical terms, he just does not notice it. Providing S with the verbal label of a functionally fixed object makes that object available for use, just as providing S with the label of another object leads him to use that object. After this initial effect, what S does will be a function of the stimulus pattern he himself partly produces. If he starts to use melted wax as an adhesive, the number of times he looks at or touches the box are fewer than if he starts to use tacks. The initial verbal response to the situation may influence later performance, but this influence is indirect. It is mediated by the sequence of manipulative and observing behaviors that S engages in.

The notion that availability of function, or lack of it (Saugstad, 1958; Staats, 1957), is the crucial variable in functional fixedness tasks receives scant support from the data obtained. Given appropriate criteria for problem solution and the label of the functionally fixed object, every S solved the problem. Each of those Ss had the appropriate solution response in his repertoire, and it is not unlikely that every S who failed to use the box to solve the problem also had that response as part of his response repertoire. If a particular functional fixedness effect results, in Duncker's terms, from a lack of perceptual signaling of the fixed object, then the name of that object eliminates that effect.

REFERENCES

ADAMSON, R. E. Functional fixedness as related to problem solving: A repetition of three experiments. *J. exp. Psychol.*, 1952, 44, 288–291.

DUNCKER, K. On problem-solving. *Psychol. Monogr.*, 1945, 58 (5, Whole No. 270).

GLUCKSBERG, S. The influence of strength of drive on functional fixedness and perceptual recognition. *J. exp. Psychol.*, 1962, 63, 36–41.

GLUCKSBERG, S. Effects of verbal behavior on problem solving: Labeling the functionally fixed object. *Amer. Psychologist*, 1964, 19, 575. (Abstract) (a)

GLUCKSBERG, S. Functional fixedness: Problem solution as a function of observing responses. *Psychon. Sci.*, 1964, 1, 117–118. (b)

JUDSON, A. J., COFER, C. N., & GELFAND, S. Reasoning as an associative process: II. "Direction" in problem solving as a function of prior reinforcement of relevant responses. *Psychol. Rep.*, 1956, 2, 501–507.

SAUGSTAD, P. Problem-solving and availability of functions. A discussion of some theoretical aspects. *Acta Psychol., Amsterdam*, 1958, 13, 384–400.

STAATS, A. W. Verbal and instrumental response-hierarchies and their relationship to problem-solving. *Amer. J. Psychol.*, 1957, 70, 442–446.

Originality

There is a rapidly growing literature in the area of creativity or creative thinking. The interest in this area is in variables that determine performance on tasks or in situations where there is no clear and agreed-upon single solution. Typically, the problems used to study creative thinking allow a variety of solutions, thereby requiring that the solutions be judged for acceptability or adequacy on one or more criteria.

As yet, there has been very little experimental research in creativity. Of the handful of studies available, most have concentrated on aspects of creativity, such as word originality or verbal cleverness, that can be defined clearly enough to be measured or judged reliably. Thus in the Christensen, Guilford, and Wilson study the major focus was on several measures of originality on each of a number of written responses. This study also uses two variables that are often of interest in creativity research, viz., instructions to be creative, and changes in originality of responses over time or repeated responding. An older area of research, the study of verbal fluency, is somewhat similar to studies of verbal originality, and it may be noted that Christensen, *et al.*, compare their data to data from fluency experiments.

Advocates of brainstorming, as a technique in creative thinking, often maintain that judgment or criticism of ideas should not be allowed during an idea-producing or brainstorming session; instead, judgment should be reserved till later. Separation of production and judgment stages and study of the effect of one stage upon the other are accomplished in the Johnson and Zerbolio article. Here Johnson has extended his method of analyzing stages separately from convergent (single-solution) thinking, as in Section Five, to divergent (multiple-solution) thinking. The findings on transfer from one process to the other support the belief that it is easier to learn to be critical than to be constructive.

Maltzman and his associates have conducted an extensive series of experiments on originality in word association. The Rosenbaum, Arenson, and Panman article (which includes the references to Maltzman's work) is an extension of this research. The experiment includes the two independent variables, instructions and training, that are typically of interest. It is often also of interest whether increased originality, if it can be produced in one task, will transfer to another task. A test frequently used to measure nonspecific transfer from one or another kind of creativity training is the Unusual Uses Test of Guilford and his associates, in which subjects are to give unusual uses for a number of common objects. In connection with their use of this test, Rosenbaum, *et al.*, present data on a problem that frequently arises in this area, viz., to what extent are increased numbers of original responses confounded by an increase in total number of responses.

Verbal association has also been used as a basis for a test of creativity, viz., the Remote Associates Test of Sarnoff and Martha Mednick. Freedman's study (which gives some of the Mednick references) shows that transfer to this test, i.e., facilitated performance, is produced by training consisting of a single trial of free association to words unrelated to those on the test. He also presents some data on an issue not directly treated in this book, viz., sex differences in performance on thinking tasks.

19. Relations of Creative Responses to Working Time and Instructions

Paul R. Christensen, J. P. Guilford, and R. C. Wilson

Most of the tests used in a recent factor analysis of creative-thinking abilities (7) are open-end tests that permit the examinee to write as many ideas or associations as he can in the allotted time. Among the scores obtained from these tests are those for fluency and originality. The fluency score in a particular test is simply the number of responses produced. Originality scores are derived from three different indicators: cleverness, remoteness of association, and uncommonness of assocation. In factor analyses, all three kinds of originality scores have appeared together projected on a factor vector that can be interpreted as *originality*, (6, 7).

In an attempt to achieve further insight as to what goes into these scores of fluency and originality, an experimental analysis was made of certain attributes of the responses in relation to time during the production period. It was expected that the results would lead to ways in which measures of both fluency and originality could be improved.

The number of recalled responses produced as a function of time has been investigated by Bousfield and Sedgewick (2) and by Johnson, Johnson, and Mark (5). Using tests that emphasize simple recall (such as naming "all the U. S. cities you can think of"), they found that the rate of producing responses was relatively high during the first part of the work period but became progressively lower as time went by.

Hypotheses. In the present study it was hypothesized that for tests that emphasize inventiveness rather than simple recall the rate of production would be relatively constant. Further, it was hypothesized that the more original responses would come later in the production period. In the case of one aspect of originality, that of cleverness, it was of additional interest to examine relative effects of instructions to write clever responses vs. instructions to write simply appropriate responses. We expected that instructions to be clever would reduce the total quantity of output of responses and raise the proportion of clever responses, but we had no hypothesis regarding the effect upon quantity of clever responses.

Reprinted by permission of the authors and the American Psychological Association from *Journal of Experimental Psychology*, 1957, 53, 82–88.

GENERAL PROCEDURE

Samples tested were Air Force aviation cadets, student officers, and college students. For some of the tests used in this study, measures of time were obtained by asking Ss to draw lines at 2-min. intervals under the last written responses. These tests are Plot Titles (clever instructions), Plot Titles (free instructions), Impossibilities, and Brick Uses. The first three were timed over a 12-min. period and the last over a 16-min. period. Other tests used in the study were Unusual Uses, Figure Concepts, and Number Associations. Further details of procedure will be described in connection with the report of each part of the study.

RESULTS

RELATION OF NUMBER OF RESPONSES TO TIME

The first results to be mentioned concern the number of responses written in the successive time increments. The four creative-thinking tests involved are labeled 1, 2, 4, and 5 in Fig. 1. In the Brick Uses test (Test 5) S writes all the uses he can think of for a brick in 16 min. Test 4 (Impossibilities) asks for all the impossible things that can be thought of in 12 min. Tests 1 and 2 present two brief stories. For each story S is allowed 12 min. in which to write as many appropriate titles as he can. In Test 2 the instructions are simply to write relevant titles. In Test 1 the instructions are to write titles that are both relevant and clever.

RESULTS

In Fig. 1 are given seven of the curves found by Bousfield *et al.* (1, 2) as well as the curves for the creative-thinking tests just described. A point on any curve shows the average number of responses produced up to that time. The list of tests at the top of the figure is in the rank order of the relative degree of curvature in the curves, those at the beginning of the list having the least curvature. This ranking is in the order of Bousfield's "m" constant, which can be interpreted as the rate at which a curve approaches its asymptote.

With the verbatim-recall tasks (such as listing makes of cars, birds, or cities) the rate of production is rapid at first but progressively slower with elapsed time. Production curves of this kind are described mathematically by Bousfield, based upon the principle that the rate of production of words at any moment is proportional to the number remaining available.

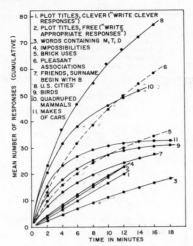

FIG. 1. Production curves of cumulative number of responses as a function of time.

For the more inventive or creative tasks there is decidedly less decrement in the number of responses produced toward the end of the time period than for verbatim recall tasks. It appears that in tests where (in contrast to simple recall) the task involves more imaginative work such as producing plot titles or naming impossibilities, the rate does not tend to vary with time, within the limits of the experimental working times.

RELATION OF UNCOMMONNESS OF RESPONSES TO TIME

Bousfield and Barclay (1) found that in recall tests the most commonly occurring words are written in the earlier stages of the production period. Their results were obtained from three subordinate-naming tasks, which called for the naming of birds, tools, and celestial bodies.

In Fig. 2 are curves from three of the creative-thinking tests. The *order* in which the responses were written is plotted on the X axis and the degree of uncommonness of occurrence in the group on the Y axis. In this study the sample was composed of approximately 400 aviation cadets and student officers.

The uncommonness values were derived empirically by determining the frequency of occurrence of every response within the group (6). Each response was rated on a scale from 1 to 5. Responses rated 1 were among the most common in the group, and those rated 5 were among the least common responses.

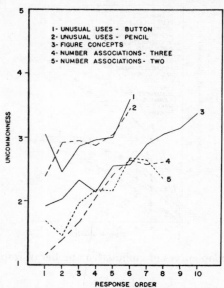

FIG. 2. Mean ratings of uncommonness vs. response order.

RESULTS

Each curve in Fig. 2 represents averages for 50 Ss, from among those Ss who wrote at least 6 responses (in the case of Curves 1 and 2), at least 10 responses (in the case of Curve 3), and at least 8 responses for the remaining two curves.

Curves 1 and 2 represent two items from the Unusual Uses test, which ask for six uses for which the object or parts of the object could serve.

Curve 3 represents the data from the Figure Concepts test, which consists of 20 simple line drawings of objects and individuals. The task is to find common features that are suggested by two or more drawings and to list these features.

Curves 4 and 5 are from the Number Associations test, in which S is asked to write synonyms, common uses, or things commonly associated with the given numbers.

In spite of the irregularities in the curves the relationship between time and uncommonness is quite clearly a positive one.

RELATION OF REMOTENESS OF RESPONSES TO TEMPORAL ORDER

A second approach to originality studied in its relation to time depends upon the degree of remoteness or indirectness of the response. For example, one of the items in the Consequences test asks "What would be the consequences if everyone in the world suddenly went blind?" Direct associations are responses such as "There would be much stumbling" or "It would be dark." Examples of more remote or indirect associations are "Those who had been blind before would become the new leaders" or "New modes of transportation would be developed."

In scoring the test, responses were assigned weights of 1, 2, or 3, depending upon degree of remoteness. One hundred of the test papers from the cadet population were used to determine whether or not remoteness of connection increases with time. A mean weight was found for the first half of the written responses and a second mean weight for the second half of the responses for each S. These means were averaged to provide a first-half mean for the 100 Ss and a second-half mean.

Four items of the Consequences test were treated in this way with a t ratio computed between the two halves in each case.

RESULTS

Three of the mean differences were found to be significant at the .01 level and the fourth at the .05 level (see Table 1).

RELATION OF CLEVERNESS OF RESPONSES TO TIME

The Plot Titles test was given under the conditions indicated in the box in Fig. 3. Two groups of college undergraduates, 26 individuals in each group, were given both stories or plots. First everyone was asked to

TABLE 1

DIFFERENCE IN MEAN REMOTENESS OF RESPONSES
OCCURRING IN THE FIRST AND SECOND HALVES
OF THE CONSEQUENCES TEST

Item	$M_2 - M_1$ (d_M)	σ_{d_M}	t
A	.281	.057	4.93
B	.366	.054	6.77
C	.208	.059	3.52
D	.129	.052	2.48

write as many appropriate titles as he could for the plot. For the succeeding plot everyone was asked to write clever titles, i.e., titles that were "interest-arousing, catchy, inviting, or novel," in addition to being appropriate. The order of presentation of the two story plots was reversed for

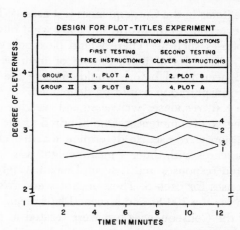

FIG. 3. Mean cleverness ratings of responses as a function of time.

the two groups as indicated in Fig. 3. The order for the two instructions, naturally, could not be effectively reversed also.

More than 1,000 different titles were obtained for each story (under both instructions), each of which was typed on a separate slip of paper. Duplicate responses were not included. Two judges (not the authors) independently sorted the responses into five ranked categories of cleverness, achieving a normal distribution. A value of 5 indicated highly clever responses while 1 indicated nonclever: The coefficients of correlation between the ratings of these two judges were .50 for both plots.

Correlations with three other judges who rated 100 selected responses indicated that the two judges who rated all the responses were sufficiently representative for the purposes of this study so that their mean rating could be used. Since the time interval in which each response occurred was known to the authors, it was possible to obtain a mean cleverness rating for the responses of each examinee by time period.

RESULTS

It would appear from the graph in Fig. 3 that the predicted increase of cleverness with time did not occur. In the analysis of variance applied to the data, the variation with time was found to be insignificant. Variation between plots was also insignificant.

RELATION OF CLEVERNESS OF RESPONSES TO TYPE OF INSTRUCTIONS

As explained in the previous section, responses under the two conditions of the Plot Titles test were rated on a five-point scale of cleverness.

RESULTS

Variation in average degree of cleverness per response due to the two different sets of instructions gives an F significant beyond the .01 point in the case of curves for Plot A, and an F significant beyond the .05 point for Plot B (see Table 2). Instructions appear to make a more pronounced difference in the cleverness for Plot A than for Plot B. Plot A presents a more concrete situation and contains within it more elements that can

TABLE 2

ANALYSIS OF VARIANCE FOR DEGREE OF CLEVERNESS PER RESPONSE
ON TWO FORMS OF THE PLOT TITLES TEST

Source of Variation	Plot A			Plot B		
	df	MS	F	df	MS	F
Between instructions	1	22.56	24.86**	1	5.93	6.48*
Between subjects in the same group	50	.91	—	50	.91	—
Between time intervals	5	.06	.38	5	.16	.91
Interaction: time intervals × instructions	5	.25	1.60	5	.07	.38
Interaction: pooled subjects × time intervals	250	.16	—	250	.18	—

* $p = .05$.
** $P = .01$.

be twisted or combined in novel ways, and it may thus provide a greater opportunity for making deliberately clever responses.

As expected, fewer total responses are produced when respondents are instructed to be clever, as shown in Fig. 1 for the two Plot Titles tests. The difference between the totals after 12 min. is significant beyond the .01 level.

Since more responses were produced under "free" instructions, there was the possibility that although the average *degree* of cleverness per response was higher under clever instructions, the total *number* of clever responses might be about the same under the two sets of instructions.

Means and SDs for the scores from the two plots were equated by linear transformation and a t test was applied, taking into account the correlation between the number of clever responses produced under the two sets of instructions. Responses were considered clever if they received an average rating of 2.5 or higher on the 5-point scale of cleverness. The resulting t was 3.98, which is significant well beyond the .01

level. A significantly greater number of clever responses was produced under the "clever" instructions even though there was a smaller average total number of responses produced under this condition.

The correlation between the *number* of clever responses under "free" instructions and under "clever" instructions was .62. This value corresponds favorably with reliability coefficients of cleverness scores obtained in other studies from two plots under identical instructions. It appears that individuals are more or less disposed toward making clever responses whether or not they are explicitly instructed to do so.

Discussion

The kind of results obtained calls for speculation concerning probable sources of the phenomena that were found and concerning their implications for measurement of fluency and originality. To be accounted for are: (*a*) the rather uniform rate of production of creative responses in contrast to the negatively accelerated rate of production of simple recall responses; (*b*) the increasing uncommonness of responses and remoteness of associations as time passes in the working period; and (*c*) the uniform level of cleverness of responses over the working time. There are also the findings that under instructions to give clever responses the effect is to decrease total quantity but to increase the number of clever responses and the average degree of cleverness. The third effect is, of course, related to the first two.

If we compare the task of simple recall of objects in a specified category with that of producing new ideas, we may describe the crucial difference in terms of the directness of the learned connections. That is, in the simple recall task all of the responses have been learned in direct connection with the stimulus, but in the production task the connections operate only by way of transfer of learning. Thus, in the latter case, the associations are indirect.

It can be hypothesized that the more direct the associations the more rapidly will they function in producing response to stimuli. It is very likely that even in the simple recall situation, associative connections differ from one another in strength because of the ordinary conditions of frequency, recency, and so on. It could be stated as one hypothesis that a skewed distribution of strengths is responsible for the negative acceleration in production, in place of or in addition to the fact that an upper limit is approached.

If an upper limit were the only reason for negative acceleration, it would seem that the curves for the productive-thinking tasks would also show the same feature. There may be, after all, a finite number of potential responses to such stimuli as have been utilized in the tests of this study. It seems more likely that the uniform rate of production of responses is due to the fact that the remote associations are, for practical purposes, of about equal strength. The curvature in the production function for the Brick Uses test is an exception. Here there are some rather familiar uses that can be produced early by simple recall. The fact of generally slower rates of production for the other four creative-thinking tests supports the hypothesis of the operation of only tenuously learned connection in those tasks.

The linear functions might be due in part to extremely large supplies of potential responses, of course. The approach to such a limit at some remote point in time might not give rise to a noticeable departure from linearity within the first few minutes of working time. It would be of interest to determine how long the same rates of production would continue, if fatigue effects could be kept out of the picture.

It was expected that, in general, later responses would be more original than earlier ones. This proved to be the case when uncommonness and remoteness of association are the criteria of originality but not when degree of cleverness is the criterion. Both uncommon and remote responses should have relatively low associative strengths and their lateness in a series of responses is therefore natural. In spite of the fact that we have demonstrated that the kind of person who gives a large number of uncommon or remotely associated responses is also likely to give more clever responses, in the single individual the relationship no longer seems to hold in terms of their relations to response time. This might suggest that clever responses are on the average just as closely associated with a stimulus as are nonclever responses. Whether they are just as common as nonclever responses is something that could possibly be determined by actual counts. The results indicate indirectly that they may be just as common, but a study on this point still remains to be done.

The decrease in quantity of total output under instructions to be clever is probably due to the self-imposed censorship of S under those instructions. Either the instruction inhibits the calling up of some of S's responses entirely or it prevents his writing responses that he rejects as nonclever. It would be a good hypothesis that both of these things occur. That the average level of cleverness is increased under instructions to be clever is an indication that this is something that can be achieved voluntarily, to some extent, at least under the circumstances of the Plot Titles test. Whether instruction to be clever induces individuals to exceed their upper limits of cleverness under the "free" instructions, is not known.

It will be noted that the temporal relationships examined were studied by using different tests for the three different types of scores—uncommonness, remoteness, and cleverness—rather than by using the same test for the different scores. It is believed, however, that since all three types of scores have been shown to be related to the factor of *originality*, the findings nevertheless have generality. It happens that each type of score is more naturally and conveniently derivable from certain kinds of tests.

One or two implications for testing practices may be seen in the results. In the measurement of fluency, it seems that testing efficiency continues at about the same level in most tests over a period of 12 min. per stimulus. This gives considerable freedom of choice between using the total time on a few items with a longer time per item vs. a larger number of items with a shorter time per item. This conclusion is based upon information regarding means, assuming that variabilities are proportional to means.

The implications for the measurement of originality are not so clear, although the indication is that longer times per item are more favorable to bringing out variance in remotely associated and uncommon responses.

The finding that fewer but relatively more clever responses are produced under instructions to be clever indicates some advantage in establishing a particular set for a group. Under the special instructions to be clever, the associative process would seem to be restricted and redirected through self-criticism. Where a score for fluency is derived from the number of nonclever responses, however, these more restrictive instructions may be less desirable.

That differential, self-imposed sets are also operating is suggested by the finding that the same individuals tend to produce the more clever responses regardless of instructions. The substantial correlation between scores under the two conditions would indicate that for selecting the more clever individuals one set of instructions would do about as well as the other. The results of the present study tell us nothing about the effects upon factor loadings. We have results from two previous studies [where the instructions were different in the two studies, (3, 4)], however, indicating that there is no appreciable difference in the *originality* loading of the tests under the two sets of instructions.

SUMMARY

This study explored relationships between the number of responses produced and the successive increments of time in which the responses were produced, for several creative-thinking tests. Other dimensions explored in relation to time were three aspects of originality: cleverness, uncommonness, and remoteness. In the case of cleverness, the effects of instructions to be clever were also studied.

As for the quantity of responses produced, examination of the production curves indicates a decrease in rate with time for simple recall tasks but a relatively constant rate for more inventive or creative tasks.

For the creative-thinking tests analyzed, it was found that two of the three aspects of originality increased with time. These were uncommonness and remoteness. Cleverness, as measured in this study, was found to be independent of time.

Instructions to be clever appeared to decrease the total number of responses produced but to increase the total number of clever responses and the average degree of cleverness.

Implications for the measurement of the traits of fluency and originality are indicated.

REFERENCES

1. BOUSFIELD, W. A., & BARCLAY, W. D. The relationship between order and frequency of occurrence of restricted associated responses. *J. exp. Psychol.*, 1950, 40, 643–647.
2. BOUSFIELD, W. A., & SEDGEWICK, C. H. W. An analysis of sequences restricted associative responses. *J. gen. Psychol.*, 1944, 30, 149–165.
3. GUILFORD, J. P., BERGER, R. M., & CHRISTENSEN, P. R. A factor-analytic study of planning. II. Administration of tests and analysis of results. *Rep. psychol. Lab.*, No. 12. Los Angeles: Univer. of Southern Calif., 1955.
4. GUILFORD, J. P., KETTNER, N. W., & CHRISTENSEN, P. R. A factor-analytic study across the domains of reasoning, creativity, and evaluation. II. Administration of tests and analysis of results. *Rep. psychol. Lab.*, No. 16. Los Angeles: Univer. of Southern Calif., 1956.
5. JOHNSON, D. M., JOHNSON, R. C., & MARK, A. L. A mathematical analysis of verbal fluency. *J. gen. Psychol.*, 1951, 44, 121–128.
6. WILSON, R. C., GUILFORD, J. P., & CHRISTENSEN, P. R. The measurement of individual differences in originality. *Psychol. Bull.*, 1953, 50, 362–370.
7. WILSON, R. C., GUILFORD, J. P., CHRISTENSEN, P. R., & LEWIS, D. J. A factor-analytic study of creative-thinking abilities. *Psychometrika*, 1954, 19, 297–311.

20. Relations Between Production and Judgment of Plot-Titles

D. M. Johnson and D. J. Zerbolio

It is possible to review the empirical evidence on thinking in terms of separate processes, such as preparation, production, and judgment; [1] and experimental attempts to differentiate one process from another have been reported, such as John's separation of analysis from synthesis,[2] and Johnson's isolation of preparation.[3] When judgment is considered, however, the strategy is not one of separation, because judgment of any object of thought is often separated in time and place from production of that object, and psychologists have traditionally investigated judgment and production as separate activities. The task of the present research is, rather, to show how judgment is related to the other intellectual activities. One experiment is reported on the influence of judgment on production, and another on the influence of production on judgment.[4]

Research of this kind requires S to construct products, the merits of which can be scaled on some significant dimension, and also to judge such products on the same dimension. Simple materials like lines and sounds can be conveniently produced and judged in the laboratory, but there is some advantage to using more complex materials that make greater intellectual demands and presumably have more significance for the psychology of thinking. If we turn to the factor-analysis of Wilson, Guilford, and Christensen,[5] which included a variety of tasks involving production, we find that the task with the highest loading for originality is *plot-titles* scored for cleverness. Hence, it is reasonable to hope that investigation of the relations between production and judgment of plot-titles will have some general significance for thinking.

As a preliminary test, two paragraphs were written giving the outlines of simple plots, one concerning the Gilson family, the other Lady Durden, and these were tried out on small groups. The results showed that each

Reprinted by permission of the authors and *The American Journal of Psychology*, 1961, 77, 99–105.

[1] D. M. Johnson, The Psychology of Thought and Judgment, 1955, Ch. 2.

[2] E. R. John, Contributions to the study of the problem-solving process, *Psychol. Monogr.*, 71, 1957, (No. 447), 1–39.

[3] Johnson, Formulation and reformulation of figure-concepts, AM. JOURN. OF PSYCHOL., 74, 1961, 418–424.

[4] Unpublished research by J. W. Jennings has demonstrated that a context-effect established during judgment will influence production, and the reverse.

[5] R. C. Wilson, J. P. Guilford, and P. R. Christensen, The measurement of individual differences in originality, *Psychol. Bull.*, 50, 1953, 362–370.

plot elicited a satisfactory number of titles and that graduate research assistants could rate them for cleverness with satisfactory agreement.[6] Since the two plots did not differ significantly in number of titles elicited or in ratings of the titles, they were accepted for the main research. Experiments then were arranged to test the hypothesis that practice in judging plot-titles for cleverness will facilitate the production of clever titles, and the reciprocal hypothesis that practice in producing clever titles will improve the accuracy of judgments of the cleverness of titles.

THE INFLUENCE OF JUDGMENT ON PRODUCTION

The rationale of 'brainstorming' includes the assumption that the elimination or the postponement of judgment will facilitate production. The present hypothesis is the opposite, in the sense that deliberate practice in judgment is expected to facilitate production. The timing is different, however, in that the practice in judging is prior to rather than simultaneous with the production. Our hypothesis ties in also with the custom of giving students practice in the critical examination of works of literature with the hope that such practice will facilitate production of similar works.

Looking at this hypothesis in the light of the principles of transfer, we should not expect that production would be facilitated by practice in judgment as much as by practice in production, but we should expect that practice in identifying the criterion of judgment, *i.e.* cleverness, would transfer in some degree to the second task. If, by practice in judging, S learns to recognize a clever title when he sees one, perhaps he can use this skill to write more clever titles when requested to do so. Previous research indicates that instruction to be clever decreases the number and increases the cleverness of the titles produced,[7] and it is conceivable that practice in judging cleverness may establish a set that controls production in the same way. It seems desirable to compare the effect of practice in judging with the effects of instructions to be clever.

Procedure. Students in two college classes were treated as four groups, called "Judgment-Clever" (*J-C*), "Judgment-Appropriate" (*J-A*), "Reading-Clever" (*R-C*), and "Reading-Appropriate" (*R-A*). The titles obtained from preliminary work with the Gilson plot were rated by the two expert judges, graduate research assistants with experience on the preliminary run, on a 5-point scale. From those on which the judges agreed, five at each point of the scale were selected to make a rectangular distribution of 25 titles as practice for the *J-C* and *J-A* groups. After the plot, five titles

[6] J. W. Jennings kindly assisted with these ratings.
[7] P. R. Christensen, J. P. Guilford, and R. C. Wilson, Relations of creative responses to working time and instructions, *J. exp. Psychol.*, 53, 1957, 82–88.

were presented with a rating for each and an explanation of the ratings. Then 10 titles were presented for ratings, after which the expert ratings were announced and recorded by the Ss for comparison with their own, and then 10 more titles were presented for rating. The R-C and R-A groups were given the same titles to read as examples, with no mention of judgment.

After the judgment or reading, all groups were given the Durden plot with instructions to write titles for 12 min. The J-C and R-C groups were instructed as follows: "Read the short plot below. After reading it, make up and write down as many clever titles for this plot as you can. Your titles will be judged as to the degree of their cleverness." The J-A and R-A groups were instructed as follows: "Read the short plot below. After reading it make up and write down as many appropriate titles for this plot as you can. Appropriate titles are those that fit the plot."

The materials and instructions were printed in booklets, hence little oral instruction was required. One college class was divided into J-C and

TABLE I

MEANS FOR FOUR GROUPS ON THREE MEASURES OF PRODUCTION
OF PLOT-TITLES

Groups	N	Number of titles	Cleverness-rating	Number of high-quality titles
Judgment-Clever	23	12.0	2.55	2.52
Judgment-Appropriate	22	13.0	2.43	2.73
Reading-Clever	23	14.7	2.42	2.52
Reading-Appropriate	24	14.8	2.35	2.25

J-A groups of 23 and 22 Ss. Another class was divided into R-C and R-A groups of 23 and 24 Ss.

Results. The 1254 titles were typed on separate sheets, randomized, and given to the two expert judges for independent rating on a 5-point scale. The agreement between the judges, computed over single titles, is represented by a correlation-coefficient of 0.35. Three scores were calculated for each S: number of titles written, mean rating of the cleverness of these titles, and number of titles of high quality. The agreement between the judges, computed over means of Ss, is represented by a correlation-coefficient of 0.64. Since the ratings of both judges were used, the effective reliability is somewhat above this value. The criterion of high quality was 7 or higher for the sum of the two judges' ratings of cleverness.

It is clear from Table I that the differences between the groups are negligible. The only statement that can be made at the 5% level of confidence is that the two groups with practice in judgment wrote fewer titles than the two groups with practice in reading. This finding raises the question of whether the practice in judging was effective, and a comparison of the first and second halves of the judging-practice in respect to agreement with the experts showed that both groups moved in the expected direction, but that neither difference approached significance.

The Influence of Production on Judgment

The hypothesis that practice in production will improve the accuracy of judgment may lie behind the assumption that book reviewers and editors should have some experience in writing. The effort to write to meet a certain criterion, such as cleverness, might improve ability to recognize cleverness when one sees it. Current doctrine on transfer suggests, however, that judgment would not be improved as much by practice in production as by practice in judgment.

Procedures. Three groups were used, named according to the sequence of activities: "Judgment-Judgment" (*J-J*), "Judgment-Production-Judgment" (*J-P-J*), and "Production-Judgment" (*P-J*). The materials were the same as in the first experiment. In all groups, the last task was the reading of a plot and judgment of a standard series of 25 titles. The *J-J* group first had practice in judgment just as in the first experiment. The *J-P-J* group also had practice in judgment first followed by practice in production, and then the standard judging task. The *P-J* group had the same practice in production, then the standard judging task. The two plots of the first experiment were used for judgment, but for production the *J-P-J* and *P-J* groups were given a similar plot supplied by Professor Guilford. These Ss were instructed to write clever titles, but the output was not analyzed.

Half the Ss in each group received the Gilson plot for the final judgment and half the Durden plot. The other plot was used for the initial judgment in the *J-J* and *J-P-J* groups. Three college classes formed the three groups, and, since the results were encouraging, three more classes were run in the same way.

Results. With the ratings of the expert judges as the standard, errors of judgment were computed as the difference between S's judgment and that of the experts. The errors were summed without regard to sign to get a measure of total error for each S. These scores could range from 0-80, and a total error of 25 would be an average of one point on the 5-point scale for 25 judgments. The two classes in each group gave similar results and therefore were combined. To check on the equivalence of the two plots, the two subgroups that judged the Gilson plot first ($N = 85$) and the two that judged the Durden plot first ($N = 86$) were compared as to total error. Since the difference was small and far from significant, error-scores for the two plots were combined, and the mean of the errors on the initial judgments (34.9) taken as the baseline against which to evaluate the effects of practice. Three other comparisons also indicate that the two plots did not differ on final judgments.

The results after these consolidations are shown in Table II. It is evident that practice in judgment did not significantly improve judgment. The J-P-J sequence improved the final judgments significantly, but the greatest improvement, that of the P-J group, is due to production alone. Furthermore, the final judgments of the P-J group are significantly more accurate at the 5% level than those of the J-J group.

DISCUSSION

The results demonstrate that, with suitable materials, two intellectual activities, previously treated separately, can meaningfully be investigated together. What these two activities have in common in the present experiments is not the overt response but an abstract dimension or quality; namely, cleverness, which is a specification of the titles to be produced and the basis of judgment of the titles to be rated.

There are several possible reasons why the expected difference due to instructions did not appear. The exact wording of the instructions may be

TABLE II

Errors on Initial and Final Judgments of Plot-Titles
for Three Groups with Different Programs
of Practice

	N	Mean error	Diff.	P
Initial judgments (J–J and J–P–J)	171	34.9		
Final judgments (J–J)	89	33.4	1.5	n.s.
Final judgments (J–P–J)	82	31.8	3.1	.05
Final judgments (P–J)	86	29.7	5.2	.01

important, hence the critical portions of the instructions for the first experiment are quoted above. Another consideration is that each S of the present experiment had only one set of instructions, while Christensen and co-workers used both instructions for the same Ss, and the latter technique may maximize the difference in their effects. In the present experiment, furthermore, all Ss had some kind of practice before beginning production, and it is possible that this practice minimized the effect of differences in instructions.

The striking fact to be explained is that practice in production improved the accuracy of judgment, while practice in judgment did not improve either production or judgment. The most obvious explanation, consistent with other evidence on learning, is that production is a more active kind of practice. The periods of practice for both activities were equally short (about 12 min.) but S probably has to think more actively to write a title, even a poor one, than to write a number from 1–5. It is also possible, since the hypothesis of the first experiment was not supported, to retain the assumption of brainstorming that practice in judgment engenders a critical attitude that interferes with improvement. The difference between the J-P-J group and the P-J group is consistent with this assumption. Another possibility is that, in selecting a task which is a good measure of individual differences in originalty, we have selected one that resists improvement. Christensen and co-workers found no improvement in plot-titles scored for cleverness over a 12-min. period of production. Meadow and Parnes found improvement on several tests of production, including plot-titles scored for number of low-quality titles, after a course in Creative Problem Solving, but the improvement in plot-titles scored for high quality did not reach significance.[8] The findings of the present experiments may not apply to other tasks in which the factor of originality is less prominent.

If we ask what is learned and transferred from production to judgment, the answer cannot be "a simple habit," for the writing of titles is quite different from the writing of numbers in blank spaces. On the basis of research in military training, Gagné has questioned the familiar principle that direct practice on a task is the best way to learn it and has emphasized the importance of analysis of the task for the design of training sequences that will maximize transfer.[9] The component of production that transfers to judgment in the present experiment is most likely the common dimension of both tasks—the quality of cleverness. This concept is familiar to college students, of course, but the practice in production could sharpen this concept and permit it to be used with more discrimination. Like some of the military research cited by Gagné, the present study shows that to improve in judgment, one should practice something else.

SUMMARY

The relation of production and judgment was studied in this experiment. Plot-titles were used because they afford a good test of originality,

[8] Arnold Meadow and S. J. Parnes, Evaluation of training in creative problem solving, *J. appl. Psychol.*, 43, 1959, 189–194.

[9] R. M. Gagné, Military training and principles of learning, *Amer. Psychologist*, 17, 1962, 83–91.

and because they are suitable for both production and judgment. The hypotheses tested were that practice in judgment improves production and that practice in production improves judgment.

College students read short plots and practiced judging the cleverness of titles for them, comparing their judgments with the judgments of experts. Then they read other plots and wrote titles for them. As compared with control groups whose members merely read the titles, there was no superiority of production due to the practice in judging. Nor were instructions to write clever titles effective, as compared with instructions to write appropriate titles.

Other Ss practiced writing titles and then judged the cleverness of a standard series of titles, which had been judged by experts. This practice improved the accuracy of judgment. A group with direct practice in judgment did not improve in judgment. Another group with practice in judgment prior to practice in production improved only slightly in judgment, possibly because of the inhibitory effects of the initial practice in judging.

These findings lead to the conclusion that it is feasible to investigate relations between intellectual activities that are grossly different. In respect to transfer, the conclusion is that it is the concept of cleverness and skill in its identification that transfer. Accuracy in judging titles is improved, not by direct practice in judgment, but by practice in the production of titles to meet the criterion involved in the subsequent judgment.

21. Training and Instructions in the Facilitation of Originality

Milton E. Rosenbaum, Sidney J. Arenson, and Richard A. Panman

A series of studies by Maltzman and his associates (Maltzman, Bogartz, and Breger, 1958; Maltzman, Simon, Raskin, and Licht, 1960) has consistently demonstrated that a training procedure designed to elicit uncommon responses will affect performance on subsequent tasks by facilitating original responses. The basic training procedure involves successive presentations of a single list of stimulus words to which the Ss are instructed to give different associations on each presentation. A control group receives only one presentation of the stimulus words. The results

Reprinted by permission of the authors and Academic Press, Inc. from *Journal of Verbal Learning and Verbal Response*, 1964, 3, 50–56.

indicate that the training procedure facilitates the elicitation of uncommon responses to a test list of new stimulus words. The training procedure also facilitates original responses on a clearly unrelated task of suggesting different uses for a common object.

A variety of variables that may be related to the elicitation of originality have been considered, and in an early study in the series (Maltzman *et al.*, 1958), the influence of instructions to be original was examined. In accord with the standard procedure, an experimental group received six presentations of the training list, while a control group was given one presentation. Half of each of these groups was instructed, prior to administration of the test list, to be original; these instructions were omitted for the remaining groups. Instruction produced a significant increase in the uncommonness of free associations on the test list, and the group that received training and instruction presented more uncommon responses than the group that received only instruction. The present study also evaluates the effects on originality of training and instructions to be original, but the instructions are introduced at the time of presentation of the training rather than at the time of test. If the training procedure has as its chief asset moving S through his hierarchy of responses to low-probability associations to the initial stimulus words, which then affects response to test materials, instructions may accomplish this goal equally as well and more efficiently and rapidly than training.

On the basis of preliminary studies, Maltzman (1961) suggests that there appear to be complex interactions between instructions to be original and originality training procedures. A factorial design is employed in the present experiment in order to assess interactions of training and instructions.

METHOD

Subjects. The Ss were 218 undergraduate students from a course in elementary psychology.

Stimulus Materials. The equating list in the present study was that used as the training list in Experiment IV reported in the monograph by Maltzman *et al.* (1960) to which the word "summer" from their test list was added to make a 25-word list. These words come principally from the Opposites Test of Woodworth and Wells (1911), who considered them equal in their tendency to evoke opposites. The 25-word training and 25-word test lists were identical with those used by Maltzman *et al.* (1958). The words in these lists were derived from norms obtained by Wilson (1942) and are the 50 words in Wilson's study which evoked the fewest different responses. The lists were responded to in booklets prepared for group administration, the number of sheets per booklet being dictated by the experimental conditions to be described below. Each sheet contained 25 numbered blank spaces. A separate booklet contained the Unusual Uses Test (Guilford, Wilson, Christensen, and Lewis, 1951).

Procedure. The experimental design required four groups: (1) training and no originality instructions (X), (2) no training and no instructions (C), (3) training and instructions (XO), and (4) no training and instructions (CO). There were eight experimental sessions which were all conducted on the same day. The Ss had selected the session in which they participated by signing up in their elementary psychology class. Groups of 25–30 Ss participated in each session. The four experimental conditions were randomly assigned to the eight sessions. Two different groups were exposed to each of the four conditions.

The equating list was administered first to all groups and was prefaced by the usual free-association instructions. The E read a stimulus word every 5 sec. The equating list was used because groups were treated differently on the first administration of the training list. Maltzman *et al.* used the first responses to the training list to assess the degree to which the various groups were equated on initial response level.

The second sheet of each booklet was used for responses to the training list. The E repeated the free-association instructions to all groups, but for the groups that received originality instructions (CO and XO) he added the sentence, "Try to be as original as possible." This sentence was not presented to the remaining groups (C and X).

The training groups (X and XO) received 5 additional presentations of the training list with instructions before each repetition to give a different response from the one(s) given before. The originality instructions were given before each presentation of the training list to the XO group. Originality instructions were given only to the CO and XO groups prior to presentations of the training list. They were not given at any other time in the experimental procedure. All groups then received the test list prefaced only by free-association instructions. At the completion of the word-association task, the training groups (X and XO) had received a total of 6 presentations of the training list, while the no-training groups (C and CO) had just one presentation. The 5-sec. rate of presentation was maintained for all word lists.

Finally, all groups were given the Unusual Uses Test. The Ss were asked to read along as the E read aloud the instructions which appeared on the first page of each test booklet. The instructions included examples of a common use for each of six different common objects. The Ss were instructed to give additional different uses for each of the objects. There was no reference to giving original or unusual responses. The test was given in two timed parts of 5 min. each. Each part included the names of three objects and their most common use with spaces for writing six other uses for each object.

RESULTS

Following the procedure of Maltzman and his associates, the frequency with which the different responses were obtained for each stimulus word in the equating, training, and test lists was determined. The frequency of the occurrence in the entire sample of each response to a stimulus word was assigned as a score to each response of an S. Each S's originality score was the mean frequency of his responses. A low score therefore indicates high originality.

The mean originality scores obtained on the equating list are presented in Table 1. They are presented in relation to the various experimental conditions to be imposed following the equating list. The variances are homogeneous as indicated by the Hartley test. Analysis of variance indicates no significant effects for Training ($F < 1.00$), Instructions ($F = 2.14$; $p > 0.05$)[1], or the Training X Instructions interaction ($F = 1.72$; $p > 0.05$). No difference is indicated, therefore, among groups prior to introduction of the experimental variables.

A comparison of the initial responses to the training list permits evaluation of the immediate effects of the instructions to be original. The mean originality scores obtained on the initial presentation of the training list by the various groups are presented in Table 1. The means obtained by the

TABLE 1

MEAN ORIGINALITY SCORES

Con-dition	N	Equating list		First training list		Test list		
		Mean	SD	Mean	SD	Mean	SD	Adj. Mean
C	54	92.09	43.80	103.39	24.34	59.52	20.66	62.54
CO	54	105.76	35.74	77.89	32.49	55.89	18.83	54.06
X	55	101.18	38.39	103.30	20.80	57.06	19.58	56.76
XO	55	102.73	32.18	72.00	30.35	44.79	18.92	44.05

two groups that received originality instructions are lower than the means of the noninstructed groups. An analysis of variance indicates a significant main effect for Instructions ($F = 57.76$; $p < 0.001$). Nonsignificant effects are indicated for Training and the interaction of the two variables.

In addition to the mean originality scores obtained by the various groups on the first presentation of the training list, Fig. 1 presents the means obtained by the two training groups on successive presentations

---

[1] The degrees of freedom for this and all subsequent F-ratios are 1 and 214.

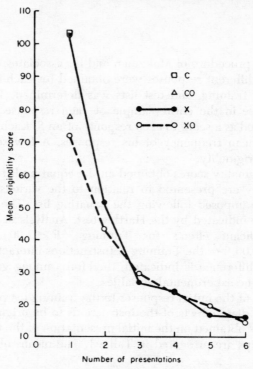

FIG. 1. Mean originality scores on the Training List for all groups as a function of the number of presentations.

of the same list. It is apparent that, eventually, lower originality scores were obtained by groups receiving the training treatment than groups that were presented with the training list only once. Although an advantage is indicated early for the XO group, this difference is no longer present by the third presentation of the training list.

In contrast to the finding of Maltzman *et al.* (1962) that the mean originality scores were highly skewed, the present distributions were essentially normal. Distributions of percentage of unique responses (those given by only one S in the sample) on each presentation of the training list were highly skewed. The occurrence of no unique responses was frequent for many Ss despite the fact that scoring of the same protocols yielded a rather low originality score in many cases. Maltzman and his associates (1958, 1960) report that from 70 to 75% of the responses of the average S on the fifth repetition of the training list were unique. The present data indicate that on the final presentation of the training list the mean percentage of unique responses was 33 for the XO group and 29 for the X group. On the first presentation of the training list the mean percentage of unique responses for all groups was 10 or below.

The mean originality score obtained on the test list are presented in Table 1. Homogeneity of variances and regression were indicated by appropriate tests, and a correlation of 0.59 was found between the equating-list and the test-list originality scores. An analysis of covariance was conducted in which the equating-list scores served as the control variable. The main effects for Training ($F = 14.13$, $p < 0.001$) and Instructions ($F = 25.41$, $p < 0.001$) were significant, but no significant interaction of the two experimental variables was indicated ($F = 1.27$). Thus, each of the independent variables affects the degree of originality obtained on the transfer task represented by the test list.

The Unusual Uses Test was scored in a manner similar to that employed for the word association test. The frequency with which the various uses appeared for each of the objects was obtained. Total number of uses, number of unique uses, and number of common uses was determined for each S. A unique use is a response that occurred no more than once in the entire sample in relation to a particular object. Common uses were responses that appeared two or more times. Table 2 presents the means for each of these response classes.

TABLE 2

Unusual Uses Test Scores

Condition	N	Unique uses		Common uses		Total uses	
		Mean	SD	Mean	SD	Mean	SD
C	54	4.61	3.43	16.72	4.86	21.33	6.44
CO	54	3.43	2.31	17.04	4.99	20.46	6.49
X	55	5.58	3.60	18.67	4.82	24.25	6.93
XO	55	5.10	3.30	19.44	5.71	24.53	7.11

The regression of these scores on the equating list scores was 0.02 or less in each instance and therefore no advantage is indicated for analyses of covariance. Analyses of variance of each type of score indicates a significant main effect for Training but no other significant terms. The F for Training in the case of Unique Uses was 8.92 ($p < 0.001$); for Common Uses, $F = 10.08$ ($p < 0.001$); and for Total Uses, $F = 14.33$ ($p < 0.001$). The F for Instructions in the case of Unique Uses was 3.58 ($0.10 > p > 0.05$), which suggests a trend in a direction opposite to that which was expected. Other results of the analyses fell far short of significant levels. It is possible that the results for Unique Uses in this and previous experiments are dependent on the total production of the Ss. To assess this possibility, correlations between Total and Unique Uses were computed. Product moment correlations for each group are as follows: C = 0.835, CO = 0.751, X = 0.744, XO = 0.616. Each of the correlations is positive and statistically significant and does not differ significantly from the others. The over-all correlation for the four groups is 0.735.

A further analysis of the responses to the Unusual Uses Test was suggested by the possibility that Common Uses occur initially to the specific test items, but as these are exhausted, Unique Uses appear. A hierarchy of response would be reflected in this succession and would favor the occurrence of Unique Uses for Ss who offer more Total Uses. In order to assess this possibility the percentage of unique responses to each item that were offered first, second, and so on up to sixth was evaluated. The percentages are as follows for the entire sample: first, 12.1; second, 17.3; third, 22.0; fourth, 29.2; fifth, 32.7; and sixth, 31.8. It should be recognized that these percentages are based on decreasing numbers of responses at each position. The reported percentages are identical in pattern for each of the groups considered individually.

Discussion

The results confirm previous findings that the standard training procedure devised by Maltzman and his associates is effective in facilitating the production of original responses on subsequent tasks. Instructions to be original have an equivalent effect on an essentially similar subsequent task but not on a rather different task.

Maltzman (1960) has offered speculations concerning the contribution of nonspecific transfer and the role of self-reinforcement in the transfer of originality training. In considering nonspecific transfer, he suggested that the resultant effects may be dependent on complex mediated generalization of intraverbal associations among uncommon responses. This interpretation leads to the expectation that the greater the degree of uncommonness achieved on the training list, the greater will be the originality in response to the test list.

It was originally expected that instructions to be original would immediately elicit a level of uncommon responding well below the dominant tendency associated with the training-list words. The instructions did produce significantly greater originality immediately, but after one demand to present different responses to a second presentation of the list, Ss in the X group presented more uncommon responses than Ss in the CO group.[2] Both the X and XO groups continued to present increasingly uncommon responses as repetition trials went on. Assuming direct transfer, the level

[2] The significance of this difference cannot be statistically evaluated because of the excessive contribution of the X group at this stage to the frequency tabulations on which the originality scores were based.

of uncommon response achieved on the training list would suggest that on the test list a training effect would appear but not an instruction effect. Alternately, an interaction effect would be possible such that instructions would be superior to no instructions only when training was not employed, but that training would be superior to no training with or without instructions. The results do not support these expectations.

Self-reinforcement is viewed by Maltzman as playing a role in the transfer of uncommon responding from the training task to the test list. The self-reinforcement may be seen as occurring when, after considerable frustration, S succeeds in producing during the training procedure a different and uncommon response. Employing both the report of Maltzman (1960) that Ss are disturbed and frustrated by the demand for repeated evocation of different responses to the same stimuli and the present evidence that instructions to be original and the training procedure produce similar test-list effects, one may derive an additional interpretation.

For the directly instructed Ss, obedience during the training period, probably in the form of rejection of a common associate, may be viewed as generalizing to the test period. For these Ss, the instructions provide some clarity as to E's intent. The disturbance and frustration of Ss in the training condition may reflect their attempts to diagnose the purpose of the task. Recognition of the necessary increase in uncommonness of their responses as training trials continued may have provided a solution to this problem and may have led to "self-instruction" to be original on the test list.

The presentation of increasingly uncommon responses by the X group may be necessary to produce self-instruction equal in potency to the explicit instructions. Congruent with this hypothesis is the finding that degree of originality tends to be directly related to number of training trials (Maltzman et al., 1960; Maltzman, 1961). The increase in trials may increase the number of Ss who employ self-instruction to be original. A parametric study involving deliberately instructed and noninstructed Ss who receive different numbers of training trials may help to examine this hypothesis.

The results of the Unusual Uses Test also replicate Maltzman's findings. An interpretation of these results is possible that may be more parsimonious than that offered by Maltzman. It should be noted that analysis of the data presented in Table 2 for unique, common, and total responses indicates that training affects all three measures similarly.

It is possible that the principal consequence of the training procedure is to increase response output on the Unusual Uses Test. As has been demonstrated, early responses are relatively common, but as output continues unique responses become relatively more frequent. Maltzman's data in published reports, although not amenable to direct evaluation, indicate at least partial support for the hypothesis that training affects total response to the Unusual Uses Test in the same way as in the present experiment. This interpretation readily accounts for the absence of an instruction effect on the Unusual Uses Test since there is no basis for expecting increased productivity.

There are difficulties in comparing the current experiment with Maltzman's studies. The administration of the equating list may have affected response to subsequent tests in unspecifiable ways. An indication that this may be so is offered by the discrepancy between the present results and Maltzman's findings for the successive trials in response to the training list. Where Maltzman has typically obtained approximately 70% unique responses after five repetitions, no more than 33% was achieved for comparable conditions in the present study. In addition, this comparison may be affected by the use of a 5-sec. response interval on training trials in the present study. The 10-sec. interval used in previous research may have allowed more time for production of uncommon associates.

SUMMARY

In order to assess the effects on originality of Maltzman's training procedure in contrast to instructions to be original, word-association lists and Guilford's Unusual Uses Test were administered. No differences among experimental groups were indicated on an initial equating association list.

On the first administration of a training list, the CO group (instructions—no training) and the XO group (instructions—training) were told to present original associations while customary word-association instructions were given to the C (no instructions—no training) group and the X (no instructions—training) group. The C and CO groups were given no further opportunities to respond to the training list. The X and XO groups responded five additional times to the training list with instructions to give a different association to each stimulus word on each occasion. In addition, the XO group continued to receive instructions to be original.

Analysis of responses to a test list indicated significant independent effects of instructions and training in facilitating originality. Training, but not instructions, resulted in signficantly more unique, common, and total responses on the Unusual Uses Test. The test-list results are discussed in terms of nonspecific transfer effects and instructionally derived response tendencies. The results of the Unusual Uses Test suggest that the demand for greater productivity during training leads to greater productivity in the transfer task, with increased originality as a secondary effect of productivity.

REFERENCES

GUILFORD, J. P., WILSON, R. C., CHRISTENSEN, P. R., AND LEWIS, D. J. A factor-analytic study of creative thinking, I. Hypotheses and description of tests. *Reports from the Psychological Laboratory, The University of Southern California*, Nov. 4, 1951.

MALTZMAN, I. On the training of originality. *Psychol. Rev.*, 1960, 67, 229–242.

MALTZMAN, I. The training of original problem solving behavior. *Tech. Rep. No. 9, Office of Naval Research*, 1961. [Contract Nonr-233 (50)].

MALTZMAN, I., BOGARTZ, W., AND BREGER, L. A procedure for increasing word association originality and its transfer effects. *J. exp. Psychol.*, 1958, 56, 392–398.

MALTZMAN, I., SIMON, S., RASKIN, D., AND LICHT, L. Experimental studies in the training of originality. *Psychol. Monogr.*, 1960, 74, No. 6 (Whole No. 493).

WILSON, D. P. An extension and evaluation of association word lists. Unpublished doctoral dissertation, Univ. of Southern California, 1942.

WOODWORTH, R. S., AND WELLS, F. L. Association tests. *Psychol. Monogr.*, 1911, 13, No. 5 (Whole No. 57).

22. Increasing Creativity by Free-Association Training

Jonathan L. Freedman

Abstract. *An experiment was conducted to test the hypothesis that facilitating S's ability to produce associations would increase his score on a test of creativity. Ss either free associated to 10 stimulus words or defined the words. Those receiving the free-association training scored significantly higher on the Remote Associates Test (RAT), a test of creativity which was administered after the training session.*

Maltzman (1960) has proposed that creative thinking consists of bringing together various associations which are novel but are also appropriate to the task. To test this idea he and his associates have conducted a series

Reprinted by permission of the authors and the American Psychological Association from *Journal of Experimental Psychology*, 1965, 69, 89–91.

of studies (Maltzman, Bogartz, & Breger, 1958; Maltzman, Simon, Raskin, & Licht, 1960) in which Ss free associate to a series of stimulus words under a variety of conditions and then take the Unusual Uses Test (Guilford, 1950). The one procedure which has been consistently successful in improving performance on the Unusual Uses Test (as compared with control groups) is presenting the stimuli a number of times and requiring Ss to give a different response to each stimulus on each presentation.

A recent experiment by Caron, Unger, and Parloff (1963) indicated, however, that this training procedure did not affect performance on the Remote Associates Test (RAT). Since Mednick (1962) has shown that Ss who have a relatively large number of associations to a given stimulus tend to score higher on the RAT than those who have fewer associations, a training technique which facilitated free associating should improve performance on the RAT. The failure of Maltzman's procedure may have been due to the fact that it is designed to increase the production of unusual associations, whereas the RAT is constructed so that the correct responses are commonly associated with the stimulus words, and are often dominant associates (e.g., MOUSE-CHEESE). Since it appears that success on the RAT depends upon the production of many associations in a short time, the present study attempted to improve performance on the RAT by a training technique specifically designed to facilitate this process.

METHOD

Subjects. The Ss were 90 students from an introductory psychology class at Stanford University. There were 20 males and 20 females in each of the two main experimental conditions, and an additional 10 males in a control condition. The Ss were run individually.

Procedure. All Ss were told that they were going to take a test designed to measure creativity and that before the test they would receive a brief warm-up exercise. The facilitation group was instructed to give their associations to each of 10 stimulus words. Each word was read aloud by E and S was told to give whatever words came into his mind, and to continue until told to stop. They were stopped after 30 sec. or when they had stopped responding. The nonfacilitation group was asked to define each of the words. The same words were used for both groups, and were chosen so that neither the words themselves nor any of their common associates were the correct responses to any of the items on the creative thinking test. The stimulus words were: BOOK, MOON, COPPER, MOVIE, BRASS, COFFEE, READ, FARM, TOGETHER, STAR.

An additional control group consisted of 10 male Ss, each of whom was paired with 1 male S in the facilitation condition. The procedure was identical to that in the facilitation condition except that the control

Ss read from a card the associations which had been given by the paired experimental S. Thus, in each pair both Ss had verbalized the same words, but the facilitation S had produced them himself, whereas the control S merely read them.

The creative thinking test was the Remote Associates Test (RAT). This test is composed of items consisting of three words, and S's task is to find a fourth word which is somehow associated with each of the three stimulus words. The test consists of 30 items and takes 40 min. It was presented in two equal parts of 15 items, and the original warm-up exercise was repeated after the first part of the test. Scores on the test consist simply of number correct. (For a more complete description of the RAT see Mednick, 1962.)

A pretest similar to the present study indicated that the experimental manipulation was more successful with men than with women. Since the pretest was run entirely by a male E, it seemed likely that female Ss were constrained in free associating in the presence of a male E. Therefore, in the present study all men were run by a male E and women by a female E.

RESULTS AND DISCUSSION

The major results are presented in Table 1, which shows the score on the RAT for facilitation and nonfacilitation groups and for male and female Ss. The means for the complete test are presented because the results are similar for the two halves of the RAT. For both men and women the

TABLE 1

MEAN SCORES ON RAT

	Males	Females
Facilitation	18.05[a]	18.60
Nonfacilitation	14.15	17.10

[a] Maximum score is 30.

facilitation group achieved higher scores than the nonfacilitation group. As may be seen in the accompanying analysis of variance (Table 2), the difference between facilitation and nonfacilitation groups is significant. Separate comparisons using the combined error term indicated that the difference is also significant for males alone; $F (1, 76) = 10.25$, $p < .01$, but not for female Ss, $F (1, 76) = 1.52$.

It is difficult to determine why the effect is so much stronger for male than for female Ss. There is, of course, a confounding of E and sex of

TABLE 2

ANALYSIS OF VARIANCE OF MEAN SCORES ON RAT

Source	df	F
Facilitation-Nonfacilitation (F–NF)	1	9.82**
Male-Female (M–F)	1	4.13*
F–NF × M–F	1	1.94
Error (MS)	76	(14.84)

* $p < .05$.
** $p < .01$.

Ss, but an extensive pretest using a single E produced essentially the same pattern of results. There were no appreciable differences in the number of associations produced by the two groups during the training session. It is possible that the difference is due to a ceiling effect for female Ss since the overall means for females are significantly higher than for males.

It could be argued that the facilitation Ss scored higher on the RAT because during the training session the former produced a large number of associations to the stimulus word whereas the latter merely defined it. Although the associations were not the exact responses necessary for the RAT, they may have indirectly strengthened the correct responses through the process of mediated generalization (Mednick & Freedman, 1960). The control group was run to assess this possibility.

The control Ss had available to them the same body of words that were available to the facilitation Ss, but the former had not actually free associated. If the availability of the words were the critical factor, the control group should have scored as high as the facilitation group on the RAT; if the act of associating were critical, the control group should score less high and should not differ from the nonfacilitation group. The latter result was found. The control group mean was 14.56 which was significantly lower than the paired facilitation group as indicated by a test for correlated means; $t(9) = 2.31$, $p < .05$, and did not differ appreciably from the nonfacilitation group. Thus, it appears that the actual act of associating is the critical factor which facilitated performance on the RAT.

Why did this training procedure have a facilitating effect when Maltzman's technique did not? The explanation does not seem to be a difference in the amount of training since the present procedure seems to have given less training than the standard Maltzman technique. The number of responses per stimulus was fewer in the present study (a mode [1] of three vs. six in Caron's study); fewer stimuli were used (10 vs. 25); and the total

---

[1] The mode is probably the most descriptive measure of central tendency since a large majority of Ss gave exactly three responses to each stimulus but a few gave a very large number of responses.

time taken by the training was considerably less (about 5 min. vs. about 20 min.).

There was probably a difference in the remoteness of the associations given during training in the two studies. Unfortunately, it is impossible to assess the remoteness of the responses given in the present study since no appropriate norms exist. The Ss did not give a number of responses to the same stimulus, but were giving a series of associations with, in most cases, only the first one being specifically to the stimulus word. It may be that this gives Ss practice associating to several stimulus words at a time, which is what he must do on the RAT.

Another possibility is that, as discussed earlier, the present technique causes Ss to produce a number of associations in a brief period whereas the Maltzman method requires only one association at a time. Since Ss probably solve the RAT problems by trying to produce many associations quickly, the present training technique is more similar to the process of solution than is Maltzman's; and the former might therefore be expected to have a greater facilitating effect than the latter.

REFERENCES

CARON, A. J., UNGER, S. M., & PARLOFF, M. B. A test of Maltzman's theory of originality training. *J. verbal Learn. verbal Behav.*, 1963, 1, 436–442.

GUILFORD, J. P. Creativity. *Amer. Psychologist*, 1950, 5, 444–454.

MALTZMAN, I. On the training of originality. *Psychol. Rev.*, 1960, 67, 229–242.

MALTZMAN, I., BOGARTZ, W., & BREGER, L. A procedure for increasing word association originality and its transfer effects. *J. exp. Psychol.*, 1958, 56, 393–398.

MALTZMAN, I., SIMON, S., RASKIN, D., & LICHT, L. Experimental studies in the training of originality. *Psychol. Monogr.*, 1960, 74 (6, Whole No. 493).

MEDNICK, S. A. The associative basis of the creative process. *Psychol. Rev.*, 1962, 69, 220–232.

MEDNICK, S. A., & FREEDMAN, J. L. Facilitation of concept formation through mediated generalization. *J. exp. Psychol.*, 1960, 60, 278–283.

time when the number corresponding to a stimulus only will of at... 20 bits).

There is probably a difference in the rapidities of the two different over-training relation in the two tables. Unfortunately, it is impossible to assess these matches in the present... even in the present work, since no appropriate... were used. The Stroke hypothesis is another factor pertinent to the same situation but requiring a profound generalization then, to meet these jobs, the first one being specifically in the sense... beyond it may be that this type, saying to... requiring to a generalization biomechanic a... which, I... which is almost too publish is very...

Another possibility is that the figure... on what the present technique enables us to produce a number of generating in a brief period when the visualizing in that requires but one association at a time. Since it is probably solves the key problem by trying to produce new associations than the present number... being... is more similar... the present and within the... and somewhat similar forms might, therefore, be expected to have a profit in dealing determines the effort.

References

CARON, A. J., GROSS, S. M., MAUROGE, M.R. A test of Maturana's theory of systematic training. Cambridge Leave & other, Brings, 1965, 1, 139-316.

CATLIN, J. J. Ghost story. Ann. Rev. Psychiat., 1935, 22, 441-94.

MARTIN, W.C. On the learning and generating. Psychol. Rep., 1880, 67, 239-245.

MARTIN, E., BOLARIN, W., & BROWN, L. A procedure for increasing word association similarity and its further effects. J. exp. Psychol., 1939, 76, 301-309.

MAUROGE, T., SIMON, S., RASSON, D., VICTOR, C. Experimental studies in the learning of originality. Paper 1, J. M. nour., 1860, 74, 119. Wholestro (1869).

MENTER, S. A. The creative basis of the creative process. Psychol. Rev., 1883, 69, 220-232.

MURACI, S. A., & FINE, JANE, P. L. Facilitation of concept formation through mediated generalization. J. exp. Psychol., 1960, 60, 278-283.

PART TWO

Concept Learning

Sections Seven through Twelve deal with the area of research variously called concept formation, or learning, or identification. The difficulty in choosing an appropriate term arises because the typical laboratory experiment in this area involves human adult subjects whose task it is to abstract certain stimulus dimensions, with which they are already familiar, from other stimulus dimensions. Some argue that subjects are not, therefore, either forming a concept or learning a concept in the sense that a child does, but rather identifying or discriminating stimuli. (Concept learning in children is not covered in this book.) Because of these arguments over terminology, the phrase "concept learning" is used here merely as a name for a research area.

Research on abstraction, as it was called originally, began in the first years of this century. Although a few good experiments, still cited as classics, were performed in the twenties and thirties, systematic investigation did not begin until after 1950. Since then, the study of concept learning has far outstripped the study of problem solving in every way. As noted earlier, in problem solving, experimentation continues to be meager and unsystematic, and theory is scarce. In contrast, there is a high rate of experimental research in concept learning, much of the experimentation is systematic, and there is a fair amount of increasingly mathematical and otherwise sophisticated theory. In selecting articles for the problem solving section, it was often difficult to find enough acceptable papers, whereas in selecting concept articles, difficult decisions had to be made as to what acceptable papers to leave out. Also, the articles within chapters and even between chapters are more interrelated in the concept section. In fact, although Sections Eight and Nine have different titles, both deal in different ways with the same topic, mediation.

Concept-Learning Theory

Several papers dealing with theory in concept learning have appeared in recent years. The three selected for inclusion here represent somewhat different approaches. Goss' article deals with the actively researched topic of mediation in concept learning and, in particular, with what is usually considered to be, for human adults, the most widely used (not necessarily the only) type of mediator, viz., words or other verbal units. Although Goss covers many aspects of mediation paradigms, the basic issue is: under what circumstances is it necessary to expand S-R units into S-r-s-R, where r-s indicates an assumed implicit response and response-produced stimulus that mediate between the overt S and the final R. As the paper indicates, several types of experiments seem to compel the mediation assumption; perhaps the most widely cited of these is the reversal-nonreversal shift method extensively used by Kendler.

As mentioned earlier, the typical concept study requires that subjects select certain cues out of some larger number. Restle's paper proposes different models for how this selection takes place, then shows that these models are basically the same and that they yield the same system of recurrent events. Some, though not all, of the implications of the basic model for concept learning are pointed out. Rather, Restle notes that most of the predictions in concept learning that were made in an earlier mathematical-theoretical paper by Bourne and Restle (see references in this paper) can be reproduced with the strategy-selection model. The issue that Restle considers in some detail, viz., additivity of cues, is related to concept learning; in fact, additivity of cues has been employed in a few concept

231

studies, but most concept experiments are concerned with what might be called subtractivity of cues, i.e., cue selection.

One indication of increasing scientific sophistication in an area is often the development of mathematical theories in the area. In this respect, concept learning theory is progressing rapidly. Levine's paper is another approach to tasks, such as discrimination and concept problems, in which it is assumed that there are a number of hypotheses available to the subjects. Hypotheses are also called by a variety of other names, including strategies, and are considered by Levine to be mediators. Noteworthy is the number of hypotheses possible with just two trials in a two-choice problem. In fact, with the more complex cues typical of concept tasks, Levine makes a simplifying assumption that subjects attempt to locate the correct cue. With this assumption, even a task with relatively few cues permits a number of hypotheses to be entertained. Most important in Levine's paper is the assumption that the hypothesis, an implicit process, not the overt choice response, is the appropriate dependent variable and is the behavior affected by the reinforcement. Thus again, mediation (hypotheses) is considered basic in concept learning.

23. Verbal Mediating Responses and Concept Formation

Albert E. Goss

Over the past five decades, verbal mediating responses and stimuli have figured as important elements in a number of stimulus-response analyses of concept formation. This paper briefly reviews these analyses as a prelude to carrying out its main purpose, which is the further explication of the role of verbal mediating responses in conceptual behavior. More specifically, spelled out first are criteria for concept formation tasks, particularly as compared with those for conventional paired-associates tasks. Then described in considerable detail are some paradigms of presumed stimulus-response relationships in concept formation. Finally,

Reprinted by permission of the authors and of the American Psychological Association from *Psychological Review*, 1961, 68, 248–274.

the paradigms are considered in conjunction with certain variables and learning principles, and sample predictions are generated.

Probably the earliest explicit stimulus-response analysis of the role of verbal mediating responses in conceptual behavior is that which Max Meyer illustrated with the concept "food" in his *Fundamental Laws of Human Behavior* (1911, pp. 213–214). The same example of the essential features of concepts was used subsequently by Weiss (1925), Dashiell (1928), and Gray (1931). Although Watson (1920, p. 102) chose a different example, his treatment of conceptual behavior also emphasized verbal mediating responses. The primary purpose of these early analyses was to show that conceptual phenomena—which had previously been thought to be impervious to behavioristic treatment—could be dealt with in stimulus-response terms. Understandably for the time, such analyses were only incidentally combined with learning principles to derive predictions about the effects of potentially significant variables on conceptual behavior, and none of the predictions was tested experimentally.

Early in the forties, Birge (1941), Miller and Dollard (1941), and Cofer and Foley (1942) made suggestions concerning the possible significance of verbal mediating responses for conceptual behavior. These treatments, however, were more concerned with defining and applying the mechanism of response-mediated similarity and generalization than with analyzing in detail the role of this mechanism in concept formation. The same is true of Gibson's (1940) development and use of the somewhat parallel notion of internal generalization and its complement, internal differentiation.

A decade later, Osgood (1953) offered *post factum* analyses of the conceptual tasks and results described by Hull (1920), Smoke (1932), Heidbreder (1946a, 1946b), and Reed (1946). These analyses, along with those of Baum (1951) and Mandler (1954), emphasized the mechanism of response-mediated similarity and generalization to the virtual exclusion of the complementary mechanism of response-mediated dissimilarity and discrimination. During the same period, Goss and his students extended their studies of the latter mechanism (e.g., Goss & Greenfeld, 1958) to the analysis and investigation of the effects of experimentally controlled verbal pretraining on conceptual sorting (e.g., Fenn & Goss, 1957), conceptual naming (Lacey, 1959), and animistic thinking (e.g., Simmons & Goss, 1957).

Hypotheses about the role of verbal mediating processes in reversal and nonreversal shifts of conceptual phenomena have been proposed and tested by Kendler and his students (e.g., Kelleher, 1956; Kendler & D'Amato, 1955), as well as by Buss (1956), Gormezano and Grant (1958), and Harrow and Friedman (1958). These proposals apparently evolved primarily from the considerable body of data and theory concerning the simple discriminative behaviors of infrahuman and preverbal human organisms to which Spence (1936) has been the major contributor, rather than from existing hypotheses and data concerning response-mediated similarity and dissimilarity. Of similar origin is Wicken's (1954) analysis of the strengthening of discriminative responses to values along one dimension of multidimensional stimuli, and his subsequent more explicit hypotheses as to how verbal mediating responses might be the vehicles of "perceptual sets" (Wickens & Eckstrand, 1954).

Pavlov's "second signal system" is essentially equivalent to mediating responses and stimuli, and it has been the basis for recent analyses of "higher nervous activity" by Soviet psychologists (e.g., Elkonin, 1957). Within this framework, Liublinskaya (1957) has described theoretical and experimental work on the role of the second signal system in the conceptual behaviors of preschool children.

Of the many analyses and studies that bear directly or indirectly on the role of verbal mediating responses and stimuli in concept formation, some have been supported solely by informal examples rather than by experimental data and principles. Those which do refer to experimental materials have often been limited to one or two relatively specific situations. And there has been a tendency to consider the nature and implications of only a few of the many possible patterns of relationships that can exist among initiating stimuli, mediating responses and stimuli, and terminating responses (Goss, 1955, 1956).[1] There is clearly need for a more comprehensive yet experimentally rooted analysis; within the limitations to be described, such an analysis is offered in this paper.

[1] A temporal sequence of stimulus-response events in which a mediating response and stimulus may be distinguished can be represented as $S_{Initiating} - R_{Mediating} \frown S_{Mediating} - R_{Terminating}$. Social situations or experimental tasks are conceived as beginning with or initiated by some stimulus "element" or "compound" and as terminating with a response which is reinforced or punished; is instrumental in altering a subject's environment; or, more generally, has simply been designated the terminating, reference, or criterion response. Any stimulus event or receptor activation might be the initiating stimulus of a sequence, though usually and practically such stimuli are social and physical events.

Ideally, two criteria must be met in order for responses and the stimuli they produce to be considered mediating responses and stimuli. The first criterion is the observation of or grounds for inferring the occurrence of one or more responses subsequent to the initiating stimulus and before the terminating response. The second criterion is the demonstration that such temporally intermediate responses and stimuli have actual or potential facilitative or inhibitory effects on one or more measures of the occurrence and strength of the terminating response. Relative covertness and some particular topography as additional criteria seem unnecessarily restrictive. However, because of the presumed greater functional significance for most complex behaviors of postverbal humans of mediating responses originally or presently involving the vocal musculature, the focus of the analyses developed here will be on such responses and the stimuli they produce—verbal mediating responses and stimuli. A more exhaustive treatment of the definition of mediating responses and stimuli and of the bases for inferring or confirming their occurrences and effects can be found in Goss (1956).

CRITERIA FOR CONCEPT FORMATION TASK

General specification of the nature of concept formation tasks is a logical starting point. Because many concept formation tasks have much in common with conventional paired-associates learning tasks, differentiation of the two types of tasks is also required.

GENERAL CRITERIA

Fundamental to the definition of concept formation tasks (conceptual behaviors) are patterns of relationships between imitating stimuli and terminating responses. More particularly, such tasks involve patterns in which two or more independently presented initiating stimuli evoke the same terminating response. It is the independent presentation of stimuli that distinguishes concept formation tasks from convergent stimulus-compound situations. Thus crudely characterized, of course, the simplest concept formation tasks are essentially identical to phenomena more often labeled primary stimulus generalization and response-mediated generalization (Dollard & Miller, 1950; Goss, 1955). Indeed, the latter phenomena might be looked on as limiting cases of the former.

Those situations *commonly* regarded as concept formation tasks, however, are more complex. Sets of initiating stimuli are partitioned into two or more subsets, at least one of which has two or more independently presented members. Usually each of the subsets has two or more members, and the learning requirement is acquisition of the same response to all members of a particular subset and of a different response for each subset.

At a descriptive level, the sets of initiating stimuli in concept formation studies have been markedly heterogeneous. Because some sets apparently require paradigms different from those for other sets, and also for simplicity, sets of initiating stimuli are divided here into three types. These three types seem sufficient both for the development of adequate one-stage and two-stage paradigms and for the representation of all sets of initiating stimuli.

In the first type of set, all members are either variations in values along one physical or psychophysical dimension, or they are combinations of values along two or more dimensions. The dimensions may be primary or derived; the combinations may be completely or incompletely orthogonal. Illustrative of such sets are four squares which are red-small, red-large, blue-small, and blue-large.

Initiating stimuli in the second type of set can be partitioned into two or more subsets on the basis that all stimuli of each subset have some physically specifiable element or relation in common. The stimuli within each of these subsets differ from each other with respect to additional features. Thus, the stimuli of each subset consist of both common and variable features, neither of which has been (or perhaps could be) completely reduced to combinations of physical or psychophysical dimensions. Four stimuli, two of which have an S-shaped form in common and two of which have a sword-shaped form in common, but whose other features differ, are representative of this type of set of initiating stimuli.

Sets of initiating stimuli which are less readily or not at all reducible to combinations of values along dimensions, or to subsets defined by common elements or relations, constitute the third type of set. Illustrative of this type are sets of words for objects, properties, or relations. Subsets of words are usually, but not necessarily, specified on the basis of observations or assumptions that all of the stimuli of each subset evoke one or more common responses, some of which differ from the common responses evoked by the stimuli of each of the other subsets. An example of such sets of initiating stimuli is provided subsequently.[2]

With this type of initiating stimuli the bases for partitioning into subsets and for assigning responses to those subsets might be entirely arbitrary or random. For example, eight consonant-vowel-consonant initiating stimuli, none of which has any letters in common, might be randomly partitioned into four subsets of two members each. As stimuli for responses, a different one of four two-digit numbers, none of which has any digit in common, might then be randomly assigned to each of the subsets of initiating stimuli, with the requirement that a different response be conditioned to each subset of initiating stimuli.

PAIRED-ASSOCIATES LEARNING TASKS AND CONCEPT FORMATION TASKS

Paired-associates learning can be regarded as referring either to a particular kind of task or to a more general *procedure* for establishing and changing stimulus-response associations. Many concept formation *tasks*, however, have employed the paired-associates *procedure* for strengthening associations betwen stimulus members and responses elicited by response members. Both conventional paired-associates tasks and such concept formation tasks may therefore be regarded as complementary

[2] The first and possibly the second of the three types of sets of initiating stimuli distinguished here and the relationships with terminating responses into which these types of stimuli enter are equivalent to what have been labeled elsewhere as conjunctive categories or concepts (Bruner, Goodnow, & Austin, 1956, pp. 41–43, 244–245). The third of the present types seems approximately equivalent to Bruner, Goodnow, and Austin's disjunctive categories or concepts. From Bruner, Goodnow, and Austin's definition of relational concepts or categories and the accompanying examples, it cannot be determined whether such relational categories overlap with the first and second of the types noted here or whether such categories involve some additional type of initiating stimuli not distinguished here.

special cases of patterns of stimulus-response associations which are strengthened by the paired-associates procedure (Metzger, 1958; Richardson, 1958).

There is only one essential difference between conventional paired-associates learning tasks and concept formation tasks in which stimulus-response associations are established by the paired-associates procedure. That difference is in the ratio of stimulus members to responses which are to be conditioned to those stimuli. For conventional paired-associates learning tasks, the ratio of stimulus members to response members has been 1:1, i.e., separate associations are established between each of mn_s different stimulus members and each of the mn_r different responses elicited by mn_r response members.

For the formation of concepts by the paired-associates procedure, however, the ratio of stimulus members to the responses which are conditioned to those stimuli has been greater than 1:1: i.e., for at least one, and usually for all of m subsets of stimulus members, $n_{sj} > 1$, where n_{sj} is the number of stimuli in the jth subset. Regardless of the type of sets of initiating stimuli, by increasing the numbers of responses to equal the number of initiating stimuli, concept formation tasks in which stimulus-response associations are established by the paired-associates procedure can be transformed into conventional paired-associates learning tasks. Conversely, by decreasing the number of responses from equality with the number of initiating stimuli the latter can be transformed into concept formation tasks.

PARADIGMS

The role of verbal mediating responses in concept formation tasks can be developed most easily and clearly by means of two-stage paradigms of presumed relationships among initiating stimuli, mediating responses and stimuli, and terminating responses for each of the three types of initiating stimuli which were distinguished in the preceding section. Inferences regarding mediating responses and stimuli are usually based on characteristics of relationships between initiating stimuli and terminating responses. Accordingly, in the first part of this section, the two-stage paradigms are developed within the framework of one-stage paradigms which involve only initiating stimuli and terminating responses. Noted in connection with the description of these paradigms are some explanatory consequences, in particular, for reversal and non-reversal shifts.

Concept formation tasks are usually complex, and mediating responses and stimuli are commonly inferred rather than observed directly. Two-stage paradigms of conceptual behaviors should, therefore, be proposed cautiously. Emphasized in the second part of this section are some precautions in the development and use of two-stage paradigms.

"Abstract set or attitude," "hypotheses," and "strategies" are notions often advanced as central to any explanations of conceptual behaviors. Moreover, they are often regarded as opposed to stimulus-response analyses of concept formation tasks. The thesis elaborated in the last part of this section, however, is that these are not opposing notions, but rather are already embodied or can be readily assimilated within the one-stage and two-stage paradigms of the present analysis.

ONE-STAGE AND TWO-STAGE PARADIGMS

One-stage paradigms of conceptual situations and behaviors involve relationships between initiating stimuli and terminating responses. Such paradigms provide baselines for the development of two-stage paradigms, which introduce verbal mediating responses and stimuli. One-stage paradigms are not merely stepping stones, however; they are useful in themselves, in that they appear to represent adequately some of the conceptual behaviors of infrahuman organisms, of preverbal humans, and of humans under conditions which preclude or short circuit verbal mediating responses.

COMBINATIONS OF VALUES ALONG DIMENSIONS

One-stage paradigms. A set of stimuli consisting of combinations of two values along each of two dimensions is the simplest case of possible sets of stimuli containing complete orthogonal combinations of m values along each of n dimensions. The four initiating stimuli of the one-stage paradigm shown in Figure 1 are combinations of two values (x_1, x_2) along an X dimension, and of two values (y_1, y_2) along a Y dimension. For example, x_1 and x_2 might be the values giving rise to the colors red and blue, respectively, along a dimension of wave length; y_1 and y_2 might be small and large areas, respectively, along a (derived) dimension of size.

The two terminating responses could be naming by means of familiar words, nonsense syllables, or manipulanda representing two different names. Or they could be sorting by placing the stimuli in groups, matching them with other stimuli, or approaching-avoiding. The two patterns of relationships between initiating stimuli and terminating responses depict the associations whose strengthening or occurrence are referred to here as concept formation. That both animals and humans can acquire such differential responses to one or some of the dimensions of multidimensional stimuli has been amply demonstrated (Kelleher, 1956; Kendler & D'Amato, 1955; Woodworth, 1958).

Determinants of the actual and potential patterns of relationships that

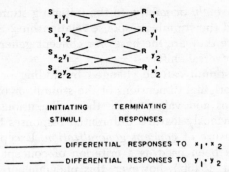

INITIATING   TERMINATING
STIMULI   RESPONSES

———————— DIFFERENTIAL RESPONSES TO $x_1 \cdot x_2$
— — — —DIFFERENTIAL RESPONSES TO $y_1 \cdot y_2$

FIG. 1. One-stage paradigm of relationships involving initiating stimuli which are combinations of two values, x_1, x_2 along an X dimension and two values, y_1, y_2 along a Y dimension. (The differential terminating responses $R_{x'_1}$, $R_{x'_2}$ are to x_1, x_2, while $R_{y'_1}$, $R_{y'_2}$ are to y_1, y_2. The X dimension might be color with values of red, x_1, and blue, x_2, and the Y dimension might be size with values of small, y_1, or large, y_2.)

will be learned include the number of fixed, relevant, and irrelevant dimensions presented, as well as the number of values selected along the relevant and irrelevant dimensions. A *fixed* dimension is exemplified by but one value along the dimension for all of the members of the set of initiating stimuli. For the stimuli shown in Figure 1, form, dimensionality, number of forms, and location of the forms on the presentation cards might be the same for each of the four initiating stimuli. They are among the fixed dimensions of those stimuli.

Should the task be to respond on the basis of red or blue, disregarding size, or to respond on the basis of small and large, disregarding color, the relevant dimensions would be color and size, respectively. More generally, the dimensions of the combinations of values to which discriminative responses are to be conditioned are the *relevant* dimensions. *Irrelevant* dimensions are those which, in the formation of some particular concept(s), involve values which must be disregarded. Such dimensions —or, more precisely, the values along such dimensions—may be completely or incompletely orthogonal with respect to combinations of values along the relevant dimensions.[3]

Once the component associations of particular patterns of relationships, such as those in Figure 1, are at a given level of strength, changes

[3] As is suggested by the overlap of the terminology employed here and that employed in classifying analysis of variance designs (e.g., Federer, 1955), such designs provide models of some of the many possible relationships between terminating responses and sets of initiating stimuli which are combinations of values along dimensions.

may occur either *singly* or *jointly*, in the initiating stimuli, the terminating responses, and the stimulus-response relationships. Such changes are important, because they are the bases for concept generalization and for reversal and nonreversal shifts.

The initiating stimuli can be changed by adding or shifting to new values along the original dimensions of the stimuli, or by adding or subtracting dimensions and values along those dimensions. The degree of occurrence of previously learned differential responses to altered sets of stimuli is the measure of *concept generalization*. Except where concept generalization has been used as a criterion of concept formation (e.g., Heidbreder, 1946a, 1946b), however, this phenomenon has not been of great experimental interest. For this reason, to elaborate on concept generalization here is considered premature.

Both the initiating stimuli and the terminating responses can remain the same, but their relationships, or the relevant and irrelevant dimensions and values, can be changed by reversal or nonreversal shifts. The effects of such shifts on conceptual behaviors, and explanations of those effects, have been among the major concerns of many recent studies of concept formation (e.g., Kendler & Kendler, 1959). It is important, therefore, to describe reversal and nonreversal shifts within one-stage paradigms for this type of initiating stimuli. Also, such description is prerequisite to the subsequent analysis of the role of verbal mediating responses and stimuli in reversal and nonreversal shifts.

With reversal shifts the values or combinations of values to which differential responses are learned remain the same, but the responses to values or combinations of values are interchanged. In Figure 1, for example, $R_{x'_1}$ might be shifted from $S_{x_1y_1}$ and $S_{x_1y_2}$ to $S_{x_2y_1}$ and $S_{x_2y_2}$; and $R_{x'_2}$ would become the reinforced response to $S_{x_1y_1}$ and $S_{x_1y_2}$ instead of to $S_{x_2y_1}$ and $S_{x_2y_2}$. Specifically, the response to red-small and red-large would be shifted to blue-small and blue-large, and the response to blue-small and blue-large would be made to red-small and red-large.

A complete nonreversal shift entails a change from differential pairings of responses with combinations of values along one or more dimensions to differential pairings of those responses with combinations of values along one or more entirely different dimensions. Thus, the pattern of relationships in Figure 1 might be changed from responding in terms of x_1 and x_2 along X, disregarding y_1 and y_2 along Y, to responding differentially to y_1 and y_2, disregarding x_1 and x_2. Only the relationships of the two responses to the initiating stimuli and not the responses themselves are changed. The relationship between $S_{x_1y_1}$ (red-small) and $R_{x'_1}$ would remain the same but that response would be changed from $S_{x_1y_2}$ (red-large) to $S_{x_2y_1}$ (blue-small). The relationship between $S_{x_2y_2}$ (blue-large) and $R_{x'_2}$ would remain the same but that response would be changed from $S_{x_2y_1}$ (blue-small) to $S_{x_1y_2}$ (red-large).

New terminating responses can be introduced. Should the old and the new responses have the same topography and, because of the time limitations imposed by the task, be prohibited from occurring in sequence, the old responses must be inhibited for the new responses to occur. Such a state of affairs has been described as a condition, if not the optimum condition, for *negative transfer*. What results is simply a shift from one one-stage paradigm to another one-stage paradigm. But if the old and new responses do not interfere with each other (have separate topographies or can occur in sequence), the old responses may not drop out but instead constitute relatively stable links—mediating responses and stimuli—between initiating stimuli and the new terminating responses. Thus, a two-stage paradigm would have emerged. This is, of course, the sequence of events which has been presumed in investigations of the effect of verbal pretraining on subsequent conceptual sorting and naming (e.g., Fenn & Goss, 1957).

Despite the usefulness and greater simplicity of one-stage paradigms, there are considerations which suggest that such paradigms are less adequate than two-stage paradigms for explanation and prediction of the conceptual behavior of verbal humans in many concept formation tasks and even, perhaps, of some of the conceptual behaviors of infrahuman organisms and nonverbal humans. These considerations include: (*a*) observations of positive transfer from verbal pretraining to subsequent conceptual sorting or naming and of facilitation due to instructions or instruction induced sets (Carey & Goss, 1957; Fenn & Goss, 1957; Gelfand, 1958; Goss & Moylan, 1958; Hunter & Ranken, 1956; Lacey & Goss, 1959), (*b*) the relatively greater ease of reversal than of nonreversal shifts for human adults (Buss, 1956; Gormazano & Grant, 1958; Harrow & Friedman, 1958; Kendler & D'Amato, 1955; Kendler & Mayzner, 1956) and for children who are fast learners (Kendler & Kendler, 1959) in contrast to the superiority of nonreversal shifts for animals (Kelleher, 1956) and for children who are slow learners (Kendler & Kendler, 1959), and (*c*) verbal humans' reports of the occurrence and use of names for dimensions and values of stimuli in the conceptual sorting of stimuli (e.g., Lacey & Goss, 1959). An additional consideration rests primarily on the results of studies employing the third type of sets of stimuli (e.g., Reed, 1946). Without the postulation of common verbal or other responses to subsets of stimuli whose members are highly dissimilar physically, generalization of a common terminating response from one stimulus of a subset to other stimuli of the subset would be precluded. Each of the associations between initiating stimuli and terminating responses would have to be strengthened separately, with a consequent increase in difficulty of mastering the task.

Two-stage paradigms. Shown in Figure 2 are some of the possible stimulus-response relationships in a two-stage expansion of the one-stage

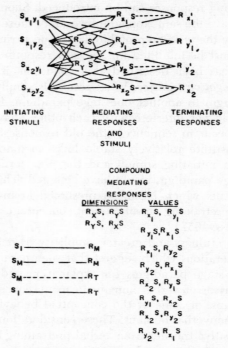

Fig. 2. Two-stage paradigm of some of the relationships possible between initiating stimuli and mediating responses, between mediating stimuli and mediating responses, between mediating stimuli and terminating responses, and between initiating stimuli and terminating responses. (In order to simplify the possible relationships of the diagram, relationships involving compound mediating responses for dimensions and compound mediating responses for values along dimensions are listed separately. The mediating responses might be differential with respect to x_1, x_2 along the X dimension or to y_1, y_2 along the Y dimension which is also the case for the terminating responses.)

paradigm presented in Figure 1. The four subsets of these relationships which should be distinguished are those: between initiating stimuli and mediating responses; between mediating stimuli and mediating responses or, more simply, between mediating responses; between mediating stimuli and terminating responses; and between initiating stimuli and terminating responses.

Within the first of these subsets of relationships, variations in the strength of two subpatterns of relationships between initiating stimuli and mediating responses may have somewhat different effects on conceptual behaviors. The first subpattern represents relationships in which responses of naming the dimensions occur. These are the associations between the initiating stimuli and R_X, R_Y. The second subpattern represents responses of naming the specific values along the dimensions. The responses of these associations are R_{x_1} for x_1; R_{x_2} for x_2; R_{y_1} for y_1; and R_{y_2} for y_2.

When the relationships between mediating stimuli and mediating responses are added, variations in the strengths of three more subpatterns of relationships can be distinguished. The first of these subpatterns is sequences of responses of naming the dimensions. These appear in the lower half of Figure 2 under "Dimensions" as $R_X S$, $R_Y S$ and $R_Y S$, $R_X S$. The second subpattern is sequences of responses of naming values along dimensions. The eight sequences of combinations and orders of two of such responses are shown in the lower half of Figure 2 under "Values." The third of these subpatterns is sequences of responses of naming both dimensions and values along dimensions. For example, combining one of the two responses of naming a dimension with one of the four responses of naming a value would generate 16 permutations of a particular dimension response with a particular value response.

Variation in the strength of each of these five subpatterns of relationships between initiating stimuli and mediating responses might have somewhat different effects on the direction and degree of: extralist response interference with both mediating responses and terminating responses, trial-to-trial variability of the stimulus patterns immediately prior to the terminating responses, response-mediated similarity, and response-mediated dissimilarity. In turn, these conditions should influence direction and degree of transfer to acquisition of associations between initiating stimuli and terminating responses. Table 1 summarizes assumptions about the effects of each of the first four subpatterns on extralist response interference, trial-to-trial variability of stimulus patterns, response-mediated similarity, and response-mediated dissimilarity. Table 1 also indicates whether these four consequences of each of the four subpatterns considered separately are expected to be facilitative $(+)$, inhibitory $(-)$, or neutral with respect to the formation of particular concepts. At present there is no way of combining the separate presumed facilitative, inhibitory, or neutral effects into a net facilitative, inhibitory, or neutral effect.

Except where precluded by prior training in the experimental situation, by selection on the basis of associations to the same or similar sets of initiating stimuli, or by instructions, each of these four subpatterns might occur both within trials and in successive trials during a good part of the course of acquiring associations between the initiating stimuli and the terminating responses. Their relative strengths at any point in learning—and, therefore, their effects on acquisition of initiating stimulus-terminating response associations—will be contingent on factors which include the following: their initial relative strengths, the values or combinations of values along one or more dimensions to which the differential terminating responses are being strengthened, time permitted to make the terminating responses, and degree of mastery of the terminating responses.

The fifth subpattern, which involves sequences of mediating responses of naming the dimension and of naming values along the dimension, may also influence acquisition of terminating responses. For example,

TABLE 1

SPECIFIC PATTERNS OF STIMULUS-RESPONSE RELATIONSHIPS

Specific Patterns Involving	Extralist Response Interference	Stimulus Variability	Response-Mediated Similarity	Response-Mediated Dissimilarity
Dimensions:				
R_X, R_Y	Reduce (+)	Reduce (+)	Increase (−)	Decrease (−)
$R_X R_Y$, $R_Y R_X$	Reduce (+)	Reduce (+)	Increase (−)	Decrease (−)
Values along single dimensions:				
R_{x_1}, R_{x_2}	Reduce (+)	Reduce (+)	Increase for $S_{x_1 y_1}$, $S_{x_1 y_2}$ and for $S_{x_2 y_1}$, $S_{x_2 y_2}$ (+ for $R_{x'_1}$, $R_{x'_2}$ and − for $R_{y'_1}$, $R_{y'_2}$)	Increase for $S_{x_1 y_1}$, $S_{x_1 y_2}$ in relation to $S_{x_2 y_1}$, $S_{x_2 y_2}$ (+ for $R_{x'_1}$, $R_{x'_2}$ and − for $R_{y'_1}$, $R_{y'_2}$)
R_{y_1}, R_{y_2}	Reduce (+)	Reduce (+)	Increase for $S_{y_1 x_1}$, $S_{y_1 x_2}$ and for $S_{y_2 x_1}$, $S_{y_2 x_2}$ (+ for $R_{y'_1}$, $R_{y'_2}$ and − for $R_{x'_1}$, $R_{x'_2}$)	Increase for $S_{y_1 x_1}$, $S_{y_1 x_2}$ in relation to $S_{y_2 x_1}$, $S_{y_2 x_2}$ (+ for $R_{y'_1}$, $R_{y'_2}$ and − for $R_{x'_1}$, $R_{x'_2}$)
Combinations of values along dimensions:				
$R_{x_1} R_{y_1}$, $R_{y_1} R_{x_1}$, etc.	Reduce (+) to Increase (−)	Reduce (+) to Increase (−)	No differential effects among initiating stimuli	

Note.—The direction of these effects are shown along with whether they are expected to have facilitative (+) or inhibitory (−) consequences. In the case of responses to values along single dimensions, whether particular initiating stimulus-mediating response relationships are facilitative or inhibitory is contingent on the relationships between initiating stimuli and terminating responses which are to be acquired.

fairly strong bidirectional associations might exist or be established between $R_X S$ and R_{x_1}, R_{x_2}, and between $R_Y S$ and R_{y_1}, R_{y_2}. Should R_X be stronger than R_Y, R_{x_1} and R_{x_2} would occur and be available for mediating discriminative terminating responses to $S_{x_1 y_1}$, $S_{x_1 y_2}$ and to $S_{x_2 y_1}$, $S_{x_2 y_2}$ rather than to $S_{x_1 y_1}$, $S_{x_2 y_1}$ and $S_{x_1 y_2}$, $S_{x_2 y_2}$. Contingent on the relationships between initiating stimuli and terminating responses which were being differentially reinforced, facilitation or inhibition of these associations might be occasioned.

The remaining two subsets of relationships, those between mediating stimuli and terminating responses and those between initiating stimuli and terminating responses, are of primary importance here because of their presumed roles in reversal and nonreversal shifts. The upper diagram of Figure 3 shows the relationships among initiating stimuli, mediating responses and stimuli, and terminating responses which might exist at appreciable levels of strength upon attainment of differential responses to the x_1 and x_2 values along the X dimension. Should there be

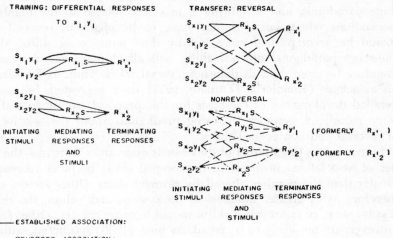

TRAINING: DIFFERENTIAL RESPONSES
TO x_1, y_1

TRANSFER: REVERSAL

NONREVERSAL

INITIATING STIMULI   MEDIATING RESPONSES AND STIMULI   TERMINATING RESPONSES

————ESTABLISHED ASSOCIATION:

——— ——REVERSED ASSOCIATION:

— — — —STRENGTHENED ASSOCIATION:

—·—·—·—WEAKENED ASSOCIATION:

Fig. 3 The paradigm for training shows conceptual responses, R_{x_1} and $R_{x'_2}$ to $S_{x_1y_1}$, $S_{x_1y_2}$ and $S_{x_2y_1}$, $S_{x_2y_2}$, respectively, after whose strengthening to some criterion level, reversal and nonreversal shifts are made. (As shown in the two paradigms for transfer, a reversal shift requires changes in only 6 associations, while a nonreversal shift may affect up to 14 associations. The terminating responses remain the same with respect to general topography and specific form—only the stimulus-response relationships into which they enter are altered. $R_{y'_1}$ and $R_{y'_2}$ of the nonreversal shift are the same responses as $R_{x'_1}$ and $R_{x'_2}$, respectively. However, the subscripts were changed to indicate that differences along the Y dimension, y_1, y_2, are the new bases for differential responses.)

introduction of differential reinforcement of R_{x_2} to $S_{x_1y_1}$, $S_{x_1y_2}$, and of R_{x_1} to $S_{x_2y_1}$, $S_{x_2y_2}$, to bring about a reversal shift, six associations might be changed: the four between the initiating stimuli and the terminating responses, and the two between the mediating stimuli and the terminating responses. In contrast, 14 associations might be affected by a nonreversal shift to the differential reinforcement of responses to the y_1 and y_2 values of Y. These are the four between initiating stimuli and R_{x_1}, R_{x_2}, which might be weakened; the four between those stimuli and R_{y_1}, R_{y_2}, which might be strengthened; the two between S_{x_1} and S_{x_2} and the terminating responses which might be extinguished while the two between S_{y_1} and S_{y_1} and those responses are established and strengthened; and are the two associations between initiating stimuli and terminating responses ($S_{x_1y_2}$ and $R_{x'_1}$; $S_{x_1y_1}$ and $R_{x'_2}$), which must be reversed.

If equal weights are assumed for the component associations of two-stage paradigms, and if shifting is inversely related to the number of associations which must or may have to be changed, reversal shifts should be accomplished more rapidly than nonreversal shifts. Within one-stage paradigms, reversal shifts will affect more associations and therefore be more difficult than nonreversal shifts. Thus, as Kendler and his associates (Kendler & D'Amato, 1955) have suggested, but without detailed development of the basis for this proposal, one-stage and two-stage paradigms generate opposing predictions about the relative ease of reversal and nonreversal shifts.

In general, as the number of dimensions and values increases, the number of associations involved in nonreversal shifts becomes increasingly greater than the number altered by reversal shifts. Other factors equal, therefore, with greater numbers of dimensions and values, the relative disadvantage of nonreversal shifts should become greater. Other factors, however, are not likely to be equal. As Buss (1956) has noted, with nonreversal shifts responses on the basis of the previously reinforced values along the no-longer-relevant dimension continue to be reinforced on 50% of the trials. The weakening of such differential responses will, therefore, be retarded, and will further contribute to the disadvantage of nonreversal shifts. But four additional conditions may serve to reduce the relative disadvantage of nonreversal shifts.

First, once some of the initiating stimuli begin to elicit the new mediating responses, when other initiating stimuli are presented these mediating responses should generalize extensively among those stimuli. One basis of such generalization would be the presence of stimuli common to each trial: i.e., those arising from the experimental situation, from postural and receptor-orienting responses, and from responses to instructions other than those aspects referring to more specific associations between initiating stimuli and mediating responses.

Second, because each of the values along the new dimension of the nonreversal shift is an element common to a subset of stimuli, the new mediating response for a subset of initiating stimuli should generalize among the members of the subset. Simultaneously, of course, the same two conditions should result in the generalization of inhibition of the relationships between initiating stimuli and the old mediating responses.

Third, though not included in the paradigms of Figure 3, the response R_X, which represents the response of naming the X dimension, might be replaced by the comparable response, R_Y, for the Y dimension. The increased frequencies of occurrence of stimuli produced by R_{y_1} and R_{y_2}, which are presumably already associated with R_Y, would be the bases of the initial evocations of R_Y. Because R_Y is only one response, however, its strengthening and generalization among the initiating stimuli should be even faster and more extensive than the strengthening and generalization of R_{y_1} and R_{y_2}. Therefore, R_Y should begin to occur first and, because of the pre-established associations between the stimuli it produced and R_{y_1} and R_{y_2}, their probabilities of occurrence relative to R_{x_1} and R_{x_2} should be increased markedly.

Fourth, successive reversals or nonreversal shifts should increase the probabilities of occurrence of mediating responses referring to a change in task. With successive reversals and nonreversal shifts, number of trials to learn the new concepts of each shift usually decreases. Some of this increasingly more rapid formation of new concepts is probably due in part to warm up or performance set in the form of familiarization with mode and rate of presentation of the initiating stimuli. Such familiarization should eliminate irrelevant competing responses as well as lead to greater stability of postural and receptor-orienting responses to thus assure more effective reception of the initiating stimuli and lower the variability of response-produced stimuli. Also, with experience, subjects should learn to recognize with greater confidence and greater accuracy that they have reached perfect or near perfect performance of discriminative responses to some subsets of stimuli. Consequently, any error then made would serve as a cue that the experimenter has shifted the concepts rather than that the concepts have not yet been learned. Further, subjects will be increasingly familiar with whether the shifts are reversal or nonreversal shifts and, if the latter, with how many dimensions have probably been shifted and even to what dimensions the shifts have probably been made. Thus, mediating responses of the form "He's changed the task" or "Something has changed" should come to control whole sets of further mediating responses which name dimensions and values along dimensions. These four conditions should reduce the net disadvantage of nonreversal to reversal shifts to margins which are much less than those suggested by simply counting the numbers of equally weighted associations which such shifts might affect.

COMMON ELEMENTS OR RELATIONS

One-stage paradigms. Figure 4 is a one-stage paradigm for concept formation with sets of stimuli, such as those constructed by Hull (1920), in which each subset requiring a common response consists of a common element accompanied by other features which vary unsystematically from instance to instance. Furthermore, the common elements are neither completely nor incompletely orthogonal combinations of values along one or more discernible physical or psychophysical dimensions. If common "relations" among the parts of complex forms are regarded as separable from the features which vary among instances exemplifying the same relation, Smoke's (1932) set of initiating stimuli and other sets that resemble his can also be represented by this paradigm.

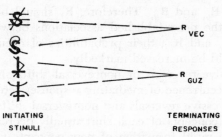

INITIATING   TERMINATING
STIMULI   RESPONSES

FIG. 4. One-stage paradigm of relationships between nonsense syllable
terminating responses and initiating stimuli which consist of two different
common elements each of which is accompanied by features which differ
from figure to figure.

Two-stage paradigms. The two-stage paradigm for the second type
of initiating stimuli is shown in Figure 5. The letters or word subscripts
of the mediating responses are possible specific pre-established mediating responses to the indicated initiating stimuli. Worth noting, because of their predictive consequences, are three major differences between this paradigm and the two-stage paradigm for sets of stimuli
composed of combinations of values along dimensions shown in Figure 2.

First, no responses of naming the component dimensions are present.
However, should the common elements of two or more subsets be at the
same spatial position, responses of orienting-toward and naming that
position might occur and be strengthened. Although such responses and
the stimuli they produce would be nondifferential with respect to the
relationships between initiating stimuli and terminating responses, their
occurrence might reduce extralist intrusions and stimulus variabilty as
well as assure more frequent reception of the elements which distinguish
one subset of figures from another.

Second, both the common element of members of a subset and the variable features of those members are likely to be made up of a fairly large
number of discriminable features, each of which elicits naming responses.
If the common element or relation which defines a particular subset of
stimuli does elicit some response which is the same for all members of
the subset, that response to each member is likely to have considerable
competition from the responses to other parts of the common element as
well as from reponses to the variable features of each member. Such responses and the further responses which they may evoke may interfere,
not only with any common mediating response to all stimuli of a subset,
but also with the terminating response for that subset. Further, few, if
any, pre-established stable patterns of associations among mediating re-

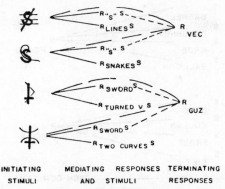

Fig. 5. Two-stage paradigm of the relationships possible between initiating stimuli, which consist of two different common elements and variable features, and both mediating and terminating responses and also between mediating stimuli and terminating responses.

sponses might exist. Such conditions should also foster high trial-to-trial stimulus variability.

Third, the variable features of stimuli with a given common element or relation may have little or no physical similarity to those features of the other subsets of stimuli with common elements. And, as already suggested, the naming responses evoked by one subset may have little overlap with those evoked by the other subsets. While reversal shifts could be instituted, such characteristics of the stimuli would severely limit or obviate nonreversal shifts.

ELICITATION OF COMMON RESPONSES

One-stage paradigms. The third kind of stimuli are those whose subsets are distinguished from each other on the basis of their members' elicitation of some common response that differs from the common responses defining each of the other subsets. Figure 6 is a one-stage paradigm and Figure 7 is a two-stage paradigm of the stimulus-response relationships presumed to be involved in the formation of concepts with such stimuli.

In the one-stage paradigm, increased frequency of arousal of each one of the common terminating responses by the stimuli of the subset is viewed as strengthening of the concept. The stronger the initial associations between the stimuli of subsets and their terminating response, and the higher the variance of those associations, the more rapid the formation of concepts (Freedman & Mednick, 1958; Underwood & Richardson, 1956). The limiting case of the formation of such concepts is

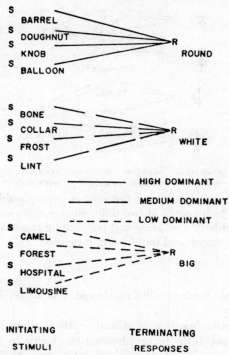

Fig. 6. One-stage paradigm of relationships between subsets of initiating stimuli each of which is defined by elicitation of a common terminating response by the stimuli. (The words used are from Underwood and Richardson's—1956—first list and are of three levels of dominance with respect to their elicitation of the terminating responses.)

the acquisition, from zero levels of initial strength, of common responses which have each been assigned to a different subset of physically dissimilar stimuli.

Two-stage paradigms. The mediating response of the two-stage paradigm (Figure 7) are those which define each of the subsets of initiating stimuli. In general, though not necessarily, the associations between initiating stimuli and terminating responses would be at zero levels initially, as would those between mediating stimuli and those responses. To the degree that each stimulus of a subset elicits the common mediating response, there will be a response-mediated increase in the similarity of those largely dissimilar stimuli; and, once the mediating stimulus is associated with the terminating response, acquisition of the concept should be facilitated by response-mediated generalization. Griffith and Spitz (1958) and Griffith, Spitz, and Lipman (1959) obtained direct

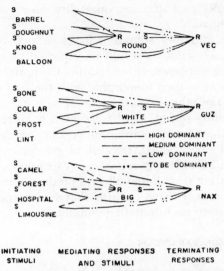

INITIATING   MEDIATING RESPONSES   TERMINATING
STIMULI   AND STIMULI   RESPONSES

FIG. 7. Two-stage paradigm of relationships possible between subsets of initiating stimuli defined by the elicitation of common responses which now function as mediating responses and stimuli in the acquisition of new associations between each of the subsets of initiating stimuli and their common nonsense syllable terminating responses. (The mediating responses should increase the similarity of stimuli within subsets and decrease the similarity of stimuli of each subset to those of the other subsets.)

relationships between correct abstractions made by normal and mentally retarded children and number of words defined by the same possible common abstractions. From these relationships they inferred that the common definition mediated the common abstractions.

The presence of different mediating response-produced stimuli, each associated with a different terminating response, might also increase the response-mediated dissimilarity and discrimination of stimuli which are members of different subsets (Fenn & Goss, 1957). Such an increase would counteract any generalization of terminating responses among subsets due to fortuitous physical resemblances among stimuli belonging to different response-defined subsets.

The relationships between initiating stimuli and terminating responses which are to be strengthened need not be isomorphic with the relationships between initiating stimuli and mediating responses. With increasing departures from isomorphism, the acquisition of terminating responses might be retarded, possibly to a degree sufficient to produce some negative transfer. Because the mediating responses might also reduce extralist response interference and stimulus variability, however, the net transfer might still be positive.

If each of the initiating stimuli belongs to two or more response-defined subsets, each stimulus would be expected to evoke two or more different mediating responses, at least during the initial trials. Unless each terminating response is then isomorphic with the two or more responses defining each of the other combinations of subsets, multiple mediating responses to initiating stimuli can be expected to increase generalization among subsets; thus some retardation of the learning of terminating responses would be occasioned. Because of greater trial-to-trial variability in stimulation preceding terminating responses, multiple mediating responses to initiating stimuli may always produce some retardation relative to the maximum positive transfer that is achievable with a single mediating response to each initiating stimulus.

USE OF TWO-STAGE PARADIGMS

Each of the preceding two-stage paradigms represents a different general case of relationships among the particular type of sets of initiating stimuli, mediating responses and stimuli, and terminating responses. The members of each of these types of sets of initiating stimuli may differ with respect to their complexity, their similarity and other properties, their number, and their probabilities of occurrence (Goss, 1955). Thus, it should be obvious that each particular concept formation task and its attendant conditions requires detailed analysis in terms of presumed stimulus-response elements and initial relationships among these elements, and also in terms of the changes in those elements and relationships which are expected to occur. The nature and strengths of both initial and changed relationships should be expressed as completely and precisely as possible. Association techniques or training controlled by the experimenter are the means of specifying the strengths of initial relationships. It should also be remembered that—except when isolated and controlled—changes in many or all of the stimulus-response relationships present probably occur, if not simultaneously, within rather small blocks of trials.

Finally, some subjects who have formed concepts correctly may not provide verbal reports of the bases for their conceptual behaviors which correspond to experimenters' specifications of the bases for forming particular concepts. When verbal mediating responses do not occur, or occur only partially, sporadically, or during the earlier phases of concept formation, appropriate verbal reports would not be expected. Should the words which constitute subjects' mediating responses differ from the labels preferred by experimenters, subjects' reports might be considered wrong or incomplete. Further, during the course of acquisition the sets of verbal mediating responses may have changed. Should subjects have failed to distinguish such changes or to indicate when they took place, their reports would seem inaccurate and confused. In addition, if subjects described the terminating responses or both mediating and terminating responses as bases for their conceptual behaviors, while experimenters' specifications were only in terms of verbal mediating responses, subjects' verbal reports would seem unsatisfactory. This would also be the case were the subjects' mediating responses nonverbal.

Differences between the labels used by subjects and those preferred by experimenters can only be determined by careful, detailed analyses of the labeling habits of subjects from a given population. Confusions between mediating and terminating responses can be minimized by ascertaining the temporal sequences of subjects' responses. Only by careful observation of locomotor-manipulative responses (and even this may be inadequate) will it be possible to determine the presence of nonverbal mediating responses.

Place of "Abstract Set or Attitude," "Hypotheses," and "Strategies" in the Framework of This Analysis

"Abstract set or attitude" (Goldstein & Scheerer, 1941; Hanfmann & Kasinin, 1942), "hypotheses" (Woodworth, 1958), and "strategies" (Bruner, Goodnow, & Austin, 1956) are terms frequently used to label some aspects of the behavior involved in acquiring concepts as well as to explain success or failure in this process. Unfortunately, these notions have certain features that limit both their experimental usefulness and their explanatory power. In general, their presence or absence is ordinarily determined on the basis of characteristics of the conceptual behaviors observed. Thus, they are post hoc descriptions which usually cannot be used predictively. Often, too, the notions are treated as primary or sole explanations of conceptual behavior when, in fact, other factors—such as types of sets of initiating stimuli, specific attributes of each type of stimuli, and amount and conditions of practice—appear to be of equal or greater importance. And, on the whole, the relationship of these terms to more general theories of behavior is tenuous at best.

In the face of such shortcomings, one course for stimulus-response analysis of concept formation consists of ignoring the terms entirely. Another course, followed here, is to attempt to assimilate what is meaningful and useful about the terms within the rather rigorous framework that this paper has presented. More specifically, it is suggested that the most meaningful and useful aspects of such notions as abstract set or attitude, hypotheses, and strategies are in part already present in this analysis, and that what is valuable but not present requires only certain translations in order to be assimilated. These aspects are considered below under the following headings: verbal mediating responses and stimuli, strengths of reactions to occurrences and extent of reversal or nonreversal shifts, sequences in which verbal mediating responses occur on single and successive trials, sequences of receptor-orienting responses, and prior habits and persistence of covert or overt verbalization and rehearsal.

VERBAL MEDIATING RESPONSES AND STIMULI

Following Fenn and Goss (1957), perhaps the simplest as well as the most common meaning of abstract set or attitude and hypotheses in concept formation is, conceived narrowly, the occurrence of verbal mediating responses and stimuli. Conceived more broadly, this meaning subsumes the largely pre-experimentally established patterns of relationships: (a) between initiating stimuli and mediating responses, where the latter are names for dimensions and values as well as for common elements or variable features, or where they are common responses or meanings that define subsets of initiating stimuli; (b) between such mediating responses and other mediating responses; and (c) between such mediating responses and terminating responses. The first part of this section on paradigms was largely devoted to an analysis of the role of these patterns of relationships in concept formation. The functional significance for concept formation of this meaning of abstract set or attitude and hypotheses has, therefore, already been considered.

REACTIONS TO SHIFTS

Also considered earlier were mediating responses that identify shifts in the task. Such responses, it was suggested, should increase in strength with successive reversal or nonreversal shifts and thus mediate changes in whole sets of further mediating responses which name dimensions and values along dimensions. These changes might be called shifts in hypotheses or strategies. And their occurrence could be taken as evidence of the presence of an abstract set or attitude.

SEQUENCES IN WHICH VERBAL MEDIATING RESPONSES OCCUR

Bruner, Goodnow, and Austin (1956, pp. 81–103, 126–147) have suggested that conditions of presentation of initiating stimuli influence trial-to-trial sequences of choice and "guess" responses. Thus, when subjects could select each successive initiating stimulus, the four sequences or strategies which were distinguished logically were simultaneous scanning, successive scanning, conservative focusing, and focus gambling. When the successive occurrences of initiating stimuli were controlled by the experimenter, they distinguished wholist (whole, focusing) and part-scanning (part) strategies or sequences. Under the condition of presentation in which subjects could select each successive initiating stimulus, the responses which were recorded were terminating responses, first in the form of a choice and then as a guess. Presumably these choices and guesses were preceded, most immediately, by mediating responses consisting of names for the combinations of values of the stimulus selected and the names of the consequent guess of the correct concept. Therefore, the sequences or strategies they distinguished, and which were found to occur to some degree in various subjects, could be regarded as providing some information about sequences of mediating responses through successive selections of stimuli. Under the condition of presentation in which the experimenter determined each successive initiating stimulus, each hypothesis written during the 10-second period following each initiating stimulus could be regarded as congruent with the just preceding mediating response. The sequences of such hypotheses, therefore, probably reflected trial-to-trial sequences of the last mediating response of each trial. No information about intratrial sequences was reported.

The two-stage paradigms of the first part of this section show each initiating stimulus as eliciting only one mediating response which is either the name for a dimension or value along a dimension, or a single combination of names for dimensions or values. Contingent on both the time subjects have to respond and on subjects' prior experiences with the same or similar stimuli, each initiating stimulus may elicit not one name or combination of names, but a sequence of names or combinations of names. For example, the subject might respond to a particular initiating stimulus with the sequence "red, small, color, size," in which "size" was the last response to occur prior to the appearance of the stimulus eliciting the terminating response to be conditioned to the initiating stimulus. Because of the shorter time interval, the terminating response might be more strongly conditioned to stimuli produced by size than to stimuli produced by the earlier mediating responses. More generally, should terminating responses be most strongly conditioned to stimuli produced by mediating responses which occurred just prior to elicitation of the terminating responses, the sequences with which mediating responses occur and whether those responses are names of values or of dimensions might have marked effects on concept formation.

Whether the effects are facilitative or inhibitory will be contingent on particular conditions. Thus, were size the relevant dimension and large and small the two values along that dimension, the sequence "color, red (or blue), size, large (or small)" should produce greater facilitation than the sequence "size, large (or small), color, red (or blue)." Similarly, sequences in which the last mediating responses were names for common elements of the initiating stimuli rather than names for their variable features should facilitate acquisition of different terminating responses to each subset of initiating stimuli with common features. Inhibitory consequences would be predicted for sequences ending with mediating responses which were names for variable features rather than for common elements. Also, occurrence of the common response to a subset of initiating word stimuli, after more specific associations to those words rather than before such associations, should facilitate; the opposite sequence should inhibit.

A further consideration would be whether the same sequence or different sequences of mediating responses occurred on each presentation of each initiating stimulus or of each member of particular subsets of initiating stimuli. With the sequence, "color, red (or blue), size, large (or small)," for example, constancy of the sequence should be most facilitative, were size the relevant dimension, and most inhibitory, were color the relevant dimension. A reduction in the percentage of times "size, large (or small)" occurred last, and a concomitant increase in the percentage of times "color, red (or blue)" occurred last, should be relatively less facilitative or less inhibitory in the formation of size or color concepts, respectively.

Modes of systematic variation of the components of sequences and of the order in which the components occur can be learned. Therefore, subjects can be expected to differ in the degree to which they have learned to vary the nature and sequences of mediating responses through successive trials. As a result subjects will not only differ with respect to the abstract set or attitude, hypotheses, and strategies with which they began but also with respect to those which are present through successive trials. Whether particular sequences or ways of varying such sequences are facilitative or inhibitory will be contingent on the particular concepts to be formed.

SEQUENCES OF RECEPTOR-ORIENTING RESPONSES

Receptor-orienting responses and their consequences may sometimes be functionally equivalent to mediating responses and stimuli (Goss, 1955). For this reason, abstract set or attitude, hypotheses, or strategies may also be conceived as sequences of receptor-orienting responses.

When initiating stimuli which are relatively small in size are presented at the same place, one at a time, receptor-orienting responses may be of little importance. Possible exceptions are initiating stimuli composed of combinations of common elements or relations and variable features for which the common element or relation of all members of a particular subset have the same location. Should there be some favored point of initial fixation for individual subjects, or for groups of subjects, whether the common element or relation of a particular subset was at that location or at other locations might influence acquisition of the concepts.

Simultaneous presentation of all initiating stimuli or groups thereof, however, might increase the importance of sequences of receptor-orienting responses. Both arrangement of initiating stimuli on the display, and the subjects' pre-experimental and subsequent experimental experiences, should determine the particular sequence of receptor-orienting responses on a given trial. The initial and subsequent fixation points might maximize focusing on successive stimuli whose combinations of values and changes in those combinations were optimal for the formation of particular concepts. If so, such sequences of receptor-orienting responses should facilitate concept formation. For other arrangements of initiating stimuli the same sequences might be inhibitory.

PRIOR HABITS OF VERBALIZATION, REHEARSAL, AND PERSISTENCE THEREIN

Included in Dollard and Miller's (1950, pp. 116–119) set of factors in "social training in the use of higher mental processes" is "training to stop and think." Adolescent and adult subjects explicitly instructed to use verbal mediating responses may differ little, if at all, in the degree to which such responses are activated. However, without such explicit instructions—and therefore largely dependent on the subjects' past experiences with similar tasks—they may or may not stop and think: i.e., they may or may not make overt or covert verbal mediating responses prior to occurrences of terminating responses to the initiating stimuli. Furthermore, some subjects may rehearse such responses between trials while others may think of other things; the latter subjects may in other words, fail to attend to the task continuously. Finally, in the face of initial failures, some subjects may persist in stopping and thinking and in rehearsing while other subjects may temporarily or permanently stop both activities. Up through adolescence the strengths of such habits should be directly related to age. Awaiting detailed determination, however, are both the nature of the relationships of habits of verbalization and rehearsal to age and the effects of such habits on probabilities of occurrence of verbal mediating responses.

In summary, conceived analytically rather than simply as names for certain instructions or for certain changes in terminating responses, the notions of abstract set or attitude, hypotheses, and strategies apparently refer to one or more of the preceding classes of relationships among the stimuli and responses of concept formation tasks. Some of the classes of relationships include mediating responses and stimuli; those which do not can be expected to have indirect effects on relationships that do involve mediating responses and stimuli.

PRINCIPLES AND PREDICTIONS

Though referred to occasionally—and always assumed—in the preceding section, little direct attention has yet been given to the classes of variables and of general principles involving those variables which enter into explanations of the strengthening, generalization, and weakening of the stimulus-response associations entailed in the one- and two-stage paradigms that have been described. Of obvious relevance are the classes of principles that concern effects on associations or on performance of classes of variables such as: schedules of practice and reinforcement-punishment, the number and both absolute and relative strengths of conflicting responses, the number of stimuli associated with the same response and the strength of those associations, and the degree of similarity among initiating stimuli and among mediating stimuli. Setting limits to the operation of these classes of variables are the patterns of relationships among initiating stimuli, mediating responses and stimuli, and terminating responses and also conditions of stimulus presentation, such as whether initiating stimuli are presented simultaneously or successively (Bruner et al., 1956) and whether they are all positive, negative, or both positive and negative (Hovland, 1952; Hovland & Weiss, 1953).

It is not the purpose of this paper to make an exhaustive enumeration of the consequences predicted by the application of each class of potentially relevant variables and the principles involving them to the several paradigms or to the various patterns of relationships the paradigms contain. In order to show explicitly how such variables and principles may be profitably combined with the paradigms, however, this final section deals with certain aspects of predictions of the effects of three important classes of variables for which some data are available. These are: strength of associations between initiating stimuli and mediating responses; patterns of relationships among initiating stimuli, mediating responses and stimuli, and terminating responses; and similarity of initiating stimuli. In each case, pertinent experimental studies are described.[4]

---

[4] Not considered, however, are those studies of the relative effects of reversal and nonreversal shifts which were noted in the first part of the second section. Also ignored are studies (Bensberg, 1958; Carey & Goss, 1957; Fenn & Goss, 1957; Hunter & Ranken, 1956; Wickens & Eckstrand, 1954) which were primarily demonstrations of positive transfer from verbal pretraining to subsequent conceptual behaviors; these demonstrations served as bases for inferences about the functional significance of verbal mediating responses in conceptual behaviors. Several additional experiments (Attneave, 1957; Rhine & Silun, 1958; Shepard & Shaeffer, 1956; Sigel, 1953, 1954; Solley & Messick, 1957; Staats & Staats, 1957; Wulff & Stolurow, 1957) have been exluded because they did not involve either experimentally controlled verbal pretraining or conventional concept formation criterion tasks.

STRENGTHS OF ASSOCIATIONS BETWEEN INITIATING STIMULI AND MEDIAT-
ING RESPONSES

The strengths of associations between initiating stimuli and verbal
mediating responses will be determined by conditions of practice such as
the number and distribution of trials or degree of mastery of those relationships prior to undertaking transfer or criterion tasks. In general, any
condition of practice and reinforcement-punishment known to increase or
decrease the strengths of stimulus-response associations of multiunit tasks
are, through their effects on strengths of associations between initiating
stimuli and mediating responses, potential determinants of subsequent
performance on transfer or criterion tasks.

In Figures 2 and 7, the relationships between initiating stimuli and
mediating responses, and between the initiating stimuli in combination
with mediating stimuli and terminating responses, can be described as
isomorphic. Put another way, for each different mediating response to a
subset of initiating stimuli, there is one and only one terminating response, each of which is different from the terminating response paired
with any other mediating response. For such isomorphic patterns of relationships, it is predicted that rate of acquisition of associations between
initiating stimuli and terminating responses would be a direct function
of strengths of associations between initiating stimuli and mediating responses. Because of generalized responses (errors of generalization, confusions, intralist intrusions), trials to learn associations between initiating
stimuli and terminating responses should be related to trials in learning
associations between initiating stimuli and mediating responses by an
ogival function or by curves showing some slight initial negative transfer
rather than being negatively accelerated throughout (Goss, 1955).[5]

Pertinent to this prediction are two recent investigations (Goss & Moylan, 1958; Lacey & Goss, 1959) of the relationship between transfer to
conceptual behaviors and strengths of associations between initiating
stimuli and presumed verbal mediating responses. In both investigations,
the initiating stimuli were 16 blocks, each of which was tall or short, black
or white, in combination with top and bottom areas which were large or
small, square or circular. In the Goss and Moylan study, nonsense syllable
responses or familiar word responses were conditioned to subsets of tall-
large, tall-small, short-large, and short-small initiating stimuli. Lacey and
Goss used only nonsense syllable responses. The transfer task of both
studies was sorting by height-size, and in both the number of blocks
sorted by height-size was directly related to degree of mastery of associations between initiating stimuli and presumed mediating responses, as well

---

[5] Murdock (1958) argues that with appropriate allowance for generalization responses, the function is negatively accelerated throughout.

as to members of trials in learning those associations. Unfortunately the resultant curves were not adequate for more precise specification of functions relating direction and degree of transfer to degree of mastery of associations between initiating stimuli and mediating responses, or to trials in learning these associations.[6] As suggested elsewhere for paired-associates learning tasks (Goss, 1955), such specifications are further complicated by the likelihood that the functions are contingent on parameters such as patterns of relationships among initiating stimuli, mediating responses and stimuli, and terminating responses, as well as on the degree of similarity of initiating stimuli.

PATTERNS OF RELATIONSHIPS

Within two-stage paradigms, regardless of the type of sets of initiating stimuli, it is useful to distinguish four extreme patterns of relationships among subsets of initiating stimuli, mediating responses and stimuli, and terminating responses, because each pattern should result in somewhat different conceptual behaviors involving the terminating responses. Figure 8 shows these four patterns. In Patterns A and B, the relationships between mediating responses and subsets of initiating stimuli are isomorphic with those between terminating responses and subsets of initiating stimuli plus mediating stimuli. This isomorphism does not hold for Patterns C and D. Pattern C is characterized by a common mediating response to both subsets of initiating stimuli and by two terminating responses, one of which is to stimulus compounds consisting of stimuli from the first subset plus the mediating stimulus, and the other of which is to stimulus compounds consisting of stimuli from the second subset plus the mediating stimulus. Pattern D is characterized by a different mediating response to each subset of initiating stimuli, and by a common terminating response both to compounds consisting of the stimuli in the first subset plus the stimulus produced by the mediating response to those stimuli, and to compounds consisting of the stimuli in the second subset plus the stimulus produced by the mediating response to those stimuli.

For concept formation tasks involving the relationships of Patterns A and B, prior acquisition of the associations between subsets of initiating stimuli and a common mediating response should facilitate acquisition of associations between the subsets of initiating stimuli and a common terminating response; prior acquisition of different mediating responses should facilitate acquisition of associations between initiating stimuli subsets and

---

[6] An alternative suggestion (Lacey & Goss, 1959) is that greater mastery of experimentally established associations between initiating stimuli and nonsense syllable responses increases the likelihood of arousal of pre-experimentally established associations between initiating stimuli and names for dimensions and values along dimensions. Such names might then serve as the actual verbal mediating responses of the transfer or criterion task.

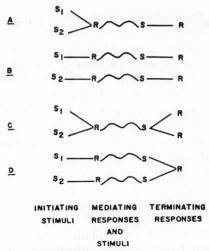

<table>
<tr><td>INITIATING</td><td>MEDIATING</td><td>TERMINATING</td></tr>
<tr><td>STIMULI</td><td>RESPONSES</td><td>RESPONSES</td></tr>
<tr><td></td><td>AND</td><td></td></tr>
<tr><td></td><td>STIMULI</td><td></td></tr>
</table>

FIG. 8. Four possible extreme patterns of relationships among subsets of initiating stimuli, mediating responses and stimuli, and terminating responses.

different terminating responses. Greater response-mediated similarity and generalization is the basis for the prediction for Pattern A, and greater response-mediated dissimilarity and discrimination is the basis for the prediction for Pattern B.

For Pattern C, in contrast, the greater similarity of the subsets of initiating stimuli (based on the presence of a common mediating stimulus) should retard acquisition of a different terminating response to each subset. For Pattern D, greater dissimilarity of the subsets of initiating stimuli (based on the presence of a different mediating stimulus for the stimuli of each subset) should slow the learning of a common terminating response to each subset.

Lacey (1959) tested each of these predictions. His stimuli were eight line drawings of faces or houses, each of which was printed on pink, light blue, light yellow, and light green paper. Eight to 11 year old children first learned either a common or different nonsense syllable mediating response to two subsets of initiating stimuli. The transfer or criterion task was acquisition of a new set of nonsense syllable responses as either a common or different terminating response to those same subsets of initiating stimuli. Thus the relationships of terminating responses to initiating stimuli and to mediating responses and stimuli were those of Patterns A, B, C, or D.

Measured against the performance of control groups, whose prior training controlled for facilitation due to warm up and receptor-orienting responses, positive transfer was obtained with Patterns A and B and negative transfer occurred with Patterns C and D. Therefore, as predicted, the pattern of relationships among subsets of initiating stimuli, mediating responses and stimuli, and terminating responses determined whether positive or negative transfer occurred. Lacey's results also suggested that Pattern B might produce greater relative positive transfer, though no greater absolute positive transfer, than Pattern A. Patterns C and D, however, did not seem to differ with respect to either relative or absolute amounts of negative transfer.

SIMILARITY OF INITITIATING STIMULI

For Patterns A, B, C, and D, similarity of sets of initiating stimuli might influence amount and perhaps direction of transfer from verbal pretraining to subsequent conceptual behaviors. For Patterns A and D, disregarding mediating responses and stimuli, similarity within and between subsets of initiating stimuli should be directly related to ease of learning associations between those stimuli and a common terminating response. Patterns B and C involve acquisition of discriminative terminating responses to initiating stimuli. Rate of acquisition of those associations should be directly related to similarity of stimuli within subsets of initiating stimuli and inversely related to similarity between those subsets. When verbal mediating responses and stimuli are considered, similarity of initiating stimuli might modify the expected positive transfer with Patterns A and B and the expected negative transfer with Patterns C and D.

Present data and theory do not warrant attempts to develop more exact predictions of the influence of similarity of initiating stimuli on direction and amount of transfer. However, since the second variable of Lacey's (1959) experiment was two degrees of similarity of the members of the sets of face and house stimuli, some pertinent data are available.

For Patterns A and D together, disregarding verbal mediating responses and stimuli, similarity was directly related to mastery of associations between initiating stimuli and terminating responses; inverse relationships were obtained with Patterns B and C together. For Pattern A, while absolute amount of positive transfer was directly related to similarity, an inverse relationship was obtained for relative amount of transfer. For Pattern D, both absolute and relative amounts of positive transfer were inversely related to similarity. For Patterns B and C, both absolute and relative amounts of positive transfer were directly related to similarity. However, since most of the relationships for each pattern separately were not statistically significant, at best they provide hypotheses for replicatory investigations.

In general, for concept formation tasks involving prior strengthening of presumed mediating responses, the findings presently available suggest that conceptual behaviors involving terminating responses are influenced by: strengths of associations between initiating stimuli and mediating responses; patterns of relationships among initiating stimuli, mediating responses and stimuli, and terminating responses; and similarity of initiating stimuli. Furthermore, these findings are reasonably consistent with predictions based on two-stage paradigms in combination with principles of the role of these and other classes of variables in the strengthening, generalization, and weakening of stimulus-response associations.

Summary

The purpose of this paper was to analyze the role of verbal mediating responses in concept formation. First summarized was the historical development of stimulus-response analyses of conceptual behaviors which have emphasized the role of mediating responses and stimuli, particularly verbal mediating responses. The influence of Max Meyer and Watson on the behavioristic analyses of the 1920s was noted. Although Birge, Miller and Dollard, Cofer and Foley, and Gibson furthered such analyses in the early 1940s, only the more detailed recent analyses of Baum, Osgood, Mandler, Goss, Kendler, and others have led to hypotheses which have been tested experimentally.

The first section provided a general specification of concept formation tasks and described the relationship between concept formation and conventional paired-associates tasks. The second section first described the structures and some explanatory consequences of one-stage and two-stage paradigms of conceptual behaviors with each of three types of sets of initiating stimuli. Some precautions in the use of these paradigms were then noted, and assimilation within the present analysis of the notions of abstract set or attitude, hypotheses and strategies was proposed. The third section showed the complementary relationship between the one-stage and two-stage paradigms and classes of variables and principles involving those variables which enter into explanations of the strengthening, generalization, and weakening of the component stimulus-response associations. Two-stage paradigms in combination with some of these principles were then used to generate sample predictions of effects on concept formation of: strengths of relationships between initiating stimuli and mediating responses; some patterns of relationships among initiating stimuli, mediating responses and stimuli, and terminating responses; and relative similarity of initiating stimuli.

REFERENCES

ATTNEAVE, F. Transfer of experience with a class-schema to identification-learning of patterns and shapes. *J. exp. Psychol.*, 1957, 54, 81–88.

BAUM, M. H. A study in concept attainment and verbal learning. Unpublished PhD dissertation, Yale University, 1951.

BENSBERG, G. J., JR. Concept learning in mental defectives as a function of appropriate and inappropriate "attention sets." *J. educ. Psychol.*, 1958, 49, 137–143.

BIRGE, J. S. The role of verbal responses in transfer. Unpublished PhD dissertation. Yale University, 1941.

BRUNER, J. S., GOODNOW, J. J., & AUSTIN, G. A. *A study of thinking*. New York: Wiley, 1956.

BUSS, A. H. Reversal and nonreversal shifts in concept formation with partial reinforcement eliminated. *J. exp. Psychol.*, 1956, 52, 162–166.

CAREY, J. E., & GOSS, A. E. The role of verbal labeling in the conceptual sorting behavior of children. *J. genet. Psychol.*, 1957, 90, 69–74.

COFER, C. N., & FOLEY, J. P., JR. Mediated generalizations and the interpretation of verbal behavior: I. Prolegomena. *Psychol. Rev.*, 1942, 49, 513–540.

DASHIELL, J. F. *Fundamentals of objective psychology.* Boston: Houghton Mifflin, 1928.

DOLLARD, J., & MILLER, N. E. *Personality and psychotherapy.* New York: McGraw-Hill, 1950.

ELKONIN, D. B. The physiology of higher nervous activity and child psychology. In B. Simon (Ed.) *Psychology in the Soviet Union.* Stanford: Stanford Univer. Press, 1957.

FEDERER, W. T. *Experimental design: Theory and application.* New York: Macmillan, 1955.

FENN, J. D., & GOSS, A. E. The role of mediating verbal responses in the conceptual sorting behavior of normals and schizophrenics. *J. genet. Psychol.*, 1957, 90, 59–67.

FREEDMAN, J. L., & MEDNICK, S. A. Ease of attainment of concepts as a function of response dominance variance. *J. exp. Psychol.*, 1958, 55, 463–466.

GELFAND, S. Effects of prior associations and task complexity upon the identification of concepts. *Psychol. Rep.*, 1958, 4, 568–574.

GIBSON, E. J. A systematic application of the concepts of generalization and differentiation to verbal learning. *Psychol. Rev.*, 1940, 47, 196–229.

GOLDSTEIN, K., & SCHEERER, M. Abstract and concrete behavior: An experimental study with special tests. *Psychol. Monogr.*, 1941, 53(2, Whole No. 239).

GORMEZANO, I., & GRANT, D. A. Progressive ambiguity in the attainment of concepts on the Wisconsin Card Sorting Test. *J. exp. Psychol.*, 1958, 55, 621–627.

GOSS, A. E. A stimulus-response analysis of the interaction of cue-producing and instrumental responses. *Psychol. Rev.*, 1955, 62, 20–31.

GOSS, A. E. University of Massachusetts conference on problem solving. Amherst, Massachusetts, June 19–21, 1956.

GOSS, A. E., & GREENFELD, N. Transfer to a motor task as influenced by conditions and degree of prior discrimination training. *J. exp. Psychol.*, 1958, 55, 258–269.

GOSS, A. E., & MOYLAN, M. C. Conceptual block-sorting as a function of type and degree of mastery of discriminative verbal responses. *J. genet. Psychol.*, 1958, 93, 191–198.

GRAY, J. S. A behavioristic interpretation of concept formation. *Psychol. Rev.*, 1931, 38, 65–72.

GRIFFITH, B. C., & SPITZ, H. H. Some relationships between abstraction and word meaning in retarded adolescents. *Amer. J. ment. Defic.*, 1958, 63, 247–251.

GRIFFITH, B. C., SPITZ, H. H., & LIPMAN, R. S. Verbal mediation and concept formation in retarded and normal subjects. *J. exp. Psychol.*, 1959, 58, 247–251.

HANFMANN, E., & KASININ, J. Conceptual thinking in schizophrenia. *Nerv. ment. dis. Monogr.*, 1942, No. 67.

HARROW, M., & FRIEDMAN, G. B. Comparing reversal and nonreversal shifts in concept formation with partial reinforcement controlled. *J. exp. Psychol.*, 1958, 55, 592–598.

HEIDBREDER, E. The attainment of concepts: I. Terminology and methodology. *J. gen. Psychol.*, 1946, 35, 173–189. (a)

HEIDBREDER, E. The attainment of concepts: II. The problem. *J. gen. Psychol.*, 1946, 35, 191–223. (b)

HOVLAND, C. I. A "communication analysis" of concept learning. *Psychol. Rev.*, 1952, 59, 461–472.

HOVLAND, C. I., & WEISS, W. Transmission of information concerning concepts through positive and negative instances. *J. exp. Psychol.*, 1953, 45, 175–182.

HULL, C. L. Quantitative aspects of the evolution of concepts. *Psychol. Monogr.*, 1920, 28(1, Whole No. 123).

HUNTER, G. F., & RANKEN, H. B. Mediating effects of labeling on sorting behavior and judgments of similarity. Paper presented at Eastern Psychological Association, Atlantic City, March 1956.

KELLEHER, R. T. Discrimination learning as a function of reversal and nonreversal shifts. *J. exp. Psychol.*, 1956, 51, 379–384.

KENDLER, H. H., & D'AMATO, M. F. A comparison of reversal shifts and nonreversal shifts in human concept formation behavior. *J. exp. Psychol.*, 1955, 48, 165–174.

KENDLER, H. H., & KENDLER, T. S. Reversal and nonreversal shifts in kindergarten children. *J. exp. Psychol.*, 1959, 58, 56–60.

KENDLER, H. H., & MAYZNER, M. S., JR. Reversal and nonreversal shifts in card sorting tests with two and four categories. *J. exp. Psychol.*, 1956, 51, 244–248.

LACEY, H. Mediating verbal responses and stimulus similarity as factors in conceptual naming by school-age children. Unpublished PhD dissertation, University of Massachusetts, 1959.

LACEY, H., & GOSS, A. E. Conceptual block sorting as a function of number, pattern of assignment, and strength of labeling responses. *J. genet. Psychol.*, 1959, 94, 221–232.

LIUBLINSKAYA, A. A. Development of children's speech and thought. In B. Simon (Ed.), *Psychology in the Soviet Union*. Stanford: Stanford Univer. Press, 1957.

MANDLER, G. Response factors in human learning. *Psychol. Rev.*, 1954, 61, 235–244.

METZGER, R. A comparison between rote learning and concept formation. *J. exp. Psychol.*, 1958, 56, 226–231.

MEYER, M. F. *The fundamental laws of human behavior*. Boston: Gorham, 1911.

MILLER, N. E., & DOLLARD, J. *Social learning and imitation*. New Haven: Yale Univer. Press, 1941.

MURDOCK, B. B., JR. Intralist generalization in paired-associate learning. *Psychol. Rev.*, 1958, 65, 306–314.

OSGOOD, C. E. *Method and theory in experimental psychology*. New York: Oxford Univ. Press, 1953.

REED, H. B. Factors influencing the learning and retention of concepts: I. The influence of set. *J. exp. Psychol.*, 1946, 36, 71–87.

RHINE, R. J., & SILUN, B. A. Acquisition and change of a concept attitude as a function of consistency of reinforcement. *J. exp. Psychol.*, 1958, 55, 524–529.

RICHARDSON, J. The relationship of stimulus similarity and numbers of responses. *J. exp. Psychol.*, 1958, 56, 478–484.

SHEPARD, W. O., & SHAEFFER, M. The effect of concept knowledge on discrimination. *Child Develpm.*, 1956, 26, 173–178.

SIGEL, I. Developmental trends in the abstraction ability of children. *Child Develpm.*, 1953, 24, 131–144.

SIGEL, I. The dominance of meaning. *J. genet. Psychol.*, 1954, 85, 201–207.

SIMMONS, A. J., & GOSS, A. E. Animistic responses as a function of sentence contexts and instructions. *J. genet. Psychol.*, 1957, 91, 181–189.

SMOKE, K. L. An objective study of concept formation. *Psychol. Monogr.*, 1932, 42(4, Whole No. 191).

SOLLEY, C. M., & MESSICK, S. J. Probability, learning, the statistical structure of concepts, and the measurement of meaning. *Amer. J. Psychol.*, 1957, 70, 161–173.

SPENCE, K. W. The nature of discrimination learning in animals. *Psychol. Rev.*, 1936, 43, 427–449.

STAATS, C. K., & STAATS, A. W. Meaning established by classical conditioning. *J. exp. Psychol.*, 1957, 54, 74–80.

UNDERWOOD, B. J., & RICHARDSON, J. Verbal concept learning as a function of instructions and dominance level. *J. exp. Psychol.*, 1956, 51, 229–238.

WATSON, J. B. Is thinking merely the action of language mechanisms? Part V. *Brit. J. Psychol.*, 1920, 11, 87–104.

WEISS, A. P. *A theoretical basis of human behavior.* Columbus, Ohio: Adams, 1925.

WICKENS, D. D. Stimulus-response theory as applied to perception. In, *Kentucky symposium: Learning theory, personality theory, and clinical research.* New York: Wiley, 1954.

WICKENS, D. D., & ECKSTRAND, G. A. Transfer of perceptual set. *J. exp. Psychol.*, 1954, 47, 274–278.

WOODWORTH, R. S. *Dynamics of behavior.* New York: Holt, 1958.

WULFF, J. J., & STOLUROW, L. M. The role of class-descriptive cues in paired-associates learning. *J. exp. Psychol.*, 1957, 53, 199–206.

24. The Selection of Strategies in Cue Learning

Frank Restle

In a cue learning problem (discrimination learning, concept formation, and maze learning) the subject chooses one of two or more responses on each trial. The correctness of the response depends on some aspect of the situation at the time of response.

In this paper it is assumed that subjects have difficulty with cue learning problems to the degree that they tend to use strategies (habits, patterns of response) which conflict with the strategy intended by the

Reprinted by permission of the authors and the American Psychological Association from *Psychological Review*, 1962, 69, 329–343.

experimenter. It is often assumed that the subject must also associate correct responses with cues in the situation. However, in most cue learning experiments the subject is instructed or pretrained to make the desired responses before the cue learning process begins. Furthermore, the experimental situation constrains the subject to make exactly one of the available responses per trial. It seems reasonable to assume that cue learning is not so much a matter of the formation as of the selection of responses. The present theoretical discussion begins with a set of strategies and is concerned with the mechanisms by which the subject might select out those strategies intended, and consistently rewarded, by the experimenter.

The term "strategy" is employed in a sense related to the more common terms, "habit" and "hypothesis," to designate a particular pattern of responses to stimuli. Consider, for example, a rat being trained to jump to the larger of two white circles in a Lashley Jumping Stand. Some possible strategies include; jumping to the left side, jumping to the right side, jumping alternately left and right, jumping always to the side last reinforced, jumping to the side which last was punished, jumping in the direction the rat was placed down on the stand, jumping toward the circle with less (or more) acute curvature, jumping toward the side with more white area, jumping toward the side which reflects more total light, and so forth. Each such pattern of behavior, if it occurs in isolation for a sufficiently long sequence of trials, can be identified by the experimenter. It will be seen that there are ordinarily a large number and variety of possible strategies in a cue learning problem, and that a number of strategies may be perfectly confounded. In the example above, jumping to the circle with less acute curvature will always lead to the same result as jumping to the side which reflects more light, since these will both be jumps to the larger circle.

THREE MODELS OF THE SELECTION OF STRATEGIES

The general idea developed here is that the problem gives rise to a set of strategies. The subject uses these various strategies, which at first are selected at random, and attempts to select strategies which will consistently lead to correct responses. For simplicity the discussion is limited to problems in which there are at least some strategies which are always correct.

Let H be the set of strategies available to the subject at the beginning of the problem. Suppose that some subset C of these strategies are always correct, another subset W are always wrong, and the remainder, I, are sometimes correct and sometimes wrong. For simplicity of presentation, begin with a problem in which the strategies of I are correct and wrong, on successive trials, with independent probabilities all of which are ½, and restrict attention to the two-choice problem.

Presentation of the theory of this conventional discrimination learning problem will begin with a special case in which one strategy is used on each trial. Then an alternative theory will be proposed, in which the subject uses all strategies at once and attempts to narrow down to the correct one. Third, a model will be proposed in which the subject chooses a random sample of all strategies and attempts to narrow down to the correct strategies within his sample. These three models will be shown to be essentially equivalent, in a theorem which may be called the "indifference to sample size" theorem. Following proof of that theorem, some empirical implications of the theory will be derived and compared with relevant data.

ONE STRATEGY AT A TIME

On the first trial of the experiment, the subject selects a certain single strategy from H at random and makes the indicated response. If the response is correct, the same strategy is used on Trial 2. If it is again correct, it is used again on Trial 3, and so forth. If, on any trial, the response is incorrect, the subject returns his strategy to the set H and then chooses a strategy again at random. It is considered possible that the same strategy may be resampled, so that the sampling process is with replacement. Imagine that an error occurs on Trial 2. Then a new strategy is chosen and this strategy is used on Trial 3. If it is correct it is used again on Trial 4. If the response on Trial 3 is wrong, the subject again chooses an hypothesis at random for Trial 4.

Notice that if the subject chooses a correct strategy, he will make no more errors. The correct strategy leads to correct responses, and when the response is correct the subject does not change strategy. Thus, the learning process is terminated by the choice of a correct strategy.

Since sampling is with replacement, the probabilities of choosing a correct, a wrong, or an irrelevant strategy are constant from trial to trial. Let these three probabilities be c, w, and $i = 1 - c - w$.

At the beginning of training the subject chooses a strategy of one of the three types, which have probabilities c, w, and i. After each error he also chooses a strategy, with probabilities c, w, and i. Thus an error is an event which returns the subject to exactly the same condition (in terms of the probabilities of future events) with which he started—it resets the process and makes it begin over. Such an event is called a "recurrent event" (Feller, 1950). Since our experimental interest centers around errors and correct responses, we can limit attention to errors and thus to the theory of recurrent events.

Imagine that at some Trial n the subject makes an error. There is a certain probability f_1 that the next error occurs at Trial $n + 1$, a probability f_2 that the next error occurs at Trial $n + 2$, and in general a probability distribution f_j that the next error after Trial n occurs at Trial $n + j$. In a model of recurrent events like the present one, the distribution f_j is the same for all Trials n on which an error occurs, and is the same as the distribution of probabilities that the first error occurs on Trial 1, 2, etc.

The random process and all of its properties are specified by the distribution f_j. However, the analysis of the process from the distribution f_j will be postponed until two steps have been completed; first, calculation of the distribution f_j for the one-strategy-at-a-time model, and second, the formulation of two other models, very different in assumptions, which also lead to systems of recurrent events with the same distribution. When these steps are completed, the generality of the f distribution will be apparent, and derivations of properties of the process will be justified.

First, f_1 is the probability of an error immediately following another error. The second error can occur because a wrong strategy was chosen (with probability w) or because an irrelevant strategy was chosen and turned out to be wrong (with probability $\frac{1}{2}i$). These are mutually exclusive events and exhaust the possibilities, so that:

$$f_1 = w + \tfrac{1}{2}i.$$

An error occurring on the second trial after the last one, with a correct response intervening, cannot result from the selection of a wrong strategy for the wrong strategy would not lead to an intervening correct response. If the error does occur on the second trial we know that the strategy chosen was not correct. Hence it must be an irrelevant one which led first to a correct and then to a wrong response. In simple discrimination learning, the probability that an irrelevant strategy would lead to a correct and then a wrong response is $\frac{1}{2} \cdot \frac{1}{2} = (\frac{1}{2})^2$. The probability of choosing an irrelevant strategy which gives this sequence correct-wrong, is therefore:

$$f_2 = i(\tfrac{1}{2})^2$$

By the same reasoning, any value of f_j, $j > 2$, implies that an irrelevant strategy was chosen and then led to $j - 1$ correct responses followed by a wrong response. The probability of a string of exactly $j - 1$ correct responses each with probability $\frac{1}{2}$, followed by an error with probability $\frac{1}{2}$, is $(\frac{1}{2})^j$. Hence, for $j \geq 2$:

$$f_j = i(\tfrac{1}{2})^j$$

Summarizing the results we have the distribution:

$$f_1 = w + \tfrac{1}{2}i$$
$$f_j = i(\tfrac{1}{2})^j$$

for all $j \geq 2$. The distribution f_j is not a proper probability function because it does not sum to unity. Notice that:

$$\sum_{j=1}^{\infty} (f_j) = w + i \sum_{j=1}^{\infty} (\tfrac{1}{2})^j = w + i = 1 - c$$

In Feller's terms this means that errors are *uncertain* recurrent events, for which probability c the subject chooses a correct strategy and never makes another error. Some of the probability of the f distribution is located at the (improper) point ∞, and the proportion so located is c. This merely reflects the fact that learning occurs in the present model and the subject can eliminate errors. The fact that f_j is not a probability function does not place any serious difficulties in the way of analysis.

ALL STRATEGIES AT ONCE

We now consider a second model of a subject working on the same discrimination learning problem discussed above, with exactly the same set of strategies H divided into correct (C), wrong (W), and irrelevant (I) subsets. Since a strategy corresponds to any specific cue in the situation and these cues are numerous and finely divisible, consider that the set of strategies consists of a fairly sizeable (though finite) number of strategies, each of which is as likely to be used, and has as much influence on behavior, as every other.

In the all-strategies-at-once model we imagine that the subject begins the learning process by considering the entire set H of strategies simultaneously. In informal terms, he then attempts to narrow down to the correct strategy by a process of elimination. However, we suppose that the subject has only a limited memory and cannot remember all of the strategies at once, but only those with which he is presently concerned. The main disability of the subject in this model is that he may accidentally eliminate the correct strategies. When this happens he is unable to remember what they were, for he can remember only the ones he is still using. When the correct strategies have been lost the subject has no recourse but to begin over with the whole set of strategies. This general idea is now stated more precisely.

On the first trial the subject considers all strategies and chooses his response. The correct strategies and some of the irrelevant ones lead toward a correct response, the wrong strategies and the remainder of the irrelevant ones lead to an error. We suppose that the probability of a response is equal to the proportion of the strategies which lead to that response, so that, if we let N_c, N_w, and N_i be the numbers of strategies in sets C, W, and I, and if we let N_i^- be the number of irrelevant strategies which lead to an error on the next trial, the probability of an error is:

$$f_1 = (N_w + N_i^-)/(N_w + N_c + N_i).$$

When the subject makes this first response we suppose that he eliminates or sets aside all the strategies he does not use. Suppose, for example, that he chooses a correct response. He at the same time eliminates all the wrong strategies and the irrelevant strategies which would have led him to the opposite response. On the next trial he will have only the correct strategies and the surviving irrelevant strategies left.

To complete the discussion and generalize it somewhat we introduce notation for the set of irrelevant strategies which, following any Trial n, first lead to a wrong response on Trial $n + j$. Let $N_{n,j}$ be the number of irrelevant strategies which lead to correct responses on trials $n + 1$, $n + 2, \ldots, n + j - 1$, and an error on trial $n + j$. Now we can write the probability of an error after an error as:

$$f_1 = (N_w + N_{n,1})/(N_c + N_w + N_i).$$

After one correct response, the only strategies which will lead to an error are those $N_{n,2}$ irrelevent strategies which first lead to an error on the second trial. The total strategies left are N_c correct and $N_i - N_{n,1}$ irrelevant strategies which have not already led toward a wrong response. Thus, the probability of an error following one correct response which follows a given error is:

$$f_2 = (1 - f_1)(N_{n,2}/[N_c + N_i - N_{n,1}])$$
$$= \frac{N_c + N_i - N_{n,1}}{N_c + N_w + N_i} \cdot \frac{N_{n,2}}{N_c + N_i - N_{n,1}}$$

Extension of this line of argument shows that in general:

$$f_j = \frac{N_c + N_i - N_{n,1}}{N_c + N_w + N_i} \cdot \frac{N_c + N_i - N_{n,1} - N_{n,2}}{N_c + N_i - N_{n,1}} \cdots$$
$$\cdot \frac{N_c + N_i - N_{n,1} - \ldots - N_{n,j-2} - N_{n,j-1}}{N_c + N_i - N_{n,1} - \ldots - N_{n,j-3} - N_{n,j-2}} \cdot \frac{N_{n,j}}{N_c + N_i - N_{n,1} - \ldots - N_{n,j-1} - N_{j-1}}$$

In this expression the numerator of each term except the last cancels with the denominator of the following term, so that:

$$f_j = N_{n,j}/(N_c + N_w + N_i)$$

In our ideal experiment, $N_{n,j}$, the number of strategies which first lead to a wrong response on Trial $n + j$ after a given error on Trial n, is independent of n and is given by $N_i(\frac{1}{2})^j$. This statement follows from the idea that irrelevant strategies are correct and wrong with independent probabilities of $\frac{1}{2}$. Actually, $N_i(\frac{1}{2})^j$ is the expected number of irrelevant strategies which first lead to an error on Trial $n + j$, but the derivation to follow does not hinge on the distinction.

If we substitute $N_i(\frac{1}{2})^j$ for $N_{n,j}$ in the expression for f_j and simplify, letting i be the proportion of irrelevant strategies in H, we obtain:

$$f_j = i(\tfrac{1}{2})^j.$$

A similar substitution in the expression for f_1 gives:

$$f_1 = w + \tfrac{1}{2}i.$$

These two results are in agreement with the one-strategy-at-a-time model. We have shown that the one-strategy-at-a-time and the all-strategies-at-once models are both systems in which errors are recurrent events, and we have shown that f_j is the same in both systems. Hence, so far as errors are concerned, the two models are identical.

One remark is in order. In the one-strategy-at-a-time model, the probability of a correct response on any trial is 1, ½, or 0 depending on whether a correct, irrelevant, or wrong strategy is being used. The probability of a correct response in the all-strategies-at-once model can take a variety of values; if there are a great many strategies, the possible values of this probability are numerous and closely packed. The two models are not at all alike in the probabilities involved, and the theorem that they give indistinguishable sequences of errors is by no means obvious on intuitive grounds, even though the proof is easy.

The correspondence of the models extends to the interpretation of the parameters. In the one-strategy-at-a-time model the parameters c, w, and i are the probabilities of selecting a correct, wrong, or irrelevant strategy. In the all-strategies-at-once model the parameters c, w, and i are the proportions of correct, wrong, and irrelevant strategies, where elementary strategies are taken to have equal weight. In terms of experimental realizations of the models, these two sets of parameters are not distinguishable.

It is still possible, of course, to tell which model is more reasonable by any technique which goes beyond the choice data. One might, for example, ask human subjects which strategies they are using, or one might use memory tests to see what parts of the situation have been employed. The equivalence of the models is asserted only for the acquisition of a single problem, and only with respect to the overt choices made: the writer will suggest, in subsequent work, that recognition and transfer tests may permit differential predictions.

A RANDOM SAMPLE OF STRATEGIES

The two models discussed above are extremes. One would intuitively imagine that the subject would use, not all strategies and not just one, but some sample of strategies. The third model, called the random-sample-of-strategies model, supposes that on the first trial and after each error the subject draws a random sample of all strategies. So long as he makes no errors the subject discards wrong and irrelevant strategies by the same mechanism as that invoked in the all-strategies-at-once model.

If the subject makes an error he takes a new independent sample from H and begins the process over.

The theorem to be proved is, if the sampling process is random in a strict sense to be described below and excludes the possibility that the subject might choose the empty sample, then the random-sample-of-strategies model generates a system of recurrent events which is the same as the other two models given above.

We again consider the set H of strategies, composed of equally potent elementary strategies. Suppose that there are N strategies in H of which N_c are correct, N_w are wrong, and N_i are irrelevant. We shall interpret N_c/N as c, the proportion of correct strategies, N_w/N as w, and N_i/N as i.

In a random sampling model of learning one may assign a fixed probability of being sampled to each element and let the sample size vary randomly, or assign a fixed sample-size, supposing that all such samples are equally probable (Estes, 1959). To eliminate the possibility of the empty sample it is desirable to deal with a fixed sample size n. The random-sampling specification is that all samples of size n are equally probable.

The total number of samples of size n which can be drawn from a population of N elements is:

$$\binom{N}{n} = \frac{N!}{n!(N-n)!}$$

Similarly, one can draw $\binom{N_c}{n_c}$ samples of n_c correct strategies from the population of N_c strategies. For each of these samples of n_c correct strategies, there are $\binom{N_w}{n_w}$ samples of n_w wrong strategies, so that there are $\binom{N_c}{n_c}\binom{N_w}{n_w}$ ways of drawing n_c correct and n_w wrong strategies. For each of these combinations there are $\binom{N_i}{n_i}$ ways of drawing n_i irrelevant strategies. Hence the total number of ways one could obtain n_c correct, n_w wrong, and n_i irrelevant strategies is:

$$\binom{N_c}{n_c}\binom{N_w}{n_w}\binom{N_i}{n_i}$$

where, of course, it is assumed that $n_c + n_w + n_i = n$. Since every sample of size n is assumed to be as likely as any other, the probability of drawing a sample of exactly n_c correct, n_w wrong, and n_i irrelevant strategies is:

$$P(n_c, n_w, n_i) = \frac{\binom{N_c}{n_c}\binom{N_w}{n_w}\binom{N_i}{n_i}}{\binom{N}{n}}$$

which is the three-category generalization of the hypergeometric distribution (Feller, 1950).

It was asserted, in the statement of the model, that once the subject has chosen a sample his performance follows the rules of the all-strategies-at-once model. Hence, after any error and the choice of a sample with n_c, n_w, and n_i strategies, we can construct the f_j distribution. We may write the f distribution conditional on the constitution of the sample as:

$f(j \mid$ sample with n_c, n_w, n_i strategies$)$

$$= \begin{vmatrix} (n_w + \tfrac{1}{2}n_i)/n & \text{for } j = 1 \\ (\tfrac{1}{2})^j n_i/n & \text{for } j > 1 \end{vmatrix}$$

directly from our results on the all-strategies-at-once model. To obtain the unconditional f_j we multiply each conditional f by the probability of the sample, and sum. This gives us the expectation of the conditional f. For f_1 we have:

$$f_1 = \mathrm{E}[(n_w + \tfrac{1}{2}n_i)/n]$$
$$= \mathrm{E}(n_w/n) + \tfrac{1}{2}\mathrm{E}(n_i/n)$$

However, in the hypergeometric distribution the mean proportion of wrong strategies in samples of size n is just the proportion of wrong strategies in the whole population. That is, $\mathrm{E}(n_w/n) = N_w/N = w$. Similar equations hold for irrelevant and correct strategies. Hence:

$$f_1 = w + \tfrac{1}{2}i$$

and, by the same argument:

$$f_j = (\tfrac{1}{2})^j i$$

for j greater than 1. Thus it is shown that the random-sample-of-strategies model with fixed sample size n is a system of recurrent events (this point is obvious and is not proved above) with the same f distribution found in the one-strategy-at-a-time and the all-strategies-at-once models. At this point one can see that the one-strategy-at-a-time model is a special case of the random-sample-of-strategies model with sample size $n = 1$; and similarly, the all-strategies-at-once model is a special case with sample size $n = N$.

One further generalization is possible. Since the final equations of the random-sample-of-strategies model contain no reference to the sample size n, one would get a system of recurrent events with the given f distribution from any mixture of systems which use different sample sizes. One can withdraw the assumption that the sample size is fixed, permitting the possibility that samples are of all different sizes. The only restrictions are that for any n, all samples of size n are equally likely; and there are no empty samples.

The strategy-sampling model differs from Estes' stimulus-sampling model (Estes, 1959) in an important respect. Let the total number of elements (strategies or, in Estes' case, stimulus elements or patterns) be N and the sample size be n. In Estes' formulations, n/N is analogous to the learning rate θ and controls the rate of learning and all the statistical characteristics of the acquisition data. In the present model, learning is independent of the sample size n/N and depends solely on the composition of the basic set H; namely, the proportions of correct, wrong, and irrelevant strategies in H. Thus while the sampling process invoked in this strategy-sampling theory is one of those used by Estes, its place in the theory is entirely different.

In this section it has been shown that three models of the selection of strategies all lead to the same system of recurrent events. Whether or not this is of interest depends largely on whether the resulting description fits the data of cue learning experiments, a question which is considered in the remainder of the paper.

STATISTICAL PROPERTIES OF THE RAW DATA

The discussion above has been restricted to the distribution f_j, the probability that an error follows the last error by exactly j trials. The f distribution can be estimated directly from raw data, but this is neither a conventional nor a very interesting way of describing the data of cue learning. In this section the data generated by this model are analyzed in several of the ways commonly employed by experimenters. Details are given in Restle (1961).

LEARNING CURVE(S)

Consider three versions of the learning curve. One is the succession of correct and wrong responses by an individual subject. A second is the average learning curve of a group of subjects. The third is a corrected or idealized form of the learning curve computed by adjusting a group learning curve (Vincentizing) or by averaging the data of subjects who are selected after the fact for similarity of over-all performance (Spence, 1956).

According to the present theory, the individual data are composed of a sequence of correct and wrong responses in irregular order, followed by an infinite sequence of correct responses. If $w > 0$, there will be somewhat more errors than correct responses on the resolution trials, and there will be a tendency for errors to follow other errors more often than errors follow correct responses. The probability of an error following an error will be $(w + \tfrac{1}{2}i)/(w + i)$ whereas the probability of an error following a correct response is $\tfrac{1}{2}$. An individual subject will produce such below-chance behavior for some block of trials and then abruptly, after some error, will either happen on a correct strategy (in the one-strategy-at-a-time model) or will begin a process of elimination which ends up with all correct strategies. This is an extreme form of the "discontinuous" or insightful learning curve. Unfortunately it is difficult to decide whether any individual subject does or does not exhibit this pattern, so data are usually combined.

The group learning curve is merely the average of a set of (theoretically) discontinuous individual curves. If all subjects have the same parameters c, w, and i, they will nevertheless happen to master the problem at different trials, so that the average learning curve is gradual. Its mathematical form is complex but in general appearance, the group learning from this theory resembles the common "growth" curve (Restle, in 1961).

If one selects, from a larger group of subjects, those who make the same number of total errors, or those who reach criterion at the same time, and averages their learning curves; or if one rescales learning trials as by the Vincent-curve method, the resulting curve will usually be S shaped. The writer has investigated this question by generating data which arise directly from the assumptions of the present model, by use of tables of random members. When, from a large set of such data, one selects a subgroup of "subjects" who all make the same number of errors, or who reach criterion at about the same trial, and average the performance within such a subgroup, the result is an S shaped curve. Exact Vincentizing produces a flat (stationary) learning curve before criterion.

The reason for the S shaped curves is not difficult to find; the above methods of selecting or rearranging the data tend to put the (theoretically random) times of solution close together. If the times of solution are put exactly together a step-function should result, but if the times of solution are only grouped close to one another, the step is blurred and an S shaped curve results (Spence, 1956).

SUMMARY STATISTICS OF THE DATA

In the present theory the actual trial on which learning takes place is not in any way fixed, but depends upon the random outcome of the process of selecting strategies. The result is large intrinsic variance in the acquisition phase, which can most conveniently be described in terms of the total errors made by each subject. If each subject is trained until a long sequence of consecutive correct responses has been obtained, one is reasonably sure that the number of errors made approximates the theoretical total errors.

On the first trial or after any error the subject may either make another error, sometimes later, or he may make no more errors. The probability that the subject will make at least one more error, the first one is exactly j trials, is f_j. Thus the total probability of at least one more error is:

$$\sum_{j=1}^{\infty} (f_j) = 1 - c$$

With the probability c the subject never makes another error at all. From this it is not difficult to show that the probability of exactly k errors is $(1 - c)^k c$. This is the geometric distribution which has mean:

$$E(k) = (1 - c)/c$$

and variance:

$$\mathrm{Var}(k) = (1 - c)/c^2.$$

The standard deviation of the distribution of error scores should be nearly equal to its mean, according to the theory, and the distribution should show an extreme positive skewness.

Provided that irrelevant strategies are correct just half the time at random, trials-to-criterion behaves very much like total errors.

METHODS OF ESTIMATING THE PARAMETERS W AND C

An important step in any mathematical development of a learning theory is the estimation of parameters. Fortunately, in the present model quite simple and efficient estimates are available. A maximum-likelihood estimator of c is given by:

$$\hat{c} = 1/(\bar{T} + 1)$$

where $\bar{T}$ is the mean total error score of a group of subjects. The variance of this estimate, with N subjects in the group, is:

$$\mathrm{Var}(\hat{c}) = c^2(1 - c)/N$$

It is also possible to estimate w by the maximum-likelihood method. As was mentioned earlier, a high frequency of consecutive errors in the presolution phase is an indication of a relatively large proportion of wrong strategies, whereas a chance frequency of consecutive errors is an indication that there are relatively few wrong strategies; provided that the irrelevant strategies are correct and wrong strictly at random. The method is to count "Trial 0," an imaginary trial before training begins, as an error. Then for each subject to divide this expanded set of errors into M_0 errors which are followed by correct responses and M_1 errors which are followed by errors. Then computing the means of these statistics one has:

$$\hat{w} = \frac{\bar{M}_1 - \bar{M}_0 + 1}{\bar{M}_0 + \bar{M}_1}$$

as a maximum-likelihood estimator of w (Restle, 1961).

SOME VARIATIONS OF THE BASIC MODEL

The theory stated above is so restrictive in its assumption that it cannot be applied with success to a great many experimental data. For example, with the theory above, one must expect the standard deviation of error scores to be just slightly less than their mean, and this is not observed with any great regularity. Furthermore, animal subjects often show a strong tendency to remain with one strategy even if it is wrong or irrelevant, for a fairly long string of trials. The model given above says that the subject starts over after each error, and this simply is not a plausible assumption for animal studies.[1]

PERSEVERATION

The model is quite easily generalized to take some account of perseveration of strategies. In place of the assumption that the subject always resamples after an error, one supposes that resampling occurs with some probability r, which may be considered a constant for given experimental conditions and also a constant during the presolution period. The subject chooses some strategy or sample of strategies at Trial 1, whence the probability of making zero errors is c. The probability that any actual error is the last one is only rc, the joint probability that (a) the subject resamples and (b) having resampled, hits on a correct strategy (in the one-strategy-at-a-time model) or goes into a terminal process of narrowing down (in the all-strategies-at-once or the random-sample-of-strategies models). For this model with perseveration the distribution of total error scores is:

$$P(0) = c$$
$$P(T) = (1 - c)(1 - rc)^{T-1}rc,$$

where $T > 0$. The value of this model in fitting animal data is illustrated by analyzing a set of error scores reported in detail by Harlow, Harlow, Rueping, and Mason (1960). (See Restle, 1960). Harlow's distributions show a relatively high frequency of solutions with zero errors, along with a spread to very large error scores, in original learning by baby monkeys. The result is that the standard deviations of the distributions are somewhat larger than the means. Harlow et al. remarked on the high degree of perseveration shown by some monkeys. Even more striking is Warren's investigation (Warren, 1959b) of the discrimination learning of cats, which show strong perseverative tendencies and which give distributions of error scores with standard deviations much larger than the corresponding means.

It is not at all sure that perseverative effects can be reduced to the single parameter r, and the writer's investigations are entirely insufficient to support the assumption. Within the model there are several symptoms of perseveration; a high frequency of zero error scores relative to the re-

---

[1] The writer is indebted to Marvin Levine for pointing out the importance of this factor in animal discrimination learning.

mainder of the distribution, higher standard deviation than mean errors, and consecutive runs of responses which follow a wrong or irrelevant strategy, such as a position habit, object preference, etc. One can imagine that perseverative tendencies would be strong whenever the incentive for learning is not entirely effective, or when the subjects (perhaps from partial reinforcement) have developed an expectation that rewards cannot always be attained. Something of this last effect, in college students, is suggested by the results of Morin (1955).

COMPLEXITY OF CORRECT STRATEGIES

In the model above it is tacitly assumed that the problem can be solved on the basis of a single correct strategy. This seems a reasonable assumption in the case of simultaneous discrimination. However, when two situations are presented on successive trials it is a question whether complete solution involves learning one strategy (turn right to white and left to black) or two strategies, one for each situation. If two strategies are learned independently and with the same parameters, then the distribution of errors is the distribution of the sum of two random variables (total errors in each situation) each of which has a geometric distribution. This results in a negative binomial distribution (see Restle, 1961) with mean:

$$E(T) = 2(1 - c)/c$$

and variance:

$$\text{Var}(T) = 2(1 - c)/c^2.$$

These statements follow at once from the fact that the mean of the sum of two independent variables is the sum of the means, and the variance of the sum is the sum of the component variances. With small c the standard deviation will be about $1/\sqrt{2}$ or about 0.7 of the mean.

An interesting fact can be brought forward in favor of this argument, though the writer has not been able to make an exhaustive test. In a case of successive size discrimination by college students (Restle, 1955) the writer found ratios of standard deviation/mean of 1.1 and 0.9 for two problems—both very close to unity, hence in agreement with the original model and with the notion that a single strategy is sufficient to solve the problem. In a comparable study using rats in a successive black-white discrimination, Amsel (1952) obtained data on three groups in which the ratio of standard deviation to mean was 0.65, 0.68, and 0.72. The rat results are in excellent agreement with the hypothesis that the rats had to use two separate strategies to solve the problem. One might guess that rats do not integrate the two habits, right turn to white and left turn to black, into a single cognitive structure, whereas humans might make just such an integration. The present analysis may be useful in throwing further light on the nature of successive discriminations for various species of subjects.

ADDITIVITY OF CUES

In several papers regarding another theory the writer has discussed the additivity of cues (Restle, 1955, 1957, 1958, 1959a; see also Bourne & Restle, 1959, and Trabasso, 1960). In simple terms the experiment involves three groups; one learns a problem based on a set A of cues, the second learns a problem based on the set B of cues, and the third learns a problem which can be solved using either A or B cues disjunctively. If the sets A and B are separate then the third set $A \cup B$ should have measure $m(A \cup B) = m(A) + m(B)$, (see Trabasso, 1960). Experimental results have been reconciled with an S-R theory involving adaptation of irrelevant cues (Restle, 1955).

Generally speaking, the calculations from the present model are in good numerical agreement with those from the "adaptation" model. Reanalysis of three of the most satisfactory sets of data used before, and one set not previously used, are reported here. The other data previously discussed are so fragmentary that analysis will hardly be fruitful; and Trabasso (1960) used such difficult problems that many of his subjects failed to learn at all on the more difficult problems, making analysis by the present model unsatisfactory. In general, the estimates reported below are not the maximum-likelihood estimates because the subjects were not run to a strong criterion. However, since learning was nearly complete, the approximate estimates are adequate.

Scharlock (1955; see also Restle, 1957) ran a place-versus-response experiment with rats in which the relative weight of correct place (extra-maze) and correct response (intra-maze) strategies can be estimated. He also ran one group with both place and response strategies correct, and a group with response strategies correct and no place cues present. In the calculations below it is assumed that the number of wrong strategies of a given type (place or response) equals the number of correct strategies. This is a symmetry assumption which, while not strictly appropriate for Scharlock's experiment, is needed to permit prediction, since separate estimates of wrong strategies cannot be made on the available data.

Rats learned to go to the same place (using extra-maze cues), with response cues irrelevant, making an average of 9.7 errors. Using the estimate $\hat{c} = 1/(1 + \bar{T})$, one estimates the correct place strategies make up $1/10.7 = .093$ of the total set of strategies. Other rats learned to make a constant response to different places, averaging 6.7 errors. We estimate that correct response strategies constitute $1/7.7 = .130$ of the total set.

The simplest interpretation of the experiment is that when both place and response strategies would work, the proportion of correct strategies would be the sum of the proportions of place and response strategies, since the same total set of strategies is available. One predicts that with place-plus-response learning, $c = .093 + .130 = 223$. We have the formula that the expected errors to solution is $(1 - c)/c$. Hence the expected mean errors is $.777/.223 = 3.4$; the obtained mean was 4.0, which is adequately close. The discrepancy can partly be explained by the fact that the place-learning and response-learning groups were not run to a high criterion and probably would have made more errors if tested longer. The fast-learning place-plus-response group would likely not have made more errors, since their performance was excellent at the end of the training given.

Another group learned a fixed response in the absence of any good place cues. We assume that this group simply had neither correct nor incorrect place strategies. Its predicted proportion of correct strategies is $.130/1 - 2(.093) = .130/.814 = .160$. The expected errors is $.840/.160 = 5.25$; the observed mean was 5.0. Both predictions are close to the obtained results, well within sampling deviations.

Warren (1959a) has reported data on monkeys in an experiment analogous to Scharlock's study of rats. Warren's monkeys had to learn position habits in some problems and object-discriminations in other problems. Warren also used a response-plus-object problem (object discrimination with the objects left in the same place each trial) and a pure response problem (e.g., choose the left one of two indistinguishable objects). Predictions followed the same formulas as above, and were extremely accurate; the proportions of object and response strategies were estimated from behavior on object (position-varied) and position (object-varied) problems. When these values were added to predict object-plus-position, the prediction was a mean of 0.67 errors, whereas Warren observed 0.63. For pure response learning, the model predicted 3.25 mean errors and the observed value was 3.04. These agreements between theory and data are well within the range of probable sampling error.

Similar results were obtained by analyzing Warren's experiment on the additivity of color, form, and size cues (Warren, 1953). The analysis is substantially the same as that given in a previous paper (Restle, 1958). Learning data are collected on problems involving only color, only form, or only size differences between the objects. These data are used to calculate the proportional weights of the three sources of strategies, and the resulting values are recombined to compute predicted learning rates for problems involving two or more dimensions; for example, discrimination of a red triangle from a green circle involves color plus form cues. In each calculation account is taken of the greater total number of strategies involved in problems with added cues, and it is assumed that whenever a set of correct strategies is introduced by adding cues, an equally large set of wrong strategies also enter the situation.

Calculations on Warren's (1953) data afforded four predictions of total errors to solution. The four predictions were wrong by −17, 0, 5 and 10 percent respectively, and all of the errors can reasonably be attributed to sampling variations.

The hypothesis of additivity of cues has also been applied to human learning (Restle, 1959a) in an experiment which required subjects to learn differential verbal responses to consonant syllables. The procedure was simple concept formation with individual letters of the syllables used as cues, and the same sort of additivity of cues as above. The adaptation model gave quite accurate predictions and the present model is, if anything, slightly more accurate; it predicts (given data on the two cues separately) that the added-cue group should make an average of 5.26 errors, whereas the observed mean was 5.25. Considering the variability of the data, the extreme closeness is coincidental.

COMPARISON WITH OTHER THEORIES

The three models of the selection of strategies are conceptually similar to the writer's adaption theory of discrimination learning (Restle, 1955). The "strategies" of the present model resemble the "cues" of the earlier theory. The strategy-selection model has, as a theorem, that the rate of learning depends upon the proportion of correct strategies. A similar idea is expressed in the adaptation model in which it was assumed that the rate of learning (θ) would depend upon the proportion of relevant cues.

Several of the serious faults of the adaptation theory are corrected in the theory of strategy-selection. First, in the adaptation theory the subject was supposed to begin conditioning relevant cues and adapting irrelevant cues, with a rate θ equal to the proportion of relevant cues, right from the first trial of training. Of course, at that first trial the subject has no possible way of knowing which cues will turn out to be relevant—it would be possible for the experimenter to change his mind after the first trial is complete. Hence, the adaptation theory could apply only to a prescient subject. The selection-of-strategies theory does not have the subject treat different strategies differently except on the basis of trials already completed, hence avoids the absurdity. Second, the idea that the structure of the problem (proportion of relevant cues or correct strategies) controls the rate of learning was only a simplifying assumption, with no justification, in the adaptation model; but is an inescapable theorem of strategy-selection. Third, the adaptation theory yielded a determinate learning curve in the sense that $p(n)$ was exactly specified for a given θ and $p(1)$. The variance of typical data was in large part left unexplained by the adaptation model and had to be attributed to individual differences, even though it is notoriously difficult to find any strong predictor of such learning. In the strategy-selection model learning itself is a random event and the model generates variability comparable with that obtained in the data.

Despite these important differences, the present theory is close enough to the adaptation theory to make it possible to carry over many of the theoretical insights, though in modified form. The one type of prediction discussed in this paper was additivity of cues, but other ideas such as the proposed basis of learning sets (Restle, 1958) and various quantitative relationships in concept identification (Bourne & Restle, 1959) can be re-cast in the mold of the selection of strategies. The many similarities and few differences in predictions must be studied in detail and cannot be discussed here, except to mention that most of the results of the Bourne and Restle paper can be reproduced using the strategy-selection model.

In more general terms, it may be remarked that the strategy-selection model is similar to the ideas of Lashley (1928) and Krechevsky (1932) in general intent. In comparison with stimulus-sampling theories (Restle, 1959b) the strategy-selection model is like theories of the observing response (Atkinson, 1959a, 1959b; Wyckoff, 1952), except that in the strategy-selection model there is no conditioning, only observing (selecting). The mathematical structure of the model is very close to that of Bower's (1960) one-element association model.

SUMMARY

A stochastic model for the solution of cue learning problems by the selection of strategies was stated and developed. Errors were shown to constitute a system of uncertain recurrent events in Feller's sense. Three models, one-strategy-at-a-time, all-strategies-at-once, and a-random-sample-of-strategies, were formulated and shown to yield the same system of recurrent events, to be identical in terms of data. This is the independence-of-sample-size theorem. The basic distribution of the recurrent-events system was used to generate a description of the data, and also a method for estimating the proportions of correct and wrong strategies in a problem. Variations of the model, which take account of perseveration and complex strategies, were indicated. Experimental evidence, mainly on the additivity of cues, was discussed.

REFERENCES

AMSEL, A. A rate of learning visual brightness discrimination as a function of discriminanda durations. *J. comp. physiol. Psychol.*, 1952, 45, 341–346.

ATKINSON, R. C. The observing response in discrimination learning. Technical Report No. 4, 1959, University of California, Los Angeles, Contract Nonr 233(58). (a)

ATKINSON, R. C. A theory of stimulus discrimination learning. Technical Report No. 1, 1959, University of California, Los Angeles, Contract Nonr 233(58). (b)

BOURNE, L. E. JR., & RESTLE, F. Mathematical theory of concept identification. Psychol. Rev., 1959, 66, 278–296.

BOWER, G. H. Properties of the one-element model as applied to paired associate learning. Technical Report No. 31, 1960, Stanford University, Contract Nonr 225(17).

ESTES, W. K. Component and pattern models with Markovian interpretations. In R. R. Bush & W. K. Estes (Eds.), Studies in mathematical learning theory. Stanford: Stanford Univer. Press, 1959.

FELLER, W. An introduction to probability theory and its applications. (1st ed.) New York: Wiley, 1950.

HARLOW, H. F., HARLOW, M. K., RUEPING, R. R., & MASON, W. A. Performance of infant Rhesus monkeys on discrimination learning, delayed response, and discrimination learning set. J. comp. physiol. Psychol., 1960, 53, 113–121.

KRECHEVSKY, I. "Hypotheses" in rats. Psychol. Rev., 1932, 39, 516–532.

LASHLEY, K. S. Brain mechanisms and behavior. Chicago: Univer. Chicago Press, 1928.

MORIN, R. E. Factors influencing rate and extent of learning in the presence of misinformative feedback. J. exp. Psychol., 1955, 49, 343–351.

RESTLE, F. A theory of discrimination learning. Psychol. Rev., 1955, 62, 11–19.

RESTLE, F. Discrimination of cues in mazes: A resolution of the "place-vs.-response" question. Psychol. Rev., 1957, 64, 217–228.

RESTLE, F. Toward a quantitative description of learning set data. Psychol. Rev., 1958, 65, 77–91.

RESTLE, F. Additivity of cues and transfer in discrimination of consonant clusters. J. exp. Psychol., 1959, 57, 9–14. (a)

RESTLE, F. A survey and classification of learning models. In R. R. Bush & W. K. Estes (Eds.), Studies in mathematical learning theory. Stanford: Stanford Univer. Press, 1959. (b)

RESTLE, F. A note on the "hypothesis" theory of discrimination learning. Psychol. Rep., 1960, 7, 194.

RESTLE, F. Statistical methods for a theory of cue learning, Psychometrika, 1961, 26, 291–306.

SCHARLOCK, D. P. The role of extramaze cues in place and response learning. J. exp. Psychol., 1955, 50, 249–254.

SPENCE, K. W. Behavior theory and conditioning. New Haven: Yale Univer. Press, 1956.

TRABASSO, T. R. Additivity of cues in discrimination learning of letter patterns. *J. exp. Psychol.*, 1960, 60, 83-88.

WARREN, J. M. Additivity of cues in visual pattern discriminations by monkeys. *J. comp. physiol. Psychol.*, 1953, 46, 484–486.

WARREN, J. M. Solution of object and positional discriminations by monkeys. *J. comp. physiol. Psychol.*, 1959, 52, 92–93. (a)

WARREN, J. M. Stimulus perseveration in discrimination learning by cats. *J. comp. psysiol. Psychol.*, 1959, 52, 99–101. (b)

WYCKOFF, L. B. The role of observing responses in discrimination learning. Part 1. *Psychol. Rev.*, 1952, 59, 431–442.

25. Mediating Processes in Humans at the Outset of Discrimination Learning

Marvin Levine

Abstract. *An earlier hypothesis model was extended to describe the set of mediating processes (Hs) employed by the adult human S. The model now deals with behavior during 2 types of discrimination problems: Outcome problems (e.g., E says "right" or "wrong" after each response) and Nonoutcome problems (E says nothing). 2 classes of Hs are stipulated: Predictions (determinants of attempts to maximize rewards) and Response-sets (determinants of systematic, nonsolution behavior). Analysis of data from 2 experiments show: (a) the model closely predicts behavior during Nonoutcome problems from behavior during Outcome problems, (b) the Nonoutcome problem may be used as a probe to determine the H an individual S is holding on a particular problem, and (c) the learning-set function can be predicted from knowledge of the Hs.*

The conception central to the model to be delineated has been suggested in a wide variety of sources (Bruner, 1951; Hovland, 1952; Kendler & Kendler, 1962; Restle, 1962—to name but a few recent ones). The conception is that the adult human starts a problem with a mediating process ("prediction," "hypothesis," "expectancy," "set" are alternative terms which have been employed) and that this mediating process affects the overt behavior in specifiable ways. The model will describe the set of such

Reprinted by permission of the author and the American Psychological Association from *Psychological Review*, 1963, 70, 254–276.

processes available at the outset of short discrimination problems, will lead to techniques for evaluating their frequency, and will permit the deduction of novel theorems about behavior. Later sections of this paper will present experimental tests of these theorems.

The present formulation is a development from a model (Levine, 1959) of the behavior of monkeys engaged in a series of three-trial discrimination problems. The fundamental assumption in that model was that there is a set of Hs (short for hypotheses, after Krechevsky, 1932), defined as systematic response patterns, one of which is chosen by the subject on each problem. Examples of Hs are "Position Preference" (defined as repeated response to one position), "Stimulus Preference" (defined as repeated response to one stimulus), and "Win-stay-Lose-shift with respect to the stimulus" (defined as response to the stimulus correct on the preceding trial). That model yielded a method of analysis for determining the frequency of occurrence of the various Hs. It became possible to conclude, for example, that Position Preference occurred on 18% of the problems and to decompose the learning-set function into the underlying set of H functions.

The same assumption, that there is a set of Hs among which the subject chooses, and the same general method of analysis will be applied to adult human behavior over a series of discrimination learning problems. The hypothesis, then, will continue to be the basic dependent variable, and will continue to be symbolized by H. There will be, however, a shift in the definition of this symbol. Whereas it had been previously defined as a response pattern, it will hereafter be defined as the *determinant* of a response pattern, as a mediating process which results in the particular response pattern. The rationale for such a change will become clear as the model is presented and will be discussed following the presentation of the experiments.

The human experimental situation to which the analysis will be applied incorporates the general procedures of the learning-set experiment (Harlow, 1959). In the most usual form of that experiment two stimulus objects are presented simultaneously for a few trials. Typically, the stimuli are relevant (response to one of them is consistently rewarded) for these few trials; their positions, which reverse on 50% of the trials, are irrelevant. A series of problems are presented, new stimuli being used for each problem.

The present experiments will differ from the previous experiments in one important detail: the experimenter will have two procedures instead of one. In the typical discrimination learning experiments with monkeys the experimenter uses a single procedure: one of the two responses is always rewarded, the other not. The analogous procedure with humans is that one of the responses is followed by the word "right," the other by the word "wrong." With humans, the experimenter may have a second procedure: "blank" trials may be presented, i.e., during some problems the experimenter may say nothing.

There are then two types of problems: Outcome problems (the experimenter says "right" or "wrong" after each response) and Nonoutcome problems (the experimenter says nothing after each response). The subject will have been instructed that both types of problems would occur and that he is to try to obtain 100% correct in either case. A major aim of the model will be the prediction of behavior during Nonoutcome problems from behavior during Outcome problems, and vice versa.

The model will be developed to specify the Hs with which the subjects start any problem. The description of subsequent Hs involves arbitrary assumptions about resampling of Hs and will not be considered here. As a result, behavioral data only through the first two trials of Outcome problems will be considered. The initial experiment to which the model will be applied will consist of precisely two-trial problems. The Hs at the outset of longer problems will be considered in the second experiment.

A two-trial problem, the subject's behavior, and the experimenter's behavior will be summarized by a few symbols. If the two stimuli maintain the same positions on Trials 1 and 2 the problem type will be described as "A"; if they reverse positions from Trials 1 to 2 the problem type will be described as "B." The response sequence will be described as I_s if the subject chooses the *identical stimulus* on Trial 2 to the one chosen on Trial 1. Choice of one then the *other stimulus* will be described as O_s. From knowledge of the problem type (A or B) and of the subject's sequence of stimulus selection (I_s or O_s) one may deduce his sequence of position selections. Nevertheless, it will be useful to symbolize also the sequence of position responses. Response to the same position for the two trials will be described as I_p; response to one then the other position will be described as O_p. The symbols $+_1$, and $-_1$, will be used to denote that the experimenter said "right" or "wrong," respectively, following the response on Trial 1. The symbol pair $+_1 I_s$ means that the subject chose a stimulus on Trial 1, the experimenter said "right" and the subject chose the same stimulus on Trial 2. The symbol pairs $+_1 O_s$, $-_1 I_s$, and $-_1 O_s$ are analogously defined.

The problem type (A or B) and these four symbol pairs describe all possible relevant outcome-response sequences for a single Outcome problem. On a single Nonoutcome problem the problem type and the symbols I_s and O_s describe all possible response sequences.

DISCRIMINATION MODEL

As already indicated, the basic conception will be that during any one problem the behavior of a subject is determined by an H, defined as a determinant of systematic responding, and to be interpreted as a prediction by the subject or his set. The *H*s available to a subject in a two-trial simultaneous discrimination problem will now be considered. In this situation *H*s have three characteristics. The first is that an *H* may be contingent either on the stimuli or on the positions. For example, a subject may Predict that one of the two stimuli is always correct (the subject Predicts that one of the *stimuli* is correct and will repeat) or that one of the two positions is always correct (the subject Predicts that one of the *positions* is correct and will repeat).[1] There are then two classes of *H*s, half directed toward stimuli, half toward positions. The second feature of *H*s is that they are sequence oriented. For example, a subject may Predict that one of the two stimuli is always correct (the subject Predicts that one of the stimuli is correct and will *repeat*) or that the correct stimulus changes from Trial 1 to Trial 2 (the subject Predicts that the correct stimulus will *alternate*).

The stimulus-position breakdown combined with the repeat-alternate breakdown yields four *H*s. Consideration of the third feature of *H*s will increase the number to eight. In all the examples just given it was assumed that the subject *Predicts* an event sequence for the first two trials. It is unrealistic to assume that this process is the only source of systematic behavior. It is conceivable that systematic response to a position or a stimulus may occur in other ways. Consider the following examples: The subject does not care about this experiment and wants to get out as fast as he can. He decides to choose always the stimulus on the left side; one of the two stimuli is repulsive to the subject and he will always choose the other even though the experimenter always says "wrong"; the subject decides to alternate stimuli (or positions) for want of anything better to do.

It is clear that these sets will yield systematic behavior, but it is equally clear that these processes are different from Predictions about correct events. One may also surmise that the resulting response patterns should be different from the patterns produced by Predictions. The distinction will be made, therefore, between *Prediction H*s and *Response-set H*s, the latter term referring to *H*s of the sort described in the last three examples.

The three two-way classifications (stimulus, position; perseveration, alternation; Prediction, Response-set) lead to eight *H*s, each of which may now be described. In order, however, to relate each *H* to behavior it is necessary to introduce two postulates, one describing behavior if a Prediction *H* exists, one if a Response-set *H* exists.

Prediction postulate: If a subject Predicts how a series of rewards will

---

[1] The word predict will have two usages: as subject's mediating process, or as the usual outcome of theoretical analysis. To help distinguish the two usages, the former will be capitalized.

occur he behaves so that if the Prediction were correct rewards would be maximized.

Suppose, for example, that a subject Predicts that one of the stimuli is correct and repeats, i.e., will be correct on both trials of the problem. If his Prediction is correct he can insure a "right" on Trial 2 of an Outcome Problem by following this rule: If the experimenter says "right" after Trial 1 choose the same stimulus on Trial 2; if the experimenter says "wrong" after Trial 1 choose the other stimulus on Trial 2. Thus, on Outcome Problems the Prediction that one of the stimuli is correct and repeats will lead to the behavior pattern formerly described (Levine, 1959) as "Win-stay-Lose-shift with respect to the stimulus."

On a Nonoutcome problem the Prediction postulate means simply that the subject strives to obtain 100% correct. A subject with the Prediction that one of the stimuli is correct and repeats would choose the same stimulus for all trials of the problem. No other behavior pattern can, if this Prediction is correct, yield 100% correct.

The four Prediction Hs are described below. The behavior manifestations are given for Outcome problems and for Nonoutcome problems, followed by the summary form in parenthesis:

Hypothesis a (H_a): *The subject Predicts that one of the stimuli is correct and will repeat.* Outcome-problem behavior: The subject shows "Win-stay-Lose-shift with respect to the stimulus" ($+_1I_s$ or $-_1O_s$). Nonoutcome-problem behavior: The subject chooses the same stimulus on Trials 1 and 2 (I_s).

Hypothesis a' ($H_{a'}$): *The subject Predicts that the correct stimulus will alternate.* Outcome-problem behavior: The subject shows "Win-shift-Lose-stay with respect to the stimulus" ($+_1O_s$ or $-_1I_s$). Nonoutcome-problem behavior: The subject chooses one stimulus on Trial 1 and the other stimulus on Trial 2 (O_s).

Hypothesis b (H_b): *The subject Predicts that one of the positions is correct and will repeat.* Outcome-problem behavior: The subject shows "Win-stay-Lose-shift with respect to position" ($+_1I_p$ or $-_1O_p$). Nonoutcome-problem behavior: The subject chooses the same position on Trials 1 and 2 (I_p).

Hypothesis b' ($H_{b'}$): *The subject Predicts that the correct position will alternate.* Outcome-problem behavior: The subject shows "Win-shift-Lose-stay with respect to position" ($+_1O_p$ or $-_1I_p$). Nonoutcome-problem behavior: The subject chooses one position on Trial 1 and the other position on Trial 2 (O_p).

Response-set postulate: If a subject has a Response-set H the behavior has the pattern described by that H and is independent of outcomes.

Suppose, for example, that the subject has the set that he will always choose the stimulus on the left. He will manifest a sequence of responses to the left side, no matter what kind of outcomes the experimenter presents.

The four Response-set Hs are described below. The behavior manifestation, which is the same for both Outcome and Nonoutcome problems, is given for each H, followed by the summary form in parenthesis.

Hypothesis x (H_x): *The subject has a Response-set to repeat the same stimulus.* Behavior: Stimulus Preference, i.e., the subject chooses the same stimulus on Trials 1 and 2 (I_s).

Hypothesis x' ($H_{x'}$): *The subject has a Response-set to alternate stimuli.* Behavior: The subject chooses one stimulus on Trial 1 and the other stimulus on Trial 2 (O_s).

Hypothesis y (H_y): *The subject has a Response-set to repeat the same position.* Behavior: Position Preference, i.e., the subject chooses the same position on Trials 1 and 2 (I_p).

Hypothesis y' ($H_{y'}$): *The subject has a Response-set to alternate positions.* Behavior: The subject chooses one position on Trial 1 and the other position on Trial 2 (O_p).

A detail to note is that the Hs have been paired off according to the words "repeat" and "alternate." Any such pair will be described as complementary, because both members of the pair dovetail in their manifestations, yielding all possible behavior patterns. This relation is denoted by employing for a given pair the same subscript letter and distinguishing the two by primes (for example, H_a and $H_{a'}$). The effect of complementarity will become explicit when the evaluation of the H strengths is discussed.

EVALUATION OF THE H PROBABILITIES

Corresponding to each H will be a probability denoting the theoretical proportion of times that the H is selected. The subscript letter will be employed to represent the probability, i.e., $P(H_a) = a$, $P(H_{a'}) = a'$, etc.

The assumption will be made that the Hs are mutually exclusive and exhaustive, i.e., that only one of the Hs occurs to a given subject on a given problem. This assumption permits the following statement:

$$a + a' + b + b' + x + x' + y + y' = 1.00. \qquad [1]$$

Given this additional assumption, a technique is available (Levine, 1959) for evaluating H probabilities from Outcome problem data. A set of equations is derived in which these probabilities are expressed as functions of the obtained frequencies of the outcome-response sequences. Appendix A presents this technique, in more general form than previously, as part of the attempt to solve for a, a', b, . . . y'. It is shown there that in the present case a complete solution is not possible, that there is available

only a relative solution which describes by how much one of a complementary pair of *Hs* exceeds the other. That is, one may solve only for:

$$D_a = a - a'; \quad D_b = b - b'; \quad D_x = x - x'; \quad D_y = y - y'.$$

Any of the D_i may range from -1.0 (if only one H involving alternation is employed) to $+1.0$ (if only one H involving perseveration is employed). For example, $D_a = +1.0$ means that, for the block of problems
considered, the subjects always have H_a, the Prediction that the correct
stimulus perseverates. $D_a = 0$ means that $a = a'$. They may both be 0 or
as much as .5.

PREDICTION OF RESPONSE PATTERNS

Appendix A shows that the D_i are obtained as numerical values from
the Outcome problem data. It is possible to employ these values to predict the behavior of the subjects during the Nonoutcome problems. The
theory may be developed to predict NI_s, the number of times that the
subject chooses the same stimulus for both trials of a problem in a block
of Nonoutcome problems.

Appendix B presents this development of the theory for the condition
when the number of A and B Nonoutcome problems are the same. It
is shown there that

$$NI_s = (T/2)[D_a + D_x + 1], \qquad [2]$$

where T represents the total number of Nonoutcome problems under
consideration, D_a reflects the degree to which the subject Predicts stimulus repetition (if D_a is positive) or alternation (if D_a is negative), and
D_x reflects the degree to which the subject has a Response-set to repeat
or alternate stimuli (if D_x is positive or negative, respectively).

Embodied in Equation 2 is the strategy for testing the model. It is
worth, therefore, repeating that D_a and D_x are numbers obtained from
the Outcome problems and NI_s is the theoretical number of repeated
stimulus selections in a block of Nonoutcome problems. The test consists
in comparing this theoretical number with the obtained number.

EXPERIMENT I

METHOD

Subjects. Eighty students from the introductory psychology courses at
Indiana University served as subjects.

Apparatus. The stimuli were 180 different three-letter nonsense syllables selected from Glaze's (1928) lists. Pairs of syllables were randomly selected to form the stimulus objects for a given trial, and were typed .5 inch apart on a 3 × 5 inch card. The same two syllables on a pair of cards constituted the materials for a problem, and a deck of 90 such pairs of cards constituted the materials for the experiment.

Design. A learning-set experiment consisting of 90 two-trial problems was presented under four experimental conditions to four groups of 20 subjects. The four conditions differed along a continuum defined by the experimenter's manner of reinforcement. At one end of this continuum is the standard learning-set procedure in which the experimenter selects the stimulus to be correct, and reinforces responses only to it on each trial of the problem. This procedure holds for every problem in the experiment. That is, the correct stimulus is the same for both trials on 100% of the problems. The group receiving this condition will be referred to as G-100. At the other end of the continuum is a procedure in which the stimulus designated as correct by the experimenter alternates from Trial 1 to Trial 2, a procedure first utilized by Behar (1961) and designated as an Alternation Learning-Set. The correct stimulus is never the same for the two trials of any problem, or, conversely, is the same for 0% of the problems. The group receiving this condition will be referred to as G-0. In between the two extremes the experimenter may follow one procedure or the other for as many problems as he wishes. For the two remaining conditions the correct stimulus was the same during 80% of the problems, changing during the remainder (G-80), and the correct stimulus was the same during 20% of the problems, changing during the remainder (G-20). The four groups, then, were G-100, G-80, G-20, and G-0, where the number describes the percentage of problems on which the experimenter caused the correct stimulus to perseverate.

Procedure. Each subject was shown a sample 3 × 5 inch card containing two syllables and was instructed that he would receive a deck composed of similar cards and that he was always to choose one of the two syllables on each card. He was further told that the experimenter would say "right" or "wrong" after each choice, and that he was to try to be right as often as possible. He was then given the deck face down and was instructed to turn the cards one at a time, making his response for each. The placement of cards after each trial was arranged so that they could not again be seen.

After either 5 or 10 Outcome problems the experimenter stopped the subject and instructed him that there would now be a test of how much had been learned thus far. The subject was told that during the next few cards the experimenter would not say anything, that because this was a test he was to try to get 100% correct. The subject then proceeded to choose syllables on the next 10 cards (5 problems) with the experimenter saying nothing. After these 5 problems the experimenter announced that

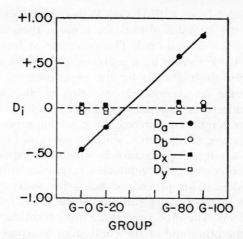

FIG. 1. The value of the D_i computed from the block of 60 Outcome problems for each group (the groups are ordered and spaced according to the percentage of problems on which the correct stimulus perseverated for the two trials).

the learning would be resumed and presented outcomes during the next 10 problems. Test instructions then followed, etc. Ten Outcome problems continued to alternate with 5 Nonoutcome problems until 90 problems—60 with, 30 without outcomes—had been presented.

RESULTS

Figure 1 shows the D_i, the difference between complementary Hs, computed from all the Outcome problems for each group. The figure shows that neither Predictions about positions nor Response-sets show greater excess in perseveration or alternation, i.e., the D_b, D_x, and D_y fluctuate around zero. The D_a, on the other hand, vary (linearly, oddly enough) from $-.47$ for G-0 (the subjects in this group Predict that the correct stimulus alternates for a minimum of 47% of the problems) to $+.80$ for G-100 (these subjects Predict that the correct stimulus repeats for a minimum of 80% of the problems).

The values of D_a and D_x may be inserted into Equation 2 to predict the number of Nonoutcome problems in which the same syllable will be selected for both trials. The prediction will be made for each group, so that T, the total number of Nonoutcome problems under consideration, will equal 600 (20 subjects × 30 Nonoutcome problems per subject). The predicted and obtained frequencies are presented in Figure 2. This figure has two noteworthy features. One is that the obtained values are exceed-

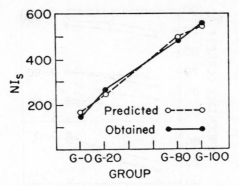

FIG. 2. Predicted and obtained NI_s for all the Nonoutcome problems for each of the four groups.

ingly close to the predicted values. None of the discrepancies from the predictions are statistically significant. The other is that there is a bias in favor of repeating syllables. If a group had been run in which the experimenter caused the correct syllables to perseverate on 50% of the problems and to alternate on the other 50%, i.e, if the experimenter had said "right" and "wrong" totally at random, then one would predict (from interpolation in Figure 2, rather than from theoretical consideration) that the subject would repeat syllables for about 360 (= 60%) of the Nonoutcome problems. The fact that with this insoluble procedure D_a would appear to be about +.15 (from interpolation in Figure 1) indicates that this repetition bias results primarily from the subject's tendency to Predict that the correct stimulus repeats rather than from a Response-set to repeat stimuli.

The validity of Equation 2 may be demonstrated in a more detailed fashion by consideration of the learning-set functions. These are typically plotted from Outcome problems as $P(+_2)$, the proportion of correct responses on Trial 2, at successive stages of the experiment. From considerations similar to those employed previously (Levine, 1959) it may be demonstrated that the theoretical proportion correct on Trial 2 for a given block of Outcome problems is given by:

$$P(+_2) = [1 + (2q - 1)D_a]/2 \qquad [3]$$

in which q is the proportion of problems on which the correct stimulus perseverates (for G-100, G-80, G-20, and G-0 the value of q is 1.0, .8, .2, and .0, respectively).

If Equation 2 is solved for D_a and the resulting expression substituted into Equation 3 the latter becomes:

$$P(+_2) = [1 + (2q - 1) \times \{(2NI_s/T) - D_x - 1\}]/2.$$

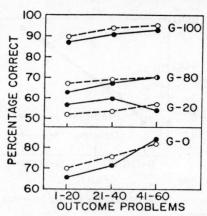

FIG. 3. Obtained (solid lines) and predicted (dashed lines) learning-set functions showing the mean percentage of correct responses on Trial 2 during blocks of 20 Outcome problems (the G-O curves were plotted on separate axes to avoid clutter).

If the assumption is now made that $D_x = 0$, i.e., that the Response-set to repeat stimuli occurs as often as the Response-set to alternate stimuli, for any block of problems considered, then the last equation becomes:

$$P(+_2) = 1 - q + \frac{NI_s}{T}(2q - 1). \qquad [4]$$

The symbols q and T are both defined by the experimenter, so that the proportion correct on Trial 2 of Outcome problems is given as a linear function of the number of repeated stimulus selections during Nonoutcome problems. Thus, from Nonoutcome problem data the conventional learning-set function can be predicted.

The predicted and obtained learning-set functions are presented in Figure 3. A prediction was separately made for each block of 20 Outcome problems from the 10 Nonoutcome problems distributed in the block ($T = 10$ problems per subject × 20 subjects = 200 problems). The pairs of points are close not only by inspection but also by statistical considerations. None of the differences between the obtained and predicted values are statistically significant at the .05 level. The largest CR, for problems 21–40 of G-20, is just short of significance ($p = .052$).

THE n-DIMENSIONAL PROBLEM

The preceding experiment demonstrates that for the two-trial simultaneous discrimination a close relationship exists between behavior during Outcome problems and during Nonoutcome problems. The model of mediating processes which has been elaborated provides a rationale for this relationship. In general, obtaining the H probabilities for one outcome condition permits a close prediction of the behavior patterns in the other condition.

The model was described, however, only for the situation in which two stimuli (for example, two different nonsense syllables) could occupy one of two positions: there were two dimensions with two values, or cues, for each dimension. The remainder of the paper will deal with transcending this limitation. It will be demonstrated how the model may be generalized to obtain H strengths at the outset of the n dimensional learning situation.

The analysis for the n-dimensional problem will be reduced relative to the analysis described in the preceding sections for the two-dimensional problem. In that analysis two general categories of Hs were described: Predictions ($H_a, \ldots, H_{b'}$) and Response-sets ($H_x, \ldots, H_{y'}$). The category of Predictions also had two types of Hs: Predictions that the correct value of one of the dimensions repeated (H_a and H_b) and Predictions that the correct value followed a sequential pattern (specifically, for the two-dimension problem, alternation: $H_{a'}$ and $H_{b'}$). The present model will be "reduced" in that it will attempt to evaluate only the first type of Prediction, i.e., only those Hs which are Predictions that one of the values of one of the dimensions is repeatedly correct. Response-set Hs and Hs which are Predictions of more complex sequential events will be ignored. In effect the assumption will be made that the most important type of mediating process which the adult human subject has at the outset of a problem of several dimensions consists in an attempt to locate the cue which is invariantly (within that problem) the basis for correct responding.

This assumption, incidentally, is not unique to the present treatment. In a common type of concept formation experiment the n-dimensional problem is employed and this assumption is more or less explicit in the analysis (for example, Bourne & Restle, 1959; Brown & Archer, 1956; Bruner, Goodnow, & Austin, 1956; Grant & Curran, 1952; Hovland, 1952). For this reason the assumption will be referred to as the concept formation (CF) assumption. The model incorporating this assumption will be referred to as the CF model.

The a priori justification for the CF assumption comes from three considerations:

1. The preceding experiment showed that the Response-set H differences, D_x and D_y, were uniformly near zero. One could have assumed that the Response-set Hs were zero without seriously altering the predictions. Also, the outright assumption that D_x was zero did not seem to impair the quality of prediction from Nonoutcome to Outcome problems (see Figure 3).

2. There is some evidence (Goodnow & Postman, 1955) that as the stimulus situation becomes multi-dimensional the subjects avoid complex sequence behaviors (resulting, for example, from single-alternation or double-alternation Predictions) in favor of locating that cue which is consistently to be chosen.

3. One may, by instructions and preexperimental demonstrations, minimize Predictions that events follow complex patterns. Several investigators of concept formation have employed this technique (Archer, Bourne, & Brown, 1955; Bruner et al., 1956; Hovland & Weiss, 1953; Oseas & Underwood, 1952).

The CF model, then, will deal with the n-dimensional problem and will focus upon Predictions by the subject concerning that dimension which defines correct responding. While the model will be presented in general form for the n-dimensional problem it will be applied specifically to a four-dimensional problem. An example of such a problem is presented in Figure 4. The dimensions are form (X versus T), position (right versus left), color (white versus black), and size (large versus small). The figure shows one possible sequence of the various levels over the four trials. This sequence has the special property that each value of each dimension appears an equal number of times with every value of every other dimension. For example, T is black twice, large letters appear on the right twice, X is small twice, etc. Problems in which the dimensions show this kind of balance will be described as *internally orthogonal*.

THE CONCEPT FORMATION MODEL

As already stated, only Predictions that the correct cue repeats from trial to trial will be evaluated. For any given dimension there is only this one H. For the problem shown in Figure 4, for example, there are four Hs corresponding to the four dimensions. If the subject has a color H at the outset of the problem he Predicts that one of the colors will be correct from trial to trial regardless of which form has that color, its size, or position. Similarly, if the subject has a size H he Predicts that one of the two sizes will be correct from trial to trial. There are also, in this problem, a position H and a form H.

One task of the model will be to show how one may evaluate individually the n Hs which correspond to the n dimensions. In addition, a residual H will be determined demonstrating the pooled effect of other mediating processes. For purposes of simplicity it will be assumed that this Residual H is the pooled strength of Predictions about dimensions which are not part of the formal structure of the problem. Such dimen-

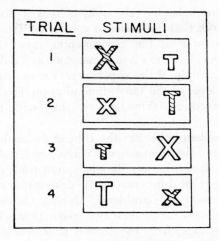

FIG. 4. Four trials of a four-dimensional problem.

sions might be movements by the experimenter, apparatus noises, a flickering light, etc.[2]

There are, then, $n + 1$ Hs to be described for the n-dimensional problem. For the four-dimensional problem described in Figure 4 there are five Hs:

H_a: The Prediction that form is the correct dimension and that the correct form will repeat.

H_b: The Prediction that position is the correct dimension, etc.

H_c: The Prediction that color is the correct dimension, etc.

H_d: The Prediction that size is the correct dimension, etc.

H_r: The Prediction that a nonrecorded dimension is correct.

The probability of any of these Hs will be denoted by the corresponding subscript symbol. Thus, $P(H_a) = a$, $P(H_b) = b$, etc.

The Hs are related to behavior solely by the Prediction postulate described for the two-trial problem (the Response-set postulate is irrelevant for the CF model). The behavioral manifestations of the ith H follow directly from this postulate:

H_i: *The subject Predicts that one level of the ith dimension is correct and will repeat.*

[2] This is an arbitrary interpretation of the Residual H. Certainly other processes could be occurring: Response-sets, more complex Predictions, periodic errors, as well as Predictions about unrecorded dimensions. The occurrence, if any, and contribution of each of these is completely unknown, nor have methods of disentangling them for the n dimensional problem been developed. The present assumption has the virtue of providing conceptual consistency and mathematical simplicity.

Outcome-problem behavior: the subject makes his best guess as to which of the levels of that dimension is correct on Trial 1. If the response is correct (for example, if the experimenter says "right") the subject chooses the same level of the same dimension on Trial 2; if the response is incorrect (for example, if the experimenter says "wrong") the subject chooses the other level of the same dimension on Trial 2. This would, in general, be described as "Win-stay-Lose-shift with respect to the ith dimension."

Nonoutcome-problem behavior: the subject makes his best guess as to which of the levels of that dimension is correct on Trial 1. He chooses the same level of that dimension on all subsequent trials of the problem.

There is an important difference in the description of the behavior for Outcome and Nonoutcome problems. During Outcome problems behavior is stipulated only for the first two trials. This is because the effects of "rights" and "wrongs" from the second trial onward involve assumptions about resampling of Hs which are beyond the scope of the present model. The limitation of relevant Outcome problem data to the first two trials makes unfeasible, in a problem with even as few as four dimensions, the solution of the H probabilities in the usual manner, i.e., from Outcome problems. The reason is, of course, that behavior patterns resulting from different Hs inevitably overlap during the first two trials, making evaluations of the Hs ambiguous. Over Trials 1 and 2 of the problem illustrated in Figure 4 for example, behavior with respect to color would be identical with behavior with respect to size, as would the behavior with respect to form and position.

During Nonoutcome problems, on the other hand, behavior is specified for all trials of a problem. In the problem of Figure 4, a subject with a form H (i.e., H_a) would respond RRLL (or LLRR; described more generally as AABB). The Prediction postulate demands precisely this behavior. No other behavior could yield 100% correct if H_a were correct. Similarly, a subject with H_b would respond AAAA; a subject with H_c would respond ABAB; a subject with H_d would respond ABBA. This freedom to observe the manifestation of the initial H over several trials of a Nonoutcome problem permits the emergence of unique response patterns corresponding to each H. In the problem shown in Figure 4, one need only observe which of the four response patterns is occurring to determine which H the subject is holding. Thus, the H held by a single subject on a single (Nonoutcome) problem may be determined. Also, if one wishes to revert to probabilistic statements about the strengths of the various Hs, one need only present the problem to a large number of subjects. The proportion of subjects showing each of the response patterns provides probability estimates of the corresponding Hs.

In an internally orthogonal four-trial problem such as that shown in

Figure 4 one may also determine when one of the class of H_r is occurring. Response patterns other than the four listed above may occur. For this problem, specifically, any combination of 3A's and 1B may also occur. Since they could not be produced by the four given Hs, these patterns will be interpreted as reflecting H_r.

By presenting a Nonoutcome problem of internally orthogonal structure, then, one may estimate the probabilities of all the various Hs described by the model. The Nonoutcome problem may be used to determine the H probabilities at a given point in a problem series. In the experiment to be described, for example, a large group of subjects receives a series of four trial problems. At various points in the series the group is subdivided, one half receiving an Outcome Problem, the other half receiving a Nonoutcome Problem. From the latter condition one may determine the probability of the Hs at the outset of the problem. The model assumes that these are also estimates of the initial H probabilities for the subjects facing the Outcome problem. The validity of this assumption will be demonstrated.

EXPERIMENT II

METHOD

Subjects. The subjects were 255 students from the experimental psychology courses at Indiana University. None of these subjects had participated in Experiment I.

Apparatus. Pairs of consonants of the alphabet were randomly selected to provide the stimulus forms for a given trial. The two letters were printed as transparent forms on an opaque background on a filmstrip negative. The pair of letters was printed four times with these variations: One of the letters was large and one was small; one was on the left and one on the right; the dimensions of letter, size, and position were mutually orthogonal, i.e., each level of each dimension appeared twice with each level of the other two dimensions. A color dimension was added by randomly selecting two hues from a set of seven transparent dies. (The hues were purple, blue, green, yellow, brown, red, and white.) The two colors were applied to the four reproductions of the pairs of letters, such that color was orthogonal to the other three dimensions. This produced the set of stimuli for the type of problem exemplified in Figure 4, i.e., four pairs of stimuli constructed from four mutually orthogonal dimensions. Twenty-four such problems were constructed. With a single exception, to be noted below, they were all internally orthogonal problems. There are six different types of 4-trial internally orthogonal problems, according to which dimension double alternates with respect to position (AABB), which single alternates (ABAB), and which follows an ABBA pattern. These six were randomly assigned to the 24 problems.

The filmstrips for the 24 problems were spliced together so that the problems could be presented conveniently in sequence. A pair of letters was projected by an overhead projector (Beseler Master Vu-Graph) onto a screen. Even in a well-lit room the letters appeared brightly with the appropriate hue. The larger of the two letters was approximately 6 × 3 inches when projected; the smaller letter was half that size. The letters were 2 inches apart.

Design. The subjects were divided into two groups of 127 and 128, respectively. Each group received a preliminary demonstration problem followed by the 24 problems of the experiment proper. The demonstration problem was constructed of the four dimensions indicated but was 14 trials in length. The 24 problems which followed this preliminary problem consisted of 18 Outcome problems with 6 Nonoutcome problems interspersed. One group (Group A) received the Nonoutcome condition on Problems 2, 6, 10, 14, 18, and 22; the other group (Group B) received the Nonoutcome condition on Problems 4, 8, 12, 16, 20, and 24. This design offered two advantages. First, H strengths, which are derived from the Nonoutcome procedure, could be obtained on every other problem. This permits a fairly detailed picture of changes in H probabilities over the problem series. Second, while one group of subjects is receiving a Nonoutcome problem (for example, Group B on Problem 20) the other group, which has had an almost identical history of problem solving experience in the experiment, is receiving an Outcome problem constructed of the same stimulus materials. The model permits prediction about behavior in the latter condition from the H information obtained from the former.

The latter feature provided the rationale for the one deviation from internally orthogonal problems during the experiment proper. The group receiving an Outcome problem when, at the same point, the other group was receiving a Nonoutcome problem did not necessarily receive an internally orthogonal problem. On these problems either zero, one, two, or all three of the remaining dimensions were confounded with the correct dimension. For example, if one dimension (for example, size) were confounded with the correct dimension (for example, color: green versus blue) then all blue letters would always be large (or always small). If all four dimensions were confounded, then the same letter would be large, blue, and on the left side on every trial of the problem. This variation in confounding expanded the range over which predictions could be made.

Procedure. The 255 subjects were run in 10 classes of approximately 25 students each. The first pair of stimuli from the preliminary problem was projected on the screen before the class while the initial instructions were read. The subjects were told that they were to decide which of the two stimuli was correct, that they were to indicate their choice by filling in the appropriate side (right or left corresponding to the location of the stimulus chosen) by the first answer space of an IBM answer sheet and that the experimenter would then indicate which stimulus was correct. They were further told that there would be a series of such stimuli and that this procedure was to be followed on each presentation. After all the subjects made their first response the experimenter pointed to the correct stimulus. Following this outcome presentation the next pair of stimuli appeared. The subjects responded and the experimenter again pointed to the correct stimulus. Fourteen trials took place in this manner. The form for these preliminary trials were always the letters A and E, the colors were red and green, and the letters were of two sizes as described above. The experimenter always pointed to the larger letter on all trials for all subjects.

When the 14 trials were ended, the experimenter announced that the large letter was always correct and told the class that this was a demonstration problem. He then explicitly described the four dimensions (large or small, right or left, the two colors, and the two letters) and stated that as in the preliminary problem where the large stimulus was always correct one of these cues would always provide the correct basis for responding.

The experiment proper was then begun. Outcomes were always presented except when Nonoutcome problems were scheduled. During all Outcome problems the experimenter pointed to the correct stimulus after each trial. For Outcome Problems 1–12 one of the two colors always served as the basis for correct responding; on Problems 13–24 one of the two letters always served as the basis for correct responding. Thus, there were two concept formation learning sets: A color set followed by a form set. The second followed the first without any special announcement or break.

Before the first Nonoutcome problem (Problem 2 for Group A; Problem 4 for Group B) the experimenter announced that the next problem would be a test of how much had been learned thus far. The class was told that during the next problem the experimenter would not point to the correct stimulus after each trial, that because this was a test the students were to continue to try to get 100% correct. The next four trials followed without outcomes. These trials were followed by the next three Outcome problems. Test instructions were then given again (before Problem 6 for Group A; Problem 8 for Group B) followed by another Nonoutcome problem. Three Outcome problems continued to alternate with one Nonoutcome problem until all 24 problems had been presented.

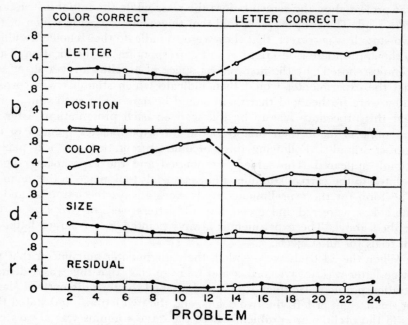

Fig. 5. The probability of occurrence of the various *H*s (the open circles are for Group A; the filled circles are for Group B).

RESULTS

The *H* probabilities on every second problem are presented in Figure 5. These probabilities are directly equivalent to the proportion of subjects manifesting the response pattern corresponding to the *H* on each Nonoutcome problem. Thus the increase in *c* over Nonoutcome Problems 2–12 means that an increasing number of subjects are showing the response pattern corresponding to the color *H* on these problems. The figure shows how the probabilities of each *H* change, first during a color learning-set series (Problems 1–12) then during a form series (Problems 13–24).

It is important to recall that each data point represented in this figure comes from a Nonoutcome problem, that the curves represent changes in response patterns recorded during problems when the experimenter is saying nothing. Furthermore, the points represent two different groups alternating on Nonoutcome problems. In spite of this unorthodox style of collecting data, the resulting curves are quite regular; the curves for *c* during Problems 2–12 and for *a* during Problems 14–24 appear very much like typical, i.e., Outcome problem, learning curves, and the curves for other *H*s show regular, gradual extinction effects.

Certain details in this graph are noteworthy. The first is that H_b scarcely ever occurs. These subjects almost never Predict that position is the basis for solution. The reasons for this effect are unclear. It may occur either because the adult human subject generally avoids response to position in such a problem or because of the particular procedures employed in this experiment. What is important, however, is that the absence of consistent response to position means not only that $b = 0$ but that there is no Response-set to position, i.e., there is no manifestation of position preference. This represents further validation of the assumption that Response-sets are negligible with this type of subject.

The second detail is that when the learning-set changes there tends to be a small increase in the strength of already extinguished Hs; i.e., when the learning set shifts from color to letter, b, d, and R show a small increment in strength. Restle (1958) suggested that this might happen. The method provides a technique for quantitative analysis of the effect.

Third, more proficiency is achieved on the first learning set than on the second (c at maximum is .84; a reaches only .60). It is possible that color is more salient than letter, but again, the particular procedures must be considered. The letter problems came in the second half of a massed, and probably tedious, procedure. There was evidence that the subjects were tiring over the experimental session. One could have demonstrated this, although it was not done, by recording the number of yawns over the experiment. They clearly increased. It is possible, then, that the depression in the second learning-set function as well as some of the irregularities found in the second half of the data might disappear with a more distributed procedure.

Figure 5 portrays the information to be gathered by going beyond mere learning representations of data. Of course, this figure describes the H strengths from Nonoutcome problems. It is necessary now to consider its relevance to what traditionally has been of more universal interest, the Outcome problem.

During any even-numbered problem of Experiment II half the subjects received an Outcome problem while the other half received a similar problem without outcomes. Since the model deals with Hs at the *outset* of the problem one may assume, as has been done throughout, that the probabilities are the same for both types of problems. Therefore, if the probabilities are known for one type of problem they are, in theory, also known for the other. In theory, Figure 5, although derived from Nonoutcome problems, also describes the H probabilities at the outset of the corresponding Outcome problems. This assertion may be tested by using the H probabilities from each Nonoutcome problem to predict percentage correct on Trial 2 of each corresponding Outcome problem. From the data in Figure 5, in effect, the model can predict the traditional learning-set function: percentage correct on Trial 2 of successive problems.

The argument is straightforward:

1. On any Outcome problem one of the dimensions, and, therefore, one of the Hs is always designated as correct. The probability of the correct H (as inferred from the Nonoutcome problem) provides an estimate of the proportion of the subjects on the corresponding Outcome problem who, because they follow this H, would be correct on Trial 2. For example, on Problem 2 $P(H_c) = .32$. This means that 32% of the subjects facing the Outcome condition on Problem 2 will make a correct response on Trial 2.

2. Zero to three dimensions may be confounded with the correct dimension during Trials 1 and 2 of the Outcome problem. Suppose, for the problem described in Figure 4, that color were the correct dimension. One dimension, size, is confounded with it over Trials 1 and 2. The probability of an H corresponding to such a confounded dimension provides an estimate of additional subjects who would be correct on Trial 2 of the corresponding Outcome problem. On Outcome Problem 2 also, size is confounded with color. $P(H_d) = .25$, so that in addition to the 32% mentioned above another 25% would be correct on Trial 2.

3. All subjects holding an H about a dimension unconfounded with the correct dimension over Trials 1 and 2 (form and position in the example of Figure 4 and on the second Outcome problem) would, because of the "Win-stay-Lose-shift" character of the behavior required by the Prediction postulate, make an incorrect response on Trial 2.

4. For the proportion of subjects holding the Residual H it will be assumed that half would be correct on Trial 2 and half would be incorrect. Since $P(H_r) = .18$ on the second problem, an additional 9% of the subjects would be correct on Trial 2 of the corresponding Outcome problem.

Thus, for Problem 2, percentage correct on Trial 2 is given as:

$$\% \text{ Correct} = P(+_2) \times 100 = (.32 + .25 + .09) \times 100 = 66\%.$$

In general,

$$P(+_2) = P(H_i) + \Sigma P(H_j) + \frac{P(H_r)}{2}$$

where $P(H_i)$ is the probability of the correct H, and $\Sigma P(H_j)$ is the sum of the probabilities of the Hs corresponding to dimensions confounded with the correct dimension over Trials 1 and 2.

Table 1 shows the dimensions which were confounded with the correct dimension during Trials 1 and 2 of the Outcome problems. It also shows in the right-hand column, the resulting formulas for determining the theoretical $P(+_2)$ for each problem. From the information in Figure 5 one may obtain the numerical theoretical values. These have been obtained as percentages and are compared to the actual percentage correct in Figure 6.

Consider first the solid line. This connects the empirical percentage correct values, i.e., $100(\# \text{ right})/N$. For all its irregularities it is a learning-set function, by definition (Percentage correct on Trial 2 over successive problems—see Harlow, 1959). The irregularities result, one should note, not from careless planning or sloppy procedure but rather, in large measure, from the deliberate confounding of dimensions. It was the task of the model to reproduce these irregularities.

TABLE 1

THE DIMENSIONS CONFOUNDED WITH THE CORRECT DIMENSIONS
OVER TRIALS 1 AND 2 OF THE INDICATED
OUTCOME PROBLEMS

Problem	Correct dimension	Confounded dimensions	Theoretical $P(+_2)$
2	color	size	$c + d + r/2$
4	color	position, size	$b + c + d + r/2$
6	color	form, position, size	$a + b + c + d + r/2$
8	color		$c + r/2$
10	color		$c + r/2$
12	color	position, size	$b + c + d + r/2$
14	form	position, size	$a + b + d + r/2$
16	form	position, color, size	$a + b + c + d + r/2$
18	form	position, color, size	$a + b + c + d + r/2$
20	form	position, size	$a + b + d + r/2$
22	form	color	$a + c + r/2$
24	form		$a + r/2$

Note.—Group B is receiving Outcome Problems 2, 6 10, etc.; Group A is receiving 4, 8, 12, etc.

The theoretical values are represented by the dashed line. The irregularities are well reproduced. Every change in direction of the curve is predicted. The H data, then, from the Nonoutcome problems permit generally good predictions of the performance at the outset of the Outcome problems. In this sense, the assertion that the H values portrayed in Figure 5 describe the values had an Outcome problem been presented receives some verification. A word of caution is needed, however. Three of the theoretical points (specifically at Problems 10, 22, and 24) are significantly different ($p < .05$ by χ^2 test) from the obtained points. The source of these differences, whether the model, or the procedure, is unknown.

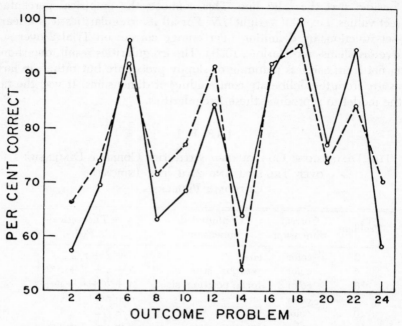

FIG. 6. The obtained (solid line) and predicted (dashed line) curves of the percentage correct on Trial 2 of successive Outcome problems.

DISCUSSION

A model has been presented which views the adult human subject as selecting, at the outset of a discrimination problem, one H from a set of Hs, where the H is defined as a mediating process. Within this general conception two variations of the model were considered. In the first the situation was restricted to the two-dimensional discrimination situation, but little restriction was imposed upon the type of H which the subject might hold. This permitted the detailed description of two classes of Hs: Predictions and Response-sets. An experiment consisting of two-trial Outcome and Nonoutcome problems effectively demonstrated that for the two-dimensional situation the model accounts for the relationship between these two types of problems. The results also suggested that Response-set Hs were not occurring.

The latter finding was employed in the second variation of the model. The omission of Response-set Hs from consideration helped simplify the model for application to the n dimensional problem. The application was restricted to the concept formation situation, i.e., to the setting in which it was assumed that the subject was attempting to locate that cue which provided the basis for correct responding. This variation permitted the specification of the H held by a single subject on any particular problem as well as statements about the probability of the Hs. A technique was demonstrated for validating the probability statements.

The general model has some special features and has uncovered some unique results which are worth stressing.

1. The H, rather than the specific choice response on a particular trial, is regarded as the dependent variable, i.e., as the unit of behavior affected by the reinforcements. This point of view has several advantages. First, as noted in the analysis of H behavior by monkeys (Levine, 1959), the learning-set effect can be treated within the context of a conditioning theory. In the typical learning-set experiment the Prediction that one of the objects is correct and will repeat is the only H which receives 100% reinforcement beyond Trial 1. This feature produces the increase in "Win-stay-Lose-shift with respect to the object" relative to the other Hs.

Second, the paradox of alternation learning is eliminated. This paradox derives from the traditional view of reinforcement as increasing the probability of the last-made choice response. Consider a subject in Group G-0 in Experiment I. He responds by choosing one of two stimuli on Trial 1 of any problem. On half of the problems the experimenter will then say "right." This outcome is virtually universally regarded as a reinforcement of the response. But does it have this function? The subject typically chooses the other stimulus on the next trial. Therefore, the experimenter has reinforced one response yet has increased the probability that the subject will make the other response—a puzzling result by most definitions of the term "reinforcement." The resolution of this paradox by the present model is that the behavior affected by the reinforcements is not the choice response but the H selected, i.e., the Prediction of how events will proceed. In this particular example a series of outcomes reinforces the Prediction that the correct stimulus alternates.

Third, Experiment II makes it clear that learning may be occurring without being manifested in the record of correct choice response, i.e., in the traditional learning curve. The obtained percentage correct on Trial 2, represented by the solid line in Figure 6, shows no clear systematic increase over problems. One must analyze the changes in H strengths, as was done in Figure 5, in order to see the learning.

2. The definition of the H has been shifted from a behavior pattern to a mediating process of which the behavior pattern is a manifestation. The former definition was employed earlier in the model for monkeys. It was possible to define the H in this way because the experimenter utilized only a single procedure (presenting outcomes) resulting, with a given H, in a single behavior pattern. It would have been superfluous to assert

that an *H* represented a Response-set or Prediction which resulted in the behavior pattern. The change was necessitated because the experimenter now employed two procedures: presenting and withholding outcomes. The behavior patterns defining an *H* previously (for Outcome problems) must, for some *H*s, necessarily change when outcomes are withdrawn. For example, a subject with a strong "Win-stay-Lose-shift" habit must change his behavior during Nonoutcome problems, since "Win" and "Lose" are not available as stimuli for staying and shifting. By transferring the definition of the *H* from the response pattern itself to the determinants of the response pattern, i.e., to the mediating process, one was able to select intuitively reasonable postulates which permitted the specification of the change in the response pattern when outcomes were withdrawn.

3. A specific relationship exists between Outcome and Nonoutcome problems. This relationship is predictable from the model, in part because of the assumption that the same set of *H*s determines behavior in both types of problems. This relationship was differently employed in the two experiments reported above. Experiment I simply demonstrated that the results predicted by the model in fact occurred. It demonstrated this for four differently treated groups receiving two-trials-per-problem learning sets.

Experiment II employed the relationship to determine *H*s in a problem series from the Nonoutcome problems. The Nonoutcome problem became a "probe" to determine, for each individual subject, the *H* he was holding at the time.

4. A distinction is explicitly made between Predictions (manifested, during Outcome problems, in behavior contingent upon outcomes) and Response-sets (manifested in behavior which is always independent of outcomes). Hypothesis analyses up until now have overlooked the distinction. Krechevsky (1932), for example, demonstrated Response-sets (position preference, stimulus preference) in rats but wrote as though the behavior were manifestations of Predictions. He characterized hypotheses as follows:

> an "hypothesis" is something that must be *verified* before it is persisted in. If the hypothesis does not lead to certain expected results it is soon dropped. "*If* this attempt is correct, *then* I should get such and such results, if I do not get such and such results then I must change my behavior." . . . The rat, in the maze or in the discrimination box, behaves in the very same way [pp. 529–530].

Note the dependence stipulated upon "results" (outcomes) as determiners of the response patterns. In fact, however, Krechevsky presented data only for behavior patterns which persist regardless of the outcomes, patterns which were Response-set manifestations.

This interpretation by Krechevsky caused Spence (1940) to retort:

hypotheses are far from what he [the writer, Spence] understands by the terms insightful and intelligent. Only *persistent* non-adaptative responses can attain the distinction of being hypotheses—for, in order to classify as a hypothesis, a response, although ineffective, must continue to be persisted in a certain minimum number of times. A maladaptive act which is speedily (intelligently?) abandoned cannot ever be a hypothesis [p. 287].

In effect, Krechevsky argued that all systematic behavior manifested an attempt by the subject to maximize his rewards; Spence's reply was that the behavior was of a different order. In terms of the analysis presented here Krechevsky was inferring Predictions from behavior patterns which are manifestations of Response-sets.

5. The prevalence of Response-sets in animals contrasts sharply with the present results. As just noted, Krechevsky found Response-sets in rats. Schusterman (1961) demonstrated similar Hs in chimpanzees, and Levine (1959) and Harlow (1950) demonstrated them in monkeys. Response-set Hs are widespread among infrahuman animals. According to the experiments reported here, adult human subjects (specifically, college students) show no Response-set Hs. Thus, one could have assumed that these Hs were zero in Experiment I without hurting the quality of prediction; the explicit assumption in Experiment II did not seem to impair the effectiveness of the model; one Response-set commonly observed among animals, position preference, was clearly absent in Experiment II.

Although the model has these above mentioned features to recommend it, it does not yet stand as a comprehensive theory. There are several problems which remain to be solved. First the model deals with Hs only at the outset of problems. This restriction was made primarily because there is currently no basis for making assumptions about the effects of outcomes beyond Trial 2. A technique for investigating these effects will be needed before the model can be generalized. Second, in going from the two-dimensional (Experiment I) to the n-dimensional (Experiment II) problem the class of Hs was restricted to Predictions that the correct cue would repeat from trial to trial. While this restriction may be satisfactory for well motivated college students it is undoubtedly not adequate for application to all subjects. Children, for example, would probably require a model which measured both Predictions and Response-sets in the n-dimensional problem. Third, the definition of the Residual H is far from settled. The treatment of this H, that it was manifested by any response pattern not strictly conforming to a recorded dimension, was simple. The chief defect with this approach, however, is that it leaves out of account momentary sources of error, "slips" by a subject who has the correct (or any other) H. Because of this, the Residual H, as now measured, would increase artifactually with longer problems. It is antic-ipated that a more satisfactory treatment of Residual response patterns will be distilled as data accumulate. Finally, the various techniques of measuring mediating processes need to be refined and compared. Experi-ment II demonstrated that, for the *n*-dimensional problem, the Nonout-come procedure may serve to determine the *H*s. M. Richter, at Indiana University, is currently developing the model to measure *H* strengths di-rectly from Outcome problems of *n* dimensions. Another technique, one which is time-honored but not tested, is to utilize verbal reports. Several researchers (Bruner et al., 1956; Heidbreder, 1924; Verplanck, 1962) have had the subject state his hypothesis before each trial or certain trials. Insufficient attempt, however, has been made to investigate the relation-ship between the verbal response and the choice responses. The three techniques need to be developed, brought within the framework of the model, and compared.

References

Archer, E. J., Bourne, L. E., Jr., & Brown, F. G. Concept identification as a function of irrelevant information and instructions. *J. exp. Psychol.*, 1955, 49, 153–164.

Behar, L. Analysis of object-alternation learning by rhesus monkeys. *J. comp. physiol. Psychol.*, 1961, 54, 539–542.

Bourne, L. E., Jr., & Restle, F. Mathematical theory of concept iden-tification. *Psychol. Rev.*, 1959, 66, 278–296.

Brown, F. G., & Archer, E. J. Concept identification as a function of task complexity and distribution of practice. *J. exp. Psychol.*, 1956, 52, 316–321.

Bruner, J. S. Personality dynamics and the process of perceiving. In R. R. Blake & G. V. Ramsey (Eds.), *Perception: An approach to per-sonality.* New York: Ronald Press, 1951. Pp. 121–147.

Bruner, J. S., Goodnow, Jacqueline J., & Austin, G. A. *A study of think-ing.* New York: Wiley, 1956.

Glaze, J. A. The association value of nonsense syllables. *J. genet. Psychol.*, 1928, 35, 255–267.

Goodnow, J. J., & Postman, L. Probability learning in a problem-solving situation. *J. exp. Psychol.*, 1955, 49, 16–22.

Grant, D. A., & Curran, J. F. Relative difficulty of number, form, and color concepts of a Weigl-type problem using unsystematic number cards. *J. exp. Psychol.*, 1952, 43, 408–413.

Harlow, H. F. Analysis of discrimination learning by monkeys. *J. exp. Psychol.*, 1950, 40, 26–39.

Harlow, H. F. Learning set and error factor theory. In S. Koch (Ed.),

Psychology: A study of a science. Vol. 2. *General systematic formulations; learning and special processes.* New York: McGraw-Hill, 1959. Pp. 492–537.

HEIDBREDER, E. An experimental study of thinking. *Arch. Psychol., N. Y.,* 1924, No. 73.

HOVLAND, C. I. A "communication analysis" of concept learning. *Psychol. Rev.,* 1952, 59, 461–472

HOVLAND, C. I., & WEISS, W. Transmission of information concerning concepts through positive and negative instances. *J. exp. Psychol,* 1953, 45, 175–182.

KENDLER, H. H., & KENDLER, TRACY S. Vertical and horizontal processes in problem solving. *Psychol. Rev.,* 1962, 69, 1–16.

KRECHEVSKY, I. "Hypotheses" in rats. *Psychol. Rev.,* 1932, 39, 516–532.

LEVINE, M. A model of hypothesis behavior in discrimination learning set. *Psychol. Rev.,* 1959, 66, 353–366.

OSEAS, L., & UNDERWOOD, B. J. Studies of distributed practice: V. Learning and retention of concepts. *J. exp. Psychol.,* 1952, 43, 143–148.

RESTLE, F. Toward a quantitative description of learning set data. *Psychol. Rev.,* 1958, 65, 77–91.

RESTLE, F. The selection of strategies in cue learning. *Psychol. Rev.,* 1962, 69, 329–343.

SCHUSTERMAN, R. J. The use of strategies in the decision behavior of children and chimpanzees. *Amer. Psychologist,* 1961, 16, 424. (Abstract)

SPENCE, K. W. Continuous versus noncontinuous interpretations of discrimination learning. *Psychol. Rev.,* 1940, 47, 271–288.

VERPLANCK, W. S. Unaware of where's awareness: Some verbal operants —notates, moments, and notants. *J. Pers.,* 1962, 30, 130–158.

APPENDIX A

The technique for evaluating the H strengths from Outcome-problem data will be presented here. The two problem types (A and B) and the four outcome-response sequences $(+_1I_s, +_1O_s, -_1I_s, -_1O_s)$ may be organized into a matrix of eight cells, in which each cell refers to one of the possible events which may occur. This matrix is presented in Table A1. After a set of Outcome problems has been presented to the subjects, the frequency with which each event has occurred may be tabulated. Each frequency will be referred to as n_{ij}, where the first subscript denotes the problem type (or row of the matrix) and the second subscript denotes the outcome-response pattern (or column of the matrix). Corresponding to the frequency will be a ratio showing the proportion of times that the same (or other) stimulus was chosen on Trial 2, given the problem type and results of Trial 1. For example,

$$p_{11} = P(I_s \mid A, +_1) = \frac{n_{11}}{n_{11} + n_{12}}.$$

Table A1 shows that the eight p_{ij} are similarly defined.

The first step in evaluating the H probabilities is to express the p_{ij} in terms of $a, a', \ldots, y'$. This will be done, by way of example, for p_{11}.

TABLE A1

FREQUENCY (n_{ij}) AND PROPORTION (p_{ij}) WITH WHICH EACH OF THE EIGHT EVENTS MAY OCCUR IN A BLOCK OF OUTCOME-PROBLEM DATA

Type	Outcome-response sequence				
	$+_1 I_s$	$+_1 O_s$	$-_1 I_s$	$-_1 O_s$	
A	$p_{11} = \dfrac{n_{11}}{n_{11} + n_{12}}$	$p_{12} = \dfrac{n_{12}}{n_{11} + n_{12}}$	$p_{13} = \dfrac{n_{13}}{n_{13} + n_{14}}$	$p_{14} = \dfrac{n_{14}}{n_{13} + n_{14}}$	$N_{1.} = \sum_j n_{1j}$
B	$p_{21} = \dfrac{n_{21}}{n_{21} + n_{22}}$	$p_{22} = \dfrac{n_{22}}{n_{21} + n_{22}}$	$p_{23} = \dfrac{n_{23}}{n_{23} + n_{24}}$	$p_{24} = \dfrac{n_{24}}{n_{23} + n_{24}}$	$N_{2.} = \sum_j n_{2j}$

Since, with this example, only Type A problems are considered, the A will be omitted from the subsequent formulas. The expression above for p_{11} becomes,

$$p_{11} = P(I_s \mid +_1) = \frac{P(+_1 I_s)}{P(+_1)}.$$

$P(+_1 I_s)$ may be expanded to:

$$
\begin{aligned}
P(+_1 I_s) &= P(H_a +_1 I_s) + P(H_{a'} +_1 I_s) + \cdots + P(H_{y'} +_1 I_s) \\
&= P(I_s \mid H_a +_1)P(H_a +_1) + P(I_s \mid H_{a'} +_1)P(H_{a'} +_1) + \cdots \\
&\qquad + P(I_s \mid H_{y'} +_1)P(H_{y'} +_1) \\
&= P(I_s \mid H_a +_1)P(H_a)P(+_1) + P(I_s \mid H_{a'} +_1)P(H_{a'})P(+_1) + \cdots \\
&\qquad + P(I_s \mid H_{y'} +_1)P(H_{y'})P(+_1).
\end{aligned}
$$

The Prediction and Response-set postulates specify $P(I_s \mid H_i +_1)$ so that the last equation may be rewritten:

$$
\begin{aligned}
P(+_1 I_s) &= 1 \cdot a \cdot P(+_1) + 0 \cdot a' \cdot P(+_1) + \cdots + 0 \cdot y' \cdot P(+_1) \\
&= P(+_1)[a + b + x + y].
\end{aligned}
$$

Therefore,

$$P(I_s \mid +_1) = a + b + x + y$$

or

$$p_{11} = a + b + x + y = \frac{n_{11}}{n_{11} + n_{12}}.$$

The other p_{ij} may be obtained in a similar manner, yielding the eight following equations:

$$p_{11} = a + b + x + y$$
$$p_{12} = a' + b' + x' + y'$$
$$p_{13} = a' + b' + x + y$$
$$p_{14} = a + b + x' + y'$$
$$p_{21} = a + b' + x + y'$$
$$p_{22} = a' + b + x' + y$$
$$p_{23} = a' + b + x + y'$$
$$p_{24} = a + b' + x' + y.$$

Because of the complementary relation between the repeat versus alternate pairs of Hs, the individual symbols may not be evaluated by any general technique. It is possible, however, to evaluate the difference between a complementary pair of Hs. It is possible, for example, to evaluate $D_a = a - a'$. This is obtained by adding p_{11}, p_{14}, p_{21}, and p_{24}, and applying Equation 1.

This yields,

$$D_a = a - a' = \frac{p_{11} + p_{14} + p_{21} + p_{24} - 2}{2}$$

$$D_b = b - b' = \frac{p_{11} + p_{22} + p_{23} + p_{14} - 2}{2}$$

$$D_x = x - x' = \frac{p_{11} + p_{21} + p_{13} + p_{23} - 2}{2}$$

$$D_y = y - y' = \frac{p_{11} + p_{22} + p_{13} + p_{24} - 2}{2}.$$

Appendix B

The determination of NI_s, the theoretical number of times that the same stimulus is selected in a block of Nonoutcome problems, will be presented here. The two problem types (A and B) and the two response sequences (I_s and O_s) may be organized into a matrix of four cells in which each cell refers to one of the possible events which may occur. This matrix is presented in Table B1.

From this table one may note that:

$$g_{11} = P(I_s \mid A) = \frac{t_{11}}{T_{1.}},$$

and that,

$$g_{21} = P(I_s \mid B) = \frac{t_{21}}{T_{2.}}.$$

Employing the mathematical arguments analogous to those in Appendix A, one obtains:

$$P(I_s \mid A) = a + b + x + y = \frac{t_{11}}{T_{1.}}$$

and

$$P(I_s \mid B) = a + b' + x + y' = \frac{t_{21}}{T_{2.}}.$$

These equations may be rewritten as:

$$t_{11} = T_{1.} \cdot (a + b + x + y)$$
$$t_{21} = T_{2.} \cdot (a + b' + x + y').$$

TABLE B1

FREQUENCY (t_{ij}) AND PROPORTION (g_{ij}) WITH WHICH EACH OF THE FOUR
EVENTS MAY OCCUR IN A BLOCK OF NONOUTCOME-PROBLEM DATA

Type	Response sequence		
	I_s	O_s	
A	$g_{11} = \dfrac{t_{11}}{t_{11} + t_{12}}$	$g_{12} = \dfrac{t_{12}}{t_{11} + t_{12}}$	$T_{1.} = t_{11} + t_{12}$
B	$g_{21} = \dfrac{t_{21}}{t_{21} + t_{22}}$	$g_{22} = \dfrac{t_{22}}{t_{21} + t_{22}}$	$T_{2.} = t_{21} + t_{22}$
	$NI_s = t_{11} + t_{21}$		

If the condition holds that $T_{1.} = T_{2.} = T/2$, i.e., if half the problems are of the A type and half are of the B type, then:

$$\begin{aligned}
NI_s &= t_{11} + t_{21}\\
&= (T/2)[2a + b + b' + 2x + y + y']\\
&= (T/2)[a + x + (a + b + b' + x + y + y')]\\
&= (T/2)[a - a' + x - x' + 1]
\end{aligned}$$

or,

$$NI_s = (T/2)[D_a + D_x + 1].$$

This last equation shows that the number of repeated stimulus selections during Nonoutcome problems may be predicted once D_a and D_x have been determined from Outcome problems. This equation is intuitively plausible, since it states that NI_s will be greater the relatively greater is the tendency either to Predict that the correct syllable repeats or to have a Response-set to repeat syllables. For this reason, this equation was used to predict NI_s. This equation, however, may be reduced to a simpler form, one which provides an interesting theorem about Outcome and Nonoutcome results.

If the equations in Appendix A for D_a and D_x are substituted into this last equation for NI_s, this equation reduces to

$$\frac{NI_s}{T} = \frac{p_{11} + p_{21}}{2}.$$

It will be recalled that $p_{11} = P(I_s \,|\, A, +_1)$; $p_{21} = P(I_s \,|\, B, +_1)$. The last equation says, essentially, that the proportion of repeats during Nonoutcome problems is equal to the proportion of repeats during Outcome problems *when the experimenter said "right" after the first response.* This may be stated in its most general form as follows:

Theorem: When a subject is trying to obtain 100% correct during Nonoutcome problems he behaves as though the experimenter were saying "right" after each response.

SECTION EIGHT

Reversal and Transfer

The technique of training an animal in a discrimination, then testing for transfer to a task in which the S-R relationships of the training task are reversed, has become a useful method to analyze concept learning in human adults. Originally, comparisons of reversal shift with various kinds of control conditions (different types of nonreversal shift, and no shift) were claimed to be of value in studying the role of mediation in concept learning and concept shifts. More recently, reversal has been brought to bear on a number of different issues. Thus, in the Bower and Trabasso article, the issue is all-or-none versus gradual learning. Whereas reversal after solution usually leads to negative transfer, reversal prior to solution had no interfering effect in their study. Bower and Trabasso conclude that this supports the all-or-none hypothesis in simple concept learning, but they are careful to point out that this may not hold for more complex concepts.

The study by Harrow shows that even reversal shift may be further analyzed into within-dimension stimulus shifts and response reversals. (It might be better to reserve the designation of within-dimension shift to the case where the stimuli are actually changed, as from yellow and blue to red and green, but Harrow also used the term when the stimuli remained red and green, but responses were reversed.) His analysis shows that it is the response reversal that is interfering, whereas stimulus shifts within the same dimension may be facilitating. It may be noted that Harrow also includes between-dimension shifts and that these are, as usual, the most difficult of all shifts.

In several earlier studies, Kendler argued that the superiority of

318

reversal over nonreversal shift in human adults suggested that mediation operated to facilitate reversal shift. The Kendler and Woerner paper further attempts to tie mediation in with a performance difference between the two types of shift by claiming that if mediation is a response that can be extinguished, then the usual advantage of reversal over nonreversal shift should be reduced. Since the stimuli were present during mediational extinction, the reduced difference that did in fact occur between shifts is perhaps attributable to the effect of extinction on Harrow's within-dimension component of reversal shifts.

Holstein and Premack use the technique of presolution random reinforcement (introduced by Levine in connection with some of his theory, as in the paper in Section Seven) to follow up the Bower and Trabasso study on presolution reversal. Although presolution random reinforcement, unlike presolution reversal, did increase trials to learn, both techniques apparently produce the same error curves characteristic of all-or-none learning, once consistent reinforcement is introduced and learning begins. Holstein and Premack make the interesting suggestion that random reinforcement increases the population of hypotheses to be sampled.

26. Reversals Prior to Solution in Concept Identification

Gordon Bower and Thomas Trabasso

Abstract. *These studies investigated the effects of reversal and non-reversal shifts before solution upon performance in a later concept identification task. In 2 experiments, a reversal or a nonreversal shift after an error on a critical trial had no interfering effect upon subsequent learning. The reversal and nonreversal groups made about the same number of errors and required as many trials to learn as did controls who were not shifted. In a 3rd experiment, 1 group of Ss received reversals on every alternate error, but still made the same number of informed errors as did*

Reprinted by permission of the authors and the American Psychological Association from *Journal of Experimental Psychology*, 1963, 66, 409–418.

controls who learned with no shifts. These results support the hypothesis that learning is insightful or an all-or-nothing event in simple concept identification.

In the typical two-category concept identification experiment, S is shown a series of complex patterns which vary in several, binary attributes. As each pattern is presented, S attempts to anticipate the correct classification; following his response, he is informed of the correct response. The patterns are divided into two mutually exclusive classes, R_1 and R_2. If, say, color (red or blue) is the relevant attribute, then red objects might be assigned to Response Class R_1 and blue objects to Class R_2. We will refer to this rule as a particular S-R assignment.

In recent studies (Bower & Trabasso, 1963a; Trabasso, 1963) of this situation with college students, Ss appeared to learn suddenly. Backward learning curves were horizontal at the chance level of 50% correct classifications over all trials until S's last error before solving. The performance of an S might be characterized by saying that on any given trial he is either in the presolution state or in the solution state, with corresponding probabilities of .50 or 1.00 of correctly classifying the stimuli. According to this two-state description of the performance, learning would be identified as a discrete, one-trial transition from the initial, presolution state into the terminal, solution state.

The theories of cue-selection learning proposed by Restle (1962) and Bower and Trabasso (1963a) imply this two-state description of individual performance. These theories assume that S is selectively attending to or sampling cues from the stimulus display and that he is testing hypotheses regarding the relevance of these cues to the correct solution. If S's response is correct, it is supposed that he continues to use the same hypothesis; if his response is incorrect, he resamples at random from the set of possible hypotheses. Assume further that the proportion of correct hypotheses is c whereas the remaining proportion $1 - c$ is irrelevant hypotheses which lead to correct and incorrect responses half the time. By these assumptions, the probability that S solves the problem after any given error is a fixed constant, c. This elementary theory has been used successfully in predicting quantitative details of several sets of data (Bower & Trabasso, 1963a).

The present studies investigate whether S acquires partial knowledge about the solution to the problem. The all-or-nothing theory supposes that he does not. Specifically, it says that when S makes an error, he has not yet learned anything of relevance regarding the correct concept. Three experiments were performed to provide tests of this assumption; the first two are described now.

Experiments I and II

Experiments I and II are identical in design; Exp. II was a replication of Exp. I with an easier problem and different stimulus materials. The design resembles that used in several animal experiments conducted on the continuity-noncontinuity issue in discrimination learning theory (e.g., Krechevsky, 1938; McCulloch & Pratt, 1934). Control Ss in Group C learned a problem with the same S-R assignments throughout (Cue A-R_1, Cue B-R_2). Two other groups worked on different S-R assignments initially and then were transferred to the assignments of the control group. This transfer occurred immediately after S made an error following a critical trial of the initial series. Group R, a reversal group, was trained initially with the opposite assignments, A-R_2 and B-R_1. Group NR, a nonreversal-shift group, was trained initially with Cues A and B present but irrelevant while another set of cues was relevant (C-R_1, D-R_2).

The question of interest is whether the initial wrong-way training retards performance of Ss in Groups R and NR who are shifted to the final, transfer problem before solving their initial problem. If Ss partially learn responses to the initially relevant cues before the shift, then such partial learning should induce negative transfer on the final problem. However, if S's error initiating the shift indicates that nothing of importance has yet been learned, then the performance on the final problem should be the same for the three groups, independent of the initial S-R assignments.

METHOD

Experimental design. A schematic outline of the design is presented in Table 1. Only two of the several stimulus attributes are represented in the left columns of Table 1. The rows give the combinations of stimulus values in the patterns and the correct responses to each pattern are listed

TABLE 1

Design for Exp. I and II

Patterns		Response Assignments			
		Initial Trials			Final Problem
Dimension 1	Dimension 2	Control	Reversal	Nonreversal	
A	C	R_1	R_2	R_1	R_1
A	D	R_1	R_2	R_2	R_1
B	C	R_2	R_1	R_1	R_2
B	D	R_2	R_1	R_2	R_2

under each condition. The Control and Reversal groups had Cues A and B relevant but they had opposite response assignments during initial training (10 trials in Exp. I and 5 trials in Exp. II). The Nonreversal group had one of the other dimensions (Cues C and D) relevant during initial training.

The Ss who made an error on Trial 10 in Exp. I or Trial 5 in Exp. II or soon thereafter were immediately shifted to the final problem listed in the right hand column of Table 1. We wished to compare on this final problem only those Ss who had not yet learned their initial problem by Trial 10 (or 5 in Exp. II). Consequently, if an S in any group began a criterion run of 16 consecutive correct responses on or before the critical trial (10 or 5), he was not shifted but was, as a result, excluded from the critical comparison between those Ss who did get put onto the final problem. According to the theory, these latter Ss were equalized at the start of the final problem since each S made an error before the shift was effected.

Procedure. The same instructions were read to all Ss. The S was to classify a set of patterns into two classes. In Exp. I, the classificatory responses were MIB and CEJ; in Exp. II, the numerals 1 and 2. The S was told that the patterns could be classified by a simple principle.

Patterns were presented one at a time on a card holder. The S paced his verbal responses and E then stated the correct classification. The S was allowed 4 sec. to view the pattern after reinforcement. A different order was presented each S by shuffling the cards before the session. Cards were reshuffled at the end of every 64 trials if S had not yet reached the learning criterion of 16 successive correct responses.

Stimulus materials. For Exp. I, patterns were constructed by sampling a single letter from each of four pairs of letters, (v or w), (F or G), (x or Y), (Q or R). Thus, vFYQ was a pattern, wvxR was not. The four letters were printed in a diamond shape on a 3 × 5 in. card. The letters appeared fixed in the order given above, but their locations at the four diamond corners rotated randomly from trial to trial. Location was an irrelevant cue. For Groups C and R, the letter pair (v, w) was relevant; the classification depended on which one of the letters was present on the card. One of the other letter pairs was selected randomly to be initially relevant for each S in Group NR, whereas (v, w) was irrelevant. The final problem was with (v, w) as the relevant cues with response assignments v-MIB and w-CEJ.

For Exp. II, the stimuli were geometric figures drawn in crayon pencil from templates on white 3 × 5 in. file cards. There were six binary dimensions: color (red or blue); size (large or small); shape (square or hexagon); number (three or four figures); position (figures arranged along right or left diagonal); and colored area within each figure (upper-right and lower-left or upper-left and lower-right quadrants). There was one relevant dimension and five irrelevant dimensions for each group. Color was relevant for Groups C and R. One of the other five dimensions was randomly selected and made relevant during initial training for each S in Group NR.

Subjects. For Exp. I, the Ss were 65 students in the introductory psychology course at Stanford University. Eleven Ss began a criterion run on or before Trial 10; there were 4, 3, and 4 Ss in Groups C, R, and NR, respectively. These Ss do not enter into the comparison on the final problem since they were not transferred. Setting aside these Ss, 18 Ss (13 males and 5 females) remained in each group.

For Exp. II, the Ss were 46 students in the introductory psychology course at Stanford University. Since the problem was easier, a larger proportion of Ss was expected to solve within a few trials. Hence, fewer initial training trials (five) were used so that the majority of Ss would not have to be set aside. Sixteen Ss, 5 in Group C, 4 in Group R, and 7 in Group NR, began a criterion run on or before Trial 5. These Ss were excluded from comparisons on the final problem. There remained 10 Ss (6 males and 4 females) in each group for comparison on the final problem.

RESULTS

In Exp. I, one S in Group C and one in Group NR failed to reach criterion within 140 trials on the final problem; all other Ss solved within 140 trials. In Exp. II, all Ss solved the final problem. Comparisons among groups on final-problem performance refer to trials following the error trial that initiated the shift to the final problem for a given S. Average errors and trial of last error are shown in Table 2 for the three conditions in both experiments.

The group differences on mean errors and mean trial of last error on the final problem were negligible in both experiments. The learning-parameter estimates (reciprocal of mean errors) are shown in Table 2; a likelihood ratio test for equality of c's was nonsignificant in both experiments. Further, a likelihood ratio test that each S's learning parameter, c_i, was equal to a common c was tested for all 65 Ss in Exp. I and for all 45 Ss in Exp. II. In each case, the null hypothesis could not be rejected—for Exp. I, $\chi^2 (64) = 53.3$, $p > 05$; for Exp II, $\chi^2 (45) = 42.4$, $p > .05$ (Bower & Trabasso, 1963b). Thus, the data were consistent with the hypothesis of a common c for Ss in each experiment; the differences among Ss' error scores could be attributed to the variability inherent in the theoretical process.

The lack of group differences indicates that performance on the final problem was unrelated to the response assignments reinforced during the initial series. Correspondingly, there was no evidence for partial learning of the relevant cues or partial elimination of irrelevant cues (cf. Group NR). Effectively, we may rely upon a single error by S to indicate that he is "naive" about the correct solution. An error in this situation has the properties of an uncertain recurrent event (Restle, 1962); when S commits an error, we may, so to speak, reset him back to the starting point from which he began working on the problem. It should be noted that the null effects of reversal and nonreversal shifts before solution differ from the effects of such shifts after initial solution has occurred (Kendler and Kendler, 1962). What differs in the two cases is that after

TABLE 2

MEAN ERRORS AND TRIAL OF LAST ERROR, SDs, AND c ESTIMATES
FOR THE FINAL PROBLEM

Group	N	c	Mean Errors	SD	Mean Trial of Last Error	SD
			Exp. I			
Control	18	.052	19.11	19.01	38.33	32.50
Reversal	18	.052	19.11	16.42	39.56	32.27
Nonreversal	18	.055	18.28	19.28	36.94	38.23
			Exp. II			
Control	10	.078	12.90	8.42	28.60	20.82
Reversal	10	.067	14.90	9.77	29.00	19.71
Nonreversal	10	.071	14.00	14.15	26.90	26.45

solution, S has a strong bias to attend to the formerly relevant cue, whereas before solution he is sampling cues at random to test (Kendler, Glucksberg, & Keston, 1961).

Presolution analyses. The data prior to the last error of each S were analyzed according to the expectations of the all-or-none theory. In theory, the presolution responses of S may be represented as a stationary and independent binomial process. To test for a constant probability of success prior to the last error, backward learning curves (Hayes, 1953) were constructed. These were stationary near .50 in each experiment. Pooling the two experiments, the probabilities of a correct classification on Trials -1, -2 ... -8 backwards from the last error were .50, .50, .52, .53, .54, .49, .51, and .50. Furthermore, the curve was flat when analyzed in two-trial blocks for 40 trials backwards from criterion, χ^2 (19) $=19.31$, $p > .05$.

Successive correct or incorrect responses prior to the last error were also statistically independent. For Exp. I, the conditional probability of a success was .52 following a success and .53 following an error; in Exp.

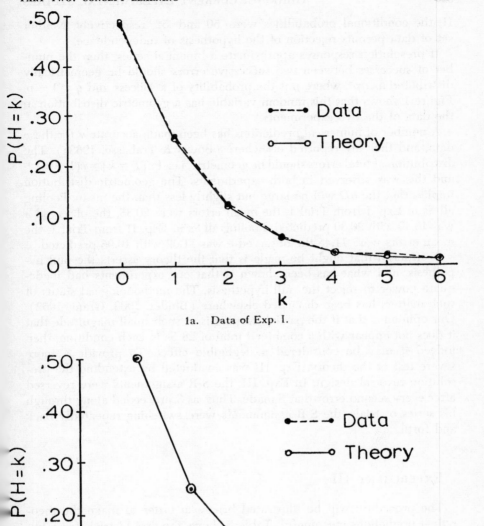

1a. Data of Exp. I.

1b. Data of Exp. II.

Fig. 1. Distribution of number of successes intervening between two adjacent errors.

II, the conditional probabilities were .50 and .52, respectively. Neither set of data permits rejection of the hypothesis of independence.

If presolution responses approximate a binomial series, then the number of successes between two successive errors should be geometrically distributed as qp^n, where p is the probability of a success and $q = 1 - p$. Figure 1 shows that this random variable has a geometric distribution in the data of the two experiments.

A number of numerical predictions has been made accurately for these data, and they are reported elsewhere (Bower & Trabasso, 1963a). The distribution of total errors should be geometric, i.e., $\Pr\{T = k\} = c(1 - c)^{k-1}$, and this was observed in both experiments. The geometric distribution implies that the SD will be large but slightly less than the mean. Pooling all Ss in Exp. I from Trial 1, the mean errors were 20.85; the observed σ was 18.49 with 20.30 predicted. Pooling all Ss in Exp. II from Trial 1, the mean errors were 11.45 the observed σ was 11.02 with 10.96 predicted.

A criticism that might be made is that the theory asserts the null hypothesis, and what has been shown is that our experiments had inadequate power to reject the null hypothesis. The methodological status of such matters has been discussed elsewhere (Binder, 1963; Grant, 1962). Our opinion is that if the partial learning is of such small magnitude that it does not appear with a combined total of 28 Ss in each condition, then indeed it may be considered a negligible effect. To provide a more severe test of the theory, Exp. III was conducted by extending the presolution reversal design. In Exp. III, the S-R assignments were reversed after every second error that S made. Thus, as S proceeded along through his series of trials, the S-R assignments were switching repeatedly back and forth.

EXPERIMENT III

The procedure will be illustrated briefly in order to make the theoretical predictions meaningful. Table 3 shows the first 14 trials for a hypothetical S. The stimulus patterns vary in five binary dimensions. Color is the relevant attribute and this S begins with the assignments "Red in Class VEK, Blue in Class CEJ." Suppose that his responses to the patterns on Trials 1 and 3 are correct according to these assignments, whereas his responses to the patterns on Trials 2 and 4 are wrong. The second error, occurring on Trial 4, initiates an immediate reversal of the S-R assignments, and S is told "Correct" for his response on Trial 4. According to the reversed assignments, the responses on Trials 4, 5, and 7 are correct whereas those on Trials 6 and 8 are errors. The second error of this subseries, occurring on Trial 8, initiates another immediate reversal back to the original S-R assignments, and the response on Trial 8 is called "Correct." The series of reversals on every second error continues in this fashion until S produces a string of 10 consecutive correct responses since his last reversal. A second group of control Ss was never reversed; they simply learned a fixed set of S-R assignments by the conventional training procedure in which they were informed of every error.

The prediction from the theory is that the number of *informed* errors (those not arrowed in Table 3) before learning for the Reversal Ss will be equal to the number of informed errors before learning made by the Control Ss. That is, no interference should result from the multiple reversals that occur during training. This prediction follows from the as-

TABLE 3

CORRECT (C) AND ERROR (E) RESPONSES OF A HYPOTHETICAL S
IN THE REVERSAL GROUP

Alternating S–R Assignments	Trials													
	1	2	3	4	5	6	7	8	9	10	11	12	13	14
Red-VEK	C	E	C	E				C	E	E			C	E
Blue-CEJ				↓				↑		↓			↑	
Blue-VEK				C	C	E	C	E		C	E	C	E	
Red-CEJ														

sumptions that learning occurs in one trial, that opportunities for giving up an irrelevant hypothesis, and hence learning, occur only after *informed* errors, and that the probability of learning following an informed error is not affected by the past S-R assignments for the relevant cues. The point of the last statement might be phrased in terms of the cues to which S is attending: if S is selectively attending to irrelevant cues and is not "noticing" the color, then his behavior when he starts noticing color is unaffected by the past history of changing correlations between the reinforced responses and the unnoticed color values. In contrast to the equality prediction above, if any one of the three assumptions is wrong, the Reversal Ss should make more informed errors than do the Control Ss.

METHOD

Subjects. The Ss were 33 paid volunteers from elementary history and psychology classes at Foothill Junior College who were randomly assigned to two groups (10 or 11 males and 6 females each).

Procedure. The instructions were the same as those used in Exp. I and II. The classificatory responses were VEK and CEJ. The learning criterion was 10 successive correct responses.

Stimuli. The patterns were identical to those used in Exp. II with the exception that the area which was colored within each figure was kept constant. Thus, there were one relevant and four irrelevant binary dimensions. Color was the relevant dimension for both groups.

Design. The Control group of 16 Ss learned a problem with fixed S-R assignments throughout. For 8 of these Ss, the assignments were Red-VEK and Blue-CEJ; the other 8 Ss had the opposite pairings. The Reversal group of 17 Ss learned the same color-relevant problem but the response assignments were reversed on every second error that each S committed. On alternate errors, S's response was confirmed (called "Correct") in accord with the instantaneous reversal of the assignments which E made as soon as S's second error of a subseries occurred. The procedure was discussed above in connection with Table 3. By this procedure, it would not be feasible to reverse S on every error since he would always be told "Correct" and E would forfeit any control over what S learns.

RESULTS

All but two Ss, one in each group, met the learning criterion. The two nonsolvers arrived late for their experimental session and had less time than the other Ss to complete the problem; therefore, they are excluded from the following analyses. Since both Ss made about the same number of errors, their exclusion does not affect the comparisons.

The remaining 16 Ss in the Reversal group averaged 7.00 reversal shifts before meeting criterion. The average numbers of informed errors were nearly equal for the two groups. For the Reversal group, the average number of informed errors was 7.81; for the Control group, it was 8.00. The SD of errors for the Control group was 8.22. Thus, the difference of .19 informed errors is not significant.

Two Ss in each group learned after only one error. As a result, two Ss in the Reversal condition were never reversed because they learned their initial response assignments. Removing these two Ss from each group, the mean number of reversals was 8.00; the mean number of informed errors was 8.79 for the Reversal group and 9.08 for the Control group, a nonsignificant difference.

On those trials where a reversal occurred, S was told "Correct" when in fact he made an error. Such a procedure should serve to maintain an irrelevant hypothesis for at least one more trial. The net effect of this procedure would be to produce more "correct" responses before the last error for the Reversal Ss than for the Controls. The mean numbers of correct responses prior to criterion for the Reversal and Control groups were 21.1 and 9.6, respectively, $t(29) = 1.99$, $p = .05$.

The mean trial of last error can be predicted for both groups once the mean errors for the Control group are known. These predictions are made to rule out the possibility that (a) length of success runs increased over trials in the Control group and (b) successive reversals tended to become more spaced out in the Reversal group over trials. For both predictions, the probability of a success prior to the last error is assumed to be constant and the a priori one-half. Let T_c be the total errors made by an S in the Control group; then his expected trial of last error is $2T_c$. The predicted mean trial of last error for the Control group was 16.00; the observed was 17.60. The difference was not significant by a matched t test, $t(14) = 1.75$, $p > .05$.

For the Reversal group, let T_r be the number of informed errors and r be the number of reversals before learning. Then the average trial of last error, n', for the Reversal group should be

$$n' = T_r + r + 1 + 2(T_r - 1). \qquad [1]$$

The first two terms, T_r and r, in Equation 1 count the number of informed error trials plus the reversal trials. The additional terms $1 + 2(T_r - 1)$ are the expected number of correct responses for an S who makes T_r informed errors in the Reversal group. The T_r informed errors partition the successes as follows: there is an average of one success before the first error, and an average of two successes between each of the $T_r - 1$ remaining informed errors. By hypothesis, the informed errors should be the same for both groups, so that $T_c = T_r$. Secondly, r is related to T_r, for if S makes T_r informed errors, then his number of reversals should be $T_r - 1$, assuming that he makes one more error after his rth and final reversal. (Note that the average number of reversals was 7, or exactly $T_c - 1$.) Substituting into Equation 1 the relations $r = T_r - 1$ and $T_c = T_r$, the following relation is obtained between T_c and the average trial of last error for the Reversal group:

$$n' = 4T_c - 2. \qquad [2]$$

Substituting the observed $T_c = 8.00$ into Equation 2, the predicted mean trial of last error (n') is 30.00. For the 16 solvers in the Reversal group, the observed value was 28.81; the SD was 26.09. The prediction is thus not significantly discrepant from the data.

The results of Exp. III favor a one-step, all-or-none interpretation of two-category concept identification in adult Ss. In addition, the results indicate that the effective information promoting learning in these problems occurs on informed error trials. Finally, the results are consistent with the notion that S's probability of solving after any given informed error is unaffected by the past history of inconsistent reinforcements to the relevant cue on which he solves.

Again the criticism may be lodged that our experiment had inadequate power to reject the null hypothesis. To provide further power for the test, we presently are running the design of Exp. III with larger groups of Ss, a different problem, and more explicit instructions to S regarding the dimensions of the stimuli, the form of the solution, etc. To date, with 24 Ss in each condition, the mean numbers of informed errors in the Control and Multiple Reversal groups are 8.22 and 7.94, respectively. Thus, the qualitative results of Exp. III are being replicated.

Discussion

The Reversal and Control conditions in Exp. I and II resemble the standard ones used with this design on the continuity-noncontinuity issue. Judging from the review by Blum and Blum (1949), nearly all of the previous studies involved rats learning simultaneous discriminations with a small number of cues. On balance, that evidence favored a continuity position supplemented by constructs such as receptor orienting acts (e.g., Ehrenfreund, 1948). Whether such results should have a crucial bearing on a situational theory of adult human concept identification is a moot question. Writing for the continuity position, Spence (1940) pointed out early that the results from the animal studies may not be directly relevant to adult human learning mediated by complex symbolic mechanisms. Such mechanisms evidently are used by adults in solving concept problems, and current theorizing emphasizes such mechanisms (e.g., Bower & Trabasso, 1963a; Hunt, 1962; Kendler & Kendler, 1962; Underwood & Richardson, 1956). Our working hypothesis is that the extent to which an S's discrimination learning fits the all-or-none as opposed to the incremental description depends on the extent to which symbolic mediating responses are available to S.

It would appear that one reason why the all-or-nothing model predicts accurately in these experiments is that the conditions promote "focus sampling" (Bruner, Goodnow, & Austin, 1956) because the memory load on S is otherwise overwhelming. The random-cue selection postulate implies that S's selection following an error of a new focus sample of cues to test is not affected by the past history of response assignments for the various cues. Such random selection of a sample focus is reasonable only if S's memory of specific past information is in some way impoverished. The experimental conditions presumably responsible for such poor memory include (a) the complexity of the stimuli, here 5 or 6 bits plus the 1-bit response, (b) the relatively rapid rate of presentation of this information (average time viewing each card was approximately 6 sec.), and (c) S has a specific set to identify the relevant cue, not to memorize and later recall the information he is seeing. In other experiments by us, direct tests of recall of specific information under these conditions showed the memory for six-card series to be very poor. Judging from the limited capacity of Ss for quickly processing and storing such large amounts of information, it is not surprising to find that they resort to focus sampling of specific cues to test.

The present results extend previous findings (Trabasso, 1963) that single-cue concept problems can be characterized as a one-step learning process. However, it is clear that not all varieties of concept learning can be so simply described. Our aim was to explore initially the most elementary form of concept learning, in a situation similar to a conventional discrimination learning procedure. Obviously, the simple all-or-nothing model must be elaborated and extended before it will account for learning of compounds of simpler concepts (e.g., conjunctions or disjunctions of several cues). Such extensions are currently under investigation (Trabasso & Bower, in press).

REFERENCES

BINDER, A. Further considerations on testing the null hypothesis and the strategy and tactics of investigating theoretical models. *Psychol. Rev.*, 1963, 70, 107–115.

BLUM, R. A., & BLUM, J. S. Factual issues in the "continuity controversy." *Psychol. Rev.*, 1949, 56, 33–50.

BOWER, G. H., & TRABASSO, T. R. Concept identification. In R. C. Atkinson (Ed.), *Studies in mathematical psychology*. Stanford: Stanford Univer. Press, 1963, in press. (a)

BOWER, G. H., & TRABASSO, T. R. Working paper on concept identification. Unpublished manuscript, Stanford University Library, 1963. (b)

BRUNER, J. S., GOODNOW, J. J., & AUSTIN, A. *A study of thinking*. Wiley: New York, 1956.

EHRENFREUND, D. An experimental test of the continuity theory of discrimination learning with pattern vision. *J. comp. physiol. Psychol.*, 1948, 41, 408–422.

GRANT, D. A. Testing the null hypothesis and the strategy and tactics of investigating theoretical models. *Psychol. Rev.*, 1962, 69, 54–61.

HAYES, K. J. The backward curve: A method for the study of learning. *Psychol. Rev.*, 1953, 60, 269–275.

HUNT, E. B. *Concept learning*. New York: Wiley, 1962.

KENDLER, H. H., GLUCKSBERG, S., & KESTON, R. Perception and mediation in concept learning. *J. exp. Psychol.*, 1961, 61, 1–16.

KENDLER, H. H., & KENDLER, T. S. Vertical and horizontal processes in problem solving. *Psychol. Rev.*, 1962, 69, 1–16.

KRECHEVSKY, I. A study of the continuity of the problem-solving process. *Psychol. Rev.*, 1938, 45, 107–133.

McCULLOCH, T. L., & PRATT, J. G. A study of the pre-solution period in weight discrimination by white rats. *Psychol. Rev.*, 1934, 18, 271–290.

RESTLE, F. The selection of strategies in cue learning. *Psychol. Rev.*, 1962, 69, 329–343.

SPENCE, K. W. Continuous versus noncontinuous interpretations of discrimination learning. *Psychol. Rev.* 1940, 54, 223–229.

TRABASSO, T. R. Stimulus emphasis and all-or-none learning in concept identification. *J. exp. Psychol.*, 1963, 65, 398–406.

TRABASSO, T. R., & BOWER, G. H. Component learning in the four-category problem. *J. math. Psychol.*, in press.

UNDERWOOD, B. J., & RICHARDSON, J. Verbal concept learning as a function of instructions and dominance level. *J. exp. Psychol.*, 1956, 51, 229–238.

27. Stimulus Aspects Responsible for the Rapid Acquisition of Reversal Shifts in Concept Formation

Martin Harrow

Abstract. *The stimulus factors responsible for the superiority of reversal over nonreversal shifts in concept formation were analyzed. 2 factors confounded in reversal shifts, within-dimension shifts and response reversals, were isolated for experimental investigation. Using card-sorting tasks, groups making only within-dimension shifts learned more rapidly than groups making both within-dimension and response reversals. Both groups learned quicker than comparable groups making between-dimension shifts. The results indicate that within-dimension shifts are an important factor in the rapid acquisition of reversal shifts, and response reversals may impede learning. In this transfer-of-training situation, positive transfer occurs when the stimulus dimension on which discrimination is based is kept constant, but the specific stimuli used are changed.*

A number of previous experiments in concept formation, using human Ss, have compared the speed of learning reversal and nonreversal shifts. The empirical results from this type of experiment often have been interpreted in terms of theoretical issues concerning the nature of certain types of human learning and concept formation (Buss, 1956; Gormezano &

Reprinted by permission of the author and the American Psychological Association from *Journal of Experimental Psychology*, 1964, 67, 330–334.

Grant, 1958; Harrow & Buchwald, 1962; Kendler & D'Amato, 1955; Kendler & Kendler, 1959; Osgood, 1953; Reese, 1962). In order to relate the results in this area to various theoretical formulations with greater exactness, there is need of a more precise analysis concerning which stimulus factors, or combination of factors, are responsible for the relatively quicker learning of reversal shifts by most older human Ss.

In the experiments using sorting tasks Ss were required to learn two successive card- or block-sorting tasks. During second-task learning, the non-reversal Ss were given a task which was based on some dimension of the stimuli which was irrelevant during first-task learning. As opposed to this, during second-task learning the reversal Ss were given a task which Es usually describe as being (in some sense) either the "opposite" or the "reverse" of the first task. A more careful analysis of the actual experimental tasks given to the "reversal" Ss, however, shows that there were at least three ways in which their tasks differed from those given to the nonreversal Ss.

1. Within-dimension shift (WDS). The second sorting task was based on the same dimension of the stimuli as was the first one (e.g., if the color of the cards was used as a basis for correct sorting during first-task learning, the color again formed the basis for correct sorting on second-task learning).

2. Response reversal (RR). The Ss were required to literally reverse the responses previously associated with each particular sorting card (e.g., if sorting Task 1 required that Response Card No. 9 be placed in Sorting Category A and Response Card No. 8 in Category B, then Sorting Task 2 required that Response Card No. 9 be placed in Sorting Category B, and Response Card No. 8 in Category A).

3. Concept reversal (CR). In several experiments (Harrow & Buchwald, 1962; Kendler & D'Amato, 1955; Kendler & Mayzner, 1956) the response cards were sorted into categories which were labeled with stimulus cards. In these experiments correct sorting depended on a systematic relationship between the response cards and the stimulus cards. Second-task learning involved a reversal of the systematic or conceptual relationship that had been used as a basis for sorting during Task 1 (e.g., response cards with stars located on them have to be sorted according to the number of stars on them. During Task 1 response cards having N stars must be sorted with the stimulus cards having $N + 1$ stars and during Task 2 response cards with N stars must be sorted with stimulus cards having $N - 1$ stars).

Thus, due to the confounding in previous experiments there were three possible factors all or some of which could have been responsible for the quicker learning of reversal shifts as compared to nonreversal shifts. There were: (a) WDSs, (b) RRs, and (c) CRs.

In the present experiment, groups of Ss making WDSs and other groups learning tasks which required both WDSs and RRs were compared for speed of learning with each other and with comparable control groups learning tasks requiring between-dimension shifts (BDSs). This permitted the separation of the effects of RRs and of WDSs from other possible influential factors.

METHOD

Subjects The Ss were 118 undergraduate students enrolled in introductory psychology courses at Indiana University. Twenty-two of them were eliminated for failure to learn the first task within 160 trials, and the data from the remaining 96 (48 males and 48 females) were used.

Materials. Three decks, each with eight response cards, were selected from the asymmetrical version of the Wisconsin Card Sorting Test. The decks of cards used for each group, as well as the experimental design, can be seen in Table 1. The experiment was carried out in a two-category card-sorting situation in which Ss had to sort response cards with one of two identical blank stimulus cards which were attached to a cardholder. There was a pocket at the top of the cardholder into which a response card could be placed. Two types of tasks (shape concepts and color concepts) were employed in the experiment. Two sets of response cards were used for each group, one for each of the two stages of the experiment.

Design. A $2 \times 2 \times 2 \times 2$ factorial design was used, with the 96 Ss being divided into 16 groups of 6 Ss (see Table 1). All experimental Ss learned two successive card-sorting tasks, with the four factors present during second-task learning being:

1. WDSs (Groups 1, 2, 5, and 6) vs. BDSs (Groups 3, 4, 7, and 8).

2. Relevant stimuli for correct discrimination not having been present during Task 1 (Groups 2, 4, 6, and 8) vs. relevant stimuli for correct discrimination having been present during Task 1 (Groups 1, 3, 5, and 7). (It should be noted in connection with this factor that the crucial aspect which distinguished RRs—Groups 1 and 5—was that the relevant Task 1 stimuli were again present and relevant during Task 2, but the specific responses to these stimuli were reversed. In contrast, the crucial factor which distinguished the groups making only WDSs, without RRs—Groups 2 and 6—was that the stimuli relevant during Task 2 had not been present during Task 1.)

3. Learning a color concept (Groups 1, 2, 3, and 4) vs. learning a shape concept (Groups 5, 6, 7, and 8).

4. Male Ss (Groups 1M, 2M, 3M, etc.) vs. female Ss (Groups 1F, 2F, 3F, etc.).

TABLE 1

Experimental Design

Groups [a]	Type of Shift [b]	Task 1			Task 2		
		Deck of Cards Used [c]	Correct Responses Category I	Category II	Deck of Cards Used [c]	Correct Responses Category I	Category II
1M & 1F	WDS & RR	A	green	red	C	red	green
2M & 2F	WDS	B	yellow	blue	C	red	green
3M & 3F	BD (Group 1 Control)	A	cross	star	C	red	green
4M & 4F	BD (Group 2 Control)	B	cross	star	C	red	green
5M & 5F	WDS & RR	A	cross	star	B	star	cross
6M & 6F	WDS	C	circle	triangle	B	star	cross
7M & 7F	BD (Group 5 Control)	A	green	red	B	star	cross
8M & 8F	BD (Group 6 Control)	C	green	red	B	star	cross

[a] M = Male Ss; F = female Ss.
[b] WDS = within-dimension shift; RR = response reversal; BD = between-dimension shift.
[c] All decks had eight cards with the following combinations: Deck A, three or four stars or crosses, colored green or red; Deck B, one or two stars or crosses, colored blue or yellow; Deck C, one or two circles or triangles, colored green or red.

Viewed from a different aspect, the eight groups of male Ss and eight groups of female Ss differed from each other in the following ways:

1. Groups 1 and 5 (WDSs and RRs). These groups made a WDS with the specific stimuli relevant during Task 2 having been present and relevant during Task 1.

2. Groups 2 and 6 (WDSs). These groups made a WDS with the specific stimuli relevant during Task 2 not having been present during Task 1.

3. Groups 3 and 7 (BDSs, controls for Groups 1 and 5). These groups made a BDS with the specific stimuli relevant during Task 2 having been present but irrelevant during Task 1.

4. Groups 4 and 8 (BDSs, controls for Groups 2 and 6). These groups made a BDS with the specific stimuli relevant during Task 2 not having been present during Task 1.

Procedure. The Ss were run individually. The standardized instructions read to S indicated that as each response card was shown to him he should point to the category he thought it belonged to and by E informing him whether he was right or wrong he would gradually find out where each response card really belonged.

The response cards were presented randomly and individually to each S by being placed in the slot which was at the top of the cardholder. The criterion of learning for both the first and second tasks was 16 successive correct responses. All Ss who met the criterion for the first task within 160 trials were required to learn a second one.

The Ss were not informed about the change in the pattern of reinforcement for the second concept. The Ss who had not learned the second concept within 160 trials were arbitrarily assigned a score of 160 for second-task learning.

Results and Discussion

Table 2 presents the results of the learning of the first and second tasks. These data represent the number of trials to learn the task involved, excluding the 16 criterion trials. To test for differences in speed of learning the first task, two separate 2 × 2 analyses of variances were computed, one for the four groups that learned a color concept for their second task (Groups 1–4) and one for the four groups that learned a number concept for their second task (Groups 5–8). The two factors present in both

TABLE 2

Number of Trials to Learn Task 1 and Task 2

Group	Type of Tasks [a]	Type of Shift [b]	N	Task 1				Task 2			
				M	SD	Mdn.	Range	M	SD	Mdn.	Range
1	C–C	WDS & RR	12	30.5	41.2	5.0	0–123	6.6	11.6	1.0	1–38
2	C–C	WDS	12	30.3	34.7	19.0	0–113	2.3	3.1	1.0	0–10
3	S–C	BD (Group 1 Control)	12	48.3	43.4	40.0	0–118	8.3	8.7	5.0	0–31
4	S–C	BD (Group 2 Control)	12	28.3	31.4	19.0	0–100	6.4	6.9	4.5	0–22
5	S–S	WDS & RR	12	34.4	33.7	20.5	1–87	8.9	10.0	6.5	1–32
6	S–S	WDS	12	22.6	23.3	18.5	0–80	4.4	9.0	1.5	0–32
7	C–S	BD (Group 5 Control)	12	59.8	58.0	45.0	0–141	31.3	44.2	19.0	3–160
8	C–S	BD (Group 6 Control)	12	26.0	36.2	8.5	2–127	38.4	48.9	18.5	2–160

[a] C = color task; S = shape task.
[b] WDS = within-dimension shift; RR = response reversal; BD = between-dimension shift.

analyses were: (a) color vs. number concept and (b) deck of cards used. Neither of the analyses showed any significant main effects or interaction, indicating that the groups were equated with each other for practice effects prior to second-task learning.

To determine the differences in speed of learning the second task, a 2 × 2 × 2 × 2 analysis of variance was carried out. To obtain homogeneity of variance the data had to be subjected to a logarithmic (1 + X) transformation (Edwards, 1950). The results of the analysis (Tables 2 and 3) show that the WDSs were learned significantly faster than the BDSs. Likewise, color concepts were learned significantly faster than shape concepts. The only significant interaction was that between the type of shift and color-shape concept. Examination of Table 2 shows that this interaction was significant because of the extremely slow learning of the BDS groups that acquired a shape concept during Task 2.

The superiority of all groups making WDSs over the comparable ones making BDSs agrees, in principle, with the results obtained by Harrow and Buchwald (1962). In the present experiment this occurred in both types of situations requiring WDSs (i.e., when WDSs occurred in conjunction with RRs and when RRs were not present).

To assess the role of RRs and to contrast them with WDSs, further analysis of the four groups making WDSs (Groups 1, 2, 5, and 6) was carried out. This was accomplished in a separate 2×2 analysis of variance, using the transformed scores ($\log 1 + X$). The two variables present (see Table 4) were: (a) type of WDS, and (b) color-shape task. The essential comparison was that for the type of WDS. This comparison was significant, indicating (Tables 2 and 4) that Groups 2 and 6,

TABLE 3

$2 \times 2 \times 2 \times 2$ ANALYSIS OF VARIANCE OF TRIALS
TO CRITERION ON TASK 2

Source	df	MS	F
Within-dim.—between-dim. shift (S)	1	4.943	25.399***
Relevant stim.-irrelevant stim. (R)	1	0.649	3.335
Color-shape concept (C)	1	2.771	14.237***
Males-females (M)	1	0.025	
S × R	1	0.413	2.121
S × C	1	0.877	4.505*
C × M	1	0.350	1.801
R × C × M [a]	1	0.210	1.077
Within groups	80	0.195	
Total	95		

Note.—Transformed scores [$\log (1 + X)$] used.

[a] The F ratios for all remaining simple and higher-order interactions were less than 1, and are omitted.

*$p < .05$.
***$p < .001$.

which only made WDSs, learned quicker than Groups 1 and 5, which made both WDSs and RRs.

The data suggest that what appears to be the facilitating effects of RRs results from their always involving WDSs. There are further indications that RRs actually retard learning as compared to WDSs.

The results from the present experiment also permit us to answer a question basic to the nature of WDSs and of importance in concept formation. That is, if WDS lead to facilitative effects in learning, is this because Ss have been trained to respond to the specific stimuli they have learned are important? The alternative hypothesis is that the advantages of a WDS occur because Ss have learned to pay selective attention to a *general* dimension of the stimuli (such as color) while learning a first task, and that they continue to pay selective attention to that aspect of the stimuli, even when the *specific* colors formerly present are no longer there. In the current transfer-of-training situation, facilitation occurred

TABLE 4

ANALYSIS OF VARIANCE OF TRIALS TO CRITERION FOR GROUPS
MAKING WITHIN-DIMENSION SHIFTS

Source	df	MS	F
Type of within-dimension shift (S)	1	1.049	6.213*
Color-shape task (C)	1	0.265	1.571
S × C	1	0.122	
Within groups	44	0.169	
Total	47		

Note.—Transformed scores [log $(1 + X)$] used.
*$p < .05$.

for the groups making WDSs when the dimension of the stimuli on which
discrimination was based was kept constant, but the specific stimuli important for correct discrimination were changed. This supports the hypothesis that the facilitative effects of a reversal shift occur because it
involves using a dimension of the stimuli which was previously relevant.

REFERENCES

BUSS, A. H. Reversal and nonreversal shifts in concept formation with
   partial reinforcement eliminated. *J. exp. Psychol.*, 1956, 52, 162–166.
EDWARDS, A. L. *Experimental design in psychological research.* New
   York: Rinehart, 1950.
GORMEZANO, I., & GRANT, D. A. Progressive ambiguity in the attainment
   of concepts on the Wisconsin Card Sorting Test. *J. exp. Psychol.*, 1958,
   55, 621–627.
HARROW, M., & BUCHWALD, A. M. Reversal and nonreversal shifts in concept formation using consistent and inconsistent responses. *J. exp.
   Psychol.*, 1962, 64, 476–481.
KENDLER, H. H., & D'AMATO, M. J. A comparison of reversal and non-
   reversal shifts in human concept formation behavior. *J. exp. Psychol.*,
   1955, 49, 165–174.
KENDLER, H. H., & MAYZNER, M. S. Reversal and nonreversal shifts in
   card-sorting tests with two or four sorting categories. *J. exp. Psychol.*,
   1956, 51, 244–248.
KENDLER, T. S., & KENDLER, H. H. Reversal and nonreversal shifts in kin-
   dergarten children. *J. exp. Psychol.*, 1959, 58, 56–60.
OSGOOD, C. E. *Method and theory in experimental psychology.* New
   York: Oxford Univer. Press, 1953.
REESE, H. W. Verbal mediation as a function of age level. *Psychol. Bull.*,
   1962, 59, 502–509.

28. Nonreinforcements of Perceptual and Mediating Responses in Concept Learning

Howard H. Kendler and Margaret Woerner

Abstract. *After college students learned to classify geometrical designs into 1 of 2 categories with a chain of behavior involving an initial perceptual-orienting response, a mediating response, and a final-choice response, they received a series of 10 nonreinforcements followed by either a reversal or nonreversal shift. The perceptual-orienting response of half of the Ss during the extinction series was not followed by the appearance of the designs. For the remaining Ss it was. Ss who had not been shown the designs exhibited the customary superiority of a reversal over a nonreversal shift. The other Ss did not, presumably because their mediational response had been extinguished.*

The purpose of this experiment was to determine the effects a series of nonreinforcements had upon a concept-learning chain that had already been acquired. The chain contained an initial perceptual-orienting response (looking to the left or right), followed in order by a mediational reaction and a terminal choice response (pressing one of two keys). A light signal, following the correct choice, had served as the reinforcement for the entire chain.

The results of a previous study (Kendler, Glucksberg, & Keston, 1961) suggested that the perceptual and mediational segments were relatively independent, that is, the mediational response was not strongly associated with the cues resulting from the orienting response but instead was connected primarily to the geometrical designs that had to be classified. If this analysis is correct, a series of nonreinforcements should have different effects depending on whether or not the perceptual-orienting response led to the appearance of the geometrical designs. If it did, the superiority of a reversal shift over a nonreversal shift should be reduced or eliminated because the mediational response, presumably responsible for this superiority (Kendler & Kendler, 1962), would be weakened by the nonreinforcements. On the other hand if the perceptual-orienting response did not lead to the appearance of the geometrical design, no opportunity for the extinction of the mediational response would occur. Under such conditions the superiority of a reversal over a nonreversal shift should be maintained.

Reprinted by permission of the authors and the American Psychological Association from *Journal of Experimental Psychology*, 1964, 67, 591–592.

Method. The experimental procedure was essentially similar to that used by Kendler et al. (1961). The S sat close to a translucent screen through which were projected for 5 msec. two geometrical figures, one at each side. The S had to learn to pay attention to the set of figures on one side only and sort them into one of two categories represented by two response keys. The major procedural modification instituted in the present study was a series of interpolated nonreinforced trials (a light indicating a correct choice never flashed on) between the learning of the two successive concepts. After learning the first concept all Ss (a total of 48 students from an introductory psychology course) received 10 trials

TABLE 1

MEAN AND MEDIAN NUMBER OF TRIALS TO LEARN
SECOND CONCEPT

Group	M	SD	Mdn.	Range
PE:R	8.8	11.3	2.5	1–43
PE:NR	31.2	37.3	19.5	0–128
ME:R	19.2	16.5	18.0	1–43
ME:NR	23.1	34.4	11.0	2–128
R [a]	4.7	4.9	2.5	1–18
NR [a]	41.4	46.0	17.5	3–128

[a] Data from Kendler et al. (1961).

in which no reinforcement was forthcoming regardless of their response. For half of the Ss (PE) a blank slide was projected on the screen. When S looked to one side he would see no geometrical figure and therefore it was assumed that the perceptual-orienting segment of the previously successful chain was weakened through nonreinforcement. The remaining half of the Ss (ME) were exposed to the same set of geometrical designs which they categorized during the learning of the initial concept. Since no reinforcement was obtained for their choice behavior, presumably their mediational response, as well as their orienting response, was being extinguished. Half of the PE and ME Ss received a reversal shift (R) following the interpolated trials while the other half were given a nonreversal shift (NR).

The relevant stimulus figure remained on the same side of the screen before and after the shift. Any S who failed to respond during one of the 10 interpolated trials was reminded to press one of the two response keys during every trial.

Results and discussion. The four groups did not differ significantly in the speed in which they learned the first concept. Table 1 reports the learning scores for the second (postshift) concept. Results of equivalent reversal and nonreversal groups *without* interpolated trials (Kendler et al., 1961) are included in the lower two lines.

The data are consistent with the expectation that failing to reinforce the perceptual-orienting response in the absence of the stimuli that evoke mediational responses would not disturb the commonly observed superiority of a reversal over a nonreversal shift. The difference between the performance of Groups PE:R and PE:NR was significant in the direction predicted at the .025 level (Mann & Whitney, 1947). In contrast there was no significant difference between the reversal and nonreversal shifts when the mediational extinction procedure was used, that is, between Groups ME:R and ME:NR.

A comparison of the present results with those of Ss who performed without interpolated nonreinforcement trials *suggests* that the mediational extinction procedure retards a reversal shift while facilitating a nonreversal shift, although the differences between Groups R and ME:R, and NR and ME:NR failed to achieve statistical significance.

These results once again demonstrate that for human adults the dominant mode of response to the present kind of problem is to execute a reversal shift. When the implicit response that mediates the reversal shift is weakened by nonreinforcements the reversal tendency loses its dominant position in the response hierarchy. The results also show that an essential segment of a problem-solving chain, in this case the perceptual-orienting response, can be weakly integrated with the succeeding links of the chain as evidenced by the fact that failing to reinforce it does not disturb the dominance of a reversal over a nonreversal shift.

REFERENCES

KENDLER, H. H., GLUCKSBERG, S., & KESTON, R. Perception and mediation in concept learning. *J. exp. Psychol.*, 1961, 61, 186–191.

KENDLER, H. H., & KENDLER, T. S. Vertical and horizontal processes in problem solving. *Psychol. Rev.*, 1962, 69, 1–16.

MANN, H. B., & WHITNEY, D. R. On a test of whether one of two random variables is stochastically larger than the other. *Ann. math. Statist.*, 1947, 17, 50–60.

29.   On the Different Effects of Random Reinforcement and Presolution Reversal on Human Concept Identification

Solon B. Holstein and David Premack

Abstract. *Levine's random reinforcement (RR) procedure was replicated using 6 as well as 2 dimensions. Contrary to a suggestion by Bower and Trabasso, RR produced as marked a decrement with 6 dimensions as with 2. However, a backward-learning curve showed post-RR learning to be essentially stationary. Both the RR decrement and the stationarity can be handled by the Bower-Trabasso model on the assumption that RR increases H, the number of S's hypothesis.*

In standard two-category concept-identification experiments, Bower and Trabasso (1963) have shown that Ss whose S-R assignments were reversed after the occurrence of every second error performed as well as controls that were never reversed. These data support the cue-selection theories of Restle (1962) and Bower and Trabasso (1963), for the effect of an error in these theories is to return S to the state he was in before he began work on the problem, so that a change in the S-R assignment after an error should have no effect.

However, Levine (1962) has shown that random reinforcement (RR), unlike presolution reversal, does have a decremental effect, though it should not according to the cue-selection theories, for both RR and pre-solution reversal involve changing the S-R assignment after S makes an error. Nevertheless, Levine has shown that starting S out with no more than six RRs before shifting him (without signal) to a consistent S-R assignment has a clear decremental effect.

Trabasso and Bower (1964) have attributed Levine's outcome to his use of only one or two irrelevant dimensions in contrast to the six which they have used. According to their theory, S attends selectively to cues from the stimulus cards and tests hypotheses regarding the relevance of the cues. If S's response is correct, it is supposed that he continues to use the same hypothesis; otherwise, he resamples at random from the set of hypotheses, and further, resamples with replacement so that his set of hypotheses remains constant in size. Bower and Trabasso suggest that when Levine used only one or two irrelevant dimensions, his Ss did not resample with replacement; rather, they were able to remember the

Reprinted by permission of the authors and the American Psychological Association from *Journal of Experimental Psychology*, 1965, 70, 335–337.

hypotheses that were disconfirmed during the RR phase. The present experiment is a test of the Bower-Trabasso interpretation; Levine's RR procedure is replicated with six as well as two irrelevant dimensions.

Method. The Ss were 160 University of Missouri students who were assigned to 16 groups and tested in individual sessions. The S's task was to learn to classify cards into two categories, VEC and NONVEC, on the basis of a single relevant dimension. Number of dimensions (2 vs. 6), number of RRs (0, 6, 20, 40), and two types of instructions (vague vs. explicit) were combined factorially to form a $2 \times 4 \times 2$ design. In the vague instructions Ss were told only that the cards could be sorted into VEC and NONVEC, and that E would tell him when his choice was "right" or "wrong"; Ss given the explicit instructions were, in addition, shown two cards that contained all values of the six dimensions, the two values of each dimension were pointed out to S, and S was told that the problem had a simple solution.

Three decks of cards were used. The dimensions were formed (diamond vs. square), color (black vs. white), size (large vs. small), direction of a diagonal passing through the figure (right vs. left), parallels bordering the figure (horizontal vs. vertical), and background (striped vs. nonstriped). All 64 possible combinations of the six dimensions were used to construct a deck of 90 cards in which the different combinations were distributed randomly throughout the deck with the restriction that no one value of a given dimension occurred more than twice in succession. Two different two-dimension decks were used to check the effect of different irrelevant dimensions; color and form, and color and size.

Training consisted of two phases. In the first and RR phase, Ss were told "right" or "wrong" after each choice according to a predetermined random schedule for either 0, 6, 20, or 40 trials, after which, without signal, all Ss were consistently reinforced on the basis of color, i.e., black-VEC, white-NONVEC. The cards were shown for either 50 trials or until S made 15 correct responses in a row.

Results. The upper panel of Fig. 1 shows that, contrary to the suggestion by Bower and Trabasso, the six-dimension case was no less subject to impairment by RR than the two-dimension case. The deficit in both cases appears to be maximal by at least 6 RR, which is in agreement with Levine's (1962) data. An analysis of variance of the trials to criterion showed that the main effects of RR and number of dimensions were both significant, $F (3.144) = 21.62$, $p < .01$; $F (1.44) = 45.85$, $p < .01$, respectively; and that neither the main effect of instructions nor any of the interactions approached the 5% level. Results for the color-form and color-size decks did not differ and were, therefore, combined in the analysis.

The lower panel shows a backward-learning curve for the two- and six-dimension groups. The essential stationarity prior to the last error was shown further in the vincentized data; percentage of success for the first

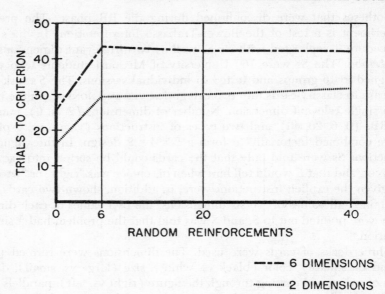

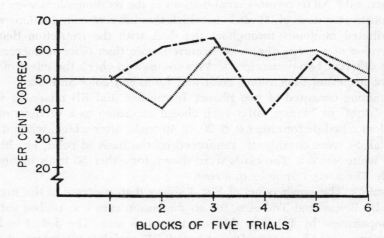

FIG. 1. Trials to criterion as a function of number of random reinforcements with separate curves for the two- and six-dimension groups (upper panel); and backward learning curve showing percentage of success prior to the last error plotted over successive blocks of five trials (lower panel).

and second halves of the trials prior to the last error was 58 and 55, respectively, for the two-dimension case, and 49 and 49, respectively, for the six-dimension case.

The stationarity data support the Bower-Trabasso model, while the

RR impairment in the six-dimension case appears to contradict the model. However, an interpretation of the effect of RR can be shown that is wholly in keeping with the Bower-Trabasso model. So far the only changes in S's hypotheses (H) that have been considered are (a) that S samples with replacement so that H remains constant, or (b) that S remembers disconfirmed hypotheses, does not sample with replacement, so that H decreases. But consider a third alternative: Error-producing operations such as RR lead to S to form new hypotheses, thus increasing the size of H. In terms of the cue selection theories, an increase in H by RR would have exactly the desired effect, viz., a lowering of the probability of learning after RR with no effect upon the all-or-none character of learning. That error-producing operations may, in fact, not only increase H but also change the character of S's hypotheses is being examined in studies aimed at getting at the composition of H.

REFERENCES

Bower, G., & Trabasso, T. Reversals prior to solution in concept identification. *J. exp. Psychol.*, 1963, 66, 409–418.

Levine, M. Cue neutralization: The effects of random reinforcements upon discrimination learning. *J. exp. Psychol.*, 1962, 63, 438–443.

Restle, F. The selection of strategies in cue learning. *Psychol. Rev.*, 1962, 69, 329–343.

Trabasso, T., & Bower, G. Presolution reversal and dimensional shifts in concept identification. *J. exp. Psychol.*, 1964, 67, 398–399.

SECTION NINE

Verbal and Mediation

Most experimental studies in concept learning have used visual stimuli such as colors and forms. Words were rarely used as stimuli until Underwood and Richardson developed scaled words for concept studies in 1956 (see reference at the end of any of the articles in this section). The availability of these verbal norms has permitted the study of a number of variables in concept learning. Furthermore, since mediation is often assumed to involve implicit verbal responses, it has seemed worthwhile to use words as overt stimuli in concept research. Both of these trends are represented in this section. The first three papers (Mednick and Freedman; Richardson; and Schulz, Miller, and Radtke) illustrate variables in concept learning that can be studied via the Underwood-Richardson norms. The last two articles (Duncan; Underwood) represent attempts to study mediation by using verbal stimulus materials of various kinds. Over-all, both this section and the preceding one largely deal with mediation in one way or another.

In the Mednick and Freedman study, subjects learned verbal S-R pairs so constructed that it was assumed that response-produced stimuli arising from the R would elicit an implicit response (another word) which would facilitate later concept learning. In the Richardson article, the reverse procedure was used; concept learning was employed to attempt to facilitate paired-associate learning. With this procedure, it was possible to test several concept conditions for different degrees of mediation to paired-associate learning. This was a worthwhile procedure, since it was found that although two conditions, mediation and example, did facilitate final learning, they did so by apparently different mediational processes.

346

Mediation involves the apprehension of an association or connection of some kind between words or other events. It would seem reasonable, therefore, that the closer in spatio-temporal contiguity the events among which mediation is possible, the greater the probability that mediation will occur. Schulz, Miller, and Radtke found this to be the case. The contiguity variable had a fairly strong effect, though not as strong as the dominance variable, i.e., the pre-experimental mediational strength among concepts.

Since mediation is usually an implicit process, researchers look for experimental procedures that will permit reliable inferences about the role of mediation. Several such procedures appear in the articles of Sections Eight and Nine. The last two articles in this section are illustrations of further methods. In the Duncan paper, mediation was measured in terms of quicker response to one member of a class as a result of reinforcement for another member of the same class. The Underwood study used the ingenious procedure of asking the subject to decide whether or not he had heard words which in fact had not been overtly presented. Thus, if the subject answered that he had, it was clear that he could only have perceived the words implicitly. It is worth noting that degree of mediation varied markedly as a function of the type of concept. Richardson also found this in his experiment.

30. Facilitation of Concept Formation Through Mediated Generalization

Sarnoff A. Mednick and Jonathan L. Freedman

Underwood (1952) has suggested a method for the study of concept formation which assumes that the attainment of a concept calls for the perception of a relationship between concept instances. The perception of this relationship is in large part dependent on the probability of the occurrence of the relevant associative responses to the concept instances.

Reprinted by permission of the authors and the American Psychological Association from *Journal of Experimental Psychology*, 1960, *60*, 278–283.

This probability is termed response dominance. The mean response dominance of all instances representing a particular concept is termed dominance level.

Underwood and Richardson (1956b) have shown that the ease of attainment of a concept is directly related to dominance level. One implication of these results and of the theory in general is that it should be possible to facilitate the attainment of a particular concept by increasing the strength of the associations between the concept instances and the correct concept response. Norms giving the response dominance of conceptual responses to 213 instances have been reported by Underwood and Richardson (1956a). However, it seems likely that by certain experimental manipulations these response probabilities could be temporarily altered. If this alteration took the form of strengthening certain chosen associations, it should result in the facilitation of the attainment of the chosen concept.

The present experiment employs a technique involving mediated generalization to increase the strength of response dominance and to facilitate concept formation. This technique is based in part on the work of Russell and Storms (1955) who attempted to demonstrate that mediated generalization would facilitate paired-associate learning. They presented Ss with two paired-associate lists, the first of which was designed to facilitate the learning of the second. For example, one pair in the first list was "cef-stem"; a pair in the second list was "cef-leaf." "Stem" elicits the associate, "flower," which in turn elicits "leaf." The assumption was that when "cef-stem" is learned, words associated with "stem" occur implicitly and the associations "cef-flower" and "cef-leaf" are also being implicitly learned. Thus the pair "cef-leaf" should be easier to learn than if S had not had experience with "cef-stem."

In the present experiment Ss are also presented with two lists, the first of which is designed to facilitate the mastering of the second. However, instead of two paired-associate lists, one paired-associate list and one concept-formation list are used. By constructing the lists in accordance with the mediated generalization paradigm we attempted to facilitate the attainment of selected concepts.

Method

Subjects. The Ss were 30 undergraduate volunteers from Harvard and Radcliffe Colleges. There were 7 men and 23 women.

Design. The design of the experiment is best explained by reference to Table 1. These are two paired-associate lists (I and II) and a concept-formation list. Paired-Associate List I is designed to facilitate the attainment of the concept "white" in the concept-formation list. Prior learning of Paired-Associate List II is designed to facilitate the attainment of the concept "soft" in the concept formation list.

The method of facilitation might best be explained by example. Thus in order to facilitate the production of the concept response "white" to the concept instance "sugar" (Table 1) prior pairing of the words "sugar-black" is given in Paired-Associate List I. It is assumed that the word "black" elicits the implicit response "white" causing the word "white" to occur in contiguity with the word "sugar," strengthening the association "sugar-white." When S is subsequently presented with the instance "sugar" in the concept-formation task the concept "white" will be attained more easily than it would have been if no pretask training had been given. That is, mediated generalization strengthens the association "sugar-white"; strengthening this association raises the response dominance of the concept instance "sugar" (since response dominance is simply the strength of association between "sugar" and "white"); raising the response dominance should facilitate the production of the concept response "white" to the concept instance "sugar." Since all of the instances of the concept "white" are facilitated in this manner by relevant associate pairs in List I we would predict that prior experience with List I would facilitate attainment of the concept "white."

For 15 Ss (3 men and 12 women) "white" was facilitated and "soft" was not facilitated (List I). For the other 15 Ss "soft" was facilitated and "white" was not facilitated (List II). Thus we could sum across the facilitated concepts ("white" preceded by learning of List I and "soft" preceded by learning of List II) and sum across the nonfacilitated concepts ("soft" preceded by learning of List I and "white" preceded by learning of List II) and compare performance on facilitated and nonfacilitated concepts knowing that any resultant differences could not be due to unique properties of the specific concepts or concept instances employed. In order to further insure that the facilitated and nonfacilitated concepts differed only with respect to the independent variable, the *responses* were kept the same in the nonfacilitated pairs of the two paired-associate lists.

The third concept, "large," was included as a buffer concept in order to increase the difficulty of the concept list. Since its appearance was not counterbalanced with respect to facilitation it could not be used as a control for facilitation.

Materials. The details of the construction of the lists follow. In making the paired-associate lists 16 words were first selected from the Minnesota Kent-Rosanoff Word Association Test norms (Russell & Jenkins, 1954). Of these 16 words, four have "white" as a common response, four have "soft," and eight have neither "white" nor "soft," as a common response. The probability of each of these associations is given in Table 1. In Paired-Associate List I the four words to which "white" is a common response were paired (as responses) with the four words that are concept instances of "white" in the concept-formation list, while the words that are concept instances of "soft" were paired with neutral words. Paired-Associate List II reversed the procedure; words that are concept instances of "soft" in the concept-formation list were paired with words which elicit "soft" as an associate, while concept instances of "white" were paired with neutral words. All instances of the concept "large" were paired with neutral words in both lists.

As is indicated in Table 1 the words designed to facilitate the attainment of the concept "soft" have a higher mean probability of response

TABLE 1

PAIRED-ASSOCIATE AND CONCEPT-FORMATION LISTS

Paired-Associate List I	
Pair	Relevant Assoc.
sugar-black	black-white (.751) [a]
hailstone-sheep	sheep-white (.009)
button-bread	bread-white (.015)
cabbage-salt	salt-white (.006)
pup-afraid	none
grape-swift	none
peach-beautiful	none
cradle-anger	none
anchor-king	none
camel-dream	none
forest-command	none
barrel-lion	none

Concept-Formation List		
Instance	Response Dominance	Concept
sugar	11	
hailstone	9	"white"
button	5	($M = 7.50$) [b]
cabbage	5	
pup	12	
grape	7	"soft"
peach	5	($M = 8.75$) [b]
cradle	11	
anchor	5	
camel	14	"large"
forest	12	($M = 9.25$) [b]
barrel	6	

TABLE 1 (continued)

Paired-Associate List II

Pair	Relevant Assoc.
sugar-afraid	none
hailstone-anger	none
button-beautiful	none
cabbage-swift	none
pup-hard	hard-soft (.674) [a]
loud-soft	loud-soft (.541)
peach-smooth	smooth-soft (.206)
cradle-comfort	comfort-soft (.069)
anchor-king	none
camel-dream	none
forest-command	none
barrel-lion	none

[a] Probability of occurrence of response term (e.g., "white") to stimulus term (e.g., "black").
[b] Mean response dominance of concept response (e.g., "white").

than those designed to facilitate the attainment of the concept "white." Due to the limited number of appropriate words available in the Minnesota norms, this inequality could not be avoided. However, the results of a study by Freedman and Mednick (1958) indicate that the polarization effect of the extremely strong association between "black" and "white" might be expected to offset this difference to some extent. In any event, since the experiment is concerned chiefly with a comparison of the facilitated and nonfacilitated concepts, and the concepts "soft" and "white" appear equally in both conditions, any difference in difficulty level which might exist would not affect the major results.

The concept-formation list (Table 1) contains three concepts ("white," "soft," and "large") each of which is represented by four nouns taken from the list of nouns for which Underwood and Richardson (1956a) have ascertained the dominance level of various responses. Based on these norms the means of response dominance of these concepts were made approximately equal. The dominance level was purposely kept quite low because it was thought that any facilitating effect would be more apparent if the lists were difficult. Also, this difficulty level of the concept list would produce a wider range of scores.

Various factors restricted the selection of concepts for the concept list: (a) it was necessary to choose concepts that could be found in the Minnesota Word Association norms as responses to the standard word association test; (b) it was important to minimize the amount of interference among the various concept instances (e.g., instances such as "rabbit" to which both "white" and "soft" were possible responses had to be avoided); (c) the concepts used had to be represented by four very low-dominant instances that could be approximately equalized in terms of mean and variance of dominance. The concepts "white" and "soft" were the only ones found that met all of these requirements.

Procedure. Each S was presented with one of the paired-associate lists and was required to learn it to a criterion of two successive perfect trials. After a slight pause during which tapes were changed, S was presented with the concept-formation instructions. It was explained to S that the list contained 12 words that could be placed in 3 groups of 4 words each, and that all of the 4 words in each of these groups could be described by the same adjective. The S was required to respond to each word with an adjective that he thought described that word. It was made clear that the adjective must describe a physical quality of the noun. When S responded E said "right" or "wrong." The S's task was to discover the three correct adjectives and to apply them to the correct nouns. The test was continued to a criterion of one perfect trial or was terminated at 18 trials. The procedure for the concept formation task has been described in more detail elsewhere (Underwood & Richardson, 1956a).

Both the paired-associate lists and the concept-formation list were presented at a 4-sec. rate in three different orders on a Gerbrands memory drum. There was an interval of 8 sec. between trials except for an interval of 20 sec. (due to a blank interval on the tape) after every three trials of the concept-formation list. To control for any effect of order of presentation of the particular words the three orders of the concept-formation list and the paired-associate lists were the same for all Ss. The orders of presentation of the *stimulus* words were kept the same in the two-paired-associate lists.

RESULTS AND DISCUSSION

The data which were subjected to analysis were the number of trials to one perfect trial on a concept (this meant giving the correct concept response to all four instances of a concept on the same trial) and the number of errors made on each concept in the entire course of the experiment. As noted above, the concept "large" was omitted from this analysis. All Ss failing to attain a concept in the 18 allotted trials were given a score of 19. Facilitated concepts ("white" preceded by learning List I, "soft" preceded by learning List II) were compared with nonfacilitated concepts ("soft" preceded by learning List I, "white" preceded by learning List II).

Table 2 presents the data for the number of Ss who attained facilitated

TABLE 2

NUMBER OF Ss ATTAINING CONCEPTS ON SUCCESSIVE BLOCKS
OF TRIALS

Concept	Trial on Which Concept Attainment Took Place				Failed to Attain	Total
	1–4	5–8	9–12	13–18		
Facilitated	7	16	4	3	0	30
Nonfacilitated	0	10	7	6	7	30
Buffer	3	13	5	2	7	30

and nonfacilitated concepts on successive blocks of trials. It can be seen that the facilitated concepts were solved earlier and that fewer Ss failed to solve them. No S failed to solve the facilitated concept whereas seven Ss failed to solve the nonfacilitated concepts. The mean number of trials taken to solve each concept was 7.17 for the facilitated concepts and 12.1 for the nonfacilitated concepts, a significant difference ($t = 3.67$, 29 df, $P < .001$). The mean numbers of errors on the facilitated and nonfacilitated concepts were 16.13 and 36.77, respectively. This difference was significant ($t = 3.4$, 29 df, $P < .005$).

Although it is evident that facilitation occurred, there is still the question of how the paired-associate learning facilitated the concept attainment. The results of a study by Freedman and Mednick (1958) suggest that the facilitation could have operated by making the first correct response to a concept occur earlier than it would have without the paired-associate learning. If the first correct response to facilitated concepts is given before the first correct response to nonfacilitated concepts, the former would be easier to attain than the latter. The mean trial on which the first correct response was given was 3.5 for facilitated concepts and 8.4 for nonfacilitated concepts. This difference was found to be significant ($t = 2.87$, 29 df, $P < .005$).

It is also possible that the facilitated concepts were easier to attain once the correct response was given. That is, the fact that the first correct response to facilitated concepts was given earlier might not be the only explanation of the facilitation; the training with the paired-associate lists might also have enabled Ss to apply the correct response (once it was given to one instance of a concept) more easily to the facilitated concepts than to the nonfacilitated concepts. The results show that the facilitated concepts were attained an average of 4.3 trials after the first correct response was given; the figure for nonfacilitated concepts is 3.7 trials. Thus, once the correct response was discovered the nonfacilitated concepts were actually attained somewhat more quickly than the facilitated concepts (but not significantly so). These results (i.e., the facilitated concepts being attained no more quickly once the correct response was known) can be explained by the fact that usually by the time the nonfacilitated concept was discovered the facilitated concept had already been attained. In addition, as might be predicted from the dominance levels, the buffer concept "large" was on the average attained earlier than the nonfacilitated concepts (mean number of trials to attainment of large was 10.2). This means that in many cases when S made his first correct response to the nonfacilitated concept he had already attained the other two concepts (facilitated and buffer). At this point only four instances remained to which the correct response was not known. Thus there was relatively little difficulty in applying the correct response to the remaining instances.

A possible objection to the present experiment might be that Ss gave the correct response to the facilitated concepts more quickly because the paired-associate learning made them aware of this response. If S were conscious of the relationship between the paired-associate list and the concept-formation task, he might be able to discover the correct response to the facilitated concept by looking for the relationship between particular words on both lists (e.g., S could question the significance of the pair "sugar-black," realize that "black" is associated with "white," and thus discover the correct response to "sugar"). In other studies demonstrating mediated association or mediated generalization (Bugelski & Scharlock, 1952; Russell & Storms, 1955), it was found that Ss were unaware of the process of mediation. Immediately following the procedures of the present experiment all Ss, except for the first four Ss, were questioned intensively about any observed relationship between the paired-associate and concept-formation lists. Of the 26 Ss interviewed, none expressed awareness of the relationship between the lists. It seems likely that the facilitation occurred "unconsciously" by strengthening of the appropriate mediating associations.

A variable that may prove to be significant is the strength of the association between the facilitating words (e.g., "black-white" is a much stronger association than "sheep-white"). Although the present study was not designed to investigate this variable, there was some indication in the data that stronger associations have a greater facilitating effect.

It might be asked whether or not it is possible to interfere with the attainment of concepts in a concept-formation test. One possible method for accomplishing this is to strengthen competing responses. For example, common responses to "grape" are "round," "juicy," "purple," and "soft." If "grape" is an instance of the concept "soft," strengthening the associations between "grape" and "juicy," "purple," or "round" should interfere with the attainment of the concept "soft" by making competing responses occur and thus cause the correct response (i.e., "soft") to be retarded. Underwood (1957) has shown that concepts represented by instances with strong competing responses are in fact more difficult to attain than concepts represented by instances that do not have strong competing responses. Therefore, by employing the paired-associate, mediated generalization method used in the present study, to strengthen interfering (i.e., competing) responses, it should be possible to make concept formation more difficult.

SUMMARY

Thirty Ss learned one of two paired-associate lists of 12 pairs and were then presented with a list of 12 nouns and were instructed to discover into what three groups the nouns could be divided and what adjectives could describe each group. The paired-associate lists were each designed by a method based on mediated generalization to facilitate a concept in the concept-formation list. The facilitated concepts were attained more quickly and with fewer errors than the nonfacilitated concepts. An explanation of the process of facilitation is offered and is supported by an analysis of the results.

REFERENCES

BUGELSKI, B. R., & SCHARLOCK, D. P. An experimental demonstration of unconscious mediated generalization. *J. exp. Psychol.*, 1952, 44, 334–338.

FREEDMAN, J. L., & MEDNICK, S. A. Ease of attainment of concepts as a function of response dominance variance. *J. exp. Psychol.*, 1958, 55, 463–466.

RUSSELL, W. A., & JENKINS, J. J. The complete Minnesota norms for responses to 100 words from the Kent-Rosanoff Word Association Test. *ONR tech. Rep.*, 1954, No. 11.

RUSSELL, W. A., & STORMS, L. H. Implicit verbal chaining in paired-associate learning. *J. exp. Psychol.*, 1955, 49, 287–293.

UNDERWOOD, B. J. An orientation for research on thinking. *Psychol. Rev.*, 1952, 59, 209–220.

UNDERWOOD, B. J. Studies in distributed practice: XV. Verbal concept learning as a function of intralist interference. *J. exp. Psychol.*, 1957, 54, 33–40.

UNDERWOOD, B. J., & RICHARDSON, J. Some verbal materials for the study of concept formation. *Psychol. Bull.*, 1956, 53, 84–95. (a)

UNDERWOOD, B. J., & RICHARDSON, J. Verbal concept learning as a function of instructions and dominance level. *J. exp. Psychol.*, 1956, 51, 229–238. (b)

31. The Learning of Concept Names Mediated by Concept Examples

Jack Richardson

A previous study (Richardson, 1960) was concerned with paired-associate lists in which each response was correct for a group of words. It was demonstrated that the difference in difficulty of the lists was due to the stimulus relationships, but ratings of associative connection among stimuli did not correspond to the difficulty of learning. It seemed, descriptively, that the nouns which were grouped on the basis of a common descriptive response and the nouns which were grouped on the basis of class membership were less difficult than would be expected from the ratings of associative connection. It was suggested that part of the transfer among the stimuli of these groups was based upon a common or mediating response.

Staats and Staats (1957) have demonstrated that pairing a nonsense syllable with words which have a common connotative meaning results in a change in the meaning of the syllable as measured by the semantic differential scale. This is considered evidence that each of the words paired with the syllable elicits a common response and that this response becomes attached to the syllable as a result of the pairing. This mediating response then determines the change in the rating of the syllable on the semantic differential.

The present study used the technique of pairing a syllable with a group of words. Syllables were paired with groups of nouns belonging to the same class and with groups of nouns which elicit a common descriptive response. The effect of this pairing on the subsequent paired-associate learning of the "name" of the nouns as a response to the syllable was determined. If the nouns function as mediating responses then the syllables should tend to elicit the names as a result of the syllable-noun pairing and there should be positive transfer to the learning of the syllable-name pairs. This procedure is comparable to the B-C, A-B, A-C, mediation paradigm where B is a group of nouns and B-C is an assumed connection between the group of nouns and the name of the group.

A pilot study with nouns from the same class demonstrated that the procedure produced strong positive transfer to learning a syllable-name list so other conditions were introduced to permit comparison with the basic mediation and control conditions. Underwood (1952) has stated

Reprinted by permission of the author and Academic Press, Inc. from *Journal of Verbal Learning and Verbal Behavior*, 1962, *1*, 281–288.

that temporal contiguity of the stimuli may be important in concept learning, so a second mediation condition provided for increased contiguity
of the presentation of the syllable-noun pairs from the same group. Porter
and Duncan (1953) have demonstrated that re-pairing the stimuli and
responses of a previously learned paired-associate list produces strong
negative transfer. A third mediation condition was provided to determine
if negative transfer would result from a comparable re-pairing in this
paradigm.

In the usual B-C, A-B, A-C, mediation paradigm with verbal materials,
B-C is a connection between a pair of words, so a fourth mediation condition was included to permit comparison of the effect of pairing a syllable with a group of nouns with the effect of pairing the syllable with
a single noun from the group. It seemed possible that both conditions
would produce positive transfer to the A-C stage of learning but that
the groups of nouns might result in more A-C learning during the A-B
pairing and thus more transfer. There was no difference between the
transfer in these two conditions, so a second experiment varied the number of pairings of the syllables and nouns prior to the syllable-name learning in order to clarify this relationship.

METHOD

EXPERIMENT I

Material. The groups of nouns selected from a class will be called class
concepts, the groups of nouns selected on the basis of a common descriptive response will be called dominance concepts, and a single noun from
a group will be called an example of that concept. The syllables, names
of the concepts, and three examples of each concept are presented in
Table 1. The eight 0% association value nonsense syllables are from Glaze
(1928) and are of minimum formal similarity. Eight groups of 14 common nouns were selected as examples of the class concepts. Three examples of each concept are presented in the second column of Table 1 to
illustrate the relationships, and the names of the class concepts are presented in the third column.

Eight groups of 14 nouns which had elicited a common descriptive
response were selected from Underwood and Richardson (1956a) as examples of the dominance concepts. Three of the 14 examples of each
dominance concept are presented in the fourth column of Table 1 and
the common descriptive response is the name in last column. The dominance values, or mean percentage of Ss who gave the name as a descriptive association to the examples, are in parentheses underneath the names.

Lists. All Ss were presented with 14 repetitions of the eight nonsense

TABLE 1

Syllables, Names, and Examples of Concepts Used in the Lists

Stimuli	Class concepts		Dominance concepts	
	Examples	Name	Examples	Name
JID	fox tiger mule	Animal	milk snow lint	White (49.79)
YIL	sweater uniform cape	Clothing	skunk cabbage goat	Smelly (49.93)
CEF	gardenia poppy daffodil	Flower	helmet balloon head	Round (49.93)
WUB	willow oak poplar	Tree	pony camel moccasin	Brown (30.00)
TOV	ivory green tan	Color	minnow bean tweezer	Small (49.79)
ZUK	lemon banana cherry	Fruit	lips belly linen	Soft (29.86)
QAP	radish potato onion	Vegetable	pail armor moon	Shiny (30.07)
GAH	plow saw hoe	Tool	rattlesnake ski limousine	Long (28.21)

syllables in Table 1 and each time the syllable was paired with an example of one of the concepts. All Ss were then requested to give a free association to each syllable and required to learn a paired-associate list with the syllables as stimuli and the names of the concepts as responses. Within each type of material, all Ss learned the same paired-associate list and the only difference in conditions was in the pairing of the syllables and examples, or in the sequence of presentation of the syllable-example pairs prior to the paired-associate learning. The five different conditions within each type of material were:

(1) Mediation—14 different examples of a single concept were paired with each of the eight syllables and the examples paired with each syl-

lable corresponded to the name which was the response to the syllable in the paired-associate learning. For example, JID was paired with fox, tiger, mule, etc., and Animal was later the response to JID in the paired-associate learning. The 112 pairs were presented in random order subject to the restrictions that a syllable should not appear more than twice in succession and that all eight syllables should appear within the last eight positions.

(2) Contiguity—the pairing of the syllables and examples was the same as in the Mediation condition and the only difference was the sequence of presentation of the syllable-example pairs. A single syllable was presented 13 times and each time appeared with a different example of the class. Another syllable was then presented 13 times, etc., until all eight syllables had appeared. The last eight pairs consisted of each syllable, paired with the 14th example of the class.

(3) Example—the sequence of presentation was the same as in the Mediation condition but each time a syllable appeared it was paired with the same example. Thus each syllable was paired 14 times with the same example instead of a single pairing with 14 different examples. Six sets, consisting of an example from each concept, were randomly selected and each set was presented to different Ss so that the results would not depend upon the particular example used in this condition.

(4) Control—the procedure was the same as in the Mediation condition except there was no systematic pairing of the syllables with examples from the same concept. Each syllable was paired with either one or two examples from each of the eight concepts and the particular examples were randomly assigned to the syllables. This condition was a control for transfer effects which were not due to the systematic pairing of a syllable with the examples of a single concept.

(5) Re-paired—the procedure was the same as in the Mediation condition except that each syllable was paired with 14 examples of a concept which was not the response to the syllable in the paired-associate learning. For example, JID was paired with willow, oak, poplar, etc., and Animal was later the response to JID in the paired-associate learning.

Procedure. The syllable-noun pairs were presented by two different methods within each condition. The syllables were always presented with a 16-mm strip-film projector but the nouns were presented by the projector and to the right of the syllables for half of the Ss, and E pronounced the nouns just after the syllable appeared for the other half of the Ss. Thus, with five conditions, two types of material, and two methods of presentation, there were 20 groups and 10 Ss were assigned to each group. The groups were listed in counterbalanced order and each of the 200 Ss was assigned to the next group as he appeared at the laboratory. The Ss were college students in introductory courses and had not served in any other verbal learning experiment. Five Ss were dropped because of difficulty with the projector or strip-film but none were eliminated for failure to learn.

Prior to the presentation of the syllables and nouns S was told that the experiment was being done to compare the simultaneous learning of non-sense syllables and words and was instructed to learn the syllables and words separately even though they were presented together. S was told to read the syllable silently but was required to pronounce the example, either read it aloud or repeat it after E. S was instructed to concentrate on the word after reading the syllable.

The 112 syllable-noun pairs were presented at a 4-sec. rate. Each syllable was then presented alone and S requested to give the first word association which occurred to him. The usual paired-associate instructions were then read to S and the pair-associate list learned by the anticipation method to a criterion of one perfect trial with a minimum of five trials. The paired-associate lists were presented in six different orders at a 2-2-sec. rate with a 4-sec. intertrial interval. They were presented with the strip-film projector and the first presentation of the paired-associate list was scored as a trial.

EXPERIMENT II

The difference between the Example and Mediation conditions was not significant in Exp. I, so comparable conditions were used in a second experiment which varied the number of pairings of syllables and examples prior to the paired-associate learning. This experiment used only the class concepts and compared the amount of transfer to the paired-associate list from pairing one example with a syllable (Example conditions) with the amount of transfer from pairing the maximum number of examples with a syllable (Mediation conditions). The paired-associate list was the same as the class concept list in Exp. I and assignment of Ss to groups, method of presentation of the paired-associate list, rate of presentation, instructions, and criterion of learning were the same as Exp. I. The syllable-example pairs were typed on 3 × 5 in. cards and presented manually at a 4-sec. rate.

Each S received either 3, 6, or 9 presentations of each of the eight syllables and each syllable was either paired with the same example on each presentation or with different examples of the same concept on each presentation. Thus there were two conditions and three numbers of presentation. Fourteen Ss were assigned to each of the six groups. Within each group, all 14 of the examples of a concept were paired with the syllable so the results would not depend upon the particular example. Fourteen different lists were presented in the three Example conditions, five different lists in the Mediation condition with three presentations, three lists in the Mediation condition with six presentations, and two lists in the Mediation condition with nine presentations. In each case there was only the minimum necessary duplication of the 14 examples between lists. Each S was presented only one of the lists. After the presentation of the syllable-example pairs the Ss were not asked for associations but went directly to the paired-associate learning.

RESULTS

EXPERIMENT I

Associations. The associations to the syllables were given after the syllable-example pairing and prior to the paired-associate learning. These associations were classified as to whether they were names of the examples which had been paired with the syllable, an example which had been paired with the syllable, or some other response including omissions. The number of each type of association for the different conditions is presented in Table 2. The number of times that a correct response was given to a syllable during the first five trials of the paired-associate learning was tabulated and the mean number of correct responses which followed each type of association is presented in the appropriate column of Table 2. It

TABLE 2

ASSOCIATIONS TO SYLLABLES AND MEAN CORRECT RESPONSES
ON THE FIRST FIVE TRIALS

	Associations to syllables					
	Names		Examples		Other	
Conditions	Number	M correct responses	Number	M correct responses	Number	M correct responses
Class						
Mediation	58	3.76	40	3.45	62	1.95
Contiguity	23	3.52	54	2.61	83	1.89
Example	0	—	127	3.32	33	1.91
Control	1	2.00	43	1.37	116	1.13
Re-paired	42	.43	52	.40	66	.39
Dominance						
Mediation	1	5.00	10	2.20	149	1.42
Contiguity	1	.00	11	2.18	148	1.32
Example	0	—	133	2.21	27	1.04
Control	0	—	49	1.84	111	1.36
Re-paired	1	3.00	29	1.90	130	1.23

should be noted that in the two Re-paired conditions the correct response for the syllable during the paired-associate learning was not the name of the examples which had been paired with the syllable. Therefore the number of correct responses during learning should not be related to the type of association in the same fashion as in the other conditions.

In general, the name associations are followed by more correct responses than the example associations, and the example associations are followed by more correct responses than other types of associations. The two Control conditions produced approximately the same number of name and

TABLE 3

MEANS AND STANDARD DEVIATIONS OF THE NUMBER OF CORRECT RESPONSES ON THE FIRST FIVE TRIALS AND TRIALS TO CRITERION

| | Trials to criterion | | | | Correct on first 5 trials | | | |
| | Class | | Dominance | | Class | | Dominance | |
Condition	M	SD	M	SD	M	SD	M	SD
Mediation	9.70	7.84	12.80	7.37	23.85	9.07	11.90	7.13
Contiguity	9.10	6.27	15.75	9.53	18.95	8.32	11.00	5.42
Example	7.20	4.96	10.40	7.06	24.25	6.62	16.10	8.83
Control	15.55	7.55	13.40	6.45	9.60	6.14	12.05	5.31
Re-paired	19.35	7.11	12.15	4.75	3.25	2.07	10.90	5.38

example associations and, as would be expected, the two Example conditions produced primarily example associations and approximately the same number. In the other conditions, the number of name associations and example associations are much greater with the class concepts.

Learning. An analysis of variance for number of trials to criterion gave Fs which did not even approach significance with the exception of Conditions ($F = 5.59$) and the interaction of Conditions and Material ($F = 5.55$) which were both significant beyond the .01 level. An analysis of variance for the number of correct responses on the first five trials of the paired-associate learning gave Fs < 1.00 with the exception of Material ($F = 13.25$), Conditions ($F = 23.02$), and the interaction of Conditions and Material ($F = 14.01$) which were all significant beyond the .01 level. The error terms were heterogeneous for both analyses. The method of presentation and the interactions were not significant, so the two methods of presentation were combined and the means ($n = 20$) and standard deviations are presented in Table 3. The significant interaction between material and conditions was the result of conditions producing a significant variation with the class concepts but not with the dominance

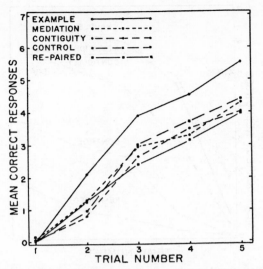

FIG. 1. Mean number of correct responses as a function of trials of paired-associate learning with dominance concepts: Exp. I.

concepts. The number correct on the first five trials seemed to be the more sensitive measure so it was used for the following comparisons. Duncan's Range Test, at the .01 level, showed that there were no significant differences between conditions within the dominance material but that all the conditions within the class materials were significantly different except the Mediation condition which was not significantly different from either the Example or Contiguity condition. The two Control conditions were not significantly different, but all other comparisons between the two types of material, within conditions, were significant.

The lack of differential transfer with the dominance concepts agrees with the distribution of the type of associations in Table 2. There was little difference in the number of example associations with the exception of the Example condition and this condition tended to show more transfer even though the differences were not significant. The means of the number of correct responses on the first five trials with the dominance concepts are presented in Fig. 1. As shown in Table 1, the dominance value of four of the concepts was approximately 50% while the dominance value of the other four was approximately 30%. An examination of the correct responses during the first five trials of paired-associate learning for the Mediation, Contiguity, and Example conditions showed no tendency for more correct responses to be given to the higher-dominance concepts than to the lower-dominance concepts. There is little indication that mediation occurred with the dominance concepts.

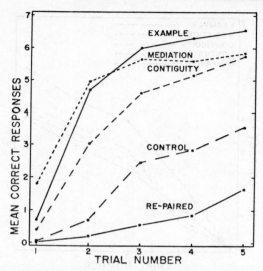

FIG. 2. Mean number of correct responses as a function of trials of paired-associate learning with the class concepts: Exp. I.

The differential transfer obtained with the class concepts also agrees with what would be expected from the associations given to the syllables. Comparing Tables 2 and 3, it is apparent that the number of "Other" responses is inversely related to the mean number of correct responses on the first five trials of paired-associate learning. The means of the number of correct responses on the first five trials for the five conditions with the class concepts are presented in Fig. 2. There was a large negative transfer in the Re-paired condition and strong positive transfer in the three mediation conditions. Contrary to the expected results, the Contiguity condition tended to produce fewer correct responses than the Mediation condition and the Example condition tended to produce more correct responses than the Mediation condition. It should be noted that there were some correct responses on the first presentation of the syllables as would be expected from the associations to the syllables. On the first trial the Mediation condition produced more correct responses than the Example condition even though there were fewer correct responses during the five trials.

EXPERIMENT II

The mean number of correct responses on the first five trials are presented in Fig. 3 for the six groups, and the two comparable groups from Exp. I are included. An analysis of variance for the six groups in Exp. II

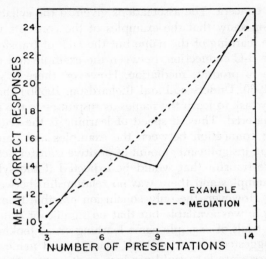

Fig. 3. Mean number of correct responses on the first five trials of paired-associate learning as a function of the number of syllable-example presentations.

gave $Fs < 1.00$ for conditions and interaction while the F for number of presentations was 2.69 ($p < .10$). Fig. 3 shows that there is no consistent tendency for pairing the maximum number of different examples with the syllable to be superior to pairing a single example with the syllable but that transfer increases as a function of number presentations. Associations were not given to the syllables in this experiment but examination of the correct responses on the first trial showed, in every case, that more correct responses were given in the Mediation condition than in the Example condition. The number of correct responses on the first trial was 4, 9, and 13 for the 3, 6, and 9 presentations respectively in the Mediation conditions, while there were 1, 0, and 1 correct responses for the comparable Example conditions.

DISCUSSION

The instructions to S to learn the syllables and examples separately and the requirement of an association to the syllable before the paired-associate learning should have produced associative arousal (Jenkins, to be published). In spite of this there was no significant transfer with the dominance concepts. Kaplan (1959) found mediation with these materials but there were many differences in the experiments, including the dominance level of the examples and the fact that the test list paired two examples of a concept. The associations given to the syllables in the Example condition show that the examples of the concepts were available to mediate the learning of the name but the lack of transfer seems to indicate that the B-C connection, between the example and name, was not strong enough to produce mediation. However, there is some evidence (Richardson, 1960; Underwood and Richardson, 1956b) that it is a comparatively easy task to learn the names as responses to the examples with this type of material. Thus, if speed of learning is the criterion, there is a fairly strong connection between the examples and names. It should be noted that an insignificant amount of positive transfer occurred instead of the negative transfer that would be expected if the syllables tended to elicit the examples and there was no relationship between the names and examples. However, the only conclusion possible from this study is that the example was available but that no significant transfer occurred. Perhaps a few trials of example-name learning or, as Jenkins (to be published) has suggested, requiring both example and name as a response in the paired-associate list would produce positive transfer.

With the class concepts, the mediated interference in the Re-paired condition agrees with results obtained with different paradigms and materials (McGehee and Schulz, 1961; Norcross and Spiker, 1958). The hypothesis that contiguity of the examples would produce more names during syllable-example pairing and thus facilitate the syllable-name learning is not supported by the results. The Mediation condition gave more name associations and tended to facilitate paired-associate learning compared to the Contiguity condition. It is possible that the Contiguity condition did facilitate production of names during the syllable-example pairing but that the names were not connected with the syllables.

In Exp. I with the class concepts, the name associations presented in Table 2 and the transfer shown in Fig. 2 are clear demonstrations of learning mediated by the concept examples. The Mediation condition did not produce more over-all transfer than the Example condition in spite of the fact that there were more name associations in the Mediation condition and that four comparisons, including Exp. II, of the two conditions showed that more correct responses were given on the first trial of the Mediation condition. The associations and the first-trial transfer suggest that during the syllable-example pairing there is more mediated learning of the syllable-name in the Mediation condition while the Example condition produces more and stronger syllable-example learning. Thus, in the Mediation condition, pairing several examples with the syllable tends to produce both names, which are correct in the paired-associate learning, and examples which mediate the learning. The Example condition, which pairs only one example with the syllable, produces only examples and the facilitation is due to the use of these examples to mediate learning during the syllable-name learning.

SUMMARY

This study paired concept examples with nonsense syllables in an attempt to produce positive transfer to learning the concept names as responses to the syllables. The results with dominance concepts were negative but there were large amounts of transfer with class concepts. When different examples of a class concept were paired with a syllable each time it was presented then the class name was often given as an association to the syllable but this did not occur when only one example of a concept was paired with a syllable. It was suggested that use of different examples of a concept tended to produce syllable-name learning while the examples were being presented and that the use of a single example of a concept simply provided a response which mediated learning when the syllable and class name was presented in a paired-associate list.

REFERENCES

GLAZE, J. A. The association value of non-sense syllables. *J. genet. Psychol.*, 1928, 35, 255–268.

JENKINS, J. J. Mediated associations: Paradigms and situations. To be published in C. N. Cofer (Ed.) *Problems and processes in verbal behavior and learning.* New York: McGraw-Hill.

KAPLAN, R. J. A study of semantic generalization through the use of established conceptual mediations. *J. exp. Psychol.*, 1959, 57, 288–293.

McGEHEE, NAN E., AND SCHULZ, R. W. Mediation in paired-associate learning. *J. exp. Psychol.*, 1961, 62, 565–570.

NORCROSS, KATHRYN J., AND SPIKER, C. C. Effects of mediated associations on transfer in paired-associate learning. *J. exp. Psychol.*, 1958, 55, 129–134.

PORTER, L. W., AND DUNCAN, C. P. Negative transfer in verbal learning. *J. exp. Psychol.*, 1953, 46, 61–64.

RICHARDSON, J. Association among stimuli and the learning of verbal concept lists. *J. exp. Psychol.*, 1960, 60, 290–298.

STAATS, CAROLYN K., AND STAATS, A. W. Meaning established by classical conditioning. *J. exp. Psychol.*, 1957, 54, 74–80.

UNDERWOOD, B. J. An orientation for research on thinking. *Psychol. Rev.*, 1952, 59, 209–220.

UNDERWOOD, B. J., AND RICHARDSON, J. Some verbal materials for the study of concept formation. *Psychol. Bull.*, 1956, 53, 84–95. *a*

UNDERWOOD, B. J., AND RICHARDSON, J. Verbal concept learning as a function of instructions and dominance level. *J. exp. Psychol.*, 1956, 51, 229–238. *b*

32.   The Role of Instance Contiguity and Dominance in Concept Attainment

Rudolph W. Schulz, Robert L. Miller, and Robert C. Radtke

In 1952 Underwood postulated that instance contiguity was a critical variable in determining the rate at which concepts will be attained and that there would be a direct relationship between degree of contiguity and performance. Support for this contention has been found by Newman (1956) with concepts based on the azimuth of lines and the position of three dots accompanying each line, and by Kurtz and Hovland (1956) whose concepts consisted of simple geometric patterns. The present study investigated instance contiguity as a variable in the rate at which concepts based on relations among words are attained. The dominance level (Underwood and Richardson, 1956a) of the concepts was also varied.

METHOD

Lists. The three concept lists constructed by Underwood and Richardson (1956a) were employed. Each list contains six concepts (sense impressions), two at each of three levels of dominance. Dominance, it will be recalled, refers to the percentage of 153 Ss that gave a particular sense-impression response (e.g., red) as an association to the present words (Underwood and Richardson, 1956b). Thus, it may be regarded as an index of the strength of the relationship between a given instance and the name of the concept. There are four instances (nouns) of each concept. Considering all three lists, the concepts (*round, small, white, smelly, soft,* and *big*) are represented once at each of the three dominance levels —high (74.8%), medium (40.7%), and low (16.1%). The lists and other details regarding their construction may be found in the report by Underwood and Richardson.

Three levels of instance contiguity were defined as follows. High contiguity (HC) meant that all four instances of a given concept were presented in succession throughout training. For medium contiguity (MC) concepts, two of the four instances of a given concept were presented successively throughout training while one or more instances of another concept intervened between presentations of the two other instances. Un-

Reprinted by permission of the authors and Academic Press, Inc. from *Journal of Verbal Learning and Verbal Behavior*, 1963, *1*, 432–435.

der low contiguity (LC) conditions, no two instances of a given concept were ever presented successively, one or more instances of another concept always intervening between presentations of instances of an LC concept. Contiguity was manipulated within lists. For a given S, two concepts were HC, two MC, and two LC. Contiguity was balanced with respect to dominance level and concepts; thus, there were three "versions" of each of the three basic lists, nine lists in all. The 24 items on each list were presented in four different random orders, with the restriction that contiguity conditions remain appropriately defined.

In brief, the design consisted of three factors: list, dominance, and contiguity. The data are amendable to statistical treatment via Lindquist's (1953) Type IV analysis of variance.

Subjects and Procedure. The Ss were 36 undergraduates at the University of Iowa. Four Ss were randomly assigned to each of the nine lists, the Nth S not being assigned to a given list until all other lists had been assigned N—1 Ss. The instructions were those described as *partially restricted* by Underwood and Richardson (1956a) where S is told that the concepts to be learned are sense impressions. Acquisition consisted of 12 trials, with a trial consisting of one presentation of all 24 instances, at a 4-sec. rate of presentation on a Stowe Memory Drum. The intertrial interval was 4 sec. The Ss were told *right* or *wrong* by E after each response.

RESULTS AND DISCUSSION

Figure 1 shows acquisition, in terms of mean number of correct responses, as a function of contiguity. It is clear from Fig. 1 that the expected direct relation between contiguity and performance was obtained. Statistically, contiguity was a reliable source of variance ($F = 8.52$, $df = 2/54$, $P < .01$). The means for total number of correct responses during the 12 acquisition trials are plotted in Fig. 2 as a joint function of contiguity and dominance. The standard errors of these means ranged from 3.49 to 7.41. In agreement with Underwood and Richardson (1956a), performance was directly related to dominance ($F = 37.65$, $df = 2/54$, $P < .01$). The trend toward interaction between contiguity and dominance in Fig. 2 was not statistically significant either as a "between" Ss ($F = 1.73$, $df = 2/27$, $P > .10$) or as a "within" Ss effect ($F < 1$). There was, however, a significant interaction between dominance and lists ($F = 3.34$, $df = 4/54$, $P < .05$). The fact that dominance had a greater effect on performance with List 2 than with the other two lists appears to be the primary source of this interaction. An explanation for this result is not apparent in the present data. The remaining Fs did not approach significance.

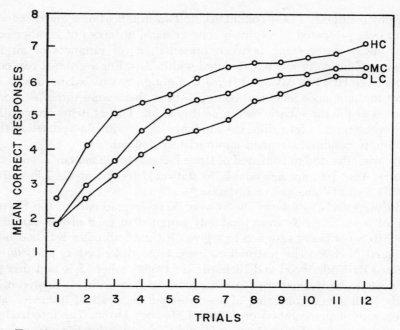

FIG. 1. Concept acquisition as a function of contiguity and trials.

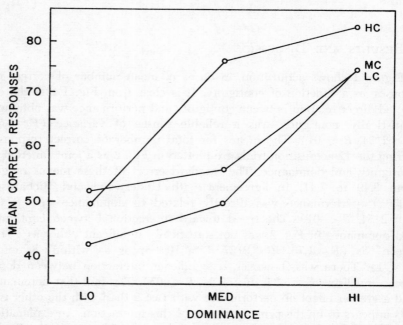

FIG. 2. Means of total numbers of correct responses during 12 trials as a function of instance contiguity and dominance.

TABLE 1

NUMBER OF CONCEPTS ATTAINED ON SUCCESSIVE BLOCKS OF FOUR
TRIALS AS A FUNCTION CONTIGUITY AND DOMINANCE LEVEL

		Trials			
Contiguity	Dominance	1–4	5–8	9–12	Not attained
High	High	16	4	3	1
	Medium	17	3	3	1
	Low	16	4	2	2
	Σ	49	11	8	4
Medium	High	10	9	2	3
	Medium	8	5	4	6
	Low	1	8	9	6
	Σ	19	22	15	15
Low	High	6	7	2	9
	Medium	4	9	3	8
	Low	3	5	6	10
	Σ	13	21	11	27

Performance, in terms of the number of concepts attained on successive blocks of four trials, is shown in Table 1. As can be seen from Table 1, contiguity and dominance are directly related to performance; hence, the results for this measure agree with those for correct responses.

Analysis of overt errors revealed similar agreement. Since with the present instructions Ss respond on almost every presentation, the relationships between errors and contiguity and dominance are essentially the inverse of those for correct responses, and need not be presented.

The present results are in full agreement with expectations regarding the effect of dominance and contiguity on performance in learning concepts based on relations among nouns which elicit the same sense impression. These results, when considered in conjunction with those of Newman (1956) and Kurtz and Hovland (1956) for concepts based on "physical" relations among simple geometric patterns, would appear to establish the relationship between instance contiguity and rate of concept attainment as a relationship with considerable generality.

SUMMARY

Three levels of instance contiguity (high, medium, and low) were investigated to determine the effect of instance contiguity on the attainment of concepts, based on relations among words, as a function of concept dominance level (high, medium, and low). Lists containing six concepts, four instances per concept, were presented at a 4-sec. rate for 12 trials to 36 Ss on a memory drum while E told S *right* or *wrong* after each of S's responses. The concepts were: *round, small, white, smelly, soft,* and *big.* Contiguity was manipulated in terms of the number of successive presentations of instances of the same concept without interpolation of instances of another concept during training (4, 2, and 0 for high, medium, and low contiguity, respectively).

Performance, in terms of correct responses and number of concepts attained in successive four-trial blocks, was directly and significantly related to both contiguity and dominance. The interaction between contiguity and dominance was not significant.

References

Kurtz, K. H., and Hovland, C. I. Concept learning with differing sequences of instances. *J. exp. Psychol.,* 1956, 51, 239–243.

Lindquist, E. F. *Design and analysis of experiments in psychology and education.* Boston: Houghton-Mifflin, 1953.

Newman, S. E. Effects of contiguity and similarity on the learning of concepts. *J. exp. Psychol.,* 1956, 52, 349–353.

Underwood, B. J. An orientation for research on thinking. *Psychol. Rev.,* 1952, 59, 209–220.

Underwood, B. J., and Richardson, J. Verbal concept learning as a function of instructions and dominance level. *J. exp. Psychol.,* 1956, 51, 229–238. (*a*)

Underwood, B. J., and Richardson, J. Some verbal materials for the study of concept formation. *Psychol. Bull.,* 1956, 53, 84–95. (*b*)

33.   Mediation in Verbal Concept Learning

Carl P. Duncan

In a typical concept-learning task with two or more dimensions or classes of stimuli, and with two or more stimuli in each class, S may or

Reprinted by permission of Academic Press, Inc. from *Journal of Verbal Learning and Verbal Behavior* 1965, 4, 1–6.

may not be told in advance what stimuli will be presented. Even if he is told, he does not know which class of stimuli will be positively reinforced (relevant). Concept learning of this kind is here assumed to involve two somewhat dissimilar processes. These processes are also considered to be stages of acquisition. The first stage is chiefly occupied by the process of problem solving or response discovery. In this stage, which largely precedes occurrence of the first correct response, S must find out as best he can some one of the stimuli in the relevant class. It is likely that performance in this initial problem-solving stage will be influenced by such variables as whether or not S is told in advance what stimuli will be presented, by the total number of stimuli (the population to be searched), and by the pre-experimental hierarchies existing, for S, among the stimuli (e.g., Heidbreder, 1949; Underwood and Richardson, 1956b).

The second stage involves the process of concept mediation. Presumably, this process can begin only after S's first reinforcement, i.e., his first correct response. Reinforcement for responding to one member of a relevant stimulus class should, of course, increase the probability that S will again respond to that same stimulus when it next appears. But that same reinforcement may also increase the probability that S will respond to any other member of the relevant stimulus class whenever one is presented, even though S has not yet been reinforced, in the experimental situation, for responding to any other member. This latter additional effect of reinforcement will here be called mediation. Defined in this or in a similar way, mediation in concept learning has come in for much recent discussion (Goss, 1961; Isaacs and Duncan, 1962; Kendler, 1961; Kendler and Kendler, 1962; Levine, 1963).

The purpose of the experiments to be reported here is to study mediation by varying the degree to which it should occur. One way to accomplish this, presumably, would be to vary the extent to which mediation can take place among the stimuli of the reinforced class. But S's concept learning might also be influenced by whether or not mediation is possible among the stimuli of negatively reinforced or irrelevant dimensions. These considerations suggest the basic design that is used in all three experiments to be reported. In one condition, Ss are reinforced for stimuli (words) that already (it is assumed) belong to a class; these stimuli should permit mediation to occur among the various members of the class. In another condition, Ss are reinforced for words that cannot, a priori, be put in any one class, so there should be little or no opportunity for mediation to occur among such words. Within each of these conditions, the irrelevant words also will either belong or not belong to classes. Over-all concept learning performance, and a more direct measure of mediation to be developed later, should vary as a function of these four conditions.

Experiment I

Stimuli. There were three pairs of Cl (class) words: *Circle* and *Square*, *Two* and *Four*, and *Red* and *Blue*. There were also three pairs of Ncl (nonclass) words: *Method* and *Lift*, *Wait* and *Give*, and *Done* and *Place*. (Although Ncl words could presumably be paired in any manner, only these pairs were used.) All of these words are of either A or AA frequency in the Thorndike-Lorge (1944) count. In any one condition, S was presented with three of the six pairs of words, e.g., one Cl pair, two Ncl pairs. One word from each of the three pairs needed for a given experimental condition was typed on a 3 × 5-inch card, e.g., *Circle*, *Method*, *Wait*. The three words were typed in a vertical column on the card. Eight cards were needed to present all possible trios of three pairs of words. In addition, each word appeared equally often in each of the three vertical positions on a card, so a total of 24 cards made up the deck to be presented to S.

Conditions. There were four conditions. In Condition Cl-Cl, all three pairs of words were Cl pairs. Half the Ss were reinforced for *Circle* and *Square*, with *Two* and *Four*, and *Red* and *Blue*, being irrelevant. The other half of the Ss were reinforced for *Two* and *Four*, so *Circle* and *Square*, and *Red* and *Blue* were irrelevant.

In Condition Cl-Ncl, one pair of words was Cl, and the other two pairs were Ncl. For all Ss in this condition, the Cl words were reinforced; the Ncl words were irrelevant. For this condition two decks of stimulus cards were used. In one deck, *Circle* and *Square* (the reinforced pair) appeared with *Method* and *Lift*, and *Done* and *Place*. In the other deck, *Two* and *Four* (reinforced) appeared with *Wait* and *Give*, and *Done* and *Place*. One deck was used with half the Ss, the other deck with the other half.

In Condition Ncl-Cl, one pair of words was Ncl and the other two pairs were Cl. The Ncl words were reinforced for all Ss in this condition; the Cl words were irrelevant. Two decks of stimulus cards were used. In one deck, *Method and Lift* (reinforced) appeared with *Circle* and *Square*, and *Red* and *Blue*. In the other deck, *Wait* and *Give* (reinforced) appeared with *Two* and *Four*, and *Red* and *Blue*. Each deck was used with half the Ss.

In Condition Ncl-Ncl, all three pairs of words were Ncl. Half the Ss were reinforced for *Method* and *Lift*, with *Wait* and *Give*, and *Done* and *Place* irrelevant. The other half of the Ss were reinforced for *Wait* and *Give*, with *Method* and *Lift*, and *Done* and *Place* irrelevant.

Subjects. The Ss were 188 students enrolled in introductory psychology courses. Students in these courses are required to serve in experiments.

The Ss were assigned to the four conditions in turn; there were 47 Ss per condition.

Procedure. The *E* and the *S* sat on opposite sides of a table and were separated from each other by a large vertical panel mounted on the table. In the center of the panel was a small window behind which the stimulus cards could be presented.

The *S* was instructed that he would see cards each containing three words, that one of the three words on each card was correct, and that he was to discover which word was correct on each card.

The 24 cards in a deck were presented in a fixed random order with the following restrictions: (a) the first two cards presented revealed to *S* all six words in the deck, and (b) no trio of words (no one card) appeared more than once within a block of eight cards.

The *S* responded by saying aloud which word he thought was correct on the card in the window. The *E* told him whether his response was correct or incorrect, and removed the card. The deck of cards was held against the window by a spring, so removing one card immediately revealed the next card. The experiment proceeded at whatever pace was convenient for *S* and *E*.

Each *S* was taken to a criterion of six successive correct responses. One *S* in Condition Ncl-Ncl did not reach criterion in 48 trials; another *S* was run as a replacement.

Results. The number of trials (number of responses, correct and incorrect) to learn, not including the six criterion responses, was taken as the measure of over-all learning. The means for each of the four groups on this measure are shown in the left column of Table 1. As the means show, learning was fairly rapid on this rather easy task. The ordering of the means, from Group Cl-Cl with the fastest learning to Group Ncl-Ncl with the slowest, is more or less what one might expect, but the differences, on this measure at least, are not great. The means were analyzed in a 2×2 analysis of variance with reinforced words (Cl vs. Ncl) as one variable and irrelevant words (Cl vs. Ncl) as the other variable. Since the distributions for all groups were positively skewed, the raw scores were converted to log $(X + 1)$. Analysis of the log scores gave $F = 3.99$, $df = 1/184$, $p < .05$ for reinforced words. For irrelevant words F was less than one, and for the interaction $F = 1.38$; neither F was significant.

Although the results suggest some advantage when Cl words are reinforced, gross learning is not all that is of interest here. A measure that may be more sensitive to mediation is also desired. The measure chosen was as follows: the number of errors made *after* the first correct response and prior to the criterion responses. These may be called unnecessary errors. If mediation operates perfectly, the first correct response, at least to a class word, should cue *S* to respond to, and only to, other members of the class. The measure actually analyzed was the ratio of unnecessary errors to the total responses, correct and incorrect, occurring between the first correct response (not counted) and the final six criterion responses.

The mean unnecessary error ratios are shown in the right column of Table 1. These four means have the same order as the means for total trials with one exception: Group Cl-Ncl has the lowest mean error ratio (this group also had the lowest mean log trials). In the 2 × 2 analysis of variance of error ratios, the F for reinforced words was 20.50 ($df = 1/184$, $p < .001$); the error ratio was lower when Cl rather than Ncl words were

TABLE 1

MEAN TRIALS TO LEARN AND MEAN UNNECESSARY ERROR
RATIOS IN EXPERIMENT I

Group	Trials	Error ratios
Cl-Cl	4.51	.391
Cl-Ncl	4.91	.239
Ncl-Cl	5.15	.482
Ncl-Ncl	6.25	.643
	$\sigma_m = .825$[a]	$\sigma_m = .055$[a]

[a] Computed from the within-groups mean square of the analysis of variance.

reinforced. The F for irrelevant words was less than one, and the interaction F was 8.22 ($df = 1/184$, $p < .01$). The means for individual groups in Table 1 reveal the chief source of the interaction: when the reinforced words were Cl, the error ratio was lower with Ncl irrelevant words, but when reinforced words were Ncl, the error ratios was lower with Cl irrelevant words.

EXPERIMENT II

The task in Exp. I was fairly easy. The purpose of Exp. II was to so change the task that mediation would be made more difficult. It was assumed that one way this could be accomplished was to add another stimulus class.

Procedure. Two more Cl words, *Pigeon* (34) and *Crow* (37), and two more Ncl words, *Brother* (AA) and *Cup* (AA), were used. Values in parentheses are Thorndike-Lorge frequencies. Each stimulus card contained four words, one word from each of four pairs of words, so 16 cards were required to present all combinations of our words. All other procedures were the same as in Exp. I. Since the same pairs of words were reinforced in Exp. II as in Exp. I, addition of the new pairs of words amounted to adding irrelevant pairs.

There were 60 Ss in each of the four groups. One S in Condition Ncl-Cl did not reach criterion in 48 trials and was replaced.

Results. Mean trials to learn, not including the six criterion trials, are shown in the left column of Table 2. The ordering of these means is the same as that found in Exp. I for mean log scores, i.e., Group Cl-Ncl learned most rapidly, followed by Groups Cl-Cl, Ncl-Cl, and Ncl-Ncl in order of progressively slower learning. Since the distributions were positively skewed, analysis of log scores was carried out. For reinforced

TABLE 2

MEAN TRIALS TO LEARN AND MEAN UNNECESSARY ERROR
RATIOS IN EXPERIMENT II

Group	Trials	Error ratios
Cl-Cl	6.30	.450
Cl-Ncl	5.60	.398
Ncl-Cl	6.67	.543
Ncl-Ncl	7.95	.521
	$\sigma_m = .838$	$\sigma_m = .049$

words, F was 7.64 ($p < .01$), for irrelevant words, F was less than one, and for the interaction, $F = 7.23$ ($p < .01$). Thus, there is the same pattern of results as in Exp. I.

In the right column of Table 2 are the means for unnecessary error ratios. The order of these means is the same as that for Exp. I except that in Exp. II, Group Ncl-Cl, rather than Group Ncl-Ncl, has the highest mean. Analysis of variance gave $F = 4.93$ ($df = 1/236$, $p < .01$) for reinforced words; the mean error ratios were lower when Cl words were reinforced. The Fs for irrelevant words and the interaction were both less than one. Thus, as in Exp. I, Group Cl-Ncl showed the most rapid mediation, as measured by the lowest unnecessary error ratio. Unlike in Exp. I, there was no interaction in the error measure, between reinforced and irrelevant words.

EXPERIMENT III

In Exps. I and II there were only two words in a reinforced set. A correct response to one of the words left only one other word to be discovered. Experiment III was a further test of the role of mediation by increasing the number of words in each set from two to three.

Procedure. As in Exp. I, only three sets of Cl words and three sets of Ncl words were used. The Cl pairs used in Exp. I were increased to trios by including *Triangle* (8) with *Circle* and *Square*, *Six* (AA) with *Two* and *Four*, and *Green* (AA) with *Red* and *Blue*. The Ncl trios were obtained by including *Able* (AA) with *Method* and *Lift*, *Brother* with *Wait* and *Give*, and *Cup* with *Done* and *Place*. There were three words on each card, one from each of three trios of words, so a deck of 27 cards was needed for all possible combinations. All other details of procedure were

TABLE 3

MEAN TRIALS TO LEARN AND MEAN UNNECESSARY ERROR
RATIOS IN EXPERIMENT III

Group	Trials	Error ratios
Cl-Cl	5.38	.381
Cl-Ncl	4.22	.205
Ncl-Cl	7.50	.340
Ncl-Ncl	10.95	.463
	$\sigma_m = 1.19$	$\sigma_m = .055$

the same as in Exp. I, including the criterion of six consecutive correct responses even though there were three instead of two reinforced words.

There were 40 Ss in each of the four groups. Two Ss in Condition Cl-Cl, and three Ss in Condition Ncl-Ncl did not reach criterion and were replaced.

Results. The mean trials to learn, excluding criterion trials, are shown in the left column of Table 3. The ordering is the same as in Exp. II. In the analysis of log scores, F was 18.40 ($df = 1/156$, $p < .001$) for reinforced words; as usual, learning was faster when Cl rather than Ncl words were reinforced. The F for irrelevant words was less than one, and the F was 6.54 ($df = 1/156$, $p < .025$) for the interaction.

The right column of Table 3 shows means for unnecessary error ratios (these errors were again measured as all errors after the first correct response to any of the three reinforced words, and prior to the six criterion responses). It may be noted, by comparing Table 3 with Table 1, that mean trials to learn were somewhat higher with word trios (Exp. III) than with word pairs (Exp. I), but that mean unnecessary error ratios were slightly lower in Exp. III. Analysis of variance of the error ratios in Table 3 gave $F = 3.91$ ($df = 1/156$, $p < .05$) for reinforced words, F less than one for irrelevant words, and $F = 7.48$ ($p < .01$) for interaction. Thus, as has usually been the case, error ratios were lower when Cl rather than Ncl words were reinforced, while Cl vs. Ncl among irrelevant words has had no effect as a main variable. However, the interaction reveals that whether irrelevant words are Cl or Ncl is important, depending upon which type of words is being reinforced.

DISCUSSION

When the variable, class vs. nonclass, applied to positively reinforced words, both mediation and over-all concept learning occurred most readily, on the whole, with class words. The unnecessary error measure is taken as the most direct evidence for the operation of mediation as the term is used here, i.e., the increase in probability of response to one member of a class as a result of positive reinforcement for responding to some other member of the same class. When class words were reinforced, responses subsequent to the first reinforcement contained a lower proportion of error responses to irrelevant words than when nonclass words were reinforced. This difference may have resulted in part from a facilitating effect of mediation among class words, and in part from an interfering effect of mediation among nonclass words in those conditions in which nonclass words were the correct responses. Positive reinforcement of a nonclass word may increase the strength of extra-task words that could interfere with discovery of the other correct nonclass words.

When the variable, class vs. nonclass, was applied to irrelevant, negatively reinforced words, there was no significant main effect. Initially, it had seemed reasonable to expect that if mediation operated among class words when class words were positively reinforced, mediation might also operate among class words when such words were negatively reinforced. This would be mediation of nonresponse; being informed that a class word was wrong might reduce the probability of responding to other members of that class. However, in none of the three experiments was class vs. nonclass among irrelevant words significant as a main variable on any measure. It may be noted, however, that a process that seems similar to, and that would have similar facilitating effects on performance as, mediation of nonresponse has already been suggested by Kendler and Karasik (1958). They say that S must respond to relevant words with a common implicit response and must also respond to irrelevant words with a different implicit response. Using words from Underwood and Richardson (1956a), they provide strong evidence that implicit response differentiation does occur and does facilitate performance.

The significant interaction that occurred in most cases between reinforced and irrelevant words in all three experiments may provide some evidence for mediation of nonresponse. For the pair of conditions where the correct words were nonclass, i.e., Ncl-Cl and Ncl-Ncl, in nearly every comparison performance was better under Ncl-Cl, where the irrelevant words could be put in classes. However, if it is assumed that there is both mediation of response when class words are relevant, and mediation of nonresponse when class words are irrelevant, then in the other pair of conditions, Cl-Cl and Cl-Ncl, performance should have been better under Cl-Cl. Although this had been the expectation, in fact the opposite was true, although the differences in favor of Cl-Ncl were usually small the significant interaction among the four conditions was chiefly due to the fact that when class words were relevant, performance was better when nonclass words were irrelevant; but when nonclass words were relevant, performance was better when class words were irrelevant. Perhaps it is harder to discriminate relevant from irrelevant words when all words either are or are not members of classes than when some words are class members and some are not.

So far, the three experiments have been discussed as if there were no differences among them. This was not the case, as comparison of Tables 1–3 show. Descriptively, performance, in terms of trials to learn, was better in Exp. I (two pairs of irrelevant words) than in Exp. II (three pairs of irrelevant words). This finding is in line with a study by Reed (1946b), who also found poorer performance as the number of irrelevant words was increased. Although Exp. III (three relevant, two trios of irrelevant, words) differs from Exps. I and II in a number of ways, it may be worth noting that the performance difference in favor of relevant class words, as compared with conditions where nonclass words were relevant, was considerably greater, numerically, in Exp. III than in either Exps. I or II. This finding tends in part to confirm another study by Reed (1946a) that, as the number of relevant words per concept was increased, the number of promptings required for learning showed a relative decrease. This greater difference in Exp. III betwen class and nonclass relevant words may imply both that learning of class words is made easier by increasing the number of class words, and that learning of nonclass words is made harder by increasing the number of nonclass words, even if in each case the proportion of relevant to irrelevant words is kept constant.

Summary

In a study of mediation in verbal concept learning, words that are members of known classes, and words that could not readily be classed with other task words, were each used both as relevant and as irrelevant stimuli. These four conditions were studied in three experiments that varied in the number of relevant and irrelevant words presented. The results were the same, on the whole, in all three experiments, both in terms of trials to learn, and with an error measure assumed to be sensitive to mediation. Among relevant words, class words were more rapidly learned, and showed more evidence of mediation, than nonclass words. Among irrelevant words, there was no difference, as a main effect, between class vs. nonclass words. There was a significant interaction such that when class words were relevant, performance was usually better with nonclass irrelevant words, but when nonclass words were relevant, performance was better with irrelevant class words. It was suggested that there was evidence for mediation of response when class words were positively reinforced, and perhaps for mediation of nonresponse when class words were negatively reinforced.

REFERENCES

Goss, A. E. Verbal mediating responses and concept formation. *Psychol. Rev.*, 1961, 68, 248–274.

Heidbreder, E. The attainment of concepts: VII. Conceptual achievements during card-sorting. *J. psychol.*, 1949, 27, 3–39.

Isaacs, I. D., and Duncan, C. P. Reversal and nonreversal shifts within and between dimensions in concept formation. *J. exp. Psychol.*, 1962, 64, 580–585.

Kendler, H. H., and Karasik, A. D. Concept formation as a function of competition between response produced cues. *J. exp. Psychol.*, 1958, 55, 278–283.

Kendler, H. H., and Kendler, T. S. Vertical and horizontal processes in problem solving. *Psychol. Rev.* 1962, 69, 1–16.

Kendler, T. S. Concept formation. *Ann. Rev. Psychol.*, 1961, 12, 447–472.

Levine. M. Mediating processes in humans at the outset of discrimination learning. *Psychol. Rev.*, 1963, 70, 254–276.

Reed, H. B. The learning and retention of concepts. II. The influence of length of series. III. The origin of concepts. *J. exp. Psychol.*, 1946, 36, 166–179. (a)

Reed, H. B. The learning and retention of concepts. IV. The influence of the complexity of the stimuli. *J. exp. Psychol.*, 1946, 36, 252–261. (b)

Thorndike, E. L., and Lorge, I. *The teacher's word book of 30,000 words.* New York: Columbia Univer. Press, 1944.

Underwood, B. J., and Richardson, J. Some verbal materials for the study of concept formation. *Psychol. Bull.*, 1956, 53, 84–96. (a)

Underwood, B. J., and Richardson, J. Verbal concept learning as a function of instructions and dominance level. *J. exp. Psychol.*, 1956, 51, 229–238. (b)

34. False Recognition Produced by Implicit Verbal Responses

Benton J. Underwood

Abstract. *200 words were read to 100 Ss at a 10-sec. rate. For each word S decided whether it had or had not been read earlier. Critical stimulus words were inserted in the list, these words being presumed to elicit specified implicit responses. Later in the list the assumed implicit response words were presented. For these latter words for 3 of 5 classes of words, false recognition was much higher than for control words. The greater the prior frequency of elicitation of the implicit response the greater the likelihood of false recognition.*

In the development of conceptual schemes to incorporate verbal-learning phenomena, implicit responses are being given more and more prominent roles. Two examples may be cited. The studies of mediation in transfer evolved from two basic assumptions, namely, that implicit responses to verbal stimuli occur and that these implicit responses will serve as mediators. When conceptual similarity within a paired-associate list is found to produce interference it seems appropriate to account for this in part by assuming that the instances of a category (e.g., DOG, COW, HORSE) may all elicit the same implicit response (ANIMAL), which, in this situation, is a nondifferentiating response.

A distinction must be made between two kinds of implicit responses made to a verbal unit. There is first the response made to the unit itself as the act of perceiving it. This implicit response has been called the *representational response* by Bousfield, Whitmarsh, and Danick (1958), and will be abbreviated here as RR. The second kind of implicit response, the one with theoretical relevance, is produced by the stimulus properties of the RR. This implicit response may be another word which is associated with the actual word presented and will be called the *implicit associative response* (IAR). The particular IAR to a given word is often assumed to be the most frequent associate produced to the word in word-association procedures. Or, as in a mediating transfer situation, the IAR is assumed to be the word which S had learned as a response to a given stimulus in a previous list. That other nonverbal implicit responses (such as affective responses) may occur to the RR cannot be denied, but, for the present purposes, need not be considered.

It must be clear that IAR, in most theoretical formulations, is conceived

Reprinted by permission of the author and the American Psychological Association from *Journal of Experimental Psychology*, 1965, 70, 122–129.

of as actually occurring. This is to say, it is not a hypothetical construct. It is hypothetical only in the sense that it is assumed to occur in a particular situation where it cannot be observed directly, and this assumption is made because it *has* been observed to occur overtly with a certain frequency in other situations (e.g., word-association procedures). The validity of the assumption is tested by experimental procedures wherein a given phenomenon is predicted *if* specific IARSs are occurring. The present study fits into this framework.

The rationale of the experiment may be understood by examining the task presented Ss. A total of 200 words was read to S at a 10-sec. rate. As each word was read, S made a decision as to whether or not the word had been read to him earlier in the list. Thus, the general procedure is that devised by Shepard and Teghtsoonian (1961) in their study of memory for 3-digit numbers. In the present list of 200 words were critical words assumed to elicit particular IARs. At a later point in the list, therefore, the words assumed to be IARs to earlier RRs were in fact presented to S. If S responded by saying that these words had been read earlier in the list we would conclude that the IARs had occurred to the critical words at the time these critical words were read. For example, if a critical stimulus word is UP, and if later the assumed IAR (DOWN) had occurred earlier in the list, we assume that DOWN had occurred as an IAR to the RR to the word UP, and that S subsequently confused an IAR with an RR.

METHOD

Words. Four different types of words must be distinguished.

Critical Stimulus Words (CS Words): These words were assumed to elicit particular IARs.

Experimental Words (E Words): These were the words representing the assumed IARs to the CS Words.

Control Words (C Words): These words were used as controls for the E Words and were assumed not to have been preceded in the list by words for which they were IARs.

Filler Words (F Words): These words were presumed to be neutral with regard to the E Words and were used to build up a specific repetition frequency.

There were 20 E Words (hence, 20 C Words) as may be seen in Table 1. There were five different classes of CS Words labeled A1, A3, CV, SO, and SI in Table 1. Each of these classes must be explained. Classes A1 and A3 consisted of words for which the E Word (assumed IAR) was an antonym of the CS Word. Thus, TOP is assumed to be the IAR to BOTTOM, TAKE to GIVE, and so on. In forming A1 and A3, 16 pairs of antonyms

TABLE 1

CRITICAL STIMULUS WORDS, EXPERIMENTAL WORDS, AND CONTROL WORDS

Class	Critical Stimulus Words	E Word	Position	C Word
A1	BOTTOM	TOP	113	DOWN
	GIVE	TAKE	135	GOOD
	DAY	NIGHT	170	LOW
	MAN	WOMAN	188	RICH
A3	ROUGH	SMOOTH	154	WEAK
	FALSE	TRUE	162	DIRTY
	HARD	SOFT	178	SHORT
	SLOW	FAST	192	GIRL
CV	BUTTER, CRUMB	BREAD	129	BRIDGE
	BED, DREAM	SLEEP	155	SMILE
	SUGAR, BITTER, CANDY	SWEET	147	SALT
	ANIMAL, CAT, BARK	DOG	182	HORSE
	DARK, HEAVY, LAMP, MATCH	LIGHT	175	LEG
	WARM, CHILL, FREEZE, FRIGID, HOT, ICE	COLD	196	CLOUD
SO	MAPLE, OAK, ELM, BIRCH	TREE	123	FISH
	COTTON, WOOL, SILK, RAYON	CLOTH	158	FRUIT
	ROBIN, SPARROW, BLUEJAY, CANARY	BIRD	189	FLOWER
SI	BARREL, DOUGHNUT, DOME, GLOBE, SPOOL	ROUND	146	SHARP
	ATOM, CABIN, GERM, GNAT, VILLAGE	SMALL	165	FAT
	BANDAGE, CHALK, MILK, RICE, SNOW	WHITE	179	RED

were divided randomly into four subgroups of four pairs each. Two of these subgroups were then assigned randomly to A1 and A3 as CS Words and E Words, the second member of the pairs of the other two subgroups as C Words. However, for these C Words, no CS Word appeared earlier in the list. Thus, when S was confronted with the C Word DOWN, this had not been preceded by UP. On the other hand, when S was confronted with the E Word TOP, it had been preceded by the CS Word, BOTTOM. The rationale of the study predicts that S will be more likely to say that TOP rather than DOWN had occurred earlier in the list.

The CS Words for the A1 class were presented only once; those for the A3 class were each presented three times prior to the appearance of the E Word. A comparison between these two classes will provide evidence on the role of frequency of IARs.

The third class of CS Words in Table 1 is CV, an abbreviation for converging associations. Each of the CS Words on a line is known to elicit the E Word with appreciable frequency in word-association norms. Thus,

BREAD is a frequent response to both BUTTER and CRUMB, SLEEP a frequent response to both BED and DREAM, and so on. In selecting words for the first three classes in Table 1, major use was made of the Connecticut word-association norms as given by Bousfield, Cohen, Whitmarsh, and Kincaid (1961) with minor use of the Minnesota norms (Russell & Jenkins, 1954).

The fourth class of CS Words in Table 1 is labeled SO (superordinates). Each of the CS Words on a given line is a specific instance of the category which becomes the E Word. These Words were taken from Cohen, Bousfield, and Whitmarsh (1957). In actual fact these investigators asked Ss to give specific instances to the category name. However, we are assuming that the instances will in turn elicit the category name as an IAR with appreciable frequency. Some justification for this assumption is found in word-association norms. For example, the Connecticut word-association norms show that 50% of the Ss responded to the stimulus word CANARY with BIRD.

The final class in Table 1 is SI (sense impressions). Taken from Underwood and Richardson (1956), each word on a line is known to elicit the E Word with appreciable frequency when the associations are limited to sense impressions by instructions and training.

The CS Words on a given line are not completely without associates to E Words on other lines. There are two fairly obvious instances. The CS Word DOUGHNUT in the SI class also elicits word SWEET with appreciable frequency, SWEET being an E Word in the CV class. So also SNOW leads to COLD. Such "contamination" would, according to the notions in the introduction, tend to increase the number of false recognitions of the appropriate E Words.

The column labeled "Position" in Table 1 represents the position in the series of 200 words occupied by each E Word. The position of a given C Word was always two positions away from the position of its corresponding E Word. Thus, the C Word DOWN occurred at Position 111. Taken as a whole, the C Words occurred after the E Words half the time and before the E Words half the time.

The CS Words were scattered throughout the positions with the last occurring at Position 151. However, it may be of value to indicate the number of positions between the last CS Words and the E Words of the classes. For A1, the range for the four words was from 86 to 104 positions, with a mean of 96. For A3, the range was 36–89, with a mean of 53; for CV, a range of 30–60, with a mean of 42; for SO, from 27–68, with a mean of 50, and finally, for SI, 27–73, with a mean of 53.

There were 47 F Words. Of these 42 occurred twice, 4 occurred three times, and 1 occurred only once. Therefore, the 200 positions are accounted for as follows: CS Words, 63; E Words, 20; C Words, 20; and F Words, 97. The actual repetition was arranged so that in the first quarter (first 50 words) 5 words had occurred earlier, with 19, 16, and 18 having occurred earlier in each of the remaining three quarters.

Procedure and Ss. The instructions and the words were presented by magnetic tape recorder. The Ss were given a single sheet of paper on which 200 numbered blanks occurred. The instructions required S to record a plus if he believed the word had occurred earlier in the list, a minus if he believed it had not. The instructions indicated that if S was in doubt a decision had to be made; a plus or minus had to be recorded for each blank. The words were read at a 10-sec. rate, each being spoken twice in immediate succession. The trial number was indicated after every tenth word to avoid any confusion as to the particular number of the word at the moment.

A total of 107 Ss records was completed in four group sessions. All Ss were college students taking introductory psychology courses at Northwestern. Seven of the records were eliminated on a random basis, so the data to be presented are based on 100 Ss.

RESULTS

Table 2 shows the number of plusses (hence, percentage of Ss) recorded for each E Word and its corresponding C Word. Also shown are the subtotals for each class of words. Looking at these subtotals it may be quickly noted that for Classes A1 and SI, expectations are not supported but that for Classes A3, CV, and SO, frequency of plusses for the E Words is much greater than for the C Words. However, we may first make an overall statistical evaluation without regard to classes of words. For each S the total number of plusses made to the 20 E Words was determined and also the total number made to the 20 C Words. The E Words produced a mean of 4.43 plusses, the C Words a mean of 2.53. The difference ($1.90 \pm .23$) gives a t of 8.26. It must be concluded that Ss responded more frequently to the E Words than to the C Words.

A statistical analysis of differences in frequency for E and C Words by classes of items is difficult by conventional methods since many Ss did not respond with a plus to any of the words within a class. Even in the above analysis there were 8 Ss with a zero entry for the 20 E Words and 24 Ss with a zero entry for the C Words. However, certain simple computations allow some fairly firm conclusions about the statistical significance of the responses by classes of words, a matter to which we will turn shortly.

We may ask about the frequency of plusses for all words except E Words when they first occurred. This determination across the entire series of words provides a measure of the "false-alarm" or "false-positive" rate. The 200 words were divided into eighths and the number of false

TABLE 2

NUMBER OF PLUSSES GIVEN TO EACH E AND C WORD
BY 100 Ss WITH SUBTOTALS FOR
EACH CLASS OF WORDS

Class	E Word	No. of Plusses	C Word	No. of Plusses
Al	TOP	9	DOWN	20
	TAKE	11	GOOD	5
	NIGHT	24	LOW	27
	WOMAN	5	RICH	10
	Total	49		62
A3	SMOOTH	28	WEAK	9
	TRUE	12	DIRTY	9
	SOFT	37	SHORT	25
	FAST	49	GIRL	9
	Total	126		52
CV	BREAD	21	BRIDGE	28
	SLEEP	23	SMILE	10
	SWEET	24	SALT	11
	DOG	20	HORSE	7
	LIGHT	42	LEG	13
	COLD	39	CLOUD	15
	Total	169		84
SO	TREE	19	FISH	9
	CLOTH	18	FRUIT	11
	BIRD	38	FLOWER	11
	Total	75		31
SI	ROUND	7	SHARP	9
	SMALL	14	FAT	7
	WHITE	3	RED	8
	Total	24		24

alarms determined for each of these eight sections. The number of words which first occurred (hence, could result in false alarms) in each successive eighth was 23, 22, 16, 15, 18, 9, 10, and 9. The mean numbers of plusses (false alarms) per word in each eighth are plotted as filled dots in Fig. 1 with a straight line drawn through them. It is clear that there is an increase in false alarms as the number of prior words increases; in the eighth section the 100 Ss averaged 11.2 false alarms for the nine words which first occurred in that section; in the first section the corresponding value was 0.5.

The plusses or false alarms for each E Word are also plotted in Fig. 1,

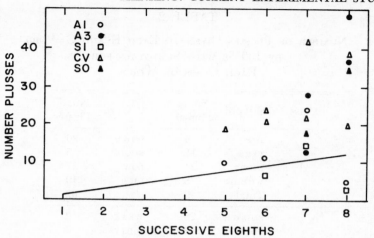

Fig. 1. False-alarm rate (number of plusses) within each successive block of 25 positions across the 200 words and number of plusses for each of the 20 E Words.

above the eighth in which it occurred. The statistical question is whether or not the E Words of various classes can be considered to come from the population of words represented by the false-alarm rate of all non-E Words when they first occurred. Clearly, Classes A1 and SI could come from this population. It can be shown, however, that it is highly improbable that the E Words in each of the other three classes could have come from this population of false alarms for control words. The sum of the plusses for the three E Words in the SO class is 75; how probable is it that this sum would be equaled by any three control words used to derive the false-alarm rate in Fig. 1? To determine this the number of plusses for the 46 words used to derive the last half of the false-alarm curve were each listed. From this listing 100 samples of three each were drawn (using a table of random numbers) and the sum of the plusses for each sample determined. In drawing the samples, replacement was immediate; that is, the same value (representing the number of plusses for a given word) could have been drawn so as to constitute all three entries in a sample. The means of this distribution of 100 sums was 30.71, with a standard deviation of 12.04. The maximum summed value obtained for any one sample was 71. Since the E Words in the SO class produced a sum of 75, we conclude that it is quite unlikely that these three E Words could come from the control population. This is to say, therefore, that the frequency of false alarms given to these E Words must have been influenced by the earlier presence of the CS Words. Or, to say this another way; S apparently confused the RR of the E Word with the IAR made earlier to the CS Word.

The above procedure could be repeated for the A3 and CV classes and the same conclusion would be reached. However, this is quite unnecessary. The maximum frequency of plusses for any word used in obtaining the control false-alarm rate was 28 (for BRIDGE, a C Word). Multiplying this value by 4 (112) does not yield a frequency as high (126) as the frequency produced by the four E Words in the A3 class. Multiplying 28 by 6 does not result in a frequency as high as that produced by the six E Words in the CV class.

In summary, therefore, the evidence indicates that RRs were confused with IARs for three classes of words. Among the 13 E Word-C Word comparisons in these three classes there is only one instance in which the frequency of the plusses for the C Word was higher than for the E Word (Class CV, BRIDGE vs. BREAD). The maximum frequency of false alarm for any E Word was 49; 49% of the Ss indicated that the word FAST had occurred earlier in the list when in fact it had not. It is of some interest to compare this value with that of the lowest frequency of detection of a repeated word. The F Word HOME appeared in Position 13 and again in Position 118 at which time only 51% of the Ss indicated it had occurred earlier. Overall, however, the correct detection of repeated words was 85.0%. It is evident, therefore, that S is far more likely to recognize a repeated word than to give a false alarm to a nonrepeated word even when we attempt to confuse him.

Other relationships. The Ss showed appreciable consistency in their tendency to report that a word had occurred earlier when in fact it had not. The product-moment correlation across the 100 Ss for number of plusses for the 20 E Words and for the 20 C Words was .62. A total of 102 of the 200 positions was held by CS Words and by the first occurrence of F Words. The correlation between the number of plusses made to these 102 words and the number made to the E Words was .60, and to the C Words, .67. On the other hand, the ability to detect a repetition is not related to the tendency to indicate that a word had occurred earlier when it had not. There were 58 positions held by repeated words. The correlation across the 100 Ss between the number of plusses assigned these 58 positions and the number of plusses assigned the 102 positions when words first occurred was −.02. A scatter plot gives no indication of curvilinearity.

DISCUSSION

Three of the classes of E Words produced results in conformance with the notion that RRs may be confused with IARs that occurred earlier; two classes did not. The fact that words in the A1 class did not produce false alarms beyond the control rate while those in A3 did, indicates that frequency of IARs is a critical variable. It would seem quite reasonable to presume that if an IAR occurs three times it has more of the properties of an RR than if it occurs only once. Indeed, it is precisely this fact which Deese (1959) has demonstrated by a sharp relationship between the appearance of an intrusion (a word which had not appeared in the list) in recall and the associative strength of the intruding word to the words actually in the list. However, in the case of the A1 words vs. the A3 words in the present study, another factor might be involved. As noted in the procedure section, on the average the number of words occurring between the CS Words and the E Words was greater for A1 than for A3. Perhaps the IARs to the CS Words in A1 are, therefore, forgotten or interfered with more than those produced by the CS Words in A3. While this possibility cannot be ruled out entirely, there is evidence against it. In the A3 class a total of 89 words occurred between the last presentation of the CS Word HARD and its E Word SOFT, yet 37% of the Ss indicated they had heard the word earlier. For two of the cases in the A1 class, 86 and 89 words occurred between the CS Word and the E Word, yet the E Words produced only 11% and 5% plusses. Furthermore, an examination of the results for the CV class indicates that those cases where four and five CS words occurred (and were presumed to elicit a common associate) produced more false alarms than did the cases in the CV class where only two and three CS words were used, and this occurred when the number of words between the last CS and the E Word was essentially the same for all cases. Thus, the evidence points strongly to frequency of IAR as a variable in producing confusion between IARs and RRs.

The SI class of words gave completely negative results; frequency of false alarms to the E Words in this class was no greater than for the C Words. As will be remembered, a given set of CS words in the SI class will, under appropriate instructions and training, elicit the common response which was here used as the E Word. It is possible that within the context of the present series of words these sense-impression responses occur as IARs with low frequency. However, in the Connecticut word-association norms (Bousfield et al., 1961) four of the five CS Words presumed to elicit the E Word ROUND do in fact elicit ROUND with some frequency (10% 9%, 9%, and 28%). Nevertheless, these frequencies are much lower than the frequencies in the other classes. We may tentatively conclude that the negative results in the SI class are due to the failure of the CS words to elicit the common IARs with appreciable frequency.

The logic of the experiment was that the RR to the word of the moment would lead to S to say that the word had occurred earlier if this RR was the same as an IAR produced by a word or words earlier in the list. This scheme might be reversed to say that the IAR to the word of the moment, if the same as an RR to an earlier word, would lead S to say that the present word had occurred earlier. Thus, if the word of the moment was DOWN, and if it elicits the IAR UP, and if UP occurred earlier in the list, S might believe that DOWN had occurred earlier. Such a mechanism might indeed handle the results for A3, for antonyms are bidirectionally associated. And, such a mechanism might account for the failure for the SI items, since the E Words do not elicit the CS Words with appreciable frequency in available norms. However, it cannot account for the results for the CV and SO classes. The positive effects produced in these classes must be due to the elicitation of the same IAR by two or more different CS Words, otherwise positive results would have been obtained in the A1 class. The IAR of the word of the moment cannot be confused with two or more different RRs of previous words such as would be necessary by the alternative scheme. Of course, it is possible that both mechanisms may be involved but until this is clearly demonstrated we will conclude that the original scheme presented is most appropriate; the RR to the word of the moment is confused with the common IAR produced by two or more previous words. This is essentially the same conclusion reached by Mink (1963) as a result of his studies on semantic generalization. And it should be noted that the present study could be classified as a study of secondary or semantic generalization.

Figure 1 showed that the frequency of false alarms increased throughout. Although this increase may be due to the same mechanisms presumed to operate for the E Words, another factor may be in part responsible. It is possible that the greater number of words S heard the more likely he would believe that a repetition would occur. Thus, if in doubt late in the list he would be more likely to signify that a repetition had occurred than if in doubt early in the list. This could be true in spite of the fact that the objective repetition was held constant over the last three quarters of the list. Nevertheless, certain of the C Words produced false alarms with such high frequency that an examination of possible causes was made. Some may have been produced by high formal similarity of RRs. For example, LOW produced 27 false alarms. The word LAW occurred as an F Word earlier in the list. The high frequency for SHORT may have been due to the appearance of SHARP earlier in the list. The C Word which produced the highest number of false alarms was BRIDGE. No previous word was high formal similarity and, when BRIDGE is thought of as a structure spanning water, no previous word would seem to elicit it as an IAR. If these Ss are avid players and followers of the game of bridge, such words as MASTER and MAJOR (which occurred three times) may have elicited BRIDGE as an IAR. In any event, it is apparent that we were unsuccessful in the attempt to establish homogeneity in false-alarm rates to control words.

REFERENCES

BOUSFIELD, W. A., COHEN, B. H., WHITMARSH, G. A., & KINCAID, W. D. The Connecticut free association norms. Technical Report No. 35, 1961, University of Connecticut, Contract Nonr-631 (00), Office of Naval Research.

BOUSFIELD, W. A., WHITMARSH, G. A., & DANICK, J. J. Partial response identities in verbal generalization. *Psychol. Rep.*, 1958, 4, 703–713.

COHEN, B. H., BOUSFIELD, W. A., & WHITMARSH, G. A. Cultural norms for verbal items in 43 categories. Technical Report No. 22, 1957, University of Connecticut, Contract Nonr-631 (00), Office of Naval Research.

DEESE, J. On the prediction of occurrence of particular verbal intrusions in immediate recall. *J. exp. Psychol.*, 1959, 58, 17–22.

MINK, W. D. Semantic generalization as related to word association. *Psychol. Rep.*, 1963, 12, 59–67.

RUSSELL, W. A., & JENKINS, J. J. The complete Minnesota norms for responses to 100 words from the Kent-Rosanoff Word-Association Test. Technical Report, No. 11, 1954, University of Minnesota, Contract N8 onr-66216, Office of Naval Research.

SHEPARD, R. N., & TEGHTSOONIAN, M. Retention of information under conditions approaching a steady state. *J. exp. Psychol.*, 1961, 62, 302–309.

UNDERWOOD, B. J., & RICHARDSON, J. Some verbal materials for the study of concept formation. *Psychol. Bull.*, 1956, 53, 84–95.

SECTION TEN

Task Variables

As was the case in problem solving, variation of characteristics of the concept tasks usually produces considerable effects on performance. The articles in this chapter represent a number of different task variables that have been of interest in studying concept learning.

Application of information theory to concept learning is not covered specifically in this book, but the Hovland and Weiss paper is one example of an approach involving manipulation of a task variable, viz., type of instance, in order to vary the amount of information transmitted. The issue here, which might be called "what the concept is versus what the concept isn't," is related to the issue of the size of the population to be searched in problem solving. The number of characteristics that must be specified to define a concept are usually fewer, often extremely fewer, than the number of characteristics that the concept is not. Note that, as was done in the Hovland and Weiss study, the total possible population of stimuli (number of dimensions and number of values on each) has to be specified in order to define clearly what is meant by a negative instance.

Since the subject, in concept learning, must learn to respond to at least one relevant (reinforced) dimension and not respond to one or more irrelevant dimensions, there has been considerable research on variations of, and comparisons among, characteristics of relevant and irrelevant dimensions. In the Gormezano and Grant article, partial reinforcement of irrelevant stimuli clearly interfered with learning the relevant stimuli. But the nonreversal shift, where a previously irrelevant dimension becomes relevant in a transfer task, did not yield clear results. The variables influencing performance in nonreversal shift are still not well known.

Another approach to comparisons of relevant and irrelevant dimensions appears in the study of Walker and Bourne. Here it is clear that as the number of different characteristics needed to define a concept (number of relevant dimensions) increases, performance rapidly decreases, but a similar increase in number of irrelevant dimensions is much less interfering. This is also a paper in which the task and the variables are such that the data can be tested for fit to a mathematical theory.

Pollack's experiment represents a quite different approach to basic task variables in grouping. Number of categories corresponds most closely to what is called, in other studies, number of relevant dimensions. Number of words per category corresponds to number of values on a dimension. There is nothing in Pollack's study to correspond to irrelevant dimensions, e.g., words that were to be ignored and not classified. The finding that an increase in number of categories considerably slowed performance corresponds well with Walker and Bourne's results for increasing the number of relevant dimensions.

35. Transmission of Information Concerning Concepts Through Positive and Negative Instances

Carl I. Hovland and Walter Weiss

In the widely known conceptual learning studies of Smoke (6, 7) an attempt was made to determine the contributions of "positive instances" (where the required characteristics of the concept are included in the stimulus figure) and "negative instances" (where one or more of the required characteristics is absent), in the acquisition of concepts. The conclusion was reached that negative instances do little to facilitate the learning of concepts. No data, however, are presented as to *what* information was transmitted by the negative instances. Thus one cannot tell whether the low efficiency of the negative instances is attributable to the fact that they communicated little information beyond that already con-

Reprinted by permission of the second author and the American Psychological Association from *Journal of Experimental Psychology*, 1953, *43*, 175–182.

veyed by the positive instances, or is caused by greater difficulty in assimilating information transmitted in the form of negative instances.

It is difficult to separate the effects of the two alternatives just mentioned when one employs the unstructured type of situation used by Smoke, since the information conveyed by each type of instance cannot be assessed accurately in the absence of knowledge of the hypotheses considered by S. Accordingly, for experimentation on this problem it is preferable to use a situation where S knows the structure of the concept and the dimensions involved. One can then determine how many of each type of instance are required from a logical standpoint to specify completely the characteristics of the concept.

A mathematical analysis of the number of positive and negative instances required to communicate concepts under various specified conditions has been made by Hovland (2). The theoretical model he analyzes is one in which each concept involves a combination of certain specific values along two or more stimulus dimensions. Form, color, quantity, and size are examples of "dimensions" and within each dimension there may be a number of "values," e.g., red, green, and yellow within the color dimension. As an example, one can transmit a concept through successive presentations of Weigl-type cards. The S will be told that the possible stimulus dimensions will be form, color, and size and that there will be three possible values of each. If he is also told that the concept will consist of a combination of one value of each of two dimensions [giving concepts such as that of a "black square"] it will take a minimum of *two* positive instances or of *ten* negative instances to define the correct combination. If positive instances are used and the first card contains a medium-sized red triangle and the second contains a medium-sized green triangle, S could deduce that the concept is a *medium-sized triangle* (of any color). Alternatively the same concept can be completely defined by stating that the following are incorrect ("negative instances"): small red square, medium green circle, small green triangle, large red circle, medium yellow square, large red triangle, large green square, medium red circle, small yellow circle, large yellow triangle. These ten instances rule out all other combinations of single values of two dimensions. Knowing that the correct concept can be transmitted by either two positive or ten negative instances permits one to raise the experimental question as to whether S will derive the correct answer with equal ease from the two sets of instances. To obtain information on this point is one of the principal purposes of the present set of experiments.

Additional problems are raised concerning the transmission of concepts by combinations of positive and negative instances. From the standpoint of the information transmitted a positive instance followed by two negative instances conveys the same amount of information concerning the characteristics of the concept as two negative instances followed by a positive. But from the standpoint of the assimilation of the information by S it is quite possible that the two sets have different effectiveness. One reason for hypothesizing a difference is that in a mixed positive and negative series the effect of positive instances is to greatly reduce the number of hypotheses which must be considered, while negative instances specify which of the alternatives can be discarded. If the positives come first, S would only have to keep in mind a limited number of possibilities; whereas, when the negatives come first, only a few possible hypotheses are eliminated and therefore S must retain quite a few alternatives until the positive instance finally defines the correct choice. Thus it might be expected that the former arrangement would be superior to the latter in ease of concept attainment.

For both types of problem, knowledge of the information transmitted by positive and negative instances enables one to hold the amount of information communicated constant in order to study experimentally the "psychological" factors affecting the manner in which information is assimilated. Differences in difficulty of learning concepts from negative instances as compared with positive instances can then be attributed to differences in the nature of the psychological processes rather than to differences in the amount of information about the concept conveyed by the two types of instances.

Experiment I

Purpose. This experiment was designed primarily to compare the learning of concepts when the necessary information is conveyed by series of instances which are exclusively positive or exclusively negative. The effect of the order of presentation of mixed positive and negative instances was also investigated.

Procedure. The S's task was to derive the combination of characteristics defining a concept on the basis of stimulus figures which either included all the requisite characteristics (positive instances) or lacked one or more of the essential characteristics (negative instances). Stimulus figures were constructed using the following dimensions: form, color, quantity, and size. The values of the form dimension were the figures X, H, O, and 8. Values of the color dimension were blue, red, and black. For the size dimension the following values were employed: small (½ in. high), medium (1 in.), and large (1½ in.). Finally, there were four values of the quantity dimension, 1, 2, 3, or 4 identical figures being used. In some of the series three dimensions were used, in others, four. From two to four values of each factor were employed in any particular series. The numbers of dimensions and values for each series are specified in the tables below.

The S was first instructed as to the meaning of the term "concept" as it would be used in the experiment. He was told before the presentation of each problem how many different dimensions he would have to consider, the number of these which would be relevant, the number of possible values for each dimension, and the number of values which would be correct for each relevant dimension (cf. 2). S was given some practice examples to solve, illustrative of each of the several ways of presenting the information needed to define the concept. The E would indicate any errors that had been made in the practice problems.

The procedure for an individual S on a particular series may be illustrated by an example: S would be told that three dimensions, color, form, and quantity, would be used; that two values of each would be involved: red or black for color, square or circle for form, and one or two for quantity; that the concept would consist of one value of each of two dimensions; that five cards showing examples of what the concept "was not" would be given. Card 1, containing *one red square*, was then exposed. Card 2 contained *two black circles;* Card 3, *one black circle;* Card 4, *two red circles;* Card 5, *two red squares.* [Correct answer—*black square.*]

Because of the likelihood that some dimensions would be more difficult than others, the dimensions and values for the various problems were rotated in such a way that for the experiment as a whole the all-positive and all-negative series involved the same dimensions and values. The order of positive and negative series was also counterbalanced.

Twelve Yale College students served as Ss. Each came for two 1-hr. sessions. The figures, printed on 3 × 5-in. cards, were exposed one at a time for 5 sec. on a table in front of S. Positive instance cards were labelled "Right" and negative "Wrong." For each series the minimum number of cards needed to specify completely the given concept was employed. After the set of cards for a particular concept was presented, S was given 20 sec. to give his answer.

Additional cases were secured under group experiment conditions from a section of the elementary psychology course at Yale ($N = 95$). Here the cards were flashed one at a time on a screen by means of an opaque projector. Each card was exposed for 5 sec., and 20 sec. was allowed at the end to write down the answer.

Results. The percentages of Ss able to define the concept correctly after being exposed to a series of positive or a series of negative instances are presented in Table 1. The number of instances of either type was the minimum number needed logically to define the concept. So in terms of the information presented, equally precise answers could be given in either case if Ss were able to absorb the presented information equally well. The results indicate that under the conditions studied it is considerably harder to define a concept on the basis of a series of instances showing what the concept "is not" than on the basis of a series of in-

TABLE 1

PERCENTAGE OF Ss ATTAINING CORRECT CONCEPT WITH ALL-POSITIVE
vs. ALL-NEGATIVE INSTANCES (SUCCESSIVE PRESENTATION)

Stimulus Series						Per Cent of Ss Attaining Concept		
Total No. Dimensions	Total No. Values	No. Dimensions Relevant	No. Values Correct	No. Pos. Instances Required	No. Neg. Instances Required	All-Positive Instances	All-Negative Instances	p_{χ^2}
3	3	2	1	2	10	100.0 ($N = 24$)	16.7 ($N = 24$)	< .001
3	2	2	1	2	5	100.0 ($N = 24$)	16.7 ($N = 24$)	< .001
4	2	2	1	2	5	(a) 95.8 ($N = 24$)	4.2 ($N = 24$)	< .001
						(b) 94.7 ($N = 95$)	13.7 ($N = 95$)	< .001

TABLE 2

PERCENTAGE OF Ss ATTAINING CORRECT CONCEPT WITH VARYING
SEQUENCES OF POSITIVE AND NEGATIVE INSTANCES
(SUCCESSIVE PRESENTATION)

Stimulus Series				Per Cent of Ss Attaining Concept		
Total No. Dimensions	Total No. Values	No. Dimensions Relevant	No. Values Correct	Positive, Negative, Negative	Negative, Negative, Positive	p_{χ^2}
4	2	2	1	37.5 ($N = 24$)	45.8 ($N = 24$)	.55
3	4*	2	1	(a) 50.0 ($N = 24$)	(a) 45.8 ($N = 24$)	.80
				(b) 21.1 ($N = 95$)	(b) 22.1 ($N = 95$)	.85

* Except for color, where only three values were used.

stances showing what the concept "is." Chi-square tests show that the difference in percentage of Ss attaining the concept from the two types of instance is significant at better than the .001 level for all series.

Table 2 compares the ease of learning concepts when the sequence is first positive and then negative as compared with that when the sequence is first negative and then positive. Series were used where one positive and two negative instances were required, so the sequences compared were positive-negative-negative *vs.* negative-negative-positive. Both series are equal in the amount of information about the concept which they contain and completely specify the concept. The data provide no suggestion of any difference in difficulty under the present circumstances, so the initial hypothesis that the series with positive instances first would be superior is not confirmed.

Experiment II

Purpose. In the preceding experiment only two positive instances were required to specify the concepts, whereas either five or ten negative instances were required to define them with equal precision. One possible contributory factor in the obtained greater difficulty of learning concepts from negative instances than from positive instances might therefore be difficulty in remembering the longer list of items required for the former. Accordingly, the first experiment was repeated on a second sample of Ss with the modification that all of the instances in any series were exposed

TABLE 3

PERCENTAGE OF Ss ATTAINING CORRECT CONCEPT WITH ALL-POSITIVE
AND ALL-NEGATIVE INSTANCES (SIMULTANEOUS PRESENTATION)
$N = 12$

Stimulus Series						Per Cent of Ss Attaining Concept		
Total No. Dimensions	Total No. Values	No. Dimensions Relevant	No. Values Correct	No. Pos. Instances Required	No. Neg. Instances Required	All-Positive Instances	All-Negative Instances	$p\chi^2$
3	3	2	1	2	10	100.0	50.0	$< .02$
3	2	2	1	2	5	100.0	83.3	0.12
4	2	2	1	2	5	100.0	66.7	0.10

simultaneously. Data were also secured on the effectiveness of combinations of positive and negative instances.

Procedure. The method paralleled closely that used in the first experiment except that the entire series of cards was exposed at once. Twelve Yale College students were employed as Ss. They were seen individually on two separate occasions of about 1-hr. duration each, separated by at least a day.

Results. A comparison of the number of Ss attaining concepts correctly when they are transmitted by an all-positive or an all-negative series is shown in Table 3. As in the case of successive presentation there is a consistent superiority for the all-positive series, although this set contains the same amount of information about the concept as the all-negative one. When the results for all three series are combined, the difference is significant at better than the .001 level ($\chi^2 = 16.3$, $df = 3$). However, it will be seen that the percentage of Ss able to attain the concept from the all-negative series is substantially higher than the number under the equivalent successive conditions (Table 1). This supports the prediction of Underwood (8), which he based on contiguity considerations. With positive instances the number of Ss answering correctly is so high even with successive presentations that no marked difference is obtained between the two temporal arrangements.

Table 4 presents a comparison of the percentage of Ss attaining the correct concept when two negative instances are substituted for one of the positive instances (giving one positive and two negative instances), as compared with a series in which only the two positive instances are employed. In none of the comparisons are as many Ss able to reach the

TABLE 4

PERCENTAGE OF Ss ATTAINING CORRECT CONCEPT WITH ALL-POSITIVE
AS COMPARED WITH MIXED POSITIVE AND NEGATIVE INSTANCES
(SIMULTANEOUS PRESENTATION)
$N = 12$

Stimulus Series				Per Cent of Ss Attaining Concept		
Total No. Dimensions	Total No. Values	No. Dimensions Relevant	No. Values Correct	Two Positives	One Positive; Two Negatives	p_{x^2}
3	*	2	1	100.0	83.3	.12
4	†	2	1	100.0	91.7	.30
				Three Positives	Two Positive; Two Negatives	
3	*	2	2	91.7	50.0	.07
4	†	2	2	75.0	33.0	.10

* Four for quantity and form, three for color.
† Four for quantity and form, three for color and size.

concept when mixed positives and negatives are used as when only positive instances are employed. In the easier series with one value correct, the differences are not significant, but significant differences do obtain for the more difficult series with two values for each dimension correct. When the results for the two more difficult series are combined, the difference between the all-positive and mixed positive and negative results is significant at better than the .01 level ($\chi^2 = 11.2$, $df = 2$).

EXPERIMENT III

Purpose. The results of Exp. II indicate that although the difference between positive and negative instances is reduced when memory factors are minimized by simultaneous presentation, a significant superiority for the positive instances remains. But comparison of the number of instances suggest another possible factor: In both Exp. I and II more negative than positive instances were necessary to completely convey the concept. The greater difficulty of negative instances might be due to the fact that it is more difficult to assimilate the larger number of instances. By appropriate selection of cases it is possible to transmit concepts by an equal number of positive, negative, and mixed instances. In this experiment, therefore, series were employed in which the same amount of information was conveyed and the same number of instances were used for all positive, all negative, and mixed positive and negative series.

Procedure. The general method employed was very similar to that used in Exp. II. Again, simultaneous exposure of all the instances needed for a particular problem was used. The problems, however, were selected in such a way that four instances would completely specify the concept for each type of problem (2). Three types of series were used, involving four positive, four negative, or two positive and two negative instances.

Instead of a single set for each concept as in the previous experiments three different sets were prepared, so that three "trials" were permitted. The first set of four was exposed and S attempted an answer. If he did not get the concept correctly, a second set of four different instances of the same concept was presented. If he failed on the second set, a third set of instances was shown. The time limit on each presentation was 3 min.

For this experiment a newly developed series of flower designs (3) was employed instead of the Weigl-type cards used in the two other experiments. The flower designs allowed the use of four values of each of four dimensions: four types of blossom were employed; each could be colored red, yellow, blue, or white; one of four differently shaped leaves could be used; and from one to four identical leaves were placed on the stem. In one series of problems all four dimensions were included, in the other, three. Counterbalancing to rotate the dimensions and values for the three conditions was employed as in the earlier experiments. In this way any differences between the groups could not be attributed to differences in the difficulty of the dimensions involved.

Twenty-four Yale College Ss were employed; none of them had taken part in any of the earlier experiments. They were seen individually in a session lasting about 1 hr.

Results. Table 5 presents the cumulative percentages of Ss able to specify the concept correctly after one, two, and three presentations of the all-positive, all-negative, and mixed positive and negative series of instances. For both the three- and four-factor series there is a clear difference between the all-positive and all-negative series in the percentage of Ss attaining the concept after one, two, and three presentations of the series (each $p_{\chi^2} = .001$ or less). When the results for the three- and four-factor series are combined, there is a significant difference on the first trial between the combined positive and negative and the all-positive series ($p_{\chi^2} = .001$) and between the combined and all-negative series ($p = .01$). On the third trial the difference between the positive and the mixed series is still significant ($p_{\chi^2} = <.001$) but that between the all-negative and mixed series is no longer sizeable ($p_{\chi^2} = .13$).

In a recent article Underwood (8) has suggested that one would expect that concepts will be learned more slowly when a greater number of stimuli are involved. A test of this can be made by comparing series where

TABLE 5

Concept Attainment on First, Second and Third Presentation
of All-Positive, All-Negative, and Mixed Positive
and Negative Instance Series
$N = 24$

Stimulus Series				Cumulative Per Cent of Ss Attaining Concept			
Total No. Dimensions	Total No. Values	No. Dimensions Relevant	No. Values Correct	Presentation	All Positive	Positive and Negative	All Negative
				1	79.2	54.2	20.8
3	4	2	3	2	95.8	70.8	41.7
				3	100.0	79.2	54.2
				1	91.7	37.5	12.5
4	4	2	3	2	95.8	45.8	33.3
				3	95.8	58.3	50.0

four dimensions are involved with the series where there are only three. The same number of values was employed and the same number of instances was required. In seven of the nine possible comparisons learning is more rapid for the three-dimension series than for the four-dimension series, but the tests are not completely independent. The likelihood that the number of dimensions is important, however, is increased by the fact that similar results were obtained in the other two experiments, particularly for the negative series (Tables 1 and 3). A similar conclusion can be drawn from the experiment of Reed (5).

DISCUSSION

While a machine could be constructed which would arrive at the correct concept with equal ease on the basis of the positive or negative instances, the results of the present experiment clearly indicate that the human organism does not operate similarly on a strict probability basis. For all of the conditions examined, more Ss arrive at the correct concept when the instances are positive than when they are negative, even though each series transmits the same amount of information. At the same time, the data disprove the generalization often cited that negative instances have no value in the learning of concepts. Under appropriate conditions over half of the Ss were able to reach the correct solution solely on the basis of negative instances.

A major research task remains, however, that of determining the factors responsible for the greater effectiveness of positive instances. Perceptual factors undoubtedly play some role in the explanation. Positive instances have the required characteristics directly perceptible. Negative instances, on the other hand, do not have the correct combination of characteristics in direct view. Closely related is a difference in the characteristics of the correct concept and the one delineated by the negative instances. The positive instances define a coherent, well-structured combination of characteristics of the concept, while the negative instances are in effect positive instances of what the concept "is not." They thus lack an organized, unitary quality, except for the limiting situation where only a single dimension is involved.

A number of limitations of the present research must be mentioned. First, it is based on only one of a number of possible concept models. Second, it is concerned only with concept *formation,* and does not consider concept *generalization,* i.e., applying the learned concept to new examples. Finally, it covers only how a single concept is learned, and does not treat the frequent situation where a positive instance for one concept serves simultaneously as a negative instance for other concepts in the list (e.g. 4). Here additional factors, such as stimulus generalization, are needed to account for interactions between items (1).

SUMMARY

Smoke (6, 7) reported that negative instances are rather ineffective in the learning of concepts. The question arises as to whether this is because negative instances convey little information or because it is difficult for Ss to assimilate material presented in this form. In the present experiments the amount of information about a concept was equated for the two types of instance, so that any differences in learning the concepts could be attributed to differences in difficulty of assimilating information concerning what the concept "is" as compared with assimilating information concerning what it "is not." Data derived from the analysis of Hovland (2) were used to determine the minimum number of positive and negative instances needed to specify completely any particular concept.

In the first experiment Ss were shown *successively* a series of Weigl-type cards conveying a concept by all-positive instances or by all-negative instances. In the second experiment equivalent series of all-positive and all-negative instances were presented simultaneously, to minimize possible memory effects. In the third experiment a series of flower design cards (3) were selected in such a way that transmission of the concept required an identical number of positive, negative, or mixed positive and negative instances.

Under the experimental conditions employed the results indicate:

a. The correct concept is attained by a higher percentage of Ss when transmitted by all-positive instances than by all-negative instances.

b. Mixed positive and negative instances are intermediate between all-positive and all-negative series in difficulty of learning.

c. When the negative instances are displayed simultaneously, the accuracy of concept attainment is higher than when they are presented successively.

The all-negative instances are thus shown to be consistently inferior to all-positive. At the same time, the results disprove the generalization that concepts cannot be learned from negative instances, since under appropriate conditions over half of the Ss were able to arrive at the correct concept exclusively on the basis of negative instances.

REFERENCES

1. BAUM, M. H. A study in concept attainment and verbal learning. Ph.D. dissertation, Yale Univer., 1951.
2. HOVLAND, C. I. A "communication analysis" of concept learning. *Psychol. Rev.,* 1952, 59, 461–472.
3. HOVLAND, C. I. A set of flower designs for concept-formation experiments. *Amer. J. Psychol.,* 1953, 66, in press.
4. OSEAS, L., & UNDERWOOD, B. J. Studies of distributed practice: V. Learning and retention of concepts. *J. exp. Psychol.,* 1952, 43, 143–148.
5. REED, H. B. The learning and retention of concepts. V. The influence of form presentation. *J. exp. Psychol.,* 1950, 40, 504–511.
6. SMOKE, K. L. An objective study of concept formation. *Psychol. Monogr.,* 1932, 42, No. 4 (Whole No. 191).
7. SMOKE, K. L. Negative instances in concept learning. *J. exp. Psychol.,* 1933, 16, 583–588.
8. UNDERWOOD, B. J. An orientation for research on thinking. *Psychol. Rev.,* 1952, 59, 209–220.

36. Progressive Ambiguity in the Attainment of Concepts on the Wisconsin Card Sorting Test

Isidore Gormezano and David A. Grant

The purpose of this investigation was to determine the difficulty of sorting for color and number in the Wisconsin Card Sorting Test (WCST) (5, 6, 7) when the irrelevant dimensions of number and form, respectively, were intermittently reinforced 0%, 25%, 50%, or 75% of the time. The study was also concerned with determining the transfer effects on number sorting of having intermittently reinforced the irrelevant number dimension during color sorting.

In concept formation S is generally confronted with a variety of stimuli objects each of which includes relevant and irrelevant elements. Relevant elements are consistently reinforced, but no such constant relationship holds for irrelevant elements. Some studies have attempted to determine the effects on concept formation of systematically varying the number of irrelevant elements (1, 12). Others have investigated the relative effectiveness of positive (relevant) and negative (irrelevant) instances on concept formation (8, 13), and some work has been done to assess the effects of the degree of intermittent reinforcement of the irrelevant elements which usually occurs in these experiments (3, 4, 9). These studies of intermittent reinforcement have concentrated on its possible role in the superiority of reversal shifts (where the relevant dimension stays the same, but the positive and negative signs are reversed) over nonreversal shifts (where a formerly irrelevant dimension becomes relevant). Buss (3) suggested that intermittent reinforcement of the formerly correct dimension impeded nonreversal shifts, but Kendler and D'Amato (9) and Buss (4) found that elimination of the intermittent reinforcement did not eliminate the *superiority of the reversal shift*. Their experiments were not designed to eliminate the possibility that intermittent reinforcement might enhance the *difficulty of the nonreversal shift* just as Buss conjectured. The present study provides evidence on this point.

Kendler and D'Amato (9) and Buss (4) interpret their findings as virtually requiring a mediational S-R theory (11, pp. 392–412) which assumes that in conceptual behavior S makes an implicit response which serves as the cue for the overt conceptual response. This theory, although it introduces some equivocation, supposedly permits an S-R continuity framework (11, pp. 446–455) to account for apparent noncontinuity

Reprinted by permission of the authors and the American Psychological Association from *Journal of Experimental Psychology*, 1958, 55, 621–627.

where abstract behavior (5, 6) or verbal behavior (10) is involved. If intermittent reinforcement of an incorrect or irrelevant dimension during the initial stage of the present experiment leads to positive transfer on a second stage, where the formerly irrelevant dimension becomes relevant, the need for a mediational theory would be lessened as the results could be accounted for by conventional S-R theory. Absence of such positive transfer would tend to support the mediational position. The adequacy of the mediational theory, depending as it does on unobserved implicit responses which are postulated to behave in a rather peculiar manner, has not been tested. The theory hence remains an *ad hoc* and untested solution to the continuity—noncontinuity difficulty.

PROCEDURE

General procedure. The WCST, conventionally, involves the use of decks of 64 response cards (5, 6). In the present investigation, however, decks of 48 response cards of the "unsystematic" type (7) were used. Each card contained one to four figures of a single color. There were four colors—red, green, yellow, and blue; and four figures—triangles, stars, crosses, and circles. Each card could therefore be sorted according to the color, form, or number of the figures.

In the test situation a gray sorting tray with four double compartments was placed on a table before S. Four stimulus cards consisting of one red triangle, two green stars, three yellow crosses, and four blue circles were placed from left to right in the upper halves of the four double compartments. Two decks of response cards, differing in composition, were placed in a partitioned box fastened to one of the legs of the table, facing E and out of view of S.

The S was instructed in the following standard manner: "I am going to present you with a series of cards similar to those you see before you [E points to the stimulus cards]. Every time I give you a card I want you to place it in the compartment underneath the card to which you think it belongs. Each time you place a card I will tell you whether you are 'right' or 'wrong'." If S asked questions—i.e., whether to sort for color, number, or form, etc.—he was simply told: "I will tell you whether you are 'right' or 'wrong'." The E then selected a response card from one of the compartments and handed it to S. The response cards were always presented to S in a standardized manner and order. Initially the category color was called "correct," but after S had sorted 10 consecutive cards correctly according to color, E then began selecting response cards from the second deck, shifting the correct category to number. Care was taken to insure that S had no cue for the shift other than E's statement of "right" or "wrong." After 10 correct number responses the experimental session was terminated. If S did not attain the criterion within 48 sortings in either stage of the experiment, his data were discarded.

Experimental design. In the first stage S was assigned to one of four groups, each of which received one of four response card decks of 0%, 25%, 50%, or 75% number ambiguity; i.e., 0, 12, 24, or 36 of the 48 response cards, when sorted correctly by S on the basis of color and accordingly called "correct," would also have been "correct" on the basis of number. Each of the four initial groups was subdivided into four more groups in the second stage. Each of these four subgroups was given one of four response card decks of 0%, 25%, 50%, or 75% form ambiguity.

The decks of 64 response cards normally used in the WCST consist of all possible combinations of figures, colors, and numbers. In the present investigation, however, it was found that decks of 48 response cards (or multiples thereof) permitted the formation of eight decks of varying degrees of ambiguity that were balanced with regard to the various combinations of figures, colors, and numbers.

The experimental paradigm utilized in the present investigation is basically a complex variation of that of transfer of training, with a simple between-groups design of 4 groups, 40 Ss in a group, in the first stage and a 4 × 4 factorial design, 10 Ss in a cell, in the second stage. The virtues of the experimental design are several. First, the effect of degree of number ambiguity on color sorting in the first stage can be evaluated by a simple between-groups analysis of variance; second, the variation between columns of the 4 × 4 factorial design permits a determination of the effect of degree of form ambiguity on number sorting that is independent of any possible transfer effects of color sorting in the first stage; third, the between-rows variation provides a means of assessing the transfer effects to the second stage of the degree of number ambiguity during the first stage, which effects are again assessed independently of any transfer effects of color sorting.

Subjects. The Ss were 160 men and women in elementary psychology courses at the University of Wisconsin. Ten Ss for each of the 16 cells satisfactorily completed the experiment. In addition there were 29 "failures" to complete either the first or second stage. These "failures" were distributed unsystematically over all experimental conditions, and the results obtained from these "failures" were discarded from the analysis.

RESULTS

Each S's performance in two stages of sorting was recorded in terms of the following scores: (*a*) *total errors;* (*b*) *total trials,* i.e., total number of sortings required to attain the criterion, including the last 10 "criterion" cards; (*c*) the *total correct responses,* i.e., the number of correct sortings

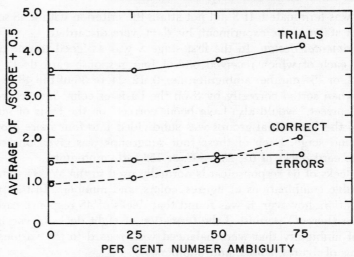

FIG. 1. The effect of increasing number ambiguity in color sorting upon total trials, total correct responses, and total errors.

made by S before he began his criterion sequence of 10 successive correct responses; and, on the second stage only, (d) the number of *perseverative errors*, i.e., the number of incorrect responses which would have been correct in the first stage, except for the initial perseverative error which presumably served to inform S that a shift had taken place; and (e) the number of *nonperseverative errors*, i.e., the responses that also would have been wrong in the first stage of the experiment. By definition, there can be no perseverative errors in the first stage and nonperseverative errors simply become total errors.

The results of the experiment are summarized in Fig. 1, 2, and 3. In each of these figures the averages of all scores, after a square-root transformation, are plotted against the four levels of ambiguity.

Figure 1 presents the effect of increasing number ambiguity on color sorting. It can be seen from the average number of trials and correct responses that 25% number ambiguity had little effect on color sorting, but as number ambiguity increased to 50% and 75%, sorting for color became more difficult. The total number of correct responses required to attain the criterion indicates the number of reinforcements or reminders needed to confirm or establish the color response and has been considered a measure of the difficulty of sorting (7). The total errors appear to be unaffected by increasing number ambiguity. It is worth noting, however, that as number amgibuity is increased there is less opportunity for S to make errors, i.e., at 0% number ambiguity each time S sorts on the basis of number an error is recorded, whereas at 75% ambiguity if

S "erroneously" sorts all cards on the basis of number, only 25% of the responses could be recorded as errors.

Statistical analysis of the first stage of sorting was carried out by means of a simple analysis of variance, and that of the second stage by a rows-by-columns analysis of variance. Because all scores were frequency measures, it was considered desirable to use the transformation $g = \sqrt{x + .5}$ where g was the score analyzed and x the original score. This rational transformation serves to reduce the skewness of the frequency data, making them more amenable to the analysis of variance (2).

TABLE 1

ANALYSES OF VARIANCE OF SCORES ON COLOR SORTING IN STAGE 1

Source of Variation	df	F Ratios		
		Total Trials	Total Correct	Total Errors
Progressive number ambiguity (between-groups)	3	10.9261*	13.5999*	.2423
Error	156	(.4075)	(.7353)	(.5237)

Note.—Numbers in parentheses are error mean squares.
* $P = .001$.

The summary of the simple analysis of variance of the three scores used to measure the effects of increasing number ambiguity on color sorting during the first stage is given in Table 1. Only the F ratios are presented, except for the error mean squares which appear in parentheses at the bottom of each column. The variation between groups was significant at the .001 level for total trials and correct responses, but the F for total errors was not significant.

Figure 2 depicts the effect of 0%, 25%, 50%, and 75% form ambiguity on number sorting in the second stage. Inspection of the figure indicates that all scores increased as form ambiguity went from 0% to 25%. However, only the total correct responses score demonstrates a uniformly progressive relationship to increasing form ambiguity. Thus as form ambiguity increased from 0% to 75%, more correct responses or reinforcements were required for S to attain the criterion of 10 successive number sortings. The total trials, total errors, and perseverative errors showed no change as form ambiguity increased from 25% to 50%, whereas non-perseverative errors and total correct responses showed a rise. As form ambiguity went from 50% to 75%, total errors, perseverative errors, and nonperseverative errors decreased, but total trials and correct responses increased.

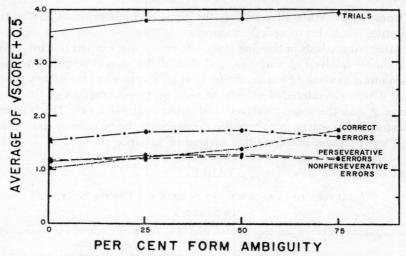

Fig. 2. The effect of increasing form ambiguity in number sorting upon total trials, total correct responses, total errors, perseverative errors and nonperseverative errors.

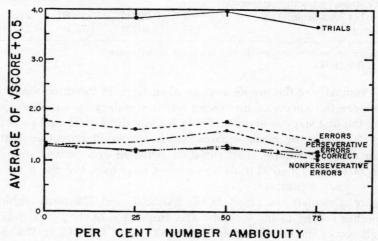

Fig. 3. The transfer effect of increasing number ambiguity in Stage 1 (color sorting), upon number sorting (Stage 2), for total trials, total correct responses, total errors, perseverative errors and nonperseverative errors.

Figure 3 presents the effect of degree of intermittent reinforcement of number responses during Stage 1 (color sorting) upon subsequent number sorting (Stage 2). Except for total trials and total correct responses which show a slight rise, all scores used show a decrease as intermittent reinforcement of number rose from 0% to 25%. At 50% ambiguity all scores show an increase, indicating that 50% intermittent reinforcement of number responses in Stage 1 made number sorting in Stage 2 more difficult. At 75% ambiguity, however, all scores show a decrease below that of 0% number ambiguity.

Table 2 gives the summary of the analysis of variance for each of the five scores considered in the second stage of sorting. In Row 1, the source of variation tested is that shown in Fig. 2, the effect of degree of form ambiguity during Stage 2 on number sorting. Only the F for total correct responses is significant. Row 2 of this table shows that for all scores,

TABLE 2

ANALYSES OF VARIANCE OF SCORES ON NUMBER SORTING IN STAGE 2

Source of Variation		*F* Ratios				
		Total Trials	Total Correct	Persev-erative Errors	Non-persev-erative Errors	Total Errors
1. Progressive number ambiguity in Stage 1 (row)	3	1.5407	1.8058	.2252	.6255	1.4066
2. Progressive form ambiguity in Stage 2 (columns)	3	1.3711	4.8072*	.4815	.1356	.5278
3. Progressive number and form ambiguity (rows × columns)	9	1.1536	.7546	1.6544	.4543	1.6333
4. Error	144	(.5826)	(.8157)	(.4334)	(.2836)	(.7524)

Note—Number in parentheses are error mean squares.
* $P = .01$.

the degree of intermittent reinforcement of number responses in Stage 1 of sorting had no statistically significant effect on number sorting in Stage 2 as was indicated in Fig. 3. In Row 3 the interactions between the Row 1 and Row 2 factors are tested. No significant interaction was found for any score.[1]

DISCUSSION

The three principal findings of this study are: (*a*) increasing the degree of number ambiguity made sorting for color more difficult in Stage 1 of the experiment; (*b*) increasing the degree of form ambiguity made sorting for number more difficult in Stage 2; and (*c*) increasing the degree of number ambiguity and hence increasing the amount of intermittent reinforcement of the number responses on Stage 1, when Ss were made to sort for color, had no significant transfer effect on number sorting in Stage 2.

[1] A second analysis of the data of Fig. 3 was carried out, using a covariance adjustment for total correct responses and total trials during the first stage to correct the second stage scores. This refinement led to no change in the significance levels of the F's reported in Table 3.

The interpretation of the first two findings is straightforward. When the percentage of ambiguity is increased, this means an increase in the amount of intermittent reinforcement given the irrelevant dimension. The only basis S has for learning the correct sorting response is via the reinforcement or nonreinforcement of each of his responses. The relevant dimension is always reinforced, but with increasing ambiguity an irrelevant dimension is reinforced up to 75% of the time. Hence, increasing ambiguity makes it increasingly difficult for S to learn which of the two dimensions is correct. Buss (3) is therefore quite correct in assuming that intermittent reinforcement of an irrelevant dimension in a nonreversal shift would impede learning of the new response. Although intermittent reinforcement can hardly account for all of the superiority of reversal shifts over nonreversal shifts (4, 9), it can account for part of it.

The third finding was a negative one; it can become definitive only if the null hypothesis can be proved. Although this cannot be done, it is proper to point out that with 160 Ss the power of the experiment is considerable, so that if intermittent reinforcement of an irrelevant concept affects future learning it must not affect it very much. This indicated failure of the overt responses to follow the continuity principle makes a mediational theory necessary to the S-R approach, but the S-R theorist must face the problem of noncontinuity in the implicit (verbal) mediating responses.

SUMMARY

An investigation was made of the difficulty of sorting for color and number in the Wisconsin Card Sorting Test when the irrelevant dimensions of number and form, respectively, were intermittently reinforced 0%, 25%, 50%, or 75% of the time. The experimental design used also permitted a determination of the transfer effects on number sorting, of having intermittently reinforced the irrelevant number dimension during earlier color sorting. The design was basically a complex variation of that of transfer of training, with a simple between-groups design of 4 groups, 40 Ss in a group, in Stage 1, and a 4 × 4 factorial design, 10 Ss in a cell, in Stage 2. The results and conclusions were as follows:

1. As number ambiguity was increased from 0% to 75% on Stage 1, sorting for color became more difficult.

2. Sorting for number became more difficult as form ambiguity was similarly increased on Stage 2.

3. Increasing number ambiguity or intermittent reinforcement of number-sorting responses in Stage 1 of sorting had no statistically significant transfer effect on number sorting in Stage 2.

4. It was concluded that intermittent reinforcement probably plays a

supplementary role in the superiority of reversal shifts over nonreversal shifts in concept formation, and that the mediational S-R theory is supported although noncontinuity in the learning of the implicit mediating responses requires further explanation.

REFERENCES

1. ARCHER, E. J., BOURNE, L. E., & BROWN, F. G. Concept identification as a function of irrelevant information and instruction. *J. exp. Psychol.*, 1955, 49, 153–164.
2. BARTLETT, M. S. The use of transformations. *Biometrics*, 1947, 3, 39–52.
3. BUSS, A. H. Rigidity as a function of reversal and nonreversal shifts in the learning of successive discriminations. *J. exp. Psychol.*, 1953, 45, 75–81.
4. BUSS, A. H. Reversal and nonreversal shifts in concept formation with partial reinforcement eliminated. *J. exp. Psychol.*, 1956, 52, 162–166.
5. GRANT, D. A., & BERG, E. A. A behavioral analysis of degree of reinforcement and ease of shifting to new responses in a Weigl-type card-sorting problem. *J. exp. Psychol.*, 1948, 38, 404–411.
6. GRANT, D. A., & COST, J. R. Continuities and discontinuities in conceptual behavior in a card sorting problem. *J. gen. Psychol.*, 1954, 50, 237–244.
7. GRANT, D. A., & CURRAN, J. F. Relative difficulty of number, form, and color concepts of a Weigl-type problem using unsystematic number cards. *J. exp. Psychol.*, 1952, 43, 408–413.
8. HOVLAND, C. I., & WEISS, W. Transmission of information concerning concepts through positive and negative instances. *J. exp. Psychol.*, 1953, 45, 175–182.
9. KENDLER, H. H., & D'AMATO, M. F. A comparison of reversal shifts and nonreversal shifts in human concept formation behavior. *J. exp. Psychol.*, 1955, 49, 165–174.
10. KUENNE, M. R. Experimental investigation of the relation of language to transposition behavior in young children. *J. exp. Psychol.*, 1946, 36, 471–490.
11. OSGOOD, C. E. *Method and theory in experimental psychology.* New York: Oxford Univer. Press, 1953.
12. REED, H. B. The learning and retention of concepts: IV. The influence of complexity of stimuli. *J. exp. Psychol.*, 1946, 36, 252–261.
13. SMOKE, K. L. Negative instances in concept learning. *J. exp. Psychol.*, 1933, 16, 583–588.

37.   The Identification of Concepts as a Function of Amounts of Relevant and Irrelevant Information

Clinton M. Walker and Lyle E. Bourne, Jr.

Several recent studies have shown that the efficiency of concept-identification depends upon the complexity of the stimulus-patterns to be categorized. Specifically, mean errors to attainment of the concept increased linearly with complexity in these studies.[1] Complexity was quantified in terms of the number of binary dimensions, e.g. color (red-green), within which the patterns could vary. Any such dimension was either relevant to solution, i.e. necessarily used in classifying the patterns, or irrelevant, hence useless for correct identification of the patterns. As the number of dimensions increased, the number of alternative patterns increased along with the information contained in each alternative. The amount of information (in bits) was defined as $\log_2 x$, where $x =$ the number of possible patterns.[2] Since each dimension was binary, each contributed one bit of information.

In previous studies of the effects of complexity, the amount of relevant information was held constant (two bits) while the irrelevant information was varied (one through six bits). Performance, however, should depend upon the amount of information necessarily used in solution as well as upon the amount irrelevant to solution. The purpose of the present experiment was to investigate the relationship between concept-identification and the amount of relevant stimulus-information under varying conditions of irrelevant information.

While an increase in irrelevant information increases the complexity of each stimulus-pattern, it has no effect upon the number of categories into which the patterns must be sorted. An increase in relevant information, however, results in an exponential increase in the number of categories,

Reprinted by permission of the second author and the American Journal of Psychology from American Journal of Psychology 1961, 74, 410–417.

[1] E. J. Archer, L. E. Bourne, Jr., and F. G. Brown, Concept identification as a function of irrelevant information and instructions, J. exp. Psychol., 49, 1955, 153–164; Bourne, Effects of delay of information feedback and task complexity on the identification of concepts, ibid., 54, 1957, 201–207; L. E. Bourne, Jr., and R. B. Pendleton, Concept identification as a function of completeness and probability of information feedback, ibid., 56, 1958, 413–420; F. G. Brown and E. J. Archer, Concept identification as a function of task complexity and distribution of practice, ibid., 52, 1956, 316–321.

[2] C. E. Shannon, A mathematical theory of communication, Bell Syst. tech. J., 27, 1948, 379–423; 623–656.

this number being 2^k for k-binary *independent*, relevant dimensions. Bits of stimulus-information, either relevant or irrelevant, might not be independent but rather *redundant* to a certain degree. If the levels of any two or more dimensions are perfectly correlated, the information they contain would be fully redundant and, in the case of relevant information, the categories required by one dimension would be identical for the others. Indications as to how redundant dimensions affect concept-identification have been reported.[3] The present study concerns the effect of variation in independent dimensions only.

Restle has proposed a mathematical theory of discriminative learning in which the stimulus-situation is described as a set of cues, either relevant or irrelevant to a particular response.[4] By assuming (a) that relevant cues are conditioned to a correct response, (b) that irrelevant cues are neutralized and rendered non-functional in the course of learning, and (c) that the probability of a correct response is proportional to the number of cues conditioned to it, he achieved some success in predicting the results of experiments on two-choice discriminative learning. The proportion of relevant cues, θ, was assumed by Restle equal to the rate of learning and was typically estimated from part of the data gathered in any experiment. A parameter, similar to θ, can be obtained directly from the content of the stimulus-series used in a study of concept-identification, if it is assumed that the number of relevant and irrelevant cues is a function of the amount of relevant and irrelevant information in the patterns. With appropriate modification of Restle's Equation [8], the following function is applicable for predicting approximate number of errors to solution under any condition of stimulus-content, assuming independent bits of information:

$$E_t \cong d \left\{ \frac{1}{2} + \frac{1}{2} \left[\frac{\log \theta'}{(1 - \theta') \log (1 - \theta')} \right] \right\}, \qquad [1]$$

where θ' is the ration of relevant to total stimulus information. For a more complete development of this argument, see Walker.[5]

A matrix portraying the relationship between stimulus-content and performance, enveloping Equation [1], can be constructed as a model. The *location* of an element within the matrix denotes the degrees of relevant and irrelevant information in the treatment yielding that element. The *value* of the element is the predicted mean error-score for that treatment. Allowing the first digit of each element to represent amount of relevant

[3] L. E. Bourne, Jr., and R. C. Haygood, The role of stimulus-redundancy in the identification of concepts, *J. exp. Psychol.*, 58, 1959, 232–238.

[4] Frank Restle, A theory of discrimination learning, *Psychol. Rev.*, 62, 1955, 11–19.

[5] C. M. Walker, Concept identification as a function of relevant and irrelevant information, Unpublished Doctoral dissertation, University of Utah, 1957, 4–18.

information and the second amount of irrelevant information in bits, the general model can be schematized as follows:

$$E_t \cong \begin{cases} 1\text{--}1 & 1\text{--}2 & 1\text{--}3 & \cdots \\ 2\text{--}1 & 2\text{--}2 & 2\text{--}3 & \cdots \\ 3\text{--}1 & 3\text{--}2 & 3\text{--}3 & \cdots \\ \cdots & & & \\ \cdots & & & \\ \cdots & & & \end{cases} \qquad [2]$$

In this model, the theoretical number of errors to solution, E_t, for a given θ' is based upon an experimentally determined parameter of pattern-discriminability, d, the value of which must be estimated from part of the data.

METHOD

Task. As in earlier studies of concept-identification, S was presented with a series of geometric patterns, each of which was a combination of the levels of x-relevant and y-irrelevant stimulus-dimensions. To identify the category to which a pattern belonged, S responded by pressing one of two, four, or eight buttons, depending upon the number of independent, relevant stimulus-dimensions. The buttons corresponded to the levels (or combinations of levels) of the relevant binary dimension(s). A dimension was relevant to solution if it necessarily was used in correct identification of the patterns. If a dimension was irrelevant, it appeared at each of its two levels within the series of patterns but could not be used to classify the patterns correctly. The criterion of problem-solution was 16 consecutively correct identifications. For a more complete discussion of the task, see Bourne.[6]

Design. A $3 \times 3 \times 2$ factorial design was used with three levels of relevant information (1, 2, and 3 relevant dimensions), three levels of irrelevant information (1, 2, and 3 irrelevant dimensions), and two different problems (defined in terms of the actual dimensions used as relevant and irrelevant).

Stimulus-lists. Both the relevant and the irrelevant dimensions were selected from a population of six simple binary attributes, viz. color (red or green), number (one or two figures), size (large or small), form (square or triangle), orientation (upright or tilted), and horizontal position (on the left or right). Since there were two levels on each dimension, the amount of information in the stimulus-objects could be quantified simply. Since the number of alternative stimulus-patterns doubled with the ad-

[6] Bourne, *op. cit.*, 201.

dition of each dimension, evaluation of $\log_2 (2^N)$, where N is the number of dimensions, shows that the number of bits of information is equivalent to the number of stimulus-dimensions present. In the problems studied, then, there were 1, 2, or 3 bits of relevant and 1, 2, or 3 bits of irrelevant information. The number of response categories was equal to the number of alternative relevant stimulus-combinations. Therefore one, two, and three relevant dimensions required, respectively, the learning of two-, four-, and eight-categories.

Eighteen series of patterns were prepared on loops of white-vellum tape to present problems at the nine relevant-irrelevant conditions with two sets of relevant and irrelevant dimensions. Nine lists used size, size and number, or size, number, and horizontal position to display relevant information. The other nine lists used color, color and form, or color, form, and orientation as relevant. The irrelevant information was displayed by the color-group when the size-group was relevant and vice versa.

Apparatus. The stimulus-patterns were presented to S at a rate of one every 6 sec. on a Gerbrands memory-drum. S sat at a distance of about 2 ft. from the drum with the response-board before him. The buttons on S's board activated lights on a control-panel located behind a partition and out of S's view. Thus E could record each response and in turn inform S as to the correctness of each response. Only during the first 3 sec. of the 6-sec. trial did the stimulus-pattern remain in the window of the drum. The movement of the drum to a blank position was S's signal to respond. Information was given by a light-panel placed directly above and about 4 in. from the keys on the response-unit. The panel consisted of a row of eight jewelled lamps, one directly above each of the eight response-keys. Regardless of S's response, the lamp above the correct key for any given pattern was lighted during the last second of the trial. A covering for certain of the lamps and keys was used when the number of categories was less than eight, *i.e.* with one and two relevant dimensions.

Subjects. The Ss (162 in number) were students in courses in elementary psychology and were assigned in order of appearance to solve one of the problems in one of the nine relevant-irrelevant combinations. Every S was presented at the outset with detailed instructions as to the nature of the task, the operation of his controls, the meaning of the lights, and the criterion of problem-solution.

RESULTS AND DISCUSSION

Two response-measures were used: trials to solution and number of errors. Due to the high correlation between these measures ($r = 0.91$)

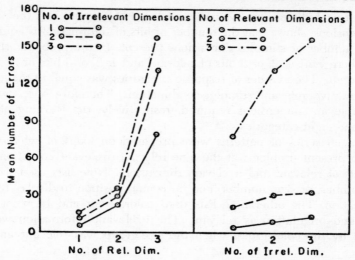

FIG. 1. Mean Errors to Solution as a Function of Amount of Relevant and Irrelevant Information (Every point represents the data from 18Ss.)

and the fact that instructions to S stressed accuracy in problem-solving, number of errors was considered the main dependent variable.

The following is a 3 × 3 matrix which portrays the obtained errors to solution, E_o, under the various conditions of relevant and irrelevant information:

$$E_o = \begin{pmatrix} 5.3 & 8.6 & 13.0 \\ 21.2 & 30.5 & 32.5 \\ 78.7 & 131.8 & 155.1 \end{pmatrix}.$$

Columns represent 1, 2, and 3 bits of irrelevant information and rows 1, 2, and 3 bits of relevant information (two-, four-, and eight-choice learning, respectively). An analysis of variance was performed on these data. Two main effects, amount of relevant and irrelevant information, were significant at the 1% level ($F = 118.66$ and 8.60, respectively, $df. = 2$ and 144). The significance of the amount of irrelevant information is consistent with all earlier studies and indicates that the number of errors made in solving this type of problem is an increasing function of the complexity of the pattern. Fig. 1 shows that this increase nearly follows a straight line. In an orthogonal polynomial analysis applied to the relationship, only the linear term reached the 1% level of significance.

Amount of relevant information produced a greater effect on performance. As can be seen in Fig. 1, errors increased at a positively accelerated rate with relevant information. An orthogonal polynomial analysis of this curve statistically confirmed its curvilinearity; the quadratic component reached significance at the 1% level.

Somewhat inconsistent with earlier results was the failure of the variance identified with problems to reach significance ($F = 3.48$, 1 and 144 $df.$, $P > 0.05$). The effect of problems has, however, always been small and dependent on the discriminability between the levels of the dimensions used as relevant.

The effect of amount of relevant information depended on the level of irrelevant information employed in a problem. This is evidenced by the lack of parallelism among the sets of curves in Fig. 1 and by the significance of the interaction of relevant by irrelevant information ($F = 7.72$, $df. = 4$ and 144, $P < 0.01$). This interaction itself was somewhat dependent upon which of the two sets of problems was used, $i.e.$ the interaction of relevant information, irrelevant information, and problems was significant ($F = 6.06$, $df. = 4$ and 144, $P < 0.01$).

With trials to solution as the measure, essentially identical results were found; the analysis of variance showed the same sources of variance to be significant.

The matrix of obtained errors can be reduced by extraction of the overall trend when the amounts of relevant and irrelevant information are equal. The result is the product of a diagonal and a residual matrix:

$$E_o = \text{diag. } (5.3, 30.5, 155.1) \begin{pmatrix} 1.0 & 1.6 & 2.4 \\ 0.7 & 1.0 & 1.1 \\ 0.5 & 0.9 & 1.0 \end{pmatrix}.$$

For comparison, computations using Equation [1] yield the following theoretical array:

$$E_t \cong 1.5d \begin{pmatrix} 1.0 & 1.7 & 2.5 \\ 0.7 & 1.0 & 1.3 \\ 0.6 & 0.8 & 1.0 \end{pmatrix}.$$

Examination of the diagonal multiplier-matrix from the data indicates that its elements form a power sequence. The scalar multiplier of the model, $1.5d$, should be replaced by the sequence, $(1.5d)^n$, where n is the number of (equal) relevant and irrelevant dimensions, in order to describe the data adequately. Using the obtained errors from the condition with one relevant and one irrelevant bit of information, $d = 3.53$. The theoretical diagonal matrix is then diag. (5.3, 28.1, 148.9). The closeness of this fit should allow the tentative formulation of a simple equation for predicting errors to solution in a concept-identification problem with equal relevant and irrelevant information:

$$E_t \cong (1.5d)^n.$$

It is perhaps worth noting that a simple transformation, $x' = 1/x$, applied to the elements, x, above the main diagonal in the residual error matrix reduces the range of those elements to that of the elements below the diagonal, *i.e.* 0 to 1. But, more interesting, symmetric matrices result.

$$E_t \cong \text{diag.} \, [(1.5d), (1.5d)^2, (1.5d)^3] \begin{pmatrix} 1.0 & 0.7 & 0.4 \\ 0.7 & 1.0 & 0.8 \\ 0.6 & 0.8 & 1.0 \end{pmatrix},$$

and

$$E_o = \text{diag.} \, (5.3, 30.5, 155.1) \begin{pmatrix} 1.0 & 0.7 & 0.4 \\ 0.7 & 1.0 & 0.9 \\ 0.5 & 0.9 & 1.0 \end{pmatrix}.$$

The results of this experiment clearly support several hypotheses generated from the proposed model. As predicted, and as has been shown in earlier studies, the difficulty of the task was affected by variation in the amount of irrelevant information in the patterns. Performance was an inverse linear function of irrelevant information. Amount of relevant information, however, had a much greater effect on difficulty. As the amount of information necessarily used to classify the patterns increased, performance decreased exponentially. Close fits of the predictions to the data clearly support the assumption that θ, the proportion of relevant stimulus-cues, is functionally related to the proportion of relevant stimulus-information. Bricker found results similar to these with an experiment designed to investigate the effect of both independent and redundant relevant information in a different task.[7] It is important to note that relevant information, as varied in the present experiment, is information that S must use to classify any given pattern. An experiment reported earlier, investigated concept-identification as a function of redundant, relevant stimulus-information.[8] Each bit of relevant information in the sequence of stimulus-patterns was redundant with the first, *i.e.* added no new stimulus-information necessarily used in the correct classificatory scheme. As might be expected in this case, increases in relevant information enhanced performance since S could use any one of the relevant bits to categorize correctly.

SUMMARY

Theoretical formulations of Restle coupled with modifications suggested by information-theory were used to construct a matrix-model for concept-identification.[9] Simply stated, this model holds that performance,

---

[7] P. D. Bricker, The identification of redundant stimulus-patterns, *J. exp. Psychol.*, 49, 1955, 73–81.

[8] Bourne and Haygood, *op. cit.*, 232.

[9] Restle, *op. cit.*, 15.

measured by total errors to concept-attainment, is a function of stimulus-discriminability and number of relevant and irrelevant bits of information in the stimulus-patterns.

An experiment, in which the independent variables were relevant and irrelevant information, was conducted as a test of the model. A $3 \times 3 \times 2$ factorial design, with three levels of relevant information, 1, 2, and 3 bits, three levels of irrelevant information, 1, 2, and 3 bits, and two different problems, was used. Each of 162 Ss served individually and learned to categorize visually presented geometric patterns.

The model predicted, and the results confirmed, a linear decrement in performance with increased irrelevant information. This finding corroborated earlier experimental evidence. In addition, an exponential performance-decrement resulted from increased relevant information as predicted.

38. Speed of Classification of Words into Superordinate Categories

Irwin Pollack

The classification task—that of assigning objects to defined categories—provides a critical examination of stimulus and response factors in human information processing. Specifically, it permits us to ask whether the speed of information processing is primarily determined by: (a) the number of different response categories that S must employ; or by (b) the number of different examples per category. The first factor is related to response diversity; the second factor is primarily related to stimulus diversity.

The present tests explore the speed of classifying words into defined superordinate categories as a joint function of the number of defined categories and of the number of examples available per category.

METHOD

Test lists, experimental group. Lists of words were typed in the format of 48 words to a single vertical column. A given list is designated by:

Reprinted by permission of the author and Academic Press, Inc. from *Journal of Verbal Learning and Verbal Behavior*, 1963, 2, 159–165.

TABLE 1

RESPONSE CATEGORIES AND EXAMPLES OF EACH CATEGORY

Response category	Examples of response category			
	(a)	(b)	(c)	(d)
animal	goat	pig	lion	leopard
measure	inch	rod	centimeter	gallon
car	Vauxhall	Consul	Simca	Fiat
boy	Robert	Harold	Peter	Thomas
illness	measles	smallpox	dysentery	impetigo
clothes	hat	tie	slacks	jacket
tree	spruce	oak	mahogany	elm
subject	Psychology	Astronomy	Statistics	Astronomy
money	farthing	lire	guilder	florin
music	piano	drum	saxophone	bagpipe
city	London	Glasgow	Berlin	Moscow
color	red	brown	grey	yellow
vegetable	lettuce	carrot	cabbage	beans
sport	football	lacrosse	badminton	boating
country	England	Yugoslavia	Germany	Netherlands
river	Thames	Volga	Amazon	Rhine
fruit	apple	strawberry	banana	plum
bird	crow	cockatoo	pheasant	peacock
fish	cod	kipper	haddock	shrimp
body	eye	teeth	tongue	stomach
girl	Alice	Pauline	Jennifer	Elizabeth
religion	Christian	Methodist	Dominican	Lutheran
flower	crocus	tulip	zinnia	chrysanthemum
job	doctor	ironmonger	mechanic	glassblower

(a) the number of response categories, and (b) the number of possible examples per category. List 4–2, for example, designates a list of 48 items consisting of the examples furnished by 4 response categories with 2 examples per category.

Table 1 lists the response categories and examples employed. Specifically, *red* is an example of the defined response category of *color*. The response categories are listed in the first column. Four examples of each category are presented in the second through the fifth columns.

Sections from five lists are presented in Table 2. List 2–1 consists of one example of each of two response categories. A correct processing of List 2–1 would proceed as "animal, animal, measure, animal, measure, etc.," List 3–2 as "car, animal, measure, animal, measure, etc.," List 24–1 "fish, sport, job, animal, etc.," and List 24–24 as "boy, music, body, job, etc."

The vocabulary of category names was successively incorporated within previously learned names. For example—noting Tables 1 and 2—two-category lists consisted of examples of *animal* and *measure;* three-category lists consisted of examples of *animal, measure,* and *car;* and four-category lists as examples of *animal, measure, car,* and *boy;* etc. Lists of 2, 3, 4, 5, 6, 8, 12, 17, and 24 categories were so constructed. An

TABLE 2

ILLUSTRATIVE EXAMPLES OF PORTIONS OF THE WORD LISTS EMPLOYED

List 2-1	List 3-2	List 24-1	List 2-24	List 24-24
goat	Consul	cod	yard	Peter
goat	goat	football	mile	bagpipe
inch	rod	doctor	furlong	stomach
goat	pig	goat	lion	glassblower
inch	rod	Psychology	gallon	Amazon
inch	inch	spruce	cheetah	grey
inch	Vauxhall	Alice	tiger	Berlin
goat	pig	England	baboon	slacks

additional set of two-category lists was constructed consisting of the third and fourth response categories. These lists, designated as 2*-reponse categories, consisted primarily of polysyllabic examples with a monosyllabic response. This contrasts with the other two-category tests which consisted primarily of shorter examples, but with a polysyllabic response.

In a parallel manner, tests with a larger number of examples incorporated previously learned examples. Specifically, tests with one example per category employed the examples of column (a) of Table 1; tests with two examples per category employed the examples of columns (a) and (b); tests with four examples per category employed the examples of columns (a) and (b) plus two other examples per category. For instance —noting Tables 1 and 2—one-example tests (with three response categories) employed *goat, inch,* and *Vauxhall;* two-example tests employed *goat, pig, inch, rod, Vauxhall, Consul,* etc.

It is important to note that only a single list of 48 items was available for each of 42 testing conditions. Thus, when the product of the number of response categories by the examples per category exceeded 48, a sampling from the set of possible items was necessary. Specifically, List 24–24 consisted of 48 items sampled out of a total pool of $24 \times 24 = 576$ items. The particular sampling of 48 items for List 24–24 is presented in columns (c) and (d). (Two examples have been modified to permit description of the test lists for the Control Group, below.)

Test lists, control group. An additional set of 42 lists was constructed in order to determine whether the obtained results were specific to the particular ordering of the categories or examples employed. In the control tests, the response categories of Table 1 were employed in an ascending, rather than a descending, order. Specifically, two-category control tests employed examples of *job* and *flower;* three-category control tests employed examples of *job, flower, religion,* etc. In a parallel manner, the examples of column (d) served in the one-example control tests; the examples of columns (d) and (c) served in the two-example control tests, etc. Because of the balanced symmetry of the lists with respect to the Experimental and Control Groups, Lists 24–2E and 24–24C (Control Group) were nearly identical as were Lists 24–24E and 24–2C.

Test procedure, classification tests. Before exposure of each list, the number of response categories and the number of examples per response category were announced. The response categories were enumerated for lists with a small number of response categories. The additional response categories, newly introduced relative to previous lists, were enumerated for lists with a large number of response categories. The examples of each response category were also enumerated for lists with a small number of examples per category.

In the main body of tests, 42 conditions were examined. Four successive series of the 42 conditions were completed by each of 17 Ss. In Series 1 and 3, successive tests were carried out with an ascending number of response categories. In Series 2 and 4, lists were completed with a larger number of response categories before lists with a smaller number of response categories, in order to take advantage of the practice developed in Series 1 and 3. Following the completion of the four test series, 15 of the Ss completed tests with 48 response categories in a separate session. Thus, the results obtained with 48 response categories are not directly comparable with those provided by 2–24 response categories.

The S was instructed to classify the words of each list as quickly as possible, consistently with a low rate of error. Before each test run, S inspected the list of examples. At the beginning of the test series, the inspection of the list was usually very detailed. With successive periods of practice, S typically glanced at the list only briefly. Attention was drawn to ambiguous and difficult examples. A small number of runs were terminated by Ss who expressed inability to classify some of the words. These runs were then repeated. Mild prompting by E, approximately 3 sec. after the previous response, reduced the seriously blocked responses in the initial trials. The percentage of promptings and of detected errors was negligibly small in the fourth test series. At the end of each test, the time score was announced and compared with previous tests. Improvements in time scores were highly praised.

The procedure with the Control Group was identical to that of the main body of tests.

Reading tests. After completion of Series 3, each S read all lists with 2 and 24 response categories. This procedure was repeated following completion of Series 4. The time score was announced at the end of each test and compared with previous tests.

Selection of results. Analysis of the results will be confined to the fastest of the four scores obtained by each S for each experimental condition. This arbitrary selection probably more clearly approaches a terminal skilled performance level than the more reliable average of several test scores. The bulk of the selected scores came from the fourth testing series, especially for the faster Ss who tended to improve uniformly with successive testing series.

Subjects. British Royal Naval Ratings served as Ss in the experimental and control tests. Each S served for two periods of 20–30 min. a day for 10 days over a 2-week period. For purposes of analysis, the 17 Ss of the main Experimental Group were rank-ordered in terms of the sum of their fastest times required for classification of all lists, except lists of 48 response categories. On the basis of the total classification time, the 17 Ss of the main Experimental Group fell into three reasonably demarked groups, with six Ss in the lowest and middle groups and 5 Ss in the fastest group.

Correlations of average classification times with intelligence-test scores (Parts I and II of Heim Group Test of General Intelligence) and with personality-test scores (Heron Neuroticism and Sociability Scales) were uniformly low with this small, selected group of Ss.

Six additional British Royal Navy Ratings served as Ss in the control tests.

Limitations. It is important to consider the limitations imposed by the experimental procedures. Whereas the ideal experiment would have employed a well-trained experimental group for each of the 42 experimental conditions, the same Ss here served under all conditions. The interactions resulting from the diversity of experimental conditions available to the same Ss are not known. The order of presentation attempted to combine training and performance trials, especially with respect to lists with a larger number of response categories and with a larger number of examples per category. Further, since only a single list was available for each testing condition, conditions with a large number of response categories or with a large number of examples per category may have been favored over a smaller number of possible categories or examples. On the other hand, familiar examples were deliberately selected for tests with a small number of examples per category which may have operated to favor a small number of examples per category.

It is impossible to state precisely what state of transitional performance is represented by the present results. The following notes may be pertinent: The differences between the time scores associated with the third and fourth series were small in comparison with the differences between the first two series. What started as a halting, jerky, hesitating series of responses ended as a smooth, relatively unbroken recitation.

RESULTS AND DISCUSSION

Results, experimental group. The average classification and reading times, in second per word, are summarized in Fig. 1 as a function of: the number of response categories (parameter), and the number of examples per category (abscissa). The three sections of the graph represent the results for the slow, middle, and fast Ss, respectively. The ordinate has been displaced in order to display the reading times with less confusion.

Figure 1 suggests the following qualitative findings:

(1) Classification time is substantially more sensitive to the number of response categories than to the number of examples per category. Specifically, the distance along the ordinate subtended by any one curve between 2 and 24 examples per category is considerably less than the distance subtended by a vertical section through the family of curves along a fixed number of examples per category.

(2) Classification time is increasingly sensitive to the number of examples per category as the number of response categories is increased. Specifically, the slopes of the empirical functions, as a function of the number of examples per category, increase with the number of response categories.

(3) Between 2 and 24 examples per category, classification time increases roughly with the logarithm of the number of examples per category.

(4) The results with tests with one example per category are not necessarily consistent with the results with 2 to 24 examples per category. For a small number of response categories, perhaps 2, 3, and 4 response categories, the difference between the times for the one- and two-example tests is considerably greater than that expected by linear extrapolation from the logarithmic relation from 2 to 24 examples. For a larger number of categories, especially for the middle and fast Ss, there is little difference between the results of the one- and two-example tests. The difference is considerably smaller than expected by extrapolation from 2 to 24 examples.

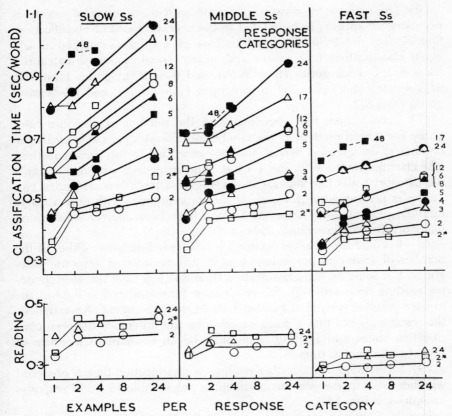

FIG. 1. Average classification-time scores (ordinate) for three groups of Ss as a joint function of the number of response categories (parameter) and as a function of the number of examples per category (abscissa). The lower section presents the corresponding average reading time scores for the same group of Ss.

(5) The increase in classification time with the number of response categories may not be continuous. For example, with the fastest Ss, the time scores with 4 and 5 response categories are nearly equal, as are the time scores with 6, 8, and 12 categories, as are the time scores with 17 and 24 categories. With the slowest Ss, however, only the time scores for 3 and 4 response categories appear to be nearly equal. That the groupings of equal time scores differ for Ss of different average proficiency suggests that the particular response categories employed were not entirely responsible for the obtained groupings.

(6) The increase in classification time with the number of examples per category appears to be related to the average speed of classification. Specifically, the following combinations of conditions yielded nearly equal classification time scores and nearly equal slopes: 2 categories (slow Ss), 3–4 categories (middle Ss), and 6–8–12 categories (fast Ss); or 3–4 categories (slow Ss), 5 categories (middle Ss), and 17–24 categories (fast Ss).

(7) Classification time increases with the number of response categories for a fixed product of the number of examples per category by the number of categories. There is only one exception to this generalization: The classification time for the 4–1 test (four categories with one example per category) was less than for the average 2–2 test (two categories, two examples per category) for each of the three groups. With only a single example per category, however, Ss may have been merely substituting one word for another word, without classification.

(8) Reading time (lower section) is relatively insensitive either to the number of examples per category or to the number of response categories. For some Ss, the classification time was less than the corresponding reading time, although this result must be considered in light of the greater practice with classification tests in the experiment. Nevertheless, the result suggests that a score based upon the difference between classification times and reading times may be an inadequate measure of "pure" classification time.

(9) Little difference in either reading or classification time is observed whether the response was monosyllabic or polysyllabic (2 vs. 2* response categories in Fig. 1).

Results, Control Group. The results of the Control Group were nearly identical with the results exhibited by the middle group of experimental Ss in Fig. 1. That is, the effects of the number of categories and the number of responses per category upon the control tests closely mirrored the effects with the experimental Ss.

A more detailed comparison between the experimental and control group 24–24C). For every single member of the experimental group (N = 17) and for every single member of the Control Group (N = 6), classification time was longer with the respective 24–24 test than upon the corresponding 24–2 test. Since Lists 24–2E and 24–24C were nearly identical, as were Lists 24–24E and 24–2C, these differences suggest that the results of Fig. 1 are not specific to the particular categories and examples initially employed. The differences in classification time are maintained despite a consistent difference in reading times for the two lists: List 24–2E or 24–24C yielded faster reading times for every S than List 24–24E or 24–2C.

Discussion. One generalization that emerges from the vast literature relating stimulus information and speed of response is that the speed of response will be sensitive to information primarily to the extent that recoding operations are required by the observer. (An excellent discussion of the effect of recoding operations and an extensive review of the effect of response uncertainty upon reaction time may be found in Fitts and Switzer, 1962; also see Leonard, 1960.) Thus, for extremely well-practiced responses, with a well-learned one to one correspondence between stimulus and response, there is little effect of stimulus information. A case in point is the reading of familiar words as shown in Fig. 1, and previously observed by many workers, e.g., Pierce and Karlin (1957), and Sumby and Pollack (1954). With a less practiced response, without a one to one correspondence between stimulus and response, the effect of the number of response alternatives may be expected to be more marked. A case in point is the classification of words as shown in Fig. 1.

The additional point of the present paper is the examination of the role of the number of examples per response category in the classification task.[1] With a small number of response categories, the number of possible examples per category appears to play only a negligible role in the classification task. Yet, with a larger and larger number of response categories, the number of examples per category plays an increasingly important role.

In terms of the initial questions about the roles of stimulus and response diversity, word classification time is clearly more sensitive to the diversity of the required response than to the diversity of the stimulus input. How far this result can be generalized beyond word classification is presently unclear because the answer may depend upon the complexity of the required coding operations for response. Empirical definition of the boundary conditions of the generalization would appear to be a desirable undertaking.

---

[1] In this respect, the author's role was entirely dictated by historical circumstances. He was privileged to attend a talk by Patrick Rabbit (1961) of the Applied Psychology Research Unit on the speed of classification of playing cards. Among many of Rabbit's interesting results was that the number of different cards was relatively unimportant when card sorting was into a small number of response classes, but not when sorting was among a large number of classes. Rabbit's result made sensible a result obtained several years ago by my colleague, William Sumby. Sumby (1958) had found little difference in the speed of sorting word-examples of birds and fishes whether the number of different birds and fishes was large or small. It remained for the author merely to extend Sumby's work to a larger number of response categories as suggested by Rabbit's results.

A detailed comparison with Rabbit's still unpublished results would be unfair to the forthcoming presentation of his excellent and extensive study. His work also includes the effect of age, irrelevant information, and several other variables. It is sufficient here to note that there is no major disagreement obtained between his results with the classification of playing cards and the present results on the classification of words.

SUMMARY

The speed of classifying words into defined superordinate categories was examined. The classification test was chosen in order to differentiate between the effects of stimulus and response diversity upon the speed of information processing. Word lists were presented which differed with respect to the number of possible response categories, e.g., colors; and with respect to the number of available examples per category, e.g., red, green, or blue.

Classification time was found to increase primarily with response diversity, i.e., with the number of possible response categories; and only secondarily with the number of available examples per category, i.e., stimulus diversity. The latter factor, however, becomes more important as the number of response categories is increased.

REFERENCES

FITTS, P. M., AND SWITZER, G. Cognitive aspects of information processing. 1. The familiarity of S–R sets and subsets. *J. exp. Psychol.*, 1962, 63, 321–329.

LEONARD, J. A. Choice reaction time and information theory. Applied Psychology Research Unit, Cambridge, England, Report 381, 1960.

PIERCE, J. R., AND KARLIN, J. E. Reading rates and the information rate of a human channel. *Bell Syst. tech. J.* 1957, 36, 497–516.

RABBIT, P. Personal communication, 1961.

SUMBY, W. Personal communication, 1958.

SUMBY, W., AND POLLACK, I. Short-time processing of information. Operational Applications Laboratory Report HFORL TR–54–6, 31 Jan. 1954.

SECTION ELEVEN

Induction

An area of research related to concept learning is that in which the task involves learning of a principle by induction from a series of positive and negative instances of the principle. The principle to be discovered is usually broader than a specific dimension or stimulus as in the typical concept task. The principle-induction kind of task has not been studied systematically until very recently, and the literature is sparse.

Smedslund's study deals with a principle, or concept, correlation which is usually learned, if learned at all, from textbooks. Detection of the presence or absence of correlation (without doing calculations) from raw data (instances) is, however, quite another matter, and, in fact, it turned out to be a very difficult task, at least for his subjects. (It is not unlikely that even subjects who had taken a course in statistics, including correlation, would do little better on the particular task Smedslund used.) The paper also shows, in its two experiments, a point of method: instances can be presented to the subject, who observes passively, or the subject may be allowed a more active role in manipulating or even creating instances (see Duncan paper). The finding that subjects seemed to deal only with the true positive cell is similar to the usual report that subjects find positive instances easier in concept learning.

In the Duncan study, an attempt was made, in the first experiment, to reduce the potentially large number of wrong hypotheses that subjects can entertain by restricting in certain ways their choice of instances. Whether or not this procedure was successful, it was clear that discovery of the principle occurred more quickly when subjects were free to create whatever instances they wished. The second experiment in this study should be compared with the experiments on processes in Section Twelve since it chiefly consisted of an analysis of subjects' responses to determine if consistent modes of behavior could be detected. It may be noted again that a problem is hard to solve or a principle is difficult to discover when the population of potential solutions to be searched is large and that this population is often made large by the great number and variety of wrong hypotheses that subjects can conjure up.

The paper by Summers and Hammond is one of a series of studies (see their references) in a systematic investigation of induction. This body of work also goes beyond other literature in the important respect of studying nonlinear as well as the usual linear correlations between cues and criterion. The article printed here includes linearity-nonlinearity as one variable and another independent variable, instructions. The instructions, in the form of information about the task, clearly reduced the population of hypotheses or responses to be searched. With a good deal of information, subjects managed to handle even the difficult nonlinear cue fairly well.

39.   The Concept of Correlation in Adults

Jan Smedslund

Abstract. *In the first of two experiments on the concept of correlation in adult subjects, the subjects' frequency estimates and inferences of relationship were studied relative to five different 2 × 2 distributions each presented in a fixed sequence. In experiment II, the subjects' spontaneous strategies in subdividing and analyzing one 2 × 2 distribution were studied in a free situation. It is concluded that adult subjects with no statistical training apparently have no adequate concept of correlation (based on the ratio of the two pairs of diagonal frequencies), and that, in so far as they reason statistically at all, they tend to depend exclusively on the frequency of ++ cases in judging relationship. The need for studies involving ordinal scale and fully quantified variates is stressed.*

Reprinted by permission of the author and of the Scandinavian Journal of Psychology from *Scandinavian Journal of Psychology*, 1963, 4, 165–173.

Two experiments will be reported, aimed at determining whether normal adults, with no training in statistics, have a concept of correlation. The concept of correlation in its elementary logical form is the ratio of the sum of two diagonal cell frequencies in a fourfold table, and the sum of the other two diagonal cell frequencies, or the total sum. It involves the categorization of events as conforming or not conforming to an hypothesis of equivalence, $A = B$, i.e. A and B are either both present or both absent. In order to combine the two diagonal frequencies $f(A \cdot B)$ and $f(A \cdot - B)$, the subject must realize that they both support the hypothesis $A = B$, although in opposite ways (reciprocals). Likewise, the other two diagonal frequencies $f(-A \cdot B)$ and $f(A \cdot -B)$ are reciprocals, and support the hypothesis AwB (exclusive disjunction), which is the negation of $A = B$. AwB asserts that either A is present and B is absent, or A is absent and B is present. In the case of negative correlations the frequency of events supporting AwB is higher than the frequency of events supporting $A = B$.

If the subject, explicitly or implicitly, reasons according to the above mentioned logical structure, and if his concept of frequency entails a ratio scale, he will be said to have an elementary concept of correlation.

The presence vs. absence of a concept of correlation is reflected in the subject's strategies of data gathering, and in his inferences from the data. There are at least three main symptoms of the presence of a concept of correlation:

1. In situations requiring a selective strategy, the subject with a concept of correlation will order the data in four categories, and count or estimate the frequency in each.

2. In situations requiring a receptive strategy, the subject with a concept of correlation will attempt to distribute his attention equally over the four categories in order to estimate their respective frequencies. Two important indices of distribution of attention are time spent observing each event, and accuracy in judging the different event frequencies. The latter measure is employed in this study.

3. The subject with a concept of correlation will base his estimates on the ratio of the sum of two diagonal cell frequencies and the sum of the two other diagonal cell frequencies. This will be reflected in accurate judgments of presence vs. absence of correlation, in accurate orderings of several materials according to degree of correlation, and, most importantly, in the subject's own explanations of his judgments. Symptom 3 is necessary and sufficient for inferring the presence of a concept of correlation, whereas the two first symptoms are necessary, to the extent that they can be reliably observed, but not sufficient.

EXPERIMENT I

In this experiment the receptive strategies of adult subjects were studied, as well as their inferences of degree of relationship. It was assumed that equal distribution of attention over the four event categories would result in approximately equal accuracy in judging the respective frequencies. Conversely, focusing on one category or ignorance of one category should result, respectively, in increased and decreased accuracy in judging the corresponding frequencies. The receptive strategy of a subject may also be reflected in his explanations and comments. Finally, the possibility of various systematic distortions in the frequency estimates was considered.

TABLE 1

THE FREQUENCY DISTRIBUTIONS FOR THE COMBINATIONS
OF PRESENCE / ABSENCE OF A AND F

	Packs									
	I		II		III		IV		V	
	−A	A	−A	A	−A	A	−A	A	−A	A
F	35	35	15	15	15	35	35	15	25	25
−F	15	15	35	35	35	15	15	35	25	25

Materials. Five packs of one hundred cards each were used, the cards measuring $3\frac{7}{16}$ in. x $2\frac{1}{8}$ in. On top of each card was typed 'Patient No.' (from 1 to 100), and the cards were ordered according to these numbers. The upper part of each card contained the word 'Symptoms' and beneath it four different capital letters, taken from the group A, B, C, D, and E (on each card one of these letters was absent). The four letters B, C, D, and E were assigned randomly to the four positions. On the cards where A was present, the one of the other four letters that should have taken its place was suppressed. In all five packs A was present on 50 cards.

The lower part of each card contained the word 'Diagnosis' and beneath it four different capital letters, taken from the group F, G, H, I, and J (on each card one of these letters was absent). The four letters G, H, I, and J were assigned to the four positions in a randomized manner. On the cards where F was present, the one of the other four letters that should have taken its place was suppressed. The frequency distributions in the five packs are shown in Table 1.

Procedure. Sixty-seven student nurses at the University of Colorado Medical Center in Denver, and 19 student nurses from Ullevål Hospital,

Oslo, served as subjects. They were seen individually in one 15-minute session. They were assigned to one of five groups differing in the pack of cards presented. Group I was given pack I, group II pack II, and so on. The Norwegian student nurses formed group V. Each subject was asked to read the following instructions:

'We are interested in learning how well beginner students of nursing are able to form an opinion about the practical usefulness of a symptom in diagnosis.

'The pack of cards represents excerpts from the files of 100 patients. The patients are numbered from 1 to 100 in the order in which they were admitted to the hospital.

'The upper part of the cards contains four letters, representing different specific symptoms of the patient. The lower part of the cards contains four letters representing specific diagnoses made by the hospital.

'You are to concentrate entirely on symptom A and diagnosis F. Your task is to look through the pack of cards once, and form an impression of the extent to which A is a useful symptom in the diagnosis of F. In other words, do you think A is a symptom one should pay attention to in trying to determine whether or not the patient is likely to be diagnosed as F?

'Take the cards in your left hand, look at them one at a time and place them face down on the table. You are not allowed to go back to cards you have already seen.

'Read through this once more, and ask questions if anything is unclear.'

After the subject had looked through the pack of cards, the following questions were asked and the answers recorded.

1. Do you think there is a connection or relationship between symptom A and diagnosis F? Tell me about it! (In group V the subjects were, in addition, asked to indicate the strength of the relationship on a seven-point scale from 'perfect' to 'zero'.)

2. How many cards do you think there are with both A and F?

3. How many cards do you think there are without A but with F?

4. How many cards do you think there are with A but without F?

5. How many cards do you think there are without A and without F?

6. Consider yourself an experienced nurse, having reviewed these hundred cases. What would you tell another nurse, with no experience in this area, about the usefulness of symptom A in relation to the diagnosis F? (This question was omitted in group V.)

The following additional task was presented to the subjects in groups III and IV:

'Below are shown the number of the various combinations of presence and absence of A and F in eight other packs of cards.

'Your task is to look at the numbers for each pack and decide whether A and F are related (correlated) in this pack. A relationship may exist, although it may not be perfectly reliable.

'The first row shows the number of cards with the various combinations in Pack I. First, the number of cards with both A and F, then the number with A but not F, then the number with F but not A, and finally the number of cards with neither A nor F.'

	Both A and F	Only A	Only F	Neither of them
Pack 1	50	0	0	50
Pack 2	35	15	35	15
Pack 3	0	50	50	0
Pack 4	25	25	25	25
Pack 5	15	35	35	15
Pack 6	15	35	15	35
Pack 7	50	0	50	0
Pack 8	35	15	15	35

Finally, the subjects in group V were given the following written instructions:

'a to g below show the number of cards with the different combinations of presence and absence of A and F in seven other packs. Rank the seven materials according to the degree of relationship between A and F. Write the letter for the material with the strongest relationship first, then the letter for the material with the second strongest relationship, and so on. If you think two relationships have the same strength, then write them side by side.'

Example of a ranking (with other letters):

j.   (strongest)
i.m. (equally strong)
l.
h.o. (equally strong)
p.   (weakest)

Number of cards with:

	A and F	A but not F	F but not A	Neither A nor F
a.	40	4	16	40
b.	45	5	35	15
c.	70	30	0	0
d.	30	2	33	35
e.	55	15	30	0
f.	50	10	0	40
g.	60	20	5	15

At the end of the session the subjects in group V were also asked about their background with respect to the concept of correlation, and were

TABLE 2

Real Values (R), Significance of Tendency (T) to Overestimate
(+) or Underestimate (−), and accuracy (σ^2 of Real Minus
Estimated Values), for the Cell Frequencies in the Five Groups

Significance of over- and underestimations computed by means of the sign test. * and
** indicate significance at the 0.05 and 0.01 levels, respectively.

							Groups								
	I			II			III			IV			V		
	R	T	σ^2	R	T	σ^2	R	T	σ^2	R	T	σ^2	R	T	σ^2
AF	35	+	216.3	15	±	115.4	35	−*	230.1	15	−	158.2	25	+	233.7
A−F	15	+**	187.1	35	−	214.3	15	+**	232.3	35	−	103.0	25	−	354.5
−AF	35	−*	284.6	15	+	103.9	15	+*	478.0	35	−*	199.4	25	+	332.5
−A−F	15	−	100.0	35	−	303.1	35	−	276.1	15	+**	345.1	25	−	166.6

asked to describe it in terms of one of the following alternatives.
(1) Course(s) in statistics, where the concept of correlation was treated.
(2) Read book(s) in statistics, where the concept of correlation was
treated. (3) Read chapters or passages in other books, where the concept
of correlation was treated. (4) Have encountered the concept, but have
never seen it defined. (5) Have never heard the word correlation before.

Results. The data on tendencies to over- and underestimate cell frequencies and on the accuracy of estimates in the five groups are presented in Table 2. The accuracy scores show no unambiguous relationship
with type of event category. There are several statistically significant
tendencies to over- or underestimate frequencies, but they are not clearly
linked with type of event category.

The judgments and explanations of the subjects may be roughly classified into the following categories:

Four or five of the subjects gave formulations which rather clearly expressed a *particularistic* concept of relationship, and several others probably also had this type of concept. Examples: 'In most cases there was
no connection'; 'When neither symptom nor diagnosis was present, no
relationship'; 'No relation in most of the cases.' These subjects appeared
to think that a relationship was present in the AF cases, and absent in the
others.

Closely related to the particularistic concept, but more statistical, is
the notion that the strength of the relationship depends simply on f(AF).
More than half of the subjects gave formulations clearly expressing this
point of view. Examples: 'Counted after card 27 and found about 11 with
both A and F. Think it is a fairly strong relation'; 'To a slight extent;
I counted 14 out of 100 (AF's)'; 'There seems to be about ⅓ with A and
F'; 'No, not too many AF's.' Another concept, frequently hard to distinguish from the preceding, is that amount of relationship is the percentage or proportion of times F appears with A, or A with F. Examples:

'F has turned up about 24 per cent of the time (A was given)'; 'A accompanies F a third of the time, the rest of the time it isn't there'; 'A lot of times A is there but F isn't.' This category did not occur very frequently.

In addition to these categories of reasoning, there were indications of certain intellectual difficulties in coping with the task. Sometimes the subjects referred to the relationship as a causal one. 'I don't think there could be a causal relationship; there might be some other letter that with A could cause F, but not a direct relationship.' There were complaints about the task, like 'It's kind of abstract', and attempts to make it more concrete: 'I'll say symptom A is something that occurs in many illnesses, such as headache. Since it did occur sometimes, I think its an important factor for diagnosis.'

Not a single subject gave any indication of having understood that the degree of relationship is determined by the ratio of the sum of the AF's and −A−F's and the sum of the −AF's and the A−F's.

Groups III and IV were asked to judge whether or not there was a relationship between A and F in eight numerically presented distributions. The results are given in Table 3.

TABLE 3

NUMBER OF SUBJECTS IN GROUPS III AND IV WHO THOUGHT
A RELATIONSHIP WAS PRESENT FOR EACH OF EIGHT NUMERICALLY
PRESENTED DISTRIBUTIONS ($N = 35$)

Distributions				Number of subjects
AF	A−F	−AF	−A−F	
50	0	0	50	34
35	15	35	15	28
0	50	50	0	4
25	25	25	25	21
15	35	35	15	16
15	35	15	35	14
50	0	50	0	31
35	15	15	35	34

The numbers in Table 3 have a certain ambiguity, since the individual subjects apparently set different limits to when a relationship was present. Some subjects apparently thought there was a relationship when $f(AF) > 0$, others when $f(AF)$ was ≥ 0.25, and still others when $f(AF)$ was ≥ 0.50. Finally, a few subjects seemed to think there was a relationship when $f(AF) > f(A - F)$. In spite of this ambiguity there is a very high correlation in Table 3 between $f(AF)$ and the number of subjects who think there is a relationship.

The subjects in group V judged the strength of the relationship between A and F in the given pack of cards. The results are presented in Table 4,

TABLE 4

The Distribution of Estimates of Strength of Relationship
in Deck V (N = 19)

Perfect	0	Weak	3
Very strong	0	Very weak	2
Strong	3	Zero	1
Medium	10		

indicating that the subjects generally had no understanding of the complete lack of relationship between A and F in pack 5. The single subject who thought there was no relationship, based this judgment on an estimated distribution of 50 AF, 20 A − F, 25 − AF, and 5 − A − F, but gave no intelligible explanation.

Finally, the subjects in group V were asked to rank-order seven numerical distributions, constructed in such a way that the rank orders corresponding to a genuine correlation concept, a concept based on $f(AF)$, and a concept based on $p(F/A)$ would be maximally different. The results turned out quite negative. The 19 subjects ranked the distributions in 19 different ways with no apparent clustering around common types. Only one subject had a rank order corresponding to a concept of relationship based on $f(AF)$, and no subject had a rank order corresponding to a genuine correlation concept or to a concept based on $p(F/A)$. Judging from the subjects' general behavior and comments, it appeared that the ranking procedure, in spite of repeated explanations and simplifications, exceeded their intellectual capacity. As to their previous knowledge of the concept of correlation, the results showed that ten subjects had never heard of the concept, six of them had encountered the word, but never had it explained, and only three had read chapters or passages in books containing a treatment of the concept. However, these three subjects did not perform better than the others.

Experiment II

In experiment I the subjects were given the essentially passive role of observing the cards once in a fixed order, and the arrangement of letters on the cards made it fairly exacting to register the presence and absence of A and F. These conditions put a heavy strain on the information processing and information storing capacity of the subjects, and may have prevented a maximal unfolding of their actual reasoning power.

Experiment II was intended to create optimal conditions for the occurrence of an understanding of the concept of correlation. The subjects were left free to arrange and sort the cards in any way they wanted to, they were allowed to look at them an unlimited number of times, and they were given pencil and paper to make notes. Also, the cards were simplified to contain only +A or −A and +F or −F.

Procedure. A pack of one hundred cards was used. On the upper part of each card was written in black ink either +A or −A, on the lower part either +F or −F. There were 37 cards with +A+F, 33 with −A+F, 17 with +A−F, and 13 with −A−F.

Twenty-eight nurses at Ullevål Hospital, Oslo, participated in one 10-minute session each. The following written instructions were presented:

'We are interested in learning how well students of nursing are able to form an opinion about the practical usefulness of a symptom in diagnosis.

'The pack of cards represents excerpts from the files of 100 patients. The upper part of the cards contains either a +A or a −A. +A means that the patient had symptom A, and −A means that the patient did not have symptom A. The lower part of the cards contains either a +F or a −F. +F means that the illness F was found, and −F means that the illness F was not found.

'Your task is to find out whether there is a relationship (connection) between the symptom A and the illness F. You may study and order the material in any way you wish, and you may make notes. Try to work as fast as possible. Read the instructions once more, and ask questions if anything is not clear.'

The experimenter recorded the subject's spontaneous behavior and his conclusions. If the subject did not spontaneously explain his conclusions, the experimenter asked questions of the type 'How do you know that?', 'How did you arrive at that?'

Results. The data may be divided into spontaneous procedure, conclusion, and justification. Despite repetitions, attempts at clarification, and concrete exemplification, the subjects generally found it hard to understand the task, and more than one third of them complained that they did not understand. Seventeen of the 28 subjects went through the material placing the cards together in one pile. Some of them asked whether one was supposed to sort the cards, but being told they were free to do anything they wished, they nevertheless placed the cards in one pile. Three subjects did not even look through the entire material, and one subject sorted the +A+F's in one pile, and the rest in another. Five subjects sorted the cards in four categories, one subject sorted them in five (two piles of −A−F's), and one sorted them in seven apparently unsystematic piles. No subject used the paper and pencil offered.

Twenty-four subjects thought there was a relationship between A and F, two subjects thought there was no relationship (correct), and two subjects gave up and did not answer this question.

The explanations may be roughly categorized according to whether they referred to frequencies or not. In the former group (18 subjects) fourteen said that there was a relationship because the number of +A+F's was the largest or was large. One subject said there was a relationship because there were more +F's than −A's, and another subject said there was no relationship because the −A+F's were the most frequent cards. Two subjects referred both to the +A+F and the −A−F categories. This may indicate a dawning understanding of correlation, but not very developed, since these two subjects sorted in respectively one and seven piles, and both were confident that there was a substantial relationship between A and F.

The ten subjects who did not refer to frequencies, either gave up without answering (three), said they felt it 'intuitively' (two), or gave vague explanations like 'Every symptom must indicate an illness'; 'If the symptom is present, the illness will come'; 'If the illness was found, there had to be symptoms present.' There were also a few particularistic statements like 'There is no relationship, because when one finds "+" on one and "−" on the other, there can be no relationship.'

DISCUSSION

The data on the subjects' inferences, and on their selective strategies, all point to an absence of correlational reasoning. The complex data on frequency estimates offer no clear evidence concerning the subjects' receptive strategies. The lack of a clear relationship between the accuracy of frequency estimates and event category either means that accuracy is not, in this context, a good measure of attention distribution, or that no simple theory of attention distribution is adequate. However, the existence of pronounced variations and accuracy and in tendency to over- or underestimate means that there may exist important regularities to be discovered by more extensive and refined experimentation.

The apparent main finding of these experiments, then, is that normal adults with no training in statistics do not have a cognitive structure isomorphic with the concept of correlation. Their strategies and inferences typically reveal a particularistic, non-statistical approach, or an exclusive dependence on the frequency of + + instances.

This conclusion is supported by Wason's (1960) finding that very few psychology undergraduates spontaneously searched for negative evidence in a simple conceptual task. If an hypothesis repeatedly gave positive results, they tended to accept it without investigating whether alternative hypotheses would lead to negative results. This corresponds directly to the lack of understanding of the relevance of the −A−F cases in the present experiments. However, it should be noted that the absence of adequate reasoning may occur primarily when the situation is fairly complex. By drastically lowering the frequencies involved, by making the cases directly and simultaneously observable, and by selecting one's subjects with respect to training and intellectual capacity, it may be possible to elicit somewhat more frequent symptoms of an understanding of correlation. This is exemplified by a study of Inhelder & Piaget (1958). They report fairly frequent occurrences of the correlation concept in 14- to 15-year-old subjects, in very simple situations with small numbers of simultaneously visible faces with brown vs. fair hair, and brown vs. blue eyes.

The findings may be interpreted relative to Piaget & Inhelder's (1951) theory of the development of the concepts of chance and probability in children. According to these authors, children before 7–8 years have no concepts of chance and probability, since they have not yet differentiated the ideas of necessity and possibility. In the absence of logical structure, there are no compelling deductions of what has to be or cannot be the case, and consequently no discovery of the non-necessary, i.e. merely possible. In the widest connotation of the word chance, it is the realm of things whose occurrence is neither implied by, nor excluded by one's assumptions. From around 7–8 years the development of concrete reasoning introduces necessity, and thereby the complementary notions of possibility and chance. However, reasoning concerning the latter requires the manipulation of possibilities in a combinatorial system (formal reasoning), and only develops after 11–12 years. Probability estimates presuppose an ability to determine the structure of possibilities entailed by the given situation, and this lies outside the scope of concrete reasoning, which functions only on the basis of actually observed events. For example, eight-year-old children may correctly estimate that a frequency of 3 out of 4 entails a higher probability than 2 out of 4, but may then proceed to argue that 3 out of 6 is more probable than 2 out of 3, thus revealing that their estimates are based on absolute rather than relative frequencies. The concept of correlation represents a rather late and complex development of formal reasoning.

The present data lead to the following interpretation of the Piaget-Inhelder theory: The analyses in this theory are seen as referring to the *optimal performance* at each developmental stage. Thus, a child capable of concrete reasoning in some situations may be functioning at a prelogical level in others, but will never reason at a formal level. An adult who is able to apply correlational reasoning in a highly simplified situation may regress to a particularistic or to an absolute frequency approach in many everyday life situations. Briefly, it is assumed that the developmental stages are descriptive of different levels of cognitive functioning, and that adults may, at various times, function at any of these levels, although under optimal conditions they are capable of formal, hypothetico-deductive reasoning. The empirical problem in each case is to determine under what range of conditions a given person will function at a given level. The present data support the hypothesis that this range is very restricted, or even non-existent, in most adults as far as the concept of correlation is concerned.

There are two important objections to this conclusion. One of them concerns the fact that nurses are thoroughly trained to adopt a strictly deterministic approach to symptoms and illnesses. Their comments frequently appear to reflect a reluctance to regard chance as an element in this connection. Some of them explicitly argue that one A—F and/or one —AF is enough to disprove the hypothesis of a one-to-one causal connection, and one or two even speculate about possible multiple causes. It is theoretically possible that this refusal to reason statistically reflects a preference rather than an incapacity. However, this argument is weakened by the fact that none of those who *did* accept a statistical approach seemed to have a concept of correlation.

Another object to the conclusion that most adults completely lack a concept of correlation, stems from the restriction of the reported experiments to dichotomous variates. Although dichotomous presence/absence variation is elementary from a logical point of view, it may not be so psychologically. Indeed, the history of correlational analysis, as well as the customary textbook introductions of correlation by means of a scattergram, suggest that ordinal scale or fully quantified variates may yield the easiest access to an understanding of the concept. No data are available to settle this important question.

REFERENCES

INHELDER, B. & PIAGET, J. (1958). *The growth of logical thinking from childhood to adolescence.* New York: Basic Books.

PIAGET, J. & INHELDER, B. (1951). *La genèse de l'idée de hasard chez l'enfant.* Paris: Presses Univ. France.

WASON, P. C. (1960). On the failure to eliminate hypotheses in a conceptual task. *Quart. J. exp. Psychol.,* 12, 129–140.

40. Induction of a Principle

Carl P. Duncan

Abstract. *Two experiments are reported in which student subjects attempted to discover a principle obtaining among pairs of numbers and letters. In the first experiment, subjects were more successful when they were free to select whatever number-letter pairs they wished than if they were restricted in whole or in part to pairs specified by the experimenter. In the second experiment, subjects who did discover the principle were compared to those who did not. Successful subjects were shown to be slightly more systematic in their approach to the task, to work at a faster pace, to write down more positive instances, and to have a much stronger tendency to vary only one variable of the task at a time.*

Wason (1960) reported a study in which subjects tried to discover a principle applying to instances each of which consisted of three numbers. He discovered that subjects mostly showed enumerative rather than eliminative induction, i.e. they made little use of instances that would have enabled them to eliminate wrong hypotheses. Wetherick (1962) found that by modifying Wason's procedure to certain ways, enumerative behaviour was reduced and the subject's chance of discovering the principle was increased. Elimination of hypotheses remained infrequent.

In the Wason study, the subject was free to write down, for each instance, any three numbers he wished, i.e. his choice of instances was not restricted in any way. This may account in part for the behaviour Wason observed. In the first experiment to be reported here, the subject is restricted, in various degrees, in his choice of instances, to determine whether the principle is discovered more (or less) readily under such restriction.

EXPERIMENT I

Task. The task consisted of pairing the numbers 1–8 with the 10 letters A–J. The principle was that any of the four odd numbers could be paired with any of the last five letters (F–J), and any of the even numbers could be paired with any of the first five letters (A–E). Thus, of

Reprinted by permission of the Quarterly Journal of Experimental Psychology from *The Quarterly Journal of Experimental Psychology*, 1964, *16*, 373–377.

the 80 possible number-letter pairs, 40 were instances of the principle, the other 40 were not.

The task was presented on a sheet of paper at the top left of which the eight numbers were dittoed in normal order in a horizontal row. At the top right were the 10 letters in a row in normal order. The rest of the sheet contained 80 blanks, numbered consecutively from 1–80, in four columns. There were two forms of this sheet. In one, the blanks contained neither numbers or letters. In the other, each blank already had printed in it one of the eight numbers. Each number appeared once in each block of eight blanks. The order of assignment of numbers to blanks was random within each block.

Conditions. There were four conditions, representing different degrees or kinds of restriction in the subject's choice of numbers and letters to create pairs. (A pair always consisted of a number followed by a letter.) A different group of subjects worked under each condition. In Group U (unrestricted), the subject, using the sheet with nothing in the blanks, chose both the number and the letter to write in each blank. In Group RL (restricted letters), the subject, using the same sheet as Group U, chose numbers to write in the blanks, but the experimenter told the subject what letter to write in after each number. In Group RN (restricted numbers), the subject used the data sheet with numbers already entered in the blanks, but was free to choose letters. In Group RNL (restricted numbers and letters), the subject also used the sheet with the numbers in blanks, and the experimenter told the subject what letter to write after each number.

Subjects. The subjects were students from classes in introductory psychology. They were required to serve in experiments as part of the course work. Students were assigned to the four conditions in turn. There were 50 subjects in each of the four groups.

Procedure. The experimenter gave each subject a pencil and the sheet needed for the condition to which the subject had been assigned. Then the experimenter pointed to the numbers and letters at the top of the sheet and said, "See these numbers and letters. They have been paired according to a certain principle. I want you to try to discover what that principle is. This is the way we will do it." At this point, the experimenter inserted instructions (see below) appropriate for each group. Then the experimenter concluded, "As soon as you have any idea as to what the principle is, tell me. If you are wrong, or only partly right, I will tell you so, and we will continue with pairs until you want to make another guess as to what the principle is. Try to discover the principle as soon as possible. As soon as you discover the principle, the experiment is finished."

In Group U, the subject was told to write any number and any letter in a blank and to state the number and letter aloud. Then the experimenter would tell him whether the pair thus created was or was not an instance of the principle. In all groups, the subject was told to make a check mark after pairs that were instances of the principle, to help them remember.

In Group RL, the subject was told to write any number in a blank, and state the number aloud. Then the experimenter told the subject what letter to write after the number, and when the subject had done so, told the subject whether the pair was an instance of the principle. The experimenter had a key which specified what letter to give the subject for every pair, and whether the pair was or was not to be an instance of the principle. Whether a pair was to be a correct instance or not had been decided by flipping a coin, with the restriction that within a block of 40 pairs, half would be correct, half incorrect. In so far as possible, the experimenter used each letter once, in giving letters to the subject, within each block of 10 pairs.

In Group RN, the experimenter pointed out to the subject that a number, selected from those listed at the top of the sheet, had already been printed in each blank. The subject was told to write any of the letters after the number, and state both number and letter aloud. Then the experimenter told the subject if the pair was an instance of the principle.

In Group RNL, the experimenter also pointed out to the subject that there was a number in each blank, and told the subject to say the number aloud. Then the experimenter told the subject what letter to put after the number, and when the subject had done so, told the subject if the pair was an instance of the principle. The key used for giving letters to the subject, and determining whether each pair was to be a correct instance or not, was the same as that for Group RL.

The subject was allowed to work at his own pace. He could guess at the principle at any time and as often as he wished. He had to state the principle completely to be considered correct. Statement of the particular numbers and letters that could be paired, without, e.g., using phrases such as "odd numbers," was allowed. If the subject had not stated the principle correctly at the end of 25 min. of work, he was stopped and was recorded as a nonsolver.

RESULTS AND DISCUSSION

Two measures reflecting attainment of the principle are shown in Table I. One is the number of solvers, those subjects in each group that stated the principle correctly. The other is the median number of pairs (of numbers and letters) to solution (scores for nonsolvers were considered to be infinity). The results are quite similar with both measures. Numerically, the best performance is by the least restricted group (U), next best

TABLE I

NUMBER OF SUBJECTS WHO DISCOVERED THE PRINCIPLE AND MEDIAN
NUMBER OF PAIRS TO SOLUTION IN EXPERIMENT I

Group	N	Solvers	Median pairs
U	50	43	39.5
RL	50	26	92.0
RN	50	27	82.0
RNL	50	37	60.0

by the most restricted group (RNL). Poorest, and essentially equivalent, performance was by the two partially restricted groups (RL and RN).

Statistical analysis reveals the following: In number of solvers, Group U was significantly different from Group RL ($\chi^2 = 11.97$, $p < 0.001$, 1 $d.f.$), and from Group RN ($\chi^2 = 10.71$, $p < 0.01$), though not from group RNL ($\chi^2 = 1.56$). Group RNL had significantly more solvers than Group RL ($\chi^2 = 4.29$, $p < 0.05$). Other comparisons were not significant.

Each group was compared to every other group by a median test on median pairs to solution. Group U differed significantly from Groups RL ($\chi^2 = 10.24$, $p < 0.01$), RN ($\chi^2 = 12.96$, $p < 0.01$), and RNL ($\chi^2 = 9.00$, $p < 0.05$). No other comparison was significant.

Examination of the number of incorrect (including partly correct) attempts to state the principle revealed no clear differences among the four conditions. The mean number of such attempts was 1.3, 0.7, 1.3, and 1.3 for Group U, RL, RN, and RNL, respectively. These means are based on all 50 subjects (solvers and nonsolvers) in each group. As might be expected, nonsolvers made somewhat more incorrect guesses (overall mean = 1.5) than solvers (mean = 1.0), since all guesses of nonsolvers were incorrect. However, it is clear that nonsolvers did not fail simply because they hesitated to make overt guesses and so failed to get information.

The results of Experiment I seem fairly clear. More subjects induced the principle, and in fewer pairs, when they were left free to create any pairs they wished. When a subject is unrestricted, he has the advantage that he can work on any hypothesis he chooses to entertain, and can switch at any time from one hypothesis to another. On the other hand, subjects in the unrestricted condition can get wrong sets or inadequate methods, such as working with too few of the numbers and letters, and there is no guidance, from external sources, away from such self-defeating response tendencies. It had originally been thought that a degree of control over the subject's choices, as exemplified by the various restricted conditions, would be advantageous since the subject would be prevented, to some extent, from persisting too long on wrong hypotheses. The results merely suggest that extreme restriction (as in Group RNL where the subject had no choices to make), though inferior to the unrestricted condition, may have had some advantage over partial restriction (Groups RL and RN).

In the unrestricted condition, the percentages of correct and incorrect pairs may deviate considerably from the 50:50 split imposed upon the restricted conditions. As will be shown in Experiment II below, the number of correct pairs increases as subjects begin to discover the principle. It is known that subjects tend to prefer positive to negative instances (Hovland and Weiss, 1953), and to exhibit enumerative instead of eliminative behaviour (Wason, 1960). Thus, the restricted conditions force the subject to deal with more incorrect instances than he would probably like, and prevent him from achieving the "success" of a long string of positive instances.

Experiment II

Examination of the pairs listed by Group U in Experiment I showed that a portion of the subjects apparently used some systematic approach in their selections of numbers and letters (such as pairing every letter with one number before changing to another number), while other subjects appeared to be quite unsystematic. Also, the fact that the numbers and letters were printed on the subject's sheet in normal order suggested, to certain subjects, various systems to be tried out. Experiment II is in part an attempt to learn something more about the role of systematic vs. unsystematic approaches in inducing a principle. In addition, certain analyses of the instances will be reported for what they may reveal about the induction process.

Method

The task, instruction, and procedure were the same as for Group U in Experiment I, with the following exceptions. There were three forms of the sheet given to the subject, on which he wrote number-letter pairs. One form was the same as in Experiment I; the numbers and letters were listed in horizontal rows at the top of the sheet in normal order. For the other two forms of the sheet, both numbers and letters were also listed in rows, but in random orders, with a different random order for each sheet. The orders were: 3 8 6 5 2 7 1 4 with D F C A E H B J G I, and 6 1 8 3 7 5 4 2 with H E G D J C I A F B. The three sheets were handed to the subjects in turn so one-third of the subjects was run with each sheet.

Any subject who had not discovered the principle in 20 min. (vs. 25 min. in Experiment I) was recorded as a nonsolver. At the end of the experiment, but while the subject still had his sheet in front of him, the experimenter questioned every subject, solver or nonsolver, as follows: The experimenter said, "Now would you go back to the first few pairs you wrote down (the experimenter pointed toward the first two or three pairs). I would like to ask you why you selected the pairs you did when you first started. Your first pair was (number and letter were stated). Try to remember what you were thinking about. What I'm trying to find out is, did you have any plan, any reason, no matter how vague, for choosing the first few pairs you did." The experimenter took notes on what the subject said.

The subjects were 135 students from introductory psychology classes.

RESULTS

There were 75 subjects who discovered the principle. The remaining 60 subjects were nonsolvers. The analyses to be reported chiefly involve comparisons of these two groups, solvers vs. nonsolvers. It may be noted in passing that the task was easier when the numbers and letters were listed in normal order; 35 of the 45 subjects with the normal-order sheet solved, whereas 40 of the 90 subjects with random-order sheets solved.

In the postexperimental inquiry, 43 solvers and 21 nonsolvers reported that they had had some plan or system in mind when they began to write down pairs. Of those subjects who said they had had no system, 32 were solvers, 39 were nonsolvers. Thus, although the differences are not great, the two largest frequencies are systematic solvers and unsystematic nonsolvers. In a test of independence of the four categories, $\chi^2 = 5.81$, $p < 0.05$, 1 $d.f.$

Incorrect attempts to state the principle were recorded for both solvers and nonsolvers. The mean for solvers was 1.13; for nonsolvers, the mean was 1.28. The difference is not significant. Furthermore, the frequencies are so low (by far the most frequent number was 1) that no relationships could be found between incorrect attempts and the measures reported below.

Differences between solvers and nonsolvers show up in certain measures based on the pairs (of numbers and letters) the subjects wrote. Even though each solver worked only until he discovered the principle, while all nonsolvers kept working for 20 min., solvers wrote a mean of 38.0 pairs, while for nonsolvers the mean was only 31.6 pairs. The difference between the means yields $t = 1.89$. If one nonsolver with a score of 137 pairs is excluded, the nonsolvers' mean becomes 29.8, and the t becomes 2.81.

The proportion of the pairs that were correct, were instances of the principle, was computed for each subject. The mean proportion for the solvers was 0.62, for nonsolvers the mean was 0.56. These means differ significantly; $t = 3.00$.

A final measure expresses subjects' tendency to vary only one factor at a time. As the subject writes down a pair, he can use both a different number and a different letter from the immediately preceding pair ("double change"), or he can vary only one of these elements by continuing to use the same number or letter he used in the preceding pair. For each subject the proportion of changes over successive pairs that were double changes was determined. The mean proportion was 0.45 for solvers, 0.61 for nonsolvers. The difference was highly significant; $t = 5.03$.

DISCUSSION

The differences found, in Experiment II, between those subjects who did, and those who did not, discover the principle are, of course, only associated with solving or not solving; causal status is not implied. With this limitation, the results can be examined for what information they provide about the task of inducing a principle from positive and negative instances.

It is clear that an approach that has some plan or system (if we can take the subject's word as to whether or not he had a plan) is not a great deal more successful than the reported absence of a systematic approach. The difference between solvers and nonsolvers on this characteristic was not great. One problem is that some plans actually make it more difficult for the subject to discover the principle, especially if the subject persists on a wrong hypothesis.

The fact that solvers wrote somewhat more pairs in less time than did nonsolvers shows, of course, that solvers' rate of overt response was faster. Perhaps nonsolvers spent too much time thinking instead of writing down pairs (although they did not make fewer attempts to state the principle). It has recently been argued (Duncan, 1963) that taking time to stop and think is worthwhile for some aspects of problem solving, but not for all.

A higher proportion of the number-letter pairs written by solvers were positive instances of the principle than was the case for nonsolvers. But this difference might have occurred simply because solvers find out, at some point, which pairs are positive instances. However, examination of the pairs at various points in practice showed that solvers had a slightly higher proportion of positive instances than did nonsolvers throughout the entire session. In their last few pairs, just before they stopped and announced the principle, solvers showed a sharp increase in proportion of positive instances (mean of 0.79 in the last tenth of instances), thus apparently exhibiting enumerative behaviour as described by Wason (1960).

Perhaps the most revealing difference between solvers and nonsolvers was in the "double change" measure. There was a clear difference in favour of solvers in tendency to hold one element, number or letter, constant in successive pairs, and vary only the other element. Examination of the pairs at various stages revealed that early in practice, both solvers and nonsolvers were showing mean proportions of double changes of approximately 0.60–0.65. As their over-all mean (0.61) shows, nonsolvers remained at about this level throughout the session. But in solvers, the proportion dropped rapidly from this high until in the last half of the session solvers were averaging only about 0.36 double changes. Thus, in their attempts to induce a simple law, solvers learned to use, and made much more use of, the advantageous device of varying only one thing at a time.

A final point seems worth noting. The present task, dealing with numbers and letters, permits subjects to entertain many wrong hypotheses. Despite the fact that one aspect of the subject's behaviour is overt (the pairs he writes down), it is clear, from the subject's incorrect attempts to state the principle, that there is very little control over his thinking. He is free to consider, implicitly, an almost infinite variety of ways that numbers and letters might be paired. This large population of wrong hypotheses seems to be the chief reason many subjects do not discover the principle.

REFERENCES

DUNCAN, C. P. (1963). Effect of instructions and of information on problem solving. *J. exp. Psychol.*, 65, 321–7.

HOVLAND, C. I., and WEISS, W. (1953). Transmission of information concerning concepts through positive and negative instances. *J. exp. Psychol.*, 45, 175–82.

WASON, P. C. (1960). On the failure to eliminate hypothesis in a conceptual task. *Quart. J. exp. Psychol.*, 12, 129–40.

WETHERICK, N. E. (1962). Eliminative and enumerative behaviour in a conceptual task. *Quart. J. exp. Psychol.*, 14, 246–9.

41. Inference Behavior in Multiple-Cue Tasks Involving Both Linear and Nonlinear Relations

David A. Summers and Kenneth R. Hammond

The purpose of this experiment was to study multiple-cue probability learning in tasks involving nonlinear as well as linear cue-criterion relations. The experiment has relevance for studies of concept formation as well.

Multiple-cue probability learning. Fundamental to Brunswik's (1956) probabilistic functionalism is the concept that the organism responds to and integrates the data afforded by probabilistic cues to a distal, or criterion, variable. Recent investigations of performance in multiple-cue probability tasks are confirmatory; they have demonstrated that Ss not only learn to make inferences from multiple cues (Smedslund, 1955; Summers, 1962; Todd & Hammond, 1965; Uhl, 1963), but that in such tasks Ss can achieve optimal cue ranking and approach the optimal least-squares prediction strategy (Peterson, Hammond, & Summers, 1965b). It is important to note, however, that in certain of these studies (Summers, 1962; Uhl, 1963), the cue-criterion variance was completely determined by linear relations ($R^2 = 1$), whereas in others (Smedslund, 1955; Todd & Hammond, 1964; Peterson, Hammond, & Summers, 1965a, 1965b), the cue-criterion variance was not completely determined ($R^2 < 1$); the residual variance in the latter studies being attributable to random error.

The empirical investigation of Ss' performance in tasks in which the residual variance $(1 - R^2)$ is attributable to systematic nonlinear (rather than random) cue-criterion relations has not yet been carried out, although there have been descriptive studies (Hammond, Hursch, & Todd, 1964; Hoffman, 1960) as well as methodological ones (Hammond & Summers, 1965; Hursch, Hammond, & Hursch, 1964). The present study is concerned with the experimental analysis of (*a*) Ss' inductive achievement and (*b*) Ss' cue dependence in tasks where the residual variance $(1 - R^2)$ is *systematic* rather than *random*. Therefore, both linear and nonlinear cue utilization are necessary if S is to achieve perfect inferential accuracy.

The effects of task properties (linear vs. nonlinear task variance) upon inductive achievement and cue dependence have yet to be investigated. Formal analysis (Hursch et al., 1964) indicates that tasks which contain both linear and systematic nonlinear cue-criterion relations permit vary-

Reprinted by permission of the authors and the American Psychological Association from *Journal of Experimental Psychology*, 1966, *71*, 751–757.

ing degrees of inferential accuracy through the utilization of (or dependence upon) either or both relations. If S utilizes both task relations, and if all criterion variance is accounted for by systematic linear and nonlinear cue-criterion relations, then S can achieve perfect predictive accuracy. If S's predictions are determined by dependence upon only linear task relations, the accuracy correlation (i.e., the correlation between S's responses and the criterion values) can be as large as the task multiple R; the accuracy correlation yielded by dependence upon only nonlinear task relations can be as large as $\sqrt{1 - R^2}$. Thus, if task linearity is *high* (R^2 approaches unity), optimal dependence upon only linear task relations will result in a high, though less than perfect accuracy correlation. Conversely, if task linearity is *low* (R^2 approaches zero), optimal dependence upon only nonlinear task relations will likewise result in a high, though less than perfect, accuracy correlation. A task defined by *equal portions* of linear and nonlinear criterion variance requires utilization of both for high accuracy; dependence upon either linear or nonlinear relations alone provides a maximum accuracy correlation of only .71 in this situation. (See Hursch et al., 1964, for a mathematical analysis of the limits of achievement under various task conditions.)

While formal analyses indicate the importance of task *properties,* empirical studies have shown the relevance of task *instructions* to S's performance in multiple-cue tasks. Thus, Peterson et al., (1965b) report that when Ss were instructed that the task was linear and cue validities were stationary, S's accuracy reached asymptote within 100 trials; in addition, if Ss are instructed that random error prevents perfect prediction, Ss approximate the optimal linear "maximizing" strategy. Similarly, when Ss received feedback about task properties (Todd and Hammond, 1965), performance exceeded that observed under conditions of traditional outcome feedback. Using a single task involving both linear and nonlinear relations, Hammond & Summers (1965) found that when Ss were instructed that linear and nonlinear relations were present, and were further instructed which cue was associated with each relation, achievement exceeded that observed for Ss who were provided less information. Moreover, both cues were utilized only under maximum information conditions; other conditions produced mainly single, linear cue dependence. It remains to be shown, however, that instructions relevant to task properties are uniformly effective over different conditions of linear and nonlinear task variance.

Concept formation. There are strong similarities between the task presented to Ss in this experiment and tasks used in the traditional concept-formation (or concept-identification) situation. In both, Ss were presented with a series of multidimensional stimulus patterns, each of which requires some inferential or predictive response indicating its value (or category), and from which S must infer a general rule or principle for responding. Concept-identification studies have focused on the effect of number of relevant cues (Walker & Bourne, 1961), memory load (Bourne, Goldstein, & Link, 1964), etc., but aside from "mis-information" studies (Bourne, 1963; Pishkin, 1960) they have been restricted to tasks in which the correlation between cue and criterion is zero for irrelevant cues and 1.00 for relevant cue(s). In the effort to meet Brunswik's criticism that the confinement of task properties to these conditions restricts the inductive generality of the findings, the present study includes both indeterminate and determinate properties. Thus, the relation between each cue and the criterion variable is less than perfect (as in the multiple-cue probability paradigm), but when the cues are combined according to the appropriate rule the relation between both cues and the criterion is perfect (as in the concept-formation paradigm).

The present study is thus concerned with the effects of different levels of linear and nonlinear task variance and different task instructions upon (a) S's inductive achievement, and (b) S's cue dependence in a task which requires the utilization of both linear and nonlinear cue-criterion relations if perfect accuracy is to be achieved.

METHOD

Design and subjects. The Ss were studied under three conditions of task linearity (high, moderate, and low) and three conditions of task instructions with repeated measurements over five blocks of trials, yielding a $3 \times 3 \times 5$ factorial design. Ninety University of Colorado undergraduates were assigned randomly to the experimental conditions.

Task conditions. All tasks were constructed so that the following conditions would hold: Cond. 1. One cue (X_1) related to the criterion (Y) in a linear manner; the other cue X_2 related to the criterion (Y) in a non-linear manner. Cond. 2. The criterion partly, but not perfectly, predictable from either cue alone. Cond. 3. The criterion perfectly predictable from correct utilization of both cues.

Differing levels of linear and nonlinear task variance were generated by specifying that cue values should be the whole numbers 1 through 10, and by combining each of the possible 100 X_1, X_2 cue values according to the following rules [1]:

$$Y = \tfrac{2}{3}(2X_1 + \text{sine } X_2)$$
$$Y = (X_1 + \text{sine } X_2)$$
$$Y = \tfrac{2}{3}(X_1 + 2 \text{ sine } X_2)$$

[1] Two of the equations were weighted by ⅔ in order that criterion (Y) values be identical over all conditions. This additional weighting will not be reflected in Ss' performance because the measure of achievement (r_a) is a correlation measure, and is therefore not affected by systematic over- or underestimation of the criterion.

where "sine X_2" indicates an approximation of one half of a sine curve. According to this approximation, the transformation rule for sine X requires that S substitute the values 2, 4, 6, 8, 10, 9, 7, 5, 3, and 1 for the stimulus X_2 values of 1 through 10.[2] This procedure results in cue intercorrelations of zero, a criterion range of 2–20, and the following task linearity (R^2) values for each equation: (a) .80 (*high linearity*), (b) .51 (*moderate linearity*), and (c) .22 (*low linearity*). The residual variance $(1 - R^2)$ in each condition is entirely accounted for by the nonlinear relationship between X_2 and the criterion (Y). Each 100-item task was divided into five blocks of 20 trials in such a way that cue-criterion correlations remained approximately constant (within $\pm.06$) over blocks.

Instructions. Instruction conditions were generated according to the amount of information conveyed regarding the sources of criterion variance. The Ss in Cond. 1 were instructed only that X_1 and X_2 determined the criterion values; Ss were told also the range of the criterion values. In addition to the information provided Ss in Cond. 1, Ss in Cond. 2 were provided *illustrations* of prediction from both linear and nonlinear (sine) relations; Ss were instructed that both types of prediction were necessary for perfect accuracy in this task. In addition, Ss in Cond. 3 were told *which* cue was linear and *which* cue was nonlinear. The Ss in all conditions were told that perfect prediction was possible.

The instructions are placed in better perspective if related to studies of concept identification or rule learning (Haygood & Bourne, 1965) in which S's task is to discover the rule which correctly embodies the relations between attributes. Thus, Cond. 1 identifies attributes and asks S to find the rule Cond. 2 includes 1 and also describes the functional relations (linear and nonlinear sine function) which exist between attributes and criterion; Cond. 3 includes 1 and 2 and also specifies which functional relation exists between each attribute and criterion.

Response measures. The accuracy of each S's performance is measured by r_a, the correlation between S's judgments and the criterion (Y) values. The S's dependence upon the linear cue is measured by the correlation between S's judgment and the X_1 cue values; S's dependence upon the nonlinear cue is measured by the correlation between S's judgments and the sine X_2 values.

Apparatus. Cues were presented on 3½ × 6 in. cards and consisted of 2 vertical bars marked off in 10 equal units; cue values were indicated by the number of bar units blacked in. In all conditions, cues (linear vs. nonlinear) were counterbalanced with regard to position on the stimulus cards. A total of 100 stimulus cards was employed in the task.

Procedure. On each of 100 trials, S (a) observed the stimulus cue values

---

[2] Because cue values and transformation values are restricted to whole numbers, the correlation between X_2 and Y is not exactly zero; however, this correlation contributes no more than .03 to the task R^2 for any given block of trials.

on a single card, (b) predicted the criterion, and (c) observed the correct criterion value on the reverse of the stimulus card. Prior to the task, each S read instructions as described earlier.

RESULTS

Correlations between Ss' judgments and (a) criterion values, and (b) X_1, sine X_2 cue values were transformed into Fisher's Z coefficients. Accuracy correlations were analyzed according to a 3×3 factorial anal-

TABLE 1

MEAN ACCURACY CORRELATIONS (IN FISHER Zs) FOR BLOCK V
ACCORDING TO TASKS AND INSTRUCTIONS

Instruction Conditions	Task Linearity					
	Low		Moderate		High	
	$\bar{Z}r_a$	SD	$\bar{Z}r_a$	SD	$\bar{Z}r_a$	SD
1	.22	.30	.84	.52	.59	.43
2	.44	.61	1.18	.93	1.05	.51
3	1.42	.53	1.87	.66	1.58	.47

ysis of variance with repeated measurements over five blocks of trials; cue-dependence correlations were analyzed according to a 3×3 factorial analysis of variance with repeated measurements over two types of cue dependencies (linear vs. nonlinear).

Accuracy correlation (r_a). Analysis of variance revealed that r_a varied significantly according to Tasks, $F (2, 81) = 6.24$, $p < .01$; Instructions, $F (2, 81) = 34.82$, $p < .001$; and Blocks of Trials, $F (4, 324) = 25.82$. $p < .001$. The Tasks $\times$ Blocks interaction was also significant, $F (8, 342) = 2.42$, $p < .05$. Individual comparisons revealed that for the final block of trials (see Table 1), Ss in both moderate and high linearity task conditions performed significantly better than did Ss in the low linearity task condition $(t = 3.03$, $p < .01$; $t = 2.16$, $p < .05)$, while the difference between moderate and high linearity task conditions was not significant. As expected, Ss in instruction Cond. 3 were more accurate than Ss in both Cond. 2 $(t = 4.20$, $p < .01)$ and Cond. 1 $(t = 7.78$, $p < .001)$; mean r_a's for Cond. 2 and 1 likewise differ in the expected direction $(t = 2.05$, $p < .05)$. The Blocks $\times$ Tasks interaction indicates that although Ss in all conditions improved significantly over trials, Ss in the moderate linearity task condition showed greater improvement from Block I to Block V than

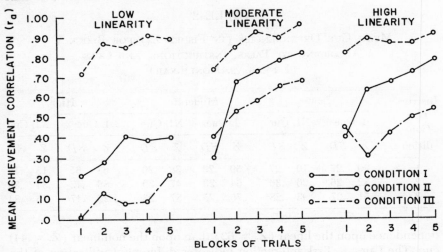

Fig. 1. Mean achievement correlations (r_a) according to Task and Instruction conditions.

did Ss in both high linearity ($t = 3.22$, $p < .01$) and low linearity ($t = 3.52$, $p < .01$) task conditions.

Mean accuracy correlations are plotted over blocks of trials in Fig. 1. Note that the data in Fig. 1 clearly demonstrate that some Ss utilized *both* the linear and nonlinear cues. In both high and low linearity conditions, any r_a over .89 is possible only through utilization of both cues; in the moderate linearity condition, any r_a over .71 likewise requires dependency on both cues.

Cue dependence. Mean cue dependencies for the final block of trials are presented in Table 2. Cue dependence differs according to Tasks, $F(2, 81) = 7.67$, $p < .01$; Instructions, $F(2, 81) = 25.20$, $p < .001$; and Cues, $F(1, 81) = 18.84$, $p < .001$. Significant interactions are found for Tasks × Cues, $F(2, 81) = 6.96$, $p < .001$, and Tasks × Instructions × Cues, $F(4, 81) = 3.36$, $p < .05$.

Individual comparisons of mean cue dependencies reveal that while the difference between moderate and high linearity task conditions is not significant, both conditions result in greater cue dependence than does the low linearity condition ($t = 2.29$, $p < .05$; $t = 2.41$, $p < .01$, respectively). With regard to instructions, mean cue dependence for Cond. 3 is greater than that evidenced by both Cond. 2 ($t = 4.15$, $p < .01$) and Cond. 1 ($t = 4.41$, $p < .01$); Cond. 1 and 2 do not differ ($t = 1.2$). The significant F due to the effect of Cues is attributable to the greater overall

TABLE 2

MEAN CUE DEPENDENCIES (IN FISHER ZS) FOR BLOCK V
ACCORDING TO TASKS, INSTRUCTIONS, AND CUES
(LINEAR VS. NONLINEAR)

Instruction Condition	Low				Moderate				High			
	L Cue		NL Cue		L Cue		NL Cue		L Cue		NL Cue	
	$\bar{Z}$	SD	$\bar{Z}$	SD	$\bar{Z}$	SD	$\bar{Z}$	SD	$\bar{Z}$	SD	$\bar{Z}$	SD
1	.29	.27	.10	.27	.59	.23	.38	.29	.63	.65	.15	.18
2	.32	.26	.26	.36	.64	.23	.47	.30	.88	.42	.34	.38
3	.51	.27	.93	.28	.76	.25	.87	.23	1.26	.47	.45	.34

dependence upon the linear ($\bar{Z}_r = .63$) than upon the nonlinear ($Z_r = .44$) cue. The Cues × Task interaction indicates differential utilization of the linear cue according to tasks; both moderate and high linearity task conditions evidence greater dependence upon the linear cue than does the low linearity task condition ($t = 4.61$, $p < .01$; $t = 4.75$, $p < .01$), and dependence upon the linear cue is likewise greater in the high linearity than in the moderate linearity task condition ($t = 2.30$, $p < .05$). Similarly, the greatest mean absolute difference between linear and nonlinear cue dependence is found in the high linearity condition ($\bar{d}_z = .72$); mean absolute differences of .26 and .38 are found in the moderate and low linearity conditions, respectively. (Differential cue dependence analyzed according to task conditions yields a Kruskal-Wallis $H = 14.10$, $p < .01$).

DISCUSSION

The major findings of this study are that (a) both achievement and cue dependence are affected by task information and task properties, and that (b) Ss can learn to make inferences from nonlinear as well as linear task relations.

The results concerning a suggest that task information makes possible the elimination of erroneous hypotheses concerning cue-criterion relations and irrelevant cues (e.g., sequence), thus leading to higher inferential achievement. The cue-dependency analysis shows that when instruction content is most relevant to task properties, the magnitude of cue-related judgments is greatest.

The finding that Ss in the low linearity condition were less accurate than were Ss in either of the other two task conditions indicates that nonlinear inductions are more difficult to learn. Further evidence for this conclusion is provided by the greater dependence upon the linear cue than upon the nonlinear cue, as well as the finding that overall cue dependence was least in the low linearity condition.

With regard to the effects of task conditions upon differential cue utilization, in both the high and moderate linearity conditions cue weightings approach those appropriate to the task; i.e., high dependence upon the linear cue in the high linearity condition, and near-equal cue dependence on the moderate linearity condition. In the low linearity condition, however, appropriate weighting of the nonlinear cue is found only under conditions of maximum task information.

The finding b that Ss can utilize both linear and nonlinear cues confirms earlier results and indicates that investigation of Ss' inference processes need not be restricted to linear relations. On the contrary, investigations of both multiple-cue probability learning and concept formation should take into account Ss' capacity to attain accurate inferences in tasks involving nonlinear as well as linear cue-criterion relations, and indeterminate as well as determinate properties.

References

BOURNE, L. E., JR. Long-term effects of misinformation feedback upon concept identification. *J. exp. Psychol.*, 1963, 65, 139–147.

BOURNE, L. E., JR., GOLDSTEIN, S., & LINK, W. E. Concept learning as a function of availability of previously presented information. *J. exp. Psychol.*, 1964, 67, 439–448.

BRUNSWIK, E. *Perception and the representative design of experiments.* Berkeley, California: Univer. California Press, 1956.

HAMMOND, K. R., HURSCH, C. J., & TODD, F. J. Analyzing the components of clinical inference, *Psychol. Rev.*, 1964, 71, 438–456.

HAMMOND, K. R., & SUMMERS, D. A. Cognitive dependence upon linear and nonlinear cues. *Psychol. Rev.*, 1965, 72, 215–224.

HAYGOOD, R. C., & BOURNE, L. E., JR. Attribute- and rule-learning aspects of conceptual behavior. *Psychol. Rev.*, 1965, 72, 175–195.

HOFFMAN, P. J. The paramorphic representation of clinical judgment. *Psychol. Bull.*, 1960, 57, 116–131.

HURSCH, C. J., HAMMOND, K. R., & HURSCH, J. Some methodological considerations in multiple-cue probability studies. *Psychol. Rev.*, 1964, 71, 42–60.

PETERSON, C., HAMMOND, K. R., & SUMMERS, D. A. Multiple probability learning with shifting weights of cues. *Amer. J. Psychol.*, 1965, 4, 660–663. (a)

PETERSON, C. R., HAMMOND, K. R., & SUMMERS, D. A. Optimal cue-weighting in multiple probability learning. *J. exp. Psychol.*, 1965, 70, 270–276. (b)

PISHKIN, V. Effects of probability of misinformation and number of irrelevant dimensions upon concept identification. *J. exp. Psychol.*, 1960, 59, 371–378.

SMEDSLUND, J. *Multiple probability learning.* Oslo, Norway: Akademisk Forlag, 1955.

SUMMERS, S. The learning of responses to multiple weighted cues. *J. exp. Psychol.*, 1962, 64, 29–34.

TODD, F. J., & HAMMOND, K. R. Differential feedback in two multiple-cue probability learning tasks. *Behav. Sci.*, 1965, 10, 429–435.

UHL, C .N. Learning interval concepts: I. Effects of differences in stimulus weights. *J. exp. Psychol.*, 1963, 66, 264–273.

WALKER, C. M., & BOURNE, L. E., JR. Concept identification as a function of amounts of relevant and irrelevant information. *Amer. J. Psychol.*, 1961, 74, 410–417.

SECTION TWELVE

Processes and Types

As in problem solving, there has always been some research in concept learning devoted to the processes by which subjects attain concepts. Also, since concepts are often classified into different types, such as color, number, and form, or conjunctive vs. disjunctive, etc., a related area of research is concerned with comparisons of performance as a function of types. In the Hunt and Hovland paper, conjunctive concepts, as well as another type called relational, were selected more frequently than disjunctive. This is consistent with other research in which conjunctive concepts have been learned more rapidly. Since it has sometimes been found that color, number, and form stimuli differ in difficulty, it is noteworthy that in Hunt and Hovland's experiment these stimulus types did not interact with concept types.

The Sechrest and Wallace experiment demonstrates that it is worthwhile to examine subjects' behavior in detail even when rate of learning, as measured by number of trials or instances, did not vary as a function of the independent variable. Redundancy, strategies used, and other quantifiable characteristics of behavior during concept learning may vary as a function of conditions even though an over-all measure of learning does not.

In the same way that Hovland and Weiss (Section Ten) equated positive and negative instances for amount of information transmitted, Conant and Trabasso equated conjunctive and disjunctive concepts in information transmitted by card choices. In spite of this, subjects did better on positive instances, and on conjunctive concepts. Conant and Trabasso were also able to show, by fine-grain analysis of subjects' behavior, that the differing types of strategies associated with the two concept types were not equally easy to learn and use.

461

Laughlin's paper is an example of detailed study of strategies as a function of a number of independent variables. (One of his variables, individual versus two-man groups, touches upon the area of group problem solving or concept learning, which is not covered in this book.) One of the problems in studying processes or strategies is deciding what measures will be used to define a particular strategy. Laughlin explicitly states his rules for the focusing strategy. (Unfortunately, there is no guarantee that the same definition of this or any other behavioral process will be used by other authors; this is a problem that continually plagues the study of processes.) In Laughlin's experiment focusing strategy, once defined, turned out to be a sensitive measure, differentiating among conditions that did not differ on the over-all measure, number of card choices.

42. Order of Consideration of Different Types of Concepts

Earl B. Hunt and Carl I. Hovland

In the learning of some types of concepts individuals acquire the correct classification without any conscious or clear-cut plan of attack. This is typical of much of our perceptual learning and even of many simple conceptual tasks. But in other types of situations, for example those that are involved in scientific analysis, individuals characteristically go about the task of finding the concept by some type of deliberate strategy. This was the most common type of approach in the acquisition of concepts involving geometrical figures in the studies of Hovland and Weiss (1953) and of Bruner, Goodnow, and Austin (1956). These studies fostered deliberate approaches because of the tasks chosen and the nature of the instructions. For such problems one can logically distinguish a number of different kinds of concepts, derived from the types of classifications of instances described by the logical operations "and" and "or." In the *conjunctive* type all of the instances have features in common, so the concept is one where each instance possesses Characteristics A *and* B, or A *and* B *and* C, etc. In the case of *disjunctive* concepts, all instances have one

Reprinted by permission of the first author and the American Psychological Association from *Journal of Experimental Psychology*, 1960, 59, 220–225.

or another feature (cf. Bruner, Goodnow, and Austin's [1956] example of the concept "strike" in baseball, where a strike is defined as either a pitched ball which crosses the plate between the batter's knees and his shoulders *or* is alternatively any pitch struck at by the batter which fails to be sent into the field). The authors just mentioned found this type of concept exceedingly difficult to learn. The third type of concept, discussed most extensively by Smoke (1935), is *relational,* in which the common properties are sets of relationships rather than common specific stimulus elements. For example, the concept of isosceles triangle involves the common relationship of equality between two of the sides, and the positive instances may have widely differing size and shape.

Subjects typically structure a concept problem in one or another of these ways and sometimes pursue their initial formulation until the evidence for its being unsuitable for the problem becomes overwhelming. In machine simulation of human concept learning it then becomes important to know the order in which solutions of each type will be tried (cf. Hovland, 1959). Since there may be individual differences in the order in which alternatives are considered it may also become necessary to establish the frequency of appearance of a particular order for different segments of the total population.

Order of attack may also be influenced by the perceptual characteristics of the stimuli to be classified. Within a single type of concept (conjunctive), variations in order of consideration have been demonstrated by Heidbreder and her associates (1945) and by Grant (1951). The Ss in these experiments first tried to classify on the basis of form; when this was unsuccessful they tried color and, finally, number of figures. One might also anticipate an interaction between stimulus characteristics and type of concept selected such that when certain dimensions are used conjunctive concepts would be considered first whereas with others, disjunctive or relational concepts would be tried first.

The present experiment was designed to obtain a systematic comparison of the frequency with which Ss choose each of the three concept types as their initial basis for organizing instances. A series of geometrical forms labeled as positive or negative instances was presented to S. The instances were chosen in such a way that they could be organized with equal logical validity on a conjunctive, disjunctive, or relational basis. Which type of concept S utilized was determined on the basis of which of a series of test instances he selected as positive instances of the concept which he had derived from the training series. Each S was given one of three different series of positive and negative instances in which color, form, and number dimensions of the stimuli were rotated as appropriate bases for particular types of concept. This design made it possible to evaluate any interaction between stimulus characteristics and type of concept utilized.

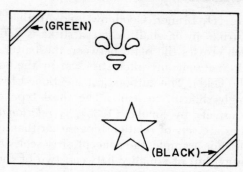

Fig. 1. Illustrative stimulus pattern.

Method

Stimuli. The stimuli were designs of the type illustrated in Fig. 1. The figures were in purple ditto ink; the stripes in the upper left and lower right corners were colored by crayon.

The stimuli involved six dimensions: color of the top stripe, color of the bottom stripe, number and form of the upper figure, number and form of the lower figure. The values used were: color (red, green, light brown, black); number (one through four); figure (triangle, cross, fleur-de-lis, and star). The sets of 15 stimuli each used during training were reproduced on 8½ x 11-in. sheets; two contained six instances each, the third three. Assignment of stimuli to a particular location and page was random. The 16 similar stimuli used in testing were presented eight to a page.

Design. Each S was randomly assigned to one of three conditions corresponding to the set of stimuli to be used in training. During training each S received a set of positive or negative instances from which one conjunctive, disjunctive, or relational concept could be derived. The three training sets provided rotation of the dimensions used for each type of concept. Following the training set S selected concept exemplars from a test set consisting of unlabeled stimuli.

Each training set contained nine positive instances (labeled "Alpha") and six negative instances (labeled "not Alpha"). These completely defined one conjunctive, one relational, and one disjunctive concept, provided S's hypotheses involved less than three dimensions.[1] The sets of

[1] Examination of the pattern of selection of test instances by Ss showed that Ss did not use categorizing rules based on three or more dimensions.

instances used in each of the three training series are presented in Table 1. It will be seen that in Training Series I the conjunctive concept "upper red stripe and lower black stripe" would be consistent with this set of

TABLE 1

DESCRIPTION OF STIMULI[a]

	Set I						Set II						Set III					
	Upper Half			Lower Half			Upper Half			Lower Half			Upper Half			Lower Half		
	Fig.	No.	Stripe Color	Fig.	No.	Stripe Color	Fig.	No.	Stripe Color	Fig.	No.	Stripe Color	Fig.	No.	Stripe Color	Fig.	No.	Stripe Color
Training: Positive Instances																		
1.	C	4	R	F	4	Bk	C	2	G	C	3	Br	S	1	Bk	T	4	Bk
2.	T	4	R	F	4	Bk	C	2	Bk	C	3	Br	S	3	Bk	T	4	Bk
3.	C	1	R	C	1	Bk	S	2	G	S	3	R	S	1	R	T	1	R
4.	C	1	R	T	1	Bk	S	2	G	S	3	Br	S	1	R	T	4	R
5.	C	3	R	S	3	Bk	F	2	G	F	3	G	S	1	G	T	3	G
6.	C	2	R	S	2	Bk	T	2	G	T	3	Br	S	1	G	T	4	G
7.	C	2	R	T	2	Bk	T	2	G	T	3	Bk	S	2	Br	T	3	G
8.	F	2	R	F	3	Bk	F	2	R	F	3	Br	S	4	Br	T	4	Br
9.	S	1	R	F	1	Bk	S	2	Br	S	3	Br	S	4	R	T	4	R
Training: Negative Instances																		
1.	T	1	R	S	4	G	S	2	Bk	C	4	Gr	S	2	R	S	1	Bk
2.	T	2	G	T	4	Bk	T	2	Bk	C	3	Bk	C	2	Gr	T	1	Bk
3.	S	1	R	T	3	Br	T	2	Br	F	3	Bk	F	3	Gr	F	2	Br
4.	S	3	Br	C	2	G	F	2	R	F	3	G	S	3	R	T	2	G
5.	F	3	R	C	1	Bk	F	2	R	S	1	R	S	4	Br	C	3	R
6.	F	4	Bk				C	1	R	T	3	R	T	4	Bk			
Test Instances																		
A.	F	1	G	S	1	Bk												
B.	T	2	Br	S	3	G												
C.	S	2	Bk	T	2	Br												
D.	S	1	R	S	4	Bk												
E.	S	3	R	T	2	Bk												
F.	C	4	R	C	2	R												
G.	T	4	R	C	4	Br												
H.	S	3	Br	T	3	G		(Test instances same for all groups)											
I.	T	1	R	T	4	Bk												
J.	S	4	R	T	1	Bk												
K.	F	2	Bk	S	3	Bk												
L.	T	2	R	C	3	R												
M.	C	4	G	F	3	Br												
N.	F	3	Bk	F	1	Bk												
O.	C	2	G	F	1	Br												
P.	C	2	Bk	C	3	R												

[a] In the training set, positive and negative instances were interspersed randomly. The description code for the figures is S—star, C—cross, F—fleur-de-lis, T—triangle. For colors it is R—Red, G—Green, Br—Brown, Bk—Black.

positive and negative instances. The relational concept "same number of upper and lower figures" would be equally correct, as would the disjunctive concept "crosses in the top row and/or fleur-de-lis in the bottom row."

Following presentation of the training series Ss were given the test set: 16 stimuli of the same type, but without labels. A description of these stimuli is given in the lower portion of Table 1. This set was the same for all Ss. Subjects were instructed to pick out those instances in the test set which they considered to be positive instances of the concept they had derived from the training set. One set of four instances would be selected if S had derived a conjunctive concept from the training series, another set of four if he had utilized a disjunctive one and a third set of four if it were relational. If the reader directs his attention to the relationship between the test set and Training Series I he will see that four of the patterns (D, E, I, J) are further instances of the conjunctive concept of this training series, four others (A, C, G, H) are positive instances of the relational concept, and four others (F, M, N, O) are positive instances by the disjunctive definition. In addition four "dummy" instances (B, K, L, P) were included which could not be considered as positive instances by any of the three categorizing rules derivable from the training series. Similar relationships between training and test stimuli obtained for the other two series.

The Ss could choose as many "positive" instances as they wished. If the majority of the test stimuli selected by S were consistent with the conjunctive definition he was categorized as having utilized a conjunctive concept; a similar categorization was applied for relational and disjunctive concepts. If the majority of S's choices were of "dummy" instances or if he did not place a majority of his choices in one of the other three categories he was classified as "inconsistent."

Subjects. Thirty-seven students from the New Haven College day school and 25 from the night school served as paid Ss. One S in each group had to be dropped for failure to understand the instructions. No S had previously participated in a concept formation experiment.

Procedure. Each S was handed an instruction sheet and an envelope containing the test and training series. The E read the instructions, answered specific questions, and described the six dimensions. The S then read the training sheets, returned them to the envelope, took out the test sheets, selected his choice of instances, and handed in the material. This procedure made it possible to present all training sets to the group and to randomly assign Ss to each training set.

RESULTS

The S's utilization of a particular concept type was evaluated in terms of the number of stimuli of each type which he indicated as exemplars. As stated above, each S could select from zero to four test instances which would be consistent with a particular concept derivable from the training set. The experiment can be analyzed as a $2 \times 3 \times 4$ "mixed" design corresponding to Lindquist's (1953) Type III. Each S is involved in one "treatment" of schools, one of "training set" and all measures for the learning of a particular concept type. In this analysis it is necessary to have proportional numbers of Ss in each of the three conditions (types of training sets) across schools. For this reason the number of cases for each training series within schools was randomly reduced to 11 (for the day school) and seven (for the night school). Analysis of variance methods were used although scores within each treatment were not normally distributed and the range of scores was curtailed. This makes a conservative interpretation of significance levels mandatory. It will be seen that the differences presented in Table 2 are large. There is no evidence that the two school populations differed on the measures taken.

TABLE 2

ANALYSIS OF VARIANCE OF CHOICES OF INSTANCES ON THE TEST SERIES

Source	df	MS	F
Between Ss	53		
Schools	1	.26	.20
Training sets	2	7.59	5.97*
Stimulus × Schools	2	.83	.65
Error (between)	48	1.27	
Within Ss	162		
Concepts	3	32.01	14.28*
(Relational and conjunctive) vs. (Disjunctive and error)	1	96.00	42.84*
Relational vs. conjunctive	1	.02	.01
Disjunctive vs. error	1	.02	.01
Concepts × Schools	3	.70	.31
Concepts × Training Sets	6	.74	.33
Concepts × Schools × Training Sets	6	3.82	1.70
Error (within)	144	2.24	

* P < .01.

The mean numbers of instances selected by Ss, by concept type and training set are presented in Table 3. For the three training sets there was a tendency to check different numbers of instances. Possibly this related to problem difficulty and the degree of certainty felt by Ss after they had seen a particular training set. It will be remembered that an S who learns, with absolute certainty, one categorizing rule will check exactly four instances. The major part of the variance was due to Ss concentrating their choices on relational and conjunctive concept exemplars much more frequently than any other type of instance in the test series.

The frequency of choice of particular types of concept exemplars did not vary with training set, as is shown by the nonsignificant Concepts × Training Set interaction.

TABLE 3

MEAN NUMBER OF INSTANCES CHOSEN FROM THE TEST SERIES

Training Set	Type				Mean Total
	Relational	Conjunctive	Disjunctive	"Inconsistent"	
Day School (N = 33)					
I	1.73	2.00	1.09	.91	5.73
II	1.46	1.82	.09	.00	3.37
III	1.82	1.27	.45	.36	3.90
Night School (N = 21)					
I	3.43	1.71	.43	.29	5.86
II	1.43	1.29	.00	.14	2.86
III	1.14	2.56	.57	.86	5.14

Mean total by training set: I = 5.78, II = 3.17, III = 4.39.
Mean total by schools: Day = 4.33, Night = 4.57.

The analysis of mean number of instances of each type of concept chosen by Ss is supported by an examination of Ss concentration of choices of instances which are consistent with a particular type of concept derivable from the training set. Four Ss concentrated their choices on disjunctive instances, eight on "dummy" instances (or had no majority), 24 concentrated on conjunctive choices and 24 concentrated on relational choices. There was no difference in frequency of choice concentrations between training sets or between the day- and night-school Ss.

DISCUSSION

The above results provide a tentative answer to the question concerning the order in which different types of concepts are considered. Under our experimental conditions both conjunctive and relational concepts are selected significantly more frequently than disjunctive ones. Accordingly, we plan to program our initial computer simulations so that conjunctive possibilities are considered alternately with relational ones. Only when both have been explored without success will the program of the computer consider possible solutions involving disjunctive concepts. The present experiment does not provide information as to what determines an S's initial choice of conjunctive or relational concept. This information will be needed to specify which of two alternative programs should be applied to simulate the behavior of a particular individual on a given concept learning problem.

A number of limitations on the generality of the present results must be considered. One concerns the population of concepts from which the limited set used in the present experiment was derived. Are our relational concepts, for example, typical of the population of such concepts or is there some tendency for investigators to select ones which are particularly easy to learn? And are our results in which "sameness" was used for the relational concept equally applicable to relationships such as "subordinate to" or "bigger than"?

There may be some question as to whether the three types of concepts are distinctive psychologically. For example, some Ss use *and* and *or* interchangeably, some describing a particular class of stimuli as consisting of red *or* green triangles while others describe the same grouping as red *and* green triangles. Similarly, when pairs of large and small circles and triangles are the stimuli some derive the concept of "two large triangles *or* two small triangles" (a disjunctive concept) while others speak of a grouping in which "the triangles are both the same size" (a relational concept).

Another restriction on generality may arise from the use of college students in the present experiment. It is possible that the preference for conjunctive and relational concepts is a product of learning and that children may tend to select disjunctive concepts more frequently than adults.

No evidence was obtained of interaction between the perceptual characteristics of the stimuli and the type of concept chosen, although interaction effects had been anticipated. It is felt that further exploration of this problem is indicated with other quite different types of stimulus material, including some where the dimensions are more difficult to discriminate. But until evidence for interaction is obtained it does not appear necessary to provide alternative computer programs for different types of stimuli in simulation studies.

SUMMARY

The Ss in a visual concept formation task could derive a correct concept from the instances presented on a conjunctive, disjunctive, or relational basis. It was found that conjunctive and relational solutions were utilized much more frequently than disjunctive ones. No significant interaction effects were obtained between the particular aspects of the stimulus involved (color, number, or type of figure) and the frequency of utilization of the different types of concept. The experiment is discussed in relation to machine simulation of human concept learning.

REFERENCES

BRUNER, J. S., GOODNOW, J. J., & AUSTIN, G. A. *A study of thinking.* New York: Wiley, 1956.

GRANT, D. A. Perceptual versus analytic responses to the number concept of a Weigl-type card sorting test. *J. exp. Psychol.*, 1951, 41, 23–29.

HEIDBREDER, E. Towards a dynamic psychology of cognition. *Psychol. Rev.*, 1945, 52, 1–22.

HOVLAND, C. I. Computer simulation techniques in behavioral science research. Talk given on *Voice of America*, 1959. (Mimeo.)

HOVLAND, C. I., & WEISS, W. Transmission of information concerning concepts through positive and negative instances. *J. exp. Psychol.*, 1953, 45, 175–182.

LINDQUIST, E. F. *The design of experiments in psychology and education.* Boston: Houghton Mifflin, 1953.

SMOKE, K. L. An objective study of concept formation. *Psychol. Monogr.*, 1932, 42, (4, Whole No. 191).

43. Assimilation and Utilization of Information in Concept Attainment under Varying Conditions of Information Presentation

Lee Sechrest and John Wallace

Abstract. *Concept attainment by 151 Ss was studied under 4 conditions of information transmission equated in value: (a) initial positive instance, (b) initial positive instance plus list of possible hypotheses remaining, (c) initial positive instance plus list of hypotheses eliminated, and (d) initial positive instance and exposure to array comprised only of positive instances of possible remaining hypotheses. The task was attainment of a single 2-attribute concept by means of free selection from an array completely visible to S. Results indicated: (a) groups did not differ in number of instances required for solution or in relevance of 1st verbalized hypotheses; (b) inefficient performance was not attributable to failure of information assimilation, but Ss did not utilize all available information; (c) Conditions III and IV resulted in a significantly greater number of redundant hypotheses.*

Recent research in concept attainment has sharply delineated the necessity for control of the amount of information available to subjects

Reprinted by permission of the authors and the American Psychological Association from *Journal of Educational Psychology*, 1962, 53, 157–164.

exposed to different experimental conditions (Hovland, 1952; Hovland & Weiss, 1953; Wallace & Sechrest, 1961). Failure to equate the amount of information across treatments yields equivocal results in which presumed treatment effects are hopelessly confounded with differential amounts of information. While control of objective information is clearly a desideratum, scant attention has been paid to the possible influence of the formal method of information transmission in concept attainment research. Cahill and Hovland (1960) have shown that successive presentation of instances results in a poorer performance than simultaneous presentation of instances. Since the objective amount of information transmitted to subjects was the same regardless of experimental condition, Cahill and Hovland concluded that the method of transmission was significantly related to performance. Subjects serving in the successive instances condition were required to retain previous instances in memory rather than having such information directly available for inspection as did subjects serving in the simultaneous instances condition.

The major purpose of the present investigation was to compare subjects' assimilation and utilization of information under varied conditions of information transmission. Although in a closed system of concepts an initial positive instance eliminates many possible concepts, if all the information inherent in the instance is used, it is by no means certain that subjects will recognize and employ all the information available to them. However, an imperfect or less-than-maximally efficient performance may be attributed either to a failure to use all available information from an initial positive instance or to the subsequent utilization of inefficient strategy, e.g., redundant choices. In this investigation four methods of information transmission were employed. Condition I consisted simply of presentation of a single positive instance of the concept to be attained. Condition II, in addition to a single positive instance of the concept to be attained, included the presentation of a printed list of the remaining possible hypotheses as to the nature of the concept. Similarly, Condition III included both a single positive instance and a printed list of hypotheses. However, the list of hypotheses included in Condition III comprised the hypotheses which were eliminated by the first positive instance. In Condition IV a single positive instance was again presented, but the array of instances shown to the subject was reduced by eliminating all instances which were negative for all the possible hypotheses remaining after the initial positive instance. It should be noted that while the subjects in Conditions II and III received lists of hypotheses, this information was theoretically redundant in that the printed material contained the same information objectively transmitted by a single positive instance. Thus, formal method of transmission varied cross conditions but objective amount of information transmitted was identical.

METHOD

Materials. The materials employed in this study consisted of arrays of cards constructed in a manner suggested by Bruner, Goodnow, and Austin (1956, p. 42). The full array employed in Conditions I, II, and III consisted of 81 instances, all possible combinations of four attributes exhibiting three values each as follows: *form* (square, triangle, cross), *color* (red, yellow, black), *number* (one, two, three), and *borders* (one, two, three). The attributes were displayed on white cards, 3″ × 1½″. The reduced array employed in Condition IV consisted of 33 instances. The instances comprising the reduced array consisted of those relevant to the six possible hypotheses remaining after the presentation of a single positive instance. Each instance of this array was a positive exemplar of at least one of the remaining six hypotheses. The reduced array was included in the present study to investigate the effects, if any, of restriction of the range of stimulus materials to instances relevant to hypotheses remaining after an initial positive instance. For example, the reduced array prevented a subject from making totally uninformative choices, at least on the first choice. The array was also reduced in apparent complexity by the elimination of so many of the stimulus cards. Both the reduced array and the full array included nine positive exemplars of the concept to be attained. However, the probability of selection of a positive exemplar of the concept was 1/9 in the full array and 3/11 in the reduced array and the full array included nine positive exemplars of the concept of selection of instances considerably removed from the remaining possible hypotheses following an initial positive instance.

The printed lists of hypotheses employed in Conditions II and III were single spaced, typed sheets of regular 8½″ × 11″ white typing paper. For each condition all of the hypotheses were listed on a single sheet of paper. In the case of Condition III the 48 hypotheses eliminated by the initial positive instance were grouped systematically by attributes and values.

Procedure. General instructions for all the subjects as well as instructions given to the subjects in Condition I were as follows:

[General instructions] This is an experiment in what is called concept attainment. Throughout this session you will be asked to try to discover *concepts* (different ways of grouping the materials) which I will have in mind.

The materials we will be using are these cards you see before you. Notice that each of these cards displays a square, cross, or triangle. Also, these figures may be red, black, or yellow and are enclosed by one, two, or three borders. Notice that there are one, two, or three figures on each card.

These features that I have just pointed out to you are called attributes. In this collection of cards there are four attributes. These are (*a*) type of figure (square, cross, or triangle), (b) color of figure (red, yellow, or black), (c) number of borders (one, two, or three), and (d) number of figures (one, two, or three).

It is possible to combine these attributes in many different ways forming categories in which a number of cards may be placed. For example, *all cards with two crosses* is a category or concept to which you would assign all of the cards which have on them, two crosses. These categories are the concepts you will be asked to find. In each case, as in the example given, you will be asked to find categories involving only two attributes at a time. For example, you will not be asked to discover a category such as all cards with *two red crosses* since this would involve three attributes, number of figures, color of figures, and type of figures.

Now, can you make up a category using these cards? Remember, it should involve only two attributes.

If a subject misses the point, correct his mistake, re-explain the nature of the task, and ask him to make up another category. If the subject shows that he understands the task by correctly devising a two attribute category, proceed by saying:

Now show me a few cards which describe the concept which you have made up.

If the subject is again correct, say:

Good, I think you have the idea of the type of concept we will be using in the experiment.

[Specific instructions—Condition I] In the following problem I will begin by showing you a card which will be a positive example of the concept that I have in mind. After I show you the card you will be asked to select more cards from the board in front of you. After each one of your selections I will tell you whether the card you have chosen is positive or negative. If it is positive, you then know that both of the attributes that define the concept are present on the card. If it is negative, you know that both of the attributes that define the concept are *not* present together on the card. You may take as many cards as you wish and you may offer one suggestion as to what you think the concept is that I have in mind after each one of our selections. Your task is to try to figure out what the concept is that I have in mind using as few of these cards as possible. Try to avoid guessing and make a real attempt to use information you get from the cards in a logical manner. There are no tricks. Do you have any questions? If not, let's begin. Here is the first card and it is a positive example of the concept which I have in mind.

After explanation as to the type of concepts with which they would deal, the subjects were asked to discover the nature of a single two attribute conjunctive concept which the experimenter had in mind. The array of instances as well as instances selected from the array remained in full view throughout the experiment. Each subject, regardless of particular condition, was presented with a single positive instance of the concept to be attained. Subjects serving in Condition II were given the list of six remaining hypotheses while Condition III subjects were given the list of 48 eliminated hypotheses. The single positive instance accompanied the lists in both conditions. Condition IV subjects were given the single positive instance and introduced to the reduced array without comment by the experimenter as to how the array differed from the full array.

A subject was instructed to select instances from the array and after each of his selections was told whether he had selected a negative or positive exemplar of the concept. After each of his selections the subject could offer one and only one hypothesis as to the nature of the concept. Each hypothesis was either confirmed (in which case the experiment was ended) or invalidated by the experimenter. Experimenter responses to verbalized hypotheses were appropriately, "correct" and "no, that is not the concept that I have in mind." Selection of cards from the arrays continued until the subject verbalized the correct concept.

While general instructions were identical for all subjects, additional instructions appropriate to each condition were included for Conditions II, III, and IV. While all subjects received the same initial positive instance, three red squares with two borders, the concept to be attained was systematically varied. In both arrays, full and reduced, a single positive instance eliminated all but six hypotheses as to the nature of the concept. These six remaining two-attribute conjunctions were as follows: red square, red and two borders, square and two borders, three red, three squares, three and two borders. The concept to be attained was systematically selected from this pool of remaining concepts following a single positive instance in such a manner that each appeared equally (approximately) often in each condition. This procedure was thought desirable in order to avoid unintentional but nevertheless, possible communication among subjects from a common source and to sample more widely from the population of concepts available. In addition, systematic varying of the concept to be attained permitted an independent comparison of concepts qua concepts with regard to possible inherent levels of difficulty. This was thought to be, in itself, an interesting problem.

Subjects. The subjects were 151 college students, 76 males and 75 females, enrolled in undergraduate introductory psychology courses. Thirty-eight subjects, evenly divided with regard to sex, were randomly assigned to Conditions II, III, and IV. Thirty-seven subjects, 19 males and 18 females, served under Condition I.

RESULTS

The analysis of variance on number of instances required to attain the concept is reported in Table 1, while means and standard deviations are given in Table 2. The results of this analysis are clearly not significant

TABLE 1

SUMMARY OF ANALYSIS OF VARIANCE ON NUMBER
OF INSTANCES REQUIRED FOR SOLUTION

Source	df	MS	F
Between	3	7.15	1.06
Within	147	3.65	
Total	150		

and indicate that the methods of transmission failed to produce reliable differences between conditions on number of instances required for solution. With full recognition of current controversy over multiple comparisons following over-all F tests, the two most extreme means were com-

TABLE 2

MEANS AND STANDARD DEVIATIONS FOR NUMBER OF INSTANCES
FOR CONDITIONS AND CONCEPTS

Instance	N	M	SD
Condition			
I	37	3.32	1.91
II	38	3.16	1.64
III	38	3.26	2.27
IV	38	4.10	1.77
Concept			
Three red	26	3.85	2.46
Three squares	24	3.40	1.62
Red two borders	24	3.00	1.75
Red square	27	3.96	2.49
Square two borders	24	3.25	1.82
Three two borders	25	3.12	1.54

pared through use of the new Duncan multiple range test (Edwards, 1960). This analysis was nonsignificant, and further pair-wise comparisons between means were not conducted. It should be noted that among available multiple analyses, the Duncan test is regarded as least conservative.

While the analysis of variance on number of instances to solution was nonsignificant, it was thought that a more sensitive analysis might reveal differences among subjects in assimilation and utilization of information. For this reason, the first verbalized hypotheses were categorized as either relevant or as representing inference errors. A hypothesis was considered relevant if it were one of the six possible hypotheses remaining after a single positive instance. On the other hand, a hypothesis was considered as constituting an inference error if it were not one of these six hypotheses. It is most interesting to note that out of 151 first verbalized hypotheses as to the nature of the concept sought, only four constituted inference errors. Two inference errors were committed by Condition I subjects, none by Condition IV subjects, and one subject each in Conditions II and III. Approximately 50% of the subjects verbalized a first hypothesis after one selection from the array and roughly 75% of the subjects after their second selection. The almost complete lack of inference errors in the total sample suggests that a majority of the subjects made good use of available information quite early in the process of attainment.

In addition to the analysis of inference errors, an analysis of individual selections and hypotheses was conducted. At each point in the attainment process, selections and hypotheses were categorized as informative or redundant. A redundant selection was defined as one that failed to permit a subject to eliminate one additional hypothesis not eliminated by prior information. A hypothesis was considered redundant if it had been logically eliminated by a prior selection. The number of tenable hypotheses remaining after each selection and after each hypothesis was computed.

With regard to influence of methods of transmission, differences among groups in the number of redundant selections on the first trial are critical. Significant differences among groups in number of redundant first selections did not obtain. In the entire sample only one subject selected a totally redundant first instance. With the exception of Condition IV, reduced array, the probability of a redundant selection by chance was 5/8. If the initial information presentations had conveyed no information at all, redundant first selections would have been expected for 70 subjects. The expected number of redundant first selections was computed on 113 subjects in Conditions I, II, and III. Condition IV subjects were excluded from this computation since the probability of a redundant first selection in this group was zero.

Groups did not differ in mean number of tenable hypotheses remaining after each selection nor after each hypothesis. However, the groups did differ in the number of redundant hypotheses emitted. An analysis of variance for the number of redundant hypotheses yielded an F significant at the .05 level. A X^2 for the number of subjects in each group who emitted redundant hypotheses was significant beyond the .01 level. Conditions II and IV were nearly equal and high in emission of redundant hypotheses while Conditions I and III were nearly equal and low. There were no differences in the total number of hypotheses emitted.

The analysis of inference errors, in addition to constituting further evidence for the nonsignificance of methods of transmission, raises the interesting question of the efficiency of the subjects in general with regard to the utilization of information. The failure to obtain significant differences in number of instances prior to solution between subjects given a single positive instance and subjects given direct verbal information is critical. This suggests that while the subjects *assimilated* information efficiently, improper *utilization* of information was an important factor in producing less than perfect performance. In other words, in this experiment subjects' strategies in the utilization of information appeared to be more highly related to performance than assimilation of objectively transmitted information. The virtual absence of inference errors suggests that utilization was quite high. However, remembering the fact that a sizable minority of the subjects did not verbalize a first hypothesis until *or* after their third selection, the following analysis was conducted in order to assess the extent to which the subjects *utilize* information.

Assume a group of perfectly logical subjects who assimilate and utilize perfectly all available information. Taking into account probabilities of chance solutions on successive trials and reasoning from the standpoint of a maximally efficient (one which affords the opportunity of progressive elimination of the greatest numbers of erroneous hypotheses) strategy, it is possible to compute expected group performance at successive stages of performance. Given an initial positive instance, in both full and reduced array conditions, the probability of a correct solution prior to the first selection from the array is 1/6. (A single positive instance eliminates all but six equally possible hypotheses.) Under the present experimental conditions, the optimal strategy is that of varying a single attribute at a time (conservative focusing). A subject who followed this strategy would have been able to eliminate three additional hypotheses by his first selection, positive or negative, from the array. Thus, after the first selection and prior to the second selection, the probability of a correct solution is reduced to 1/3. Subsequent selections under this strategy reduce remaining hypotheses by two in the case of a negative selection and one per selection in the case of a positive selection. A negative selection on Trial 2 reduces the probability of solution to certainty while a positive selection further reduces the probability of solution to ½. Regardless of selection on Trial 2, negative or positive, under the assumptions outlined above, all the subjects should be expected to reach a solution after their third selection and prior to their fourth selection.

Comparison of expected performance with actual performance suggests that subjects as a group do not make full use of objectively available information. Whereas the expected number of subjects reaching solution after their third selection is 151, only 80 subjects achieved solution at this point. Furthermore, since the subjects were permitted to verbalize a hypothesis after each selection, the expected performance as computed above is conservative. This is possible since utilization of experimenter feedback constitutes an additional source of information and if used non-redundantly permits the elimination of one hypothesis per *invalidation*. Of a total of 755 hypotheses eliminated, 145, or approximately 19%, were eliminated through nonredundant experimenter feedback.

TABLE 3

SUMMARY OF AN ANALYSIS OF A VARIANCE ON NUMBER OF INSTANCES REQUIRED TO ATTAIN SPECIFIC CONCEPTS

Source	df	MS	F
Between	5	3.96	1.02
Within	145	3.86	

With regard to possible differences in difficulty levels of concepts, since methods of transmission were nonsignificant, it was possible to collapse the methods dimension forming six conditions of concepts containing approximately 25 subjects in each. Table 3 presents a summary of an analysis of variance of total number of instances required to attain six different concepts, each subject solving only one. As Table 3 shows, this analysis was also nonsignificant and indicated that, for the concepts employed in this experiment, differences in difficulty level did not obtain.

DISCUSSION

Bearing in mind the essential ambiguity of attempts to prove the null hypothesis, the failure to obtain significant effects by the methods of information transmission employed in this experiment is most interesting. The subjects were able to assimilate and utilize information transmitted by a single positive instance of a two-attribute conjunctive concept as effectively as the subjects given identical information via direct verbal methods. This equality of performance was apparent in the total number of instances required for solution as well as in the relevance of first verbalized hypothesis and number of inference errors. However, it is most interesting to note that while assimilation of information was apparently highly efficient, the subjects, as a group, failed to utilize all objectively available information. Of particular interest is the failure of the many subjects to take advantage of the experimenter as an additional source of information. Since the subjects were allowed a single hypothesis after each selection from the array, each invalidation by the experimenter, if utilized properly, permitted the elimination of an additional hypothesis. While virtually all subjects verbalized a relevant first hypothesis, it is interesting to note that a sizable minority of 48 subjects did not verbalize a hypothesis until after three or more selections from the array. The possible advantage given by an active search for a solution as evidenced by *hypothesis spewing* in conjunction with utilization of the experimenter as a validational source is suggested by the fact that a clear linear relationship was obtained between number of instances prior to verbalization of the first hypothesis and total instances to solution. In other words, the earlier the subject ventured a hypothesis as to the nature of the concept, the fewer total instances he required for solution. Since this analysis was obviously post hoc, a formal analysis of data is not reported and the following remarks are offered in the spirit of suggestions for future research.

Taking into account the informational advantages that accrue to the subject who seeks validation from the experimenter, as well as the possibility of a chance solution not available to the subject who does not emit hypotheses, it is not at all surprising that a relationship exists between the point of appearance of the first hypothesis and the total number of instances to solution. However, differences among subjects in the point of appearance of the first hypothesis (number of prior selections of instances) is curious. The most parsimonious explanation is simply that differential intellective ability among the subjects is related to both the point of appearance of the first hypothesis as well as total instances to solution. In addition, it is possible that some subjects took the "avoid guessing" instructions much more seriously than others.

Considering the as yet unresolved problem of explication of large individual differences routinely obtained in concept attainment studies, a plausible but slightly more complicated conjecture involves differential sets toward validation responses of the experimenter. Subjects who establish an "information focus" could conceivably perceive the experimenter's invalidations or possible invalidations as a source of information useful in solution and as such, positively reinforcing. On the other hand, subjects set to perceive experimenter's invalidations as punishment establish an expectancy of negative reinforcement and, reluctant to engage in hypothesis spewing, persist in the selection of instances from the array until virtually certain of solution. Whatever the reason for the subjects' delays in verbalizing hypotheses, the data indicate that for approximately 66% of the subjects, solution was achieved with only one, or no, instance after the first verbalized hypothesis regardless of the point of appearance.

It is not completely clear why Conditions II and IV emitted more redundant hypotheses, but the result was that they had more opportunities for confirmation during the attainment process. Across all measures obtained, Condition IV, reduced array, was so consistently different from the other conditions in the direction of reduced efficiency that it is the writers' belief that Condition IV was very likely different in its effect from the other conditions. It may well be that the negative and redundant instances removed from the array have in some way an informative or confirming effect when they are present.

As mentioned above, these tentative remarks are offered as suggestions for future research. Since active search for solution through hypothesis spewing appears as a possible advantageous strategy in concept attainment studies involving experimenter feedback, possible differential expectancies toward the experimenter's validational responses appear important. At any rate, all factors effecting active overt hypothesis formation by the subjects constitute important areas of investigation.

REFERENCES

BRUNER, J. S., GOODNOW, J. J., & AUSTIN, G. A. *A study of thinking.* New York: Wiley, 1956.

CAHILL, H. E., & HOVLAND, C. I. Memory in the acquisition of concepts. *J. exp. Psychol.,* 1960, 59, 137–144.

EDWARDS, A. L. *Experimental design in psychological research.* New York: Holt, Rhinehart & Winston, 1960.

HOVLAND, C. I. A communication analysis of concept learning. *Psychol. Rev.,* 1952, 59, 461–472.

HOVLAND, C. I., & WEISS, W. Transmission of information concerning concepts through positive and negative instances. *J. exp. Psychol.,* 1953, 45, 175–182.

WALLACE, J., & SECHREST, L. Relative difficulty of conjunctive and disjunctive concepts. *J. psychol. Stud.,* 1961, 12, 97–104.

44. Conjunctive and Disjunctive Concept Formation under Equal-Information Conditions

Michael B. Conant and Tom Trabasso

Abstract. *College students learned sets of conjunctive and inclusive disjunctive concepts in which the minimum number of choices necessary for solution was equated. The disjunctive concepts were more difficult to master. Selection of instances and redundancy in choices indicated that Ss learn to use a positive-focusing strategy within a conjunctive problem sooner than they learn to use a negative-focusing strategy within a disjunctive problem.*

In a discussion of the logical structure of concepts, Bruner, Goodnow, and Austin (1956) made particular note of the difference between conjunctive and disjunctive concepts. A conjunctive concept is defined by the joint presence of several values. An example of a conjunctive concept is "blue-eyed *and* red-haired men." A disjunctive concept, on the other hand, is defined by the presence of one or another value (e.g., "tall *or* thin men"). Hunt (1962) makes a further distinction between inclusive and exclusive disjunctivity. In an inclusive disjunction, either value or both may occur; in an exclusive disjunction, either value but not both may occur.

In studies of concept formation, Bruner et al. found that Ss have difficulty working with disjunctive concepts; the authors suggested that this was due, in part, to the necessity of using negative instances in order to solve disjunctive problems most efficiently. Indirect evidence for this hypothesis came from an earlier study by Hovland and Weiss (1953), who found that Ss are inefficient in using negative instances to solve conjunctive problems. Hunt and Hovland (1960) studied problems in which conjunctive, relational (e.g., larger than), and disjunctive solutions were equally correct. They found conjunctive and relational solutions are more frequently offered than disjunctive ones. These authors suggest that the frequency of each type of solution may be an indication of its relative difficulty. Recently, Wells (1963) obtained transfer of training from disjunctive concept formation to choice problems where either a conjunctive or a disjunctive solution was possible, indicating that prior learning of concept types is a factor in the difficulty of concept

Reprinted by permission of the authors and the American Psychological Association from *Journal of Experimental Psychology*, 1964, 67, 250–255.

learning. Wells' training procedure apparently modified prior habits of focusing on positive instances and thereby facilitated disjunctive concept formation.

The purpose of the present study was to obtain a direct comparison between conjunctive and disjunctive problems given to the same Ss. This aim was accomplished by constructing conjunctive- and disjunctive-concept problem sets which were structurally, perceptually, and informationally equivalent.

METHOD

Stimuli. The stimuli consisted of two colored figures drawn on white 3 × 5 in. file cards. On each card there was a triangle on the left and a circle on the right. The figures varied independently in two dimensions, size (large or small) and color (red or green), making 16 different patterns.

Procedure. The 16 cards used throughout the experiments were placed in a 4 ×4 array before S at the start of each problem. The dimensions and values were described to S, and appropriate instructions were read before each conjunctive and disjunctive set of problems; it was ascertained that S knew the general nature of the relevant concept type by having him pick out all positive and negative example cards associated with a sample concept of each type. To begin a problem, E presented S with 1 of the 16 cards as either a positive or negative example of an unknown concept. The S then selected single cards and was told each time whether his choice was a positive or negative instance. The S grouped the selected cards according to class, and a problem was completed when he verbalized the concept. Premature verbal solutions were discouraged.

At the opening of a session, the following instructions were read:

> This is an experiment to see how you think. As you can see, there are 16 cards laid out on the table. Each card contains one circle and one triangle. Circles and triangles vary both in size and color. For instance, a circle is large or small and red or green. The same holds for triangles.
> For purposes of this experiment, a concept will be considered to be a certain set of these cards. A concept about these cards has been chosen. Your job will be to find out the concept as efficiently as possible, in a manner that will be described to you.

Then, before a set of conjunctive problems was given to S, the following three paragraphs were read:

> An example of the type of concept we are dealing with might be all those cards which contain *both* large triangles and green circles.

Would you please point out all the cards here which have the property of having both large triangles and green circles?

That is correct. Four of the 16 cards have this property, and with the type of concepts we will now deal with, 4 of the cards will always be examples of the concept, and 12 will not.

Please keep in mind that with the type of concepts we are now dealing with, just one property of the circles is required (red, large, green, or small), and one property (red, large, green, or small), not necessarily the same, is required for triangles. In other words, small red triangles is not a concept we are dealing with, because this has two properties of one figure. Each concept, again, requires that its examples have just one property of the circles *and* one property of triangles. Do you have any questions about this?

Before the set of inclusive disjunctive problems, the following three paragraphs were read:

An example of the type of concept we are dealing with might be all those cards which contain *either* large triangles or green circles or both. Would you please point out all the cards here which have the property of having either large triangles or green circles or both? That is correct. Twelve of the 16 cards have this property, and with the type of concepts we will now deal with, 12 of the cards will always be examples of the concept, and 4 will not.

Please keep in mind that with the type of concepts we are now dealing with, just one property of circles is required (red, large, green, or small) and one property (red, large, green, or small), not necessarily the same, is required for triangles. In other words, small red triangles is not a part of a concept we are now dealing with, because this has two properties of one figure. Each concept requires that its examples have just one property of circles *or* one property of triangles. Do you have any questions about this?

Following each set of conjunctive or disjunctive instructions, all Ss were told:

I will give you a card that is or is not (and you will be told which) an example of the concept. Your job will be to try other cards, one at a time. I will tell you after each choice whether or not these are examples of the concept. You may guess at the concept at any point, but wrong guesses will result in a subtraction from your score. However, there is obviously no penalty for picking particular cards which are not examples of the concept. Your score will be dependent on how few cards you have to try before you are sure of what the concept is. When you have arrived at the concept, tell me what it is. If you are correct, that problem will be finished and we will go on to another concept. Time is not a factor, only the number of cards you have to try. Work efficiently, but do not hurry. You may take as long as you wish. You may rearrange the cards during trials in any way that may be helpful to you. We will make two rows at the side, one for cards that are examples of the concept, and a row for those that are not. Do you have any questions?

Design. A $2 \times 2 \times 2$ design was used with the following variables: (*a*) two sets of three problems, a conjunctive set (C) and an inclusive disjunctive set (D); (*b*) two presentation orders, C-D and D-C; and (*c*) sex. Each S was given both C and D sets and was randomly assigned to one of the two presentation orders.

Problems. Table 1 summarizes the two sets of three C and D problems along with the example card given before each problem for Exp. I (for

TABLE 1

CONJUNCTIVE AND INCLUSIVE DISJUNCTIVE SETS USED IN EXP. I

Problem	Concept			Example		
	Triangle		Circle	Triangle	Circle	Instance
C1	G	and	L	S, G	L, R	Positive
C2	L	and	R	S, G	S, R	Negative
C3	R	and	S	L, R	L, G	Negative
D1	L	and/or	R	L, G	L, G	Positive
D2	G	and/or	G	L, R	S, R	Negative
D3	S	and/or	L	S, R	S, G	Positive

Note.—The values of the stimuli were G (Green), L (Large), S (Small), and R (Red).

the problems of Exp. II, see below). Given the instructions and the stimuli, there are 16 possible triangle-value and circle-value solutions for each problem. If an example card is positive for a C problem or negative for a D problem, 12 of these possible solutions are eliminated. Similarly, if an example card is negative for a C problem and positive for a D problem, 4 of the possible solutions are eliminated. Thus, positive C instances and negative D instances yield the most information and their respective selection would lead to the most efficient C or D problem solving. When the example card was positive, a C problem could be solved in two card choices, and a D problem in three or four choices, depending upon S's first card choice. When the example card was negative, a D problem required two choices and a C problem, three or four. The C and D sets of three problems each were equated as to the minimum number of choices necessary for solution, 8–10 choices for Exp. I, and 9–12 choices for Exp. II.

Experiments. Two experiments were performed. In the second experiment, the D problems in Table 1 were made C problems and vice versa.

Thus, all C example cards became negative and all D example cards became positive. The second experiment was conducted to assess whether or not the particular value-value pairs contributed to any possible differences observed in Exp. 1.

Subjects. For Exp. I, the Ss were 24 volunteers, 12 males and 12 females, from psychology classes at Columbia University. For Exp. II, there were 12 volunteers, 6 males and 6 females, from the same student population.

RESULTS AND DISCUSSION

Efficiency was first evaluated by comparing the number of choices required to solve all three problems of a concept set. Table 2 summarizes the analysis of variance for each experiment.

TABLE 2

ANALYSIS OF VARIANCE ON CHOICES TO SOLUTION

Source	Exp. I			Exp. II		
	df	MS	F	df	MS	F
Between Ss	23			11		
Sex (S)	1	6.02	.21	1	15.04	2.00
Order (O)	1	20.02	.72	1	.37	.05
S × O	1	1.69	.06	1	11.81	1.57
Error (b)	20	28.46		8	7.53	
Within Ss	24			12		
Concepts (C)	1	336.02	23.40**	1	92.04	7.20*
C × S	1	3.52	.25	1	15.05	1.18
C × O	1	35.02	2.44	1	.21	.02
C × S × O	1	3.69	.26	1	5.21	.41
Error (w)	20	14.36		8	12.81	

* $p < .05$.
** $p < .01$.

In both experiments, the D set required more choices to solution than the C set. In Exp. I, the mean total choices were 19.04 for the D set and 13.75 for the C set. For Exp. II, these values were 19.00 and 15.05, respectively. No other main effect or interactions were significant and no transfer between concept types was observed. Product-moment correlations between S's number of choices required on each of the two problem sets were not significant. No S required all cards to solve a problem; the maximum number selected by an S for a D problem was 14 and for a C problem, 11.

The mean number of choices per problem is reported in Table 3. Relative transfer within each set cannot be properly evaluated because

TABLE 3

MEAN NUMBER OF INSTANCES CHOSEN PER PROBLEM

	Problems					
	Exp. I			Exp. II		
Concept	1	2	3	1	2	3
C	4.17	5.21	4.37	5.48	5.25	4.32
D	7.00	5.75	6.29	6.91	5.76	6.33

of confounding with the class of example cards and inconsistencies in trend.

If S selects instances at random throughout a problem, then the proportion of positive instances chosen should be near .25 for C concepts and .75 for D concepts. However, if S uses a "positive-focusing strategy" (cf. Bruner et al., 1956) which is efficient for C problems and, conversely, a "negative-focusing strategy" which is efficient for D problems, these respective proportions should be higher or lower. To study this, each S's problem was divided into halves and the number of Positive C and negative D instances chosen per half was counted. These Vincentized percentages were nearly equal for the two experiments and were pooled for the summary presented in Table 4.

TABLE 4

PROBABILITY OF A POSITIVE C AND A NEGATIVE D CHOICE

	Proportion per Half					
Problems	Positive C			Negative D		
	First	Second	Trials	First	Second	Trials
1	.24	.56	72	.19	.32	117
2	.22	.61	84	.17	.36	92
3	.22	.64	76	.21	.37	107
Total	.22	.62	232	.20	.35	316

Summing over all problems, the proportion of positive C choices and of negative D choices was above chance expectations. The first- and second-half comparisons in Table 4 indicate that S learns to select, *within a problem,* a positive instance under C conditions more rapidly than a negative instance under D conditions. The S would appear to solve C concepts sooner since he learns to choose positive instances within a C problem more rapidly than negative instances within a D problem. Since the improvement in selection occurs only during the second half of the problem and not over successive problems, there is no apparent transfer of either a positive- or negative-focusing strategy. The tendency to choose more informative instances may result from the information obtained on initial choices. That is, a positive C card may be easier to find once S has selected a few cards, be they positive or negative.

TABLE 5

PROBABILITY OF POSITIVE AND NEGATIVE FINAL CARDS

Instance	Concept			
	C		D	
	Choices	Redundant	Choices	Redundant
Positive	.85	.66	.64	.84
Negative	.15	.75	.36	.65

An information analysis was performed on the card choices with respect to the number of redundant and nonredundant card selections to solution. A card choice was defined as redundant if it could not eliminate at least one further incorrect solution beyond those already eliminated by the example card, preceding card choices and, if verbalized by S, wrong hypotheses. Admittedly, one does not know exactly what solutions were tried by an S but this analysis provides indirect evidence for informational use.

According to this analysis, nearly all incorrect solutions were eliminated by card choices. Eighty-seven percent of the problems were solved with all incorrect solutions eliminated; the remainder were solved with three or less incorrect solutions still possible. The average nonredundant choices were nearly equal: for Exp. I, they were 9.04 for C problems and 8.75 for the D set, and for Exp. II, these values were 10.57 for the C set and 11.20 for the D set. However, more redundancy in choice occurred on D problems. For Exp. I, mean redundant choices were 4.71 for the C set and 10.29 for the D set, $F(1, 20) = 32.02$, $p < 01$; and for Exp. II, these values were 4.48 for the C set and 7.80 for the D set, $F(1, 8) = 7.61$, $p < .05$. No other main effect or interaction was significant.

The relative frequencies with which an S chose positive and negative instances on the final card for a problem are summarized in Table 5. The percentage of these choices which were redundant is also reported.

The very high proportion of positive C instances selected as the last card and the above-chance selection of negative D instances are consistent with use of positive- and negative-focus strategies within a problem. Last-choice redundant negatives are more frequent for the C set, whereas redundant positives are more frequent for the D set. This is expected since these selections are more likely to be redundant when chosen later in the series.

Since there is no difference, between C and D classifications except for the labels S is forced to apply, the form which S's verbal hypothesis must take may be the critical variable. If an S is unfamiliar with the language of a D concept, he may be reluctant to proffer a statement until doubly, hence, redundantly certain. To test this possibility, the trial upon which the first hypothesis (correct or incorrect) was offered was compared in the two sets and no significant differences were obtained. In Exp. I, the mean trial of the first hypothesis per C problem was 3.82 and per D problem was 4.28 matched t (23) $= 1.28$, $p > .05$; and in Exp. II, the respective values were 4.55 and 4.69, matched t (11) $= .32$, $p > .05$. Of the first hypotheses offered, 75% of the Cs and 56% of the Ds were correct.

An alternative interpretation of the redundancy data can be made on the basis of S's choice behavior. With C concepts, a negative choice following a positive is more likely to be redundant than a positive choice following a negative. The reverse is true for D concepts. For the C set, the conditional probability of a negative following a positive was .52; whereas for the D set, the conditional probability of a positive following a negative was .66. Therefore, in C learning, the fewer redundant choices result from both the lower number of choices to solution and the higher incidence of informationally rich positive choices. In D learning, the redundancy results from the larger number of choices and the high incidence of low-information positive choices. An S appears to be more efficient in using positive C choices than negative D choices, even though both instance types yield the same high information. In particular, comparing Problems C1 and D2 of Exp. I, where C1 began with a positive example and D2 with a negative, the ratio of redundant to nonredundant choices in D2 was twice that of C1.

REFERENCES

BRUNER, J. S., GOODNOW, J., & AUSTIN, G. *A study of thinking*. New York: Wiley, 1956.

HOVLAND, C. I., & WEISS, W. Transmission of information concerning concepts through positive and negative instances. *J. exp. Psychol.*, 1953, 45, 175–182.

HUNT, E. B. *Concept learning*. New York: Wiley, 1962.

HUNT, E. B., & HOVLAND, C. I. Order of consideration of different types of concepts. *J. exp. Psychol.*, 1960, 59, 220–225.

WELLS, H. Effects of transfer and problem structure in disjunctive concept formation. *J. exp. Psychol.*, 1963, 65, 63–69.

45. Selection Strategies in Concept Attainment as a Function of Number of Persons and Stimulus Display

Patrick R. Laughlin

Abstract. *The selection strategies of individuals and 2-person cooperative groups were investigated in 5 concept-attainment problems. 2 types of stimulus displays were used: (a) form displays, consisting of geometric forms varying in 6 attributes with 2 levels of each, (b) sequence displays, consisting of 6 plus and/or minus signs in a row. The arrangement of cards in the stimulus displays was ordered or random. The principal results were: (a) 2-person groups used the focusing strategy more, required fewer card choices to solution, and required more time than individuals; (b) form displays resulted in more use of the focusing strategy than sequence displays, with no difference in number of card choices; (c) no difference between ordered and random arrays in use of the focusing strategy or number of card choices.*

Bruner, Goodnow, and Austin (1956) distinguish the two basic selection strategies of focusing and scanning in concept attainment. In focusing S tests the relevance of all the possible hypotheses involved in a particular attribute or attributes by choosing a card differing in one (conservative focusing) or more (focus gambling) attributes from a positive focus card. In scanning he tests specific hypotheses, either singly (successive scanning) or all at once (simultaneous scanning) or some intermediate number. In general, focusing is a more successful strategy, which Bruner et al. (1956) interpret as due to the more difficult memory requirements of scanning. This interpretation is supported by later experiments demonstrating the important effects of memory in concept learning by Cahill and Hovland (1960) and Hunt (1961). In a study of individual

Reprinted by permission of the author and the American Psychological Association from *Journal of Experimental Psychology*, 1965, 70, 323–327.

vs. group memory, Perlmutter (1953) found better memory for groups. From these considerations of memory effects in concept learning and in individuals vs. groups, the present study hypothesized that two-person cooperative groups would (*a*) use the focusing strategy more than individuals, and (*b*) solve concept-attainment problems in fewer card choices than individuals. If memory is a relevant variable, individuals should have more repetitions of card choices, more hypotheses, more repetitions of hypotheses, and more untenable hypotheses than groups.

Concept-attainment research typically has used stimulus displays with simple geometric forms such as triangles or squares, varying in several attributes such as color or size. These displays present S with one unified perceptual object having several attributes of variability. In applying a focusing strategy, attributes are successively abstracted from the unified object and the set of hypotheses involved tested for applicability to the concept. The S may thus be set to use a focusing strategy because of the nature of the stimulus display. However, if the attributes were not in a single perceptually unified figure, but rather in a series of separate figures, S might perceive the situation as a problem in the permutations of discrete objects and thus be set to use a scanning strategy by directly testing specific hypotheses. Thus, the present experiment used two types of stimulus displays: (*a*) the typical geometric forms with six attributes (*b*) a sequence of six plus signs and/or minus signs in a row. It was hypothesized that the form displays would result in more use of the focusing strategy than sequence displays, and thus in fewer card choices.

METHOD

Design. A $2 \times 2 \times 2$ factorial design was used with the following variables: (*a*) number of persons (individual or two-person group), (*b*) stimulus display (form or sequence), (*c*) array (ordered or random).

Subjects. Twelve male introductory psychology students were randomly assigned to each of the four individual conditions and 24 to each of the four group conditions.

Stimulus displays. The problem materials were 24, 28×44 in. white posterboards, each containing an 8×8 array of 64, $2\frac{1}{2} \times 4$ in. cards drawn in colored ink with dark outlines. The 64 cards represented all possible combinations of six attributes with two levels of each.

Form displays consisted of the following attribues and values: (*a*) shape: square or triangle (*b*) size: large or small (*c*) number: one or two (*d*) color: red or green (*e*) pattern: striped or solid (*f*) borders: one or two. Sequence displays consisted of all combinations of six plus and/or minus signs in a row. In order to facilitate reference to the six positions, each was a different color, so that the color name was the attribute and plus or minus the value of each color. The attributes and values were listed on a reference card which S could use throughout the experiment. All cards were numbered from 1 to 64 by rows in the upper right corner.

The stimulus displays were arranged in six ordered arrays, in which the position of each card varied systematically in relation to the other cards, and six random arrays. For example, on the first ordered array the top four rows of cards had one border and the bottom four rows two. Each attribute occupied a different position on each of the six arrays. Within each treatment condition two replications were randomly assigned to each of the six arrays, and within each array one replication was randomly assigned to two-attribute and one to three-attribute concepts.

Problems. All Ss within form or sequence displays received the same five problems in the same order. The two-attribute form display problems were: (a) striped, triangle (b) small, solid (c) one figure, two borders (d) two figures, large (e) green, square. Three-attribute problems added the values (a) large (b) square (c) large (d) red (e) one border, to the corresponding two-attribute problem. The two-attribute sequence display problems were: (a) green minus, red plus (b) black minus, yellow minus (c) orange plus, red plus (d) blue minus, green plus (e) blue plus, black plus. The three-attribute problems added the values (a) yellow plus (b) blue minus (c) green minus (d) orange minus (e) red plus, to the corresponding two-attribute problem.

Procedure. The instructions explained the meaning of conjunctive concepts and the nature of the task, pointed out the attributes and values and the ordered or random arrays, and emphasized that the problems were to be solved in as few card choices as possible, regardless of time (Laughlin, 1964).

RESULTS

The means for the eight treatment groups for focusing strategy, number of card choices to solution, and time to solution over all five problems are given in Table 1. Focusing strategy was scored according to three rules: (Rule 1) Each card choice had to obtain information on one new attribute. New information was obtained if the card choice altered only one attribute not previously proven irrelevant (conservative focusing) or, if more than one attribute was altered (focus gambling), the instance was either positive or the ambiguous information correctly resolved on the next card choice by altering only one attribute. (Rule 2) If a hypothesis was made it had to be tenable considering the information available. Untenable hypotheses were of two types: (a) a hypothesis for a value of an attribute when the other value had previously occurred on a positive

TABLE 1

MEAN NUMBER OF CARD CHOICES TO SOLUTION, FOCUSING STRATEGY, AND TIME TO SOLUTION OVER FIVE PROBLEMS

	Form Displays		Sequence Displays	
	Ordered	Random	Ordered	Random
Individual				
Focusing Strategy	3.48	3.20	2.89	2.50
Card Choices to Solution	36.83	32.58	34.08	34.67
Time in Minutes	16.50	19.20	12.60	15.20
Group				
Focusing Strategy	4.19	3.88	3.62	3.38
Card Choices to Solution	26.08	30.42	26.58	25.08
Time in Minutes	22.70	27.00	20.10	29.10

Note.—Maximum focusing strategy is 5.00.

instance, e.g., the hypothesis "red square" when a green instance had been positive; (b) a hypothesis for a value which had previously occurred on a negative instance, e.g., the hypothesis "red square" when an instance with a red square had been negative. (Rule 3) Neither the card choice nor hypothesis could be a repetition of a previous card choice or hypothesis. Each card choice and accompanying hypothesis (if given) that satisfied these three rules was counted as an instance of focusing, and the total number of such instances was divided by the total number of card choices to give a continuous focusing score from .00 to 1.00.

Two-person groups used the focusing strategy more than individuals at the .001 level, $F(1, 88) = 23.02$, and required fewer card choices to solution at the .001 level, $F(1, 88) = 14.37$. Groups required more time to solution at the .001 level, $F(1, 88) = 17.13$. Form displays resulted in more use of the focusing strategy than sequence displays at the .001 level, $F(1, 88) = 14.07$. There was no difference between form and sequence displays on number of card choices to solution, $F(1, 88) < 1$. The differences between ordered and random arrays on number of card choices to solution and focusing strategy were not significant, $F(1, 88) < 1$ and $F(1, 88) = 3.88$, respectively. None of the interactions of any variable were significant.

The means for the eight treatment groups for the number of repetitions of card choices, hypotheses, reptitions of hypotheses, and untenable hypotheses over all five problems are given in Table 2.

Individuals had more repetitions of card choices than groups at the .05 level, $F(1, 88) = 5.78$; more hypotheses at the .001 level, $F(1, 88) = 13.09$; more repetitions of hypotheses at the .05 level, $F(1, 88) = 4.40$; and more

TABLE 2

MEAN NUMBER OF REPETITIONS OF CARD CHOICES, HYPOTHESES,
REPETITIONS OF HYPOTHESES, AND UNTENABLE HYPOTHESES
OVER FIVE PROBLEMS

	Form Displays		Sequence Displays	
	Ordered	Random	Ordered	Random
Individual				
Repetitions of Card Choices	2.08	4.83	1.77	5.57
Hypotheses	15.08	19.92	14.00	16.67
Repetitions of Hypotheses	1.33	2.42	.83	1.83
Untenable Hypotheses	3.83	5.58	2.83	2.75
Group				
Repetitions of Card Choices	1.08	2.08	1.08	.67
Hypotheses	11.75	12.75	11.67	10.00
Repetitions of Hypotheses	.92	1.33	.42	.33
Untenable Hypotheses	1.58	2.25	1.58	.33

untenable hypotheses at the .01 level, $F(1, 88) = 7.99$. None of the interactions of any variable were significant.

Since the six ordered and six random arrays and the two-attribute vs. three-attribute concepts were essentially control variables of secondary interest, they were analyzed across all conditions by a one-way analysis of variance rather than as orthogonal effects in the factorial design. There were no significant differences between either the six ordered arrays or the six random arrays for either focusing strategy or number of choices, $F(5, 42) < 1$ for all four. There were thus no gross board-position effects. There was no significant difference between two-attribute and three-attribute concepts on number of choices, $F(1, 94) < 1$, but three-attribute concepts results in more use of focusing at the .025 level, $F(1, 94) = 6.38$.

As hypothesized, two-person groups required fewer card choices to solution and used the focusing strategy more than individuals. However, as in all individual vs. group problem solving, the objection may be made that this result is merely an artifact, due to the greater probability of one person in each pair of group conditions being above the overall mean in ability. If these persons dominate the problem solving, group superiority is merely an artifactual function of their greater ability. In order to test this objection, the correction model of Taylor and McNemar (1955) was used. Two-person "groups" were formed by randomly pairing all the 48 Ss in individual conditions, and giving each pair the score obtained by the better of the two individuals. The procedure was repeated with another random pairing to obtain another 24 scores, and the 48 scores were compared with the actual group scores by a one-way analysis of variance. This analysis showed no difference between actual and artificial groups for number of card choices to solution, $F(1, 46) < 1$. The actual groups used the focusing strategy more than artificial groups at the .001 level, $F(1, 46) = 23.37$.

DISCUSSION

The difference between two-person groups and individuals on number of card choices to solution was not upheld with the Taylor and McNemar (1955) correction model, so the most parsimonious conclusion is that it is merely an artifactual function of the better individual in each pair. However, the greater use of the focusing strategy by groups was upheld with the correction model, so that two persons working together used the strategy more than they would have working alone. This seems to be due to better memory for the groups, as indicated by significantly fewer repetitions of card choices, hypotheses, repetitions of hypotheses, and untenable hypotheses for groups than individuals. In addition, the opportunity for discussion in the groups may have aided them in the realization that focusing is a strategy designed to reduce memory requirements and insure a constant increment of information on each card choice.

As hypothesized, form displays resulted in more use of focusing than sequence displays. This seems to reflect a difference in the perception of the two displays. The form displays would seem to be perceived as unified figures with several attributes of variation, which may set S to use focusing by successively abstracting attributes and testing the set of hypotheses involved in each attribute. The sequence displays would seem to be perceived as a series of different discrete objects, which may set S to consider the problem in terms of the permutations of many objects. Thus, he would tend to use a scanning strategy in order to test specific hypotheses directly. However, despite the difference in the use of focusing, the hypothesis that form displays would require fewer card choices to solution was not supported.

The greater use of focusing with three-attribute concepts than with two-attribute concepts is only suggestive because it was based on a one-way analysis of variance rather than a factorial effect. However, it does reflect the relative efficiency of focusing vs. scanning for the two types of concepts. With focusing, three-attribute concepts can be solved in a maximum of four choices, while two-attribute concepts require a maximum of five. On the other hand, scanning is more difficult with three-attribute concepts, because, given the initial positive focus card, there are 20 possible three-attribute concepts and only 15 possible two-attribute concepts.

Contrary to the results of Bruner et al. (1956), there were no differences in the use of focusing or number of card choices between ordered and random arrays. Since random arrays only complicate an already complex situation, it would seem better to limit future research on strategies to ordered arrays.

REFERENCES

BRUNER, J. S., GOODNOW, J. J., & AUSTIN, G. A. *A study of thinking.* New York: Wiley, 1956.

CAHILL, H. E., & HOVLAND, C. I. The role of memory in the acquisiton of concepts. *J. exp. Psychol.*, 1960, 59, 137–144.

HUNT, E. B. Memory effects in concept learning. *J. exp. Psychol.*, 1961, 62, 598–604.

LAUGHLIN, P. R. Speed versus minimum-choice instructions in concept attainment. *J. exp. Psychol.*, 1964, 67, 596.

PERLMUTTER, H. V. Group memory of meaningful material. *J. Psychol.*, 1953, 35, 361–370.

TAYLOR, D. W., & McNEMAR, O. W. Problem solving and thinking. *Annu. Rev. Psychol.*, 1955, 6, 455–482.

Name Index

Subject Index

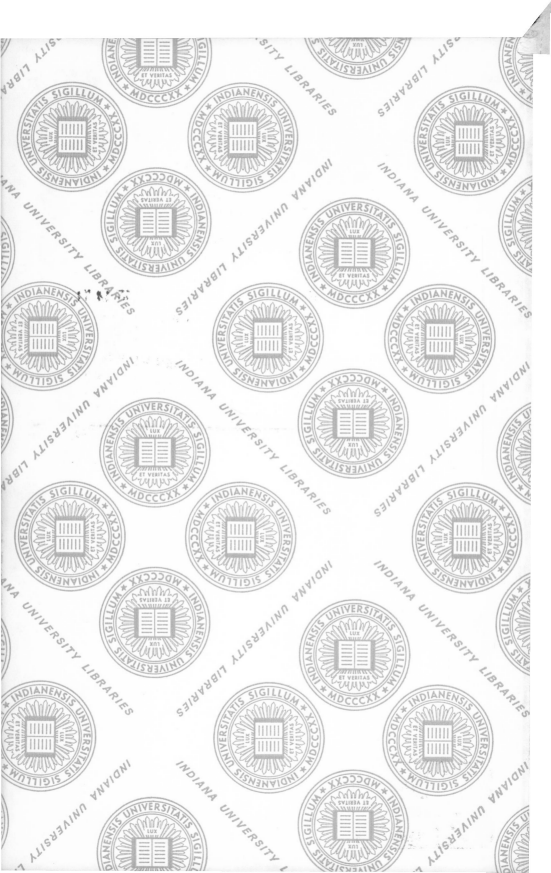